RESEARCH HANDBOOK ON COMPLEX PROJECT ORGANIZING

T0327648

Research Handbook on Complex Project Organizing

Edited by

Graham M. Winch

Professor of Project Management, Alliance Manchester Business School, UK

Maude Brunet

Assistant Professor, Department of Management, HEC Montréal, Canada

Dongping Cao

Associate Professor, Department of Construction Management and Real Estate, School of Economics and Management, Tongji University, China

EE Edward **Elgar**
PUBLISHING

Cheltenham, UK • Northampton, MA, USA

Published by
Edward Elgar Publishing Limited
The Lypiatts
15 Lansdown Road
Cheltenham
Glos GL50 2JA
UK

Edward Elgar Publishing, Inc.
William Pratt House
9 Dewey Court
Northampton
Massachusetts 01060
USA

Paperback edition 2024

A catalogue record for this book
is available from the British Library

Library of Congress Control Number: 2022948495

This book is available electronically in the **Elgar**online
Business subject collection

http://dx.doi.org/10.4337/9781800880283

ISBN 978 1 80088 027 6 (cased)
ISBN 978 1 0353 3735 4 (paperback)
ISBN 978 1 80088 028 3 (eBook)

Printed and bound by CPI Group (UK) Ltd, Croydon, CR0 4YY

Contents

Figures

Tables

Contributors

Kirsi Aaltonen, Associate Professor of Management of Projects and Complex Systems, Faculty of Technology, Industrial Engineering and Management, University of Oulu, Finland.

Fran Ackermann, John Curtin Distinguished Professor, School of Management and Marketing, Faculty of Business and Law, Curtin University, Australia.

Monique Aubry, Associate Professor, Department of Management, Université du Québec á Montréal, Canada.

Sihem BenMahmoud-Jouini, Associate Professor, Innovation Management, HEC Paris, France.

Tyson R. Browning, Professor of Operations Management, Neeley School of Business, Texas Christian University, USA.

Maude Brunet, Assistant Professor, Department of Management, HEC Montréal, Canada.

Dongping Cao, Assistant Professor, Department of Construction Management and Real Estate, School of Economics and Management, Tongji University, China.

Lisa Carlgren, Division Digital Systems, Prototyping Societies, RISE Research Institutes of Sweden, Sweden.

Stewart Clegg, Professor, School of Project Management, University of Sydney, Australia and Visiting Professor, University of Stavanger Business School, Norway.

Eric Daniel, Professor of Project Management, Centrale Lille, France.

Pierre A. Daniel, Associate Professor of Project Management, SKEMA Business School, Université Côte d'Azur, France.

Therese Dille, Associate Professor, School of Business, University of South Eastern Norway, Norway.

David John Edwards, Professor of Plant and Machinery Management, Birmingham City University, UK.

Faris Elghaish, Lecturer in Construction Project Management, School of Natural and Built Environment, Queen's University Belfast, UK.

Juliette Engelhart, Doctoral Student in Supply Chain Management, School of Management, University of Bath, UK.

Karim Farghaly, Lecturer in Facilities Management, Bartlett School of Sustainable Construction, University College London, UK.

Hans Georg Gemünden, Professor Emeritus for Technology and Innovation Management, Berlin Institute of Technology, Technische Universität Berlin, Germany.

Burak Gozluklu, Research Affiliate, MIT Sloan School of Management, Massachusetts Institute of Technology, USA.

Markus Hällgren, Professor of Management, Umeå School of Business and Economics, Umeå University, Sweden.

Tor Hernes, Professor of Organization Theory, Department of Organization, Copenhagen Business School, Denmark.

M. Reza Hosseini, Associate Head of School, School of Architecture and Built Environment, Deakin University, Geelong, Australia.

Pierre-André Hudon, Assistant Professor, Department of Management, Université Laval, Canada.

Martina Huemann, Professor, Department Strategy and Innovation, Vienna University of Economics and Business, Austria.

Lavagnon A. Ika, Professor of Project Management, Telfer School of Management, University of Ottawa, Canada.

Klaudia Jaskula, Marie Skłodowska-Curie Early-Stage Researcher, Bartlett School of Sustainable Construction, University College London, UK.

Anne Keegan, Full Professor of Human Resource Management, College of Business, University College Dublin, Ireland.

Christof Kier, Doctoral Student, Department Strategy and Innovation, Vienna University of Economics and Business, Austria.

Alexander Kock, Professor, Department for Technology and Innovation Management, Technische Universität Darmstadt, Germany.

Jere Lehtinen, Postdoctoral Researcher, Industrial Engineering and Management, Aalto University and University of Oulu, Finland.

Roine Leiringer, Associate Professor, Department of Real Estate and Construction, University of Hong Kong, China.

David Lowe, Professor of Commercial Management, School of Energy, Geoscience, Infrastructure and Society, Heriot Watt University, UK.

Weisheng Lu, Professor of Construction Management, Department of Real Estate and Construction, University of Hong Kong, China.

Stephan Manning, Professor of Strategy and Innovation, University of Sussex Business School, University of Sussex, UK.

Igor Martek, Senior Lecturer in Construction, School of Architecture and Built Environment, Deakin University, Australia.

Miia Martinsuo, Professor of Industrial Management, Department of Industrial Engineering and Management, Tampere University, Finland.

Eunice Maytorena-Sanchez, Senior Lecturer in Project Management, Alliance Manchester Business School, University of Manchester, UK.

Ata Ul Musawir, Assistant Professor of Project Management, Riphah School of Business and Management, Riphah International University, Pakistan.

Johan Ninan, Assistant Professor, Faculty of Civil Engineering and Geosciences, Delft University of Technology, The Netherlands.

Eleni Papadonikolaki, Associate Professor in Digital Innovation and Management, Bartlett School of Sustainable Construction, University College London, UK.

Nicolas Paquet, Doctoral Student, Faculty of Planning, Architecture, Art, and Design, Université Laval, Canada.

Peerasit Patanakul, Professor of Management, Black School of Business, Pennsylvania State University, Behrend College, USA.

Jeffrey K. Pinto, Andrew Morrow and Elizabeth Lee Black Chair in Technology Management and Professor of Management, Pennsylvania State University, Behrend College, USA.

Julien Pollack, Associate Professor, School of Project Management, University of Sydney, Australia.

Jens K. Roehrich, Professor of Supply Chain Innovation, School of Management, University of Bath, UK.

Luca Sabini, Associate Professor of Project Management, School of Civil Engineering, University of Leeds, UK.

Natalya Sergeeva, Associate Professor, Bartlett School of Sustainable Construction, University College London, UK.

Shiting Shao, Doctoral Student, Department of Construction Management and Real Estate, School of Economics and Management, Tongji University, China.

Qian Shi, Professor, Department of Construction Management and Real Estate, School of Economics and Management, Tongji University, China.

Gilbert Silvius, Professor of Project and Programme Management, HU University of Applied Sciences Utrecht, The Netherlands, and University of Johannesburg, South Africa.

Anders Söderholm, Research Scholar, Ronin Institute for Independent Scholarship, Sweden.

Jonas Söderlund, Professor, Department of Leadership and Organizational Behavior, BI Norwegian Business School, Norway   .

Brian Squire, Professor of Operations Management, School of Management, University of Bath, UK.

John Sterman, Professor of Management, MIT Sloan School of Management, Massachusetts Institute of Technology, USA.

Jörg Sydow, Professor of Inter-firm Cooperation, Department of Management, School of Business and Economics, Freie Universität Berlin, Germany.

Rodney Turner, Visiting Professor, School of Civil Engineering, University of Leeds, UK.

Anne Live Vaagaasar, Associate Professor, Department of Leadership and Organizational Behaviour, BI Norwegian Business School, Norway.

Alfons van Marrewijk, Full Professor of Construction Cultures, Department of Management in the Built Environment, Delft University of Technology, The Netherlands.

Guangbin Wang, Professor, Department of Construction Management and Real Estate, School of Economics and Management, Tongji University, China.

Jennifer Whyte, Professor of Project Management, School of Project Management, University of Sydney, Australia.

Graham M. Winch, Professor of Project Management, Alliance Manchester Business School, University of Manchester, UK.

Chao Xiao, Assistant Professor, Department of Construction Management and Real Estate, School of Economics and Management, Tongji University, China.

Jinying Xu, Post-Doctoral Fellow, Department of Real Estate and Construction, University of Hong Kong, China.

Huijin Zhang, Doctoral Student, Department of Construction Management and Real Estate, School of Economics and Management, Tongji University, China.

Shanjing Zhou (Alexander), Research Postgraduate, Department of Civil and Environmental Engineering, Imperial College London, UK.

Foreword

Rodney Turner

Projects are becoming increasingly complex. In a common model, projects have two dimensions: technical complicatedness and organizational, social and political complexity. It is the social and behavioural elements of the project that make it complex. The Betuweroute is a freight line from the Port of Rotterdam to the German border. Apart from two elements, the project to construct the line was technically quite simple. But, it is considered very complex. The project manager said he found himself playing on four chess boards. The first involved the relationship between the local stakeholders and politicians. Dutch people can be very vociferous, and they lobbied national and local politicians. It was said that every time a Dutch member of parliament visited the site it resulted in a change in scope. The second was the relationship with the Ministry of Transport. Both the ministry and project organization were dependent on each other for success but had different definitions of failure. The third was the interface with the rail systems in other European countries, particularly Germany. Dutch and German systems had to be compatible. The fourth was the relationship with the contractors. In one of the technically complicated areas, the technical difficulty was enhanced by the way the project organization and contractors had to interact. The solution was an alliance contract. The solution was the way the project was organized.

Much has been written recently about the organization of projects, particularly the book *Organizational Project Management* by Ralf Müller, Nathalie Drouin and Shankar Sankaran. However, there has been less investigation into the organization of complex projects. Organization can be both a cause of complexity and a vehicle for ameliorating it. This book aims to enhance our current understanding of the organization of complex projects, identifying our current knowledge and opening avenues for future research and development.

There are four parts. Part I covers four inherent elements essential for understanding complexity on projects: uncertainty, complexity itself, projectivity and the temporality of projects. Then there are three parts covering what we can learn from mainstream research in organization and management theory, the challenges of organizing complex projects and new directions for the organization of projects responding to modern technology, labelled Project Organizing 4.0.

In Part II, mainstream organizational theory introduces us to systems dynamics and complex adaptive systems. Complex adaptive systems introduce us to the VIO approach: vision-implementation-organization. The vision consists of goals, objectives and deliverables. Goals are the long-term definition of how we desire the world to improve as a result of doing the project. On complex megaprojects that is often economic development. The objectives are medium-term outcomes that will improve people's lives. That means being able to do things differently, but on complex megaprojects it includes societal benefits such as improved health, safety and environment. Goals and objectives include the common PESTLE: political, economic, societal, technical, legal and environmental. The goals will also influence the project organization itself. There are, for instance, chapters on the influence of transaction costs on project organization, and on how governmentality can influence collaboration and social interaction on projects. Deliverables are the project outputs that deliver the desired outcomes. Implementation describes how the needs of critical stakeholders are converted into the project deliverables, and organization describes how relationships between the stakeholders are governed to enable the work of the project to take place. A key element of project organizing is to deal with conflicting objectives of stakeholders. A chapter explores non-human actors. People were bemused when Actor-Network Theory considered Coquilles St Jacques. On the Gotthard Base Tunnel, the tunnel through the Swiss Alps connecting Milan and Zurich, the geology had a significant impact on the way the project was organized. But, our project organization is influenced by the tools we use, the rules we follow and the communication systems we use.

Part III considers challenges of complex project organizing (CPO). In two classical military quotations, Helmuth von Moltke from the late nineteenth century said, 'The battle plan never survives first contact with the enemy', and General Dwight D. Eisenhower said, 'In preparing for battle, I have always found that plans are useless, but planning is indispensable.' President Eisenhower is saying the battle plan will not survive first contact with the enemy, but through planning, we can create scenarios and narratives for how the battle might evolve, which help us understand what is happening as the battle evolves, and to deal with situations as we encounter them. On complex projects, the plan will often not survive first contact with reality and perhaps the project organization will not either. Several chapters consider the challenges of CPO, particularly the role of governance, defining relationships between stakeholders, which is a role of governance, and the complexities created by megaprojects. One chapter deals with the creation of narratives and storytelling. The authors have previously considered the importance of narratives in project governance. That also leads onto sensemaking and sensegiving, important in the early stages of scenario planning, making sense of the complexity faced, and giving sense to the uncertainty creating it.

Finally, in Part IV, project organizing faces a radically different future under technological changes. The Internet of Things, social media, artificial intelligence, robotics and blockchain will make project organizing unrecognizable from our old models. One chapter considers the impact of digitalization. This has been happening for 40 years now, but information modelling is changing how projects are organized. That includes the Internet of Things and social media, which are now constantly changing the way people communicate on projects, and access information. Artificial intelligence and robotics are changing the way work is done, and therefore also changing the relationship between stakeholders. These are non-human actors, which change the way human actors work, and how they relate to each other through the project organization. Blockchain is creating new complexities but also creating new organizational solutions. The final chapter of the book suggests we need a revolution in CPO, adopting previously unimagined solutions. We need to open up new avenues of research and development.

Acknowledgements

Preparing this *Handbook* has been an enormous collaborative effort. We first wish to thank the tremendous efforts by all the authors who have submitted chapters – without them this book could not exist! We also thank warmly the reviewers for each chapter, some of whom were not contributors. Finally, we thank Dr Sandra Schmidt, without whose project management and copy-editing skills the final push to collate and submit all the chapters would probably have overwhelmed us. Thanks everyone!

1. Introduction to the *Research Handbook on Complex Project Organizing*

Graham M. Winch, Maude Brunet and Dongping Cao

1.1 WHY COMPLEX PROJECT ORGANIZING?

Our society increasingly faces challenges when we look at the drastic climate change causing floods, migrant flows and displacements; massive fires; geopolitical struggles and wars; and our need for transiting to a net-zero economy to remain sustainable. Those grand challenges call for urgent transitions in our socio-technical regimes for energy, mobility and shelter (Geels, 2010). Indeed, the central spine of one framework for addressing global challenges (George et al., 2016, figure 2) can be read as mapping onto the project life-cycle through 'articulating and participating in grand challenges' (project shaping), 'multilevel actions' (project delivery) and 'impacts and outcomes' (benefits realization). On one estimate, achieving net zero alone will entail a 60 per cent increase in capital investment in the short and medium terms above our existing rate of capital investment, mainly in complex projects (McKinsey, 2022), but we face enormous challenges in delivering on these investments aimed at transitioning to zero carbon. For example, the Muskrat Falls megaproject in Canada turned from a promising hydroelectric sustainable energy facility into one of the most impressive and notorious megaproject failures (LeBlanc, 2020). Although project organizing is highly relevant for delivering the solutions (Kaufmann & Danner-Schröder, 2022) to grand challenges, it still seems overlooked or ignored (Winch, 2022).

The assertion that we now live in a volatile, uncertain, complex and ambiguous (VUCA) world is a familiar trope (Bennett & Lemoine, 2014). At the heart of this world, we suggest, is complexity, which has long been investigated within CPO (Geraldi & Söderlund, 2018). Recent research has addressed this theme through various lenses. These include systems engineering to improve project governance and performance (Gorod et al., 2018; Locatelli et al., 2014) and the specific setting of megaprojects (Davies & Mackenzie, 2014; Hu et al., 2015; Pitsis et al., 2018). Project leaders and stakeholders have to tackle complexity, depending on how they perceive it (Fisher et al., 2018; Mikkelsen, 2020), and to develop strategies accordingly (Floricel et al., 2016).

Despite abundant research on the topic, we felt that there was a missing thread behind these various contributions. Therefore, with this *Research Handbook on Complex Project Organizing*, we seek to develop a guiding path to help academics – both established and early career – and research students navigate through these important topics, and envision how to respond to the grand challenges we all face. Our aim with this *Handbook* is to provide a state-of-the-art review of the main studies conducted in complex project organizing (CPO) research, and to suggest fruitful avenues for future research. The editorial team is both interdisciplinary and geographically widespread, and we have sought contributions from leaders in project studies to address various facets of complexity. Before presenting the contents of this

Handbook in more detail, it will be useful to provide a brief history of CPO research to provide context for the following contributions.

1.2   RESEARCH ON COMPLEX PROJECT ORGANIZING: A BRIEF HISTORY

We now present briefly an intellectual history of research on CPO. This is not a history of CPO; rather, we sketch out three research perspectives on CPO research and trace their origin back to attempts to understand the organizational innovations associated with United States (US) weapons acquisition programmes in the 1950s (Johnson, 1997). While our field has its own urtext (Defoe, 1697), little was written in the ensuing 350 years outside professional and technical publications (Pinney, 2001) until scholars from US business schools began to take an interest in weapons acquisition. We can identify three distinct, but complementary, traditions of research over the last 60 years:

- In organization theory, early contributions addressed the challenges of organizational coordination under complexity around the concept of matrix organization, which evolved into the theory of temporary organizations in a projects-as-coordination perspective.
- In systems theory, early contributions heavily influenced by general systems theory evolved into concerns around complexity, system dynamics and complex adaptive systems in a projects-as-systems perspective.
- In commercial theory, early work from the perspective of institutional economics evolved into perspectives derived from transaction cost economics in a projects-as-contracts perspective.

The focus of this *Handbook* is on organizing, so we will not discuss the fourth stream of research that emerged during the 1950s in management science providing increasingly sophisticated tools for decision-making on projects, especially for schedule and risk. We call this the projects-as-planning perspective, also known as the optimization school (Söderlund, 2011; Turner et al., 2013).

The scale and complexity of US weapons acquisition programmes during the 1950s, complemented by the later success of the Apollo programme that applied the new organizational innovations, led to innovative contributions to the projects-as-coordination stream of enquiry. At the core of these contributions was the concept of the matrix organization which broke with the principle of the unity of command in organizations (Fayol, 1918) – a principle which fails to address the complex 'tangled fabric' (Gulick, 1937, p. 20) of organizations. The characterization of the project manager 'in the middle' (Gaddis, 1959) initiated this line of enquiry; supported by research on Boeing (Galbraith, 1970) and NASA (Sayles & Chandler, 1971), it became a standard element in the contingency theory of organizations (Chapter 6) and promised a strong research agenda (Ford & Randolph, 1992). Fundamentally, this line of enquiry addressed the advantages of matrix organization in addressing the core organizational problem of coordination (Mooney, 1937; Okhuysen & Bechky, 2009; Puranam, 2018), where the increasing complexity of business processes and products generated growing organizational differentiation and so a greater need for organizational coordination (Lawrence & Lorsch, 1967).

It is perhaps ironic that as the projectification (Midler, 1995) of manufacturing organizations gathered pace in the 1990s (Chapter 5), interest in matrix organization waned to be replaced by interest in projects as temporary organizations (Bakker, 2010; Bryman et al., 1987; Burke & Morley, 2016). In one way, this new focus provided an important clarification of the matrix organization concept because research had shown that project-oriented matrix organizations were the most effective (Ford & Randolph, 1992), and a rich body of research developed. However, it was not long before the issue of the relationship to the permanent organizations which supplied the temporary organization with resources arose (Bakker et al., 2016). This suggests to us that the theoretical concerns of the analysts of matrix organization remain relevant for the analysts of temporary organization – one example is in project leadership research (Merrow & Nandurdikar, 2018).

The projects-as-systems perspective draws on the application of general systems theory to organizations and their 'project systems' (Johnson et al., 1964) which was enthusiastically taken up in the seminal text of the field (Cleland & King, 1968). This combined systems concepts, investment appraisal techniques and Fayol's life-cycle of strategic planning (prévoyance) > organization > coordination > control to provide a coherent, if partial, theory of CPO. Later editions expanded the systems perspective to include more formal life-cycle analysis (King & Cleland, 1983), matrix organization and stakeholder management (Cleland, 1986). This projects-as-systems perspective has been enormously influential, and still provides the conceptual foundations of basic education in the field (Kerzner, 2017). It is reflected in some of its multiple dimensions in Chapters 3, 7 and 14.

The projects-as-contracts perspective addresses the acquisition, or procurement, process. The sheer complexity of the new generation of weapons systems meant that owners in the form of the US Air Force and Navy had enormous problems of managing commercial relationships with their private-sector suppliers. Attempts by researchers to address these issues (Peck & Scherer, 1962; Williamson, 1967) drew on concepts from industrial economics to argue that it was a case of market failure under high levels of uncertainty. Theoretical developments in economics in the 1970s (Williamson, 1975) enabled the application of transaction cost economics (TCE) to the problem (Masten et al., 1991; Stinchcombe, 1985). However, this stream of enquiry remained largely separate from the other two for reasons that remain puzzling; after all, 'projectizing' (Peck & Scherer, 1962) was central to the acquisition process on the owner side. TCE has now become the main starting point for analysing commercial relations in CPO and more generally (Cuypers et al., 2021); these concerns are reflected in Chapters 8, 21 and 22.

More recently, there have been attempts to bring together these perspectives to provide a more integrative one. An elegant combination of the theory of temporary organization with the life-cycle aspects of the systems perspective (Lundin & Söderholm, 1995) has been very influential. The integration of commercial issues with a matrix theory of temporary organization (Winch, 2014) is more recent. Within both the coordination and system perspectives, there has been considerable evolution with the rethinking project management initiative (Winter et al., 2006) being identified as a point of inflection (Padalkar & Gopinath, 2016) from a hard to a soft paradigm (Pollack, 2007) and greater attention to the dynamic aspects of complexity (Cooke-Davies et al., 2007). This shift encouraged a focus on behavioural issues (the 'nominalist' quadrants of Figure II.1) in projects-as-coordination and a focus on complex adaptive systems (Chapter 14) in projects-as-systems. Recent developments in the projects-as-contracts perspective have moved beyond the focus on discrete transactions and articulated a broader set of challenges around procuring complex performance (Caldwell & Howard, 2011) and inter-organizational coordination trajectories (Oliveira & Lumineau, 2017). However, the perspective still remains relatively isolated from mainstream CPO research (von Danwitz, 2018).

An important concern of any research field is the balance between fragmentation and specialization (Söderlund, 2011). While the kind of pluralism displayed, particularly in Parts II and III, is the sign of a healthy, self-renewing field of research, it can lead to a perception of fragmentation when viewed from the perspective of other fields of research which are then not sure what it specifically contributes to the development of management research overall. During the 1960s, this contribution was clear; it was how (US) society created novel complex systems to meet the urgent challenges of the day (the Cold War arms race). As such, it became part of the mainstream of management research. Few contemporary researchers would be happy with such a narrow research domain and the projectification process (Chapter 5) shows that concepts generated in that original body of research have a wide, if problematic, applicability. Yet, the field has become marginal in the wider development of research in management (Jacobsson & Söderholm, 2020). We suggest that this is partly because it is not presently seen to be addressing contemporary urgent societal challenges in the way it was in the 1960s. For instance, CPO is not seen as part of the research agenda for the sustainability transitions that are essential to meet the challenges of achieving net zero (Köhler et al., 2019), nor does it feature strongly in other research debates around meeting the challenges of the fourth industrial revolution (Winch, 2022).

1.3   THE FUTURE CHALLENGES FOR COMPLEX PROJECT ORGANIZING

Despite substantial developments during the past decades, CPO delivery remains plagued by diverse, long-standing performance problems (Flyvbjerg et al., 2003; Merrow, 2011) and by several emerging new threats (Whitmore et al., 2020; Winch, 2022). Among the most prominent of these are the increasing uncertainty and complexity of project delivery environments. Since the turn of the millennium, exploding technological progress compounded by dramatic ecological disasters, geopolitical conflicts and economic turbulence have disrupted our economic and social life with unprecedented pace and scale. It is becoming ever more difficult for project managers to make informed decisions and effectively manage project scope, schedule and resources based on fixed plans throughout a project life-cycle (Levitt, 2011). With the arrival of the COVID-19 pandemic as a 'Black Swan' event in the VUCA world, for example, we have witnessed the impending needs to develop emergency field hospitals with unprecedented agility and to deliver the 'Operation Warp Speed' vaccine development programme at an unprecedented pace (Winch et al., 2021). The increasing volatility, uncertainty, complexity and ambiguity of project delivery environments derived from these disruptions – and also the return of war to Europe – prompt us to rethink the effectiveness of current CPO practices, which we characterize as centralized planning, formalized controlling and fixed-price contracting, to manage complex projects in this new era.

The United Nations climate agreements have committed to transforming the worldwide development trajectories towards sustainability through achieving global net-zero carbon emissions by 2050 and projects will play a critical role in the transformation. This is not only due to the distinctive energy-extensive nature of many project-based sectors – for example, construction alone contributes about 23 per cent of the total carbon dioxide emissions produced by global economic activity (Huang et al., 2018) – but also because of their centrality for the sustainability transitions of non-project-based sectors such as energy. As such, the net-zero transition requirements have a great potential to reshape the landscape of CPO through changing the practices of both 'sustainability of the project' and 'sustainability by the project' (Huemann & Silvius, 2017). This includes the addition of sustainability criteria to traditional business-as-usual projects, the mitigation projects that are required to build resilience against the effects of climate change and the advance of energy development projects and technology research projects that promise new ways of energy generation and consumption (Winch, 2022).

The development of CPO is also challenged by the strengthened public concerns for human-centred issues such as equality, mental health and wellbeing in the new era. Despite the increasing projectification tendency in diversified industries (Schoper et al., 2018), project activities in many industries are still organized in distinctive labour-intensive manners with relatively harsh working environments. For example, among the 53.67 million employees in the project-based Chinese construction sector in 2020, about 97.38 per cent are rural migrant workers and about 26.40 per cent of these migrant workers are above the age of 50 (National Bureau of Statistics of China, 2021). With the strengthened public concerns for these human-centred issues, the success of CPO should no longer be measured simply as meeting arbitrary objectives on project delivery cost and schedule but needs to include the value brought to the people that deliver the projects (Whitmore et al., 2020).

At the heart of the fourth industrial revolution is the rapid development of emerging digital technologies, including internet of things and artificial intelligence, which hold the promise to enable an almost real-time and intelligent connection between physical and digital systems (Schwab, 2016). While these digital innovations have a great potential to reshape CPO through transforming project life-cycle information processes towards a more integrated, intelligent and real-time capability, they will not act as a 'panacea' to address the grand challenges automatically. They may also generate new sustainability or human-centrality problems such as excessive automation, expanded energy consumption and privacy disclosure. The integration of emerging digital technologies within CPO could result in a range of organisational adjustments, such as the redistribution of benefits and risks at the inter-organisational level, the integration of multiproject resources at the organisational level and the governance of resistance behaviours at the individual level (Cao et al., 2022; Oraee et al., 2019; Whyte, 2019). Collectively shaped by the enabling digital technologies and the inhibiting disruptions in the new era, project organising practices hold a great potential to evolve into the Project Organising 4.0 paradigm (in analogy to Industry 4.0) that is more capable of agility, sustainability and human centrality. We hope this *Handbook* contributes to a deepened understanding of this wave of paradigm evolution as well as potential future research directions in this area.

1.4 THE STRUCTURE OF THE BOOK

We opened this introductory chapter with an assessment of the scale of the challenges we face, and how much more we need to do to ensure that the investments that will provide solutions to those challenges actually deliver. How does the content of this *Handbook* start to address these questions? In Part I, we identify four core concepts of CPO that, we suggest, provide the conceptual foundations of research on CPO. Two of these are familiar – uncertainty and complexity – but often misunderstood, while the other two are implicit in CPO but rarely articulated explicitly. There is an emerging body of research on temporality in project organizing, but less attention has been paid to projectivity. This is surprising given that fundamentally projects are about how we achieve desired future states defined as outputs that realize outcomes for the investors in the project. Reading these four chapters together, we suggest that, in interaction (Figure I.1), they constitute a distinctive configuration for CPO research as the only management research discipline that fully integrates the four concepts with the exception of strategy. In comparison to strategy, though, CPO has a much longer time horizon than most strategy research, which, we suggest, makes it particularly appropriate for researching the achievement of grand challenges.

Theory is central to high-quality research in any management discipline, including CPO. Theory allows both the clear positioning of the contribution of any particular study and showing the broader implications of the empirical analysis for both practice and further theory development. In Part II, therefore, we offer 11 chapters that each present a different theoretical perspective that is relevant for CPO research (Figure II.1). Some of the perspectives were developed initially during the original heyday of CPO research in the 1960s, yet remain fully relevant today. A second group reflects the range of going perspectives that have evolved since the paradigm shift in the mid-2000s identified above and can now be considered collectively as the nominalist 'mainstream' in contemporary CPO research. Finally, a smaller group of theoretical perspectives is discussed which are less established but, we believe, offer new approaches to CPO research with considerable promise. There is a richness of theory across these chapters – and indeed across other perspectives that we were not able to include in this *Handbook* – which is a sign of a vibrant research community. However, one downside of this diversity could be that researchers outside the field do not see it as having a distinctive contribution to make as it 'borrows' theoretical perspectives from other fields and 'applies' them to CPO. If CPO is to escape the 'straightjacket', then it surely needs to be developing distinctive theoretical framings that can be applied more broadly in management research?

Part III gets to the heart of empirical research in CPO, and by addressing the various areas of enquiry our empirical knowledge will grow that allows distinctive theoretical framings to develop. We therefore offer a set of 15 chapters on a diverse range of topics, all of which have attracted considerable research attention in recent years. We focus on four overarching themes to address challenges of CPO research: organizational structures, inter-organizational relationships, stakeholders and project value creation. While each topic gathers several chapters which may address distinctive facets of complexity, they are presented in a continuum from more static system complexity (organizational structures), through socio-political complexity (inter-organizational relationships and stakeholders), to finish with more subjective complexity (project value creation as a state of mind).

Finally, we turn to the prospects for CPO research in the context of the fourth industrial revolution (Figure IV.1) in Part IV and suggest that we are now moving towards Project Organizing 4.0 (Figure IV.2). Myriad new technologies are now on offer to enhance the performance of complex projects. At the very least, they offer multiple lines of enquiry within the projects-as-planning perspective, particularly for the development of project controls. However, they also have important implications for the other perspectives: blockchain has the potential to change significantly the governance of the commercial interface for the projects-as-contracts perspective; and model-based definition offers considerable opportunities for projects-as-coordination. Perhaps most significantly, the projects-as-systems perspective can be renewed through the much enhanced information-processing capabilities of complex project organizations. All these fourth industrial revolution technologies will transform CPO over the coming years and deserve much greater research attention from an organizational perspective than they have received to date from researchers in the field.

1.5   INVITATION TO COMPLEX PROJECT ORGANIZING RESEARCH

We hope you find our *Handbook* helpful in developing your own research in CPO. We have been able to entice many of the most able scholars in the research field to contribute to this *Handbook*; not only established names but also rising stars. Some scholars were unable to contribute due to their personal diary pressures, and publishers set limits on the length of books they will publish. Were we to start again on this collaborative editorial enterprise, we would likely have included a chapter on value in Part I (but see Chapter 28), socio-materiality in Part II (but see Chapter 15) to support research on the technologies covered in Part IV and leadership in Part II (but see Chapters 25 and 27). Nevertheless, we hope that this *Handbook* can further stimulate the debate about the distinctive nature of CPO; how CPO can contribute theoretically to the development of management research and teaching more generally; and, most importantly, how CPO can contribute to addressing the grand challenges we all face across the globe and the sustainability transitions that are going to enable us to reach our collective aspirations for a sustainable planet.

Enjoy!

REFERENCES

Bakker, R. M. (2010). Taking stock of temporary organizational forms: A systematic review and research agenda. *International Journal of Management Reviews*, 12(4), 466–486.

Bakker, R. M., DeFillippi, R. J., Schwab, A., & Sydow, J. (2016). Temporary organizing: Promises, processes, problems. *Organization Studies*, 37(12), 1703–1719.

Bennett, N., & Lemoine, J. (2014). What VUCA really means for you. *Harvard Business Review*, 92(1/2), 27.

Bryman, A., Bresnen, M., Beardsworth, A. D., Ford, J., & Keil, E. T. (1987). The concept of the temporary system: The case of the construction project. *Research in the Sociology of Organizations*, 5, 253–283.

Burke, C. M., & Morley, M. J. (2016). On temporary organizations: A review, synthesis and research agenda. *Human Relations*, 69(6), 1235–1258.

Caldwell, N., & Howard, M. (2011). *Procuring complex performance: Studies of innovation in product-service management*. Routledge.

Cao, D., Shao, S., Huang, B., & Wang, G. (2022). Multidimensional behavioral responses to the implementation of BIM in construction projects: An empirical study in China. *Engineering, Construction and Architectural Management*, 29(2), 819–841.

Cleland, D. I. (1986). Project stakeholder management. *Project Management Journal*, 17, 36–44.

Cleland, D. I., & King, W. R. (1968). *Systems analysis and project management*. McGraw Hill.

Cooke-Davies, T., Cicmil, S., Crawford, L., & Richardson, K. (2007). We're not in Kansas anymore, Toto: Mapping the strange landscape of complexity theory, and its relationship to project management. *Project Management Journal*, 38(2), 50–61.

Cuypers, I. R. P., Hennart, J.-F., Silverman, B. S., & Ertug, G. (2021). Transaction cost theory: Past progress, current challenges, and suggestions for the future. *Academy of Management Annals*, 15(1), 111–150.

Davies, A., & Mackenzie, I. (2014). Project complexity and systems integration: Constructing the London 2012 Olympics and Paralympics Games. *International Journal of Project Management*, 32(5), 773–790.

Defoe, D. (1697). *An essay upon projects*. Cockerill.

Fayol, H. (1918). *Administration industrielle et générale*. Dunod.

Fisher, C. M., Pillemer, J., & Amabile, T. M. (2018). Deep help in complex project work: Guiding and path-clearing across difficult terrain. *Academy of Management Journal*, 61(4), 1524–1553.

Floricel, S., Michela, J. L., & Piperca, S. (2016). Complexity, uncertainty-reduction strategies, and project performance. *International Journal of Project Management*, 34(7), 1360–1383.

Flyvbjerg, B., Bruzelius, N., & Rothengatter, W. (2003). *Megaprojects and risk: An anatomy of ambition*. Cambridge University Press.

Ford, R. C., & Randolph, W. A. (1992). Cross-functional structures: A review and integration of matrix organization and project management. *Journal of Management*, 18(2), 267–294.

Gaddis, P. O. (1959). The project manager. *Harvard Business Review*, 37(3), 89–97.

Galbraith, J. R. (1970). Environmental and technological determinants of organizational design. In J. W. Lorsch & P. R. Lawrence (Eds), *Studies in organization design* (pp. 113–139). Irwin-Dorsey.

Geels, F. W. (2010). Ontologies, socio-technical transitions (to sustainability), and the multi-level perspective. *Research Policy*, 39(4), 495–510.

George, G., Howard-Grenville, J., Joshi, A., & Tihanyi, L. (2016). Understanding and tackling societal grand challenges through management research. *Academy of Management Journal*, 59(6), 1880–1895.

Geraldi, J., & Söderlund, J. (2018). Project studies: What it is, where it is going. *International Journal of Project Management*, 36(1), 55–70.

Gorod, A., Hallo, L., & Nguyen, T. (2018). A systemic approach to complex project management: Integration of command-and-control and network governance. *Systems Research and Behavioral Science*, 35(6), 811–837.

Gulick, L. (1937). Notes on the theory of organization. In L. Gulick and L. Urwick (Eds), *Papers on the science of administration* (pp. 3–45). Institute of Public Administration.

Hu, Y., Chan, A. P. C., Le, Y., & Jin, R. (2015). From construction megaproject management to complex project management: Bibliographic analysis. *Journal of Management in Engineering*, 31(4), 1–11.

Huang, L., Krigsvoll, G., Johansen, F., Liu, Y., & Zhang, X. (2018). Carbon emission of global construction sector. *Renewable and Sustainable Energy Reviews*, 81(P2), 1906–1916.

Huemann, M., & Silvius, G. (2017). Projects to create the future: Managing projects meets sustainable development. *International Journal of Project Management*, 35(6), 1066–1070.

Jacobsson, M., & Söderholm, A. (2020). Project studies beyond the straitjacket: An escape artist's manual. *Project Management Journal*, 51(4), 411–419.

Johnson, R. A., Kast, F. E., & Rosenzweig, J. E. (1964). Systems theory and management. *Management Science*, 10(2), 367–384.

Johnson, S. B. (1997). Three approaches to big technology: Operations research, systems engineering, and project management. *Technology and Culture*, 38(4), 891–919.

Kaufmann, L. J., & Danner-Schröder, A. (2022). Addressing grand challenges through different forms of organizing: A literature review. *Research in the Sociology of Organizations*, 79, 163–186.

Kerzner, H. (2017). *Project management: A systems approach to planning, scheduling, and controlling* (12th ed.). Wiley.

King, W. R., & Cleland, D. I. (1983). Life cycle management. In D. I. Cleland & W. R. King (Eds), *Project management handbook*. Van Nostrand Reinhold.

Köhler, J., Geels, F. W., Kern, F., Markard, J., Onsongo, E., Wieczorek, A., … Boons, F. (2019). An agenda for sustainability transitions research: State of the art and future directions. *Environmental Innovation and Societal Transitions*, 31, 1–32.

Lawrence, P. R., & Lorsch, J. W. (1967). Differentiation and integration in complex organizations. *Administrative Science Quarterly*, 12(1), 1–47.

LeBlanc, R. D. (2020). *Muskrat Falls: A misguided project*. Queen's Printer for Newfoundland and Labrador.

Levitt, R. E. (2011). Towards project management 2.0. *Engineering Project Organization Journal*, 1(3), 197–210.

Locatelli, G., Mancini, M., & Romano, E. (2014). Systems engineering to improve the governance in complex project environments. *International Journal of Project Management*, 32(8), 1395–1410.

Lundin, R. A., & Söderholm, A. (1995). A theory of the temporary organization. *Scandinavian Journal of Management*, 11(4), 437–455.

Masten, S. E., Meehan, Jr., J. W., & Snyder, E. A. (1991). The costs of organization. *Journal of Law Economics and Organization*, 7, 1–25.

McKinsey. (2022). *The net-zero transition: What it would cost, what it would bring*. McKinsey & Co.

Merrow, E. W. (2011). *Industrial megaprojects: concepts, strategies, and practices for success*. Wiley.

Merrow, E. W., & Nandurdikar, N. (2018). *Leading complex projects: A data-driven approach to mastering the human side of project management*. Wiley.

Midler, C. (1995). 'Projectification' of the firm: The Renault case. *Scandinavian Journal of Management*, 11(4), 363–375.

Mikkelsen, M. F. (2020). Perceived project complexity: A survey among practitioners of project management. *International Journal of Managing Projects in Business*, 14(3), 680–698.

Mooney, J. D. (1937). The principles of organization. In L. Gulick & L. Urwick (Eds), *Papers on the science of administration*. Institute of Public Administration.

National Bureau of Statistics of China. (2021). *Report on the rural migrant workers monitoring survey in 2020*. NBSC.

Okhuysen, G. A., & Bechky, B. A. (2009). Coordination in organizations: An integrative perspective. *Academy of Management Annals*, 3(1), 463–502.

Oliveira, N., & Lumineau, F. (2017). How coordination trajectories influence the performance of inter-organizational project networks. *Organization Science*, 28(6), 1029–1060.

Oraee, M., Hosseini, M. R., Edwards, D. J., Li, H., Papadonikolaki, E., & Cao, D. (2019). Collaboration barriers in BIM-based construction networks: A conceptual model. *International Journal of Project Management*, 37(6), 839–854.

Padalkar, M., & Gopinath, S. (2016). Six decades of project management research: Thematic trends and future opportunities. *International Journal of Project Management*, 34(7), 1305–1321.

Peck, M. J., & Scherer, F. M. (1962). *The weapons acquisition process; An economic analysis*. Harvard University.

Pinney, B. W. (2001). *Projects, management and protean times: Engineering enterprise in the United States 1870–1960*. PhD, Massachusetts Institute of Technology.

Pitsis, A., Clegg, S., Freeder, D., Sankaran, S., & Burdon, S. (2018). Megaprojects redefined – complexity vs cost and social imperatives. *International Journal of Managing Projects in Business*, 11(1), 7–34.

Pollack, J. (2007). The changing paradigms of project management. *International Journal of Project Management*, 25(3), 266–274.

Puranam, P. (2018). *The microstructure of organizations*. Oxford University Press.

Sayles, L. R., & Chandler, M. K. (1971). *Managing large systems: Organizations for the future*. Harper and Row.

Schoper, Y. G., Wald, A., Ingason, H. T., & Fridgeirsson, T. V. (2018). Projectification in Western economies: A comparative study of Germany, Norway and Iceland. *International Journal of Project Management*, 36(1), 71–82.

Schwab, K. (2016). *The fourth industrial revolution*. World Economic Forum.

Söderlund, J. (2011). Pluralism in project management: Navigating the crossroads of specialization and fragmentation. *International Journal of Management Reviews*, 13(2), 153–176.

Stinchcombe, A. L. (1985). Contracts as hierarchical documents. In A. L. Stinchcombe & C. A. Heimer (Eds), *Organization theory and project management: Administering uncertainty in Norwegian offshore oil* (pp. 121–171). Oslo University Press.

Turner, J. R., Anbari, F., & Bredillet, C. (2013). Perspectives on research in project management: The nine schools. *Global Business Perspectives*, 1(1), 3–28.

von Danwitz, S. (2018). Managing inter-firm projects: A systematic review and directions for future research. *International Journal of Project Management*, 36(3), 525–541.

Whitmore, D., Papadonikolaki, E., Krystallis, I., & Locatelli, G. (2020). Are megaprojects ready for the fourth industrial revolution? *Proceedings of the Institution of Civil Engineers – Management, Procurement and Law*, 174(2), 49–58.

Whyte, J. (2019). How digital information transforms project delivery models. *Project Management Journal*, 50(2), 177–194.

Williamson, O. E. (1967). The economics of defence contracting: Incentives and performance. In R. McKean (Ed.), *Issues in defense economics* (pp. 217–256). National Bureau of Economic Research.

Williamson, O. E. (1975). *Markets and hierarchies: Analysis and anti-trust implications*. Free Press.

Winch, G. M. (2014). Three domains of project organising. *International Journal of Project Management*, 32(5), 721–731.

Winch, G. M. (2022). Projecting for sustainability transitions: Advancing the contribution of Peter Morris. *Engineering Project Organization Journal*, 11(2).

Winch. G. M., Cao, D., Maytorena-Sanchez, E., Pinto, J. K., Sergeeva, N. & Zhang, S. (2021). Operation Warp Speed: Projects responding to the COVID-19 pandemic. *Project Leadership and Society*, 2.

Winter, M., Smith, C., Morris, P., & Cicmil, S. (2006). Directions for future research in project management: The main findings of a UK government-funded research network. *International Journal of Project Management*, 24(8), 638–649.

PART I

CORE CONCEPTS OF COMPLEX PROJECT ORGANIZING

INTRODUCTION TO PART I

Graham M. Winch

The aim of this part is to present four core concepts of complex project organizing (CPO) research. Two – uncertainty and complexity – are widely used, but with limited awareness of their conceptual history. As a result, there is often little clarity as to how the concept is being used or the assumptions implied in that use. The other two concepts – temporality and projectivity – are emerging concepts in sociological and organizational theory that, we suggest, have the potential to enrich research in CPO. This introduction therefore discusses two themes around these core concepts. One is the importance of concept clarity and how these four chapters can enable researchers to improve concept clarity in their research. The second is more ambitious; it is to suggest a new positioning for CPO research in relationship to organizational research more generally to achieve a much improved level of exchange between the fields and to show how – in combination – these four core concepts of CPO have the potential to provide an exciting new research agenda.

Concept clarity – or as some prefer construct clarity – is central to the scientific endeavour. A 'concept' is a cognitive symbol that has meaning for the scientific community that uses it (Podsakoff et al., 2016). Concepts are, therefore, abstractions that capture explanatory aspects of the phenomenon under investigation within both positivist and hermeneutic methodologies. Lack of concept clarity inhibits theoretical development and the communication of those developments to a wider scientific audience, particularly because, over time, concepts develop 'surplus meaning' and need 'concept clean-ups' (Suddaby, 2010). Clear concepts allow the crisp identification of presence or absence of the phenomenon of research interest and its relationship to other phenomena, whether causal or not. This is an urgent requirement for CPO research because 'uncertainty' and 'complexity' are frequently confounded, leading to weak theory-building (Padalkar & Gopinath, 2016).

Our intent in this part is not to clean up familiar definitions of concepts such as uncertainty and complexity or to provide less familiar concepts fully formed for your consideration. Rather it is to support the first phase of clear concept development, which is identifying the potential attributes of the concept by reviewing its intellectual history (Podsakoff et al., 2016) so that CPO researchers can develop their own conceptual frameworks. We suggest that these four concepts are core because most CPO researchers deploy them – either implicitly or explicitly – in their research and so an understanding of their intellectual history is essential for the further development of CPO research. An example of this process is the definitions of uncertainty and complexity developed for a recent textbook on strategic project organizing (Winch et al., 2022). They do not claim to be 'correct' in some fundamental sense, but they are (hopefully!) clear and concise and allow readers to know how they are used in the argument.

A particular issue that emerges in all four of the chapters in this part is whether the phenomenon captured conceptually is subjectively or objectively conceived. That is to say, for instance, is temporality conceptually a state of mind or a state of nature? It should be noted that this distinction is not the same as the ontological one between nominalists and realists – see Figure II.1 – but an epistemological one. More precisely, it is the distinction, to give one example, between defining uncertainty as cognitive or behavioural. This distinction comes from the 'cognitive revolution' in psychology, in which cognitive phenomena such as beliefs and memories are considered to be real even if they cannot be measured directly (Greenwood, 1999). In cognitive approaches, typically an information-processing metaphor is used for decision-making. It is perfectly possible to deploy a cognitive concept within a realist ontology and positivist methodology. The classic exemplar is neoclassical economics. The economic actor – *homo economicus* – is assumed to act rationally with perfect information, yet the required information is about future states and so is not available. This issue was resolved with the subjective revolution in economics (Chapter 2) in which the rationality is defined in terms of subjective probabilities of expected utility (Savage, 1954; Schoemaker, 1982) and the probabilities of an event are not the outcome of repeated plays but the subjective non-transitive perceptions of likelihood. Once defined thus, the full panoply of positivism can be deployed (Friedman, 1953). Later, this cognitive formulation also allowed the incorporation of psychological research on biases away from rationality (Kahneman et al., 1982) to be incorporated into *homo economicus*.

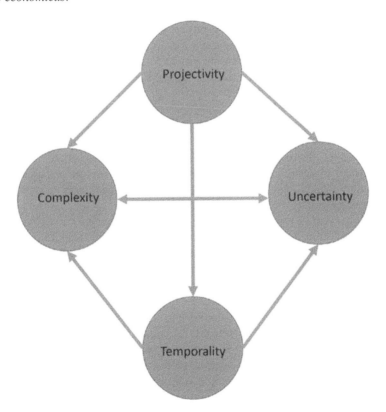

Figure I.1   *The core concepts of complex project organizing*

Chapter 2 shows how the epistemology of uncertainty – what we can know about the future – has moved from an objective to a subjective one over the last four centuries, driven by the cognitive revolution in economics. However, it goes on to argue that attempts to incorporate a psychological dimension into *homo economicus* are inadequate, and that uncertainty about the future has much more profound consequences for CPO. Chapter 3 then turns to static complexity, showing that it has a very different and more recent intellectual history from uncertainty and how an objective epistemology of 'complexity' is distinguished from a subjective epistemology of 'complicatedness'. More dynamic conceptions of complexity are presented in Chapters 7 and 14.

Turning to the less established core concepts, Chapter 4 discusses the importance of temporality in CPO, and presents the classic distinction in temporality research between objectively comprehended linear time and subjectively comprehended non-linear temporality as applied to CPO. Both are central to CPO research and practice – project scheduling takes an inherently objective stance, while more subjective senses of time are captured in processes such as entrainment. Chapter 5 turns to projectivity, or the process of achieving desired future states. This is inherently subjective because, as Aristotle (1974) pointed out, the future is neither true nor false because it has not happened yet, so any claims about the future can only be subjectively perceived.

Our argument is that these four core concepts are central – or ought to be central – to CPO research, but how do they relate? We suggest a way in Figure I.1. We assert that all complex projects are about achieving a desired state projected into the future. Thus, future-perfect thinking by actors with access to the necessary financial resources is the driver of projecting. It is only in the context of such a desired future state that uncertainty and complexity become tractable analytically. It is only in the context of such an aspiration that questions can be asked, for instance, around what information is missing about how that future state will be achieved (uncertainty) and how many elements will interact as it is achieved (static complexity). It also follows that this is an inherently temporal process of mobilizing past understandings in the present to conceive of desired future states, and then to mobilize the resources required to achieve that future state through time. Temporality also gives uncertainty and complexity their dynamic, emergent aspects.

As illustrated in Figure I.1, projectivity is the process by which we – individuals, organizations and societies – think about the future, identify desired future states and project how we are going to organize to achieve that desired future state. Projectivity is therefore, we suggest, the driver of all CPO. The articulation of the desired future state then allows the scoping of the levels of uncertainty and complexity associated with projecting towards that desired future state. Uncertainty can be around both means and ends (Turner & Cochrane, 1993), but it lies at some point on the spectrum between certain and impossible (Keynes, 1921) as neither certain nor impossible. As Knight argued, uncertainty is characterized by 'neither entire ignorance nor complete and perfect information, but partial knowledge' (1921, p. 199). Temporally, uncertainty is progressively reduced by learning (Winch et al., 2022) as information regarding means and ends is acquired through the project life-cycle.

A similar argument applies to complexity, where the challenge of complexity in CPO is defined as dealing with 'a sizeable number of factors which are interrelated into an organized whole' (Weaver, 1948, p. 539). Projectivity answers the question of where this 'whole' comes from in CPO; it is only possible to define a system as simple, complicated or complex once the rough bounds of the system are known. Similarly, complexity is resolved by learning through the project life-cycle (Pich et al., 2002). Thus, both uncertainty and complexity are bounded by projectivity and resolved temporally by learning through the project life-cycle. However, they are not the same constructs, so the question of whether complexity is a component of uncertainty or uncertainty is a component of complexity is otiose (Padalkar & Gopinath, 2016). Uncertainty defines the processes of decision-making on the project while complexity captures the structure and dynamics of the project organization (Daniel & Daniel, 2018). In the terms of Figure II.1, uncertainty is about agency, and complexity is about structure and we argue that they are similarly mutually constituted (Chapter 15) in CPO.

Temporality has been taken for granted in CPO, yet research in the field is split between those who espouse an objective view of time and those who espouse a subjective view of temporality (Winch & Sergeeva, 2022). Temporality is fundamental to projectivity which draws on cognitive resources (knowledge and learning) from the past to project in the present to the desired future state (Emirbayer & Mische, 1998). Moreover, temporality in its life-cycle aspect is fundamental to the processes of resolving complexity and uncertainty to achieve desired project outcomes. We therefore propose the conceptual model shown in Figure I.1 as a mutually constitutive set of core concepts for research in CPO. We further propose that the CPO research field is the only one across business and management generally which combines these four concepts with the exception of strategy, and that the temporal horizon in CPO is much further ahead than in strategy. CPO research, therefore, has a distinctive contribution to make to business and management research in general and to organization theory in particular.

REFERENCES

Aristotle. (1974). *Categories and de interpretatione*. Clarendon.
Daniel, P. A., & Daniel, C. (2018). Complexity, uncertainty and mental models: From a paradigm of regulation to a paradigm of emergence in project management. *International Journal of Project Management*, 36(1), 84–197.
Emirbayer, M., & Mische, A. (1998). What is agency? *American Journal of Sociology*, 103(4), 962–1023.
Friedman, M. (1953). *Essays in positive economics*. University of Chicago Press.
Greenwood, J. D. (1999). Understanding the 'cognitive revolution' in psychology. *Journal of the History of the Behavioral Sciences*, 35(1), 1–22.
Kahneman, D., Slovic, P., & Tversky, A. (1982). *Judgment under uncertainty: Heuristics and biases*. Cambridge University Press.
Keynes, J. M. (1921). *A treatise on probability*. Macmillan.
Knight, F. H. (1921). *Risk, uncertainty and profit*. Houghton Mifflin.
Padalkar, M., & Gopinath, S. (2016). Are complexity and uncertainty distinct concepts in project management? A taxonomical examination from literature. *International Journal of Project Management*, 34(4), 688–700.
Pich, M. T., Loch, C. H., & Meyer, A. D. (2002). On uncertainty, ambiguity, and complexity in project management. *Management Science*, 48(8), 1008–1023.
Podsakoff, P. M., MacKenzie, S. B., & Podsakoff, N. P. (2016). Recommendations for creating better concept definitions in the organizational, behavioral, and social sciences. *Organizational Research Methods*, 19(2), 159–203.
Savage, L. J. (1954). *The foundations of statistics*. John Wiley and Sons.
Schoemaker, P. J. H. (1982). The expected utility model: Its variants, purposes, evidence and limitations. *Journal of Economic Literature*, 20(2), 529–563.
Suddaby, R. (2010). Editor's comments: Construct clarity in theories of management and organization. *Academy of Management Review*, 35(3), 346–357.
Turner, J. R., & Cochrane, R. A. (1993). Goals-and-methods matrix: Coping with projects with ill defined goals and/or methods of achieving them. *International Journal of Project Management*, 11(2), 93–102.
Weaver, W. (1948). Science and complexity. *American Scientist*, 36(4), 536–544.

Winch, G. M., Maytorena-Sanchez, E., & Sergeeva, N. (2022). *Strategic project organizing*. Oxford University Press.

Winch, G. M., & Sergeeva, N. (2022). Temporal structuring in project organizing: A narrative perspective. *International Journal of Project Management*, 40(1), 40–51.

2.   Uncertainty

Graham M. Winch

I compare fortune to one of those violent rivers which, when they are enraged, flood the plains, tear down trees and buildings, wash soil from one place to deposit in another. Everyone flees before them, everybody yields to their impetus, there is no possibility of resistance. Yet although such is their nature, it does not follow that when they are flowing quietly one cannot take precautions, constructing dykes and embankments so that when the river is in flood it runs in to a canal or else its impetus is less wild and dangerous. So it is with fortune. She shows her power where there is no force to hold her in check: and her impetus is felt where she knows there are no embankments and dykes built to restrain her.

(Machiavelli, 1961, p. 130)

2.1   INTRODUCTION

Machiavelli's advice to a new prince is a distinctively modern one as decision-makers began to see fortune no longer as the whim of gods, but something to be mastered through investment projects and other actions (Machiavelli, 1961). The concepts of uncertainty and risk have played a central role in this development over the past six centuries, yet two distinct schools of thought, which we will elaborate as the analytic and cognitive perspectives, use them very differently. Note that these perspectives are distinct from the widely used aleatory and epistemic definitions of probability, where 'aleatory' refers to calculating risk from observed probabilities and 'epistemic' refers to calculating risk from revealed preferences. As we will see, the analytic perspective evolved into applying aleatory methods to epistemic degrees of belief. We will show how the analytic perspective came to be paradigmatic by the end of the twentieth century, and how its failings have recently encouraged more attention to the cognitive perspective, which has been obscured by the dominance of the analytic perspective.

Machiavelli's advice begs the principal questions of investment appraisal such as which flood defences where, and how much to spend? Answering these questions within the analytic perspective has led to the development of the risk management industry with a sophisticated toolbox at its disposal, yet these tools have often been found wanting in investment appraisal where projects continually overrun their schedules and budgets, and fail to deliver the expected outcomes (Flyvbjerg et al., 2003). We turn first to discussing the genesis of the analytic school and how it defines uncertainty and risk before we identify some of its weaknesses. We then discuss the cognitive perspective and its rather different definitions of uncertainty and risk, and attempt to assess whether these can provide the basis for a rather different approach to investment appraisal appropriate for the grand challenges of the twenty-first century. We thereby attempt to advance decision theory in complex project organizing (CPO) as 'the theory of deciding what to do when it is uncertain what will happen' (Hacking, 2006, p. 64).

2.2   THE ANALYTIC PERSPECTIVE

The analytic perspective has its roots in the development of probability and statistical inference starting with the importation of Arabic numbers into Renaissance culture by Fibonacci. Pacioli and Cardano – near contemporaries of Machiavelli – developed this new numeracy to analyse gambling problems as well as, in Pacioli's case, double-entry bookkeeping (Bernstein, 1996). Thus, the founding principles of the analytic perspective – quantification and the ludic model – were set out. Pascal and D. Bernoulli took the analysis further by considering not only the probability of an event occurring, but also its utility for the decision-maker, while J. Bernoulli and Bayes established the principles by which uncertainty could be 'measured', on the condition that the future was like the past (Bernstein, 1996; Hacking, 2006). As the nineteenth century wore on, the emphasis upon measurement as the foundation for decision-making increased with major contributions from the likes of Jevons in economics and Galton in statistics.

However, none of these developments addressed the fundamental problem of quantification and the ludic model. This is that they depend on empirical observation to calculate the risks around choices, but data from measurements are inevitably historical while the decision problem is future-orientated. Only by maintaining the deep assumption that the future will be like the past can historical data – even if near real time – be the basis for quantitatively accurate predictions of future outcomes as in the ludic model. The analytic school broke from this 'objectivist' trap with the development of subjective probabilities and the utility function (Savage, 1954). This proposed that all the tools developed by the analytic school could be deployed in the absence of data so long as a decision-maker's revealed preferences for utility were transitive and stable – that is, arranged in a logical order which stayed in that order between related decisions (Von Neumann & Morgenstern, 1944). In addition to providing the theoretical micro-foundation for neoclassical economics, subjective probabilities provided the basis for the development of management science as a decision theory. Together, these constituted the expected utility (EU) paradigm, in which uncertainty is either synonymous with risk, or more usually, uncertainty is defined as the probability of a specified risk occurring (Aven & Renn, 2009; Schoemaker, 1982).

The concept of a subjective (or personal) probability starts with a conundrum – is the 50 per cent probability of a fair coin landing tails a property of the coin or the decision-maker? Clearly the coin is not making any decisions, but the confidence of the decision-maker that there is a 50 per cent probability of tails is derived from empirical observations of actual events (past tosses of the coin). Yet, the decision-maker is making a decision about something that does not yet exist – the orientation of the coin after the next toss. It follows logically that it is a property of the decision-maker – the consequences of any decision 'might appropriately be called states of the person, as opposed to states of the world' (Savage, 1954, p. 12). This insight, when married to Pascal's utility theory, allows the development of a theory of decision-making based on subjective probabilities in which the personal perceptions of the utility associated with each future state presented for a decision held by the decision-maker can be transitively rank ordered to form the basis of rational decision-making with full information.

Savage provides a theoretical exploration of how decision-makers might be induced to reveal their preferences for option A over option B over option C by 'behavioral interrogation' (Savage, 1971). His fundamental assumption is that given appropriate incentives to be both honest and dispassionate in revealing a personal probability usable data will result. Subjective probabilities with expert judgment have since developed into sophisticated methodologies for obtaining the data required for quantitative risk analysis along the lines proposed by Savage. A review (Spetzler & Stael von Holstein, 1975) identified a number of tools for eliciting probabilities.

The challenges of providing the infrastructure for the growing economies of the late nineteenth century stimulated important developments in investment appraisal in the United States and France (Porter, 2020). Concerned about 'logrolling' in which local political representatives exchange favours when voting for national budget appropriations that favour their own constituencies, national agencies responsible for infrastructure development developed new cost-benefit analysis (CBA) tools that purported to provide 'objective' means to identify the most beneficial investments and rank order them in line with available budgets. While originally developed by engineers, these tools were soon incorporated into the EU paradigm (Persky, 2001). CBA also applied a distinctive form of subjective utility measure revealed by the 'willingness to pay' of a beneficiary when the benefits were not directly monetized (Ramsey, 1990).

There are many practical difficulties in eliciting subjective probabilities (Vick, 2002), but these do not necessarily undermine the analytic perspective's value as a normative perspective on decision-making under uncertainty (Schoemaker, 1982). It is a normative model of how decision-makers ought to behave, and deviations from that model can be cast as biases to be corrected by improved practice (Kahneman et al., 1982). However, there have been growing challenges to the analytic perspective, which place it in question.

The first challenge is the behavioural assumption that decision-makers actually calculate in terms of subjective probabilities when making decisions. Decision-makers are 'boundedly rational' with incomplete information rather than fully rational with complete information (Simon, 1955). The classic response has been that behavioural reality does not matter so long as the theory predicts observed outcomes (Friedman, 1953). A second line of critique came from prospect theory (Kahneman & Tversky, 1979), developing into the heuristics and biases line of enquiry (Gilovich et al., 2002; Kahneman et al., 1982, 2021). This work is largely based on experimental psychology in which participants are asked to make a judgement to which the experimenters know the correct answer, and then the extent and type of 'bias' from, or 'noise' around, that correct answer is measured. Prospect theory showed how decision-makers were loss-averse and intransitive in their choices thereby violating the micro-foundations of EU theory.

A third line of critique is the 'ludic fallacy' (Taleb, 2007) because the EU paradigm remains fundamentally based on the probabilistic model of repeated games. For instance, it is argued that the EU model holds even if decision-makers do not calculate as the model expects, just as billiard players do not do all the calculations that the laws of physics require when they play a shot (Friedman & Savage, 1948). However, this is to fall into the ludic fallacy of comparing decision-making under uncertainty to a game where there is no uncertainty – all the information required for the billiard shot is literally on the table. Known deviations from this model stimulate calls for better practices in decision-making with better tools in support (Kahneman, 2011) and greater professional probity in eliciting subjective probabilities (Vick, 2002). However, an alternative view is that the 'fallacy of misplaced concreteness' (Whitehead, 1926) haunts the elicitation of subjective probabilities where something that is not real is believed to be real.

A set of issues also applies specifically to CBA, both practical and technical. The main practical issue is that it is simply not used effectively (Coyle & Sensier, 2020; Flyvbjerg & Bester, 2021). The technical issues (Vickerman, 2007, 2017) include its reliance on marginal analysis derived from EU theory for very lumpy investment decisions, its inability to include network effects in interaction with existing infrastructure assets and a very limited ability to take into account spillover costs and benefits. Whether this is considered to be due to delusion and deception (Flyvbjerg et al., 2009) or to our fundamental lack of knowledge about the future is likely a function of whether one subscribes to the analytic or cognitive school.

The analytic perspective presupposes that the principal problem with eliciting subjective personal probabilities is that experts and other decision-makers know what the objective probabilities of an event are, but are poorly motivated to elicit them rigorously and then to communicate them to others who could use the information. There is no consideration within this perspective of whether the probabilities elicited from the decision-maker bear any relation to the underlying patterns of events in the real world. In other words, the analytic perspective treats uncertainty as an epistemological problem (Dunn, 2008) with which decision-makers struggle more (Chapman & Ward, 2011) or less (Kahneman, 2011; Kahneman et al., 2021) successfully to understand a stable world. We now turn to the cognitive perspective, which holds that uncertainty is an ontological problem of an unstable world in which subjective probabilities are of little help in decision-making, and that a very different decision-making approach is required for investment appraisal.

2.3   THE COGNITIVE PERSPECTIVE

It may not be a coincidence that the first major breaks (Keynes, 1921; Knight, 1921) with the developing analytic tradition were both originally published in the same year following the chaos of the First World War and the collapse of nineteenth-century confidence that the future would be more of the past (Bernstein, 1996). At the heart of the contribution of both Keynes and Knight is the assertion that not all probabilities are measurable. Keynes is keen to retain the concept of 'probability' as a logical proposition for both the measurable and the unmeasurable rational belief in a future outcome in the knowledge of the weight of evidence available for and against the proposition. He is clear that this is a logical relationship independent of the actual beliefs of the decision-maker, which may or may not be rational (Keynes, 1921). He builds on this treatise when he makes a central assertion in his general theory originally published in 1936:

> If we speak frankly, we have to admit that our basis of knowledge for estimating the yield ten years hence of a railway, a copper mine, a textile factory, the goodwill of a patent medicine, an Atlantic liner, a building in the City of London amounts to little and sometimes nothing. (Keynes 1961, p. 149)

Keynes goes to the heart of Machiavelli's decision problem of which flood defences, where and how much to spend – we simply do not and cannot know with any measurable level of certainty.

Knight addresses the same problem and offers us the useful distinction between risk, which is insurable because it is based on measurable probabilities, and uncertainty, which is not because appropriate measures are not available (Runde, 1998). Rather, it is based on 'the sheer brute fact that the results of human activity cannot be anticipated' (Knight, 1921,

p. 310). Knight integrates uncertainty more thoroughly into his analysis of capitalist development (Dunn, 2008), showing how the dynamism of the competitive process itself generated ontological uncertainty and what was later called 'creative destruction' (Schumpeter, 1942). Both Keynes and Knight saw entrepreneurship as the principal means for decision-making under uncertainty. While Keynes' notion of 'animal spirits' is often associated with financial markets (Shiller, 2015), Keynes actually uses it as an explanation of why an entrepreneur would invest in fixed assets through a 'spontaneous urge to action rather than inaction, and not as an outcome of a weighted average of quantitative benefits multiplied by quantitative probabilities' (Keynes, 1961, p. 161). This line of enquiry generates concepts such as 'entrepreneurial error' (Sawyer, 1952) and the 'hiding hand' (Hirschman, 1967) application of the 'hidden hand' of market benefice (Smith, 1776) to infrastructure development. This treatment of uncertainty is ontologically different from Simon's bounded rationality (Dunn, 2008) because Simon (1955) is focused on epistemological limitations in assessing uncertainty, not the ontological impossibility of doing so.

A major limitation of the contributions of Knight and Keynes is that they leave a large gap in our knowledge of how entrepreneurs actually do make investment decisions. Indeed, they are obliged to fall back in their writing on the observation that entrepreneurs in practice extensively use probability-like calculations in their decision-making (Keynes, 1937) and a 'convention' that the future is like the past (Keynes, 1961) in what Knight calls 'estimates' which have the 'form' of probability calculations (Knight, 1921, pp. 224–232). This has led some (LeRoy & Singell, Jr., 1987) to argue that Knight (unlike Keynes) actually accepted the principle of subjective probabilities seminally formalized by Savage, much of which was developed in critique of Keynes (Feduzi et al., 2014; Ramsey, 1990). We suggest, rather, that Keynes and Knight were struggling with the empirical question of entrepreneurial decision-making under 'radical' (Kay & King, 2020) uncertainty about which they only had available casual observation rather than empirical research.

Since 1921, considerable advances have been made within the cognitive perspective that, in our view, break cleanly with the analytic perspective and start to provide a plausible alternative. One important contribution is that of scenario analysis (Schoemaker, 1995; Wack, 1985), characterized as a 'disciplined method for imagining possible futures' (Schoemaker, 1995, p. 25). Alternative plausible futures are prepared and evaluated through a disciplined process and strategies can be 'stress-tested' (Westgaard et al., 2021) against those scenarios, in order to answer the question of which of those scenarios it would survive. Another important development is the development of cognitive mapping (or 'causal mapping') in which perceptions of possible future events are elicited together with the possible relations between those events to enhance sensemaking about the future (Chapter 26). Cognitive mapping is part of a broader set of 'problem-structuring methods' (Rosenhead & Mingers, 2001) that can address some of the 'wicked problems' facing decision-makers.

A third is the development of 'reference narratives' (Kay & King, 2020), which articulate a forward direction and a reference point for subsequent decision-making. Research on 'project narratives' (Chapter 27) shows how future-orientated narratives articulating desirable future states rather than present-orientated narratives based on CBA more easily mobilize investment resources. They also identify the importance of understanding the interplay between ante-narratives and counter-narratives to the reference project narrative. Narratives are an important means of 'stabilizing the future' under uncertainty (Vaara et al., 2016).

Finally, more attention is being paid to 'naturalistic' decision-making (Klein, 2017), stressing the importance of intuition and experience in effective decision-making. Psychologists are also starting to explore how people think about the future (Baumeister et al., 2016), and the heuristics they use to make decisions about that future (Gigerenzer & Todd, 1999). Crucially, in the cognitive perspective, attention is paid to what people actually do when making decisions rather than how fallible they are in relation to some theoretically derived norm that is the thrust of the analytic perspective.

There are important criticisms of what we have defined as the cognitive perspective. A first challenge is the lack of 'decomposability' (Vick, 2002) of 'animal spirits' and 'estimates'. While it is clear that both Keynes and Knight were thinking in terms of levels of uncertainty across a spectrum of decision-making problems that included risks, they did not take this much further. A number of frameworks have been proposed in the investment project context (De Meyer et al., 2002; Ramasesh & Browning, 2014; Winch & Maytorena-Sanchez, 2011). While these are valuable, lack of agreement on the terminology of the various cognitive states described hampers progress on research and application in practice. Much further work is required on articulating these cognitive states.

Others argue that the cognitive perspective is simply inadequate for the challenges of investment appraisal. One argument is that the hiding hand is more malevolent than beneficial (Flyvbjerg, 2016). While the data set supporting this argument is impressive, the argument does little to solve the challenge of investment appraisal beyond doubling down on CBA by including private participation in public projects (Flyvbjerg et al., 2003) and implementing reference class forecasting (Lovallo & Kahneman, 2003). This critique implicitly treats uncertainty in investment appraisal as an epistemological problem rather than an ontological one. That said, the critique is a powerful one – the cognitive perspective has yet to add up to an adequate decision theory either as a micro-foundation for entrepreneurial decision-making, or as a guide to improving infrastructure investment. This is a large research agenda. The challenge, we suggest, is to gain much deeper insight into the cognition – and hence motivation – behind animal spirits and to how such entrepreneurs in both the public and private sectors can be supported to make better estimates of the relationship between costs and benefits in infrastructure investment appraisal. A first step might be empirical research on investment decision-making, perhaps building on the projects-as-practice (Chapter 11) line of enquiry, while some of the theoretical implications are explored in Chapter 4.

2.4   CONCLUSIONS

We have sketched out the principal axioms of the analytic and cognitive schools of thought on risk and uncertainty showing their strengths and limitations. We do not see these two schools as alternatives; rather they are complements. Just as Newtonian mechanics still works most of the time, despite being surpassed by quantum mechanics, EU theory and its behavioural developments have much to recommend them for many routine decision problems (Ramsey, 1990). Similarly, Keynes (1961) argues that most decision-makers fall back on a convention that the future is like the past with inevitable consequences when comparing outcomes with aspirations. Where past data are available (Knight's statistical probability) and it can be reasonably assumed that they forecast the future, then EU-derived decision theory works. However, the inherent dynamics of capitalism mean that this is very unlikely to hold for business data for anything but the short term; on the other hand, it does hold in the case of engineering data in the absence of complexity. Where these conditions do not hold, then uncertainty is at the heart of the decision problem, Savage's axiom is implausible and we need to fall back on the cognitive school to gain any traction. Of course, knowing which of these two information states one is in is part of the decision problem! Where we agree with Savage is that this is an inherently subjective problem, and hence both an ontological and epistemological challenge.

We opened this chapter with an epigraph from Machiavelli on the infrastructure investment problem under uncertainty. This problem is, when exponentially scaled, the problem of addressing climate change through investment in both alternative green technologies and coping mitigations. We simply do not have the investment appraisal tools for investment choice under the radical uncertainty of what the world will be like in 10 or 20 years' time. Machiavelli's own response to the challenges posed by 'fortune' was 'virtù', which has many dimensions in his thought (Hannaford, 1972; Skinner, 2000; Wood, 1967). However, one positive view is that those whose decisions are imbued with virtù are those who

> were directed towards public political purposes – state service, the establishment of legitimate 'political' authority, and the maintenance of the highest and noblest conceptions of classical liberty and citizenship. At the same time, they were able to put aside the purposelessness of private tyranny, despotism, conspiracy, calumny, corruption, licence and ambition. (Hannaford, 1972, p. 187)

Or, as Defoe (1697, p. 35) puts it:

> the Honest Projector is he, who having by fair and plain principles of Sense, Honesty, and Ingenuity, brought any Contrivance to a suitable Perfection, makes out what he pretends to, picks nobody's pocket, puts his Project in Execution, and contents himself with the real Produce as the profit of his Invention.

We are going to need a lot of those qualities in order to address the grand challenges we all face globally in the face of the inherent uncertainty of the future.

REFERENCES

Aven, T. & Renn, O. (2009). On risk defined as an event where the outcome is uncertain. *Journal of Risk Research*, 12(1), 1–11.

Baumeister, R. F., Vohs, K. D. & Oettingen, G. (2016). Pragmatic prospection: How and why people think about the future. *Review of General Psychology*, 20(1), 3–16.

Bernstein, P. L. (1996). *Against the gods: The remarkable story of risk*. John Wiley and Sons.

Chapman, C. & Ward, S. (2011). *How to manage project opportunity and risk* (3rd ed.). Wiley.

Coyle, D. & Sensier, M. (2020). The imperial treasury: Appraisal methodology and regional economic performance in the UK. *Regional Studies*, 54(3), 282–295.

De Meyer, A. C. L., Loch, C. H. & Pich, M. T. (2002). Managing project uncertainty: From variation to chaos. *MIT Sloan Management Review*, 43(2), 60–67.

Defoe, D. (1697). *An essay upon projects*. Cockerill.

Dunn, S. P. (2008). *The 'uncertain' foundations of post Keynesian economics: Essays in exploration*. Routledge.

Feduzi, A., Runde, J. & Zappia, C. (2014). De Finetti on uncertainty. *Cambridge Journal of Economics*, 38(1), 1–21.

Flyvbjerg, B. (2016). The fallacy of beneficial ignorance: A test of Hirschman's hiding hand. *World Development*, 84, 176–189.

Flyvbjerg, B. & Bester, D. W. (2021). The cost-benefit fallacy: Why cost-benefit analysis is broken and how to fix it. *Journal of Benefit-Cost Analysis*, 12(3), 395–419.

Flyvbjerg, B., Bruzelius, N. & Rothengatter, W. (2003). *Megaprojects and risk: An anatomy of ambition.* Cambridge University Press.

Flyvbjerg, B., Garbuio, M. & Lovallo, D. (2009). Delusion and deception in large infrastructure projects: Two models for explaining and preventing executive disaster. *California Management Review*, 51(2), 170–194.

Friedman, M. (1953). *Essays in positive economics.* University of Chicago Press.

Friedman, M. & Savage, L. J. (1948). The utility analysis of choices involving risk. *Journal of Political Economy*, 56(4), 279–304.

Gigerenzer, G. & Todd, P. M. (1999). *Simple heuristics that make us smart.* Oxford University Press.

Gilovich, T., Griffin, D. & Kahneman, D. (2002). *Heuristics and biases: The psychology of intuitive judgement.* Cambridge University Press.

Hacking, I. (2006). *The emergence of probability* (2nd ed.). Cambridge University Press.

Hannaford, I. (1972). Machiavelli's concept of virtù in *The prince* and the discourses reconsidered. *Political Studies*, 20(2), 185–189.

Hirschman, A. O. (1967). *Development projects observed.* Brookings Institution.

Kahneman, D. (2011). *Thinking fast and slow.* Penguin.

Kahneman, D., Sibony, O. & Sunstein, C. R. (2021). *Noise: A flaw in human judgment.* William Collins.

Kahneman, D., Slovic, P. & Tversky, A. (1982). *Judgment under uncertainty: Heuristics and biases.* Cambridge University Press.

Kahneman, D. & Tversky, A. (1979). Prospect theory: An analysis of decision under risk. *Econometrica*, 47(2), 263–291.

Kay, J. & King, M. (2020). *Radical uncertainty: Decision-making for an unknowable future.* Bridge Street Press.

Keynes, J. M. (1921). *A treatise on probability.* Macmillan.

Keynes, J. M. (1937). The general theory of employment. *Quarterly Journal of Economics*, 51(2), 209–223.

Keynes, J. M. (1961). *The general theory of employment, interest and money.* Macmillan.

Klein, G. (2017). *Sources of power: How people make decisions* (20th Anniversary ed.). MIT Press.

Knight, F. H. (1921). *Risk, uncertainty and profit.* Houghton Mifflin.

LeRoy, S. F. & Singell, Jr., L. D. (1987). Knight on risk and uncertainty. *Journal of Political Economy*, 95(2), 394–406.

Lovallo, D. & Kahneman, D. (2003). Delusions of success. *Harvard Business Review*, 81(7), 56–63.

Machiavelli, N. (1961). *The prince.* Penguin.

Persky, J. (2001). Cost-benefit analysis and the classical creed. *Journal of Economic Perspectives*, 15(4), 199–208.

Porter, T. M. (2020). *Trust in numbers: The pursuit of objectivity in science and public life* (2nd ed.). Princeton University Press.

Ramasesh, R. V. & Browning, T. R. (2014). A conceptual framework for tackling knowable unknown unknowns in project management. *Journal of Operations Management*, 32(4), 190–204.

Ramsey, F. P. (1990). *Philosophical papers.* Cambridge University Press.

Rosenhead, J. & Mingers, J. (2001). *Rational analysis for a problematic world: Problem structuring methods for complexity, uncertainty, and conflict* (2nd ed.). John Wiley and Sons.

Runde, J. (1998). Clarifying Frank Knight's discussion of the meaning of risk and uncertainty. *Cambridge Journal of Economics*, 22(5), 539–546.

Savage, L. J. (1954). *The foundations of statistics.* John Wiley and Sons.

Savage, L. J. (1971). Elicitation of personal probabilities and expectations. *Journal of the American Statistical Association*, 66(336), 783–801.

Sawyer, J. E. (1952). Entrepreneurial error and economic growth. *Explorations in Economic History*, 4(4), 199.

Schoemaker, P. J. H. (1982). The expected utility model: Its variants, purposes, evidence and limitations. *Journal of Economic Literature*, 20(2), 529–563.

Schoemaker, P. J. H. (1995). Scenario planning: A tool for strategic thinking. *Sloan Management Review*, 36(2), 25–50.

Schumpeter, J. A. (1942). *Capitalism, socialism, and democracy*. Harper and Brothers.

Shiller, R. J. (2015). *Irrational exuberance*. Princeton University Press.

Simon, H. A. (1955). A behavioral model of rational choice. *Quarterly Journal of Economics*, 69(1), 99–118.

Skinner, Q. (2000). *Machiavelli: A very short introduction*. Oxford University Press.

Smith, A. (1776). *An inquiry into the nature and causes of the wealth of nations*. Strahan & Cadell.

Spetzler, C. S. & Stael von Holstein, C.-A. S. (1975). Probability encoding in decision analysis. *Management Science*, 22(3), 340–358.

Taleb, N. N. (2007). *The black swan: The impact of the highly improbable*. Random House.

Vaara, E., Sonenshein, S. & Boje, D. (2016). Narratives as sources of stability and change in organizations: Approaches and directions for future research. *Academy of Management Annals*, 10(1), 495–560.

Vick, S. G. (2002). *Degrees of belief: Subjective probability and engineering judgment*. ASCE Press.

Vickerman, R. (2007). Cost-benefit analysis and large-scale infrastructure projects: State of the art and challenges. *Environment and Planning B: Planning and Design*, 34(4), 598–610.

Vickerman, R. (2017). Beyond cost-benefit analysis: The search for a comprehensive evaluation of transport investment. *Research in Transportation Economics*, 63(C), 5–12.

Von Neumann, J. & Morgenstern, O. (1944). *Theory of games and economic behavior*. Princeton University Press.

Wack, P. (1985). Scenarios: Uncharted waters ahead. *Harvard Business Review*, 63(5), 73–89.

Westgaard, S., Fleten, S.-E., Negash, A., Botterud, A., Bogaard, K. & Verling, T. H. (2021). Performing price scenario analysis and stress testing using quantile regression: A case study of the Californian electricity market. *Energy*, 214(C), 118796.

Whitehead, A. N. (1926). *Science and the modern world*. Cambridge University Press.

Winch, G. M. & Maytorena-Sanchez, E. (2011). Managing risk and uncertainty on projects: A cognitive approach. In P. W. G. Morris, J. K. Pinto & J. Söderlund (Eds), *The Oxford handbook of project management* (pp. 345–364). Oxford University Press.

Wood, N. (1967). Machiavelli's concept of virtù reconsidered. *Political Studies*, 15(2), 159–172.

3. Complexity

Tyson R. Browning

3.1 INTRODUCTION

Complexity is an increasingly prominent characteristic of contemporary society, business, and work. Even so, the term complexity is often sloppily overused as a catch-all descriptor for project challenges; in particular, it is often conflated with project uncertainty. Based on systems theory, complexity is primarily an objective, structural characteristic of any system. Closely related to complexity is the concept of complicatedness, a subjective, observer-dependent characteristic relative to a system. Complexity and complicatedness are both increased by various factors, and both in turn cause increased uncertainty in projects. 'Simplicity' implies a low degree of complexity or complicatedness. Drawing heavily from two prior sources (Ramasesh & Browning, 2014; Browning & Ramasesh, 2015), this chapter discusses how these factors increase project complexity and complicatedness – all with the objective of providing project managers with a better understanding of how to manage them rather than be managed by them.

This chapter takes a relatively static view of complexity and complicatedness, although both will evolve over the course of a project. Some have made this explicit by using terms such as 'dynamic complexity' (Brady & Davies, 2014) and emphasizing the importance of the speed or pace of the change (Shenhar & Dvir, 2007). Actually, a project fulfils the criteria for being not just a dynamically complex system but a complex adaptive system (CAS), a system composed of independent but connected agents who collectively adapt and self-organize, causing the overall behaviour of the system to emerge over time (e.g., Holland, 1992; Kauffman, 1993; Chapter 14). Even where such has been noted (e.g., Kurtz & Snowden, 2003), the attributes distinguishing a CAS from a merely complex system are not explicitly highlighted but rather lumped into a definition of project complexity. Due to limitations of space, this chapter will avoid such conflations and keep the focus on static complexity, while calling for further work to define a dynamic project explicitly as a CAS (e.g., Lévárdy & Browning, 2009; Daniel & Daniel, 2019). Furthermore, this chapter positions complexity and complicatedness as contributors to project uncertainty, rather than the other way around.

3.2 PROJECT SUBSYSTEMS

A project system includes at least five important subsystems (or domains) – result, process, organization, tools, and goals (Browning et al., 2006; Browning & Ramasesh, 2015). Each subsystem consists of related elements. A project's result is the thing it produces – such as a new product, service, or deliverable – which consists of related parts of the project's deliverable(s) (e.g., product components, service actions, sections of a report, etc.). A project's process is the network of all of the activities done to get its result. These activities have input–output relationships that create dependencies. A project's organization is the individuals and teams doing the work (executing the process); they relate in terms of communication, at least. A project's tools are the non-human resources and tools (including software) used to accomplish the work; these may also have input–output relationships (e.g., data import/export). And a project's goals are the requirements and objectives for its result, how that is achieved (process), who is involved (organization), and the means at their disposal (tools); goals may be reinforcing or competing, implying relationships among them. Thus, a project contains subsystems of interrelated elements – components, activities, organizational units, tools, and goals – all contributing to its complexity.

3.3   COMPLEXITY

Complexity theory provides useful insights on sources and types of complexity and the behaviour of complex systems, including the emergence of unanticipated behaviours. Hence, complexity is typically defined in the context of systems. Weaver (1948), Simon (1962), and Warfield (2002) provided some of the foundational works on complexity theory which, like systems theory (but unlike concepts of uncertainty and risk), formally originated in the twentieth century. It is currently impossible to characterize the complexity of large physical, biological, and sociological systems in a way that allows us to recognize and fully understand all of their elements and relationships. Weaver distinguished 'disorganized complexity' – such as that manifest by a large number of gas molecules in a chamber, where the overall behaviour of the system can be described statistically and predicted probabilistically – from 'organized complexity', where the number of elements is smaller (but not small), but the relationships give rise to less easily describable and predictable (emergent) behaviour. Bar-Yam (1997) explained how a system's complexity depends on the amount of information required to describe it, governed by its number of distinct possible states.

Complexity has been studied in a variety of contexts and defined and characterized in a variety of ways. Homer-Dixon (2000) discussed complexity in a non-technical, managerially relevant way. The most widely acknowledged notions of complexity base it upon a system's number of elements and their interconnections or relationships (Simon, 1962; Kauffman & Levin, 1987). These two properties set a foundation for a more nuanced definition of complexity as a function of both its elements and their relationships, as determined by the factors explained below.

3.3.1   Element Complexity

Element complexity is prominent in the complexity science literature. For example, many have discussed the influence of the number and variety of elements on complexity (e.g., Simon, 1962; Kauffman & Levin, 1987; Baccarini, 1996; Bar-Yam, 1997; Frizelle, 1998; Shenhar, 2001; Chu et al., 2003; Geraldi et al., 2011; Jacobs & Swink, 2011; Vidal et al., 2011). Simply put, having many more elements of the same type increases complexity somewhat, as does having even a few elements of different types, while having both many and different elements increases complexity geometrically. Ceteris paribus, a project with a greater number and/ or variety of components in its result (e.g., function points), activities in its process, people/ teams/locations/cultures in its organization, tools, and/or goals (e.g., requirements, use cases) is more complex.

However, the factors commonly accepted as measures of system complexity, such as the numbers of elements and relationships, depend on the chosen model of a system – i.e., on the definitions of the elements and relationships. One model might break a system down into ten elements (e.g., a process composed of ten activities), whereas another model might represent the same system in terms of only five elements (e.g., the same process in terms of five larger activities). These are different maps of the same territory, drawn to different scales. However, when used to operationalize measures of system complexity, the model with ten elements and 20 relationships will yield a different result than the model with five elements and six relationships. Any overly simplistic approach to modelling system complexity (such as one that depends only on the numbers of elements and relationships) would be expected to have low inter-rater reliability. Hence, to adjust for these differences, one must account for the internal complexity of both the elements and the relationships. If the second model (with five elements and six relationships) was explicit that each of its elements and relationships was more complex than those in the first model, then both models of the same system would be more likely to yield similar overall measures of complexity. Internal complexity is thus a nested factor to account for the frequent impossibility of defining system elements uniformly.

Lack of robustness accounts for the pressures faced by elements (result components, process activities, organization units, particular tools, and various goals) to change over the course of a project. Whether or not they must indeed change to accommodate this pressure depends on their robustness, their ability to provide a desired result across a broad range of situations. For example, best practices in software development make source code modules robust against spurious inputs. Similarly, project activities that can achieve their desired result despite variations in inputs, resources, and circumstances make projects less complex and more predictable. Buffers, safety margins, and slack help insulate against changes and can contribute to robustness, while drives towards greater efficiency may remove these protections, making projects brittle and leading to emergent problems (Lawson, 2001).

3.3.2   Relationship Complexity

As with the number of elements, the number of relationships that exists among them influences a system's complexity. Systems with more relationships among their elements have an increased chance of propagating causal effects (Simon, 1962; Kauffman & Levin, 1987). Chu et al. (2003) and Jacobs and Swink (2011) pinpointed connectivity among system elements as a fundamental cause of complexity. A project with more dependencies and constraints among its people, tasks, and tools is more complex than one whose various components are relatively independent.

Again, the variety of relationships among elements also matters. A system of five elements with the same type of relationship is less complex than a system of five elements with many possible relationships, from which a greater variety of behaviours could emerge. The latter system requires more information to describe (Bar-Yam, 1997). For example, a project activity that provides the same report to ten recipients has a less complex job than one having to provide a different, customized report to each. A software tool that must exchange data in different ways with each of eight other tools presents a more complex situation than if the interfaces all used the same standard or protocol.

Relationship criticality, where some relationships matter more than others, also contributes to complexity. Not all relationships affect complexity to the same extent. For example, in a project's activity network (process), non-redundant arcs (dependencies) have a greater effect than redundant ones (Browning & Yassine, 2010). In the result, spatial relationships among components are especially important, because other types of relationships, such as data transfer, can be easier to establish over distances (Eppinger & Browning, 2012). In the organization, information asymmetry implies that some organizational units have more valuable information (and more power) than others, which in turn can diminish camaraderie and trust (IRGC, 2010). The types of relationships that matter most may very well differ by project subsystem. Across varied subsystems, however, Chu et al. (2003) identified any non-linear relationships as particularly salient. As the number and extent of critical, sophisticated relationships among its elements increases, so does a project's complexity.

The relationships among the elements of a system may result in particular patterns that increase or decrease complexity and emergent behaviour. Three such patterns are modules, cycles, and hubs. Simon (1962) described how a system's decomposition into subsystems (modules) affects its behaviour, particularly with more 'nearly decomposable' (nearly modular) systems having relatively strong intra-subsystem relationships and relatively weak inter-subsystem relationships. In contrast, tightly coupled systems are highly related, meaning that a change in one element can have rapid, multiple effects on others, sometimes causing the system to overreact. For example, Perrow (1984) noted the drastically different response to someone shouting 'fire' at a crowded beach versus in a packed stadium, because the latter is a tightly coupled system, constraining the people inside to leave through a small number of exits, forcing many interactions. See Engel et al. (2017) for a recent example of leveraging a result architecture in terms of modularity.

In organizations, Thompson (1967) distinguished between dependent (unilateral) and interdependent (bilateral or coupled) relationships among elements, of which the latter are particularly influential (e.g., Geraldi et al., 2011) because they spawn feedback loops, iterations, or cycles that are non-linear and counterintuitive (Forrester, 1971; IRGC, 2010) and that propagate perturbations – e.g., in the product (e.g., Clarkson et al., 2004), process (Lévárdy & Browning, 2009), and goal (Vidal et al., 2011) subsystems. Hirschi and Frey (2002) found that the time required for humans to solve a coupled parameter design problem increased geometrically as the number of coupled elements increased linearly. Sosa et al. (2013) found that software components involved in architectural cycles (coupling interrelationships among two or more code modules) were significantly more likely to contain bugs. These examples highlight the challenges posed by the increased complexity caused by cycles in system architectures.

Hubs may also affect a system's complexity and behaviour. Unlike random networks, where each element's number of relationships is normally distributed, scale-free networks contain a few dominant hub elements, each with a relatively large number of relationships, their elements' number of relationships follows a power-law distribution, and vicious cycles of feedback within them exacerbate cascading failures (Homer-Dixon, 2000). For example, in software development projects, Sosa et al. (2011) found that the presence of hubs in the result (software code) had a highly significant effect on its likelihood of containing bugs: architectures with more hubs had fewer bugs, up to a point. In the project organization, hubs are centralized individuals or teams with significant influence over the network, and the abrupt removal of a hub person could cause project failure. Consequential patterns of relationships such as hubs, cycles, and modules can engender complexity.

Relationships among elements may also differ in their internal complexity. Complex relationships, such as those in a supply chain or between countries, can amplify the effects of the other factors driving relationship complexity. One complex dyad can generate more complex behaviours for a system than several simple relationships. In a project, a complex relationship between two important result components, two large teams in the organization, or two competing goals can result in greater complexity than several simple and more straightforward relationships. For example, a multifaceted, ongoing relationship with a single supplier can cause more project complexity than several simple purchasing arrangements with commodity suppliers. Similarly, relationships among elements in a project's five subsystems will vary in their internal complexity.

Since many project elements link to its external context or environment, external relationships also affect complexity. The greater the number, variety, criticality, and internal complexity of such relationships, the greater the possibility that the external context will affect the internal elements, thereby amplifying complexity. Chu et al. (2003) referred to this situation as 'radical openness' and 'contextuality', both of which 'make the control and prediction of complex systems very difficult'. Note that defining the boundary of a complex system is a challenging task in itself. In modelling a complex system, one defines arbitrary boundaries around it, often implicitly by the very act of naming it. Large, complex projects might contain several segments dispersed across geographical regions, markets, political situations, and regulatory agencies (de Weck & Eckert, 2007). The resulting diversity of external interfaces increases complexity in the process, organization, and goal subsystems, at least.

3.4   COMPLICATEDNESS

The factors of complexity presented above are intrinsic and largely objective characteristics of a system (albeit depending on one's definition of an element in each subsystem, which can be subjective). In contrast, we can distinguish complicatedness (or cognitive complexity) as the more subjective, observer-dependent aspect of complexity. Using an example from Tang and Salminen (2001), a car with an automatic transmission is more complex than one with a manual transmission, because the former has more parts and intricate linkages. Yet its complicatedness differs between drivers (to whom the automatic transmission seems less complicated) and mechanics who must fix them (to whom the automatic transmission seems more complicated). A software application's complex code may be hidden by a simple and elegant user interface. A stereotypical professor's office, stacked with books and papers, looks like a complete mess to a visitor, but somehow the professor knows exactly where to find things. These examples show us that there is more to consider about complexity than the objective, intrinsic properties of a system: it also exists in the eye of the beholder. A system can be more or less well organized and/or hidden from various observers, and these observers have varying capabilities to understand the system, so they will deem it more or less complicated, apart from its underlying complexity. Although complexity and complicatedness may correlate and interact, they do not have a generalizable causal relationship. Suh (2001) thus distinguished 'real' and 'imaginary' complexity as orthogonal dimensions. Simon (1956) used the analogy of scissors, where one blade represents the structure of the environment and the other the cognitive limitations of the observer. Complexity can be a desirable property of projects – often as the price of increased capabilities – but increased complicatedness is seldom (if ever) desirable. Separating complicatedness from complexity improves the clarity by which projects can be described and analysed. Thus, we use complicatedness as an orthogonal construct to complexity.

We are especially interested in the perceptions of the project manager, a project's main decision maker. Again, we can explore these with respect to each of a project's five subsystems: the result (e.g., a product design is unprecedented or unintuitively structured), the process (e.g., the project's activities are unusual or grouped unclearly), the organization (e.g., the project's participants have not worked together before or are not fluent in the same language), the tools (e.g., the project is using new software for the first time), or the goals (e.g., the project's requirements are unfamiliar and unclear).

Encapsulated interactions group a system's inputs and outputs into a limited number, type, and variety, such as a limited number of knobs, buttons, or options for operating a system or a limited number of states resulting from its use. Encapsulation often implies that the system includes mechanisms for robustly suppressing diverse behaviours into limited classes of output – meaning that it is tougher to 'mess it up'. Compared with a manual transmission in an automobile, an automatic transmission is an example of encapsulated interaction. (Note that such encapsulation can also affect the objective complexity of a system by increasing the robustness of its elements and/or decreasing the variety of their relationships, but the addition of internal mechanisms to accomplish this can also increase the number and variety of elements.) A project manager might manage a large project at the level of only a few major work packages, a few major deliverables, and a few large teams, and the status reports provided for reviews might be 'high-level' documents with only 'big picture' statements. The project may thus appear less complicated, whereas exposing more of the details would make it seem more so.

Intuitive organization of its elements and relationships makes a system seem simpler to an observer. Returning to the example of the professor's messy office, the same number of items (books, papers, etc.), filed and organized by topic, would seem less complicated to a typical observer. Similarly, if the elements and relationships in a project's subsystems seem disorganized, or if the organization scheme does not allow for easy extraction of the information needed to support managerial decisions, then the project will seem more complicated. A process flowchart with many crossing lines (as opposed to a much cleaner one with the same number of lines but without any of them crossing) or an organization chart with unclear titles and reporting relationships are both examples of system representations more likely to befuddle an observer.

Novelty is another subjective, observer-dependent attribute of a project (Brockhoff, 2006). As an observer gains experience with a system, s/he develops intuition and learning about its structure and behaviour: the system becomes more familiar. The observer can identify the system's components, relationships, and behaviours and better anticipate cause-and-effect relationships (Schrader et al., 1993). Novelty represents a lack of such experience and familiarity (Rosenkopf & McGrath, 2011). Tatikonda and Montoya-Weiss (2001) found that a higher level of technology novelty leads to greater task uncertainty (process subsystem). Sauser et al. (2009) noted that novelty is related to a product's (result's) uniqueness in its relation to the market and to the uncertainty in its goals. Novelty also pertains to the relationships in the organization – e.g., the classic 'storming, forming, and norming' phases (Tuchman, 1965). Interestingly, overspecialization (less novelty in one area) can create situations of increased novelty with respect to other aspects of a project outside an observer's area of expertise. Increased novelty makes a project more complicated.

Observer capability. Some observers relate better to some systems than to others and will understand some systems more readily than others. If an observer has a high aptitude for understanding a particular system, and if the system's behaviours seem logical and intuitive, then he or she is in a position to 'get down the learning curve' faster. Other variables, such as an observer's relative attention to a system, could also be identified and included, but here we subsume aptitude, attention, and related aspects into observer capability.

Very large scale-up. When a system exceeds a certain size, an observer will have difficulty accounting for all of its elements and relationships. The threshold will vary by observer, but it has been noted to occur at about 7±2 elements (Miller, 1956). As system size increases, an observer's mental model of the system becomes increasingly abstracted and disconnected from the details. Long-time horizons also pose challenges. For example, feedbacks loops can be especially pernicious when they take a long time to occur, because they inhibit observers from connecting causes and effects (Forrester, 1971; IRGC, 2010). In such situations, a system's complexity (element and relationship) can increase its complicatedness.

Divergent viewpoints. The famous Asian fable of the blind men and the elephant (Linton, 1878, pp. 150–152) illustrated how complex systems are seen and (partially) understood from multiple perspectives, each of which may contain some validity (i.e., equifinality, e.g., Beven, 2006). Contemporary projects include many specialists. For example, a product development project may include specialists in reliability, sustainability, usability, safety, supportability, cost, security, quality, supplier selection, production, marketing, etc. The greater the diversity of these viewpoints, the greater the complicatedness of the project (Jones & Anderson, 2005), because discussions among project stakeholders may not confirm and validate an individual's mental model; rather, such discussions may raise additional questions and even create confusion. This situation may be desirable when it serves to dispel ignorance and catch problems, but shepherding project participants and stakeholders towards mutual understanding and eventual agreement takes time and effort. Meetings, conversations, common processes, interactive tools, communication and visualization capabilities, and other integrative mechanisms may all contribute to alignment. Although specialists often develop their own jargon to communicate more efficiently among themselves, it is tedious to develop the common frame of reference needed for multidisciplinary endeavours such as projects, so this effort is often short-changed. If the diverse viewpoints of the project participants and stakeholders, which can add value initially, fail to converge for the purposes of the project, then these divergent viewpoints will increase complicatedness.

3.5   PROJECT CONTEXT

Every project exists within a larger context. A project may be part of a larger portfolio of projects, or it might have multiple stakeholders who have competing visions and requirements for success. A project's ideal software tools might be consistent with its parent organization's standards for multiproject commonality, or they may be completely incompatible. A project's context contains many social, technical, political, economic, and environmental elements (e.g., Maylor & Turner, 2017) that influence the elements in each of its five subsystems. Although such contextual aspects fall outside a project's boundary and thus do not directly determine its internal complexity or complicatedness, additional complexity or complicatedness in a project's environment do indirectly affect these within a project by causing additional activities, goals, relationships, etc. (as described above).

3.6   CONCLUSION

Project complexity and complicatedness often impede project success. Managers must find ways to appreciate, visualize, and manage both to deliver value to stakeholders. Several factors drive project complexity and complicatedness, and understanding them provides a step towards better management. Complexity and complicatedness may often correlate, but there are many exceptions to this (such as the example of the automatic transmission) that managers may exploit. These factors can occur within and between at least five key subsystems as well as with its context. Modelling all of these elements and relationships requires advanced techniques such as multidomain matrices (Eppinger & Browning, 2012) and architecture frameworks (Browning, 2013). Unfortunately, many reviews of project complexity mix the five subsystems and the factors driving complexity and complicatedness into a single list, thereby confounding multiple dimensions into one and oversimplifying a complex phenomenon. Where appropriate, simplicity (e.g., Siegel & Etzkorn, 2013) is a welcome antidote to both complexity and complicatedness, albeit while remembering Einstein's caveat to 'keep things as simple as possible, but not simpler'.

REFERENCES

Baccarini, D. (1996). The concept of project complexity – a review. *International Journal of Project Management,* 4(4), 201–204.

Bar-Yam, Y. (1997). *Dynamics of complex systems.* Addison-Wesley.

Beven, K. (2006). A manifesto for the equifinality thesis. *Journal of Hydrology,* 320(1–2), 18–36.

Brady, T. & Davies, A. (2014). Managing structural and dynamic complexity: A tale of two projects. *Project Management Journal,* 45(4), 21–38.

Brockhoff, K. (2006). On the novelty dimension in project management. *Project Management Journal,* 37(3), 26–36.

Browning, T. R. (2013). Managing complex project process models with a process architecture framework. *International Journal of Project Management,* 32(2), 229–241.

Browning, T. R., Fricke, E. & Negele, H. (2006). Key concepts in modeling product development processes. *Systems Engineering,* 9(2), 104–128.

Browning, T. R. & Ramasesh, R. V. (2015). Reducing unwelcome surprises in project management. *MIT Sloan Management Review,* 56(3), 53–62.

Browning, T. R. & Yassine, A. A. (2010). A random generator of resource-constrained multi-project network problems. *Journal of Scheduling,* 13(2), 143–161.

Chu, D., Strand, R. & Fjelland, R. (2003). Theories of complexity: Common denominators of complex systems. *Complexity,* 8(3), 19–30.

Clarkson, P. J., Simons, C. & Eckert, C. (2004). Predicting change propagation in complex design. *Journal of Mechanical Design,* 126(5), 788–797.

Daniel, E. & Daniel, P. A. (2019). Megaprojects as complex adaptive systems: The Hinkley Point C case. *International Journal of Project Management,* 37(8), 1017–1033.

de Weck, O. & Eckert, C. (2007). *A classification of uncertainty for early product and system design.* Working Paper, ESD-WP-2007-10. Massachusetts Institute of Technology, Engineering Systems Division.

Engel, A., Browning, T. R. & Reich, Y. (2017). Designing products for adaptability: Insights from four industrial cases. *Decision Sciences,* 48(5), 875–917.

Eppinger, S. D. & Browning, T. R. (2012). *Design structure matrix methods and applications*. MIT Press.

Forrester, J. W. (1971). Counterintuitive behavior of social systems. *Technology Review*, 73(3), 52–68.

Frizelle, G. (1998). *The management of complexity in manufacturing: A strategic route map to competitive advantage through the control and measurement of complexity*. Business Intelligence.

Geraldi, J., Maylor, H. & Williams, T. (2011). Now, let's make it really complex (complicated): A systematic review of the complexities of projects. *International Journal of Operations & Production Management*, 31(9), 966–990.

Hirschi, N. W. & Frey, D. D. (2002). Cognition and complexity: An experiment on the effect of coupling in engineering design. *Research in Engineering Design*, 13(3), 123–131.

Holland, J. H. (1992). *Adaptation in natural and artificial systems*. MIT Press.

Homer-Dixon, T. (2000). *The ingenuity gap*. Alfred A. Knopf.

IRGC (2010). *The emergence of risks: Contributing factors*. International Risk Governance Council.

Jacobs, M. A. & Swink, M. (2011). Product portfolio architectural complexity and operational performance: Incorporating the roles of learning and fixed assets. *Journal of Operations Management*, 29(7–8), 677–691.

Jones, B. S. & Anderson, P. (2005). Diversity as a determinant of system complexity. *GIST Technical Report*, 2005-1, Glasgow School of Art.

Kauffman, S. A. (1993). *The origins of order: Self-organization and selection in evolution*. Oxford University Press.

Kauffman, S. A. & Levin, S. (1987). Towards a general theory of adaptive walks on rugged landscapes. *Journal of Theoretical Biology*, 128(1), 11–45.

Kurtz, C. F. & Snowden, D. J. (2003). The new dynamics of strategy: Sense-making in a complex and complicated world. *IBM Systems Journal*, 42(3), 462–483.

Lawson, M. B. B. (2001). In praise of slack: Time is of the essence. *Academy of Management Executive*, 15(3), 125–135.

Lévárdy, V. & Browning, T. R. (2009). An adaptive process model to support product development project management. *IEEE Transactions on Engineering Management*, 56(4), 600–620.

Linton, W. J. (1878). *Poetry of America: Selections from one hundred American poets from 1776 to 1876*. William Clowes and Sons.

Maylor, H. & Turner, N. (2017). Understand, reduce, respond: Project complexity management theory and practice. *International Journal of Operations and Production Management*, 37(8), 1076–1093.

Miller, G. A. (1956). The magical number seven, plus or minus two: Some limits on our capacity for processing information. *Psychological Review*, 63(2), 81–97.

Perrow, C. (1984). *Normal accidents: Living with high-risk technologies*. Basic Books.

Ramasesh, R. V. & Browning, T. R. (2014). A conceptual framework for tackling knowable unknown unknowns in project management. *Journal of Operations Management*, 32(4), 190–204.

Rosenkopf, L. & McGrath, P. (2011). Advancing the conceptualization and operationalization of novelty in organizational research. *Organization Science*, 22(5), 1297–1311.

Sauser, B. J., Reilly, R. R. & Shenhar, A. J. (2009). Why projects fail? How contingency theory can provide new insights – a comparative analysis of NASA's Mars Climate Orbiter loss. *International Journal of Project Management*, 27(7), 665–679.

Schrader, S., Riggs, W. M. & Smith, R. P. (1993). Choice over uncertainty and ambiguity in technical problem solving. *Journal of Engineering and Technology Management*, 10(1), 73–99.

Shenhar, A. (2001). One size does not fit all projects: Exploring classical contingency domains. *Management Science*, 47(3), 394–414.

Shenhar, A. & Dvir, D. (2007). *Reinventing project management*. Harvard Business School Press.

Siegel, A. & Etzkorn, I. (2013). When simplicity is the solution. *Wall Street Journal*, 29 March. www.wsj.com/articles/SB10001424127887324000704578386652879032748.

Simon, H. A. (1956). Rational choice and the structure of the environment. *Psychological Review*, 63(2), 129–138.

Simon, H. A. (1962). The architecture of complexity. *Proceedings of the American Philosophical Society*, 106(6), 467–482.

Sosa, M. E., Mihm, J. & Browning, T. R. (2011). Degree distribution and quality in complex engineered systems. *Journal of Mechanical Design*, 133(10).

Sosa, M. E., Mihm, J. & Browning, T. R. (2013). Linking cyclicality and product quality. *Manufacturing and Service Operations Management*, 15(3), 473–491.

Suh, N. P. (2001). *Axiomatic design: Advances and applications.* Oxford University Press.

Tang, V. & Salminen, V. (2001). *Towards a theory of complicatedness: Framework for complex systems analysis and design.* Conference presentation, 13th International Conference on Engineering Design, Glasgow, 21–23 August.

Tatikonda, M. V. & Montoya-Weiss, M. M. (2001). Integrating operations and marketing perspectives of product innovation: The influence of organizational process factors and capabilities on development performance. *Management Science*, 47(1), 151–172.

Thompson, J. D. (1967). *Organizations in action.* McGraw-Hill.

Tuchman, B. W. (1965). Developmental sequence in small groups. *Psychological Bulletin*, 63(6), 384–399.

Vidal, L.-A., Marle, F. & Bocquet, J.-C. (2011). Measuring project complexity using the analytic hierarchy process. *International Journal of Project Management*, 29(6), 718–727.

Warfield, J. N. (2002). Understanding complexity: Thought and behavior. AJAR Publishing Company.

Weaver, W. (1948). Science and complexity. *American Scientist*, 36, 536–544.

4. Projectivity
Graham M. Winch

4.1 INTRODUCTION

We largely take for granted in research on complex project organizing (CPO) what projects are. The Project Management Institute's succinct definition does the heavy lifting for most purposes: 'a temporary endeavor undertaken to create a unique product, service or result'. However, this tells us little about what projects do and how they do it. In other words, what roles do projects play in socio-economic processes more generally? There is a variety of proximate answers to this question, including:

- They are fundamental to economic development (Hirschman, 1967).
- They are the means of strategy implementation (Shenhar & Dvir, 2007).
- They create value (Winter & Szczepanek, 2008).
- They are creating new forms of society (Lundin et al., 2015).

These role definitions are largely complementary even if they come from different theoretical perspectives. In this chapter contributing to the core concepts of CPO, we build on these definitions to argue that projects are fundamentally about how we (individually and collectively) create the future.

In order to do this, we introduce a new concept to research on CPO that we suggest is core to developing a full analysis of what projects do as they create the future: projectivity (Emirbayer & Mische, 1998). We argue that we need this addition to the conceptual armoury of CPO because it makes meaningful the other three core concepts of CPO as discussed in the introduction to Part I. We suggest that the projectivity concept includes two dimensions: future-perfect-thinking (Schutz, 1967a), as the cognitive process of conceptualizing a desired future state, and projecting (Defoe, 1697; Schutz, 1967b), as the dialogic process of articulating that desired future state to others through narrating. These processes, we suggest, are the micro-foundations of project shaping (Miller & Lessard, 2000) and therefore the essential precursors to the socio-economic process of mobilizing resources (financial, technological, and human) to deliver those desired future states.

In order to introduce this new concept, we first present a framework from the sociology of action that locates projectivity in the broader context of human activity. This establishes future-perfect-thinking and projecting as the micro-foundations of project shaping which we illustrate with some empirical examples of projecting. Second, we turn to the macro-level of analysis and show that projecting is also important conceptually for understanding the socio-economic implications of projectivity. We then present the argument that CPO has become such an important part of economy and society that we are witnessing a projectification (Midler, 1995) towards a different type of society – a project society (Lundin et al., 2015).

4.2   PROJECTIVITY AS ACTION

We suggest that the concept of 'projectivity' allows us to theorize the proposition that projects are about how we create the future. The principal theoretical concern of Emirbayer and Mische (1998) is the nature of human agency. They argue that it is fundamentally temporal with a 'chordal triad' of the 'iterative' which reflects on the past, the 'projective' which generates the future, and the 'evaluative' in which experience is contextualized in the present. Within this triad, they define projectivity as 'the imaginative generation by actors of possible future trajectories of action, in which received structures of thought and action may be creatively reconfigured in relation to actors' hopes, fear and desires for the future' (1998, p. 971).

Emirbayer and Mische draw heavily on the phenomenology of future-perfect-thinking (Schutz, 1967a, 1967b) in developing their argument. Schutz argues that all purposive action, as opposed to reactive behaviour, has the nature of a 'protention' or a vision of a completed future state that gives present meaning to the subsequent action which will bring forth that future state. Thus, while the protention is cognitive in that it exists as a perceived future state, it is qualitatively different from a 'retention' which is inherently a perception about the past. However, because the protention, like a retention, is perceived as completed, 'the planned act has the temporal character of pastness' (1967a, p. 61) and is therefore thought of in the future-perfect tense formulated as 'will have been' in English.

In developing this perspective, Schutz emphasizes the motivational aspect of future-perfect-thinking, showing how it provides the future-oriented 'in-order-to' motive for an action in the present, rather than the present-oriented and past-oriented 'because' motive for behaviour. He thereby distinguishes action that is proactive and future-oriented, and behaviour that is reactive and past-oriented. He is also careful to distinguish future-perfect-thinking from pure fantasy by the criterion of the feasibility of the act assessed in the knowledge of similar projections by others. However, the projection remains 'empty'; it is an abstraction, which indicates the direction of travel, but not the journey whose steps remain to be filled in: 'Projecting like any other anticipation carries along its empty horizons which will be filled in merely by the materialization of the anticipated event. This constitutes the intrinsic uncertainty of all forms of projecting' (Schutz, 1967b, p. 69).

For CPO, we can think of this materialization process of 'filling in' as project delivery constituted by successive cycles of 'future-making' (Comi & Whyte 2018; Winch & Sergeeva, 2022). We also clarify Schutz's use of 'projecting' as dialogic in distinction and complement to the cognitive process of future-perfect-thinking. Thus, in our definition, projectivity captures the cognitive and dialogic processes of imagining and articulating desired future states in which time's arrow flows from right to left. This then stimulates the related process of filling in how we achieve that future state in which time's arrow flows from left to right (Winch & Sergeeva, 2022). This results in the materialization of the anticipated event in the form of a valued asset. How does this micro-level of analysis relate to what projects do in socio-economic terms? We suggest that the link is through project narratives defined as words that do things (Austin, 1962) with performative intent (Sergeeva & Winch, 2021).

4.3   PROJECTING AS NARRATING

If future-perfect-thinking is about convincing oneself of the viability of a project, projecting is about convincing others (Winch & Sergeeva, 2022). It is therefore an essential part of what project leaders do (Winch et al., 2022). Projecting in this sense can be seen in these statements from the promotors – the people Defoe (1697) called 'projectors' – of some successful complex projects:
Joseph Roebling on the Brooklyn Bridge:

> The completed work, when constructed in accordance with my designs, will not only be the greatest bridge in existence, but will be the greatest engineering work of the continent, and of the age. (Cited in Shapira & Berndt, 1997, p. 339)

V. I. Lenin on electrification and economic development:

> Communism is Soviet power plus the electrification of the whole country. Otherwise the country will stay a small-peasant country. (Speech to the 8th All Russia Congress of Soviets, 22 December 1920)

John F. Kennedy on the Apollo programme:

> I believe that this nation should commit itself to achieving the goal, before this decade is out, of landing a man on the moon and returning him safely to the Earth. No single space project in this period will be more impressive to mankind, or more important for the long-range exploration of space; and none will be so difficult or expensive to accomplish. (Speech to a joint session of the US Congress, 25 May 1961)

Boris Johnson on achieving net zero:

> The coming industrial revolution is green power plus the electrification of the whole country. (Speech before the Annual Conference of the Confederation of British Industry, 22 November 2021)

One can also see in these quotations, particularly from Roebling and Kennedy, the aspiration for the 'technological sublime' of awesome architectural and engineering achievement (Frick, 2008), which is an important part of projecting. They also have meme-like qualities as indicated in the relationship between the Lenin and Johnson narratives.

We can see from these quotations from projectors the importance of articulating a desired future state for mobilizing the resources required for CPO from resource-rich stakeholders. Research on recent United Kingdom (UK) rail projects (Ninan & Sergeeva, 2021; Sergeeva & Winch, 2021) shows how the articulation of a desired future state was essential for the successful shaping of three recent major projects – even if delivery was another matter – and is playing a key part in the shaping of a fourth. For instance, in the case of the Elizabeth Line, a favourable cost-benefit calculation based on the present benefit of easing congestion for commuters did not mobilize adequate resources. It was only when a newly elected mayor advocated a vision of London in 2076 that resources were mobilized for a reconfigured project that connected to London's Heathrow Airport (Sergeeva & Winch, 2021). Similarly, the cost-benefit case for the HS2 project was widely criticized as weak, and it was only when the future-oriented benefit of 'levelling up' the UK economy was articulated that the project finally received the go-ahead (Oakervee, 2020). Thus, we can argue that the use of cost-benefit analysis (CBA) is inherently evaluative in the sense defined above, and therefore can only provide a *because-motive* for investment in a project, while the level of resources required for large complex projects requires a strong *in-order-to* motive for investment provided by projectivity. The two in combination are perhaps the most powerful.

This observation suggests that leadership by projectors, and the project narratives they articulate (Sergeeva & Winch, 2021), is worthy of greater research attention. However, we also suggest that a focus on projectors as individuals is limited, because such individuals work in social networks to mobilize the resources they need. This can be seen, for instance, from case studies of United States (US) advanced technology projects such as the ARPANET and Atlas programmes (Hughes, 1998). The ways in which urban elites across the public and private sectors mobilized around two bids for the Olympic Games in Manchester (Cochrane et al., 2002) which were never likely to succeed but did provide the basis for a successful 2002 Commonwealth Games (the second largest global sporting event) demonstrates the social nature of projecting in the twenty-first century. We need to move beyond projecting being just what project leaders do to its socio-economic implications at the macro-level that is Defoe's focus – what we might call *macro-projecting*. We do this by exploring two broad themes. One is about the contribution of projects – particularly infrastructure projects – to economic and social development. The second is about the implications for work and society of the increased 'projectification' of organizations.

4.4   PROJECTS AND SOCIETY

Capital investment projects are a fundamental – probably the fundamental – contributor to socio-economic development, but that investment must produce net benefits for that development to happen. If investment projects do not realize net benefits, then social and economic decline ensues. An important critique of transportation infrastructure investment argues that often such investment is wasted because of distortions in the investment appraisal process due either to optimism bias or to strategic misrepresentation (Flyvbjerg et al., 2003). The former is the result of delusion and the latter of deception in investment decision-making (Flyvbjerg et al., 2009), and the solution is held to be much greater rigour in investment appraisal and greater professionalism in CBA. However, as argued above, CBA is better at providing a because-motive for project shaping, while projecting the likes of Manchester's 'Olympic dreams' provides an in-order-to motive for project shaping. CBA's contribution is to help distinguish possibility from fantasy in those projections. Thus, an alternative view is that the inherent uncertainties of investment appraisal mean that the 'animal spirits' of investors are required as discussed in Chapter 2 rather than improved CBA practice. Many such investment projects will fail (Sawyer, 1952), but the overall net effect to the economy will be beneficial thanks to the 'hiding hand' of economic development projects (Hirschman, 1967). Here Hirschman evokes Smith's (1776) 'hidden hand' to the effect that individual profit-oriented activity has beneficial social outcomes. Both were apparently channelling Defoe's contention that a good investment has 'both the Essential Ends of a Project in it, Publick Good, and Private Advantage' (1697, p. 28).

Macro-projecting played an enormously important role in the first globalization during the latter part of the nineteenth century to 1914 known as the 'age of empire' (Hobsbawm, 1987). This was particularly true of transportation infrastructure (Linder, 1994; Middlemas,

1963) where colourful characters such as Thomas Brassey, Ferdinand de Lesseps, and Henry Meiggs built canals, ports, and railways across the world. As the energy intensity of the global economy deepened during the twentieth century, project-based firms (Chapter 17) such as Bechtel helped international owners in places like the Middle East to find the capital to invest in oil and gas and nuclear power projects and actively projected. Their strategy was 'if there's no project, we'll try to find one; if there's no client we'll try to assemble one; if there's no money we'll try to get them some' (cited Denton, 2016, p. 209). Most recently, China's Belt and Road Initiative (BRI) is a systematic attempt to project Chinese influence through infrastructure development projects (Hillman, 2020). In this, China is emulating the global activities of the European powers during the latter half of the nineteenth century and the US in the period after 1945.

Global projectivity has a dark side, however. As the normally prosaic *Engineering News Record* commented in 1921, a 'railway is a strategic tool of a foreign power and not a means, except incidentally, of developing the country through which it passes' (cited in Linder, 1994, frontispiece). Dam projects, in particular, have received widespread criticism, both within the US (Reisner, 1986) and globally (Scudder, 2017). BRI has come under criticism for generating unsustainable levels of debt in partner countries (*Financial Times*, 2021). A major challenge in the research agenda on projects and society is to address these issues while moving beyond the geopolitical posturing of the major international players in infrastructure development finance.

4.5   PROJECTIFICATION

An important trend over the last 30 years or so has been the growing 'projectification' (Midler, 1995) of many organizations, which has led to the development of the concept of a 'project society' (Lundin et al., 2015) as a society in which project forms of organization dominate economic activity. At one level this is a truism, because any economy that is growing and changing will have relatively high levels of capital investment, and the faster the growth the higher the proportion of capital investment and hence projects in society to deliver that investment. However, this macro-level observation hides an important organizational-level trend, which is the growing adoption of the routines associated with the type of project management that evolved on US aerospace projects as part of the 'project economy' (Nieto-Rodriguez, 2021). Driven by the increasing differentiation within organizations which in turn requires increasing integration (Morris, 1973), it is noticeable how this projectification process accelerated during the 1990s. Examples include new product development in the auto industry (Clark & Fujimoto, 1990; Cusumano & Nobeoka, 1998) in complement to the development of lean manufacturing in operations management (Womack et al., 1990), pharmaceuticals (Pisano, 1997), and manufacturing more widely (Bowen et al., 1994; Giard & Midler, 1993; Winch, 1994).

Presently, projectification is spreading to the public sector where, it is argued, the major challenges of delivering on new policy initiatives – often through spectacular failures in digital transformation projects (King & Crewe, 2013) – are being addressed through a much more project-orientated approach (Hodgson et al., 2019). In the case of the UK, this process of projectification includes the establishment of a public-private partnership to promote standardized project management methodologies and certifications against them (www.axelos.com); the development of strong, centralized project and programme governance processes (www.gov.uk/government/

organisations/infrastructure-and-projects-authority); and the formation of the project delivery profession as a distinctive career pathway (www.gov.uk/government/organisations/civil-service -project-delivery-profession) within the civil service. There are a few empirical studies of the projectification process in particular organizations – Midler (1993) provides the case of Renault, and for not-for-profit sectors see Winch et al. (2012) and Jałocha et al. (2019). We need many more studies to understand this important trend.

4.6   PROJECTING THE FUTURE OF PROJECTIVITY

Projectivity is at the heart of action on the grand challenges presently facing economy and society. Projectivity was fundamental to the exit from the suppression of economic and social activity in response to the COVID-19 pandemic. The rapid acceleration of vaccine development relied upon both sophisticated project portfolio management by government owners responsible for healthcare systems such as Operation Warp Speed in the US, the Vaccine Task Force in the UK, and intensive schedule compression at the level of individual vaccine development projects by suppliers around the world (Winch et al., 2021). Once licensed, national mass vaccination programmes were then organized with varying success across the globe to move from the outputs of efficacious vaccines to the outcomes of immunized populations and the attendant health benefits.

A globally agreed future-perfect state of 'holding the increase in the global average temperature to well below 2°C above pre-industrial levels and pursuing efforts to limit the temperature increase to 1.5°C above pre-industrial levels' was agreed in Paris in 2015, supported by persuasive projecting on its vital importance for humanity. Yet while there is no doubt about the undesirable future we all want to avoid, there is little agreement on the specifics of how we are going to get there. Clearly, our future-perfect will involve an extraordinary range of projects including, for example, infrastructure projects for new sources of energy generation, storage, and distribution; electrification of transportation; upgrading of existing housing and infrastructure to ensure resilience; and much more, but which ones and in what order of priority? One recent estimate is for a 50 per cent increase in capital investment projects to address global warming (McKinsey, 2022). Yet, there has been remarkably little debate on what this means for research in CPO (Winch, 2022). How, then, might our argument on projectivity, future-perfect thinking, and projecting help?

Two recent contributions suggest one way forward. One argument is that the achievement of the United Nations' 17 Sustainable Development Goals (SDGs) inherently involves major projects that complement the technological sublime with a 'sustainability sublime' (Sankaran et al., 2020). More generally, it is argued that the economy as a whole should become 'mission-orientated' in order to address the societal grand challenges captured in the SDGs (Mazzucato, 2021). The argument draws on the example of the Apollo programme – perhaps the most iconic project of the latter half of the twentieth century (Winch, 2022) – as an example of what can be achieved by projecting. However, observation of the response to the COVID pandemic suggests that this implicit reliance on monolithic complex projects to deliver desired futures is misguided in many cases. A first issue is that whatever the reasons – and they are hotly debated – megaprojects have a consistent tendency to overrun their schedules and budgets by serious amounts (Denicol et al., 2020; Flyvbjerg et al., 2003). A second is that the Apollo programme was embedded in a very specific stakeholder context (Horwitch, 1987).

The third issue is that the lessons from the COVID response suggest that the fundamental challenge is not project or programme organizing, but portfolio organizing (Winch et al., 2021).

This last point suggests another way forward. One approach to vaccine development relied on strong portfolio management by owners (governments responsible for healthcare systems) stimulating solution providers (pharmaceutical companies) to radically compress project stage gates. This was enabled by radically transformed commercial interfaces so that the financial threat of project failure was borne largely by governments as owners, and not the vaccine developers as suppliers, in a reversal of the normal risk allocations (Winch et al., 2021). There are much wider lessons here for the organization of complex projects to address the challenges of global warming and the SDGs more generally. Whichever way forward is chosen we need to find a way to move from generalized projecting towards more closely articulated project narratives that can mobilize the resources required to deliver feasible projects.

4.7   CONCLUSIONS

In this chapter on projectivity as a core concept of CPO, we addressed the question of what projects do and how they do it at the micro-level and the macro-level. At the micro-level we introduced the core concept of *projectivity* with its dimensions of the cognitive process of *future-perfect-thinking* and dialogic process of *projecting*. These, we suggested, are the micro-foundations of project shaping. We believe that projectivity is an important addition to the conceptual armoury of CPO research to complement the more established ones of complexity, temporality, and uncertainty (Chapters 2, 3, and 5). Projectivity provides an explanation of why uncertainty and complexity are inherently high on major projects because the future is inherently unknown as it does not yet exist (Aristotle, 1975), and inherently complex because we cannot understand the interactions between entities in that unknown future. We also suggest that it complements the concept of temporality as the flow of past, present, and future by emphasizing the distinctively future orientation of CPO compared to other forms of organizing such as operations management, which are inherently about present performance.

In order to achieve desired (or avoid undesired) future-perfects, projectors need to shape their aspirations into project narratives which perform and thereby change the future (Sergeeva & Winch, 2021). It is through articulating persuasive project narratives that projectors move from the micro-level to the macro-level of analysis encompassing what projects do for socio-economic development. In this perspective, projecting in Schutz's sense and projecting in Defoe's sense are the micro-level and macro-level of the same process of achieving our desired futures. At the macro-level we identified two underdeveloped research themes – issues of the relationship between projects and the societies in which they are embedded, and the projectification of organizations in the public, private, and third sectors. At the micro-level we identified the processes of future-perfect-thinking and projecting. We suggest that the concept of projectivity will help to raise the profile of research on these two important levels of analysis that are connected by project narratives and the ensuing project life-cycle processes of future-making. This will complement the current research on CPO that focuses largely on the delivery of projects, programmes, and portfolios rather than their shaping.

The framework here does not address the meso-level of the projects, programmes, and portfolios that deliver desired future states that are the focus of this research handbook. There is growing interest in project shaping and the associated front-end definition in CPO research (Babaei et al., 2021; Williams et al., 2019). Yet, project-shaping research remains largely descriptive and so we propose that one important potential contribution of the projectivity concept is to provide a theoretical basis for research on project shaping in CPO. The micro-level of analysis of projectivity can support theory development in project shaping and front-end definition research while the macro-level perspective on projecting can provide a perspective for analysing the context in which, and for which, complex projects are shaped. We will thereby obtain a deeper understanding of what projects do to complement our existing understanding of what they are.

REFERENCES

Aristotle. (1975). *Categories and de interpretatione*. Clarendon.

Austin, J. L. (1962). *How to do things with words*. Harvard University Press.

Babaei, A., Locatelli, G. & Sainati, T. (2021). What is wrong with the front-end of infrastructure megaprojects and how to fix it: A systematic literature review. *Project Leadership and Society*, 2, 100032.

Bowen, H. K., Clark, K. B., Holloway, C. A. & Wheelwright, S. C. (1994). *The perpetual enterprise machine: Seven keys to corporate renewal through successful product and process development*. Oxford University Press.

Clark, K. B. & Fujimoto, T. (1990). *Product development performance: Strategy, organization, and management in the world auto industry*. Harvard Business School Press.

Cochrane, A., Peck, J. & Tickell, A. (2002). Olympic dreams: Visions of partnership. In J. Peck & K. Ward (Eds), *City of revolution: Restructuring Manchester* (pp. 95–115). Manchester University Press.

Comi, A. & Whyte, J. (2018). Future making and visual artefacts: An ethnographic study of a design project. *Organization Studies*, 39(8), 1055–1083.

Cusumano, M. A. & Nobeoka, K. (1998). *Thinking beyond lean: How multi-project management is transforming product development at Toyota and other companies*. Free Press.

Defoe, D. (1697). *An essay upon projects*. Cockerill.

Denicol, J., Davies, A. & Krystallis, I. (2020). What are the causes and cures of poor megaproject performance? A systematic literature review and research agenda. *Project Management Journal*, 51(3), 328–345.

Denton, S. (2016). *The profiteers: Bechtel and the men who built the world*. Simon and Schuster.

Emirbayer, M. & Mische, A. (1998). What is agency? *American Journal of Sociology*, 103(4), 962–1023.

Financial Times. (2021). Hidden debt on China's Belt and Road tops $385bn, says new study. September 26.

Flyvbjerg, B., Bruzelius, N. & Rothengatter, W. (2003). *Megaprojects and risk: An anatomy of ambition*. Cambridge University Press.

Flyvbjerg, B., Garbuio, M. & Lovallo, D. (2009). Delusion and deception in large infrastructure projects: Two models for explaining and preventing executive disaster. *California Management Review*, 51(2), 170–194.

Frick, K. T. (2008). The cost of the technological sublime: Daring ingenuity and the new San Francisco–Oakland Bay bridge. In H. Priemus, B. Flyvbjerg, & B. van Wee (Eds), *Decision-making on megaprojects: Cost-benefit analysis, planning and innovation* (pp. 239–262). Edward Elgar Publishing.

Giard, V. & Midler, C. (1993). *Pilotages de projet et entreprises: Diversités et convergences*. Economica.

Hillman, J. E. (2020). *The emperor's new road: China and the project of the century*. Yale University Press.

Hirschman, A. O. (1967). *Development projects observed*. Brookings Institution.

Hobsbawm, E. J. (1987). *The age of empire, 1875–1914*. Weidenfeld and Nicolson.

Hodgson, D., Fred, M., Bailey, S. & Hall, P. (2019). *The projectification of the public sector*. Routledge.

Horwitch, M. (1987). Grands programmes: L'expérience américaine. *Révue Française de Gestion*, March–May, 54–69.

Hughes, T. P. (1998). *Rescuing prometheus: Four monumental projects that changed the modern world*. Vintage.

Jałocha, B., Góral, A. & Bogacz-Wojtanowska, E. (2019). Projectification of a global organization: Case study of the Roman Catholic church. *International Journal of Managing Projects in Business*, 12(2), 298–324.

King, A. & Crewe, I. (2013). *The blunders of our governments*. Oneworld.

Linder, M. (1994). *Projecting capitalism: A history of the internationalization of the construction industry*. Greenwood Press.

Lundin, R. A., Arvidsson, N., Brady, T., Ekstedt, E., Midler, C. & Sydow, J. (2015). *Managing and working in project society: Institutional challenges of temporary organizations*. Cambridge University Press.

Mazzucato, M. (2021). *Mission economy: A moonshot guide to changing capitalism*. Allen Lane.

McKinsey. (2022). *The net-zero transition: What it would cost, what it would bring*. McKinsey & Co.

Middlemas, R. K. (1963). *The master builders*. Hutchinson.

Midler, C. (1993). *L'auto qui n'existait pas*. InterEditions.

Midler, C. (1995). 'Projectification' of the firm: The Renault case. *Scandinavian Journal of Management*, 11(4), 363–375.

Miller, R. & Lessard, D. R. (2000). *The strategic management of large engineering projects: Shaping institutions, risks, and governance*. MIT Press.

Morris, P. W. G. (1973). An organisational analysis of project management in the building industry. *Build International*, 6(6), 595–616.

Nieto-Rodriguez, A. (2021). *Harvard Business Review project management handbook*. Harvard Business Review Press.

Ninan, J. & Sergeeva, N. (2021). Labyrinth of labels: Narrative constructions of promoters and protesters in megaprojects. *International Journal of Project Management*, 39(5), 496–506.

Oakervee, D. (2020). *Oakervee review*. Department for Transport.

Pisano, G. P. (1997). *The development factory: Unlocking the potential of process innovation*. Harvard Business School Press.

Reisner, M. P. (1986). *Cadillac desert: The American West and its disappearing water*. Viking.

Sankaran, S., Müller, R. & Drouin, N. (2020). Creating a 'sustainability sublime' to enable megaprojects to meet the United Nations Sustainable Development Goals. *Systems Research and Behavioral Science*, 37(5), 813–826.

Sawyer, J. E. (1952). Entrepreneurial error and economic growth. *Explorations in Economic History*, 4(4), 199–204.

Schutz, A. (1967a). *The phenomenology of the social world*. Northwestern University Press.

Schutz, A. (1967b). *Collected papers 1: The problem of social reality*. Martinus Nijhoff.

Scudder, T. (2017). The good megadam: Does it exist, all things considered? In B. Flyvbjerg (Ed.), *The Oxford handbook of megaproject management* (pp. 428–450). Oxford University Press.

Sergeeva, N. & Winch, G. M. (2021). Project narratives that potentially perform and change the future. *Project Management Journal*, 52(3), 264–277.

Shapira, Z. & Berndt, D. J. (1997). Managing grand-scale construction projects: A risk-taking perspective. *Research in Organizational Behavior*, 19, 303–360.

Shenhar, A. J. & Dvir, D. (2007). *Reinventing project management: The diamond approach to successful growth and innovation*. Harvard Business School Press.

Smith, A. (1776). *An inquiry into the nature and causes of the wealth of nations*. Strahan and Cadell.

Williams, T., Vo, H., Samset, K. & Edkins, A. (2019). The front-end of projects: A systematic literature review and structuring. *Production Planning and Control*, 30(14), 1137–1169.

Winch, G. M. (1994). *Managing production: Engineering change and stability*. Oxford University Press.

Winch, G. M. (2022). Projecting for sustainability transitions: Advancing the contribution of Peter Morris. *Engineering Project Organization Journal*, 11(1).

Winch, G. M., Cao, D., Maytorena-Sanchez, E., Pinto, J., Sergeeva, N. & Zhang, S. (2021). Operation warp speed: Projects responding to the COVID-19 Pandemic. *Project Leadership and Society*, 2.

Winch, G. M., Maytorena-Sanchez, E. & Sergeeva, N. (2022). *Strategic project organizing: A three domains approach*. Oxford University Press.

Winch, G. M., Meunier, M.-C., Head, J. & Russ, K. (2012). Projects as the content and process of change: The case of the health and safety laboratory. *International Journal of Project Management*, 30(2), 141–152.

Winch, G. M. & Sergeeva, N. (2022). Temporal structuring in project organizing: A narrative perspective. *International Journal of Project Management*, 40(1), 40–51.

Winter, M. & Szczepanek, T. (2008). Projects and programmes as value creation processes: A new perspective and some practical implications. *International Journal of Project Management*, 26(1), 95–103.

Womack, J. P., Jones, D. T. & Roos, D. (1990). *The machine that changed the world*. Rawson Associates.

5. Temporality

Anne Live Vaagaasar, Therese Dille and Tor Hernes

5.1   INTRODUCTION

Over the past decade or so, we have witnessed a proliferation in research on time and temporality in organizational research. While this research is increasingly accepted in project management research, scholars still call for more studies examining the role of temporality in project organizing (Bakker et al., 2016; Braun & Lampel, 2020). In an attempt to broaden the understanding of the potential of temporality in project management research, we discuss temporality with respect to three selected project phenomena: temporariness, life-cycle, and entrainment. As will hopefully be clear from our chapter, temporal aspects of complex project organizing will benefit from taking a strong process view, drawing on the ontology of temporality and working with situated temporal views.

5.2   TEMPORALITY

The linear assumption in project management research inherent in the ontology of time is widespread, but also problematic. The ontology of temporality, rooted in non-linear time conceptions, allows present, past and future to be understood as mutually constitutive rather than sequentially ordered. The distinction between the ontology of time and the ontology of temporality will inform the discussion throughout this chapter. The distinction between time and temporality is important insofar as the two terms address different ontologies. Hussenot, Hernes and Bouty (2020) argue that whereas in the ontology of time, time is a standardized and external dimension from which organizational phenomena can be measured or managed, the ontology of temporality refers to the situated and emergent activity of (re)enacting present, past and future.

Scholars have tended to work from dichotomies of time, such as clock time versus process time or objective versus subjective time. Whereas such dichotomies have served the field in the past, they are not very helpful to advance time research to capture the complexity of temporary organizing. It is assumed in a temporal ontological view that all temporal experience is basically 'subjective' and that we all experience time differently. For example, some perceive it as 'time passing' and others as 'time dragging' (McGrath & Kelly, 1986). Some perceive and talk of time as moving towards them (using a time-moving frame) while others talk about how they move in time (an ego-moving frame) (Crilly, 2017). Hence, time research includes studies of how actors perceive time differently and what can be called temporal personality variables, i.e. how actors understand, explain and react to time (Ancona et al., 2001b). In a temporal ontology, every unique and individually experienced moment feeds into a collectively experienced sense of time, which becomes structured socially, as noted by Orlikowski and Yates (2002), and mediated through materiality (Hernes et al., 2020). Temporality refers to the qualitative experience of being in the flow of time (Hernes, 2014) whereby the subjective experience becomes embedded in practices and expressed through social interaction (Emirbayer & Mische, 1998). In this view, inspired by process theory, practice theory, pragmatist philosophy, to name but a few streams of thought, distinctions such as clock versus process time or objective versus subjective time become superfluous.

Whereas it is true that clock time refers to quantitative measuring of continuous time, people do not experience the measured time as such. Our judgement of duration depends on the number and connectivity of activities taking place within the duration we are judging, in the sense that the busier we are, the faster we think time passes (Hicks et al., 1976). One second for a pilot landing on an aircraft carrier is not felt the same way by someone working in an office. We do not feel the duration of 60 minutes, but we have a sense of what 60 minutes represents in terms of activities. A duration of activity may have taken place in the past, we might be in the middle of it or it may be expected to take place in the near future. A temporal view would include that second as part of an event, which then has connotations of the experience of things moving faster or slower. Whereas it is also true that when involved in novel activity we tend to perceive and remember the time as unique (Butler, 1995), the uniqueness is constructed socio-materially as part of the collective trajectory through time (Hernes, 2017). Hence, a temporal view, rather than rejecting clock time, translates clock time into the social experience of time defined through the lens of activity. As an integral part of activity, temporality is not just concerned with present-past-future dynamics, but also with sequencing of activity. It recognizes that some activities or events precede other activities or events, but also assumes that it matters whether some activities/events are in the past, the future or are being carried out in the present.

In a temporal view, time is not understood as independent of human action, but nor is it considered exclusively limited to human action. Rather, it emerges through reflexive interplay between temporal structures and human action (Orlikowski & Yates, 2002, p. 684). Neither of them can determine the other – time and practices are co-produced. In practice, we use this interplay, more or less consciously, as we move through time. Social activity will always have temporal effects. *Temporal structuring*, which refers to 'a sociotemporal ordering that guides, orients, coordinates … work [activities]' (Skade et al., 2020, p. 108), is key to understanding behaviour in temporary organizing. Temporal structuring may include elements such as pacing, deadlines and rhythm, which become features that vary from one temporary organization to another.

Whereas the temporary organization may be considered a temporal structure in itself, there are other forms of temporal structuring that extend beyond the temporary organization to influence actors' behaviour (Stjerne & Svejenova, 2016). Such temporal structures may typically take the form of events (Hernes, 2014) that actors connect into their respective trajectories. From within projects, for example, actors enact events that took place before the beginning of the project as well as events they see as taking place after the project's end. Using the concept of temporal translation, Hernes and Schultz (2020) discuss explicitly how actors enact distant events through their temporal structures to makes sense of, or transform, the temporal structures within which their activities take place. In the context of project organizing, the establishment of a formal scheduled event in a project plan comes about as a result of 'the process of creating socially shared meaning' (Ancona et al., 2001a, p. 649). As project practitioners start practising based on these temporal structures, they reproduce the very same structures (Orlikowski & Yeats, 2002), while translating past and future events into the temporal structures of the project. Enactment of temporal structures can happen at individual or collective level (groups, institutions, societies) and even develop into cultural variances in relating to time. These variances can create tensions when actors move between regimes or collaborate across them (Reinecke & Ansari, 2015), for example in inter-organizational projects (Dille et al., 2018, 2019; Dille & Söderlund, 2011).

5.3 KEY ASPECTS OF TEMPORALITY IN PROJECT ORGANIZING

There are several interesting aspects of temporality with respect to project phenomena such as temporariness, life-cycle and entrainment.

5.3.1 Temporariness – Predefined Duration

The notion of temporariness is inherent in all theorizing of project organizing as it denotes the mere fact that projects are established only to endure within a certain, ex ante defined time span (Janowicz-Panjaitan et al., 2009; Lundin & Söderholm, 1995). Despite variations in goals, size, duration and other features, they have in common that they are temporary in the sense of a predefined duration. This is also the case when their actual and planned duration differs (significantly) (Flyvbjerg, 2011) and their final deadline is postponed over and over again (Biesenthal et al., 2018). This key feature of being temporary, and the sense of transience that often follows it, affects both the inner life of projects (Engwall, 2003, p. 790) as well as their interaction with more permanent organizations. Discussions of the temporariness and duration of project organizations often mirror the project as something 'opposite' to the permanent organization (Sydow et al., 2004) where time is 'eternal' (Lundin & Söderholm, 1995). Various conceptions are used for this mirroring, for example temporary-permanent (Lundin & Söderholm, 1995) or determinate-indeterminate (Winch, 2014).

Temporariness makes temporal matters quite paradoxical in the context of projects. On the one hand, there has been a tendency to assume that projects gain their distinct temporality because of being bracketed off from the social and historical context (Engwall, 2003). Time bracketing means to create beginnings and ends, and while it can enable action (Jacobsson & Söderholm, 2022) it may also create a misconception of projects being 'sheltered from the past, present and future' (Bakker & Janowicz-Panjaitan, 2009, p. 126). In such reasoning, projects have been understood as 'timeless' operating under conditions of a-temporality (Kenis et al., 2009). On the other hand, the acknowledgement of temporariness has put temporality at the core of temporary organizing and project management (Bakker, 2010; Burke & Morley, 2016; Lundin & Söderholm, 1995).

A consequence of the temporariness of projects is that they will always move towards the end of their duration, and the actors involved will find that 'time is always running out' (Lundin & Söderholm, 1995, p 439). Inevitably, their lingering past is increasing while their pending future is diminishing. Bergson (1922, p. 5) described the passing of time as a process of 'continuous progress of the past which gnaws into the future'. Therefore, a fundamental question in project organizing research is how the fact of moving towards the end affects organizing.

Temporariness affects actors and organizing in several ways. Firstly, this characteristic implies a compression of time and therefore projects are often considered efficient means to accelerate tasks and activities (Wenzel & Koch, 2018). Secondly, as a response to time compression, project practitioners engage in temporal structuring to organize, coordinate and account for activities (Bakker, 2010), as well as to drive up their speed (Bluedorn, 2002). Detailed schedules and plans are commonly applied in projects or processes of shorter duration and event-based structures for projects and processes of (relatively) long duration (Jones & Lichtenstein, 2008). And, thirdly, as we come back to the end, when outlining the situated temporal view, it also affects the ability to make changes.

5.3.2 Project Life-Cycle

The awareness of the deliberate dismantling of the project organization at a specified point in time makes it relevant to conceptualize time as a life-cycle in the context of projects (Lundin & Söderholm, 1995; Morris, 1994). The concept of life-cycle refers to the anticipated progression of certain phenomena – for example, human life where youth comes before adolescence (Ancona et al., 2001b). Projects typically progress from their beginning to their end through a set of designated phases succeeding each other. Artefacts, such as project plans, often display this as a linear journey in the form that key project processes and governance activities are to take place during the different phases. It is a widespread understanding that the project life-cycle starts with a concept stage, followed by a development stage, an execution stage, and finally the termination stage. Focusing on the particular actions at the different stages in the life-cycle can enable our understanding of the nature and development of temporary organizations. According to Lundin and Söderholm's (1995) much cited theory, projects move through their life-cycle undergoing a sequence of four action phases that can, to some extent, overlap. The first phase is action-based entrepreneurialism (in the concept stage), and then fragmentation for commitment-building (the development stage). The third phase is planned isolation to get the work done (the execution stage), and finally the phase of institutionalized termination (termination stage). Each of these four phases dominates the project activities at a certain point and their importance is contingent upon where the project is in its life-cycle (Lundin & Söderholm, 1995).

Knowledge of where one is in the life-cycle can illuminate inner processes of projects; for example shifts in the nature of work and relationships between project team members (Burke & Morley, 2016; Bygballe et al., 2016). Gersick (1988) demonstrates how project groups often experience a midpoint crisis when they are halfway through their life-cycle. As the midpoint crisis of the project hits, a transition occurs that includes a display of more strategic reflection among the participants on what they are doing, and why and how they are doing it, and a display of turn-around behaviour. Gersick (1995, p. 145) calls it 'breaking the spell'. Thus, the life-cycle is both a conceptualization of time describing the progression from beginning to end, and a way for actors to relate to their perceptions of both time and appropriate action – and link their present behaviour with past and future events. Project scholars have pointed to how certain deadlines during the life-cycle offer glimpses of clear-sightedness (Lindkvist et al., 1998, p. 947) that trigger moments of sudden change (Engwall & Westling, 2004) or revolutionary episodes of turn-around (Geraldi et al., 2010) that change the path forward. This means that project phases can shift around in relative order as well as be repeated. We will come back to this in our reflections on situated temporality at the end of the chapter.

To improve our understanding of project organizing, it is important to move beyond the single project life-cycle. Since Engwall (2003, p. 789) stated that 'no project is an island' it has become widely acknowledged that projects are not sheltered phenomena, but rather socio-historically embedded in networks of more indeterminate relationships, such as 'permanent' organizations or networks of projects feeding into each other (Lundin et al., 2015; Stjerne & Svejenova, 2016; Sydow & Staber, 2002). For example, it has been demonstrated that actors in projects actively link their present project activity to the past and future, for example long-term strategies or norms (Engwall, 2003), to mobilize knowledge (Grabher & Thiel, 2015), resources and legitimacy (Engwall, 2003; Stjerne & Svejenova, 2016), and trust (Swärd, 2016). Taking a network perspective, different life-cycles of projects are nested together in networks of relations that stretch far beyond the different projects in time (Lundin et al., 2015; Manning & Sydow, 2011). Each project life-cycle becomes an episode in a long-term trajectory (Grabher, 2002).

5.3.3   Entrainment

Entrainment refers to how activity cycles of one system adjust to those of a more dominant system (Khavul et al., 2010) by synchronizing tempo and/or pace. Organizations, both determinate and indeterminate, face the challenge of adapting to dominant macro-cycles typically put into place by industry leaders or governing bodies, for example budget and audit cycles, or reporting dates. These macro-cycles provide contingencies for the activity cycles of project-based organizations that again provide cycles to which the project is expected to adjust. In the context of complex project organizing, we can talk about entrainment at different levels.

The tempo of activities or the phase of activity cycles can be entrained with cycles that are chosen at the project level, at the level of the organizations initiating the projects, or other macro-cycles and/or political pressures (van Berkel et al., 2016). External political pressure can lead to increased project tempo, which in turn creates issues when trying to entrain with slower-paced, more permanent organizations (van Berkel et al., 2016) that typically have a quite multi-faceted temporality whose inter-connectedness varies with the nature of the organization (Dawson & Sykes, 2016). Projects facing pressure to speed up activities tend to respond by adhering to a singular temporal logic of intensive sequencing that creates tensions in entraining with more permanent organizations (Dille et al., 2019; Geraldi et al., 2020).

The matter of entrainment is even more complicated in the context of megaprojects, in particular those that are inter-institutional (Dille & Söderlund, 2011; Pemsel & Söderlund, 2020). Organizations that are embedded in the same institutional field tend to grow alike and develop similar activity cycles (Dille & Söderlund, 2011). When organizations from different institutional fields need to entrain, such temporal differences can create tensions and collaboration problems (Dille & Söderlund, 2011; Dille et al., 2018, 2019).

Interestingly, Blagoev and Schreyögg (2019) note that the theoretical perspective of entrainment creates a view of temporal structuring that is not representative because it backgrounds asynchrony, treating it as inferior to synchrony. Contrary to entrainment theory, Blagoev and Schreyögg (2019) discuss how organizations that choose to entrain with one rhythm might have to desynchronize from other rhythms and activate positive feedback dynamics that support their choice. This can lead to a 'lock-in' in the chosen rhythm that hinders entrainment with other dominant rhythms, as entrainment scholars commonly assume (Khavul et al., 2010), over time. Thus we can question the whole idea of striving for entrainment to coordinate actors in complex projects and suggest that coordinating in this context may be better understood as different forms and degrees of temporal translation between actors.

5.4   THE SITUATED TEMPORAL VIEW

While the main systems paradigm in project organizing promotes an objective time view (Winch & Sergeeva, 2022), an increasing number of scholars no longer consider project organizing as temporally sheltered, but rather as a highly temporally embedded phenomenon. A temporal view assumes that rather than view projects from the outside, we view projects from within and follow actors as the project unfolds. There is the argument about each project being an episode in long-term trajectories, and there is the argument that actors, on their journey from a project's beginning to its end, link their present activities to past and future events. Both arguments lead us to the issue of how things are situated in time – and emerging over time. This is in line with Winch and Sergeeva's (2022) suggestion of project organizing emerging as actors make use of the present and the past to formulate narratives about desired future states. Narratives can thereby mobilize the resources required to realize the desired future states. In this sense, project organizing is both goal-orientated and emergent at the same time (Winch & Sergeeva, 2022).

Sergi et al. (2020) advocate studies on the nature of project organizing as the actors involved in the project perceive the unfolding of processes through time. A temporal ontology of time helps to understand this phenomenon (Vaagaasar et al., 2020). The situated temporal view is based on the argument that organizations are caught in multiple temporal flows in which they weave past, present, and future together (Hernes, 2014). The manner of weaving changes as projects move from the beginning towards the end. Throughout its duration, the project experiences an ongoing present from within which sense is made of past and future events. This can be illustrated by moving along a road and 'from every new rise the landscape that stretches behind us becomes a different landscape' (Mead, 1932, p. 42, in Hernes et al., 2013, p. 5).

The practice-based approach to time, as presented by Orlikowski and Yates (2002), acknowledged already 20 years ago that actors and structures co-create one another, so what does the situated temporal view add? The situated temporal view enables researchers to explore how the effects of temporal structures on complex project organizing can change over time as the project moves towards the end. It allows accounts of the effects of the changing relationship between past and future during project execution (Dille et al., 2019), where agency always lies in the present (Hernes, 2014), and 'how actors' changing temporal orientations influence their emerging action patterns and the possibilities for making changes as deadlines approach' (Vaagaasar et al., 2020, p. 420). This enables the study of an interesting challenge in project organizing: the closer the project comes to its projected ending the more difficult it becomes for actors to effect changes. This can lead the actors to persist in reproducing dysfunctional action patterns (Vaagaasar et al., 2020) and to mistranslations and temporal decoupling whereby the project collaboration breaks down.

Along with the situated temporal view, we urge researchers to enact an ontology of temporality as Hussenot et al. (2020) suggest. Under conditions of discontinuity in complex project organizing actors continuously review their past in the light of an emerging future, thus defining opportunities and constraints for how to act in the present enables a fuller view of time to be accounted for in complex project organizing research.

REFERENCES

Ancona, D. G., Goodman, P. S., Lawrence, B. S. & Tushman, M. L. (2001a). Time: A new research lens. *Academy of Management Review*, 26(4), 645–663.

Ancona, D. G., Okhuysen, G. A. & Perlow, L. A. (2001b). Taking time to integrate temporal research. *Academy of Management Review*, 26(4), 512–529.

Bakker, R. M. (2010). Taking stock of temporary organizational forms: A systematic review and research agenda. *International Journal of Management Reviews*, 12(4), 466–486.

Bakker, R. M., DeFillippi, R. J., Schwab, A. & Sydow, J. (2016). Temporary organizing: Promises, processes, problems. *Organization Studies*, 37(12), 1703–1719.

Bakker, R. M. & Janowicz-Panjaitan, M. (2009). Time matters: The impact of 'temporariness' on the functioning and performance of organizations. In P. Kenis, M. Janowicz-Panjaitan & B. Cambré (Eds), *Temporary organizations: Prevalence, logic and effectiveness* (pp. 107–127). Edward Elgar Publishing.

Bergson, H. (1922). *Creative evolution: An alternate explanation for Darwin's mechanism of evolution.* Macmillan.

Biesenthal, C., Clegg, S., Mahalingam, A. & Sankaran, S. (2018). Applying institutional theories to managing megaprojects. *International Journal of Project Management*, 36(1), 43–54.

Blagoev, B. & Schreyögg, G. (2019). Why do extreme work hours persist? Temporal uncoupling as a new way of seeing. *Academy of Management Journal*, 62(6), 1818–1847.

Bluedorn, A. C. (2002). *The human organization of time: Temporal realities and experience.* Stanford University Press.

Braun, T. & Lampel, J. (2020). Introduction: Tensions and paradoxes in temporary organising: Mapping the field. In T. Braun & J. Lampel (Eds), *Tensions and paradoxes in temporary organizing.* Emerald Publishing.

Burke, C. M. & Morley, M. J. (2016). On temporary organizations: A review, synthesis and research agenda. *Human Relations*, 69(6), 1235–1258.

Butler, R. (1995). Time in organizations: Its experience, explanations and effects. *Organization Studies*, 16(6), 925–950.

Bygballe, L. E., Swärd, A. R. & Vaagaasar, A. L. (2016). Coordinating in construction projects and the emergence of synchronized readiness. *International Journal of Project Management*, 34(8), 1479–1492.

Crilly, D. (2017). Time and space in strategy discourse: Implications for intertemporal choice. *Strategic Management Journal*, 38(12), 2370–2389.

Dawson, P. & Sykes, C. (2016). *Organizational change and temporality: Bending the arrow of time.* Routledge.

Dille, T., Hernes, T. & Vaagaasar, A. L. (2019). *Coordinating multiple organizational actors: The temporal challenge of temporary organizations.* Paper presented at the European Group for Organization Studies, Edinburgh.

Dille, T. & Söderlund, J. (2011). Managing inter-institutional projects: The significance of isochronism, timing norms and temporal misfits. *International Journal of Project Management*, 29(4), 480–490.

Dille, T., Söderlund, J. & Clegg, S. (2018). Temporal conditioning and the dynamics of inter-institutional projects. *International Journal of Project Management*, 36(5), 673–686.

Emirbayer, M. & Mische, A. (1998). What is agency? *American Journal of Sociology*, 103(4), 962–1023.

Engwall, M. (2003). No project is an island: Linking projects to history and context. *Research Policy*, 32(5), 789–808.

Engwall, M. & Westling, G. (2004). Peripety in an R&D drama: Capturing a turnaround in project dynamics. *Organization Studies*, 25(9), 1557–1578.

Flyvbjerg, B. (2011). Over budget, over time, over and over again: Managing major projects. In P. W. G. Morris, J. Pinto & J. Söderlund (Eds), *The Oxford handbook of project management* (pp. 321–344). Oxford University Press.

Geraldi, J. G., Lee-Kelley, L. & Kutsch, E. (2010). The Titanic sunk, so what? Project manager response to unexpected events. *International Journal of Project Management*, 28(6), 547–558.

Geraldi, J., Stjerne, I. & Oehmen, J. (2020). Acting in time: Temporal work enacting tensions at the interface between temporary and permanent organisations. In T. Braun & J. Lampel (Eds), *Tensions and paradoxes in temporary organizing, Vol. 67: Research in the sociology of organizations* (pp. i–xviii). Emerald Publishing.

Gersick, C. (1988). Time and transitions in work teams: Toward a new model of group development. *Academy of Management Journal*, 31(1), 9–41.

Gersick, C. (1995). Everything new under the gun creativity and deadlines. In C. M. Ford & D. A. Gioia (Eds), *Creative action in organizations* (pp. 142–148). Sage.

Grabher, G. (2002). Cool projects, boring institutions: Temporary collaboration in social context. *Regional Studies*, 36(3), 205–214.

Grabher, G. & Thiel, J. (2015). Projects, people, professions: Trajectories of learning through a mega-event (the London 2012 case). *Geoforum*, 65, 328–337.

Hernes, T. (2014). *A process theory of organization*. Oxford University Press.

Hernes, T. (2017). Process as the becoming of temporal trajectory. In H. Tsoukas & A. Langley (Eds), *Sage handbook of process organizational studies* (pp. 601–607). Sage.

Hernes, T., Feddersen, J. & Schultz, M. (2020). Material temporality: How materiality does time in food organising. *Organization Studies*, 42(2), 351–371.

Hernes, T. & Schultz, M. (2020). Translating the distant into the present: How actors address distant past and future events through situated activity. *Organization Theory*, 1(1), 1–20.

Hernes, T., Simpson, B. & Söderlund, J. (2013). Managing and temporality. *Scandinavian Journal of Management*, 29(1), 1–6.

Hicks, R. E., Miller, G. W. & Kinsbourne, M. (1976). Prospective and retrospective judgments of time as a function of amount of information processed. *American Journal of Psychology*, 89(4), 719–730.

Hussenot, A., Hernes, T. & Bouty, I. (2020). Studying organization from the perspective of the ontology of temporality. In J. Reinecke, R. Suddaby, A. Langley & H. Tsoukas (Eds), Time, temporality, and history in process organization studies. Oxford University Press.

Jacobsson, M. & Söderholm, A. (2022). An essay on 'Homo projecticus': Ontological assumptions in the projectified society. *International Journal of Project Management*, 40(4), 315–319.

Janowicz-Panjaitan, M., Bakker, R. M. & Kenis, P. (2009). Research on temporary organizations: The state of the art and distinct approaches toward 'temporariness'. In P. Kenis, M. Janowicz & B. Cambré (Eds), *Temporary organizations: Prevalence, logic and effectiveness* (pp. 56–85). Edward Elgar Publishing.

Jones, C. & Lichtenstein, B. B. (2008). Temporary inter-organizational projects. In S. Cropper, M. Ebers, C. Huxham & P. S. Ring (Eds), *The Oxford handbook of inter-organizational relations* (pp. 231–255). Oxford University Press.

Kenis, P., Janowicz, M. & Cambré, B. (Eds) (2009). *Temporary organizations: Prevalence, logic and effectiveness*. Edward Elgar Publishing.

Khavul, S., Pérez-Nordtvedt L. & Wood, E. (2010). Organizational entrainment and international new ventures from emerging markets. *Journal of Business Venturing*, 25(1), 104–119.

Lindkvist, L., Söderlund, J. & Tell, F. (1998). Managing product development projects: On the significance of fountains and deadlines. *Organization Studies*, 19(6), 931–951.

Lundin, R. A., Arvidsson, N., Brady, T., Ekstedt, E., Midler, C. & Sydow, J. (2015). *Managing and working in project society*. Cambridge University Press.

Lundin, R. A. & Söderholm, A. (1995). A theory of the temporary organization. *Scandinavian Journal of Management*, 11(4), 437–455.

Manning, S. & Sydow, J. (2011). Projects, paths, and practices: Sustaining and leveraging project-based relationships. *Industrial and Corporate Change*, 20(5), 1369–1402.

McGrath, J. E. and Kelly, J. R. (1986). *Time and human interaction: Toward a social psychology of time*. Guilford Press.

Morris, P. W. G. (1994). *The management of projects*. Thomas Telford.

Orlikowski, W. J. & Yates, J. (2002). It's about time: Temporal structuring in organizations. *Organization Science*, 13(6), 684–700.

Pemsel, S. & Söderlund, J. (2020). Who's got the time? Temporary organising under temporal institutional complexity. In T. Braun & J. Lampel (Eds), *Tensions and paradoxes in temporary organizing, Vol. 67: Research in the sociology of organizations* (pp. 127–150). Emerald Publishing.

Reinecke, J. & Ansari, S. (2015). When times collide: Temporal brokerage at the intersection of markets and developments. *Academy of Management Journal*, 58(2), 618–648.

Sergi, V., Crevani, L. & Aubry, M. (2020). Process studies of project organizing. *Project Management Journal*, 51(1), 3–10.

Skade, L., Stanske, S., Wenzel, M. & Koch, J. (2020). Temporary organizing and acceleration: On the plurality of temporal structures in accelerators. In T. Braun & J. Lampel (Eds), *Tensions and paradoxes in temporary organizing, Vol. 67: Research in the sociology of organizations* (pp. 105–125). Emerald Publishing.

Stjerne, I. S. & Svejenova, S. (2016). Connecting temporary and permanent organizing: Tensions and boundary work in sequential film projects. *Organization Studies*, 37(12), 1771–1792.

Swärd, A. (2016). Trust, reciprocity, and actions: The development of trust in temporary inter-organizational relations. *Organization Studies*, 37(12), 1841–1860.

Sydow, J., Lindkvist, L. & DeFillippi, R. (2004). Project-based organizations, embeddedness and repositories of knowledge. *Organization Studies*, 25(9), 1475–1489.

Sydow, J. & Staber, U. (2002). The institutional embeddedness of project networks: The case of content production in German television. *Regional Studies*, 36(3), 215–227.

Vaagaasar, A. L., Hernes, T. & Dille, T. (2020). The challenges of implementing temporal shifts in temporary organizations: Implications of a situated temporal view. *Project Management Journal*, 51(4), 420–428.

van Berkel, F. J., Ferguson, J. E. & Groenewegen, P. (2016). Speedy delivery versus long-term objectives: How time pressure affects coordination between temporary projects and permanent organizations. *Long Range Planning*, 49(6), 661–673.

Wenzel, M. & Koch, J. (2018). Acceleration as process: A strategy process perspective on startup acceleration. In M. Wright & I. Drori (Eds), *Accelerators: Successful venture creation and growth* (pp. 21–36). Edward Elgar Publishing.

Winch, G. M. (2014). Three domains of project organising. *International Journal of Project Management*, 32(5), 721–731.

Winch, G. M. & Sergeeva, N. (2022). Temporal structuring in project organizing: A narrative perspective. *International Journal of Project Management*, 40(1), 40–51.

PART II

PERSPECTIVES FROM ORGANIZATION THEORY

INTRODUCTION TO PART II

Graham M. Winch

Our premise for this part is that 'research must go beyond description and must be reflected against theory' (Thompson, 1956, p. 102). In doing so, research on complex project organizing (CPO) draws heavily on the social sciences (Winch, 1990), with a particular influence from sociology which is usually mediated through organization theory. As an applied research field, this influence *from* the social sciences *to* CPO is usually a one-way process, but the ambitions of this *Handbook*, as described in Chapter 1, are both to enhance this application process and to do it in such a way that there is a flow of ideas in both directions. Any such interactive influencing requires 'reflexive meta-theories' which allow such translations to take place (Davies et al., 2018). The content of this part provides a number of potential such meta-theories. They range from some very established theories that are now the cornerstones of teaching in our field and hence our textbooks, through a rich body of work that is now dominant in the pages of our research journals, to some theoretical perspectives that could well shape future CPO research.

The deep influence of sociology on the organization theory applied to CPO suggests that the sociological paradigms typology (Burrell & Morgan, 1979) in an updated format is appropriate for our purposes of framing the presentation of the chapters in this part. The sociological paradigms typology builds from two dimensions. The first addresses the nature of social science in the subjective/objective ontological dimension between the nominalists who argue that all social phenomena are comprehended through perceptions and the realists who hold that society exists independently of those perceptions. Each of these dimensions is typically associated with distinctive epistemologies such as hermeneutics for the nominalists and positivism for the realists.

The second dimension addresses the nature of society in the order/conflict dimension in terms of whether the fundamental driver of social phenomena is order or conflict, capturing the differences between mainstream sociology and Marxist sociology, respectively. Debates since the late 1970s have, however, tended to emphasize the underpinnings of the order/ conflict dimension in the actor/system dimension (Dawe, 1970), which is also known as the agency/structure dimension, rather than order/conflict as such. So, we adopt that formulation here. This dimension captures whether the analytic emphasis is upon the ways in which agents shape social phenomena or the ways in which social structures shape what agents do. The first is usually dubbed the interpretivist or constructivist paradigm, and the latter the structural-functionalist paradigm (Burrell & Morgan, 1979). These two dimensions are used in Figure II.1.

We also need to extend the application of the paradigm to the other social sciences, not only sociology, in order to capture comprehensively the full range of contributions to research in CPO. Work within economics has made very important contributions to CPO (Merrow, 2011), as has work in anthropology (Van Marrewijk et al., 2016) and psychology (Buehler et al., 2010). We can suggest that the tradition of economics as applied to CPO is typically structural-realist; similarly, psychology is typically agential-realist, and anthropology typi-

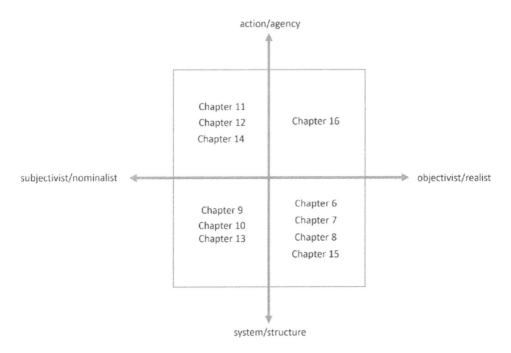

Figure II.1   *The four paradigms of complex project organizing*

cally subjectivist whether agential or structural. A further important limitation of this typology is that some of the major theoretical developments in sociology over the last 40 years since Burrell and Morgan wrote have attempted to address the agency/structure dichotomy. In their different ways both structuration theory (Giddens, 1984) and morphogenetic theory (Archer, 1995) address the dichotomy by putting structure and agency into mutually constitutive interaction – the principal difference between them is on the subjectivist/objectivist dimension. As an alternative critique, some streams of practice theory (Schatzki et al., 2001) and actor-network theory (Latour, 2005) espouse a 'flat' ontology which argues that the agency/structure dichotomy is a false one while focusing on the flow of agency. Additionally, the subjective/objective dimension has been challenged by critical realism (Bhaskar, 1998) as a philosophy of science that combines a realist ontology with a subjectivist epistemology.

However, we believe it is useful for our purposes here to use this adaptation of the sociological paradigms typology to frame the contributions to this part in relation to each other, which we do in Figure II.1. The first group of chapters present long-established perspectives in CPO research that still demand attention. Chapter 6 presents a brief history of organization theory before presenting the contribution of contingency theory to comparing different types of projects. Chapter 7 draws on a rather different tradition in the study of organizations – systems theory – which has played a vital part in the development of the field (Cleland & King, 1968), showing how systems dynamics gives us unique insights into project delivery. Chapter 8 turns to the commercial interface and the contribution of transaction cost economics to CPO research. All three of these perspectives fall into the structural/realist category in Figure II.1.

The next two groups of chapters present theoretical perspectives that have become highly influential – and collectively dominant – in recent CPO research. Chapter 9 covers neo-institutional theory, which is currently dominant in organization theory (Grothe-Hammer & Kohl, 2020), showing how individual projects and programmes are embedded in larger institutional structures, but also how institutional projects can change those structures. Chapter 10 moves to the concept of governmentality and its relevance for CPO research, particularly on the governance interface. Both theoretical perspectives can be most usefully categorized as subjectivist/structural. While they emphasize how social structures are created through the actions and interactions of agents, the analytic focus is more on the structures created than the individual agents. The remaining two subjectivist perspectives focus, by contrast, more on agency. Chapter 11 presents projects-as-practice, which is part of a wider movement around practice theory that is, arguably, challenging the dominance of neo-institutional and network theory in organization theory. Chapter 12 presents actor theory with its distinctive inclusion of non-human 'actants' within its explanatory scope, which is particularly useful for analysing primordial stakeholders (Driscoll & Starik, 2004).

Finally, we have a group of perspectives that offer the prospect of new directions in CPO research – one in each of our categories. Chapter 13 draws on network theory, which is the other dominant perspective currently in organization theory, but little used in CPO research. Chapter 14 takes a rather different approach to systems analysis from Chapter 6, showing how we can conceptualize complex adaptive systems, particularly when analysing project shaping in contrast to project delivery. Chapter 15 presents a perspective from morphogenetic theory that is particularly useful for analysing the achievement of project outcomes through digital transformations. Finally, Chapter 16 presents design thinking which shares its theoretical roots with transaction cost economics in the Carnegie School (Gavetti et al., 2007; Simon, 1996) and, again, has been little used in CPO research. We hope that you will find the theories presented in these chapters useful in positioning your own research contribution.

REFERENCES

Archer, M. S. (1995). *Realist social theory: The morphogenetic approach*. Cambridge University Press.

Bhaskar, R. (1998). *The possibility of naturalism: A philosophical critique of the contemporary human sciences* (3rd ed.). Routledge.

Buehler, R., Griffin, D., & Peetz, J. (2010). The planning fallacy: Cognitive, motivational, and social origins. In M. P. Zanna & J. M. Olson (Eds), *Advances in experimental social psychology*, Vol. 43 (pp. 1–62). Elsevier.

Burrell, G., & Morgan, G. (1979). *Sociological paradigms and organisational analysis: Elements of the sociology of corporate life*. Heinemann.

Cleland, D. I., & King, W. R. (1968). *Systems analysis and project management*. McGraw-Hill.

Davies, A., Manning, S., & Söderlund, J. (2018). When neighboring disciplines fail to learn from each other: The case of innovation and project management research. *Research Policy*, 47(5), 965–979.

Dawe, A. (1970). The two sociologies. *British Journal of Sociology*, 21(2), 207–218.

Driscoll, C., & Starik, M. (2004). The primordial stakeholder: Advancing the conceptual consideration of stakeholder status for the natural environment. *Journal of Business Ethics*, 49(1), 55–73.

Gavetti, G., Levinthal, D., & Ocasio, W. (2007). Perspective – neo-Carnegie: The Carnegie School's past, present, and reconstructing for the future. *Organization Science*, 18(3), 523–536.

Giddens, A. (1984). *The constitution of society: Outline of the theory of structuration*. Polity Press.

Grothe-Hammer, M., & Kohl, S. (2020). The decline of organizational sociology? An empirical analysis of research trends in leading journals across half a century. *Current Sociology*, 68(4), 419–442.

Latour, B. (2005). *Reassembling the social: An introduction to actor-network-theory*. Oxford University Press.

Merrow, E. W. (2011). *Industrial megaprojects: Concepts, strategies, and practices for success*. John Wiley and Sons.

Schatzki, T. R., Knorr-Cetina, K. D., & Savigny, E. v. (2001). *The practice turn in contemporary theory*. Routledge.

Simon, H. A. (1996). *The sciences of the artificial* (3rd ed.). MIT Press.

Thompson, J. D. (1956). On building an administrative science. *Administrative Science Quarterly*, 1(1), 102–111.

Van Marrewijk, A., Ybema, S., Smits, K., Clegg, S., & Pitsis, T. (2016). Clash of the Titans: Temporal organizing and collaborative dynamics in the Panama Canal megaproject. *Organization Studies*, 37(12), 1745–1769.

Winch, G. (1990). The social sciences and construction management: Overview and applications. *Habitat International*, 14(2–3), 205–215.

6. Contingency theory and its applications to complex project organizing

Peerasit Patanakul

6.1 INTRODUCTION

Contingency theory has been widely applied to complex project organizing, particularly the understanding of different project types and the adaptation of project management approaches with respect to those project types. To review the applications of contingency theory to complex project organizing, this chapter summarizes what contingency theory is in a context of mainstream organization theory. The chapter highlights the principal contributions of contingency theory to complex project organizing. In addition, the chapter reviews some of the frameworks, suggested by several researchers, used to categorize projects into the different types. These frameworks represent the applications of contingency theory to project management. The chapter also reviews some of the project management approaches deemed to be appropriate for different types of projects. Furthermore, the contribution of contingency theory on strategic project management is discussed. At the end of the chapter, potential research opportunities are suggested.

6.2 ORGANIZATION THEORY: CONTINGENCY SCHOOL AND OTHER SCHOOLS OF THOUGHT

The focus of this section is to introduce contingency theory and its development and application in complex project organizing research. In doing so, other relevant organization theories are also reviewed. One of the early contributors of what is currently known as organization theory was Max Weber, considered the 'father of organization theory' (Wren, 1972). Built around rational decision making, Weber suggested bureaucracy as a form of organization. Knowledge and ability were proposed as the basis for organization over favouritism. Later on, scholars from many disciplines contributed to the development of organization theory, resulting in several major schools of thought, as discussed by Hodge and Anthony (1988). Among them are the classical school (1890–1930), the behavioural school (1930–1960), the systems school (1960–present), and the contingency school (1965–present). The following sections briefly highlight the different schools of thought. The contingency school is particularly emphasized.

6.2.1 Different Schools of Thought

In the classical school, the theorists put their attempts to generating rational techniques used in creating process and structure offering the coordinated set of relationships among an organization's components (Hodge & Anthony, 1988). Their focus was on the appropriateness in work allocation to people and machines, including the formation of functional processes, organizational structure, and control. The classicists emphasized the way to build an organization that centres around work and the processing of information necessary to perform that work in the most efficient way. They emphasized the benefits of specialization and the existence of 'one best way' to perform the work. Since task performance is at the centre of the classical view, the classicists tend to hold human element relatively constant (Hodge & Anthony, 1988).

The behavioural school sought to improve the understanding of organization behaviour by accounting for the human element in a theory of organizations. With behavioural views, researchers studied the behaviours of organizations' members in different organization settings, enabling management to better understand the members' behaviours and modify them to benefit organizations' effectiveness. Some prominent research in this area includes Abraham Maslow's hierarchy of human needs (Maslow, 1943) and Frederick Herzberg's two-factor theory of motivation (Herzberg et al., 1959). Other research encompasses the studies of group dynamics, role performance, and leadership, for example. While human element was accounted for and included in a theory of organization, the behaviourists did not consider the total set of functional relationships of the organization. Nonetheless, the works of the behaviourists greatly contributed to the present understanding of organization theory (Hodge & Anthony, 1988).

The systems school took a macro perspective to analyse organizations. The focus was on how the organization functions and how it interacts with its environment. With the systems approach, the systems scholars viewed an organization as an integrated set of components or resources combined together with the aim of accomplishing some purposes (Bertalanffy, 1968; Boulding, 1956). This includes investigations of organization components, functioning together as a unit and inter-organization linkages. Within the systems school, the scholars suggested two views. A closed system operates independently from its environment or outside influences. With this definition, the classical view of organizations was considered a closed system (Hodge & Anthony, 1988). On the contrary, the open systems view takes the context of the organization into consideration when performing an analysis of organizations. The contributions of the systems school have significantly influenced the contingency school. Several concepts developed by the systems school were used as the basis for the contingency theory (Hodge & Anthony, 1988).

6.2.2   Contingency School of Thought

The contribution of the contingency school centres around the proposition that the relationship between an organization and its economics and social contexts depends on the situation. With an adaptive view of the organization, the contingency school rejects the constructs developed from the static view of the classical school. The organization theorists within the contingency school believe that the open-systems concept must be used as a basis for organization theory (Hodge & Anthony, 1988).

Early researchers within the contingency school attempted to understand what impacts an organization's performance. Joan Woodward (1965) studied the impact of technology on the organization. Her attempt was to understand the reason why, despite having an organizational structure built on classical foundations, firms were not always the most successful from a commercial aspect. Woodward found that organizations should be structured to address the different kinds of demands from different technologies on individuals and organizations. The commercially successful firms seemed to be the ones that were structured in such a way that complemented those demands.

In addition to Woodward, Jay Galbraith (1970) viewed an organization as an information processor that kept in alignment with the demand of its task environment by properly processing decision information. The more certain the task, the more amount of activity could be planned, leading to a reduction in the need for continuous information flows through the organization. Galbraith also suggested that the organization should tie in with its environment and that changes in its environment require more effort and coordination among various organization components to process information in order to react to the changes. Galbraith contributed significant work on organization design (Galbraith, 2014).

The contribution of James D. Thompson (1967) centres on his indication of the necessity to analyse an organization as an open system. His research focused on the forces of technology and open environmental systems affecting the organization. He suggested that an organization should be built with the consideration of the impact of technology and environment affecting it. Thompson's contribution was significant and was considered a landmark in the evolution of organization theory (Hodge & Anthony, 1988).

The work of Lorsch and Lawrence (1970) was among the first that focused on the contingent relationship between an organization and its environment. Lorsch and Lawrence suggested that successful organizations were structured in such a way that was consistent with the demands from the environment. This work was significant as it clearly put forward the impact of the environment on organizations. To address this impact, the organizations must differentiate and integrate activities and orientations in a particular or contingent fashion.

6.2.3   Contingency Theory and Complex Projects

Contingency theory has significantly impacted research on complex project organizing. Many researchers have relied on contingency theory as a basis for their studies. Several approaches have been suggested for managing projects, including an adaptive approach for organizing complex projects (Shenhar & Dvir, 2007).

An adaptive project management approach was developed based on the premise that projects are not only the collection of activities that need to be managed to accomplish time, cost, and performance goals. Projects include uncertainty and complexity (see Chapters 2 and 3). Therefore, projects should be managed in a flexible and adaptive way. Project management styles must be adapted accordingly with a 'one size does not fit all' principle. This, however, does not mean that traditional project management should be ignored. Adaptive project management merely complements it.

In order to manage projects in a flexible and adaptive way, project managers must first understand that projects are different from one another and, second, they must have a way to distinguish projects. Many researchers have proposed frameworks to categorize projects. One of the frameworks, a diamond-shaped framework suggested by Shenhar and Dvir (2007), is discussed in the next section.

6.3   MANAGING A PROJECT ACCORDING TO ITS TYPE

The Diamond Framework (Shenhar & Dvir, 2007) can be used to distinguish projects. The framework includes four dimensions: novelty, technology, complexity, and pace, also referred to as the NTCP model (Shenhar, 2001; Shenhar & Dvir, 1996; Shenhar et al., 2005). Shenhar and Dvir argue that this framework provides a disciplined tool for analysing a project's benefits and risks. Project managers can, therefore, develop a set of protocols for managing each project type.

6.3.1   Assessing Project Types

As one of the four dimensions of the Diamond Framework, *novelty* represents the uncertainties associated with the project. These uncertainties come from the project's goal or market, or both. Novelty is measured in terms of the newness of a project's product to the customers, users, or the market in general. It also represents the level of clarity of the initial product requirement. Three types of novelty are used in the framework, according to the degree of product newness. They are derivative, platform, and breakthrough. Derivative projects create products that extend or improve existing products or services. For this types of project, the degree of newness of the project's product is relatively low. Platform projects create products that are considered the new generation of existing product lines or provide new services to existing or new markets and customers. The degree of newness of the project products is considered medium. Breakthrough projects introduce a novel product or concept, a new idea, or a new use for a product that customers have never thought of before. The degree of newness of the project products is relatively high.

Technology is another dimension of the Diamond Framework. It represents the level of technological uncertainty associated with the project. The more new technologies required for the project, the higher the technological uncertainty of the project. Four categories are used in the framework with respect to the degree of technological uncertainty. They are low tech, medium tech, high tech, and super high tech. Low-tech projects use only existing, well-established, and mature technologies. Medium-tech projects mostly use existing technologies with limited use of new technologies or new features. The majority of the technologies used in high-tech projects are new or recently developed. For super-high-tech projects, key project technologies do not exist at the time of project initiation.

The third dimension of the Diamond Framework is *complexity*. It represents the complexity of the product, tasks, and project organization. Three types of complexity are included in the framework. They are assembly, system, and array (system of systems). Assembly projects involve a single component or device, or a complete assembly. Such projects create products that are either independent and self-contained that function on their own or products that function within a larger system. System projects involve multiple systems and require system integration. Array projects involve a dispersed collection of systems that function together to achieve a common purpose. Array projects can be referred to as system of systems. They are typically large in scale.

The last dimension is *pace*. It represents the urgency of the project. In other words, given the project's scope, how much time is required to complete the project. Four categories of pace are used in the framework. These are regular, fast/competitive, time-critical, and blitz. Regular projects are projects where the time to complete them is not critical to organizational success. Missing the deadline may be tolerated. If the project completion time is important to an organization's competitive advantage, the projects are considered fast/competitive. These projects are typically initiated to address a market opportunity or to create a strategic positioning. Time-critical projects are the ones that need to be completed by a specific completion date that cannot be changed. These projects are typically initiated in response to a specific window of opportunity. Failing to meet the time goal means project failure. Blitz projects are the one with the highest urgency. These projects must be completed as soon as possible since they are typically initiated to address a crisis or an unexpected event.

Winch et al. (2022) proposed a similar model to understand a type of project. Their four-dimensional model includes technological complexity, organizational complexity, novelty, and pace as dimensions. The Diamond Framework and the four-dimensional model can be used to assess the type of project (see Figure 6.1). Using the Diamond Framework as an example, Project A can be categorized as a platform project on the novelty dimension because it creates a new generation of product for an existing product line. Project A is also a medium-tech project since it mostly uses existing technologies and a few new technologies. It is an assembly project on the complexity dimension. It creates a simple and self-contained product. Project A is a time-critical project on a pace dimension because its product should be launched to the market prior to the upcoming holiday season.

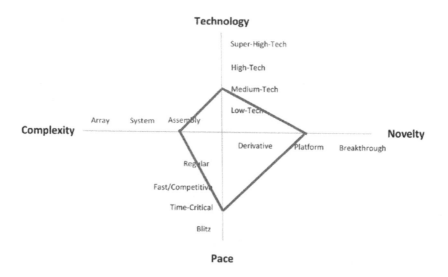

Figure 6.1   *An example of the use of the Diamond Framework to assess project type*

6.3.2   Managing Different Project Types

Understanding project type by using the Diamond Framework allows a project manager to manage the project accordingly. On the novelty dimension, a derivative project, for example, should be managed differently from a platform or breakthrough project. Breakthrough projects need fast product prototyping to obtain customer or market feedback and very late freeze of the requirements. Derivative projects, on the other hand, may have earlier freeze of product requirements, perhaps right after project initiation, since the understanding of requirements is clearer. As for platform projects, the project team needs to invest in defining products and involve customers in the process prior to making the decision to freeze the requirements, perhaps mid-project.

On the technology dimension, project managers should also manage projects contingently on the project type. For example, project managers can utilize a rigid 'get it done' approach when managing low-tech and medium-tech projects. However, flexibility and readiness to accept changes should be used for high-tech and super-high-tech projects. While the linear development approach with phase overlapping may be used for low-tech and medium-tech projects, it is not recommended for high-tech and super-high-tech projects where the spiral development approach is recommended.

Project managers should use different approaches to manage projects with different degrees of complexity. While the informal management style can be used to manage assembly projects, it may not be appropriate for system and array projects. The project managers of system projects may need to utilize a more formal style and be aware of political and inter-organizational issues. They also need to focus on system requirements, system design, and system integration. As for array projects, program and project managers have to have a high awareness of political, environmental, legal, and social issues. They also have to have a strong focus on program policy coordination and political decision making.

As for the pace dimension, projects with different pace requirements should be managed differently. Regular projects can be managed by following established processes and procedures. While following structured procedures is significant for fast/competitive projects, project managers should seek new concepts or methods to shorten project duration. Time-critical projects need tight schedule control with the focus on meeting the deadline. Blitz projects should be managed without bureaucracy. Contingency should be prepared, planned, and ready to be utilized for blitz projects.

Project managers can use the Diamond Framework to assess their projects such that they can manage the project accordingly. Failure to manage projects according to their type may have some negative impact on project success. In addition, the framework can be used to evaluate whether the actual management style fits with the style that is required for the project.

6.4   STRATEGIC PROJECT MANAGEMENT

Another research area where researchers have applied concepts from the contingency school is strategic project management. In essence, researchers suggest that since projects are initiated as part of an organization's strategy execution, projects should be managed according to the strategic category they serve. In this research area, projects are categorized based on the strategic context. Some of the research in this area is highlighted in this section.

6.4.1   Project Management Systems

Cooke-Davies et al. (2009) explored the impact of the underlying drivers of an organization's strategy on the nature of the projects that have been selected for implementation, and the approaches used to manage the projects. They proposed a Strategic Project Management Systems–Value Driver Portfolio Model that can be used to link specific types of projects to a specific pattern of strategic value drivers, derived from a specific strategy. They suggested four contexts of the value drivers based on the need to improve economics of process and the need for differentiation.

Context 1

Low process economics driver/low differentiation driver. Organizations operating in this context are likely to be operations-based and in a relatively stable market environment. Project initiation in these organizations tends to be on an *ad hoc* basis. A rigorous and well-structured project management system may not be needed for managing projects in these organizations.

Context 2

High process economics driver/low differentiation driver. Organizations operating in this context are likely to compete on a low-cost basis. They need to create and launch products to the market with the lowest price in accordance with quality requirements. With this, efficient project implementation processes are needed for managing projects.

Context 3

Low process economics driver/high differentiation driver. Organizations operating in this context are innovation-driven organizations. Projects within these organizations are initiated to create new innovative products or services to the market. With the high degree of uncertainties associated with the project and its product, the organization needs to implement project management systems that can address highly uncertain processes.

Context 4

High process economics driver/high differentiation driver. Organizations operating in this context can be categorized as entrepreneurship and intrapreneurship. This leads to the need to be both operationally and innovatively excellent. Leadership excellence with a high degree of entrepreneurial autonomy should be the focus of project management systems in these organizations. Cooke-Davies et al. (2009) conclude that more research is needed to study an appropriate project management system for this context.

6.4.2   Project Strategy

Contingency theory has some influence on the concept of project strategy. In essence, scholars propose that project managers should not manage every project the same way. They should develop a project strategy for each project and use the strategy to lead the project to its success. Different project strategies are used due to the different demands from the business environment of the project under consideration. The concept of project strategy has been proposed by many researchers.

Artto et al. (2008, p. 8) defines project strategy as 'a direction in a project that contributes to the success of project in its environment'. They suggest that the strategy of each project depends on the project's position in its environment. As for innovation projects, they found four types of project strategies depending on the degree of the complexity of stakeholder environment and the level of project autonomy. These projects have different project strategies and different ways of strategy development. Subordinate projects are those with a low degree of complexity in the stakeholder environment and a low level of project autonomy. These projects create their own project strategy by taking the direction from the firm's strategy. Autonomous projects are those with a low degree of complexity in the stakeholder environment and a high level of project autonomy. The purpose of these projects is to transform the parent organization or its business. The strategy of these projects may, therefore, contradict the strategy of the parent organization. Projects with a weak position in a complex stakeholder environment are those with a high degree of complexity in the stakeholder environment and a low level of project autonomy. These projects typically originate from a consortia of multiple organizations. The project strategy depends on the result of the negotiations of the surrounding stakeholder network. Autonomous projects in a complex stakeholder environment are those with a high degree of complexity in the stakeholder environment and a high level of project autonomy. The strategy for these projects emerges from the active contribution of the stakeholders.

Patanakul and Shenhar (2012, p. 7) suggest that the project strategy is 'the project perspective, position, and guidelines for what to do and how to do it, to achieve the highest competitive advantage and the best value from the project'. Three elements of project strategy are suggested: perspective, position, and plan. Perspective represents the background, the environment, the reason why the project is initiated, including the overall objective, and the strategic concept that will guide the project's experience. Position represents the competitive position the company will achieve after the project has completed. Plan represents action to achieve the project results, including the behaviour needed to complete the project. These three elements represent the 'why', 'what', and 'how' of project strategy. By addressing these elements, project managers should be able to formulate a project strategy for their projects. A later empirical study by Patanakul et al. (2012) identified three types of project strategy for new product and software development projects: product superiority strategy, product time-to-market strategy, and customer intimacy strategy. Product superiority strategy is used when project teams focus on developing a product with superior quality, functionalities, features, etc. A product time-to-market strategy leads project teams to focus more on project completion time and product launch date either within the window of opportunity or by being first in the market. Customer intimacy strategy directs project teams to focus on the development of close relationships with their customers. Such relationships could lead to future business opportunities. The research findings revealed that projects may need different project strategies to be able to address different demands from their business environment.

6.5　MOVING FORWARD

Contingency theory has had a significant impact on project management research. Using contingency theory as a foundation, many research studies proposed project management frameworks, methods, and approaches, including tools and techniques that can be used to manage different project types and to address different business environments. Besides the research studies outlined as examples in the previous sections, contingency theory is also prominent in other areas of project management research, particularly project leadership. Many researchers suggested that project managers should possess an adaptive leadership style that can be used to lead different projects and teams with different characteristics; in other words, project managers should use a leadership style that suits the characteristics of the projects and teams they lead (Shenhar & Dvir, 2007; Tyssen et al., 2014). Moving forward, there are several potential research themes studying the applications of contingency theory to project management.

It has been accepted by project management scholars that different projects should be managed differently. In addition, several scholars have proposed ways to categorize projects into different types. It is time to revisit this research area to further identify project management approaches that are appropriate for different types of projects. Shenhar and Dvir (2007), for example, have identified project characteristics associated with different project types for each dimension of the Diamond Framework – novelty, technology, complexity, and pace. They have also identified the impact of different project types on project success and managerial approaches with regards to the technology dimension. More work needs to be done on the novelty, complexity, and pace dimensions.

Future research studies can also be conducted to expand the area of strategic project management. There is a research opportunity to extend the work of Cooke-Davies et al. (2009), who propose four contexts of value drivers based on the need to improve economics of process and the need for differentiation. Further research can extend their work by identifying appropriate project management approaches for each context. Context 4 (high process economics driver/high differentiation driver), in particular, is under-researched, both in terms of the type of project that fits in this context and the managerial approaches that are appropriate for it.

Another research opportunity in the area of strategic project management is research related to project strategy. Using contingency theory as a foundation, researchers can identify project strategies that are appropriate for different project types. By using the definition of project strategy, proposed by Patanakul and Shenhar (2012) as a basis, future studies can be conducted to identify appropriate project strategies for different project types on each dimension of the Diamond Framework. For instance, on a pace dimension, which project strategies are appropriate for regular, fast/competitive, time-critical, and blitz projects? Pursuing this research topic will be a significant endeavour. The research scope and plan need to be well thought out.

REFERENCES

Artto, K., Kujala, J., Dietrich, P. & Martinsuo, M. (2008). What is project strategy? *International Journal of Project Management*, 26(1), 4–12.

Bertalanffy, L. V. (1968). General systems theory: A critical review. In W. Buckley (Ed.), *Modern systems research for the behavioural scientists* (pp. 11–30). Aldine.

Boulding, K. E. (1956). General systems theory: The skeleton of science. *Management Science*, 2(3), 197–208.

Cooke-Davies, T. J., Crawford, L. H. & Lechler, T. G. (2009). Project management systems: Moving project management from an operational to a strategic discipline. *Project Management Journal*, 40(1), 110–123.

Galbraith, J. (1970). Environmental and technological determinants of organization design. In J. W. Lorsch & P. R. Lawrence (Eds), *Studies in organization design*. Richard D. Irwin and The Dorsey Press.

Galbraith, J. (2014). *Designing organizations*. Jossey-Bass.

Herzberg, F., Mausner, B. & Snyderman, B. (1959). *The motivation to work*. John Wiley and Sons.

Hodge, B. J. & Anthony, W. P. (1988). *Organization theory*. Allyn and Baron.

Lorsch, J. W. & Lawrence, P. R. (1970). *Studies in organization design*. Richard D. Irwin and The Dorsey Press.

Maslow, A. H. (1943). A theory of human motivation. *Psychological Review*, 50(4), 370–396.

Patanakul, P. & Shenhar, A. J. (2012). What project strategy really is: The fundamental building block in strategic project management. *Project Management Journal*, 43(1), 4–20.

Patanakul, P., Shenhar, A. J. & Milosevic, D. Z. (2012). How project strategy is used in project management: Cases of new product development and software development projects. *Journal of Engineering and Technology Management*, 29(3), 391–414.

Shenhar, A. J. (2001). One size does not fit all projects: Exploring classical contingency domains. *Management Science*, 47(3), 394–414.

Shenhar, A. J. & Dvir, D. (1996). Toward a typological theory of project management. *Research Policy*, 25(4), 607–632.

Shenhar, A. J. & Dvir, D. (2007). *Reinventing project management*. Harvard Business School Press.

Shenhar, A. J., Dvir, D., Milosevic, D. Z., Mulenburg, J., Patanakul, P., Reilly, R., Ryan, M., Sage, A., Sauser, B., Srivannaboon, S., Stefanovic, J. & Thamhain, H. (2005). Toward a NASA-specific project management framework. *Engineering Management Journal*, 17(4), 8–16.

Thompson, J. D. (1967). *Organizations in action*. McGraw-Hill.

Tyssen, A. K., Wald, A. & Spieth, P. (2014). The challenge of transactional and transformational leadership in projects. *International Journal of Project Management*, 32(3), 365–375.

Winch, G. M., Maytorena, E. & Sergeeva, N. (2022). *Strategic project organizing: A three domains approach*. Oxford University Press.

Woodward, J. (1965). *Industrial organization: Theory and practice*. Oxford University Press.

Wren, D. A. (1972). *The evolution of management thought*. Ronald Press.

7. System dynamics to understand and improve the performance of complex projects

Burak Gozluklu and John Sterman

7.1 COMPLEX PROJECTS: LATE, EXPENSIVE, AND WRONG

Complex projects are chronically LEW: late, expensive and wrong, failing to meet quality standards and customer needs. A 2019 Gartner survey (2019) found only 11 per cent of organizations met their initial launch targets, with 45 per cent reporting delays. Projects often appear to be going smoothly until near the end, when errors made earlier are discovered, necessitating costly rework, overtime, unplanned hiring, expediting, schedule slippage, or reductions in project scope and quality. The result is poor profitability, loss of market share and reputation, and, often, costly litigation between customers and contractors.

A typical reaction to project failure is to blame someone. As a senior executive in a large company the second author studied said, 'Around here we don't ask the "5 why's" [when there's a problem] … we ask the "5 who's"'. But the prevalence and persistence of project pathologies suggest it is not a matter of 'a few bad apples'. System dynamics stresses that the structure of the systems in which we work powerfully conditions our behaviour (Sterman, 2000). The vast majority of people are honest, capable, and hard-working. But the complexity of the systems in which we are embedded far exceeds our ability to understand the many feedbacks and interactions that create their dynamics. Consequently, people facing intense pressure to hit cost, schedule, and quality targets make decisions in good faith that, perhaps helpful in the short run, worsen performance later, further intensifying the pressures they face (Repenning & Sterman, 2001, 2002).

7.2 SYSTEM DYNAMICS IN PROJECT MANAGEMENT

System dynamics has been used successfully in project management for over 40 years, both for dispute resolution (Cooper, 1980; Cooper & Reichelt, 2004; Eden et al., 2000; Stephens et al., 2005) and, more importantly, to avoid the problems that lead to disputes (Cooper & Lee, 2009; Godlewski et al., 2012). Lyneis and Ford (2007) and Ford and Lyneis (2020) provide an extensive bibliography; see also Abdel-Hamid and Madnick (1991), Ford and Sterman (1998a, 1998b), and Williams et al. (1995). A key concept is the rework cycle, first described by Cooper (1980); see also Rahmandad and Hu (2010).

Figure 7.1 presents a simplified representation of the core structure for a project phase. Project scope determines the initial base work to be completed (e.g., defining customer requirements, pouring concrete, or coding software). The stock of base work remaining falls as work is completed. Work completion depends on the workforce, workweek, and labour productivity, along with resources such as equipment, materials, and the work product of

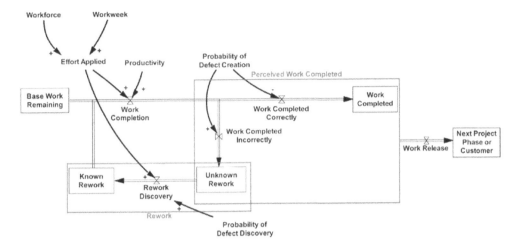

Figure 7.1   *The rework cycle*

Note: Stocks (rectangles) are connected by flows of work; arrows with polarities show the causal factors that control the flows.
Source: Sterman (2000).

upstream phases. For example, the construction of a building depends on construction drawings, equipment, permits, materials, etc.

Not all work is done correctly. The gross flow of work completed splits into work completed correctly and work completed incorrectly, according to the probability of defect creation. 'Defects' include outright errors – bugs in code, bad welds, errors in construction drawings – and any attribute of the work that does not meet customer requirements even if it is not technically flawed (e.g., software that runs, but too slowly).

Work done correctly accumulates in the stock of work completed. Work done incorrectly accumulates in a stock of unknown rework. The stock of undiscovered rework is drained as errors are discovered. But errors are not detected immediately. The detection delay depends on the nature of the project and the effort applied to inspection and testing. Some defects can be found quickly. Others cannot be detected despite careful testing until a full prototype is built and tested. And defects are sometimes deliberately concealed from others on the project team, delaying rework recognition and harming project performance (Ford & Sterman, 2003a). The probability of defect discovery depends on the resources for and thoroughness of testing. Defect discovery adds to the stock of known rework until those tasks are reworked. Reworked tasks can be done correctly or incorrectly. Consequently, numerous unplanned iterations often occur as tasks flow around the rework cycle multiple times before they are ultimately completed correctly (Ford & Sterman, 2003b).

By definition, unknown rework is work believed to have been done correctly. The sum of the work completed and unknown rework is the work perceived to be completed. The total rework required is the sum of the known and undiscovered rework. Consequently, true progress will be overestimated and rework requirements underestimated, often leading to insufficient time and resources allocated to the project. If project timeline, budget, and resources do not account for the rework cycle – a common situation – then projects will quickly fall behind. The resulting schedule and cost pressure then forces managers and workers into unplanned actions to get the project back on track. These actions may help in the short run, but often trigger reinforcing feedbacks that act as vicious cycles that further degrade schedule, cost, and quality. We now describe some of these feedback processes.

7.2.1   Responses to Schedule Pressure: Overtime and Corner Cutting

Overtime and long hours are perhaps the most commonly used method to boost progress when a project falls behind (Figure 7.2).

Overtime and corner cutting respond to schedule pressure, the ratio of the rate at which work must be completed to finish the project by the deadline to the rate work can be completed given the workforce, standard workweek, and current estimate of productivity. High schedule pressure leads to overtime, speeding work completion through the balancing overtime feedback.

Individual workers can also speed progress by cutting corners. They can work faster by taking less care on each task, skipping steps, and failing to document their work, coordinate with others on the team, or train inexperienced team members. All carpenters know they should 'measure twice, cut once', but under schedule pressure they can speed progress by measuring once. The balancing *cutting corners* feedback can quickly boost progress and reduce schedule pressure. Corner cutting is common because it is often difficult to detect and enables people to hit their deadlines without excessive overtime.

Similarly, high schedule pressure can lead people to cut testing. By testing less thoroughly, or skipping some tests, the probability of discovering defects falls. The stock of known rework will be less than it would have been, reducing the perceived work remaining and easing schedule pressure, the balancing *cutting testing* feedback. All these responses to schedule pressure

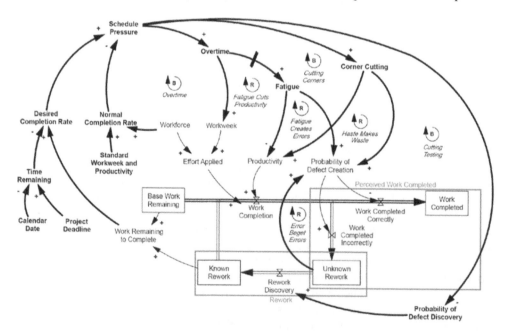

Figure 7.2   Overtime, cutting corners, and cutting testing

operate swiftly and help late projects get back on track. They are all locally rational but all create the possibility of unintended harms.

Extended overtime causes both knowledge workers and labourers to become tired or exhausted, worsening schedule pressure through the self-reinforcing *fatigue cuts productivity* and *fatigue creates errors* feedbacks. Fatigue also eventually leads to burnout and increases employee attrition, creating another vicious cycle when a project falls behind (not shown) by reducing progress, intensifying schedule pressure, and leading to still longer hours.

Cutting corners increases errors: carpenters who measure once often cut to the wrong length. More work is done incorrectly. When those defects are discovered, known rework rises, increasing schedule pressure and pressure for still more corner cutting, forming the vicious *haste makes waste* cycle.

Further, the defects not found accumulate in the stock of undiscovered rework, where they become the basis for subsequent work, which leads to still more defects. The result is another vicious cycle, the reinforcing *error begets error* feedback.

7.2.2   Unplanned Hiring

Unplanned hiring is another common response to high schedule pressure. Expanding the project team increases work completion, easing schedule pressure. But new hires are less effective than veterans, and only gradually gain experience and build relationships with others on the team. Thus, the first impact of hiring is a reduction in average experience and skill. The result is lower productivity, more defects, and lower chances of defect discovery. The project falls further behind, creating pressure for still more hiring – additional vicious cycles that contribute to delay and disruption.

High schedule pressure causes some overworked and overstressed team members to transfer to other projects or quit. Hiring can replace these losses, but the new hires are inexperienced, further eroding productivity, work quality, and testing, creating another set of reinforcing feedbacks. Additional harms from unplanned hiring include increased worksite congestion and team coordination problems, further harming productivity, quality, and defect detection (see http://bit.ly/ProjectCLDs for diagrams showing these and related feedbacks).

These effects are most severe when new hires are truly inexperienced, but also arise when veterans are brought in. Obviously, poaching experienced people from other projects causes those projects to suffer (see Repenning, 2000, 2001). But even if veterans with top skills could be hired without harming other projects, they don't know the project they are joining and lack the personal relationships that build the trust required for effective collaboration, high productivity, and quality work.

7.2.3   Increasing Concurrency: Working out of Sequence

Another common response to get a late project back on track is doing tasks best done sequentially in parallel. Such 'concurrent project management', 'concurrent engineering', or 'fast tracking' can be effective – if the organization redesigns the process and builds stronger capabilities for cross-functional collaboration and coordination. Doing so, however, takes time and effort. All too often, managers of a project behind schedule increase concurrency without investing in the capabilities needed for it to be effective. Increased concurrency immediately boosts work completion, easing schedule pressure. But lacking the capabilities for enhanced concurrency, doing more work out of sequence increases defect creation as team members must make assumptions about the work product of others they need in order to do their own work correctly but that is not yet available. The result is another vicious cycle that increases schedule pressure further as lower work quality eventually increases rework.

7.2.4   Scope Creep

Project scope often changes during the project. Late scope changes can be proposed by customers, the marketing team, or the project team (Figure 7.3). Demands for new features accrue in a backlog of pending feature requests. Project managers or organization executives decide whether to add those features to the scope.

The larger the backlog of pending requests for new features, the greater the pressure to add those changes. Agreeing to do so is an intendedly rational response that eases the pressure, shown as the balancing feedback *addressing customer demand.*

The direct costs of the new features are usually added to the project budget (but often not to the timeline). However, accepting new features also frequently requires reworking some previously completed tasks, increasing the work remaining beyond the direct impact of the late scope changes. The increase in base work and rework of tasks previously completed increases the total work remaining, delaying completion. The longer the project lasts, the greater the likelihood that still more new features will be proposed. Accepting them increases work remaining still more. The project can become stuck in another vicious cycle through the reinforcing feedbacks *scope changes cause rework* and *delays cause more late changes.* Further, managers seeking to ease the growing cost and schedule pressure may cut scope by eliminating features deemed less essential. But scope cuts also require more previously completed tasks to be reworked, creating additional vicious cycles, not shown, that further worsen delay.

The later a scope change is made, the more previously completed work requires rework and the later the project will become. This obvious fact suggests that scope changes should be few, and should cease before detailed design and other phases get under way. Often, however, the opposite occurs.

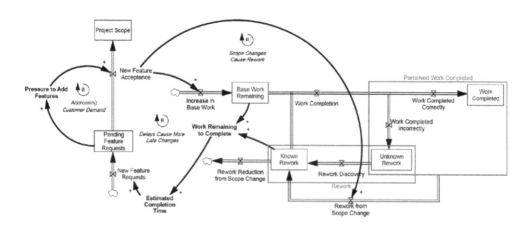

Figure 7.3   *Impact of late specification changes*

7.2.5   Why Would People Continue to Request New Features Even When Doing So Causes Further Delay and Disruption?

It is difficult to identify all the rework caused by late changes. Figure 7.3 shows only one project phase, but scope changes also force rework in other phases, particularly when they occur after some design work has been released to other phases (Parvan et al., 2015). The rework triggered by scope changes induces still more rework elsewhere, especially in projects with tight interdependencies across phases. The resulting 'avalanche of changes', 'ripple effects', or 'snowball effects' (Terwiesch & Loch, 1999; Ullah et al., 2016) have been at the heart of many project management applications of system dynamics (Lyneis & Ford, 2007). Rahmandad and Weiss (2009) describe a system dynamics model showing how these feedbacks undermined the competitiveness of a major firm; Cooper and Lee (2009) and Godlewski et al. (2012) used a system dynamics model to identify these problems and proactively avoid them at construction giant Fluor.

More importantly, project delays lead to still more late changes. Consider commercial product development. Every day brings the possibility of changes in technology, consumer preferences, and competing products. The longer a project takes, the more new features are likely to be suggested. Christensen's (1997) study of medical device maker Medtronic provides an example. At the time, Medtronic was losing market share due to late product launches. A Medtronic executive explained, 'The problem then fed on itself ... the development people would tell me that they could never get anything to market because marketing kept changing the product description in the middle of the projects. And the marketing people would say that it took so long for engineering to get anything done, that by the time they got around to completing something, the market demands would have changed ... it becomes a vicious spiral' (Christensen, 1997, p. 3).

The diagrams and discussion here illustrate only a few of the many feedbacks created by common managerial responses to projects in distress (an expanded set of causal diagrams is available at http://bit.ly/ProjectCLDs). Readers are encouraged to explore others, e.g., slipping the deadline or soft launch. For each, first seek the intended impact – how it could improve performance – then ask what unintended consequences might arise and what feedback processes these create.

7.3   SUMMARY: MULTIPLE INTERACTING FEEDBACKS CREATE DELAY AND DISRUPTION

Several lessons emerge from the dynamic feedback perspective on project performance outlined here. First, each common response to a project in trouble, whether overtime, corner cutting, unplanned hiring, increasing concurrency, or accepting late customer changes, is intendedly rational. Each creates a balancing feedback that attempts to speed progress, control costs, or better meet customer and market needs. In almost all cases, these interventions are undertaken in good faith by well-intentioned people who sincerely seek to improve project performance.

Second, each of these actions creates unintended consequences including scope creep, stress, fatigue, skill dilution, work done out of sequence, and others. These unintended impacts cut productivity, increase errors, and erode testing quality, slowing progress and triggering multiple reinforcing feedbacks that act as vicious cycles, leading to cumulative delay and disruption far larger than expected. Each reinforcing feedback may be relatively weak, but their joint impact can be far larger than people anticipate. The increase in errors caused by fatigue, by itself, may not outweigh the benefits of longer hours, but the joint impact of fatigue on errors, productivity, test quality, worker attrition, and other impacts can overwhelm the benefits of longer hours.

Third, these effects are non-linear and often delayed. Increasing the workweek from 40 to 48 hours immediately boosts output and may not harm productivity, quality, or worker retention, but further increases sharply worsen them. The harm manifests after delays, that, when unrecognized, can lead people who sincerely seek to improve performance to inadvertently worsen it.

Finally, these feedbacks are not captured in most project management tools. Gantt charts, critical path methods, and project management software represent work activities in great detail, but the planned duration, resource requirements, and costs of each activity are specified exogenously. They do not capture the feedback processes identified above. As a result, the unintended impact of, say, a late customer specification change on overtime, fatigue, productivity, error rates, error detection, unplanned hiring, and so on are not captured. Consequently, project management software will underestimate the impact of the changes, often dramatically.

System dynamics is complementary to traditional scheduling and project management tools: where traditional tools are useful to deal with the combinatorial complexity of complex projects with multiple parallel and sequential activities, system dynamics is useful to deal with the dynamic complexity created by the interdependencies, feedbacks, time delays, and non-linearities in large-scale projects.

Rigorously accounting for these interactions requires simulation models that capture these interactions with sufficient granularity for the purpose, and with parameters and relationships grounded in evidence. The system dynamics literature describes how such models can be developed, estimated, and tested, and how they have been used successfully to improve projects. Chapter 37 presents the interactive MIT Sloan Project Management Simulator, including policies for the successful management of complex projects.

REFERENCES

Abdel-Hamid, T. & Madnick, S. (1991). *Software project dynamics: An integrated approach.* Prentice-Hall.

Christensen, C. M. (1997). *We've got rhythm! Medtronic corporation's cardiac pacemaker business.* Harvard Business School Press.

Cooper, K. (1980). Naval ship production: A claim settled and a framework built. *Interfaces,* 10(6), 20–36.

Cooper, K. & Lee, G. (2009). *Managing the dynamics of projects and changes at Fluor.* Ken Cooper Associates.

Cooper, K. & Reichelt, K. (2004). Project changes: Sources, impacts, mitigation, pricing, litigation, and excellence. In P. W. G. Morris & J. K. Pinto (Eds), *The Wiley guide to managing projects* (pp. 743–772). John Wiley and Sons.

Eden, C., Williams, T., Ackermann, F. & Howick, S. (2000). The role of feedback dynamics in disruption and delay on the nature of disruption and delay (D&D) in major projects. *Journal of the Operational Research Society,* 51(3), 291–300.

Ford, D. & Lyneis, J. (2020). System dynamics applied to project management: A survey, assessment, and directions for future research. In B. Dangerfield (Ed.), *System dynamics: Encyclopedia of complexity and systems science series* (pp. 285–231). Springer.

Ford, D. & Sterman, J. (1998a). Expert knowledge elicitation for improving mental and formal models. *System Dynamics Review*, 14(4), 309–340.

Ford, D. & Sterman, J. (1998b). Dynamic modeling of product development processes. *System Dynamics Review*, 14(1), 31–68.

Ford, D. & Sterman, J. (2003a). The liar's club: Concealing rework in concurrent development. *Concurrent Engineering: Research and Applications*, 11(3), 211–220.

Ford, D. & Sterman, J. (2003b). Overcoming the 90% syndrome: Iteration management in concurrent development projects. *Concurrent Engineering: Research and Applications*, 11(3), 177–186.

Gartner Group (2019). *Gartner survey finds that 45% of product launches are delayed by at least one month.* Press release, 9 September. www.gartner.com/en/newsroom/press-releases/2019-09-09-gartner-survey-finds-that-45-percent-of-product-launches-are-delayed-by-at-least-one-month.

Godlewski, E., Lee, G. & Cooper, K. (2012). System dynamics transforms Fluor project and change management. *Interfaces*, 42(1), 17–32.

Lyneis, J. & Ford, D. (2007). System dynamics and project management: A survey, assessment and directions for future work. *System Dynamics Review*, 23(2/3), 157–189.

Parvan K., Rahmandad H. & Haghani, A. (2015). Inter-phase feedbacks in construction projects. *Journal of Operations Management*, 39(1), 48–62.

Rahmandad, H. & Hu, K. (2010). Modeling the rework cycle: capturing multiple defects per task. *System Dynamics Review*, 26(4), 291–315.

Rahmandad, H. & Weiss, D. (2009). Dynamics of concurrent software development. *System Dynamics Review*, 25(3), 224–249.

Repenning, N. (2000). A dynamic model of resource allocation in multi-project research and development systems. *System Dynamics Review*, 16(3), 173–212.

Repenning, N. (2001). Understanding fire fighting in new product development. *Journal of Product Innovation Management*, 18(5), 285–300.

Repenning, N. P. & Sterman, J. (2001). Nobody ever gets credit for fixing problems that never happened: Creating and sustaining process improvement. *California Management Review*, 43(4), 64–88.

Repenning, N. P. & Sterman, J. (2002). Capability traps and self-confirming attribution errors in the dynamics of process improvement. *Administrative Science Quarterly*, 47(2), 265–295.

Stephens, C., Graham, A. & Lyneis, J. (2005). System dynamics modeling in the legal arena: Meeting the challenges of expert witness admissibility. *System Dynamics Review*, 21(2), 95–122.

Sterman, J. (2000). *Business dynamics: Systems thinking and modeling for a complex world.* Irwin/McGraw-Hill.

Terwiesch, C. & Loch, C. (1999). Managing the process of engineering change orders: The case of the climate control system in automobile development. *Journal of Product Innovation Management*, 16(2), 160–172.

Ullah, I., Tang, D. & Yin, L. (2016). Engineering product and process design changes: A literature overview. *Procedia CIRP*, 56, 25–33.

Williams, T., Eden, C., Ackerman, F. & Tait, A. (1995). The effects of design changes and delays on project costs. *Journal of the Operational Research Society*, 46(7), 809–819.

8. Transaction cost economics: governing the commercial interface

David Lowe

8.1 INTRODUCTION

This chapter explores the influence of concepts from the transaction cost economics (TCE) stream of research in institutional economics and organisation studies on complex project organising (CPO) research. It starts by classifying the concept of 'governance' in CPO research into two different streams of research with little synergy between them. One is focused on the governance of the relationship between the owner and its projects – the governance interface – and the other on the relationship between the owner and its suppliers – the commercial interface. The focus here is on the commercial interface. The chapter then briefly outlines the core concepts of TCE, relational contract theory (RCT), and reviews key early applications to the commercial interface on projects and how they have influenced theory development in commercial management. More recent contributions are then reviewed before a forward research agenda is proposed for the continuing application of TCE concepts to CPO research.

8.2 GOVERNANCE

Despite intensified academic interest in governance within the field of project research, project governance remains an ambiguous (Ahola et al., 2014) and fragmented concept, lacking both agreement on what it is and its underling components (Musawir et al., 2020). For example, Ahola et al. (2014) identify two discrete and comparatively independent avenues of research, which view project governance as either 'external to any specific project' or 'internal to a specific project'.

In the first instance, project governance is an activity that is 'externally, and unidirectionally, imposed by the project-based firm on the focal project'. Accordingly, its purpose is to both define standards and establish procedures that individual projects are required to follow, and to monitor their realisation (Ahola et al., 2014, p. 1325). The focus here is on the governance of the relationship between the owner and its projects, which Winch (2014) labels the 'governance interface'. This interface, therefore, addresses the 'challenge of governance' – the procedures adopted by owners to verify their project selection (decision-making) and whether these projects are proceeding as planned (performance).

The second defines 'shared practices for safeguarding, coordinating, and adapting the numerous exchanges that take place between project-based firms and (non-project-based)' organisations involved in the project. In this instance, the primary objective is to 'establish a shared set of rules and procedures that all firms participating to the project are expected to follow' (Ahola et al., 2014, p. 1325). The emphasis here is on the relationship between the owner and its suppliers, particularly their commercial relationship (Lowe, 2013; Turner,

1995), the 'commercial interface' (Winch, 2014) and from work based on TCE. This chapter therefore focuses on the second 'governance thread': the commercial interface and the application of TCE.

8.3 TRANSACTION COST ECONOMICS AND RELATIONAL CONTRACT THEORY

Inter-organisational relationships are primarily regulated simultaneously by two principal governance mechanisms (Lumineau, 2017): one focused on the use of formal contracts to safeguard against opportunism and conflict (TCE) and the other centred on relational governance, and in particular trust (RCT).

As an interdisciplinary concept, TCE fuses facets of contract law, economics and organisation theory (Cuypers et al., 2021; Williamson, 1981). Consequently, Lowe (2013, 2022) deems it highly germane to commercial management (the management of the commercial interface), providing both a theoretical framework and common vocabulary to examine and explain commercial practice. Williamson's contribution centres on economic governance and the boundaries of the firm. Governance structure relates to the institutional framework in which economic exchanges (transactions) are conducted. Principally, there are two polar options: markets (where products and services are purchased external to an organisation) and hierarchies (where the product or service is either manufactured or supplied from within an organisation) – classically referred to as the 'make or buy' decision. Between these, a number of hybrid options exist, adapted to the particular attributes of the transaction (Williamson, 1985, figure 3.2).

TCE applies the transaction as its unit of analysis and governance as the mechanism by which order is introduced to the exchange, moderating conflict and attaining reciprocal benefit. Transaction costs are generated each time a product or service is 'transferred across a technologically separable interface', leading to the development of new skills, abilities, and processes to manufacture a product or deliver a service (Williamson, 1981, p. 552). It is, therefore, the cost to an organisation of acquiring a product or service via the market in preference to manufacturing or supplying them from within. Costs incurred in an exchange (transaction) can be categorised as: selecting, contracting, monitoring (post-award contract management) and enforcing activities (Williamson, 1985). Despite TCE predominantly assuming a demand-side perspective, transaction costs are incurred by both parties; suppliers face costs of contract acquisition such as bidding.

In respect of project governance, TCE highlights the establishment of ex-post governance structures (safeguards) as its principal control mechanism to avert or kerb the opportunistic behaviour of an exchange partner. Defining opportunism as 'self-interest seeking with guile', Williamson acknowledges that many trading partners will not behave opportunistically. However, he acknowledges the difficulty in determining pre-award (ex-ante) those who will.

Maladaptation, the inability ex-post to provide appropriate or adequate adjustment, is a key aspect of TCE. Change is inevitable, particularly on, but not exclusive to, complex projects, due to unforeseen circumstances and technical advancement. The objective, therefore, is to predict during the pre-award phase potential contractual hazards, identify appropriate control mechanisms, and then incorporate these into the governance structure adopted. In a Western context, exchange transactions are primarily safeguarded using formal contracts. These can range from simple discrete to complex bespoke. The cost of drafting, negotiating, and agreeing these contracts increases significantly as one transitions from simple to complex. A point is eventually reached where the cost of creating appropriate contracts is prohibitive and integrating the activity vertically becomes more cost-effective.

TCE utilises three attributes to describe exchange transactions:

- Asset specificity: the extent to which parties can redeploy specialised/specific assets (physical, human, site, dedicated, brand name, and temporal) secured to either manufacture a product or deliver a service, and the importance of these assets to the ongoing relationship. Where a party is unable to reutilise an asset or recoup their investment in them bilateral dependency is created, increasing the potential for opportunistic behaviour.
- Uncertainty: complex and long-term contracts are inclined to change, due to unforeseen circumstances and technological change. To facilitate change, contracts incorporate mechanisms to coordinate and reconcile adaptations. Uncertainty can generate ex-ante environmental and ex-post behavioural costs.
- Frequency of transaction generates self-interest trust, encourages the preservation of relationships (due to the potential value to be derived from future exchanges) and incentivises the parties to invest in specialised governance mechanisms.

Associated with these attributes, Williamson (1975) identifies two behavioural characteristics:

- Opportunism: the pursuit of self-interest using, for example, dishonesty, double-dealing, deception, and falsifying information to achieve an organisation's objectives.
- Bounded rationality: decision-making is constrained by the availability of information, an individual's cognitive skills, and time. When combined with complex and uncertain environments, it is theorised that bounded rationality will lead to hierarchy.

To these, Winch (2001) contributes a third behavioural characteristic:

- Learning: derived from the frequency of transaction and length of relationship between the parties, resulting in a clearer understanding of the other party's requirements, aims, processes, etc. and their motivation to transact.

TCE theory maintains that transaction costs increase as transactors (parties to the exchange) invest more in specialised assets, due to the need to safeguard themselves against the potential opportunistic behaviour of the other party, and particularly when combined with a high level of uncertainty. However, Williamson (1991) asserts that the transaction costs of all governance arrangements increase with asset specificity. Prevailing governance arrangements include:

- Market governance (classical contracting): the principal governance structure for repeat and one-off transactions, where the product or service is standardised or commoditised. Scope and performance are captured in discrete terms and conditions (low uncertainty), while opportunistic behaviour is tempered by the availability of alternatives within the market (low asset specificity). Under this structure litigation is the prime dispute resolution mechanism.
- Trilateral governance (neoclassical contracting): an apt governance structure for both mixed and highly idiosyncratic infrequent transactions. For example, where there is high asset specificity and low uncertainty or high uncertainty and low asset specificity. In the

former instance, both parties are primarily motivated to deliver on their commitments due to their investment in specialised assets and potentially high switching/termination costs. Here the focus is on maintaining the relationship with third-party intervention (arbitration) used to resolve ex-post disputes.

- Transaction-specific governance (relational contracting): specialised governance structures that are frequently utilised on mixed and highly idiosyncratic, frequent, non-standard transactions. For example, where there are high asset specificity and high levels of uncertainty Williamson offers two approaches:
  - Bilateral governance (obligational contracting): where bespoke governance arrangements are established to address the specific circumstances of the exchange. Placed between markets and hierarchies, it is a hybrid, networked, third-way approach that adopts collaborative arrangements, such as project and strategic partnering, framework arrangements and alliances, and relational approaches based on trust (Powell, 1990).
  - Vertical integration: where the external supplier is brought within the boundaries of the 'purchasing' organisation.

Criticisms of TCE include its over-reliance on the protection afforded by contracts and vertical integration (Poppo & Zenger, 2002), while Ghoshal and Moran (1996) argue that when markets fail organisations are not direct substitutes for structuring efficient transactions. Additionally, they stress that TCE fails to appreciate the value-creating aspects of organisations when assessed against markets. Moreover, Cousins et al. (2008) argue that it fails to consider the limitations of hierarchies; particularly an organisation's ability to develop or acquire the prerequisite capabilities. Also, in certain contexts greater value may be generated by adopting an apparently inefficient (from a TCE perspective) exchange approach (Zajac & Olsen, 1993).

8.4   TRUST AND RELATIONAL CONTRACTING

Trust and 'self-enforcing' agreements have been proposed as an alternative mechanism to contracts. 'Trust is a psychological state comprising the intention to accept vulnerability based upon positive expectations of the intentions or behaviour of another' (Rousseau et al., 1998, p. 395).

Developed over time and grounded in social interaction, trust is considered to increase cooperation (Cook et al., 2005); although, it is a substitute for control and not a control mechanism (Rousseau et al., 1998). Moreover, trust in conjunction with collaboration, contractual flexibility, and innovation is viewed as a facilitator – a means of addressing the intrinsic risk and complexity found in projects, particularly complex projects (Davies et al., 2017). In the context of exchange transactions and the formation of long-term relationships, several forms of trust have been identified, including contractual, competence, and goodwill trust (Sako, 1992), plus socially orientated and self-interest trust (Lyons, 1995). However, as Cousins (2002) cautions, as maximisers and satisfiers 'all firms are snakes concerned with their self-interest and survival'. Their raison d'être is maximising shareholder value; therefore, they will work collaboratively with other firms when it's in their self-interest to do so but when it ceases to be they will 'bite you'.

Acknowledging criticism of classic contracting as a means of structuring transactions, Macneil (1983) advocated a perspective that emphasises the value of informal mechanisms and focuses on the behaviour of the participants in an exchange. Thus, transactions could be placed on a continuum (discrete to relational), conditional on the intensity of the relationship between the parties. Ultimately adopting the designation 'essential contract theory' (Macneil, 2000a), his approach identified ten common contract behavioural 'patterns and norms that supply a checklist for isolating all elements of the enveloping relations that might affect any transaction significantly', providing a framework by which to analyse and aid our understanding of relationships between trading partners (Macneil, 2000b, p. 893). Extant in all contracts, these norms and patterns are viewed by some as an alternative to explicit, complex contracts or vertical integration. They underpin relational contracts, adopted on recurring, collaborative business-to-business exchanges (Baker et al., 2002). Initially the operationalisation of relational contracting was illustrated using examples from the Japanese car manufacturing sector (for example, Doornik, 2006), subsequently there have been accounts of the introduction of the approach within project-based environments, particularly Heathrow Terminal 5 (Davies et al., 2016; Gil, 2009).

Criticism of RCT includes its failure to appreciate the importance of contractual consent (Barnett, 1992), moreover, as Eisenberg (2000) recognises, relational contracts are not a distinct class of contract, as virtually all contracts are relational. For a review of RCT's influence on management strategies and project outcomes, see Nwajei (2021), while Ivens and Blois (2004) provide a critical review of Macneil's contribution to the domain.

While the findings of Poppo and Zenger (2002), Arranz et al. (2011), and Chen et al. (2018), for example, validate the view that transactional and relational mechanisms are complementary, literature simultaneously supports the apparent conflicting propositions that formal contracts both undermine and support trust-based behaviour, cooperation, and incentives. However, Poppo and Zenger (2002) established that contractual complexity and relational governance have separate origins and different roles in fostering transaction performance. Lumineau (2017) suggests that these two positions are not inconsistent. Differentiating between the control and coordination aspects of contracts, he determines that researchers who established a negative relationship focused on the control function of contracts, while those who found a positive relationship focused on coordination.

8.5 EARLY APPLICATIONS OF TCE AND RCT TO THE COMMERCIAL INTERFACE

Early applications of TCE principles to the commercial interface were predominantly in construction with additional contributions from oil and gas and military contracts. The concept of 'quasi-firms' (semi-stable inter-organisational arrangements) within the construction sector was advanced by Eccles (1981), who called for the inclusion of an intermediate governance structure within TCE to account for the sector's adoption of relational contracting. Similarly, Reve and Levitt (1984) concluded that construction contracts are located between markets and hierarchies. Stinchcombe and Heimer (1985) illustrated how complex contracts transform market into hierarchy (or produce hierarchical outcomes). A conceptual framework for the governance of transactions across the project lifecycle was presented by Winch (2001), who explored the notion of the project coalition as a nexus of treaties distinguishing between vertical and horizontal transaction governance (Winch, 2006). Masten et al. (1991) established the importance of internal organisation costs, suggesting that variations in costs of organising within, in addition to between, firms should be addressed.

While ex-post opportunism reduces as contracts become more complete, this comes at the cost of increased ex-ante design expenditure (Crocker & Reynolds, 1993). The ideal level of contractual completeness/incompleteness requires a trade-off between these divergent factors. To mitigate the hazards of ex-post opportunism (hold-up problem), Chang and Ive (2007) advocate owners aligning project characteristics with the specific features of the various procurement systems. In particular, they recommend the adoption of partnering approaches. Elsewhere, Corts and Singh (2004) established that purchasers were less likely to utilise fixed-price contracts when the frequency of appointment of a particular supplier increased, arguing that robust contracts and recurring engagements can act as either substitutes or complements.

8.6   A REVIEW OF MORE RECENT CONTRIBUTIONS

Subsequent applications of TCE have centred on exploring the relationship between project governance and project performance and investigating the optimal design and selection of project governance frameworks.

Utilising TCE and relational capital theory to examine the influence of a project's governance structure on alliance project performance, Lee and Cavusgil (2006) found relational-based rather than contractual-based governance to be more significant and impactful. Moreover, they proffer that encountering environmental instability enhances the positive outcomes of relational-based governance. Likewise, Chen and Manley (2014) found that project performance is:

- predicted more by the implementation intensity of informal mechanisms (non-contractual conditions) than that of formal mechanisms (contractual conditions);
- not directly impacted by specific contract terms and conditions (their impact is facilitated by non-contractual project attributes); and
- insufficiently optimised by contractual commitments.

Subsequently, Chen et al. (2018) concluded that in an environment of high asset specificity (and/or where a supplier is strategically important) and high uncertainty, non-contractual governance becomes more important. Moreover, their analysis of collaborative infrastructure projects linked higher project performance to contracts awarded based on competition, but where the competitive emphasis was placed on profit margins and non-price criteria as opposed to those based on lowest price.

Benítez-Ávila et al.'s (2018) findings suggest that aspects of relational governance mediate the relationship, while contract governance 'partially' facilitates relational norms. Additionally, relational norms counterbalance the creation of long-term contractual governance through the establishment of routine 'collaborative micro-practices'. Contradictorily, Lu et al.'s (2015) results indicate that contractual governance is more effective in improving supplier performance, while relational governance is more effective in mitigating opportunism. Additionally, they found opportunism not to negatively influence project performance. However, Roehrich et al. (2020) found there to be a paucity of knowledge on what specific clauses in formal contracts foster coordination and adaptation, and how they influence project (exchange) performance.

In the context of megaprojects, Galvin et al. (2021) caution that the relational norms found in alliance contracts are insufficient in themselves to eradicate opportunistic behaviour. They suggest that collaboration is fostered and opportunism mitigated where the parties invest in structures that underpin governance, culture, and trust. Moreover, they conclude that governance, culture, and trust are interconnected and complementary. For example, transparency of governance was considered to enable trusting relationships to develop. They also encourage managers to establish collaborative, as opposed to self-interest-seeking, behaviours. However, they acknowledge that there is a significant cost incurred in adopting such an approach and as a result this may not be cost-effective on less complex or costly projects. Additionally, Vukomanović et al. (2021) suggest that trust and governance can be conceived as multidimensional and integrated, and that within this context the concept of trust should be employed as the preferred governance mechanism.

The design of the commercial interface between the project owner and its suppliers has received relatively little consideration in project organising research (Winch et al., 2020). Similarly, only a few examples were found that sought to integrate commercial management into the mainstream of project organising research.

Winch et al. (2020) theorise the commercial interface between the owner and the supplier domains of project organising within the context of CPO. They postulate an empirical basis for the strategic management of the commercial interface by project owners, which they term owner commercial strategy. In particular, they address opportunism and conflict, the 'dark side' of inter-organisational relationships (Oliveira & Lumineau, 2019). Adopting a pluralistic owner-based perspective to the management of the commercial interface, Winch et al. (2020, 2022) present a 'Four Forces Model', designed to enable owners to explore and map their contracting strategy for procuring complex performance from the multiple suppliers engaged on a specific project across the entire project lifecycle. To complement this model, Lowe (2022) developed a 'Contractual Governance Matrix', its dimensions comprising 'level of dependency' and 'level of uncertainty', enabling the project owner to select the most appropriate contractual governance regime from across its four quadrants. The approach is consistent with the recommendations of Davies et al. (2017), who advocate that, while under 'predictable and stable conditions' fixed-price contracts may be appropriate, under 'unexpected and rapidly changing circumstances' more flexible contracts, such as cost-plus or cost-reimbursable contracts, are needed to govern the commercial interface.

8.7   A FORWARD RESEARCH AGENDA

Project governance, and in particular the management of the commercial interface, i.e. 'Commercial Management' (Lowe, 2013; Lowe & Leiringer, 2006), is a complex and multifaceted phenomenon (Galvin et al., 2021); its analysis requiring more than one theoretical lens (Ahola et al., 2014; Winch et al., 2020). Therefore, while TCE and RCT have to a degree explained the behaviours of the parties to an exchange and offered partial governance 'solutions', these are still incomplete.

The continued application of TCE to project governance is, however, advocated to examine how project-based firms align governance structures to specific contextual dimensions, such as the level of uncertainty encountered on each project in its portfolio (Ahola et al., 2014). Further empirical work on the application of TCE to the changing nature of governance arrangements between owners and suppliers is required.

Although TCE has generally been applied to dyadic relationships, CPO involves the governance of a network of interconnected organisations and transactions. Further research is, therefore, encouraged into the application of network-level governance frameworks and the impact of discrete, dyadic arrangements on the multiple relationships within project networks (Ahola et al., 2014; Roehrich et al., 2020; Winch et al., 2020); the juxtaposition of the temporary aspect of projects with the relatively permanent nature of the project-based firm (Ahola et al., 2014; Winch, 2014); and the significance of coordination and relational governance to network relationships (Roehrich et al., 2020). To further address the managerial aspects of project governance, Galvin et al. (2021) encourage the utilisation of complementary lenses in addition to the predominant economic perspective applied to date. For example, Pitsis et al. (2014) propose the application of distributed knowledge management and learning perspectives and systems engineering approaches.

Further, specific areas of research interest include:

- Creating 'strong owners': investigating the role of powerful stakeholders (Ahola et al., 2014) and developing project owner capability (Winch & Leiringer, 2016), particularly in respect of understanding and shaping the structure of supply (Winch et al., 2020); encouraging the coordination and adaptation roles of contracts (Roehrich et al., 2020); and aligning project governance structures to specific characteristics of the project owner (Ahola et al., 2014).
- Negotiating governance frameworks: exploring the impact of pre-award contract negotiations on the implementation of projects (Ertel, 2004); post-award negotiations and project success to determine how to negotiate governance frameworks that encourage trust; establish effective relationships; and support project execution. Aligned to this is a need to determine the processes that foster and control trust in project governance, and how these may be encapsulated in governance frameworks (Vukomanović et al., 2021).
- Expanding the scope of the commercial interface (Lowe, 2013): to examine the function of project governance from project inception to asset disposal/service termination (Musawir et al., 2020) and, specifically, the alignment of project goals with the strategic intent of the participating organisations.

REFERENCES

Ahola, T., Ruuska, I., Artto, K. & Kujala, J. (2014). What is project governance and what are its origins? *International Journal of Project Management*, 32(8), 1321–1332.
Arranz, N. & Fdez de Arroyabe, J. C. (2011). Effect of formal contracts, relational norms and trust on performance of joint research and development projects. *British Journal of Management*, 23(4), 575–588.
Baker, G., Gibbons, R. & Murphy, K. J. (2002). Relational contracts and the theory of the firm. *Quarterly Journal of Economics*, 117(1), 39–84.
Barnett, R. E. (1992). Conflicting visions: A critique of Ian Macneil's relational theory of contract. *Virginia Law Review*, 78, 1175–1206.

Benítez-Ávila, C., Hartmann, A., Dewulf, G. & Henseler, J. (2018). Interplay of relational and contractual governance in public-private partnerships: The mediating role of relational norms, trust and partners' contribution. *International Journal of Project Management*, 36(3), 429–443.

Chang, C. Y. & Ive, G. (2007). Reversal of bargaining power in construction projects: Meaning, existence and implications. *Construction Management and Economics*, 25(8), 845–855.

Chen, L. & Manley, K. (2014). Validation of an instrument to measure governance and performance on collaborative infrastructure projects. *Journal of Construction Engineering and Management*, 140(5).

Chen, L., Manley, K., Lewis, J., Helfer, F. & Widen, K. (2018). Procurement and governance choices for collaborative infrastructure projects. *Journal of Construction Engineering and Management*, 144(8).

Cook, K. R., Hardin, R. & Levi, M. (2005). *Cooperation without trust?* Russell Sage Foundation.

Corts, K. S. & Singh, J. (2004). The effect of repeated interaction on contract choice: Evidence from offshore drilling. *Journal of Law, Economics, and Organization*, 20(1), 230–260.

Cousins, P. D. (2002). A conceptual model for managing long-term inter-organisational relationships. *European Journal of Purchasing and Supply Management*, 8(2), 71–82.

Cousins, P. D., Lamming, R. C., Lawson, B. & Squire, B. (2008). *Strategic supply management: Principles, theories and practice*. Pearson Education.

Crocker, K. J. & Reynolds, K. J. (1993). The efficiency of incomplete contracts: An empirical analysis of Air Force engine procurement. *RAND Journal of Economics*, 126–146.

Cuypers, I. R. P., Hennart, J.-F., Silverman, B. S. & Ertug, G. (2021). Transaction cost theory: Past progress, current challenges, and suggestions for the future. *Annals*, 15(1), 111–150.

Davies, A., Dodgson, M. & Gann, D. (2016). Dynamic capabilities in complex projects: The case of London Heathrow Terminal 5. *Project Management Journal*, 47(2), 26–46.

Davies, A., Dodgson, M., Gann, D., & MacAulay, S. (2017). Five rules for innovation in megaprojects. *MIT Sloan Management Reviews*, 59(1), 73–78.

Doornik, K. (2006). Relational contracting in partnerships. *Journal of Economics and Management Strategy*, 15(2), 517–548.

Eccles, R. G. (1981). The quasifirm in the construction industry. *Journal of Economic Behavior and Organization*, 2(4), 335–357.

Eisenberg, M. A. (2000). Why there is no law of relational contracts. *Northwestern University Law Review*, 94, 805–821.

Ertel, D. (2004). Getting past yes: Negotiating as if implementation mattered. *Harvard Business Review*, 82(11): 60–68.

Galvin, P., Tywoniak, S. & Sutherland, J. (2021). Collaboration and opportunism in megaproject alliance contracts: The interplay between governance, trust and culture. *International Journal of Project Management*, 39(4), 394–405.

Ghoshal, S. & Moran, P. (1996). Bad for practice: A critique of the transaction cost theory. *Academy of Management Review*, 21(1), 13–47.

Gil, N. (2009). Developing project client-supplier cooperative relationships: How much to expect from relational contracts? *California Management Review*, 51(2), 144–169.

Ivens, B. S. & Blois, K. J. (2004). Relational exchange norms in marketing: A critical review of Macneil's contribution. *Marketing Theory*, 4(3), 239–263.

Lee, Y. & Cavusgil, S. T. (2006). Enhancing alliance performance: The effects of contractual-based versus relational-based governance. *Journal of Business Research*, 59(8), 896–905.

Lowe, D. (2013). *Commercial management: Theory and practice*. Wiley-Blackwell.

Lowe, D. (2022). *Strategic commercial management*. Routledge.

Lowe, D. J. & Leiringer, R. (Eds) (2006). *Commercial management of projects: Defining the discipline*. Blackwell Publishing.

Lu, P., Guo, S., Qian, L., He, P. & Xu, X. (2015). The effectiveness of contractual and relational governances in construction projects in China. *International Journal of Project Management*, 33(1), 212–222.

Lumineau, F. (2017). How contracts influence trust and distrust. *Journal of Management*, 43(5), 1553–1577.

Lyons, B. R. (1995). Specific investment, economies of scale, and the make-or-buy decision: A test of transaction cost theory. *Journal of Economic Behavior and Organization*, 26(3), 431–443.

Macneil, I. R. (1983). Values in contract: Internal and external. *Northwestern University Law Review*, 78, 340–418.

Macneil, I. R. (2000a). Contracting worlds and essential contract theory. *Social and Legal Studies*, 9(3), 431–438.

Macneil, I. R. (2000b). Relational contract theory: Challenges and queries. *Northwestern University Law Review*, 94, 877–907.

Masten, S. E., Meehan, Jr., J. W. & Snyder, E. A. (1991). The costs of organization. *Journal of Law, Economics and Organization*, 7(1), 1–26.

Musawir A u, Abd-Karim, S. B. & Mohd-Danuri, M. S. (2020). Project governance and its role in enabling organizational strategy implementation: A systematic literature review, *International Journal of Project Management*, 38(1), 1–16.

Nwajei, U. O. K. (2021). How relational contract theory influence management strategies and project outcomes: A systematic literature review. *Construction Management and Economics*, 39(5), 432–457.

Oliveira, N. & Lumineau, F. (2019). The dark side of interorganizational relationships: An integrative review and research agenda. *Journal of Management*, 45(1), 231–261.

Pitsis, T. S., Sankaran, S., Gudergan, S. & Clegg, S. R. (2014). Governing projects under complexity: Theory and practice in project management. *International Journal of Project Management*, 32(8), 1285–1290.

Poppo, L. & Zenger, T. (2002). Do formal contracts and relational governance function as substitutes or compliments? *Strategic Management Journal*, 23(8), 707–725.

Powell, W. (1990). Neither market nor hierarchy: Network forms of organization. *Research in Organizational Behavior*, 12, 295–336.

Reve, T. & Levitt, R. (1984). Organization and governance in construction. *International Journal of Project Management*, 2(1), 17–25.

Roehrich, J. K., Selviaridis, K., Kalra, J., Van der Valk, W. & Fang, F. (2020). Inter-organizational governance: A review, conceptualisation and extension. *Production Planning and Control*, 31(6), 453–469.

Rousseau, D. M., Sitkin, S. B., Burt, R. S. & Camerer, C. (1998). Not so different after all: A cross-discipline view of trust. *Academy of Management Review*, 23(3), 393–404.

Sako, M. (1992). *Prices, quality and trust: Inter-firm relations in Britain and Japan*. Cambridge University Press.

Stinchcombe, A. L & Heimer, C. (1985). *Organization theory and project management: Administering uncertainty in Norwegian offshore oil*. Norwegian University Press.

Turner, J. R. (1995). *The commercial project manager: Managing owners, sponsors, partners, supporters, stakeholders, contractors and consultants*. McGraw Hill.

Vukomanović, M., Cerić, A., Brunet, M., Locatelli, G. & Davies, A. (2021). Editorial: Trust and governance in megaprojects. *International Journal of Project Management*, 39(4), 321–324.

Williamson, O. E. (1975). *Markets and hierarchies*. Free Press.

Williamson, O. E. (1981). The economics of organization: The transaction cost approach. *American Journal of Sociology*, 87(3), 548–577.

Williamson, O. E. (1985). *The economic institutions of capitalism*. Free Press.

Williamson, O. E. (1991). Comparative economic organization: The analysis of discrete structural alternatives. *Administrative Science Quarterly*, 36(2), 269–296.

Winch, G. M. (2001). Governing the project process: A conceptual framework. *Construction Management and Economics*, 19(8), 799–808.

Winch, G. M. (2006). The governance of project coalitions: Towards a research agenda. In D. Lowe & R. Leiringer (Eds), *Commercial management of projects: Defining the discipline* (pp. 324–343). Blackwell.

Winch, G. M. (2014). Three domains of project organising. *International Journal of Project Management*, 32(5), 721–731.

Winch, G. M. & Leiringer, R. (2016). Owner project capabilities for infrastructure development: A review and development of the 'strong owner' concept. *International Journal of Project Management*, 34(2), 271–281.

Winch, G. M., Maytorena-Sanchez, E. & Sergeeva, N. (2022). *Strategic project organizing*. Oxford University Press.

Winch, G. M., Sergeeva, N. & Lowe, D. J. (2020). *Managing inter-organizational relations on complex projects: Project owner commercial strategy*. Conference presentation, Proceedings of the European Academy of Management, Dublin.

Zajac, E. J. & Olsen, C. P. (1993). From transaction cost to transactional value analysis: Implications for the study of interorganizational strategies. *Journal of Management Studies*, 30(1), 131–145.

9. Organizing complex projects from neo-institutional perspectives

Jörg Sydow and Jonas Söderlund

9.1 INTRODUCTION

Projects do not have to be 'megaprojects' to be complex. Admittedly, complexity is a matter of degree and type, and it seems fair to assume that the more complex projects are, the more managing them successfully relies on institutions, internal as well as external rules and regulations, or commonly accepted practices (Biesenthal et al., 2018). Thus, in this case more than elsewhere, 'cool projects' seem to require 'boring institutions' (Grabher, 2002).

Barley and Tolbert (1997, p. 99) define institutions as being 'historical accretions of past practices and understandings that set conditions on action' in a way that 'gradually acquire the moral and ontological status of taken-for-granted facts which, in turn, shape future interactions and negotiations'. Institutions are as much an outcome of social interaction and, in particular, practices, as they in turn guide, yet not determine, practices (Giddens, 1984; Schatzki, 1996). Thus, complex projects are both a result of institutionalized practices and shape those practices; projects are 'not islands', but are embedded in their surroundings in a number of ways (Engwall, 2003; Lundin & Söderholm, 1998, Chapter 13). This demonstrates the importance of acknowledging the role of the historical, institutional, and organizational contexts of projects (Dille & Söderlund, 2011; Miterev et al., 2017; Orr & Scott, 2008).

The starting point of the discourse in project studies informed by neo-institutionalism was certainly the insight that projects need to adapt to institutional forces, but agents can do much more than adapting project practices to such forces (Manning, 2008). As we will show, this insight has been incorporated by neo-institutional theory which has become an increasingly popular perspective for analysing complex projects (Orr et al., 2011; Söderlund & Sydow, 2019; Winch & Maytorena-Sanchez, 2020). We believe, however, that the full potential of institutional theory for 'project studies' (Geraldi & Söderlund, 2018) is yet to be realized.

We summarize the major contributions of the different strands of institutional theory to project studies in Table 9.1, thereby highlighting what we know about complex projects and seeing what needs to be done to further improve our understanding. We start with neo-institutionalism that highlights structural, isomorphic forces developed in demarcation to 'old' institutionalism, before moving on to more recent, agency-oriented concepts such as institutional entrepreneurship and institutional work. In reaction to these agency-oriented perspectives, scholars moved to institutional logics and institutional complexity in order to highlight the importance of structural forces to which social systems such as projects – and the practices that produce, reproduce, and transform them – are exposed. We conclude with a short discussion of what neo-institutional perspectives can bring to practice-based approaches (Nicolini, 2012), and whether there is an opportunity to merge these theories towards either a practice-driven neo-institutionalism or an institution-sensitive practice theory.

Table 9.1   *Neo-institutional perspectives on project studies*

Neo-institutional perspective (emphasis)	Key references	Central concepts and mechanisms	Potentialities for project studies	Publications in project studies (selection)
Classic neo-institutionalism (structure)	DiMaggio and Powell (1983); Meyer and Rowan (1977); Scott (1995); Tolbert and Zucker (1983)	Organizational field, isomorphism, legitimacy, symbolic structure	Projects as organizational form, institutional embeddedness of projects, projectification, global projects	Jones and Lichtenstein (2008); Kadefors (1995); Lundin and Söderholm (1998); Miterev et al. (2017); Orr and Scott (2008); Orr et al. (2011)
Institutional entrepreneurship (agency)	Beckert (1999); DiMaggio (1988); Garud et al. (2007); Tracey et al. (2011)	Institutional entrepreneurship, embedded agency	Vanguard projects, innovative projects, institutional projects	Dille and Söderlund (2011); Dille et al. (2018); Hall and Scott (2019); Holm (1995); Morris and Geraldi (2011); Tukiainen and Granqvist (2016)
Institutional work (structure and agency, structuration)	DiMaggio (1988); Lawrence and Suddaby (2006); Lawrence et al. (2011)	Purposeful action or practices of creating, maintaining, and disrupting institutions	Institutional work, more recently enriched with the concept of institutional infrastructure (Hinings et al., 2017)	Bresnen and Marshall (2011); Esposito et al. (2021); Lieftink et al. (2019); Sydow and Staber (2002); Tukiainen and Granqvist (2016); Van den Ende and Van Marrewijk (2019)
Institutional logics and complexity (structure and agency, close to structuration)	Friedland and Alford (1991); Greenwood et al. (2011); Pache and Santos (2010); Thornton et al. (2015)	Multiple logics, tensions and contradictions, vertical and horizontal complexity	Institutional complexity to emphasize the multiplicity of logics to which institutional work is exposed	Dille et al. (2018); Hetemi et al. (2021); Matinheikki et al. (2019); Pemsel and Söderlund (2020); Qiu et al. (2019); Uriate et al. (2019); Winch and Maytorena-Sanchez (2020)
Field-configuring events (structuration)	Lampel and Meyer (2008)	Purposeful configuration and reconfiguration of a field with the help of events and actions	Organizing events with the help of projects (events as projects), but also – conceptually – events as (projects as) events	Bohn and Braun (2021); Grabher and Thiel (2015); Maoret et al. (2011); Schüßler and Müller-Seitz (2013); Schüßler and Sydow (2015); Schüßler et al. (2014)
Practice-driven institutionalism (structure and agency, close to structuration)	Smets et al. (2012, 2017)	Mundane practices as sources of creating, maintaining and disrupting institutions	Leading and managing projects as an emergent phenomenon	We expect publications here shortly

9.2   NEO-INSTITUTIONALISM, ORGANIZATIONS, AND PROJECTS

Research informed by neo-institutional theory addresses the ways in which organizations and practices of organizing come to resemble one another and, thereby, gain legitimacy among key stakeholders in their institutional environments. This could be one key reason why 'projectification' (Midler, 1995) has become a megatrend. Projectification has been a key focus for much research to better understand the underlying rationale of why certain organizations and sectors embrace the principle of project-based organizing so strongly (Lundin et al., 2015; Schoper et al., 2018). There is a range of reasons for adopting projectification as a central element of organizing, yet this stream of research centres less on the narrow rationalistic reasons and more on the institutional reasons – that organizations become projectified because other organizations are becoming projectified.

Such processes of isomorphism play an important role in a number of industries and sectors to reduce uncertainty among the actors involved (DiMaggio & Powell, 1983; Scott, 1995). If everyone follows the same template of organizing, actors are provided with a solution that establishes a taken-for-grantedness in the way organizations should behave. This means that institutions play a critical role both at the level of the organization – the way organizations are structured and managed and the extent to which they rely on projects – and also at the level of projects, i.e. how projects should operate so that they are in line with the institutional regulations and templates that govern behaviour in a particular context. This stream of research thus enhances our understanding of why organizations adopt projects as an organizational form, and addresses the essential question of why projects exist. Moreover, it sheds light on several interesting and important issues around how organizations organize their projects, particularly complex projects, as these projects tend to be more strongly governed institutionally than less complex ones.

For instance, Kadefors (1995) addressed how the construction industry is subjected to strong forces of institutionalization. Scott and colleagues (Orr & Scott, 2008; Orr et al., 2011; Scott, 2012) researched 'global projects' where actors faced unforeseen costs after failing to comprehend cognitive-cultural, normative, and/or regulative institutions in an unfamiliar host societal context. Hetemi et al. (2021) investigated the construction of two high-speed rail lines in Spain and the Netherlands, how the institutional environment in these two countries changed over the years, and how the projects responded to new legitimacy requirements.

9.3   INSTITUTIONAL ENTREPRENEURSHIP AND INSTITUTIONAL PROJECTS

Institutional change has become an important question for neo-institutionalists as organizations not only seek legitimacy and institutional support for their actions, but also aspire to influence the regulations and templates that govern their behaviour. This is also a central question for scholars within project studies who argue that projects play a particularly important role in providing mechanisms to change or create new institutions. Two strands of research seem particularly important here: the literature on institutional entrepreneurship and the literature on institutional projects.

Institutional entrepreneurship (Garud et al., 2007; Tracey et al., 2011) research not only reconnects with early work (DiMaggio, 1988), which introduced interested agency into neo-institutional theorizing, but has become an increasingly important concern in project studies. For instance, large-scale change projects and innovation projects have been framed as examples of institutional entrepreneurship (Battilana et al., 2009; Biesenthal et al., 2018; Biygautane et al., 2019). In these settings, the project is playing a key role in generating novelty with regard to institutional rules and regulations defining actors involved in such processes as 'institutional entrepreneurs' (DiMaggio, 1988). The study of projects as institutional entrepreneurship therefore tends either to view the project as such as an enabler of institutional entrepreneurship, or an arena for individuals as to act as institutional entrepreneurs. A key concept here is the 'institutional project' (Holm, 1995), focusing on the role that a particular project can play to drive change within an industry. An example is a project for inducing regulatory change, i.e. a project with the aim of changing regulations in a relatively bounded institutional setting (Tukiainen & Granqvist, 2016).

Thus, projects are not only influenced by institutional forces, but may also play a central role in driving institutional change. These studies emphasize agency and address the outward-oriented impact which projects may have on institutions (Aaltonen & Sivonen, 2009; Grabher & Thiel, 2015; Morris & Geraldi, 2011).

9.4   INSTITUTIONAL WORK AND PROJECT WORK

The study of institutional work as 'the purposive action of individuals and organizations aimed at creating, maintaining and disrupting institutions' (Lawrence & Suddaby, 2006, p. 215) highlights three key aspects: it depicts institutional actors as being reflexive, goal-oriented, and capable; it focuses on actors' practices as being the hub of institutional dynamics; and it strives to capture structure and agency and the interrelation of the two (Battilana et al., 2009; Lawrence et al., 2011).

Research on creating institutions focuses primarily on institutional entrepreneurship, drawing on the concept of institutional work only peripherally (Garud et al., 2007; Tracey et al., 2011). A few recent exceptions, however, testify to the promise of exploring the creation of institutions from a work perspective. Slager et al. (2012, p. 763), for example, conceptualize standardization as being institutional work identifying three types – 'calculative framing, engaging and valorizing' – which 'support the design, legitimation and monitoring processes whereby a standard acquires its regulatory power'. Perkmann and Spicer (2008, p. 811) examine the role of institutional work in the institutionalization of management fashions, arguing that 'fashionable management practices acquire permanence when they are anchored within fieldwide institutions', and identifying 'political work', 'technical work', and 'cultural work' as being critical to this process. Maguire and Hardy (2009) explore the institutional work associated with the deinstitutionalization of dichlorodiphenyltrichloroethane (DDT), showing how actors engage in 'disruptive' and 'defensive' institutional work, and Zietsma and Lawrence (2010) explore institutional work in the context of field-level change, arguing that two kinds – 'practice work' and 'boundary work' – are critical to this process.

Studies on how actors work to maintain institutions are close to the concept of institutional work. Previously, the role of the purposive efforts of actors in maintaining institutions was relatively neglected; a stream of research and theory devoted to understanding the dynamics of this kind of institutional work has now emerged (Dacin et al., 2010; Zilber, 2009).

In a project context, the study of institutional work would thus address how actors build, maintain, change, and disrupt institutions. The main differences between the study of institutional entrepreneurship and institutional work are not only a concern for the duality of structure and agency (Giddens, 1984), but also an interest in looking both at the maintenance and change aspects of the project, and paying more attention to the work-related micro-aspects in which individuals engage.

9.5   INSTITUTIONAL LOGICS AND INSTITUTIONAL COMPLEXITY

Research within institutional logics and complexity centres on the ways organizations respond to different institutional requirements. Like the enrichment of institutional work with the concept of institutional infrastructure (Hinings et al., 2017), this move should be understood as a response to the excessive agency focus of the institutional work and, in particular, institutional entrepreneurship approaches. This stream mainly concerns the challenges associated with coping with different and sometimes fundamentally conflicting institutional logics, i.e. institutional complexity (Pache & Santos, 2010). Most notably, it addresses the conflicts when 'hybrid' organizations are operating in both a not-for-profit and a traditional business context. In particular, it investigates how organizations structure their operations to cope with institutional complexity by either decoupling certain parts of their operations or seeking to integrate the conflicting requirements within their management control systems. For project studies, the focus on institutional logics has been adopted by scholars to address the challenges of private-public partnerships.

The challenges of institutional complexity seem particularly interesting in the context of complex projects, as these typically face requirements from multiple institutional logics and need to balance institutional complexity requirements to ensure successful project completion. Pemsel and Söderlund (2020) address the challenges of 'temporal institutional complexity', indicating that certain institutional logics are associated with different temporalities rooted in various institutional logics. They showcase different strategies by which actors engage with the challenges of temporal institutional complexity, pointing out the central role of the project organization to cope with such complexity through handling the participating organizations' different views on time, such as when things should be done, how fast things should be done, and in what order they should occur. A central concern for managing projects wrestling with such complexities is to find ways out of these differences, impose changes on the temporal order of the project, seek combinations among the stakeholders, and sometimes surf on those differences (Pemsel & Söderlund, 2020).

9.6   FIELD-CONFIGURING EVENTS AND PROJECTS

The idea of field-configuring events emerged from an interest in uncovering how particular events have the capacity to either change existing institutions or create new ones (Lampel & Meyer, 2008). This stream of research inherited the field focus from early neo-institutionalism but, because it emphasizes action or the process of 'structuration' (Giddens, 1984), is more like research on institutional entrepreneurship and institutional work, respectively. Field-configuring events are defined as temporary organizations 'that encapsulate and shape the development of professions, technologies, markets and industries' (Lampel & Meyer, 2008, p. 1026), no matter whether the configuration, reconfiguration, or the maintenance of a field is intended or not. Such events are usually not only limited in duration, but also take place in one particular location, attract actors with either homogeneous or heterogeneous backgrounds, and provide a space for formal and informal interactions. Hence research on field-configuring events looks mostly at micro-activities during an event or a series of events to explain macro-outcomes on the field level.

For project studies, this stream of institutional research is of interest for at least two reasons. First, most events, particularly those of a field-configuring (or reconfiguring or maintaining) nature, are prepared in complex, typically interorganizational projects or 'project network organizations' (Manning, 2017). These include conferences, award ceremonies, trade fairs, or festivals, often in the creative industries (Grabher & Thiel, 2015; Schüßler & Sydow, 2015). Bohn and Braun (2021) mobilized a mixed-method approach to look at the configuring impact of two projects in the field of electric mobility on the opening and closing of the public debate on this topic in Germany, thereby contributing also to the debate on projectification.

Second, some propose conceptualizing 'projects as events' (Maoret et al., 2011). Events are considered as a sequence of activities or processes occurring over a certain period of time. In the case of field-configuring events, but also of some other kinds of events such as crises or disasters, the main focus remains on the triggering effect they have (including setting up a project). In other cases, the focus lies on either the processes (e.g. collaboration within or across projects) or the outcomes (e.g. coping successfully with a crisis or attracting an audience to a festival with the help of a well-designed project). This perspective also allows the study of project dynamics, i.e. a temporary organization as a series of more or less interdependent events, and how these unfold over time and space (Maoret et al., 2011), thus connecting well to current research on time and temporality in organization studies (Reinecke et al., 2020).

9.7　OUTLOOK: MARRYING INSTITUTIONAL AND PRACTICE THEORY?

The latest stream of research inspired by neo-institutionalism and potentially relevant to project studies tries to marry research on institutions and the process of institutionalization: practice-based approaches to strategy and organization (Lundin et al., 2015; Vaara & Whittington, 2012, Chapter 11). Following the 'practice turn' in social sciences (Schatzki et al., 2001), practice-based approaches focus on the constitution of the social practices of individual or collective actors, typically conceived as recurrent activities that are enabled and restrained by structure (Giddens, 1984) and that emerge in a social system like projects, organization, networks, or fields.

The 'marriage' of these two streams of research has developed into what is called 'practice-driven institutionalism' (Smets et al., 2012, 2017). In contrast to other streams of research informed by neo-institutional theory, practice-driven institutionalism explicitly builds on Schatzki's (1996) rather than Giddens' (1984) theory of practice and tries to capture in great detail more or less emergent practices that develop into institutions or, not unlike institutional work (but with less emphasis on intentional agency), lead to the creation, maintenance, or disruption of other institutions. Advocates argue that 'practice and institutional theorists have simply been looking at opposite sides of the same coin' (Smets et al., 2017, p. 366). In consequence, most practice theories have not been particularly interested in institutions, and proponents of neo-institutional theory often speak of practices and consider them to be a kind of institution (e.g. Lounsbury & Crumley, 2007), but do not adopt practice theory as an additional theoretical lens (Meyer et al., 2021).

While progress has been made very recently (cf. Lounsbury et al., 2021), would a marriage of these two streams of research of different theoretical traditions help to better understand the praxis of complex projects? What exactly is to be expected of this marriage? Would such a perspective connect micro-activities with macro-processes and outcomes even better than that of institutional work? Would it be possible to consider not only intentional actions, but also (e.g. self-reinforcing) processes developing behind the back of the individual or collective actors? To the best of our knowledge, no study on project-based organizing has yet picked up this integrative perspective but, given the prominence of neo-institutionalism not only in management and organization studies, but also in project studies, this will only be a matter of time and once more increase the likelihood of mutual recognition and cross-fertilization of research in both domains.

REFERENCES

Aaltonen, K. & Sivonen, R. (2009). Response strategies to stakeholder pressures in global projects. *International Journal of Project Management*, 27(2), 131–141.

Barley, S. R. & Tolbert, P. S. (1997). Institutionalization and structuration: Studying the link between action and institution. *Organization Studies*, 18, 93–117.

Battilana, J., Leca, B. & Boxenbaum, E. (2009). How actors change institutions: Towards a theory of institutional entrepreneurship. *Academy of Management Annals*, 3(1), 377–419.

Beckert, J. (1999). Agency, entrepreneurs, and institutional change: The role of strategic choice and institutionalized practices in organizations. *Organization Studies*, 20(5), 777–799.

Biesenthal, C., Clegg, S., Mahalingam, A. & Sankaran, S. (2018). Applying institutional theories to managing megaprojects. *International Journal of Project Management*, 36(1), 43–54.

Biygautane, M., Neesham, C. & Al-Yahya, K. O. (2019). Institutional entrepreneurship and infrastructure public-private partnership (PPP): Unpacking the role of social actors in implementing PPP projects. *International Journal of Project Management*, 37(1), 192–219.

Bohn, S. & Braun, T. (2021). Field-configuring projects: How projects shape the public reflection of electric mobility in Germany. *International Journal of Project Management*, 39(6), 605–619.

Bresnen, M. & Marshall, N. (2011). Projects and partnerships: Institutional processes and emergent practices. In P. W. G. Morris, J. K. Pinto & J. Söderlund (Eds), *The Oxford handbook of project management* (pp. 154–174). Oxford University Press.

Dacin, M. T., Munir, K. & Tracey, P. (2010). Formal dining at Cambridge colleges: Linking ritual performance and institutional maintenance. *Academy of Management Journal*, 53(6), 1393–1418.

Dille, T. & Söderlund, J. (2011). Managing inter-institutional projects: The significance of isochronism, timing norms and temporal misfits. *International Journal of Project Management*, 29(4), 480–490.

Dille, T., Söderlund, J. & Clegg, S. (2018). Temporal conditions and the dynamics of inter-institutional projects. *International Journal of Project Management*, 36(5), 673–686.

DiMaggio, P. J. (1988). Interest and agency in institutional theory. In L. G. Zucker (Ed.), *Institutional patterns and organizations* (pp. 3–21). Ballinger Publishing.

DiMaggio, P. J. & Powell, W. W. (1983). The iron cage revisited: Institutional isomorphism and collective rationality in organizational fields. *American Sociological Review*, 48, 147–160.

Engwall, M. (2003). No project is an island: Linking projects to history and context. *Research Policy*, 32(5), 789–808.

Esposito, G., Nelson, T., Ferlie, E. & Crutzen, N. (2021). The institutional shaping of global megaprojects: The case of the Lyon-Turin high-speed railway. *International Journal of Project Management*, 39(6), 658–671.

Friedland, R. & Alford, R. R. (1991). Bringing society back in: Symbols, practices, and institutional contradictions'. In W. W. Powell & P. J. DiMaggio (Eds), *The new institutionalism in organizational Analysis* (pp. 232–226). University of Chicago Press.

Garud, R., Hardy, C. & Maguire, S. (2007). Institutional entrepreneurship as embedded agency: An introduction to the special issue. *Organization Studies*, 28(7), 957–969.

Geraldi, J. & Söderlund, J. (2018). Project studies: What it is, where it is going. *International Journal of Project Management*, 36(1), 55–70.

Giddens, A. (1984). *The constitution of society*. Polity Press.

Grabher, G. (2002). Cool projects, boring institutions: Temporary collaboration in social context. *Regional Studies*, 36(3), 205–214.

Grabher, G. & Thiel, J. (2015). Crossing boundaries: Exploring the London Olympics 2012 as a field-configuring event. *Industry and Innovation*, 22(3), 229–249.

Greenwood, R., Raynard, M., Kodeih, F., Micelotta, E. R. & Lounsbury, M. (2011). Institutional complexity and organizational responses. *Academy of Management Annals*, 5(1), 317–371.

Hall, D. M. & Scott, W. R. (2019). Early stages in the institutionalization of integrated project delivery. *Project Management Journal*, 50(2), 128–143.

Hetemi, E., Van Marrewijk, A., Jerbrant, A. & Bosch-Rekveldt, M. (2021). The recursive interaction of institutional fields and managerial legitimation in large-scale projects. *International Journal of Project Management*, 39(3), 295–307.

Hinings, C., Logue, D. & Zietsma, C. (2017). Fields, institutional infrastructure and governance. In R. Greenwood, C. Oliver, T. B. Lawrence & R. M. Meyer (Eds), *The Sage handbook of organizational institutionalism* (pp. 163–189). Sage Publishing.

Holm, P. (1995). The dynamics of institutionalization: Transformation processes in Norwegian fisheries. *Administrative Science Quarterly*, 40(3), 398–422.

Jones, C. & Lichtenstein, B. B. (2008). Temporary inter-organizational projects: How temporal and social embeddedness enhance coordination and manage uncertainty. In S. Cropper, M. Ebers, C. Huxham & P. S. Ring (Eds), *The Oxford handbook of inter-organizational relations* (pp. 231–255). Oxford University Press.

Kadefors, A. (1995). Institutions in building projects: Implications for flexibility and change. *Scandinavian Journal of Management*, 11(4), 395–408.

Lampel, J. & Meyer, A. (2008). Field-configuring events as structuring mechanisms: How conferences, ceremonies, and trade shows constitute new technologies, industries, and markets. *Journal of Management Studies*, 45(6), 1025–1035.

Lawrence, T. B. & Suddaby, R. (2006). Institutions and institutional work. In S. R. Clegg, C. Hardy, T. B. Lawrence & W. R. Nord (Eds), *The Sage Handbook of Organization Studies* (pp. 215–254). Sage Publishing.

Lawrence, T., Suddaby, R. & Leca, B. (2011). Institutional work: Refocusing institutional studies of organization. *Journal of Management Inquiry*, 20(1), 52–58.

Lieftink, B., Smits, A. & Lauche, K. (2019). Dual dynamics: Project-based institutional work and subfield differences in the Dutch construction industry. *International Journal of Project Management*, 37(2), 269–282.

Lounsbury, M., Andersen, D. A. & Spee, P. (2021). On practice and institutions. *Research in the Sociology of Organizations*, 70, 1–28.

Lounsbury, M. & Crumley, E. T. (2007). New practice creation: An institutional perspective on innovation. *Organization Studies*, 28(7), 993–1012.

Lundin, R., Arvidsson, N., Brady, T., Eksted, E., Midler, C. & Sydow, J. (2015). *Managing and working in project society: Institutional challenges of temporary organizations*. Cambridge University Press.

Lundin, R. A. & Söderholm, A. (1998). Conceptualizing a projectified society: Discussion of an eco-institutional approach to theory on temporary organisations. In R. A. Lundin and C. Midler (Eds), *Projects as arenas for renewal and learning processes* (pp. 13–23). Kluwer.

Maguire, S. & Hardy, C. (2009). Discourse and deinstitutionalization: The decline of DDT. *Academy of Management Journal*, 52(1), 148–178.

Manning, S. (2008). Embedding projects in multiple contexts: A structuration perspective. *International Journal of Project Management*, 26(1), 30–37.

Manning, S. (2017). The rise of project network organizations: Building core teams and flexible partner pools for interorganizational projects. *Research Policy*, 46(8), 1399–1415.

Maoret, M., Massa, F. G. & Jones, C. (2011). Toward a projects as events perspective. In G. Cattani, S. Ferriani, L. Frederiksen & F. Täube (Eds), *Project-based organizing and strategic management* (pp. 427–444). Emerald Publishing.

Matinheikki, J., Aaltonen, K. & Walker, D. (2019). Politics, public servants, and profits: Institutional complexity and temporary hybridization in a public infrastructure alliance project. *International Journal of Project Management*, 37(2), 298–317.

Meyer, J. W. & Rowan, W. (1977). Institutionalized organizations: Formal structure as myth and ceremony. *American Journal of Sociology*, 83(2), 340–363.

Meyer, R., Jancsary, D. & Höllerer, M. A. (2021). Zones of meaning, Leitideen, institutional logics – and practices: A phenomenological institutional perspective on shared meaning structures. *Research in the Sociology of Organizations*, 70, 161–186.

Midler, C. (1995). 'Projectification' of the firm: The Renault case. *Scandinavian Journal of Management*, 11(4), 363–375.

Miterev, M., Engwall, M. & Jerbrant, A. (2017). Mechanism of isomorphism in project-based organizations. *Project Management Journal*, 48(5), 9–24.

Morris, P. W. G. & Geraldi, J. (2011). Managing the institutional context for projects. *Project Management Journal*, 42(6), 20–32.

Nicolini, D. (2012). *Practice theory, work, and organization: An introduction.* Oxford University Press.

Orr, R. J. & Scott, W. R. (2008). Institutional exceptions on global projects: A process model. *Journal of International Business Studies*, 39(4), 562–588.

Orr, R. J., Scott, W. R., Levitt, R. E., Artto, K. & Kujala, J. (2011). Global projects: Distinguishing features, drivers, and challenges. In R. W. Scott, R. E. Levitt & R. J. Orr (Eds), *Global projects: Institutional and political challenges* (pp. 15–51). Cambridge University Press.

Pache, A. & Santos, F. (2010). When worlds collide: The internal dynamics of organizational responses to conflicting institutional demands. *Academy of Management Review*, 35(3), 455–476.

Pemsel, S. & Söderlund, J. (2020). Who's got the time? Temporary organizing under temporal institutional complexity. In T. Braun & J. Lampel (Eds), *Tensions and paradoxes in temporary organizing* (pp. 127–150). Emerald Publishing.

Perkmann, M. & Spicer, A. (2008). How are management fashions institutionalized? The role of institutional work. *Human Relations*, 61(6), 811–844.

Reinecke, J., Suddaby, R., Langley, A. & Tsoukas, H. (Eds) (2020). *Time, temporality, and history in process organization studies.* Oxford University Press.

Qiu, Y., Chen, H., Sheng, Z., & Cheng, S. (2019). Governance of institutional complexity in megaproject organizations. *International Journal of Project Management*, 37(3), 425–443.

Schatzki, T. R. (1996). *Social practices: A Wittgensteinian approach to human activity and the social.* Cambridge University Press.

Schatzki, T. R., Knorr-Cetina, K. & von Savigny, E. (Eds) (2001). *The practice turn in contemporary theory.* Routledge.

Schoper, Y., Wald, A., Ingason, H. T., Vikingur, T. & Fridgeirsson, T. V. (2018). Projectification in Western economies: A comparative study of Germany, Norway and Iceland. *International Journal of Project Management*, 36(1), 71–82.

Schüßler, E., Dobusch, L., & Wessel, L. (2014). Backstage: Organizing events as proto-institutional work in the popular music industry. *Schmalenbach Business Review*, 66, 415–437.

Schüßler, E. & Müller-Seitz, G. (2013). From event management to managing events: A process perspective on organized and unexpected field-level events. *Managementforschung*, 23, 193–226.

Schüßler, E. & Sydow, J. (2015). Organizing events for configuring and maintaining creative fields. In C. Jones, M. Lorenzen & J. Sapsed (Eds), *Oxford handbook of creative industries* (pp. 284–300). Oxford University Press.

Scott, R. W. (1995). *Organizations and institutions.* Sage Publishing.

Scott, R. W. (2012). The institutional environment of global project organizations. *Engineering Project Organization Journal*, 2(1–2), 27–35.

Slager, R., Gond, J.-P. & Moon, J. (2012). Standardization as institutional work: The regulatory power of a responsible investment standard. *Organization Studies*, 33(5–6), 763–790.

Smets, M., Aristidou, A. & Whittington, R. (2017). Towards a practice-driven institutionalism. In R. Greenwood, C. Oliver, T. B. Lawrence & R. E. Meyer (Eds), *The Sage handbook of organizational institutionalism* (pp. 365–391). Sage Publishing.

Smets, M., Jarzabkowski, P., Burke, G. T. & Spee, P. (2012). Reinsurance trading in Lloyd's of London: Balancing conflicting-yet-complementary logics in practice. *Academy of Management Journal*, 58(3), 932–970.

Söderlund, J. & Sydow, J. (2019). Projects and institutions: Towards understanding their mutual constitution and dynamics. *International Journal of Project Management*, 37(2), 259–268.

Sydow, J. & Staber, U. (2002). The institutional embeddedness of project networks: The case of content production in German television. *Regional Studies*, 36(3), 223–235.

Thornton, P. H., Ocasio, W. & Lounsbury, M. (2015). *The institutional logics perspective*. Oxford University Press.

Tolbert, P. S. & Zucker, L. G. (1983). Institutional sources of change in the formal structure of organizations: The diffusion of civil service reform, 1880–1935. *Administrative Science Quarterly*, 30(1), 22–39.

Tracey, P., Phillips, N. & Jarvis, O. (2011). Bridging institutional entrepreneurship and the creation of new organizational forms. *Organization Science*, 22(1), 60–80.

Tukiainen, S. & Granqvist, N. (2016). Temporary organizing and institutional change. *Organization Studies*, 37(12), 1819–1840.

Uriarte, T. Y., DeFilippi, R. J., Riccaboni, M. & Catoni, M. L. (2019). Projects, institutional logics and institutional work practices: The case of the Lucca Comics and Games Festival. *International Journal of Project Management*, 37(2), 318–330.

Vaara, E. & Whittington, R. (2012). Strategy-as-practice: Taking social practices seriously. *Academy of Management Annals*, 6(1), 285–336.

Van den Ende, L. & Van Marrewijk, A. (2019). Teargas, taboo and transformation: A neo-institutional study of community resistance and the struggle to legitimize subway projects in Amsterdam 1960–2018. *International Journal of Project Management*, 37(2), 331–346.

Winch, G. M. & Maytorena-Sanchez, E. (2020). Institutional projects and contradictory logics: Responding to complexity in institutional field change. *International Journal of Project Management*, 38(6), 368–378.

Zietsma, C. & Lawrence, T. B. (2010). Institutional work and the transformation of an organizational field: The interplay of boundary work and practice work. *Administrative Science Quarterly*, 55, 189–221.

Zilber, T. B. (2009). Institutional maintenance as narrative acts. In T. B. Lawrence, R. Suddaby & B. Leca (Eds), *Institutional work: Actors and agency in institutional studies of organizations* (pp. 205–235). Cambridge University Press.

10. Foucault's governmentality and the issue of project collaboration

Stewart Clegg and Johan Ninan

10.1 INTRODUCTION

Project governance involves the process of achieving project objectives by managing the different stakeholders involved and implicated in project settings. The distinction between involved and implicated is significant. Those stakeholders involved are formally recognized as such by being associated with the project's governance, participating in its delivery. Those stakeholders implicated in project governance are not necessarily formally and legitimately involved; they may be asserting a stake that is not formally recognized. Significant consequences can flow from not managing project relations with not only formal stakeholders such as investors but also those whose stakeholding may not be formally acknowledge but is, by any ethical metric, implicated.

Governance takes care of some of the formal aspects of project management. Carlsson et al. (1995) define governance as the sum of the many ways individuals and institutions, public and private, manage their common affairs. Governance is important in projects because there may be no necessary alignment between the many corporate governance doctrines that might be involved on the part of multiple partners. An overall code of governance separate from those of the firms involved may be necessary, for four primary reasons. First, complex, uncertain and creative challenges are taken up through projects (Hartman, 1998), hence projects require formal governance through measures such as project charters to achieve objectives. Second, there is a need to resolve conflict between the short-term interests of the contractor and the long-term interests of the client and end users. Third, there is a need to have in place strategies for ensuring responsible, reflexive and self-organizing project management in situ (Müller et al., 2014). Fourth, project management is a social activity with people at the centre of all interactions (Packendorff, 1995). People working for the project, such as managers and engineers, or people being affected by the project, such as communities and project-affected persons (Tutt & Pink, 2019), may need to be managed in accordance with project objectives.

The concept of governmentality has proven useful to analyse how the reflexive management of people within and without the project is conducted. In this chapter we explore the organizational theory of governmentality and its importance in project settings. First, we identify the specificity of project governance and relate it to the definition and discussion of governmentality by Michel Foucault. Following this, the use of governmentality within projects through project culture is discussed. Subsequently, the use of governmentality outside projects through social media is discussed. Finally, the chapter concludes by highlighting new directions for research with governmentality as the focal point.

10.2   FOUCAULT'S GOVERNMENTALITY

Foucault defines governmentality as an 'ensemble formed by the institutions, procedures, analyses and reflections, the calculations and tactics, that allow the exercise of this very specific albeit complex form of power' (Foucault, 1991, p. 20). The term governmentality was coined by Roland Barthes in 1957, to study the ways in which governing organizations present themselves to the public (Dean, 2010). Twenty years later, the concept gained popularity when French philosopher Michel Foucault used the concept in a narrower sense in his studies on power. Foucault introduced the term in his collection of lectures at the College de France on the Birth of Biopolitics in 1979 (Marks, 2000, p. 128). For Foucault, governmentality meant combined strategies of organizational governance in a broad sense, as well as self-governance by those made subjects of organizational governance.

Foucault used the notion of 'governmentality' to connect the idea of 'government', a term he uses in a broad sense, one not restricted to formal political institutions, with that of 'mentality', as a neologism based on a semantic merger. Foucault defines government as a specific combination of governing techniques and rationalities, typical of the modern, neoliberal period. He was pointing to a fusion of new technologies of government with a new political rationality. 'Governmentality' refers not only to new institutions of governance but also their effects. Governmentality thus refers to normatively institutionalized ways governed increasingly by standards, charters and other codes. The Project Management Institute (2021), for instance, formulates such norms, defining the practices of a successful project manager through which project managers can become 'entrepreneurs of their selves' (Cooper, 2015) by achieving project milestones. As du Gay (2000, p. 168) suggests, governmentality 'create[s] a distance between the decisions of formal political institutions and other social actors, conceive[s] of these actors as subjects of responsibility, autonomy and choice, and seek[s] to act upon them through shaping and utilising their freedom'. Such shaping of freedoms has a functional purpose; for Foucault, the concept of governmentality is premised on the active choice of subjects, rather than their domination or external control (Clegg et al., 2002). Functionally, the need for an architectonic of external control is greatly reduced if choices can be relied upon in their premises if not their specifics.

Deploying the concept of governmentality in *The birth of the clinic*, Foucault (2002) studied the ways in which a normative universe was formed by how the 'truths' of practices, such as medicine, were constructed and taken for granted. Rather than seeing power relations as a matter of different forces' positions and resources, Foucault saw it in terms of strategies, discourses and processes (Clegg, 1989). The focus was on 'the totality of practices, by which one can constitute, define, organize, instrumentalize the strategies which individuals in their liberty can have in regard to each other' (Foucault, 1988, p. 20). Subsequently, many scholars (Fleming & Spicer, 2014; Haugaard, 2012) list Foucault's governmentality as the fourth dimension of power as an extension of Lukes' (1974) three dimensions of power. People voluntarily delegate their autonomy and willingly position their subjectivity in relation to a normative force that is external to themselves (Jackson & Carter, 1998).

Foucault (2007, p. 108) describes how taken-for-granted practices, that are not idiosyncratically invented by individuals but derive from the deeply shared norms, often professionally institutionalized, create subjectification to norms and self-surveillance (Fleming & Spicer, 2014; Sewell, 1998) as these norms are situationally reproduced. The practice of governmentality aspires to create a common sensemaking frame (Colville et al., 1999; Weick, 1995) whereby project participants will voluntarily and willingly agree to be normatively governed in choices forming the subjectivity of their project selves (Barnett et al., 2014). The aspiration is that the personal ambitions of those governed will become enmeshed with those of the overall project management team through their subjectification to these norms.

Achieving a degree of collective consciousness is valuable for all forms of organizations; it is critical for project settings where there is no unitary centre of control and many stakeholders that may be implicated, although not formally recognized as such. Control of stakeholders is difficult to achieve in project settings through traditional forms of governance focused on contractual tightness and strict surveillance (Stinchcombe & Heimer, 1985). Despite this, governmentality is a relatively underexplored concept in project management. We now turn to discuss separately how governmentality was used within projects and outside projects.

10.3   GOVERNMENTALITY WITHIN PROJECTS THROUGH PROJECT CULTURE

In the past, Pitsis et al. (2003) and Clegg et al. (2002) studied governmentality creating a strong project culture in alliance contracting between a public-sector body and three private-sector contractors for the construction of a large infrastructure project in Sydney, Australia. The project was designed to prevent stormwater detritus and sewage ending up in the harbour. All parties to the alliance contract were partners in a risk/reward scheme which was based on the successful achievement of key performance indicators (KPIs) of schedule, budget, occupational health and safety, community and ecology. Normativity was instituted both through training and through the visual cues of the space in which project staff worked. A visible commitment to the KPIs was evident from observation of the head office where all the alliance partners were collocated. There were banners declaring the rhetoric of 'no-blame' culture and 'whatever is best for the project' along with glossy photography and clearly visible mission and vision statements. The walls of the staff kitchen were decorated with stories about the project that had been cut out of the local and metropolitan press. The progress of the project was displayed in charts throughout the office space. Notices were posted about forthcoming social and training events.

What characterized the project's relations with its partners, both those that were formal and (most of those) that were informal, was the attention paid to governmentality in the project. The attention was authentic, premised not upon relations of power over but about creating a culture of trust in which the power to achieve the objectives of the project were widely shared both internally between project teams and externally between stakeholders formally and informally implicated in the project. Power over and trust in are mutually opposed variables: where trust is low, projects will strive to maximize power over stakeholders by various means; where trust is high, relations of power over stakeholders can be relaxed. In relationships between project and stakeholders, trust can shift attention from self-interest to 'common interest' and help the parties share more knowledge and other resources (see, among others, Eskerod & Vaagaasar, 2014; Smyth et al., 2010). Trust reduces transaction costs in terms of control and increases the opportunity for positive interaction. Trust between the project and various stakeholders grew through repeated assessments of whether the other acted in accordance with what was agreed.

What was crucial was creating relations characterized by mutual trust that the parties in the project would perform what they were committed to doing. The risk and reward profit-sharing agreement in the project was central to this being achieved internally. Formal stakeholders included actors such as alliance partners, subcontractors, the building workers' union, the Construction, Forestry Maritime, Mining and Energy Union and clients; and informal stakeholders were the citizens in areas in which the project was being undertaken. All parties stood to benefit from cooperation and completion of the KPIs on the positive side of the risk/reward ledger, including subcontractors and employees. The communities in the areas in which the work was preceding also stood to benefit from cleaner water in the harbour. Community liaison officers were deployed in the communities affected, holding strategic conversations with residents, winning their trust and accepting ideas for project implementation that arose from their concerns.

In the wake of Pitsis et al. (2003) and Clegg et al.'s (2002) research other project management scholars considered governmentality. Renou (2017) emphasized the importance of governmentality for performance measurement and regulation in the case of water utilities in France. Müller et al. (2016) show a significant correlation between governmentality as an enabler for project governance and organizational success. Ninan et al. (2019) studied a metro rail project in which the role of governmentality for branding the project and managing the project community was vital. As we shall see in the next section, drawing on the work of Ninan and his associates, the projection of governmentality can occur not only through face-to-face contact but also through the use of social media, affordances barely visible at the time of the project in question.

10.4   GOVERNMENTALITY OUTSIDE PROJECTS THROUGH SOCIAL MEDIA

Outside projects, there are external stakeholders such as existing landholders, utilities and the community surrounding the project site, all of whom have significant impact on the delivery of the project. These external stakeholders are difficult to govern as they interact with the project across permeable boundaries, are unaccountable to the requirements of the project and cannot be governed with contractual instruments or conformance to standards, as is the case with internal stakeholders (Ninan et al., 2020). These sources of difference are exacerbated in megaprojects because of their increased scale, duration, complexity and the wide range of external stakeholders implicated.

Ninan et al. (2019) studied the practice of governmentality in an infrastructure project in India using social media. Data were collected through semi-structured interviews and observations in social media platforms such as Twitter and Facebook. Qualitative content analysis (Hsieh & Shannon, 2005) and grounded theory methods (Glaser & Strauss, 2017) were employed to open code the social media data and interview data, respectively. Each of the incidents reported in social media was assigned to a category that emerged from our data. Multiple cycles of coding, crosschecking and theoretical review was followed to derive theory from the data (Strauss & Corbin, 1990). The project had a social media strategy for communicating effectively with the stakeholders outside the project. The objective of this strategy was to build alliances with key constituencies of interest, forged through building a common sense of pride and purpose that incorporated those outside of the project upon whom its work had effects. Progress updates of the project such as work completed, progress photos and service information were regularly shared in the official social media platform of the project. The photos uploaded were glossy images depicting the inside of trains and outside of stations and did not cover any negative events such as accidents, safety issues or delays. There was an explicit focus on promoting the project using rhetoric, such as of the project 'transforming the city' and how the awards bestowed on the project were a source of pride for the city. Promotional events and awareness programmes to educate the community of the benefits of the project were conducted in parks, malls and colleges. Reports of other events such as hoisting flags for national days and celebrations of regional festivals were shared on the social media platforms. Painting competitions on the theme 'go green metro' were conducted for school children.

The use of these strategies resulted in some visible changes in the behaviour of the project community. Traffic diversions to enable the construction of the project usually cause a lot of inconvenience to the community and result in agitation from the public. However, the project in consideration did not experience any such problems as it enjoyed special preference and support from the community during construction. Akin to customer insensitivity to prices seen in branded consumer goods (Dawes, 2009), the project community was not affected by traffic diversions and hassles during the construction of the project. There was also a positive brand image for the project with community members claiming that they were proud of the project. The community members tied the project's celebration of the regional festivals to the organization becoming an icon of the identity of the city, complementing similar discourses found in the social media interactions of the organization. In addition, there were community brand advocates for the project as community members supported and defended the decisions of the project in social media. This transformation of identity occurred because the project targeted sections of the population, such as school children, specifically to enrol and translate into loyal supporters of the project.

10.5   DISCUSSION AND FUTURE AVENUES OF RESEARCH

The use of governmentality within projects (Clegg et al., 2002) and outside projects (Ninan et al., 2019) has some similarities, which affords some interesting avenues for future research in the area. Governmentality tools such as banners, rhetoric, clear vision statements, glossy photography, progress updates and social events have been employed for creating governmentality within the projects. Similarly, governmentality tools such as progress updates, photos, strategic rhetoric, awareness programmes, hoisting flags for national days, celebrations of regional festivals and painting competition events were employed for creating governmentality outside the projects.

The effect of governmentality can be seen in taken-for-granted practices. In the case of governmentality within projects reduced conflicts are the aim, while in the case of governmentality outside projects, support for project activities in both specific and general publics is the aim. The second process involves deploying knowledge via a power–knowledge nexus. In the case of governmentality within projects an appreciation of common project culture and shared consciousness is deployed, while in the case of governmentality outside projects, the key actions are building the trust and support of critical stakeholders implicated in the project's success. Developing technologies of the self, positioning personal identities of those governed, creates reflexive self-monitoring agencies in terms of the formally inculcated nexus of power–knowledge. In the case of governmentality within projects employees became subjects of responsibility, autonomy and choice, while in the case of governmentality outside projects, the

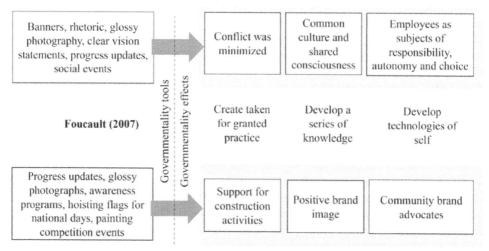

Figure 10.1   Governmentality within and outside projects

project community were recruited not as opponents but as advocates of the project. The governmentality tools and effects from governmentality within and outside projects are depicted by drawing on two research projects in which we have been involved in Figure 10.1.

The work on governmentality within projects can be extended by studying how alternate forms of governance other than contracts can be used to govern internal stakeholders efficiently. The effect of governmentality on long-term and short-term relationships amongst explicit and implicated stakeholders can be explored. With advances in technology and increases in the scale of projects, many interactions relating to projects will occur via digital platforms. Ninan et al. (2019) observed social media platforms, however, there are many other platforms where interactions outside the project are evident. Along with an exploration of other social media platforms such as YouTube, interactions outside the project are evident in news articles (Ninan & Sergeeva, 2021), which can also be explored for studying governmentality. In the modern era, along with observations of office spaces and meetings, digital platforms such as WhatsApp, Skype and Teams offer many insights into interactions within the project.

Projects worldwide, such as the HS2 project in the United Kingdom, the WestConnex project in Australia and the Statue of Unity project in India, are experiencing resistance from the project community. There is a need to explore how governmentality can be an efficient tool in mitigating community resistance. The interaction between governmentality within projects and outside projects needs further investigation. The project team and the way their normative universe is shaped as they deploy strategies to manage external stakeholders in the project community is vital (Ninan et al., 2021). The key is transparency about the project aims and progress and clear articulation of the benefits through KPIs.

10.6 CONCLUSION

The objective of this chapter has been to introduce the concept of governmentality and its applications in the domain of project management. We have discussed the use of governmentality within projects in Australia and in a project in India. In the case of governmentality within projects, conflict appears to be minimized when a common culture and shared consciousness is created and employees are transformed into subjects of responsibility, autonomy and choice. In the case of governmentality outside projects, where there is support from a community for project activities, a positive brand image needs to be created and the community transformed to become brand advocates.

Foucault's (2007) processes of governmentality capture the practices of these new approaches to governance well. While stakeholders within projects develop new identities and consciousness and take part in new disciplines and institutions, stakeholders outside the project are invited into the fold of the organization; in some contexts, this might be done digitally, in other cases through negotiation. With the advance in technology and increase in scale of projects, many interactions relating to projects occur in the digital platforms. In other cases, governmentality will be done more directly by representation and consultation. In the modern era, along with observations of meetings and training programmes, digital platforms such as WhatsApp, Skype and Teams offer many insights on interactions within the project, while platforms such as Twitter, Facebook and YouTube offer insights on interactions outside the project. Governmentality significantly affects all aspects of performance in project settings.

REFERENCES

Barnett, C., Clarke, N., Cloke, P. & Malpass, A. (2014). The elusive subjects of neo-liberalism: Beyond the analytics of governmentality. In S. Binkley & J. Littler (Eds), *Cultural studies and anti-consumerism* (pp. 116–145). Routledge.

Barthes, R. (1957). *Mythologies*. Seuil.

Carlsson, I., Ramphal, S., Alatas, A. & Dahlgren, H. (1995). *Our global neighbourhood: The report of the commission on global governance*. Oxford University Press.

Clegg, S. R. (1989). *Frameworks of power*. Sage.

Clegg, S. R., Pitsis, T. S., Rura-Polley, T. & Marosszeky, M. (2002). Governmentality matters: Designing an alliance culture of inter-organizational collaboration for managing projects. *Organization Studies*, 23(3), 317–337.

Colville, I. D., Waterman, R. H. & Weick, K. E. (1999). Organizing and the search for excellence: Making sense of the times in theory and practice. *Organization*, 6(1), 129–148.

Cooper, C. (2015). Entrepreneurs of the self: The development of management control since 1976. *Accounting, Organizations and Society*, 47, 14–24.

Dawes, J. (2009). The effect of service price increases on customer retention: The moderating role of customer tenure and relationship breadth. *Journal of Services Research*, 11(3), 232–245.

Dean, M. (2010). *Governmentality: Power and rule in modern society*. Sage.

du Gay P. (2000). Enterprise and its futures: A response to Fournier and Grey. *Organization*, 7(1), 165–183.

Eskerod, P. & Vaagaasar, A. L. (2014). Stakeholder management strategies and practices during a project course. *Project Management Journal*, 45(5), 71–85.

Fleming, P. & Spicer, A. (2014). Power in management and organization science. *Academy of Management Annals*, 8(1), 237–298.

Foucault, M. (1988). The care of the self as a practice of freedom. In J. Berbauer & D. Rasmussen (Eds), *The final Foucault*. MIT Press.

Foucault, M. (1991). Governmentality. In G. Burchell, C. Gordon & P. Miller (Eds), *The Foucault effect: Studies in governmentality*. University of Chicago Press.

Foucault, M. (2002). *The birth of the clinic*. Routledge.

Foucault, M. (2007). *Security, territory, population: Lectures at the Collège de France*. Springer.

Glaser, B. G. & Strauss, A. L. (2017). *Discovery of grounded theory: Strategies for qualitative research*. Routledge.

Hartman, F. T. (1998). Innovation in project management: Using industry as the laboratory. In R. A. Lundin & C. Midler (Eds), *Projects as arenas for renewal and learning processes* (pp. 79–88). Kluwer Academic.

Haugaard, M. (2012). Rethinking the four dimensions of power: Domination and empowerment. *Journal of Political Power*, 5(1), 33–54.

Hsieh, H. F. & Shannon, S. E. (2005). Three approaches to qualitative content analysis. *Qualitative Health Research*, 15(9), 1277–1288.

Jackson, N. & Carter, P. (1998). Labour as dressage. In A. McKinlay & K. Starkey (Eds), *Foucault, management and organization theory* (pp. 51–64). Sage.

Lukes, S. (1974). *Power: A radical view*. Macmillan.

Marks, J. (2000). Foucault, Franks, Gauls: Il faut défendre la société: The 1976 lectures at the Collège de France. *Theory, Culture and Society*, 17(5), 127–147.

Müller, R., Pemsel, S. & Shao, J. (2014). Organizational enablers for governance and governmentality of projects: A literature review. *International Journal of Project Management*, 32(8), 1309–1320.

Müller, R., Shao, J. & Pemsel, S. (2016). *Organizational enablers for project governance*. Project Management Institute.

Ninan, J. & Sergeeva, N. (2021). Labyrinth of labels: Narrative constructions of promoters and protesters in megaprojects. *International Journal of Project Management*, 39(5), 496–506.

Ninan, J., Clegg, S. & Mahalingam, A. (2019). Branding and governmentality for infrastructure megaprojects: The role of social media. *International Journal of Project Management*, 37(1), 59–72.

Ninan, J., Mahalingam, A. & Clegg, S. (2020). Power and strategies in the external stakeholder management of megaprojects: A circuitry framework. *Engineering Project Organization Journal*, 9(1), 1–20.

Ninan, J., Mahalingam, A. & Clegg, S. (2021). Asset creation team rationalities and strategic discourses: Evidence from India. *Infrastructure Asset Management*, 8(2), 1–10.

Packendorff, J. (1995). Inquiring into the temporary organization: New directions for project management research. *Scandinavian Journal of Management*, 11(4), 319–333.

Pitsis, T., Clegg, S. R., Marosszeky, M. & Rura-Polley, T. (2003) Constructing the Olympic dream: Managing innovation through the future perfect. *Organization Science*, 14(5), 574–590.

Project Management Institute (2021). *A guide to the Project Management Body of Knowledge: PMBOK guide* (7th ed.). Project Management Institute.

Renou, Y. (2017). Performance indicators and the new governmentality of water utilities in France. *International Review of Administrative Sciences*, 83(2), 378–396.

Sewell, G. (1998). The discipline of teams: The control of team-based industrial work through electronic and peer surveillance. *Administrative Science Quarterly*, 43(2), 397–428.

Smyth, H., Gustafsson, M. & Ganskau, E. (2010). The value of trust in project business. *International Journal of Project Management*, 28(2), 117–129.

Stinchcombe, A. L. & Heimer, C. A. (1985). *Organization theory and project management: Administering uncertainty in Norwegian offshore oil*. Norwegian University Press.

Strauss, A. & Corbin, J. (1990). *Basics of qualitative research: Grounded theory procedures and techniques*. Sage.

Tutt, D. & Pink, S. (2019). Refiguring global construction challenges through ethnography. *Construction Management Economics*, 37(9), 475–480.

Weick, K. E. (1995). *Sensemaking in organizations*. Sage.

11. Projects-as-practice: taking stock and moving on

Markus Hällgren and Anders Söderholm

11.1 INTRODUCTION

Projects-as-practice originated in interest in social practices and their influence on behaviours. A practice approach in social science has been discussed and debated over the years by academic giants such as Anthony Giddens (e.g., 1984) and Pierre Bourdieu (e.g., 1977). Focusing on practice emphasizes the importance of individuals' actions and the intertwined patterns formed as individuals interact. While structuralism and individualism concentrate on either larger societal systems (such as capitalism or markets) or the precise psychological foundations of social interactions, practice theory addresses an intermediate analytical level. Practice encompasses the doings and sayings of individuals, their immediate material environments, and the history, rules, and routines in which they are embedded. Taken together, practice constitutes the core of social interaction and social dynamics.

Building on the practice tradition, Theodore Schatzki has developed and promoted the practice turn in social science (Schatzki, 1996; Schatzki et al., 2001). While some theorists would suggest that multiple layers of social reality should be recognized and considered (e.g., Giddens), Schatzki, among others, claims that social structures and interactions should be treated more holistically as a single layer of social reality. If this approach is adopted, macro- and micro-level explanations merge into what is sometimes referred to as a 'flat ontology', where social practices are seen as embedded in wider contexts, rooted in ideas, rules, experiences, and intertwined with other, parallel, practices. Schatzki (2002) refers to his interpretation of a flat ontology as 'site ontology'. A site, in this framework, is not defined by macro-level phenomena or micro-level actions. Individuals are not solely defined by their personal properties, or structural properties of the context in which they act. They are regarded as making use of their experiences, what they have learned, as well as material arrangements, rules, and tales of the site. See Chapter 12 for a supporting view on flat ontology, and Chapters 9 and 15 for contrasting views.

A site is a context that may be a physical place, but is perhaps more often defined as a phenomenon that enjoys a common determination as a collective social arena for action. It may be a site for cooking a meal, grading an exam, or the work within an academic department (Schatzki, 2002, 2005). A site is fluid and dependent on inter-linked activities, common events, joint chains of action, and social meaning being assigned to actions and practices.

There are several ways to outline major elements of a site. Whittington (2006) differentiates between praxis (situated doings of individuals), practices (norms, values, policies that actions depend on) and practitioners (the people carrying out the praxis and practices). Taken together praxis, practices, and practitioners engage in episodes of action that constitute the site, are meaningful to the individuals, and available for research. Since there is only one layer of social reality, large phenomena can be unfolded through the study of sites and episodes. The large phenomena or larger structural systems only exist because they influence sites and what occurs in them. For example, capitalism or a school policy only exists if it is being reiterated at (several) sites through the execution of praxis and practices.

A focus on practice also influences the optimal research methods and designs. Schatzki (2012, pp. 24–26) touches upon this, mentioning the suitability of ethnomethodology and other micro-oriented methods, including interviews, participatory observation, and video-recording. In an overview of practice studies, Loscher et al. (2019) show that ethnographic methods are most commonly used in organizational studies based on a practice approach. The practice approach also guides empirical work in terms of suggesting the key social components, and relations among them, for research. Practice is thus not only an ontological choice. It is also a methodological choice.

Practice approaches are relevant to all aspects of social life, including organizational settings. For many reasons, an organization qualifies as a site (or a number of sites) in which social practices are carried out under the influence of rules and individual capabilities. Loscher et al. (2019) outline three areas for the application of site ontology to organizational studies:

- Micro-foundations of organizational phenomena, i.e., the daily activities and organizational phenomena that emerge through them.
- The embeddedness of organizations in the wider context, focusing on bundles of activities representing wider contextual environments.
- Temporal and spatial dimensions of organizing, enabling analysis of how organizations are built by activities delimited in time and space.

Due to this multi-dimensionality, a site can be defined and analysed in various ways depending on the chosen path and underlying research question(s). A site is not an empirical entity that is defined once and for all, but rather a strategic choice made by the researcher. The same activity can thus be part of different sites depending on the analytical focus chosen by the researcher.

In a previous article, we discussed the application of a practice approach in project studies (Hällgren & Söderholm, 2011). Two general challenges were outlined. One is the 'pattern challenge', referring to the importance of finding patterns in individual observations to connect the particular to the general. For example, if meetings are the objects of study, activities involved in meetings at different locations or situations can be analysed to find general features. The other is the 'relevance challenge', referring to the identification of the implications of the research for a certain knowledge or theoretical domain. Efforts to address the pattern challenge focus on ways to build common understanding and draw general conclusions from single observations, while the relevance challenge involves definition of focal sites in terms of one or more knowledge domains or theoretical areas that the research may extend or strengthen. In the following sections we explore how these challenges have been met in projects-as-practice studies.

Next, we present an overview of topics addressed in project-as-practice studies and the approaches adopted, covering both theoretical and methodological choices in complex project organizing research.

11.2 TAKING STOCK OF PROJECTS-AS-PRACTICE RESEARCH

We would like to highlight that there have been some excellent contributions to the projects-as-practice approach, attempts to improve its conceptualization, and identification of further required refinements. For example, Floricel et al. (2014) emphasize the need to define what 'practice' is to add further detail to the concept. Similarly, Buchan and Simpson (2020) differentiate between approaching projects-as-practice as a verb and a noun, which they regard as complementary perspectives, as a project may be regarded as being or becoming. However, as projects are emerging social phenomena treating the term as a verb is likely to yield deeper insights. In response to both contributions we agree that the practice approach requires further conceptual and methodological refinement, but we would like to stress that in research on projects-as-practice, practice should not be treated as a noun. Instead, in accordance with Weick (1979, p. 44), efforts should be made to 'stamp out the nouns and replace them with verbs and gerunds'. Van der Hoorn and Whitty (2015) extend this idea by advocating a 'Heiddegerian' 'Being and time' perspective of project phenomena.

Reviewing the literature we identify three themes. Identified themes include 'best practice', 'micro-foundations' and 'embeddedness'. Long before the concept was introduced, project studies strongly focused on best practice, and this tradition has continued after its introduction but relies on a substantially different ontological position. We therefore acknowledge their existence, but do not include them as examples of practice studies. This chapter is not intended as a full review of the extant literature but offers some insights into how the field of inquiry has developed.

11.2.1 Micro-Foundations of Temporary Organizations

The micro-foundations concept refers to key elements of the inner life of projects (cf. Loscher et al., 2019), or temporary organizations (Lundin & Söderholm, 1995) as they are often called (e.g., Addyman et al., 2020; Melkonian & Picq, 2011; Willems et al., 2020). This does not mean that every action, response, and interaction (however trivial) warrants attention, although apparently trivial actions (such as the failure to turn a valve off or on at an appropriate time, or harsh criticism) may have major consequences. As in any research, exploration of the micro-foundations must be the focus. Such focus could be on the practitioners themselves (Bredillet et al., 2015; Jacobsson & Merschbrock, 2018) and their careers (Akkermans et al., 2020), or teams thereof. For example, Sjögren et al. (2019) identified eight practices that help ad hoc teams to discover and exploit opportunities associated with emergent and initiated change requests. The eight practices include establish the root cause, proven experience, ad hoc meetings, revisiting, floating, win-win solutions, design conditions, and retrospective requests. Importantly, these practices describe everyday activities that lead to resolving the said change requests. The authors also note that it is not easy to delineate between a practice-based approach and a process-based approach, but nevertheless the findings contribute to shedding light on the benefits, rather than threats of engineering changes. For related studies see, for example, Sjögren et al. (2018), Van der Hoorn and Whitty (2017), and O'Leary & Williams' research (2012) on the practices associated with alignment-seeking. See also Lindgren and Packendorff (2011) or Jacobsson and Wilson (2014), for example, who refer to a projects-as-practice approach as a way to explore everyday activities, but take a pronounced process-based stance. In addition, see Whittington (2006) and Blomquist et al. (2010) for attempts to distinguish the process and practice approaches.

Another example of micro-foundational research is provided by Musca et al. (2014). In contrast to most other practice-based approaches (but see Alvarez et al., 2011, Melkonian & Picq, 2011, or Thibodeau & Rüling, 2018 for other exceptions), they did not focus on a traditional industry, but a challenging physical activity (mountaineering) to challenge taken-for-granted assumptions. They followed a group of mountaineers as they attempted the unprecedented crossing of Cordillera Darwin in Patagonia. Ethnographically embedded on the boat that took the team of mountaineers to their starting point, they explored how the team of professionals co-constructed their sense of the situation. When the crossing proved impossible and the boat was having trouble, they identified four discursive practices that helped the team's sensemaking: wording and rewording of the unexpected, reframing, focusing attention, and reaffirming team cohesiveness. By applying these practices the crew was able to formulate a new plan. Musca et al. (2014) argued that this contributed to a novel way of viewing project renewal. Other examples of contributions to this theme included analysis by Eriksson and Kadefors (2017) on the development of heuristics, challenges by Lenfle (2014) of the use of best practices in a major defence project, and consideration by Bygballe et al. (2016) of coordinating practices in construction projects.

In sum, key objectives in a projects-as-practice study focused on micro-foundations are to identify practices of people working in projects to describe and characterize their lived experience. Micro-foundational research draws inspiration from a wider set of industries and activities than traditional streams, which helps efforts to challenge taken-for-granted assumptions. However, the bulk of the research is still on traditional industries and commercial activities, such as construction or research and development projects.

11.2.2   Embeddedness of Temporary Organizations

While projects-as-practice studies originally focused on the micro-foundations of project organizations, the agenda has been widened to include their embeddedness within organizations and the broader society, particularly bundles of activities representing wider contextual environments. In the early 2000s, researchers began to focus increasingly on the programmes and portfolio management associated with multi-project organizations (Engwall & Jerbrandt, 2003) and project-intensive organizations (Ekstedt et al., 1999). Extension of the interest in nitty-gritty doings and sayings of single projects has led to a similar, broader interest in phenomena, including what observers have called 'governance-as-practice' (e.g., Brunet & Aubry, 2018; Hällgren & Lindahl, 2017; Sanderson, 2012), i.e., ways that governance issues are handled in projects. For example, Brunet 'advances a conceptualization for governance-as-practice' by examining what was actually done in four projects. She notes that a governance framework is 'an institutionalized artifact' (2019, p. 293) and identifies three types of governance practices: structuring, normalizing, and facilitating. In another example, Hällgren and Lindahl (2017) explore two inter-linked projects and struggles to coordinate the efforts. Due to a lack of established governance practices, the project participants had to rely on soft problem-solving, which circumvented the lack of governance structures and enabled resolution of political issues embedded in the projects. A complication was noted by Hedborg et al. (2020) in an exploration of inter-project dependencies using a theoretical framework rooted in project ecology concepts. This is that, although neglected in the literature, horizontal project interdependencies embedded in project ecosystems are important for project success, but typically beyond project managers' responsibilities (see also, for example, Clegg et al., 2018; Delisle, 2020; Petro et al., 2020).

Within this theme, we include the governance of mega-projects, as addressed for instance by Sanderson (2012), Pollack et al. (2013), and Van Marrewijk and Smits (2016). Projects of this size have larger scale than 'ordinary' projects. Their inner life is thus harder to define and, similar to the idea that a governance framework is an institutionalized artifact, mega-projects can be regarded as almost an institution by themselves, with multiple smaller but coordinated projects. Sanderson (2012) finds that past research has focused too much upon how actors behave to construct governance structures and thus neglect the life of the mega-project. In line with Sanderson's call to action, and an interest in the embeddedness approach, Van Marrewijk and Smits (2016) ethnographically explore the Panama Canal Expansion Megaproject through a cultural lens. They identify five cultural practices involved: ritualizing the public announcement of the bid winner, changing teams during the transition phases, struggling over governance structure of the works management team, labelling national cultures, and labelling organizational cultures. These practices fill the void between structural forms of governing mega-projects and the micro-processes of governing, and their recognition allows Van Marrewijk and Smits to show that '(mega-)projects need to be understood as living worlds with their own subcultures, history, rituals, symbols and practices' (2016, p. 542) which calls for broader considerations of activities on complex projects. Other authors (e.g., Parker et al., 2018) have explored the multi-dimensional effects of the agency of the multiple stakeholders in public-private partnering projects, which have similar setups to mega-projects (despite differences), and often include major undertakings with complex governing structures.

The embeddedness theme also encompasses broader institutional impacts of projects and the agency within them. For example, Buchan and Simpson (2020, p. 38) use an empirical illustration 'from a Health and Social Care Partnership in Scotland' to 'highlight the inherently emergent nature of projects as they bring about transformational change'. Another example of how institutional change can be induced or driven by projects is provided by Tukiainen and Granqvist (2016), in an exploration (based on interviews and archival data) of how the 'Innovation University Project' advanced nationwide regulatory reform of universities in Finland. As both of these studies indicate, projects can be considered more powerfully than otherwise conceived because a practice-based perspective revealed the innate power of project activities (see also e.g., Caldwell & Dyer, 2020; Jensen et al., 2018).

In sum, projects-as-practice research interested in embeddedness issues provides insights into the power of projects in changing major undertakings in society, and what organizations, structures, activities, and societies in which they are embedded may be like in the future.

11.2.3 Final Observations on Projects-as-Practice Research

A final observation that cuts across the two themes is that practice-based studies of projects are becoming increasingly broadly disseminated, including use of the associated theorization to contribute to management and organization studies more generally. Examples include the merger of project and career studies by Akkermans et al. (2020), as well as contributions to the entrepreneurship literature by Antonacopoulou and Fuller (2020) and Germain and Aubry (2019), healthcare studies by Dorant and Krieger (2017), and the strategy literature by Hidalgo and Morell (2019). Further evidence of the dissemination includes contributions published in

Table 11.1   *Relations between the identified practice themes and identified (pattern and relevance) challenges*

	Micro-foundations	Embeddedness
Pattern challenge	Explain project dynamics and intra-project dependencies	Provide understanding of the project's place in organizations and/or society at large
Relevance challenge	Intra-project topics of interest to project theories or generic social science areas	Organization and management theories with inter-project sites as a basis for analysis

journals that do not specifically focus on projects, for example, organization studies (Tukiainen & Granqvist, 2016), creativity and innovation management (Lindgren & Packendorff, 2011), and sustainability (Uribe et al., 2018).

11.3   THE PATTERN AND RELEVANCE CHALLENGES IN THE PROJECTS-AS-PRACTICE APPROACH

We have outlined the two main themes of the projects-as-practice approach, the micro-foundations theme and the embeddedness theme, which also represent two solutions to the pattern and relevance challenges discussed earlier. Both challenges are connected to the site concept and how a research site is defined and considered. To reiterate, according to the site ontology, a site is not a physical place. It may be situated in a physical place, for example, a project member's office, but it is, more importantly, a collective social arena where practice unfolds, for example, as a project member interacts with other project members imbued with norms and values (cf. Schatzki, 2002, 2005).

Possible analytical approaches are defined according to how the challenges are met and sites are defined. Focusing on the micro-foundations theme leads to attention to intra-project dynamics among practitioners, practice, and praxis, with 'the site' becoming either the temporal organization or a specific part of the organization. Finding patterns in these dynamics may be challenging, but such pattern-finding is a key objective of researchers more generally. Analysis of problem-solving mechanisms, decision-making, and group dynamics are possible avenues for research with a micro-foundation approach, which may make strong contributions to the understanding of generic issues, such as decision-making, power distribution, and negotiation.

Contributions to the embeddedness theme focus on relations between projects and their broader organizational and societal contexts: how activities associated with a project impact it, or how activities within a project impact other organizational activities. From the perspective of site ontology, established practices that impact praxis are inherent elements of the researched phenomena as institutionalized artifacts (cf. Brunet, 2019). The pattern challenge is to contribute to understanding how and why projects influence each other within an organization or society at large. The relevance challenge is to provide theoretical insights that are of interest to a broader audience, beyond the phenomena in question, including (for example) how organizational structures and project organizations interact, multi-project governance, and the project's effects on overall organizational or societal development. See Table 11.1 for a summary of how these two challenges and two themes are related.

11.4   MOVING ON

Based on the examples given and our brief analysis of how the pattern and relevance challenges have been met, we suggest three areas that need to be carefully considered when designing projects-as-practice research efforts.

First, a plethora of methods have been used, but interview-based case studies are common (e.g., Brunet & Aubry, 2018; Sjögren et al., 2019). Perhaps this is a matter of convenience as it provides reasonable closeness to the object of study and can provide valuable insights, but does not require as much time and access as an ethnographic study. However, while interviews are useful for explaining intentions, ethnographic methods are more suitable for describing what and how activities unfold (Schatzki, 2012). Thus, we would like to encourage researchers to engage in embedded, longer-term studies, if appropriate and feasible, and to develop optimized methods for the research objectives. This is a call for developing a more refined projects-as-practice epistemology.

Second, we identify a need to engage with the philosophical stance of a practice approach. Some authors have contributed to such an understanding, but many cite a practice approach to support claims that their research contributions are relevant to practitioners (and vice versa) which is a too narrow stance. Hence, there are still needs to refine site definitions and delimitations, aligning research with appropriate social models and theories of human behaviour to further strengthen the site ontology of projects-as-practice research (Schatzki 2002: 124).

Third, few researchers have engaged with the contributions to management and organization studies (see Jacobsson & Söderholm, 2011). Currently, we see rising interest in issues of temporality in management and organization studies, but few apply a project or temporary organization lens, as outlined in the project community. To honour the underlying site ontology we believe a practice approach may serve as an important tool to make contributions beyond the project literature.

Finally, we hope to see more research within the area of complex project organizing utilizing the advantages of a practice approach. However, as always, it is important to design research efforts rigorously and consider both epistemological and ontological issues carefully. It is equally important to consider these issues in relation to each other, i.e., to use methods that are aligned with the analytical purposes and objects of study. Likewise, complex projects comprise a rich empirical field, representing contemporary organizations, and their analysis can provide valuable insights that are highly relevant not only to project theory, but also, as mentioned earlier, to wider management and organizational theories!

REFERENCES

Addyman, S., Pryke, S. & Davies, A. (2020). Re-creating organizational routines to transition through the project life cycle: A case study of the reconstruction of London's Bank underground station. *Project Management Journal*, 51(5), 522–537.

Akkermans, J., Keegan, A., Huemann, M. & Ringhofer, C. (2020). Crafting project managers' careers: Integrating the fields of careers and project management. *Project Management Journal*, 51(2), 135–153.

Alvarez, J. F. A., Pustina, A. & Hällgren, M. (2011). Escalating commitment in the death zone: New insights from the 1996 Mount Everest disaster. *International Journal of Project Management*, 29(8), 971–985.

Antonacopoulou, E. P. & Fuller, T. (2020). Practising entrepreneuring as emplacement: The impact of sensation and anticipation in entrepreneurial action. *Entrepreneurship and Regional Development*, 32(3–4), 257–280.

Blomquist, T., Hällgren, M., Nilsson, A. & Söderholm, A. (2010). Project-as-practice: In search of project management research that matters. *Project Management Journal*, 41(1), 5–16.

Bourdieu, P. (1977). *Outline of a theory of practice*. Cambridge: Cambridge University Press.

Bredillet, C., Tywoniak, S. & Dwivedula, R. (2015). What is a good project manager? An Aristotelian perspective. *International Journal of Project Management*, 33(2), 254–266.

Brunet, M. (2019). Governance-as-practice for major public infrastructure projects: A case of multilevel project governing. *International Journal of Project Management*, 37(2), 283–297.

Brunet, M. & Aubry, M. (2018). The governance of major public infrastructure projects: The process of translation. *International Journal of Project Management*, 11(1), 80–103.

Buchan, L., & Simpson, B. (2020). Projects-as-practice: A Deweyan perspective. *Project Management Journal*, 51(1), 38–48.

Bygballe, L. E., Swärd, A. R. & Vaagaasar, A. L. (2016). Coordinating in construction projects and the emergence of synchronized readiness. *International Journal of Project Management*, 34(8), 1479–1492.

Caldwell, R. & Dyer, C. (2020). The performative practices of consultants in a change network: An actor–network practice perspective on organisational change. *Journal of Organizational Change Management*, 33(5), 941–963.

Clegg, S., Killen, C. P., Biesenthal, C. & Sankaran, S. (2018). Practices, projects and portfolios: Current research trends and new directions. *International Journal of Project Management*, 36(5), 762–772.

Delisle, J. (2020). Working time in multi-project settings: How project workers manage work overload. *International Journal of Project Management*, 38(7), 419–428.

Dorant, E. & Krieger, T. (2017). Contextual exploration of a new family caregiver support concept for geriatric settings using a participatory health research strategy. *International Journal of Environmental Research and Public Health*, 14(12), 1467.

Ekstedt, E., Lundin, R. A., Söderholm, A. & Wirdenius, H. (1999). *Neo-industrial organising: Renewal by action and knowledge formation in a project-intensive economy*. Routledge.

Engwall, M. & Jerbrant, A. (2003). The resource allocation syndrome: The prime challenge of multi-project management? *International Journal of Project Management*, 21(6), 403–409.

Eriksson, T. & Kadefors, A. (2017). Organisational design and development in a large rail tunnel project: Influence of heuristics and mantras. *International Journal of Project Management*, 35(3), 492–503.

Floricel, S., Bonneau, C., Aubry, M. & Sergi, V. (2014). Extending project management research: Insights from social theories. *International Journal of Project Management*, 32(7), 1091–1107.

Germain, O. & Aubry, M. (2019). Exploring processual and critical avenues at the crossroad of entrepreneurship and project management. *International Journal of Managing Projects in Business*, 12(1), 2–5.

Giddens, A. (1984). *The constitution of society: Outline of the theory of structuration*. University of California Press.

Hällgren, M. & Lindahl, M. (2017). Coping with lack of authority: Extending research on project governance with a practice approach. *International Journal of Managing Projects in Business*, 10(2), 263–294.

Hällgren, M. & Söderholm, A. (2011). Projects-as-practice: New approach, new insights. In P. W. G. Morris, J. Pinto, & J. Söderlund (Eds), *The Oxford handbook of project management*. Oxford University Press.

Hedborg, S., Eriksson, P.-E. & Gustavsson, T. K. (2020). Organisational routines in multi-project contexts: Coordinating in an urban development project ecology. *International Journal of Project Management*, 38(7), 394–404.

Hidalgo, E. S. & Morell, M. F. (2019). Co-designed strategic planning and agile project management in academia: Case study of an action research group. *Palgrave Communications*, 5(1), 1–13.

Jacobsson, M. & Merschbrock, C. (2018). BIM coordinators: A review. *Engineering, Construction and Architecture Management*, 25(8), 989–1008.

Jacobsson, M. & Söderholm, A. (2011). Breaking out of the straitjacket of project research: In search of contribution. *International Journal of Managing Projects in Business*, 4(3), 378–388.

Jacobsson, M. & Wilson, T. L. (2014). Partnering hierarchy of needs. *Management Decisions*, 52(10), 1907–1927.

Jensen, C., Johansson, S. & Löfström, M. (2018). Policy implementation in the era of accelerating projectification: Synthesizing Matland's conflict–ambiguity model and research on temporary organizations. *Public Policy and Administration*, 33(4), 447–465.

Lenfle, S. (2014). Toward a genealogy of project management: Sidewinder and the management of exploratory projects. *International Journal of Project Management*, 32(6), 921–931.

Lindgren, M. & Packendorff, J. (2011). Issues, responsibilities and identities: A distributed leadership perspective on biotechnology R&D management. *Creativity and Innovation Management*, 20(3), 157–170.

Loscher, G., Splitter, V. & Seidl, D. (2019). Theodore Schatzki's practice theory and its implications for organization studies. In S. Clegg & M. Pina e Cunha (Eds), *Management, organizations and contemporary social theory* (pp. 115–134). Routledge.

Lundin, R. A. & Söderholm, A. (1995). A theory of the temporary organization. *Scandinavian Journal of Management*, 11(4), 437–455.

Melkonian, T. & Picq, T. (2011). Building project capabilities in PBOs: Lessons from the French special forces. *International Journal of Project Management*, 29(4), 455–467.

Musca, G. N., Mellet, C., Simoni, G., Sitri, F. & De Vogüé, S. (2014). 'Drop your boat!': The discursive co-construction of project renewal. The case of the Darwin mountaineering expedition in Patagonia. *International Journal of Project Management*, 32(7), 1157–1169.

O'Leary, T. & Williams, T. (2012). Managing the social trajectory: A practice perspective on project management. *IEEE Transactions on Engineering Management*, 60(3), 566–580.

Parker, D. W., Dressel, U., Chevers, D. & Zeppetella, L. (2018). Agency theory perspective on public-private-partnerships: International development project. *International Journal of Productivity and Performance Management*, 67(2), 239–259.

Petro, Y., Ojiako, U., Williams, T. & Marshall, A. (2020). Organizational ambidexterity: Using project portfolio management to support project-level ambidexterity. *Production Planning and Control*, 31(4), 287–307.

Pollack, J., Costello, K. & Sankaran, S. (2013). Applying actor–network theory as a sensemaking framework for complex organisational change programs. *International Journal of Project Management*, 31(8), 1118–1128.

Sanderson, J. (2012). Risk, uncertainty and governance in megaprojects: A critical discussion of alternative explanations. *International Journal of Project Management*, 30(4), 432–443.

Schatzki, T. R. (1996). *Social practices: A Wittgensteinian approach to human activity and the social.* Cambridge University Press.

Schatzki, T. R. (2002). *The site of the social: A philosophical account of the constitution of social life and change.* Penn State Press.

Schatzki, T. R. (2005). Peripheral vision: The sites of organizations. *Organization Studies*, 26(3), 465–484.

Schatzki, T. R. (2012). A primer on practices: Theory and research. In J. Higgs, R. Barnett & F. Trede (Eds), *Practice-based education* (pp. 13–26). Sense Publishers.

Schatzki, T. R., Knorr-Cetina, K. & Von Savigny, E. (Eds) (2001). *The practice turn in contemporary theory.* Routledge.

Sjögren, P., Fagerström, B., Kurdve, M. & Callavik, M. (2018). Managing emergent changes: Ad hoc teams' praxis and practices. *International Journal of Managing Projects in Business*, 11(4), 1086–1104.

Sjögren, P., Fagerström, B., Kurdve, M. & Lechler, T. (2019). Opportunity discovery in initiated and emergent change requests. *Design Science*, 5(5).

Thibodeau, B. D., & Rüling, C.-C. (2018). Overcoming project inertia and gaining project momentum: Strategic adaptation in cultural facilities planning. *International Journal of Arts Management*, 21(1), 28–48.

Tukiainen, S., & Granqvist, N. (2016). Temporary organizing and institutional change. *Organization Studies*, 37(12), 1819–1840.

Uribe, D. F., Ortiz-Marcos, I., & Uruburu, Á. (2018). What is going on with stakeholder theory in project management literature? A symbiotic relationship for sustainability. *Sustainability*, 10(4), 1300.

Van Der Hoorn, B. & Whitty, S. J. (2015). A Heideggerian paradigm for project management: Breaking free of the disciplinary matrix and its Cartesian ontology. *International Journal of Project Management*, 33(4), 721–734.

Van Der Hoorn, B. & Whitty, S. J. (2017). The praxis of 'alignment seeking' in project work. *International Journal of Project Management*, 35(6), 978–993.

Van Marrewijk, A. & Smits, K. (2016). Cultural practices of governance in the Panama Canal expansion megaproject. *International Journal of Project Management*, 34(3), 533–544.

Weick, K. E. (1979). *The social psychology of organizing*. Addison-Wesley.

Whittington, R. (2006). Completing the practice turn in strategy research. *Organization Studies*, 27(5), 613–634.

Willems, T., Van Marrewijk, A., Kuitert, L., Volker, L. & Hermans, M. (2020). Practices of isolation: The shaping of project autonomy in innovation projects. *International Journal of Project Management*, 38(4), 215–228.

12. Uncovering the role of non-human actors in projects

Julien Pollack and Stewart Clegg

12.1   INTRODUCTION

Actor-Network Theory (ANT) offers a way of conducting research that has not yet received broad attention within the field of project management. However, it offers considerable opportunities to produce novel insights into the management of projects and temporary organisations. ANT is a form of sociological research, with a basis in the study of science and scientific discovery. ANT is also referred to as the sociology of translation (Law, 1992), due to its emphasis on the networks of translation and transformation often used to explore how action, artefacts, and meaning are transformed into networks of activity. The purpose of this chapter is to make ANT more accessible to those conducting research into projects and their management. We address this purpose by introducing some key concepts related to ANT and exploring how it has already been used in project management research. We then discuss how ANT could potentially be applied in future research, first through a discussion of how ANT could bring the environment to the fore in stakeholder management, followed by illustrating how ANT's use in other fields presents potential for application in project management research.

ANT does not have a unified body of literature (Cho et al., 2008) but is most closely associated with Latour (Mutch, 2002), with its early development also significantly influenced by Law and Callon (Law & Hassard, 1999). ANT has evolved into a distinct, yet complex, theoretical formulation that has many variations and interpretations (Nimmo, 2011). It's application in research 'assumes a familiarity with bodies of literature and ideas that are formidable in their range and scope' (Mutch, 2002, p. 480). Given this, a researcher should anticipate considerable range in both the ways that ANT has been used in research, as well as the areas to which it has been applied. Nonetheless, review of the literature on the use of ANT in project management research reveals some consistent themes relevant to the field of complex projects and their management.

In exploring the opportunities that ANT may present for project management research, it is important to clarify common areas of confusion. First, the term 'network' does not refer to an organisational structure in ANT (Aubry, 2011), nor to systems and processes formalised through information technology (IT), although ANT has been used to explore these kinds of networks. Neither does it refer to the relationships explored using Social Network Analysis, where the kind of relationship under study is tightly defined by the specifics of the data collection instrument. Instead, 'network' broadly refers to an association that can span technical, social and institutional categories, allowing the researcher to trace the association between otherwise qualitatively distinct phenomena.

Misunderstanding of ANT comes also from the name 'Actor Network Theory'; ANT is less a theory than a methodological approach, with elements of a unique ontology. It is a way to learn from and about actors, without the imposition of unnecessary external constructs; an approach that is comparable to ethnomethodology in its eschewal of macro-forces as the source of order (Latour, 1999). Instead, order and disorder are to be seen as emergent properties of actor networks. ANT practitioners abhor functionalist social abstractions, such as a 'central value system' or its Marxian analogue, a 'dominant ideology'. Harty (2010) describes ANT as an ontological perspective, instead of a theory, providing an ontology for enquiry into the ways that actors come together and form stable and heterogeneous networks of interaction; these networks link human actors with socio-material actants (Law, 1992) such as technologies and digital and other devices.

The original development of ANT was partially a reaction against a tendency to grant special status to human actors, separating them from other non-social aspects producing socio-material effects. ANT refuses the differentiation between humans and non-human actors in a network of interaction, taking the agency of non-humans seriously, considering the influence of humans and non-humans through the same conceptual and methodological terms. Both humans and non-humans have agency; they are more than merely simple and passive recipients of symbolic projection (Latour, 2005). The social and technical worlds are entangled and mutually defining. Using a metric contributes to defining the agency of its user as much as that of the phenomena whose abstract qualities are calculated.

ANT allows for free conceptual movement between otherwise conceptually distinct spheres such as 'nature' and 'society', assuming a symmetry between humans and non-humans (McGrath, 2002), acknowledging that it is not only possible but also desirable to use the same analytical terms to examine both the human and the non-human (Law, 1986). For ANT, actants and actors can equally assume a role as heterogeneous, multiple and complex actors/actants in everyday endeavours; humans are not assumed to have any essential ontological primacy. Such heterogeneity should be examined with the same critical intent as all other kinds of phenomena. One consequence is that the tendency to resist pre-determined classification extends in ANT to a rejection of commonly assumed dualistic distinctions, such as micro and macro (Fox, 2000; Mutch, 2002), the distinction between internal and external networks (Aubry, 2011), subject–object dualism (Nimmo, 2011), change versus stability or social versus economic forces. ANT provides a methodology with which to explore how such orderings are co-created and taken for granted (Harty, 2010). In an echo of Garfinkel's (1967) 'ethnomethodological indifference' ANT constitutes itself as 'agnostic' to all categories that members use for making sense of phenomena. This is a central aspect of its rejection of pre-determined categories and dualities commonly in use in earlier sociological studies.

From an ANT perspective, an actor or actant is any 'element which bends space around itself, makes other elements depend upon itself and translates their will into a language of its own' (Callon & Latour, 1981, p. 286). Hence a spreadsheet or a PowerPoint could be considered an actant shaping actors' networks and relations. Actors act not only alone and with others but through actants with which they are constituted in networks. Every 'actor is also, always, a network' (Law, 1992, p. 384); a network of interconnected actors can be thought of as a single actor. Hence entities such as 'the PMO' or 'the project' have effects distinguishable from the human actors involved in them and impossible without the affordances of so many actants: metrics, machines and milestones.

It is effects caused by networks that make things happen (Latour, 2005). Actors and actants are connected through networks of association that are mutually changing and affecting each other. Action is inherently context-dependent, in a constant state of reconfiguration and change, becoming rather than being, in processes affected by the network of interactions of which they are a part (Callon, 1998). Action, from this perspective should not be harmonistically associated with intention.

> Action is not done under the full control of the consciousness; action should rather be felt as a node, a knot, and a conglomerate of many surprising sets of agencies that have to be slowly disentangled. It is this venerable source of uncertainty that we wish to render vivid again in the odd expression of actor-network. (Latour, 2005, p. 44)

Latour differentiates two types of actions based on their stability and predictability: intermediaries and mediators. Intermediaries act in a predictable fashion and play a stable role in a network; although they still act and transform actions, the input to the action can be taken as a predictor of the output. With mediators, there is less certainty. 'Their input is never a good predictor of their output; their specificity has to be taken into account every time. Mediators transform, translate, distort, and modify the meaning or the elements they are supposed to carry' (Latour, 2005, p. 39). Actors may change to being intermediary or mediator based on the role that they play in the network at any time. A project management information system may be an actant that usually produces reports of little import but unexpectedly malfunctions or highlights overlooked information, shifting from intermediary to mediator. A working model of a detail in a construction project, such as a mock-up of how a window aligns with an innovative brick formation attached to a curvaceous sub-frame designed by a 'star architect' such as Frank Gehry, may shift the detail from being an intermediary in the unfolding of the project to one that becomes a mediator (Naar & Clegg, 2015, 2018), mocked up in a studio. In contrast, a new project management information system, once a mediator destabilising project processes, can shift to become an intermediary as its role in the network stabilises (Pollack et al., 2013).

ANT explores the relationships between networks of actors, each connected through a series of associations, each potentially triggering others to act. It is through networks of interaction and association that elements gain both agency and identity; qualities that are not essential attributes but are created through the network of interactions (Harty, 2010). Networks are constantly in the process of formation and reformation, stabilisation and breakdown. One of the most productive points to explore network processes is when new associations are being created, as connections are often more visible when forming. Porsander (2005) notes that examining when new connections are being created provides unique insight into the process of organising; something that is more problematic once connections have been stabilised. Projects, as deliberately temporary forms of organisation, undergo significant change throughout the project lifecycle, being formed through new associations between people, processes, materialities and technologies, temporarily stabilised in networks to be deliberately sundered on delivery. During network formation, conflicts, tensions and issues can be studied as they occur (Aubry, 2011), an aspect of ANT particularly suited to research into project management, with the next section used to explore some of the ways that ANT has addressed these issues.

12.2   USES OF ANT IN COMPLEX PROJECT ORGANISING RESEARCH

An ANT study should be open to understanding networks of association, without preconception. To Law (1992, p. 380) 'it is important not to start out assuming whatever we wish to explain'. The highly normative nature of much project management 'theory' renders this lack of assumption especially important. A significant benefit of ANT is to see the project management guides and standards as inscriptions of normative assumptions that can be potential actants. Aubry (2011) notes that while project management research has largely focused on the technical aspects of delivery it is paying increasing attention to sociological research, something reflected in prioritising practice rather than normativity (Cicmil et al., 2006) and understanding projects as networks of practices (Blomquist et al., 2010). While Leybourne (2007) notes that ANT represents an opportunity to move project management research from the technical to the social; ANT actually goes further, recognising the necessary imbrication of the social with the material. The material can be composed of both natural systems, such as terrain, ecology, climate, etc., as well as the technical systems used to work on and with the natural features.

ANT has been used to study a wide range of project phenomena. Blackburn (2002) used ANT to interpret project managers' stories about practice as a way of understanding the relationship between stakeholders, processes and project managers, noting how ANT can reveal the effects project deliverables cause. Missonier and Loufrani-Fedida (2014) note that ANT's focus on relational ontology shifts the dominant view of stakeholders to one of mutual unfolding and co-evolution with the projects in which they hold or claim a stake.

ANT provides an opportunity to look more directly at the project context than can be achieved through imposition of a priori categories or frameworks of analysis. For example, Georg and Tryggestad (2009) noted that the role of the project manager is typically conceptualised as focused on efficient delivery, with other parties focusing on project relevance. However, their ANT study uncovered the active role that project budgets, architectural drawings and other devices play as actants, entangling the project manager in a network of design activities otherwise considered outside their remit of efficient delivery. Their study raises the question of how accurately the role of the project manager is represented in normative guides. Hybrid approaches, using aspects of predictive and agile methodologies, blur interpretation of this role, shaping it in local choices of techniques, technologies and artefacts. Alliances, sustained supplier partnerships, as well as the use of contractors as an elastic semi-permanent workforce, change traditional relationships between client and contractor, introducing other actors and actants as sources of indeterminacy constructed in practice, which future studies can explore.

Aubry et al. (2007) advocated the use of ANT in project management research, later using it (Aubry, 2011) to explore the complex network of translations associated with a project status report, focusing on how these inscriptions were processes of translation of multiple viewpoints. Considered simply as an object, the project status report obscures the use of conflicts, controls and calculations. Pollack et al. (2013) used ANT to analyse multiple cases involving the roll-out and uptake of project management information systems, studying the extent to which networks stabilised in project management practice. Voordijk (2021) explored how, in the context of construction projects, digital technologies co-shape each other, mediating access to the environment. Other notable studies employing ANT focus on construction innovation

(Harty, 2010), decision-making in projects (Parkin, 1996), organisational change projects (Linde & Linderoth, 2006), healthcare information system implementation (Cho et al., 2008), the response of the London Ambulance Service when a dispatch system failed (McGrath, 2002) and e-Government IT (Heeks & Stanforth, 2007).

ANT is flexible as a research tool; for instance, Porsander (2000, 2005) used ANT in two different ways. First, ANT was used to explore a project as a whole system of associations. Second, ANT was used to understand how an IT system, as an actant, networked the project. Linderoth and Pellegrino (2005) coupled ANT to the social construction of technology approach to explain issues encountered in two case studies of IT-dependent organisational change. Other studies apply ANT in combination with other theoretical frameworks; for example, Mutch (2002) and Greenhalgh and Stones (2010) both combined ANT with structuration theory in studies that enquired into the United Kingdom National Health Service in research comparable to Linde and Linderoth's (2006) inquiry into project management of IT projects in Swedish healthcare. ANT has already been applied in various ways offering significant opportunity and potential for understanding practices and processes in future project management research.

In the next sections, we briefly explore the ways that ANT might play a role in future research into project management. We first illustrate this with discussion of how ANT could bring aspects of the environment to the fore in discussion of project stakeholder management. We then draw on a variety of related research from outside the project management literature to provide the reader with other examples of how ANT could potentially be applied.

12.3 THE PRIMORDIAL STAKEHOLDER AS AN ACTOR IN PROJECTS

Winch (2017) argues for a focus on the environment as a primordial project stakeholder (Driscoll & Starik, 2004) as part of an increasing interest in sustainable project management. Projects can have a profound and damaging ecological impact upon the material environment through both process and product. Similarly, non-human actors in the natural environment can act directly on project delivery when the project encompasses aspects of the natural environment as an objective, as Tryggestad et al. (2013) explain in their account of how frogs can become stakeholders and as Willemsen et al. (2020) discuss in the context of threatened species recovery. Callon's (1986) seminal ANT study, describing the process by which a group of scientists momentarily stabilised a network of interaction when they acted as investigators of the lifecycle of scallops, provides an example that may illustrate the process of nature as an actant. A network was constituted by the scallops, the fishermen living off the scallops and the scientists researching the lifecycle of amphibian habits, which was the major actant.

The natural environment is a project stakeholder and should be considered as such, as on the Olympic project that Pitsis et al. (2003) analysed. There is growing concern for ensuring that the way we manage projects, the materials consumed during delivery and the outputs of projects do not damage the natural environment. Despite an increasing emphasis on sustainability in project management (Sabini et al., 2019), the impact of project management on the natural environment remains a secondary actant for those many projects in which effects on nature are not a primary object of calculation.

The natural environment becomes a stakeholder in projects through different representations of it as well as by virtue of the projects' effects on salient ecological aspects (Aaltonen & Kujala, 2016). For instance, the representations made in the processes producing environmental impact statements create an actant whose inscriptions can have considerable materiality for a project, especially during the planning and approval process. Inscriptions are never stable because their meaning is always dependent on the sensemaking interpreting them. Such sensemaking is always a matter of indexical interpretation from positions of professional and organisational interest, indexing what is relevant to the actors' interpretive interests in these inscriptions, while glossing over that to which they would rather not attend (Clegg, 1975). One of the most ubiquitous stakeholder representations is the power/impact matrix, a representation providing only a singularly static perspective. Romestant's (2020) stress on non-human and non-business actants in sustainability's agency (its 'agencing') suggests the need for an open and dynamic perspective on stakeholders. Considerations of ecological impact increasingly feature in stakeholder matrices, extending relevant actor networks' entanglement with various environmental action groups and their representational work on behalf of plants, species and other mute actants, for which ANT can help untangle connections.

An ANT perspective provides a way of understanding why the natural environment is so easily ignored as a stakeholder when making design decisions. While the natural environment may not often directly act on project delivery, past a contingency for weather during delivery, it can render project designs inadequate when nature acts critically, in fire, flood and disease. Warming climates, subsequent meteorological changes and the behaviour of viral pandemics have a profound effect as actants on design practices and the nature of projects. Unanticipated frost or other environmental extremes may force momentary awareness of the natural environment upon a project by causing delay, damage or other expense. Viral pandemic made the COVID-19 virus an actant in the design process, increasing consideration of the circulation of air in zones of buildings and of co-mingling occupancy not only in construction but also in occupation. COVID-19 also became an actant in project team work, leading to increased reliance on virtual and distributed teams, causing persistent changes in collaboration practices.

Actants that do not feature at the time that they are produced, such as carbon emissions during a project's process or those that occur as a result of its product, become actants as carbon taxes increasingly take these into account (Verrender, 2021). Actants that have future effects can in retrospect, and increasingly in prospect, become powerful actors in and around the project. Nature is a major actant; the science of anthropocentric climate change is premised on this being the case in its investigation of actor-climate networks and their effects (Heikkurinen et al., 2019). Although project managers might imagine that environmental impact statements, energy efficiency reports or green building certification all provide mechanisms to ensure that the environmental impact of complex projects is included as part of the design and approval process, these measures do not limit network effects. Networks are open assemblages of systems' actants that are not foreclosed by closures of systems effected by human actors. For instance, the tsunami that caused the collapse of the nuclear power station at Fukushima demonstrated, in retrospect, that the power station's closed system was not as closed as its designers planned. The tsunami was an actant with major effects on past and future energy projects; earlier, the 1986 meltdown of the number 4 Chernobyl reactor in the Ukraine became an actant shaping the projects that were not considered in Germany, which instituted a 'no nukes' policy, creating a future path dependency in contemporary times on the Russian Nord Stream gas supply.

12.4 FUTURE RESEARCH

Having explored the way that ANT can extend consideration of stakeholder management to include consideration of non-human actants, we next draw on ANT research outside project management to suggest opportunities to extend understanding of project management through ANT. For example, Abboubi et al. (2021) used ANT to investigate how a company worked to engage other organisations with the potential benefits of voluntary corporate social responsibility certification. The approach could be extended to researching ways of engaging stakeholders in beneficial networks relating to sustainability, diversity, community or culture. These may not be directly mandated under contractual or regulatory terms, so the question of how to stabilise these networks arises (Ninan et al., 2020a, 2020b). Equally, studies could examine how seemingly entrenched patterns of damaging behaviour might be destabilised.

Postma (2010) used ANT to critique a case study of an enterprise resource planning (ERP) system. The focus was not on the project management of the ERP delivery but on the ERP system as an actant within an ecosystem of other actors, exploring how the new ERP system became part of an existing collective. Inclusion of the new ERP system was not a simple matter of system replacement but a complex rearrangement of the network, including a series of accommodations between the new system and the old; something that has implications for future research into benefits management and the way that change management practices play a role in the uptake of project outputs.

Opportunities for enquiry into the project lifecycle are also illustrated by Lancione and Clegg (2013), who used ANT to focus upon a project network that could not be characterised as a simple transition from an old to a new state but could potentially be traced as a constantly changing topology of relationships between actants. Viewing change in terms of project life-cycle phases provided little benefit in understanding how the change occurred. Instead, they traced a series of small translations, conceptualised as chronotropes, which could be seen as movement towards alignment in a common interest. The possibility for further research that questions the ubiquitous role of the project lifecycle model in understanding how projects progress over time is suggested.

Finally, Viljanen's (2020) ANT exploration of contracts also provides an interesting illustration of how ANT could be used in project management research. His aim was to describe the way that contracts act as points in a network that create behavioural change in others, identifying that it is only through the networks in which a contract operates that the contract gains efficacy. Viljanen extends the view of the contract from being a discrete entity to viewing contracts as creating and created by a network of contractual mechanisms, including conditional obligation and implied future enforcement acting upon the present. From this perspective, contracts do not act by themselves; their efficacy relies on a network of processes, roles and resources, both inside and outside the contracting parties. Obvious parallels could be drawn to research into the efficacy of other forms of project documentation.

12.5 CONCLUSION

ANT provides a unique approach, connecting people, artefacts, institutions and organisations in their socio-materiality, illuminating complex ties that might escape analysis focused exclusively on organisation, project, process or system. ANT can be used to provide an account of complex projects that engages with the complex network of associations that momentarily stabilise around organised projected intention. It does so in a way that neither assumes the project to be a closed system with a range of manipulable variables nor one in which human agency is sovereign. Project management requires recognising that much of its processes are constantly reshaped in practice by actants that act as agents of normalisation and disruption, as much as the current normative guides and professional associations do. ANT provides a lexicon, ontology and approach that can render much that is left unaccounted visible.

REFERENCES

Aaltonen, K. & Kujala, J. (2016). Towards an improved understanding of project stakeholder landscapes. *International Journal of Project Management*, 34, 1537–1552.
Abboubi, M., Pinnington, A., Clegg, S. & Nicolopoulou, K. (2021). Involving, countering, and overlooking stakeholder networks in soft regulation: Case study of a small-to-medium-sized enterprise's implementation of SA8000. *Business and Society*, 00076503211010175.
Aubry, M. (2011). The social reality of organisational project management at the interface between networks and hierarchy. *International Journal of Managing Projects in Business*, 4(3), 436–457.
Aubry, M., Hobbs, B. & Thuillier, D. (2007). A new framework for understanding organisational project management through the PMO. *International Journal of Project Management*, 25, 328–336.
Blackburn, S. (2002). The project manager and the project-network. *International Journal of Project Management*, 20(3), 199–204.
Blomquist, T., Hallgren, M. & Söderholm, A. (2010). Project-as-practice: In search of project management research that matters. *Project Management Journal*, 41(1), 1–12.
Callon, M. (1986). Some elements of a sociology of translation: Domestication of the scallops and the fisherman of St Brieuc Bay. In J. Law (Ed.), *Power, action, and belief: A new sociology of knowledge* (pp. 196–233). Routledge and Kegan Paul.
Callon, M. (1998). An essay on framing and overflowing: Economic externalities revisited by sociology. In M. Callon (Ed.), *The laws of the markets* (pp. 244–269). Blackwell.
Callon, M. & Latour, B. (1981). Unscrewing the big Leviathan: How actors macro-structure reality and how sociologists help them to do so. In K. Knorr-Cetina & V. Cicourel (Eds), *Advances in social theory and methodology: Towards an integration of micro- and macro-sociologies* (pp. 277–303). Routledge and Kegan Paul.
Cho, S., Mathiassen, L. & Nilsson, A. (2008). Contextual dynamics during health information systems implementation: an event-based actor-network approach. *European Journal of Information Systems*, 17(6), 614–630.
Cicmil, S., Williams, T., Thomas, J. & Hodgson, D. (2006). Rethinking project management: Researching the actuality of projects. *International Journal of Project Management*, 24(8), 675–686.
Clegg, S. R. (1975). *Power, rule and domination: A critical and empirical understanding of power in sociological theory and organizational life*. Routledge and Kegan Paul.
Driscoll, C. & Starik, M. (2004). The primordial stakeholder: Advancing the conceptual consideration of stakeholder status for the natural environment. *Journal of Business Ethics*, 49(1), 55–73.
Fox, S. (2000). Communities of practice, Foucault and actor–network theory. *Journal of Management Studies*, 37(6), 853–867.
Garfinkel, H. (1967). *Studies in ethnomethodology*. Prentice Hall.
Georg, S. & Tryggestad, K. (2009). On the emergence of roles in construction: The qualculative role of project management. *Construction Management and Economics*, 27(10), 969–981.
Greenhalgh, T. & Stones, R. (2010). Theorising big IT programmes in healthcare: Strong structuration theory meets actor-network theory. *Social Science and Medicine*, 70(9), 1285–1294.
Harty, C. (2010). Implementing innovation: Designers, users and actor-networks. *Technology Analysis and Strategic Management*, 22(3), 297–315.
Heeks, R. & Stanforth, C. (2007). Understanding e-Government project trajectories from an actor-network perspective. *European Journal of Information Systems*, 16(2), 165–177.

Heikkurinen, P., Clegg, S., Pinnington, A. H., Nicolopoulou, K. & Alcaraz, J. M. (2019). Managing the Anthropocene: Relational agency and power to respect planetary boundaries. *Organization and Environment*, 34(2), 267–286.

Lancione, M. & Clegg, S. (2013). The chronotopes of change: Actor-networks in a changing business school. *Journal of Change Management*, 13(2), 117–142.

Latour, B. (1999). On recalling ANT. In J. Law & J. Hassard (Eds), *Actor network theory and after* (pp. 15–25). Blackwell Publishing.

Latour, B. (2005). *Reassembling the social*. Oxford University Press.

Law, J. (1986). On the methods of long-distance control: Vessels, navigation and the Portuguese route to India. In J. Law (Ed.), *Power, action, and belief: a new sociology of knowledge* (pp. 234–263). Routledge and Kegan Paul.

Law, J. (1992). Notes on the theory of the actor-network: Ordering, strategy and heterogeneity. *Systems Practice*, 5, 379–393.

Law, J. & Hassard, J. (1999). *Actor network theory and after*. Blackwell Publishing.

Leybourne, S. (2007). The changing bias of project management research: A consideration of the literatures and an application of extant theory. *Project Management Journal*, 38(1), 61–73.

Linde, A. & Linderoth, H. C. J. (2006). An actor-network theory perspective on IT-projects. In S. Cicmil & D. Hodgson (Eds), *Making projects critical* (pp. 155–170). Palgrave Macmillan.

Linderoth, H. & Pellegrino, G. (2005). Frames and inscriptions: Tracing a way to understand IT-dependent change projects. *International Journal of Project Management*, 23, 415–420.

McGrath, K. (2002). The Golden Circle: A way of arguing and acting about technology in the London Ambulance Service. *European Journal of Information Systems*, 11(4), 251–266.

Missonier, S. & Loufrani-Fedida, S. (2014). Stakeholder analysis and engagement in projects: From stakeholder relational perspective to stakeholder relational ontology. *International Journal of Project Management*, 32(7), 1108–1122.

Mutch, A. (2002). Actors and networks or agents and structures: Towards a realist view of information systems. *Organization*, 9(3), 477–496.

Naar, L. & Clegg, S. R. (2015). *Gehry in Sydney*. Images Press.

Naar, L. & Clegg, S. R. (2018). Models as strategic actants in innovative architecture. *Journal of Management Inquiry*, 27(1), 26–39.

Nimmo, R. (2011). Actor-network theory and methodology: Social research in a more-than human world. *Methodological Innovations Online*, 6(3), 108–119.

Ninan, J., Mahalingam, A. & Clegg, S. (2020a). Power and strategies in the external stakeholder management of megaprojects: A circuitry framework. *Engineering Project Organization Journal*, 9.

Ninan, J., Mahalingam, A., Clegg, S. R. & Sankaran, S. (2020b). ICT for external stakeholder management: Sociomateriality from a power perspective. *Construction Management and Economics*, 38(9), 840–855.

Parkin, J. (1996). Organizational decision making and the project manager. *International Journal of Project Management*, 14(5), 257–263.

Pitsis, T., Clegg, S. R., Marosszeky, M. & Rura-Polley, T. (2003). Constructing the Olympic dream: Managing innovation through the future perfect. *Organization Science*, 14(5), 574–590.

Pollack, J., Costello, K. & Sankaran, S. (2013). Applying actor-network theory as an sensemaking framework for complex organisational change programs. *International Journal of Project Management*, 31(8), 1118–1128.

Porsander, L. (2000). Translating a dream of immortality in a (con)temporary order. *Journal of Organizational Change Management*, 13(1), 14–29.

Porsander, L. (2005). 'My name is Lifebuoy': An actor-network emerging from an action net. In B. Czarniawska & T. Hernes (Eds), *Actor-network theory and organizing* (pp. 14–30). Studentlitteratur.

Postma, D. (2010). *The politics of technological design and implementation*. International Conference on Information Management and Evaluation, Academic Conferences International.

Romestant, F. (2020). Sustainability agencing: The involvement of stakeholder networks in megaprojects. *Industrial Marketing Management*, 89, 535–549.

Sabini, L., Muzio, D. & Alderman, N. (2019). 25 years of 'sustainable projects': What we know and what the literature says. *International Journal of Project Management*, 37(6), 820–838.

Tryggestad, K., Justesen, L. & Mouritsen, J. (2013). Project temporalities: How frogs can become stakeholders. *International Journal of Managing Projects in Business*, 6(1), 69–87.

Verrender, I. (2021). *How the carbon tax has come back to haunt the Australian government.* www.abc.net.au/news/2021-07-26/carbon-tax-has-come-back-to-haunt-the-government/100322396.

Viljanen, M. (2020). Actor-network theory contract theory. *European Review of Contract Law*, 16(1), 74–94.

Voordijk, H. (2021). Technical mediation and digital technologies in construction practice. *Architectural Engineering and Design Management*, 1–15.

Willemsen, M., Pollack, J. & Algeo, C. (2020). The role of project management in threatened species recovery. *International Journal of Managing Projects in Business*, 13(5), 981–998.

Winch, G. M. (2017). Megaproject stakeholder management. In Flyvbjerg, B. (Ed.), *The Oxford handbook of megaproject management* (pp. 339–361). Oxford University Press.

13. Project organizing in network contexts

Stephan Manning

13.1 INTRODUCTION

Projects are often seen as highly flexible forms of organizing activities towards rather complex goals (Bakker, 2010; Lundin & Söderholm, 1995; Söderlund, 2008). Scholars have argued that projects seem more suitable than permanent organizations to take on complex tasks in creative and flexible ways, combining heterogeneous sources of knowledge and competencies (Obstfeld, 2012). However, projects are also shaped by various norms, expectations and resources provided by the social contexts projects are embedded in (Engwall, 2003; Manning, 2008). Especially in professional project businesses – or 'project-based sectors' (Sergeeva & Winch, 2020), in which projects are the primary means of value creation, such as film, construction, event organizing, complex product and system development, projects are typically embedded in multiple layers of social structure – organizations, networks and fields (Cattani et al., 2011). Such contexts both enable and constrain project organizing (Manning, 2008).

One central social context of project organizing is networks. Networks denote sets of longer-term relationships providing opportunities for initial and repeat collaboration between legally independent partners (Borgatti & Foster, 2003; Jones et al., 1997). Networks help manage risks, bundle resources and competencies and manage transaction costs particularly in highly volatile industries (Jones et al., 1997; Powell, 1990). One network form in particular has received special attention from project scholars – so-called project networks or project network organizations (PNOs). PNOs have been defined as sets of project-based relationships between legally independent individuals and organizations which get activated for temporary projects, yet sustain beyond the time limitations of any project for potential future endeavours (Manning, 2010, 2017; Windeler & Sydow, 2001).

PNOs have been studied, partly under different labels, in various project-based sectors, including film, construction, advertising, academic research and international development (see for an overview, Manning, 2017). PNOs may differ in structure and composition, but they typically share three central features: strategic coordination, core project teams and flexible partner pools (Manning, 2017). Yet, despite continuous interest in PNOs, empirical studies rarely make explicit which 'network perspective' they use when analysing PNOs. This is problematic because multiple network perspectives co-exist – networks as relational structures, networks as governance forms, networks as organizational systems – all of which help us 'see' particular dynamics while being 'blind' to others. This handbook chapter attempts to explore the comparative utility of each network perspective when applied to PNOs.

13.2 PROJECT NETWORK ORGANIZATIONS

PNOs were first studied in the film and television (TV) industry (Manning, 2005; Starkey et al., 2000; Windeler & Sydow, 2001). In this context, PNOs can be described as longer-term, yet project-based sets of relationships between film producers, TV channels or film studios, directors, script writers, actors and technical service providers. They typically emerge within regional film production clusters (Foster et al., 2015; Sydow & Staber, 2002) and are embedded in regionally bounded 'project ecologies' (Grabher, 2002, 2004). PNOs share three main features: strategic coordination; stable core project teams; and flexible pools of complementary partners (see Manning, 2017).

First, PNOs are strategically built up and maintained by film production firms and individual filmmakers who act as 'project entrepreneurs' (see e.g. DeFillippi & Arthur, 1998; Ferriani et al., 2009). Their main role is to regularly develop ideas, pitch ideas to studios and TV channels and assemble creative teams around them. Second, PNOs typically develop around core project teams that sustain beyond singular projects. In feature film, core teams are often comprised of producer, studio, directors and/or script writers, who jointly develop projects and often collaborate repeatedly over time. Core teams develop both economic and creative interdependencies and establish 'collaborative paths' that allow for both explorative and exploitative project-based learning (Manning & Sydow, 2011). Third, filmmakers and their core team members maintain rather flexible pools of potential project partners who typically work as freelancers and who get recruited on demand depending on project requirements. With each project engagement, pool participants update their status position, e.g. as preferred or next-in-line director, script writer or actor, for future projects (Blair, 2001).

PNOs exist as organizational forms not only in TV and film production, but in many professional project businesses (Manning, 2017), including event organizing, complex products and systems, construction, collaborative research and international development. Across these fields PNOs often form around a series of similar projects, such as TV series (Stjerne & Svejenova, 2016), series of events (Anand & Watson, 2004), series of complex products and systems installations for particular clients (Gann & Salter, 2000; Geyer & Davies, 2000), series of research projects (Manning, 2010) or series of development projects (Manning & Von Hagen, 2010). No matter which context, PNOs typically combine strategic coordination, core project teams and flexible partner pools. Strategic coordinators include e.g. entrepreneurial researchers (Manning, 2010), event agencies (Anand & Watson, 2004), aid agencies (Manning & von Hagen, 2010; Stadtler & Probst, 2012) and consultants in construction (Ebers & Maurer, 2016). Like in film, these project entrepreneurs maintain core teams of project collaborators as well as flexible pools of project partners they can draw from on a project-by-project basis.

13.3   THREE NETWORK PERSPECTIVES

Three major network perspectives have established in the literature – networks as relational structures, networks as governance forms and networks as organizational systems. While overlapping in some respects, they focus on different network dimensions, thus drawing attention to certain network dynamics and processes while ignoring others.

The notion of networks as relational structures is rooted primarily in formal sociology based on the work of Simmel (1992 [1908]), as well as relational sociology (Emirbayer, 1997; Wellman, 1988). In this tradition, networks are understood as structural configurations of social relationships between individual and collective actors (Cook & Whitmeyer, 1992; Wellman, 1988). These configurations both enable and constrain actions of those interconnected (Mitchell, 1969). This network perspective has been used to examine both formal and informal relational structures both between and within organizations (Smith-Doerr & Powell, 2005; Zaheer et al., 2010). It is therefore a very generic network perspective that can be used to examine relational qualities of almost any social structure, including markets, organizations and projects (see e.g. Baker, 1990; White et al., 1976). Due to its generic quality, it also constitutes the foundation of network analysis as a method (Wasserman & Faust, 1994).

This network perspective has proven useful in analysing how network structures affect project initiation and project team formation, and how in turn specific projects affect network structures between project partners longer term (Schwab & Miner, 2008; Soda et al., 2004). For example, it helps analyse the extent to which stable ties between project partners emerge and affect future collaboration (Sorenson & Waguespack, 2006) and the extent to which so-called 'structural holes' and 'bridging ties' affect project initiation and team formation (Uzzi & Spiro, 2005; Zaheer & Soda, 2009). However, this network perspective remains relatively silent about how pre-established ties and team structures can be mobilized for future projects, and which norms or practices apply in the process.

The notion of networks as governance forms is rooted in new institutional economics which focuses on institutional arrangements and mechanisms underlying economic activity (Powell, 1990; Williamson, 1985). Traditionally, market and hierarchy are distinguished as mechanisms governing economic activity. Markets are typically associated with flexible price-based coordination, whereas hierarchies provide stability through planned coordination, employment contracts and administrative structures (see e.g. Richardson, 1972). In this paradigm, Powell (1990) introduced networks as a governance form of medium flexibility in which legally independent partners with complementary strengths set up interdependent relationships. Their exchanges are not primarily based on price or hierarchical coordination, but trust and reciprocity (see also Gulati, 1995; Uzzi, 1997). Based on these 'social' mechanisms (Jones et al., 1997), networks are able to lower transaction and production costs, manage resource interdependencies and risks and ease knowledge sharing (Powell, 1990).

In project contexts, this perspective has been rarely used in its pure form. One notable exception is research in construction on how relational governance structures help manage transaction costs (Eccles, 1981; Winch, 1995). Oftentimes, elements from this perspective, such as the importance of reciprocity and trust in governing network relations, have been used to explain why stable network ties make future collaboration more likely (Sorenson & Waguespack, 2006; Larson & Wikström, 2007; Schwab & Miner, 2008). More generally, the governance view potentially helps understand why certain governance forms are used to manage exchanges and collaborations. In addition, as I detail below, it can be used to explain why in some network contexts multiple governance forms are used in combination. Yet its rather abstract and static conception of 'governance' also limits its analytical utility.

The third perspective focuses on networks as organizational systems. This one specifically looks at properties of networks as coordinated sets of inter-organizational relationships (see also Sydow & Windeler, 1998). It focuses on 'network organizations' (Borgatti & Foster, 2003) with their specific governance structures and membership rules (Provan & Kenis, 2008), rather than boundaryless networks. This perspective also allows to examine the institutional embeddedness of networks in particular regional or industry contexts (Sydow & Staber, 2002). It further looks at the ability of networks to sustain structural properties while having adaptive qualities (Kilduff et al., 2006). However, this adaptive quality is not simply an emerging property, but also an outcome of collective processes and coordinated efforts in which network participants engage (Manning, 2019). This is also why this network perspective emphasizes individual and collective agency and 'relational practices' in terms of regularized patterns of network interactions (Ness, 2009; Manning, 2010).

Applications of this network perspective in the context of project organizing are still pretty rare. However, many prior studies of PNOs (Manning, 2010, 2017; Starkey et al., 2000; Windeler & Sydow, 2001) are linked to this perspective, because they take coordination practices and reproduction dynamics within PNOs seriously (Manning, 2010; Windeler & Sydow, 2001). However, like the other network views, this one has limitations. For example, unlike the network governance view, the organizational system perspective tends to treat network organizations at least in part like any form of organization, while neglecting network properties. Also, unlike the relational structure view, the organizational system perspective often underspecifies the relational structures emerging within networks and their impact on project organizing. I therefore regard all three network perspectives as limited, yet valuable and complementary, and thus potentially useful in examining how PNOs work, as I will detail next.

13.4   HOW PROJECT NETWORK ORGANIZATIONS WORK

Next, I examine the three major properties of PNOs – strategic coordination, core project teams and flexible partner teams – from all three network perspectives, thereby illustrating strengths and limitations of each perspective. Table 13.1 provides a comparative summary.

13.4.1   Strategic Coordination

In the networks-as-relational-structures perspective, strategic agency and coordination are thought of as entrepreneurial action of network participants in response to their immediate structural position. For example, Burt (1992) conceptualized how actors can take advantage of structural holes, i.e. of being connected to actors who are not connected to each other. Similarly, Obstfeld (2005) argued that in particular contexts, such as innovation, actors may be important in bringing unconnected others together. These notions of strategic agency are instrumental in understanding relational micro-dynamics within networks. For example, in the context of PNOs, project entrepreneurs typically engage in 'nexus work' (Lingo & O'Mahony, 2010), which combines practices of exploiting and bridging structural holes. Project entrepreneurs thereby typically take central network positions, in being connected – both directly and indirectly – to more network partners than others. This perspective, however, also draws attention to the fact that for example structural holes may exist in different areas of the same network thus giving opportunities to different actors to exploit them. This may affect network and project dynamics. Thus, in this network view, no single network participant has full control over the formation and reproduction of the entire network (or the initiation of projects within a network context).

By comparison, the networks-as-governance-form view focuses on more specific coordination mechanisms project entrepreneurs may employ in PNOs. Studies in film and TV production, for example, show the importance of 'swift trust' (Meyerson et al. 1996) and reciprocity in facilitating the recruitment of project partners (see e.g. Manning & Sydow, 2011). Strategically, trust and reciprocity can be enacted by project entrepreneurs as 'relational resources' to facilitate projects. Another important feature of networks as governance forms is interdependencies between legally independent partners (Powell, 1990). Effective strategic

Table 13.1   Major properties of PNOs from different network perspectives

Dimension	Networks as relational structure	Networks as governance form	Networks as organizational system
Strategic coordination	Focuses on relational micro-dynamics of strategic coordination, such as exploiting structural holes and uniting unconnected network partners.	Effective network coordination relies on accumulation of trust and reciprocity as relational resources, and on effective management of interdependencies.	Strategic coordination combines different relational practices (e.g. making contacts, pooling partners, maintaining core partnerships) and functions: partner selection, resource allocation, evaluation and regulation.
	View also helps examine existence of multiple distributed structural holes and entrepreneurial opportunities for different network participants driving network and project dynamics.	Strategic coordinators may choose hierarchical sub-structures to better coordinate managerial resources (e.g. creative producers in film).	Strategic coordinators rely on various institutional and organizational resources to perform their roles.
Core project teams	Core teams are represented by strong ties and cliques of actors based on repeat project collaboration. Yet strong ties do not necessarily predict performance.	Network view helps examine choices of governance of core teams in different network contexts, depending on various project and collaboration properties.	Core project teams are composed based on certain principles and team-building practices that may be specific to particular field contexts.
	Strong ties may independently emerge between different network partners (sub-team structures) which may be relevant in project partner selection.	Core project teams typically feature a high degree of interdependence. Yet, in some PNOs hierarchical and network forms of governance may co-exist in managing core project teams.	Core teams may become associated with particular project types over time, whereby 'connecting practices' help connect projects and teams to allow for exploitation economies.
Flexible partner pools	Flexible pools are composed of rather weak ties that are centrally bundled by project entrepreneurs; they allow access to a variety of resources.	Partner pools represent the flexibility property of network governance. This view thus emphasizes the functionality of pools within networks.	Partner pools emerge as project entrepreneurs strategically group network contacts according to the critical criteria of team formation.
	Concept of 'network pool' does not directly exist in this view, but prior work on the relational dynamics in labour pools shows analytical potential.	Network pools are truly 'network' – based when reciprocity and trust play a major role in building and managing them.	Pool positions are affected by institutionalized status positions as collaborative practices.

coordination thus requires the ability of project entrepreneurs to identify and manage critical interdependencies with other network partners. Finally, this network view prompts us to differentiate between 'network' relationships and other – market-based or hierarchical – relationships project entrepreneurs build over time. For example, creating project-based firms as hierarchical sub-structures within PNOs may be deliberate choices of project entrepreneurs to ease coordination with certain partners. In film, producers often employ executive and creative producers to ease coordination across projects and to lower chances of opportunistic behaviour.

Finally, the networks-as-organizational-systems perspective helps examine various practices and resources project entrepreneurs employ to build and maintain PNOs over time. For example, Manning (2010) shows how a project entrepreneur in European research combines practices of 'making and renewing project-based contacts', 'pooling potential project partners' and 'maintaining core project partnerships' to build a PNO that can facilitate repeat project initiation over time. This perspective also emphasizes institutional drivers of power and legitimacy in strategic coordination, such as field status and organizational roles, rather than (just) network centrality (Manning, 2010). Finally, this perspective takes 'network membership' more seriously, as project entrepreneurs need to decide over time how to allocate 'membership status' to different partners (see below). More generally, this network perspective helps focus on issues of partner selection, resource allocation, regulation of conflicts of interest and evaluation of network performance (see e.g. Sydow & Windeler, 1998).

13.4.2 Core Project Teams

From the perspective of networks as relational structures, core project teams are mostly associated with strong ties and cliques that get reproduced over time. Strong ties as opposed to weak ties are often associated with mutual trust, familiarity and relational experience (see also Granovetter, 1973, 1974; Gulati, 1995; Uzzi, 1997). However, network studies also show that the repeated mobilization of strong ties may hamper innovation and performance (Schwab & Miner, 2008; Sorenson & Waguespack, 2006). This network perspective therefore does not automatically assume that having core teams benefits particular projects. Also, according to this network perspective, strong ties may exist in different parts of the same network. For example, in film PNOs, strong ties may independently emerge between producers and particular directors, as well as between directors, camera operators and cutters (see e.g. Manning, 2005). The potential distribution of stable tie structures across the network is an important insight, as it impacts project coordination and team formation.

The networks-as-governance-form view invites us to examine the governance of core project teams in greater detail. In this perspective, core project teams can be characterized by a strong level of interdependence between partners. Project entrepreneurs, however, have various options for how they build and manage core project teams. For example, in classical music, dance and theatre, creative teams (dance group, orchestra, etc.) are typically directly employed, thus managed 'hierarchically' (Glynn, 2000; Haunschild, 2003; Voss et al., 2000), reflecting the repetitive nature of performances and the specific investments core teams need to make (i.e. rehearsals). By comparison, core project teams in film typically collaborate more infrequently, while still being in need for the right 'creative chemistry', thus favouring relational contracts, based on a combination of trust, reciprocity and interdependence, rather than price-based coordination. That said, in some contexts, such as research, hierarchical forms of coordination, e.g. co-located research teams that repeatedly collaborate, may co-exist with network forms, e.g. international research teams (Manning, 2010). This network perspective thus helps better understand different ways of governing core project teams in different PNOs.

Finally, the networks-as-organizational-systems perspective helps better understand how core project teams are actually built and maintained in practice, and which norms and resources are used in the process. For example, it helps examine how project partners become part of core project teams. In TV production, certain script writers may become core team members for projects for certain TV channels because of their proven ability to write for the right audience (Manning & Sydow, 2011). Core teams often meet prior to the launch of projects to discuss a wider range of ideas. This perspective also helps look more dynamically at how core project teams become associated with particular types of projects and thereby develop what Manning and Sydow (2011) call 'collaborative paths'. In establishing these paths, project entrepreneurs employ 'connecting practices' that help generate linkages between different projects and help core project teams develop and exploit collaborative capabilities over time.

13.4.3 Flexible Partner Pools

From the perspective of networks as relational structures, 'partner pools' can be thought of as populations of potential network partners that are all connected to project entrepreneurs via weak project-based ties (see e.g. Manning, 2005). According to early studies by Granovetter (1973, 1974), weak ties are typically characterized by infrequent or sporadic interactions, yet they provide the opportunity to access new information and mobilize resources outside established relationships and cliques. However, this network perspective is limited in its conception of 'pools'. In fact, in his seminal work on hiring and job searches, Granovetter (1974) attempted to replace the established notion of 'labor market pools' with a relational network view in arguing that recruitment is a relational process building on combinations of strong and weak ties. However, I see potential in connecting 'pool' and 'relational' perspectives to more systematically understand the micro-dynamics underlying the use of 'network pools'.

In the networks-as-governance-form perspective, partner pools can be seen as a manifestation of the flexibility that network governance is known for. Early concepts such as 'adhocracy' (Mintzberg & McHugh, 1985), 'dynamic network' (Miles & Snow, 1986) and the 'flexible firm' (Atkinson, 1984) embody this idea. For example, Atkinson (1984) distinguishes between 'functional flexibility' provided by the 'core' (i.e. 'core project teams') and 'numerical flexibility' provided by the periphery (i.e. 'flexible partner pools'). In other words, the governance view emphasizes the flexibility potential coming from the maintenance of pools of substitute partners. In addition, this perspective helps qualify which governance mechanisms apply when using partner pools. In the more narrow sense, partner pools can only be qualified as network pools if relational trust and reciprocity play an important role in mobilizing partners. Studies suggest that this is often the case, for example when producers urgently recruit substitute script writers (Manning & Sydow, 2011). By comparison, core partner teams are much more based on co-specialization and interdependence. However, one could equally think of 'pools' of rather anonymous potential partners with no prior joint project experience. In such cases, market mechanisms may play a more central role in recruiting such partners, at least initially.

Finally, the networks-as-organizational-systems perspective helps better understand how partner pools are built and maintained in practice. For example, Manning (2010) examines how an entrepreneurial European researcher shifted over time from building a network of potential collaborators serendipitously to taking a more strategic approach, as he started coordinating projects, by grouping contacts such that all major European regions were represented in order to ease recruitment for funding purposes. In other words, following funding criteria and needs for certain expertise resulted in building 'regional pools' of potential project partners who can also be substituted in case someone becomes unavailable. This network perspective also helps examine the 'pool status' of particular partners. For example, in film production networks, certain directors and script writers might be assigned a 'preferred selection' status within their professional pools, thus also qualifying for joining core teams (Blair, 2001). Others, by comparison, may adopt the reputation of being an effective 'joker' substitute. For example, some script writers develop a particular skill as 'script doctors' in being able to improve existing scripts on demand (see study by Manning & Sydow, 2011). It can thus be critical to have such 'script doctors' in the pool of script writers to plan for project contingencies.

13.5   CONCLUSION

This chapter has applied three network perspectives – networks as relational structures, networks as governance forms and networks as organizational systems – to highlight different ways in which network contexts, specifically PNOs, establish and affect project collaboration. The study demonstrates the value and utility of each network perspective and encourages future studies to make better use of multiple perspectives in complementary ways.

REFERENCES

Anand, N. & Watson, M. R. (2004). Tournament rituals in the evolution of fields: The case of the Grammy Awards. *Academy of Management Journal*, 47(1), 59–80.
Atkinson, J. (1984). Manpower strategies for flexible organizations. *Personnel Management*, 16(8), 28–31.
Baker, W. E. (1990). Market networks and corporate behavior. *American Journal of Sociology*, 96(3), 589–625.
Bakker, R. M. (2010). Taking stock of temporary organizational forms: A systematic review and research agenda. *International Journal of Management Reviews*, 12(4), 466–486.
Blair, H. (2001). 'You're only as good as your last job': The labour process and labour market in the British film industry. *Work, Employment and Society*, 15(1), 149–169.
Borgatti, S. & Foster, P. (2003). The network paradigm in organizational research: A review and typology. *Journal of Management*, 29(6), 991–1013.
Burt, R. S. (1992). *Structural holes: The social structure of competition*. Harvard University Press.
Cattani, G., Ferriani, S., Frederiksen, L. & Taeube, F. (2011). Project-based organizing and strategic management: A long-term research agenda on temporary organizational forms. In G. Cattani, S. Ferriani, L. Frederiksen & F. Taeube (Eds), *Project-based organizing and strategic management* (pp. xv–xxxix). Emerald Group Publishing.
Cook, K. S. & Whitmeyer, J. M. (1992). Two approaches to social structure: Exchange theory and network analysis. *Annual Review of Sociology*, 18, 109–127.
DeFillippi, R. J. & Arthur, M. B. (1998). Paradox in project-based enterprise: The case of film-making. *California Management Review*, 40(2), 1–15.
Ebers, M. & Maurer, I. (2016). To continue or not to continue? Drivers of recurrent partnering temporary organizations. *Organization Studies*, 37(12), 1861–1895.
Eccles, R. G. (1981). The quasi-firm in the construction industry. *Journal of Economic Behavior and Organization*, 2(4), 335–357.

Emirbayer, M. (1997). Manifesto for a relational sociology. *American Journal of Sociology*, 103(2), 281–317.

Engwall, M. (2003). No project is an island: Linking projects to history and context. *Research Policy*, 32(5), 789–808.

Ferriani, S., Cattani, G. & Baden-Fuller, G. (2009). The relational antecedents of project-entrepreneurship: Network centrality, team composition and project performance. *Research Policy*, 38(10), 1545–1558.

Foster, P., Manning, S. & Terkla, D. (2015). The rise of Hollywood East: Regional film offices as intermediaries in film and television production clusters. *Regional Studies*, 49(3), 433–450.

Gann, D. M. & Salter, A. J. (2000). Innovation in project-based, service-enhanced firms: The construction of complex products and systems. *Research Policy*, 29(7–8), 955–972.

Geyer, A. & Davies, A. (2000). Managing project-system interfaces: Case studies of railway projects in restructured UK and German markets. *Research Policy*, 29(7–8), 991–1013.

Glynn, M. A. (2000). When cymbals become symbols: Conflict over organizational identity within a symphony orchestra. *Organization Science*, 11(3), 285–298.

Grabher, G. (2002). The project ecology of advertising: Tasks, talents and teams. *Regional Studies*, 36(3), 245–262.

Grabher, G. (2004). Temporary architectures of learning: Knowledge governance of project ecologies. *Organization Studies*, 25(9), 1491–1514.

Granovetter, M. S. (1973). The strength of weak ties. *American Journal of Sociology*, 78(6), 1360–1380.

Granovetter, M. S. (1974). *Getting a job: A study of contacts and careers*. Harvard University Press.

Gulati, R. (1995). Does familiarity breed trust? The implications of repeated ties for contractual choice in alliances. *Academy of Management Journal*, 38(1), 85–112.

Haunschild, A. (2003). Managing employment relationships in flexible labour markets: The case of German repertory theatres. *Human Relations*, 56(8), 899–929.

Jones, C., Hesterley, W. S. & Borgatti, S. P. (1997). A general theory of network governance: Exchange conditions and social mechanisms. *Academy of Management Review*, 22(4), 911–945.

Kilduff, M., Tsai, W. & Hanke, R. (2006). A paradigm too far? A dynamic stability reconsideration of the social network research program. *Academy of Management Review*, 31(4), 1031–1048.

Larson, M. & Wikström, E. (2007). Relational interaction processes in project networks: The consent and negotiation perspectives. *Scandinavian Journal of Management*, 23(3), 327–352.

Lingo, E. L. & O'Mahony, S. (2010). Nexus work: Brokerage on creative projects. *Administrative Science Quarterly*, 55(1), 47–81.

Lundin, R. A. & Söderholm, A. (1995). A theory of the temporary organization. *Scandinavian Journal of Management*, 11(4), 437–455.

Manning, S. (2005). Managing project networks as dynamic organizational forms: Learning from the TV movie industry. *International Journal of Project Management*, 23(5), 410–414.

Manning, S. (2008). Embedding projects in multiple contexts: A structuration perspective. *International Journal of Project Management*, 26(1), 30–37.

Manning, S. (2010). The strategic formation of project networks: A relational practice perspective. *Human Relations*, 63(4), 551–573.

Manning, S. (2017). The rise of project network organizations: Building core teams and flexible partner pools for interorganizational projects. *Research Policy*, 46(8), 1399–1415.

Manning, S. (2019). Building adaptive capacity in project network organizations: Project contexts, network ties and relational practices. In J. Sydow & H. Berends (Eds), *Managing inter-organizational collaborations: Process views* (pp. 39–67). Emerald Publishing.

Manning, S. & Sydow, J. (2011). Projects, paths, and practices: Sustaining and leveraging project-based relationships. *Industrial and Corporate Change*, 20(5), 1369–1402.

Manning, S. & von Hagen, O. (2010). Linking local experiments to global standards: How project networks promote global institution-building. *Scandinavian Journal of Management*, 26(4), 398–416.

Meyerson, D., Weick, K. E. & Kramer, R. M. (1996). Swift trust and temporary groups. In R. M. Kramer & T. R. Tyler (Eds), *Trust in organizations: Frontiers of theory and research* (pp. 166–195). Sage Publications.

Miles, R. E. & Snow, C. C. (1986). Organizations: New concepts for new forms. *California Management Review*, 18(3), 62–73.

Mintzberg, H. & McHugh, A. (1985). Strategy formation in an adhocracy. *Administrative Science Quarterly*, 30(2), 160–197.

Mitchell, J. C. (1969). The concept and use of social networks in urban situations. In J. C. Mitchell (Ed.), *Social networks in urban situations: Analyses of personal relationships in central African towns* (pp. 1–50). University of Manchester Press.

Ness, H. (2009). Governance, negotiations, and alliance dynamics: Explaining the evolution of relational practice. *Journal of Management Studies*, 46(3), 451–480.

Obstfeld, D. (2005). Social networks, the tertius iungens orientation, and involvement in innovation. *Administrative Science Quarterly*, 50(1), 100–130.

Obstfeld, D. (2012). Creative projects: A less routine approach toward getting new things done. *Organization Science*, 23(6), 1571–1592.

Powell, W. W. (1990). Neither market nor hierarchy: Network forms of organization. *Research in Organizational Behavior*, 12, 295–336.

Provan, K. G. & Kenis, P. (2008). Modes of network governance: Structure, management, and effectiveness. *Journal of Public Administration Research and Theory*, 18(2), 229–252.

Richardson, G. B. (1972). The organisation of industry. *The Economic Journal*, 82(327), 883–896.

Schwab, A. & Miner, A. (2008). Learning in hybrid-project systems: The effects of project performance on repeated collaboration. *Academy of Management Journal*, 51(6), 1117–1149.

Sergeeva, N. & Winch, G. M. (2020). Narrative interactions: How project-based firms respond to government narratives of innovation. *International Journal of Project Management*, 38(6), 379–387.

Simmel, G. (1992 [1908]). *Soziologie. Untersuchungen über die Formen der Vergesellschaftung.* Suhrkamp Verlag.

Smith-Doerr, L. & Powell, W. W. (2005). Networks and economic life. In N. J. Smelser and R. Swedberg (Eds), *The handbook of economic sociology* (pp. 379–402). Russell Sage Foundation and Princeton University Press.

Soda, G., Usai, A. & Zaheer, A. (2004). Network memory: The influence of past and current networks on performance. *Academy of Management Journal*, 47(6), 893–906.

Söderlund, J. (2008). Competence dynamics and learning processes in project-based firms: Shifting, adapting and leveraging. *International Journal of Innovation Management*, 12(1), 41–67.

Sorenson, O. & Waguespack, D. M. (2006). Social structure and exchange: Self-confirming dynamics in Hollywood. *Administrative Science Quarterly*, 51(4), 560–589.

Stadtler, L. & Probst, G. (2012). How broker organizations can facilitate public–private partnerships for development. *European Management Journal*, 30(1), 32–46.

Starkey, K., Barnatt, C. & Tempest, S. (2000). Beyond networks and hierarchies: Latent organizations in the UK television industry. *Organization Science*, 11(3), 299–305.

Stjerne, I. S. & Svejenova, S. V. (2016). Connecting temporary and permanent organizing: Tensions and boundary work in sequential film projects. *Organization Studies*, 37(12), 1771–1792.

Sydow, J. & Staber, U. (2002). The institutional embeddedness of project networks: The case of content production in German television. *Regional Studies*, 36(3), 215–227.

Sydow, J. & Windeler, A. (1998). Organizing and evaluating interfirm networks: A structurationist perspective on network process and effectiveness. *Organization Science*, 9(3), 265–284.

Uzzi, B. (1997). Social structure and competition in interfirm networks: The paradox of embeddedness. *Administrative Science Quarterly*, 42(1), 35–67.

Uzzi, B. & Spiro, J. (2005). Collaboration and creativity: The small world problem. *American Journal of Sociology*, 111(2), 447–504.

Voss, G. B., Cable, D. M. & Voss, Z. G. (2000). Linking organizational values to relationships with external constituents: A study of nonprofit professional theatres. *Organization Science*, 11(3), 330–347.

Wasserman, S. & Faust, K. (1994). *Social network analysis: Methods and applications.* Cambridge University Press.

Wellman, B. (1988). Structural analysis: From method and metaphor to theory and substance. In B. Wellman & S. D. Berkowitz (Eds), *Social structures: A network approach* (pp. 19–61). Cambridge University Press.

White, H. C., Boorman, S. A. & Breiger, R. (1976). Social structure from multiple networks, I: Blockmodels of roles and positions. *American Journal of Sociology*, 81(4), 730–780.

Williamson, O. E. (1985). *The economic institutions of capitalism: Firms, markets, relational contracting*. Free Press.

Winch, G. M. (1995). *Project management in construction: Towards a transaction cost approach*. Le Groupe Bagnolet Working Paper No. 1. Paris. www.chantier.net/europe.html.

Windeler, A. & Sydow, J. (2001). Project networks and changing industry practices: Collaborative content production in the German television industry. *Organization Studies*, 22(6), 1035–1060.

Zaheer, A. & Soda, G. (2009). Network evolution: The origins of structural holes. *Administrative Science Quarterly*, 54(1), 1–31.

Zaheer, A., Gözübüyük, R. & Milanov, H. (2010). It's the connections: The network perspective in interorganizational research. *Academy of Management Perspectives*, 24(1), 62–77.

14. Multi-level project organizing: a complex adaptive systems perspective
Pierre A. Daniel and Eric Daniel

14.1 FOUNDATIONS OF COMPLEX ADAPTIVE SYSTEM THEORY

Research on complexity in projects reveals the need to understand better complex non-deterministic phenomena (Padalkar & Gopinath, 2016b), and thus to contribute to a new paradigm of emergence as an alternative model to the paradigm of regulation dominant in project management (Daniel & Daniel, 2018). Past research has identified three types of complex problems – of simplicity, of disorganized complexity and of organized complexity (Weaver, 1948) – and three types of complexity – Newtonian, stochastic and emergent (McKelvey, 2004). This plurality is confirmed by the multiple systems theories used in organizational sciences to deal with complex phenomena, from deterministic models such as those of operations research (Beer, 1959; Churchman et al., 1957) and cybernetics (Wiener, 1950), to non-deterministic models such as those of second-order cybernetics (Maturana & Varela, 1992; Von Foerster, 1974) and Complex Adaptive Systems (CAS) (Gell-Mann, 1994; Holland, 1992a). CAS theory is the source of the emergence paradigm taking a growing place in organizational science over the past two decades. It brings both an interactionist perspective which extends static models of complexity such as design structure matrix (Browning, 2001) and an evolutionary perspective which extends dynamic models of the systems paradigm (Cleland & King, 1968; Forrester, 1961), such as system dynamics (SD) (Sterman, 2001; see Chapters 3 and 7, respectively). In project studies, CAS highlights a subjective temporality of project organizing as becoming by opposition to an objective temporality of project organizing as determinate (Winch & Sergeeva, 2022). CAS constitutes an original and fruitful scientific approach for project studies by its ability to redefine both project organizing dynamics and project management principles.

14.2 NON-LINEARITY

Complexity theory presents two distinct perspectives to address complex structures and dynamics: linear thinking, which is effective when systems adjust around equilibria (Manson, 2001), and non-linear thinking, which is more effective when systems are not in equilibrium (Roundy et al., 2018) and generate emergence dynamics (Meyer et al., 2005). While the theories of deterministic systems – such as cybernetics or chaos theory – are based on sets of equations that predict the evolution of the system from time t0 to t1, CAS attempts to represent unpredictable behaviours within non-deterministic systems (Anderson, 1999; Holland, 1992b). CAS theory analyses and interprets organizational behaviours and dynamics from a perspective equivalent to that applied in the natural sciences (Richardson, 2011). Used in biology, ecology and chemistry, it indicates that systems that are not in equilibrium must be studied according to specific dynamic principles (Eisenhardt & Piezunka, 2011). The application of a CAS approach in project studies would provide a new understanding of the complex non-deterministic phenomena that exist in project organizations (Padalkar & Gopinath, 2016a, 2016b). Particularly in the evolution of the ecosystems research domain, early research currents did not highlight the non-linearities, the radical changes and the discontinuities that the CAS theory made it possible to describe (Phillips & Ritala, 2019).

14.2.1 Evolution

The dynamics of change within organizations are at the centre of the questions highlighted by CAS (Girod & Whittington, 2015) which legitimizes CAS for project studies because projects are temporary organizations and sources of change and transformation for organizations (Turner & Müller, 2003). CAS reminds us that the notion of equilibrium or the search for stability is not the norm in our social systems. If an order is possible, it is subject to constant changes and evolutions (Meyer et al., 2005). The dominant model of project management (Cleland & King, 1988) is based on the principle of negative feedbacks which help to maintain an organizational system in its initial or planned equilibrium (Shewhart, 1931). SD theory has shown that projects could be subject to positive feedbacks, sources of unpredictable non-linearities for project managers (Sterman, 1992). SD then suggests that managers adapt to non-linearities with a learning approach based on SD modelling techniques. In a different way, the CAS approach seeks to describe the evolutionary dynamics of non-linearities that lead to the emergence of a new order within activities (Lichtenstein et al., 2007). The metaphorical proximity between CAS and programmes, portfolios or megaprojects is very strong as projects aim to transform organizations by provoking changes in order to achieve new strategic benefits (Breese, 2012; Serra & Kunc, 2015). Recent work on 'project society' demonstrates the role played by projects in economic and social transformations (Geraldi & Söderlund, 2018; Lundin et al., 2015).

14.2.2 Multi-Level Perspective

CAS is above all about systems open to their environment. It studies the multiple interactions that exist between the different active elements within systems (agents) and the different levels that make up these systems. Behaviours at the macro-level emerge from the micro-level and in turn influence interactions at the micro-level (Levin, 2002; Lissack & Letiche, 2002). The notion of emergence at the heart of CAS highlights the existence of relationships between lower levels and aggregate levels (Meyer et al., 2005). This micro/macro-relationship is central in project studies because it clearly appears in organizational relationships between projects (at the micro-level) and programmes, portfolios and megaprojects (at the macro-level) which represent aggregations of projects. We find this multi-level perspective (MLP) in the 'assembly project', 'system project' and 'array project' classification (Shenhar, 2001). For CAS, it is through the interactions that take place at different levels that complex systems are able to adapt to changes in the environment (Roundy et al., 2018). These mechanisms of adaptation to change are the source of the concept of emergence (Lichtenstein, 2011). The MLP is not necessarily limited to the relationship between micro- and macro-levels, but can reveal a relationship between micro-, meso- and macro-levels (Dopfer et al., 2004).

14.2.3   Agent-Based Models

Non-linearity, evolution and MLP are fundamentally linked to the nature of CAS as an agent-based theory. It focuses on the interactions between multiple independent agents who pursue a common goal in a complex environment (Holland, 1995). CAS studies how interactions between agents in the system and interactions with the environment allow the system to adapt (Webb et al., 2006). It considers that these agents are autonomous (Holland, 1992b), follow their own schemata (Anderson, 1999) and have the capacities to learn and exchange information and resources to react to changes in the environment (Hedlund, 1994; Uhl-Bien & Arena, 2017). The notion of agent refers to 'entities of action' (Nan, 2011) which, depending on the level of analysis adopted, can be aggregated and form meta-agents at a higher level (Simon, 1996). Thus, an agent can be an individual, team, division or organization (Choi et al., 2001). In the field of project studies, agents can be defined as decision-making stakeholders (micro-level) interacting within a megaproject (macro-level) (Daniel & Daniel, 2019), or as agile projects (micro-level) interacting within a portfolio of projects (macro-level) (Kaufmann et al., 2020; Sweetman & Conboy, 2018).

14.3   CAS IN PROJECT ORGANIZING THEORY

14.3.1   CAS in Organization Science

Many disciplinary fields have adopted a CAS perspective: organizations (Anderson, 1999), operations and supply chain management (Choi et al., 2001), change (Girod & Whittington, 2015; Meyer et al., 2005), entrepreneurship (Roundy et al., 2018) and ecosystems (Phillips & Ritala, 2019). These applications highlight three dynamic mechanisms that describe the way in which organizations operate, produce changes and ultimately evolve: the principle of 'self-organization', the principle of 'coevolution' and the principle of 'recombination'.

The concept of emergence is the source of the greatest theoretical breakthroughs proposed by CAS. It proposes a paradigm opposed to that of regulation which is based on linear rationality and principles of equilibrium based on the control of drifts (Daniel & Daniel, 2018). Emergence is an organizational dynamic that relies on non-linear interactions, amplified by both positive and negative feedback loops that produce unpredictable systemic effects (Kok et al., 2021). Properties at one level of the organization cannot be predicted at lower levels (Emmeche et al., 1997). Thus, interactions between agents produce continuous modifications within a system (project, portfolio, organization), which allow the system to adapt to changes and new conditions (Messier & Puettmann, 2011). These organizational adaptations take place through recombinations within systems, which has the consequence of rendering any attempt at prediction unnecessary.

14.3.2   CAS in Project Organizing Theory

Initial links with CAS were established in multi-project environments: programmes and project portfolios which behave like CAS characterized by (1) inter-relationships, (2) adaptability, (3) self-organization, (4) emergence, (5) feedback and (6) non-linearity (Aritua et al., 2009). Sweetman and Conboy (2018) show that projects can be considered as agents whose properties at the micro-level – self-organizing, common purpose, autonomy, adaptive, requisite variety, exchange of resources – generate emerging properties at the macro-level of the project portfolio – agility, performance, culture, strategy. Emerging capacities are revealed at the level of agile teams under three principles: coevolutionary change, self-organizing and exploitation/exploration synchronization (Vidgen & Wang, 2009). Recent work shows that there is a beneficial relationship between agile projects (at the micro-level) and the strategic initiatives that emerge within the project portfolio (at the macro-level), thus contributing to the organization's strategy (Kaufmann et al., 2020).

The second area of application is megaprojects. Research on Hinkley Point C has shown that organizational dynamics within megaprojects respond to key principles of CAS (Daniel & Daniel, 2019) by focusing on the interactions between the United Kingdom government and the leaders of EDF during the initial phases of the project. This study confirms the complex adaptive dynamic during the development of the megaproject: the perception of the success of the megaprojects by the stakeholders is multidimensional (agent with schemata); the sources of control are multiple and shared by the stakeholders (self-organization); the behaviours of stakeholders coevolve by adapting to observable changes at the output level (coevolution); and the structure of the megaproject is transformed, as are the relations between stakeholders (systems recombination).

14.4 PERSPECTIVES FOR MULTI-LEVEL PROJECT ORGANIZING RESEARCH

14.4.1 A Multi-Level Project Organizing Framework

CAS theory applied to project studies helps to redefine the organizational object of the project organization. It broadens project organizing theory by focusing attention on three combined characteristics: structural levels, performance levels and organizational levels.

First, CAS extends the definition of projects as temporary organizations in which projects are the evolving organizational constituents of a larger systemic structure (programme, portfolio, megaproject) open to its environment. Such a multi-project approach cannot be the simple theoretical and practical extension of a single project approach (Aritua et al., 2009). Any programme, portfolio or megaproject yields outcomes in the context of its integration into larger systems of systems, defined as large technical systems (Hughes, 1983) or socio-technical regimes (Geels, 2004). The application of CAS theory to project organizing research reveals three levels of analysis: projects (micro-level), portfolios of projects or programmes (meso level) and systems of systems (macro-level). It highlights a three-level perspective on project management: technical, strategic and institutional (Morris & Geraldi, 2011). This perspective establishes fruitful research bridges between project studies and sustainability transition studies by understanding the links between several levels of interactions and several levels of impact, starting from experimental initiatives at the micro-level and producing impacts on public policy at the macro-level (Edmondson et al., 2019; Geels, 2002; Kern et al., 2019; Markard et al., 2012).

Second, CAS highlights the need to make the link between projects and their strategic intent – their outcomes – and that project studies contributes to reflection on strategic emergence as a result of the management of programmes and portfolios (Kaufmann et al., 2020).

Such a foundation could contribute to the many studies that have already demonstrated the link between projects and strategy, considering projects as sources of medium- and long-term benefits (Artto et al., 2008; Chih & Zwikael, 2015; Eweje et al., 2012; Huemann & Silvius, 2017; Zwikael et al., 2018).

Third, CAS emphasizes the issue of agility in projects and highlights adaptation capacities within portfolios, programmes and megaprojects as central. It presents an alternative to the top-down planning paradigm of the project management cycle, built on the principles of predictability and optimization (Deming, 1986; Shewhart, 1931). It proposes to rethink the classical principles of single project management based on cybernetic regulation, in order to understand better the dynamic principles of organizational adaptation, based on collaborative learning mechanisms within project networks. CAS supposes establishing a new adaptive management paradigm at multiple levels of the project organization. This approach is confirmed in the field of project governance, which highlights that project governance processes should be studied at multiple organizational levels: project level, project management office level and organizational level (Biesenthal & Wilden, 2014).

Figure 14.1 presents a multi-level project organizing research framework based on the CAS approach. The framework is based on the three foundations presented above and is inspired by the MLP (Geels, 2002) adopted in the field of sustainability transitions research. The parallelism that is proposed makes it possible to understand better the connections that could be established between the macro-research perspective within project studies (Geraldi & Söderlund, 2018; Geraldi et al., 2020) and the growing field of sustainability transitions. The new project organizing foundations presented above call into question two important research perspectives within project studies: governance and frameworks of performance.

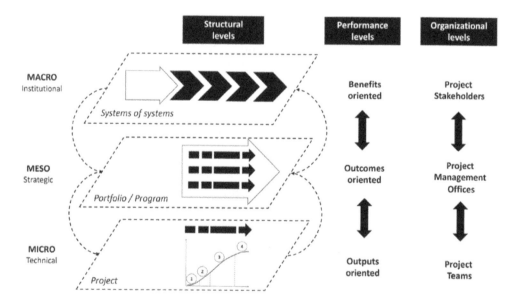

Figure 14.1   Multi-level project organizing research framework based on CAS theory

14.4.2 Revisiting Governance Theory in Project Studies

For a decade, the field of project governance has called for the development of a new theory of governance for large multi-firm projects. Theoretical renovation should take into account the fact that megaprojects are complex network structures, which function as systems open to their environment and require self-regulation mechanisms different from the classic markets and hierarchies approach (Ruuska et al., 2011). The planning function (determination of vision, goals and actions) and the control function (regulation) call for the application of a 'governance structure' based on shared planning and control, and a 'governance dynamic' based on adaptive planning and control (Daniel & Daniel, 2019). Recent work on governance in mega-event projects proposes to adopt a framework based on Evolutionary Governance Theory as better able to take into account a socio-economy that functions like CAS (Li et al., 2018). Thus, the foundations of complex project governance, challenged by non-linear and unpredictable dynamics, suppose adaptive capacities at all levels of the organization based on principles of multi-level governance systems (Duit & Galaz, 2008). Case studies from mega-event projects show that governance contexts, goals, configurations and techniques evolve during the life cycle of a megaproject (Li et al., 2018).

14.4.3 Revisiting Frameworks of Performance in Project Studies

Based on the CAS literature, theoretical work explains that projects focused on capacity development require a more eclectic managerial approach and performance analysis framework than those generally adopted by methodologies such as Result Based Management (McEvoy et al., 2016). They explain that the dominant paradigm in international development projects is the rational analysis model, built on overstatic evaluation and monitoring tools. The professional literature had already demonstrated the strength of the CAS approach in understanding the unpredictable and disorganized aspects that characterize the dynamics of capacity development within organizations and large systems (Land et al., 2009).

This orientation towards new management frameworks confirms the results coming from research on boundary objects. Boundary objects are devices that facilitate communication and improve common understanding between stakeholders (Ruuska & Teigland, 2009), acting in a logic of sensemaking, and playing the role of facilitator in the resolution of complex problems (Alderman et al., 2005; Koskinen & Mäkinen, 2009). Chang et al. (2013) show that the effective use of an Integrated Master Schedule helps to visualize complex realities such as interactions, interdependencies and emergencies in projects in order to improve communication and negotiation between stakeholders around shared goals. This work highlights the importance of developing new tools for modelling adaptive dynamics when it comes to managing multi-projects. Particular attention should be paid to the development of new decision models capable of helping the many stakeholders who constitute a control sub-system to better manage the emerging dynamics of projects which constitute a production sub-system within an uncertain and unstable environment (Daniel & Daniel, 2018). Theories on management under unforeseeable uncertainty promote iterative and dynamic project management practices based on 'selectionism' and 'trial-and-error learning' (Pich et al., 2002; Sommer & Loch, 2004), but we know still very little about the management frameworks capable of supporting the organizational learning processes related to these practices. Research on COVID vaccine development confirms the need to understand better selectionism strategies in the case of owner project portfolio management which highlight multiple levels of decision-making at the government level and the supplier level (Winch et al., 2021). The CAS perspective is able to renovate decision-making instruments and models in managerial situations of adaptation and evolution.

REFERENCES

Alderman, N., Ivory, C., McLoughlin, I. & Vaughan, R. (2005). Sense-making as a process within complex service-led projects. *International Journal of Project Management*, 23(5), 380–385.

Anderson, P. (1999). Complexity theory and organization science. *Organization Science*, 10(3), 216–232.

Aritua, B., Smith, N. J. & Bower, D. (2009). Construction client multi-projects: A complex adaptive systems perspective. *International Journal of Project Management*, 27(1), 72–79.

Artto, K., Kujala, J., Dietrich, P. & Martinsuo, M. (2008). What is project strategy? *International Journal of Project Management*, 26(1), 4–12.

Beer, S. (1959). *Cybernetics and management*. John Wiley and Sons.

Biesenthal, C. & Wilden, R. (2014). Multi-level project governance: Trends and opportunities. *International Journal of Project Management*, 32(8), 1291–1308.

Breese, R. (2012). Benefits realisation management: Panacea or false dawn? *International Journal of Project Management*, 30(3), 341–351.

Browning, T. R. (2001). Applying the design structure matrix to system decomposition and integration problems: A review and new directions. *IEEE Transactions on Engineering Management*, 48(3), 292–306.

Chang, A., Hatcher, C. & Kim, J. (2013). Temporal boundary objects in megaprojects: Mapping the system with the integrated master schedule. *International Journal of Project Management*, 31, 323–332.

Chih, Y.-Y. Y. & Zwikael, O. (2015). Project benefit management: A conceptual framework of target benefit formulation. *International Journal of Project Management*, 33(2), 352–362.

Choi, T. Y., Dooley, K. J. & Rungtusanatham, M. (2001). Supply networks and complex adaptive systems: Control versus emergence. *Journal of Operations Management*, 19(3), 351–366.

Churchman, C. W., Ackoff, R. L. & Arnoff, E. L. (1957). *Introduction to operations research*. John Wiley and Sons.

Cleland, D. I. & King, W. R. (1968). *System analysis and project management*. McGraw-Hill.

Cleland, D. I. & King, W. R. (1988). *Project management handbook*. Van Nostrand Reinhold.

Daniel, E. & Daniel, P. A. (2019). Megaprojects as complex adaptive systems: The Hinkley Point C case. *International Journal of Project Management*, 37(8), 1017–1033.

Daniel, P. A. & Daniel, C. (2018). Complexity, uncertainty and mental models: From a paradigm of regulation to a paradigm of emergence in project management. *International Journal of Project Management*, 36(1), 184–197.

Deming, W. E. (1986). *Out of the crisis*. MIT Press.

Dopfer, K., Foster, J. & Potts, J. (2004). Micro-meso-macro. *Journal of Evolutionary Economics*, 14(3), 263–279.

Duit, A. & Galaz, V. (2008). Governance and complexity: Emerging issues for governance theory. *Governance*, 21(3), 311–335.

Edmondson, D. L., Kern, F. & Rogge, K. S. (2019). The co-evolution of policy mixes and socio-technical systems: Towards a conceptual framework of policy mix feedback in sustainability transitions. *Research Policy*, 48(10), 103555.

Eisenhardt, K. M. & Piezunka, H. (2011). Complexity theory and corporate strategy. In S. Maguire & B. Mckelvey (Eds), *The Sage handbook of complexity and management* (pp. 506–523). Sage.

Emmeche, C., Køppe, S. & Stjernfelt, F. (1997). Explaining emergence: Towards an ontology of levels. *Journal for General Philosophy of Science*, 28(1), 83–117.

Eweje, J., Turner, R. & Müller, R. (2012). Maximizing strategic value from megaprojects: The influence of information-feed on decision-making by the project manager. *International Journal of Project Management*, 30(6), 639–651.

Forrester, J. (1961). *Industrial dynamics*. MIT Press.

Geels, F. W. (2002). Technological transitions as evolutionary reconfiguration processes: A multi-level perspective and a case-study. *Research Policy*, 31(8–9), 1257–1274.

Geels, F. W. (2004). From sectoral systems of innovation to socio-technical systems: Insights about dynamics and change from sociology and institutional theory. *Research Policy*, 33(6–7), 897–920.

Gell-Mann, M. (1994). Complex adaptive systems. In D. Cowan, D. Pines & D. Meltzer (Eds), *Complexity: Metaphors, models and reality* (pp. 17–45). Addison-Wesley.

Geraldi, J. & Söderlund, J. (2018). Project studies: What it is, where it is going. *International Journal of Project Management*, 36(1), 55–70.

Geraldi, J., Söderlund, J. & van Marrewijk, A. (2020). Advancing theory and debate in project studies. *Project Management Journal*, 5(4), 351–356.

Girod, S. J. G. & Whittington, R. (2015). Change escalation processes and complex adaptive systems: From incremental reconfigurations to discontinuous restructuring. *Organization Science*, 26(5), 1520–1535.

Hedlund, G. (1994). A model of knowledge management and the N-form corporation. *Strategic Management Journal*, 15(S2), 73–90.

Holland, J. H. (1992a). *Adaptation in natural and artificial systems: An introductory analysis with applications to biology, control and artificial intelligence*. MIT Press.

Holland, J. H. (1992b). Complex adaptive systems. *Daedalus*, 121(1), 17–30.

Holland, J. H. (1995). *Hidden order: How adaptation builds complexity*. Perseus Books.

Huemann, M. & Silvius, A. J. G. (2017). Projects to create the future: Managing projects meets sustainable development. *International Journal of Project Management*, 35(6), 1066–1070.

Hughes, T. P. (1983). *Networks of power: Electrification in western society, 1880–1930*. Johns Hopkins University Press.

Kaufmann, C., Kock, A. & Gemünden, H. G. (2020). Emerging strategy recognition in agile portfolios. *International Journal of Project Management*, 38(7), 429–440.

Kern, F., Rogge, K. S. & Howlett, M. (2019). Policy mixes for sustainability transitions: New approaches and insights through bridging innovation and policy studies. *Research Policy*, 48(10), 103832.

Kok, K. P. W., Loeber, A. M. C. & Grin, J. (2021). Politics of complexity: Conceptualizing agency, power and powering in the transitional dynamics of complex adaptive systems. *Research Policy*, 50(3), 104183.

Koskinen, K. U. & Mäkinen, S. (2009). Role of boundary objects in negotiations of project contracts. *International Journal of Project Management*, 27(1), 31–38.

Land, T., Hauck, V. & Baser, H. (2009). *Capacity development: Between planned interventions and emergent processes*. Policy Management Brief 22. European Centre for Development Policy Management.

Levin, S. A. (2002). Complex adaptive systems: Exploring the known, the unknown and the unknowable. *Bulletin of the American Mathematical Society*, 40, 3–19.

Li, Y., Lu, Y., Ma, L. & Kwak, Y. H. (2018). Evolutionary governance for mega-event projects (MEPs): A case study of the world expo 2010 in China. *Project Management Journal*, 49(1), 57–78.

Lichtenstein, B. B. (2011). Complexity science contributions to the field of entrepreneurship. In P. Allen, S. Maguire & B. Mckelvey (Eds), *The Sage handbook of complexity and management* (pp. 471–493). Sage.

Lichtenstein, B. B., Carter, N. M., Dooley, K. J. & Gartner, W. B. (2007). Complexity dynamics of nascent entrepreneurship. *Journal of Business Venturing*, 22(2), 236–261.

Lissack, M. R. & Letiche, H. (2002). Complexity, emergence, resilience, and coherence: Gaining perspective on organizations and their study. *Emergence*, 4, 72–94.

Lundin, R. A., Arvidsson, N., Brady, T., Ekstedt, E., Midler, C. & Sydow, J. (2015). *Managing and working in project society: Institutional challenges of temporary organizations*. Cambridge University Press.

Manson, S. M. (2001). Simplifying complexity: A review of complexity theory. *Geoforum*, 32(3), 405–414.

Markard, J., Raven, R. & Truffer, B. (2012). Sustainability transitions: An emerging field of research and its prospects. *Research Policy*, 41(6), 955–967.

Maturana, H. R. & Varela, F. J. (1992). *The tree of knowledge: The biological roots of understanding.* Shambhala Publications.

McEvoy, P., Brady, M. & Munck, R. (2016). Capacity development through international projects: A complex adaptive systems perspective. *International Journal of Managing Projects in Business*, 9(3), 528–545.

McKelvey, B. (2004). Complexity science as order-creation science: New theory, new method. *Emergence: Complexity and Organization*, 6(4), 2–27.

Messier, C. & Puettmann, K. J. (2011). Forests as complex adaptive systems: Implications for forest management and modelling. *L'Italia Forestale e Montana*, 66(3), 249–258.

Meyer, A. D., Gaba, V. & Colwell, K. A. (2005). Organizing far from equilibrium: Nonlinear change in organizational fields. *Organization Science*, 16(5), 456–473.

Morris, P. W. G. & Geraldi, J. (2011). Managing the institutional context for projects. *Project Management Journal*, 42(6), 20–32.

Nan, N. (2011). Capturing bottom-up information technology use processes: A complex adaptive systems model. *MIS Quarterly*, 35(2), 505–532.

Padalkar, M. & Gopinath, S. (2016a). Are complexity and uncertainty distinct concepts in project management? A taxonomical examination from literature. *International Journal of Project Management*, 34(4), 688–700.

Padalkar, M. & Gopinath, S. (2016b). Six decades of project management research: Thematic trends and future opportunities. *International Journal of Project Management*, 34(7), 1305–1321.

Phillips, M. A. & Ritala, P. (2019). A complex adaptive systems agenda for ecosystem research methodology. *Technological Forecasting and Social Change*, 148(November), 119739.

Pich, M. T., Loch, C. H. & De Meyer, A. (2002). On uncertainty, ambiguity and complexity in project management. *Management Science*, 48(8), 1008–1023.

Richardson, K. A. (2011). Complexity and management: A pluralistic view. In S. Maguire & B. MacKelvey (Eds), *The Sage handbook of complexity and management* (pp. 366–381). Sage.

Roundy, P. T., Bradshaw, M. & Brockman, B. K. (2018). The emergence of entrepreneurial ecosystems: A complex adaptive systems approach. *Journal of Business Research*, 86(1), 1–10.

Ruuska, I. & Teigland, R. (2009). Ensuring project success through collective competence and creative conflict in public – private partnerships: A case study of Bygga Villa, a Swedish triple helix e-government initiative. *International Journal of Project Management*, 27, 323–334.

Ruuska, I., Ahola, T., Artto, K., Locatelli, G. & Mancini, M. (2011). A new governance approach for multi-firm projects: Lessons from Olkiluoto 3 and Flamanville 3 nuclear power plant projects. *International Journal of Project Management*, 29, 647–660.

Serra, C. E. M. & Kunc, M. (2015). Benefits realisation management and its influence on project success and on the execution of business strategies. *International Journal of Project Management*, 33(4), 852–862.

Shenhar, A. J. (2001). One size does not fit all projects: Exploring classical contingency domains. *Management Science*, 47(3), 394–414.

Shewhart, W. A. (1931). *Economic control of quality of manufactured product*. Van Nostrand Publishing.

Sommer, S. C. & Loch, C. H. (2004). Selectionism and learning in projects with complexity and unforeseeable uncertainty. *Management Science*, 50(10), 1334–1347.

Sterman, J. D. (1992). *System dynamics modeling for project management*. Massachusetts Institute of Technology.

Sterman, J. D. (2001). System dynamics modeling: Tools for learning in a complex world. *California Management Review*, 43(4), 8–25.

Sweetman, R. & Conboy, K. (2018). Portfolios of agile projects: A complex adaptive systems' agent perspective. *Project Management Journal*, 49(6), 18–38.

Turner, J. R. & Müller, R. (2003). On the nature of the project as a temporary organization. *International Journal of Project Management*, 21(1), 1–8.

Uhl-Bien, M. & Arena, M. (2017). Complexity leadership: Enabling people and organizations for adaptability. *Organizational Dynamics*, 46(1), 9–20.

Vidgen, R. & Wang, X. (2009). Coevolving systems and the organization of agile software development. *Information Systems Research*, 20(3), 355–376.

Von Foerster, H. (1974). *Cybernetics of cybernetics*. Springer.

Weaver, W. (1948). Science and complexity. *American Scientist*, 36(4), 536–544.

Webb, C., Lettice, F. & Lemon, M. (2006). Facilitating learning and innovation in organizations using complexity science principles. *Emergence: Complexity and Organization*, 8(1), 30–41.

Wiener, N. (1950). *The human use of human beings: Cybernetics and society*. Houghton Mifflin.

Winch, G. M. & Sergeeva, N. (2022). Temporal structuring in project organizing: A narrative perspective. *International Journal of Project Management*, 40(1), 40–51.

Winch, G. M., Cao, D., Maytorena-Sanchez, E., Pinto, J., Sergeeva, N. & Zhang, S. (2021). Operation warp speed: Projects responding to the COVID-19 pandemic. *Project Leadership and Society*, 2, 100019.

Zwikael, O., Chih, Y. Y. & Meredith, J. R. (2018). Project benefit management: Setting effective target benefits. *International Journal of Project Management*, 36(4), 650–658.

15. From duality to dualism in complex project organizing: structuration and morphogenetic theory

Graham M. Winch

15.1 INTRODUCTION

One of the most important types of complex project organizing (CPO) is the complex information systems project (CISP) that creates digital infrastructure for organizations as the basis of digital transformations (Hanelt et al., 2021; Vial, 2019). CISP thereby interactively transform both technology and organization in order to achieve higher performance (Markus, 2004). Research to date on CISP in the information systems literature has relied heavily on structuration theory (Giddens, 1979, 1984; Jones & Karsten, 2008). While there are important differences of emphasis within this perspective (Jones, 2014), the body of literature as a whole shares a foundational reliance on structuration theory, evolving into the research theme of socio-materiality (Gaskin et al., 2014; Jones, 2014; Leonardi, 2013; Orlikowski, 1992; Orlikowski & Scott, 2008; Orlikowski & Yates, 1994; Yates & Orlikowski, 1992).

We will argue that this reliance on structuration theory for CISP research hampers its further development because it incorporates the temporal conflation of the synchronic and diachronic dimensions of social analysis (Saussure, 1959), which lies at the heart of structuration theory (Giddens, 1979). The result is that it is difficult to analyse the different temporal rhythms of the development of the technological and the organizational over time. Analysis drawing on structuration theory becomes temporally 'fused' with the technological and organizational being analysed within the same conceptual time frame (Archer, 1993). The aim of this chapter, then, is to develop the analysis of CISP by reintroducing the distinction between the synchronic and diachronic dimensions. This will allow the differing temporal rhythms of the technological and the organizational to be analysed both separately and jointly.

Morphogenetic theory has already made an important contribution to CISP research (Mutch, 2010; Volkoff & Strong, 2013; Volkoff et al., 2007) drawing on the morphogenetic critique of the 'central conflation' of structure and agency in structuration theory (Archer, 1982, 1995, 1996). We propose to advance on that work by also drawing on the morphogenetic critique of the temporal conflation of the synchronic and diachronic in structuration theory so that they are retained in a temporal dualism rather than conflated in a temporal duality. This will allow us to theorize technology and organization as both mutually constitutive and analytically distinct – each with its own temporal rhythms of development – and to show under which conditions they come together to enable digital transformation, and under which conditions they do not. Thus we use 'dualism' not in terms of polar opposition (Farjoun, 2010), but analytic distinction. Although the argument is developed in the context of CISP, we will suggest in conclusion that it is applicable across all types of CPO.

15.2 THE CRITIQUE OF STRUCTURATION THEORY AND MORPHOGENETIC THEORY

The 'two sociologies' (Dawe, 1970), addressing respectively the 'problem of order' and the 'problem of action', have riven enquiry into the 'vexatious fact of society' (Archer, 1995). Organization theory is riven along similar lines (Burrell & Morgan, 1979). Those starting from the problem of order have tended to see action as being the result of the socialization of the individual into existing social structures in a 'downwards conflation' from macro to micro (Archer, 1988). That is to say, agency is typically theorized as the outcome of structure in a more or less deterministic way. For those starting from the problem of action, structural phenomena are theorized as mere aggregates of individual agency or, in the more sophisticated versions (Berger & Luckmann, 1967), as socially constructed through agential interaction in an 'upwards conflation' from micro to macro (Archer, 1988). Structure is thereby theorized as a voluntaristic outcome of human activity. In either case, the result is typically unsatisfactory because these attempts fail to give ontological autonomy to either agency or structure (Archer, 1995), but theorize the macro as an epiphenomenon of the micro or the micro as an epiphenomenon of the macro.

Structuration theory (Giddens, 1979, 1984) made a highly influential attempt to move beyond this rift in social research and to resolve the tensions between structure and agency. In structuration theory, structure and agency are mutually constitutive of each other in the 'duality of structure' mediated through practices in which humans interact reflexively. However, structuration theory merely achieves a 'central conflation' rather than truly transcending the agency/structure dichotomy (Archer, 1982). Structuration theory has difficulty, therefore, addressing 'when' questions regarding under which conditions agency shapes structure and structure shapes agency. From the perspective of our concerns here for CISP, this leads to a crucial weakness.

One of the principal contributions of structuration theory is its bringing of space/time into social theory (Urry, 1991), but it does so only partially because of its rejection of the distinction between the synchronic and diachronic (Giddens, 1979). The result is that its time frame is entirely in the present, rather than the past or future (Archer, 1993). Thus structuration theory proposes a temporal conflation of the past, present and future in the diachronic dimension to complement its central conflation of structure and agency in the synchronic dimension. This results in the duality of structure, where agency and structure are so tightly bonded in their mutual instantiation in space/time that the possibility of structure and agency evolving through different temporal rhythms is occluded. In other words, one cannot look further backwards (or forwards) when investigating structure than when investigating agency, nor vice versa.

While the morphogenetic critique of structuration theory does not depend upon a critical realist philosophy of science, adopting such a philosophy adds considerable weight to the argument (Archer, 1995) because agency and structure can now be theorized as both ontologically distinct and epistemologically problematic. It proposes a morphogenetic theory of social stasis and change that retains structuration theory's insistence on the mutual constitution of structure and agency, while deploying a layered ontology in which the layers have emergent properties that are not properties of their constituent parts, rather than a flattened and conflated one. This implies that structure cannot be deconstructed to agency, and that agency is not a mere outcome of structure. This is achieved through an 'analytical dualism' in which structure and agency are held in analytic tension rather than conflated to each other through practice. Further, morphogenetic theory moves beyond structuration theory's approach to temporality by allowing structure and agency to evolve through different time periods rather being mutually constituted in the analytic present.

Thus the morphogenetic approach rests on two temporal axioms: (1) structure necessarily pre-dates the actions which transform it; and (2) structural elaboration post-dates these actions. In other words, actors are both constrained and enabled by the institutions (and associated rules and procedures) which were developed by others prior to their arrival on the scene and then, through their actions, leave an institutional legacy for those who come after.

The point is well illustrated by the division of labour in pin manufacture (Smith, 1970). From a morphogenetic perspective (Archer, 2000), the associated increase in productivity is emergent from the interaction between the individual workers but is the property of none of them individually and therefore cannot be reduced to their individual efforts. From an inter-pretivist perspective (King, 1999), the increased productivity is a construct of the interactions of the group of workers, and therefore cannot be reified as a property of the group alone. But this interpretivist perspective misses the elaboration phase. Once the division of labour is established, it requires coordination, and hence a managerial class to do that coordination with, therefore, an interest in maintaining that division of labour (Marx, 1976). Moreover, the division of labour then allowed the development of specialized machines leading to increased specialization and higher productivity (Smith, 1970). Once this morphogenetic cycle is mobilized, these developments constrain further groups and it becomes impossible for any one group to opt voluntaristically to reduce the division of labour significantly because it is constrained by the reality that any alternative organization of production needs to be at least as efficient as the divided one which binds both the managers (owners) and the workers. The effect of the division of labour, therefore, is to establish over time relations between productive organizations (whatever their internal group organization might be) which exogenously constrain the actions of the groups in those organizations (Porpora, 2015).

15.3   TOWARDS A MORPHOGENETIC THEORY OF CISP

This review suggests that we need to move on from a structurationist approach to research on CISPs and to follow the lead of some pioneers (Mutch, 2010; Volkoff et al., 2007) to develop a fully morphogenetic theory of CISPs that analyses the causal powers of technological and organizational structures with a strong temporal dimension. How might this insight be developed into a more general theory of the morphogenesis of organizations through complex information systems?

The theory of social change (Lockwood, 1964) underpinned by a critical realist philosophy (Archer, 1996) suggests a way forward. It distinguishes between 'social integration' and 'system integration' where 'the problem of social integration focuses attention upon the orderly or conflictual relationships between the *actors*, the problem of system integration focuses on the orderly or conflictual relationships between the *parts*, of a social system' (Lockwood, 1964, p. 245; emphasis in original). Contradictions between the structural parts of the social system and conflict between the actors of the social systems do not necessarily align, but it is only when they do align that social change is possible. This analytic (rather than philosophical) distinction between the structural 'parts' of the social system and the agency of 'actors' offers the prospect of non-conflationary theorizing of social change in which explanatory power is derived from treating parts and actors as separable in a dualism rather than fused in a duality. The interface between parts and systems is then the focus of intensive investigation. The increase in explanatory power derives from concentrating upon neither element in its own right, but rather from forging explanations in terms of their variable combinations (Archer, 1996).

Temporality is fundamental to morphogenetic theory:

> Basically, analytical dualism is possible due to temporality. Because 'structure' and 'agency' are phased over different tracts of time, this enables us to formulate practical social theories in terms of the former being prior to the latter, having autonomy from it and exerting causal influence upon it. In other words, we can talk about 'system integration' conditioning 'social integration' which necessarily confronts the former, and similarly speak of systemic elaboration being posterior to a particular sequence of social action. (Archer, 1996, p. 694; emphasis in the original)

While care should be taken in directly comparing these concepts of social and system integration at the societal level with our application at the organizational level, we can take the fundamental points that the technological and the organizational need to be held analytically distinct as a dualism; that the different temporal rhythms of their respective evolutions needs to be analysed rather than assumed and then conflated into a duality; and that the focus of our empirical research needs to be on their mutual but variable constitution through time. We further suggest that this mutual but variable constitution is central to a CISP research agenda.

One of the principal arguments for advocating the analytic distinction between the synchronic and the diachronic in research on CISPs is the evidence that even in successful implementations, organizations evolve with a different rhythm from the technologies that they deploy. Research on the implementation of computer-aided design and computer-aided manufacturing (CAD/CAM) systems in 15 United Kingdom manufacturing organizations (Winch, 1994) showed that what distinguished the five organizations that were successful in achieving alignment between organizational change and technological change from the six that had achieved neither technological or organizational change was that the former group had changed their organization because of the need to address competitive challenges before they implemented the technology, while the latter group tried to implement the technology and then to change the organization afterwards. The other four organizations had achieved either technical or organizational integration.

Research on the implementation of enterprise resource planning (ERP) in NASA (Berente & Yoo, 2012; Berente et al., 2010, 2016) shows again the independence of the organizational and technological. NASA had tried to integrate its accounting and control systems a number of times before they decided to implement a SAP ERP system. This implementation proceeded through a number of iterations but was eventually successful at achieving a higher level of organizational integration. In parallel with the ERP implementation NASA went through two different changes in organization structure, first towards a matrix of programmes and operational centres aimed at breaking down the relative isolation of the geographically dispersed centres and second towards ensuring the financial viability of the separate centres. These organizational developments were conditioned by broader strategic issues, while the SAP system played an important enabling role in achieving the organizational changes once the broader organizational changes had been achieved.

This argument is complemented by research on relationships between vendor and user organizations of CISP on the 'biography of the artefact' (Pollock & Williams, 2009; Williams

& Pollock, 2012). This shows how the development of CISP by vendors is relatively auton-omous from any one implementing organization, and how the interactions between such systems and the implementing organization are carefully calibrated by the vendor technology development organization. In the case of ERM systems such as these, the ability of the user organization – no matter how large – to influence the overall technological development of the system is highly constrained. The diachronic artefact biography is vital for understanding the synchronic implementation of that artefact in a CISP.

In these case studies we can see that changes in organization and changes in technology were relatively independent but mutually reinforcing under the right conditions. Perhaps most importantly, in the CISP implementation studies, organizational change was driven more by institutional (including market) factors than technological factors, and that alignment with technological factors was more a case of serendipity than design, particularly in the CAD/CAM case. Poor project delivery can lead to failure of both organization and technology in CISP with resulting serious financial losses (Chen et al., 2009; Markus, 2004). We therefore suggest that the alignment of technology and organization is an empirical question. We do not suggest that technology is an entirely exogenous force, but argue that our theoretical framings of the relationship between technology and organization need to be open to all positions in the entanglement of technology and organization between endogeneity and exogeneity in the co-constitution of technology and organization (Faraj & Pachidi, 2021).

This concern for the relationship between technology and organization is not just a concern for CISP projects. We are in the midst of the fourth industrial revolution (Schwab, 2018), and extraordinary new information technologies are starting to transform CPO through Project Organizing 4.0 (Part IV). CPO researchers need to develop appropriate theoretical framings for analysing both CISP projects themselves and for the deployment of new information tech-nologies as co-constituents in organizing complex projects more widely.

These cases also show the importance of moving beyond the temporal conflation inherent in structuration theory as well as the central conflation. The experience of implementing CISPs such as CAD/CAM and ERP is a lot messier and contingent than can be analysed by drawing on structuration theory, and so morphogenetic theory is to be preferred (Bygstad et al., 2016; Leonardi, 2013; Volkoff et al., 2007). Indeed, the argument applies to organizational change more generally (Herepath, 2014).

15.4   TOWARDS AN AGENDA FOR CISP RESEARCH

Critical realism is a philosophy of science, not a research methodology, so for it to enable CISP research, we need to develop and adopt appropriate methodologies within critical realism's broad epistemological flexibility. We first need to say a little more about critical realism itself. Ontologically, it holds that there is a reality 'out there', but that it is epistemologically inaccessible to us. All that can be achieved by science is conditional approximations to that reality (Bhaskar, 2008), and this applies equally to the social and natural sciences (Bhaskar, 1998). Thus science cannot access the real (what is), but only the actual (what is potentially observable) and the empirical (what was actually observed). The formulation implies that the 'generative mechanisms' which cause phenomena in the real domain may not be manifest in the actual domain because the conditions are not right, and may not be observed in the empirical domain. A classic example is the Higgs Bosun which gives mass to particles (Peters

& Peterson, 2013). It has always been there (i.e. real), but research in physics (Higgs, 1964) has only recently identified a gap in the knowledge (i.e. it has become actual), and finally it was identified experimentally using the Large Hadron Collider in 2012 (i.e. it has become empirical). This identification remains provisional, however, because physicists are inherently 'entangled' in their instrumentation (Barad, 2007).

Empirical realism (Bhaskar, 2008) is research that only addresses the empirical domain. For instance, positivistic research has selected methodologies that have focused on the micro-level of analysis because this is much more tractable empirically than the macro; interpretivists, drawing significantly on ethnography, have also tended to focus on the micro for similar pragmatic reasons (Coleman, 1986). It is simply easier to survey individuals' opinions on their immediate situation or to immerse oneself in a relatively small group context than to attempt to grapple with large macro-level entities which are inherently less observable. However, methods are available (Edwards et al., 2014). For instance, while organizational structures are not amenable to direct observation, they can be visualized. This can be done descriptively such as in an organigram (Mintzberg, 1979) or process map (Davenport, 1993) or analytically as in causal loop diagrams (Chapter 7) and social networks (Burt, 2005).

The challenge is to move beyond the empirical realism of positivist surveys and ethno-graphic hermeneutics. It can be suggested that empirical realism in the social sciences has an inherent tendency towards upwards conflation derived from its choice of methodology either through aggregation for the positivists or constructivism for the interpretivists. This pragmatic methodological choice is compounded epistemologically by an empirical realism that holds that only the observable is real. It is simply easier to observe agency in action – people doing things – than to observe structure and the causal powers that shape what they do. Thus the fundamental epistemological problem is how to empirically observe structure in its analytical dualism with agency when it can only be observed by its effects. Agency can be observed through a variety of methods ranging from psychometric scales to participant observation, yet organizational structures of various types are much less easily observable and have to be inferred by their effects on agency. In critical realism, this inferential process is called 'retro-duction' as the process of theorizing what the world must be like for the effects observed to be as they are and not otherwise (Porpora, 2015; Wynn & Williams, 2012), or more widely as 'abduction' (Van de Ven, 2007).

An important challenge in morphogenetic research deploying a critical realist philosophy of science is how to characterize technology in the dualism of organization and technology (Leonardi, 2013). In developing such a characterization, the concept of 'affordance' from environmental psychology (Gibson, 1986) is important for morphogenetic approaches to CISP research (Bygstad, et al., 2016; Volkoff & Strong, 2013). An affordance is the produc-tive potential offered by a technology to the organization that is implementing it. However, an important distinction between the natural world with which environmental psychology is concerned and the artificial world of complex information systems is that the latter are designed (Simon, 1996). In other words, a complex information system is a 'rational artefact' designed with a specific functional intent (Chapter 16) by agents drawing on experiences in both the natural and artificial worlds. This suggests that we need to think of affordances as the structural properties of the information system that has been designed to afford them and 'an affordance as an emergent property of the relation between an object (IT artefact) and an actor' (Volkoff & Strong, 2013, p. 829).

15.5　CONCLUSIONS

We argued in this chapter that research on CISP has been dominated by perspectives derived from structuration theory, but this suffers from two limitations. The first is the central conflation of agency and structure inherent in structuration theory, which means that it is not possible to analyse separately the development of technology and organization. The second limitation is the temporal conflation of the synchronic and diachronic which, we suggest, is particularly important for CISP research given the inherent temporality of CPO.

In order to overcome these limitations, we proposed that morphogenetic theory is a more appropriate theoretical perspective with which to research CISPs. This is because, unlike structuration theory, it does not conflate technology and organization into a duality but retains them as a dualism in which they are mutually constituted but analytically separable. This is particularly important for the analysis of CISPs because the inherent messiness of the relationship between technology and organization through time cannot be captured in a duality that conflates the diachronic and synchronic, but applies to research on organizations more generally as well (Frederiksen & Kringelum, 2021).

The empirical domain of CISP is only a subset of the published research on project organizing which covers the full spectrum of project-based sectors, even if it is the predominant employer of project managers, at least in the United Kingdom (APM, 2019). However, the fundamental issues raised by the debates on the relationship between technology and organization reviewed in this chapter are, we suggest, applicable across all types of complex projects as Section 15.4 shows. The inescapably intimate relationship between technology and organization on CISPs meant that the limitations of the focus of much project organizing research on delivering outputs rather than achieving outcomes (Winch et al., 2022) was appreciated at an early stage, but the point applies more generally.

In construction, buildings are mere shells unless put to purposeful activity as the futility of delivering consummately executed field hospitals to treat COVID patients in the United Kingdom without the staff to provide healthcare services in them demonstrates. Fundamentally, buildings stabilize social life (Gieryn, 2002). As Winston Churchill famously said of the Houses of Parliament, 'we make our buildings and afterwards our buildings make us' (Brand, 1994). Similarly, infrastructure is just a scar on the landscape unless it is providing infrastructure services (Kessides, 1997) for economy and society, thereby creating 'displacements' (Gellert & Lynch, 2003) in how that economy and society function. One can repeat this analysis across all the project-based sectors; the morphogenetic approach is not just applicable to CISP, but to all CPO as we increasingly research outcomes as well as outputs.

REFERENCES

APM (2019). *The golden thread: A study of the contribution of project management and projects to the UK's economy and society*. Association for Project Management.

Archer, M. S. (1982). Morphogenesis versus structuration: On combining structure and action. *British Journal of Sociology*, 33(4), 455–483.

Archer, M. S. (1988). *Culture and agency: The place of culture in social theory*. Cambridge University Press.

Archer, M. S. (1993). Taking time to link structure and agency. In H. Martins (Ed.), *Knowledge and passion: Essays in honour of John Rex* (pp. 154–173). I. B. Tauris.

Archer, M. S. (1995). *Realist social theory: The morphogenetic approach*. Cambridge University Press.

Archer, M. S. (1996). Social integration and system integration: Developing the distinction. *Sociology*, 30(4), 679–699.

Archer, M. S. (2000). For structure: Its reality, properties and powers: A reply to Anthony King. *The Sociological Review*, 48(3), 464–472.

Barad, K. M. (2007). *Meeting the universe halfway: Quantum physics and the entanglement of matter and meaning*. Duke University Press.

Berente, N. & Yoo, Y. (2012). Institutional contradictions and loose coupling: Postimplementation of NASA's enterprise information system. *Information Systems Research*, 23(2), 376–396.

Berente, N., Gal, U. & Yoo, Y. (2010). Dressage, control, and enterprise systems: The case of NASA's full cost initiative. *European Journal of Information Systems*, 19(377), 21–34.

Berente, N., Lyytinen, K., Yoo, Y. & King, J. L. (2016). Routines as shock absorbers during organizational transformation: Integration, control, and NASA's enterprise information system. *Organization Science*, 27(3), 551–572.

Berger, P. & Luckmann, T. (1967). *The social construction of reality: A treatise in the sociology of knowledge*. Penguin.

Bhaskar, R. (1998). *The possibility of naturalism: A philosophical critique of the contemporary human sciences* (3rd ed.). Routledge.

Bhaskar, R. (2008). *A realist theory of science* (2nd ed.). Verso.

Brand, S. (1994). *How buildings learn: What happens after they're built*. Viking.

Burrell, G. & Morgan, G. (1979). *Sociological paradigms and organisational analysis: Elements of the sociology of corporate life*. Heinemann.

Burt, R. S. (2005). *Brokerage and closure: An introduction to social capital*. Oxford University Press.

Bygstad, B., Munkvold, B. E. & Volkoff, O. (2016). Identifying generative mechanisms through affordance: A framework for critical realist data analysis. *Journal of Information Technology*, 31(1), 83–96.

Chen, C. C., Law, C. C. H. & Yang, S. C. (2009). Managing ERP implementation failure: A project management perspective. *IEEE Transactions on Engineering Management*, 56(1), 157–170.

Coleman, J. S. (1986). Social theory, social research, and a theory of action. *American Journal of Sociology*, 91(6), 1309–1335.

Davenport, T. H. (1993). *Process innovation: Reengineering work through information technology*. Harvard Business School Press.

Dawe, A. (1970). The two sociologies. *British Journal of Sociology*, 21(2), 207–218.

Edwards, P. K., O'Mahoney, J. & Vincent, S. (2014). *Studying organizations using critical realism: A practical guide*. Oxford University Press.

Faraj, S. & Pachidi, S. (2021). Beyond uberization: The co-constitution of technology and organizing. *Organization Theory*, 2(1), 1–14.

Farjoun, M. (2010). Beyond dualism: Stability and change as a duality. *Academy of Management Review*, 35(2), 202–225.

Frederiksen, D. J. & Kringelum, L. B. (2021). Five potentials of critical realism in management and organization studies. *Journal of Critical Realism*, 20(1), 18–38.

Gaskin, J., Berente, N., Lyytinen, K. & Yoo, Y. (2014). Toward generalizable sociomaterial inquiry: A computational approach for zooming in and out of sociomaterial routines. *MIS Quarterly*, 38(3), 849–871.

Gellert, P. K. & Lynch, B. D. (2003). Mega-projects as displacements. *International Social Science Journal*, 55(175), 15–25.

Gibson, J. J. (1986). *The ecological approach to visual perception*. Lawrence Erlbaum Associates.

Giddens, A. (1979). *Central problems in social theory: Action, structure, and contradiction in social analysis*. Macmillan.

Giddens, A. (1984). *The constitution of society: Outline of the theory of structuration*. Polity Press.

Gieryn, T. F. (2002). What buildings do. *Theory and Society*, 31(1), 35–74.

Hanelt, A., Bohnsack, R., Marz, D. & Antunes Marante, C. (2021). A systematic review of the literature on digital transformation: Insights and implications for strategy and organizational change. *Journal of Management Studies*, 58(5), 1159–1197.

Herepath, A. (2014). In the loop: A realist approach to structure and agency in the practice of strategy. *Organization Studies*, 35(6), 857–879.

Higgs, P. W. (1964). Broken symmetries and the masses of gauge bosons. *Physical Review Letters*, 13(16), 508–509.

Jones, M. R. (2014). A matter of life and death: Exploring conceptualizations of sociomateriality in the context of critical care. *MIS Quarterly*, 38(3), 895–925.

Jones, M. R. & Karsten, H. (2008). Giddens's structuration theory and information systems research. *MIS Quarterly*, 32(1), 127–157.

Kessides, C. (1997). *World Bank experience with the provision of infrastructure services for the urban poor: Preliminary identification and review of best practices*. World Bank.

King, A. (1999). Against structure: A critique of morphogenetic social theory. *The Sociological Review*, 47(2), 199–227.

Leonardi, P. M. (2013). Theoretical foundations for the study of sociomateriality. *Information and Organization*, 23(2), 59–76.

Lockwood, D. (1964). Social integration and system integration. In G. K. Zollschan & W. Hirsch (Eds), *Explorations in social change* (pp. 244–257). Routledge.

Markus, M. L. (2004). Technochange management: Using it to drive organizational change. *Journal of Information Technology*, 19(1), 4–20.

Marx, K. (1976). *Capital*. Penguin.

Mintzberg, H. (1979). *The structuring of organizations: A synthesis of the research*. Prentice-Hall.

Mutch, A. (2010). Technology, organization, and structure: A morphogenetic approach. *Organization Science*, 21(2), 507–520.

Orlikowski, W. J. (1992). The duality of technology: Rethinking the concept of technology in organizations. *Organization Science*, 3(3), 398–427.

Orlikowski, W. J. & Scott, S. V. (2008). Sociomateriality: Challenging the separation of technology, work and organization. *Academy of Management Annals*, 2(1), 433–474.

Orlikowski, W. J. & Yates, J. (1994). Genre repertoire: The structuring of communicative practices in organizations. *Administrative Science Quarterly*, 39(4), 541–574.

Peters, T. & Peterson, C. (2013). The Higgs Boson: An adventure in critical realism. *Theology and Science*, 11(3), 185–207.

Pollock, N. & Williams, R. N. (2009). *Software and organisations: The biography of the enterprise-wide system or how SAP conquered the world*. Routledge.

Porpora, D. V. (2015). *Reconstructing sociology: The critical realist approach*. Cambridge University Press.

Saussure, F. d. (1959). *Course in general linguistics*. Peter Owen.

Schwab, K. (2018). *Shaping the future of the fourth industrial revolution: A guide to building a better world*. Portfolio Penguin.

Simon, H. A. (1996). *The sciences of the artificial* (3rd ed.). MIT Press.

Smith, A. (1970). *The wealth of nations*. Penguin.

Urry, J. (1991). Time and space in Giddens' social theory. In C. G. A. Bryant & D. Jary (Eds), *Giddens' theory of structuration: A critical appreciation* (pp. 160–175). Routledge.

Van de Ven, A. H. (2007). *Engaged scholarship: A guide for organizational and social research*. Oxford University Press.

Vial, G. (2019). Understanding digital transformation: A review and a research agenda. *Journal of Strategic Information Systems*, 28(2), 118–144.

Volkoff, O. & Strong, D. M. (2013). Critical realism and affordances: Theorizing IT-associated organizational change processes. *MIS Quarterly*, 37(3), 819–834.

Volkoff, O., Strong, D. M. & Elmes, M. B. (2007). Technological embeddedness and organizational change. *Organization Science*, 18(5), 832–848.

Williams, R. & Pollock, N. (2012). Research commentary: Moving beyond the single site implementation study: How (and why) we should study the biography of packaged enterprise solutions. *Information Systems Research*, 23(1), 1–22.

Winch, G. M. (1994). *Managing production: Engineering change and stability*. Oxford University Press.

Winch, G. M., Maytorena-Sanchez, E. & Sergeeva, N. (2022). *Strategic project organizing*. Oxford University Press.

Wynn, D. & Williams, C. K. (2012). Principles for conducting critical realist case study research in information systems. *MIS Quarterly*, 36(3), 787–810.

Yates, J. & Orlikowski, W. J. (1992). Genres of organizational communication: A structurational approach to studying communication and media. *Academy of Management Review*, 17(2), 299–326.

16. The contribution of design thinking to complex project organizing

Sihem BenMahmoud-Jouini and Lisa Carlgren

16.1 INTRODUCTION

Literature in project management has acknowledged the necessity to adopt specific approaches in order to manage projects in contexts with a high degree of complexity (Morris, 2013; Shenhar & Dvir, 2004). Indeed, a contextual approach to project management has been now widely accepted in the literature. It claims that different types of projects (Shenhar, 2001) should be managed accordingly and complex projects are not an exception. Therefore, complex projects require specific methods of addressing them, i.e. complex project organizing (CPO).

In a world characterized by rapid change, intensive innovation, and increasing complexity, such projects are becoming the norm rather than the exception. We therefore aim in this chapter to investigate what design and especially design thinking (DT), which is known to be a suitable approach for addressing wicked and complex problems, can bring to research on CPO.

In fact, despite the common focus on complex problems, the literatures on DT and CPO have developed in parallel trajectories without engaging in conversation. Our intent in this chapter is to pursue such a conversation. DT and CPO are considered to be powerful approaches to address uncertainty and ill-defined problems. They are both highly associated with knowledge exploration and learning, propose a process perspective including tools and methods to apprehend uncertainty, and involve a variety of actors. We intend to build on these similarities in order to explore the reciprocal contributions and novel perspectives that they can bring one another.

In order to initiate such a conversation, we will start by presenting DT and CPO and then present the two fields through a common canvas based on three perspectives: (1) cognitive; (2) processual; and (3) organizational. The cognitive perspective will refer to the type of problems addressed and the type of knowledge required; the processual perspective will refer to the approaches (activities, methods, tools) recommended and used; and the organizational perspective will refer to the way organizations are shaped and animated. We will then explore potential correspondences and complementarities. We intend to examine CPO through the principles of DT and suggest a designerly way of CPO.

16.2 DESIGN THINKING AND COMPLEX PROJECTS

According to Simon (1969), design is the process by which we devise courses of action aimed at changing existing situations into preferred ones through the creation of artefacts – objects created by humans through creative reasoning. It is the 'science of the artificial' (Simon,

1969): it is about creativity. Early literature on design focused on products and later expanded to include services, organizations, and any situation that involves humans and requires the understanding of their behaviours, attitudes, and emotions (Auernhammer & Roth, 2021). Therefore, the outcome of a design process can be a graphic, a form, a product (tangible or intangible), a system, an interaction, an interface, or an experience. Buchanan (2015) summarized that by suggesting four domains – communication, construction, interaction, and integration – in which designers invent, judge, connect, and integrate. Therefore, design concerns not only form, aesthetics, and functionality, but also sensemaking (Verganti, 2008) and meaning: 'something must have form to be seen but must make sense to be understood and used' (Krippendorff, 1989, p. 14).

It is often argued that design addresses ill-defined problems (Rittel, 1972) and therefore consists of framing and reframing problems. In order to do so, designers are driven by specific cognition (thinking), behaviour (doing), and affect (feeling). According to Schweitzer et al. (2016), they are empathetic towards people's needs and context, collaboratively geared, embrace diversity, are inquisitive and open to new perspectives and learning, and are mindful of process and thinking modes. They also have experiential intelligence, take action deliberately and overtly, are consciously creative, accept uncertainty, practise critical questioning, are open to risk, and have the desire and determination to make a difference.

In design research, studies on DT focused on how designers think and work as they go about designing. More recently the concept of DT emerged in management debates, disconnecting the practice from the designer, suggesting that others could learn and adapt the practice (Johansson-Sköldberg et al., 2013). In this discourse, DT has been predominantly defined as a creative approach to explore ill-defined problems inspired by the way designers think and work. It is described as a deep, holistic, ethnographic user understanding, involving diverse perspectives and levels of abstraction to reframe problems, and visualizing, imagining, and prototyping as ways to explore concepts and solutions. Embracing ambiguity and being open to the unexpected are frequently repeated mantras.

Since the early 2000s, the concept has diffused across different fields, and is now applied in a variety of sectors such as healthcare, sustainability, non-governmental organizations, and even research (Brown, 2008, 2009; Liedtka, 2015; Martin, 2011). This has led to a plethora of design consultancies offering education, project support, and implementation advice as a growing number of organizations adopt DT. Based on a multiple case study of firms with long experience of using DT, and the variety of their interpretation and use of the concept, Carlgren et al. (2016) suggest that whether embodied as mindsets or enacted as structured practices and specific techniques, DT can be characterized by five general themes: human focus, problem framing, experimentation, visualization, and diversity:

- Human focus: deep understanding of people and their needs to guide all work, as well as involvement and co-creation with users and stakeholders.
- Problem framing: exploring rather than solving problems, addressing the complexity of multiple problems within a given challenge.
- Experimentation: a curious learning and maker mindset, working in many small iterations and experiments.
- Visualization: making ideas tangible by use of visual methods, stories, role play, and mock-ups to explore, communicate, develop, and make ideas concrete.

- Diversity: work is performed by diverse teams with multiple perspectives with emphasis on collaboration, dialogue, and a democratic mindset.

Research on DT has developed beyond the design community and has flourished recently in management journals (Micheli et al., 2019) without interacting with other approaches, apart from recent work that has initiated connections with agile product development, lean start-up, or effectuation (Klenner et al., 2021; Verganti et al., 2021). Cross-referencing between DT and CPO is very rare except through the field of innovation management (BenMahmoud-Jouini et al., 2016). Breakthrough innovation projects or exploration projects for which – unlike development projects – neither technologies nor customer requirements are known from the start (Lenfle, 2008) are complex projects characterized by a high level of uncertainty (Loch et al., 2008).

Indeed, complex projects are incompletely specified in advance and deal with unstructured problems with little pre-given inputs and outputs (Hatch & Cunliffe, 2012). According to Bakhshi et al. (2016), complex projects face ambiguity, uncertainty, interdependency, non-linearity, unique local conditions, autonomy, emergent behaviours, and unfixed boundaries. According to Ahern et al. (2014), complex projects are organizationally complex problems with the following characteristics: (1) the solution must serve a variety of organizational objectives; (2) there is a high degree of interdependence between parts; (3) they can't be readily understood and solved by one person or group; and (4) they include unknowns at the frontier of knowledge or at the interface arising from combining existing ideas and techniques in a new way. Even though there is no universally accepted definition of complexity (Ireland et al., 2013), we find most often the following elements: a variety of interrelated and interdependent parts such as tasks or components that require feedback loops (Chapter 3). Such elements of definition resonate precisely with the type of situations DT addresses (Liedtka, 2015).

16.3 COGNITIVE PERSPECTIVE

The cognitive perspective that we will adopt below refers to the type of problems addressed and the type of knowledge required in CPO and DT, respectively. This perspective will consider complex projects as projects dealing with complex organizational problems. As highlighted above, complex projects are characterized by interdependency and incompleteness. Thus, a crucial question is the adequate representation of the situation to be addressed: its components and their dynamics (Floricel et al., 2016). In such situations, there is not one problem to solve, rather many interconnected problems to explore and improve, nor is there one universal solution.

A potential means to address such situations lies in the use of open representations that enable the problem's emergence and dynamics. Indeed, research on complexity and uncertainty, as shown in Chapters 2 and 3, distinguishes between an objectivist approach where complexity is a state of nature and a subjectivist one where it is a state of mind dependent on the observer. Taxen and Lillieskold (2008) have shown that traditional project management tools such as critical path methods and work breakdown structures are inadequate to represent the integration of activities and dependencies that characterize complex projects. There is thus a call for representations and images that emphasize comprehensibility over formalism and rigour and are resonant with how our mental cognitive systems represent the world.

In DT, visualization has been emphasized as a crucial principle (Carlgren et al., 2016). Indeed, visual and narrative elements such as charts and graphs, storytelling, use of metaphor, and analogies all play an important role in order to get overview and to make sense of the situation and engage the members in discussions about the interconnectedness of the project's elements.

DT is generally adopted to address 'wicked' problems (Rittel, 1972): problems that lack both definitive formulations and solutions, and are characterized by high uncertainty and ambiguity. They are a class of social problems with a fundamental indeterminacy without a single solution (Buchanan, 1992). They have no definitive formulation, no stopping rules, the solutions cannot be true or false, only good or bad, there is always more than one possible explanation that depends on the designers' vision of the world, and no formulation and solution has a definitive test. Therefore, such situations require research in order to identify hypotheses to be tested.

Indeed, according to Liedtka (2015, p. 927), DT:

> is a hypothesis-driven process that is problem, as well as solution, focused. It relies on abduction and experimentation involving multiple alternative solutions that actively mediate a variety of tensions between possibilities and constraints, and is best suited to decision contexts in which uncertainty and ambiguity are high. Iteration, based on learning through experimentation, is seen as a central task.

She claims that DT addresses and mitigates the cognitive biases that strongly impact any creative process. One such bias is the project members' inability to see beyond themselves and escape their past, current state, and personal preferences. Engaging in ethnography and close interaction with users improves the ability to imagine their experiences. Another bias relates to the inability of users to articulate their needs and provide accurate feedback. Through journey mapping and participant observation, for instance, DT helps identifying users' needs. A third category of biases relates to flaws in the ability to test the hypotheses identified. By working with multiple options and reflecting on the results of real experiments, DT can help mitigate such biases.

We suggest that by acknowledging the cognitive bias experienced by the project members, DT is a human-centric approach that is similar to the subjectivist approach to complexity and uncertainty mentioned in relation to CPO. DT offers a productive mix of analytical and intuitive thinking (Martin, 2009) and is opposed to linear and analytical problem-solving approaches that are ill-suited to address complexity and uncertainty which require knowledge acquisition.

16.4   PROCESSUAL PERSPECTIVE

The processual perspective refers to the approaches (activities, methods, tools) recommended and used in DT and COP. A salient characteristic of complex projects is that the pre-given knowledge is incomplete and therefore there is a necessity to build emergent knowledge during the project. Over their life cycle, complex projects continuously create and generate emergent knowledge that is unspecifiable at the outset. Therefore, project execution is a journey of knowledge creation (Engwall, 2003): delivering the project is about learning the project.

Ahern et al. (2014) suggest that complex projects may only be 'boundedly' planned: at any moment, they consist of emergent prototypes with incomplete knowledge. External or top-down control is counterproductive and results in poor performance. Floricel et al. (2016) highlight two planning strategies that can address project complexity related to technology, organization, market, and environments: (1) the project development process dealing with knowledge, either combining pre-existing knowledge or contributing to the production of new project-specific knowledge; and (2) the process dealing with shaping the project organization either by separating and allocating, or integrating and collaborating strategies.

Complex projects are different from complicated projects for which cause–effect relationships exist but are not apparent, and that require analytical thinking and search for information to investigate available options (Snowden & Boone, 2007). A complex project, on the other hand, is in a state of flux and unpredictability: high-level patterns exist, but isolated events cannot be predicted. After the fact, one might see connections and underlying reasons, but they could not have been predicted at the time (Snowden & Boone, 2007). The approach is to learn about the system through experiments, take multiple perspectives, be patient, and not focus on a problem too early; rather, seek to understand the patterns that appear.

DT is an approach that allows precisely this: probing and learning through experiments, bringing in multiple perspectives, and reframing problems. According to Brown (2008) at the Californian design firm IDEO, DT consists of a process that passes through and loops back between three phases: inspiration, ideation, and implementation. The process is often described in three phases with iteration between the phases: (1) an initial exploratory phase focused on data gathering for inspiration, identifying user needs, and defining the problem as a hypothesis to be explored; (2) a stage of idea and concept generation; and (3) prototyping to experiment and implement the concepts proposed as an answer to the hypothesized problem (Seidel & Fixson, 2013).

A pedagogic entry point to DT is its representation through the iconic 'double diamond' (Design Council, 2005) in order to illustrate the diverging and converging nature of exploring both problem and solution spaces. In the problem space, the first step is empathizing, i.e. gaining a deep holistic user and context understanding through the use of ethnographic methods, such as interviews, observations, workshops, immersion, and interactions with actors in adjacent fields. The idea is to learn as much as possible about unspoken needs of users in their specific contexts. The vast amount of collected information is synthesized in order to identify what really aches; for example, tensions and contradictions within policies and systems that may clash with the feelings and behaviours of individuals. The idea here is to work with diverse perspectives and different levels of abstraction to reframe the problem(s) at hand. Some people find it helpful to use visual tools and frameworks as support, such as affinity diagrams, personas, and journey maps. The first diamond ends with a set of reframed problems, or design principles, represented by the narrow waist of the double diamond.

Moving into the solution space, the aim is to create, explore, and develop ideas and concepts that address the identified challenges. Different ideation techniques are used, and as quickly as possible, teams start to prototype solutions, i.e. create something tangible to communicate and develop emerging ideas and to create something testable. This means sketching, creating artefacts with simple materials such as cardboard and glue, making storyboards and wireframes, or engaging in role play. Ideation should be done in a rapid and cheap way, in order not to turn ideas into pet concepts that are hard to let go of when criticized. The use of material practices is crucial because sometimes just interacting with different materials or using the body differently can create direction and spark ideas. The team lets users test and experience the concepts by interacting with the prototypes in different ways to learn from their reactions and new ideas they might have. Testing and observing the user interacting with a prototype may become a way to understand further the problem, rather than just testing the solution.

Therefore, the process is usually rather messy and iterative with phases blurring into each other. For example, testing concepts with users may turn into both new data collection and co-creation. Synthesizing data starts in parallel with collecting them, working in iterations also within problem exploration. The problem at hand can be reframed over and over again, investigating parallel angles, understandings, and perspectives. Ideation happens simultaneously with sketching and building at the same time. While this may sound chaotic, it is a continuous exploration rather than searching for definitive solutions. It is not about finding the right problem to solve, but identifying many problems from various perspectives, and each of them can be explored both in finding creative solutions and better understanding the needs behind them. Such a process with defined steps, tools, and mindsets associated with each phase is a handrail to hold onto in complex settings.

Even if DT has its origins in the product design field, it involves learning and reasoning that are mobilized for a larger domain of applications. Indeed, while evolving within problem and solution spaces, and across abstraction and concreteness, as well as analysis and synthesis, designers deploy different learning types. Beckman and Barry (2007) show that when they draw insights from the world of practice, convert them to abstract ideas or theories, and then translate those theories back into the realm of practice in the form of artefacts or institutions, designers combine the four core experiential learning styles (diverging, assimilating, converging, and accommodating) identified by Kolb (1984). Altogether, this process enables problem and solution finding and selecting. Therefore, DT enables the reduction of uncertainty through a learning-focused, hypothesis-driven approach (Beckman & Barry, 2007; Owen, 1993; Schön, 1983). This learning associates abstract reasoning with action in order to launch a 'reflective conversation with the situation' (Schön, 1983).

DT emphasizes learning and knowledge acquisition thanks to observation, collaboration, visualization of ideas, rapid concept prototyping, and concurrent business analysis (Lockwood, 2009). It is a process dedicated to learning that is supported by methods and tools.

16.5   ORGANIZATIONAL PERSPECTIVE

The organizational perspective refers to the way organizations are shaped and animated which is usually called organization design (Galbraith, 2008). Complex project organizations consist of autonomous and independent parts as well as interconnected ones, resulting in a variety of groups. Actors in such projects are diverse and this can generate unexpected emergent behaviours (Ireland et al., 2013) including self-organization (see Chapter 14).

Therefore, one crucial mission is to build a shared understanding of the project and its challenges by uncovering and accepting the diverse perspectives that may exist, and pacing the way towards addressing them progressively. Cohesion and an open atmosphere within the team is thus crucial. Considering the importance of reactivity and flexibility over the planning in such projects, organizing complex projects is more about sharing the experience of collective action than having a shared collective meaning upfront. Collective actions will contribute to the constitution of an evolving collective meaning (Weick, 1979).

One of DT's principles is empathy (Brown, 2008): the ability to imagine the world from multiple perspectives – those of colleagues, clients, end users, customers (both current and prospective), and other stakeholders. The collective dimension is therefore crucial. Co-location, co-working, fab-labs, and living labs (Magadley & Birdi, 2009) as well as virtual tools are important ways to ensure stakeholder mobilization and understanding. Indeed, Krippendorff (2011) highlighted the necessity to develop intertwined understandings of the artefacts resulting from design activity, and of the stakeholders' understanding of these artefacts.

In order to achieve its goal, a mutual adaptation between DT and the culture of the organization adopting it is required (Elsbach & Stigliani, 2018). For that purpose, Carlgren and BenMahmoud-Jouini (2021) identified eight specific characteristics of DT that can be seen as its cultural archetype: subjective and aesthetic ways of knowing; long-term and non-linear views about time; intrinsic motivation and sense of purpose; flexibility and change; relationships, empathy, and emotions at work; collaboration and inclusion; team autonomy and informality; and external orientation. Of particular interest for complex settings are the relationships, empathy, collaboration, and team autonomy.

Indeed, the dimension 'relationships, empathy, and emotions at work' refers to a focus on social relations where empathy with peers and being open to showing emotions is crucial. DT enables playfulness and having fun that is crucial for being innovative and creating engagement. Collaboration and inclusion are the foundations for productive and efficient work, involving multi-disciplinary and diverse teams. It is often argued that an inclusive atmosphere creates a greater acceptance of diverse backgrounds and competencies as well as a dedicated physical space fostering collaboration and creative work (see Chapter 25). Regarding 'team autonomy and informality' we learn that teams need operational autonomy to make decisions about their own work, something which is only possible within a reasonably flat hierarchy that encourages engagement, (some) rule breaking, and participative behaviour.

Working on complex projects can drain energy and cause friction and tension, both within a team and with the surrounding organization. Being able to work in an atmosphere of psychological safety and where small tests and mistakes are allowed is crucial. Thus, some of the cultural traits of DT offer possibilities for working with complex problems, but they may also result in friction in an organization where the cultural gap with DT is large. For example, in an organization which is not open to complexity and ambiguity, that is short-term focused, characterized by micro-management and that only favours linear and structured work (Carlgren & BenMahmoud-Jouini, 2021), this can cause problems.

Organizing a complex project consists mainly of coordinating learning through self-organizing higher-order principles (Kogut & Zander, 1992). DT can be used to influence organizational design on micro- and macro-levels on purpose as well as being a result of using DT over time. Indeed, it has sometimes been used to tackle problems that affect the organization such as redesigning internal policies that were hindering day-to-day work, bridging silos of the organization to establish discussion and transversality, or redesigning employee assessment systems that favour collaboration rather than individual effort.

In particular, DT has been increasingly adopted to design innovative organizational forms (Magistretti et al., 2021) that are able to reinvent themselves. DT is therefore considered a dynamic capability in its own right (Liedtka, 2020). As such, recent research has addressed how organizations can nurture such a capability (Sahakian & BenMahmoud-Jouini, 2021).

16.6 CORRESPONDENCES AND COMPLEMENTARITY BETWEEN DESIGN THINKING AND COMPLEX PROJECT ORGANIZING

Having adopted three perspectives (cognitive, learning, and organizational) in the presentation of the two fields (DT and CPO), we have initiated a conversation that we summarize in Table 16.1 where we highlight the characteristics of complex projects and the elements of DT that can contribute to CPO.

Table 16.1   A conversation between complex project organizing and design thinking

Complex project organizing	Design thinking
Cognitive perspective	
- Representation of interdependent, interrelated, and incomplete elements	- Divergent and iterative thinking
	- Framing and reframing
- Necessity for an open and dynamic representation	- Subjective ways of knowing through intuition and by being human centric
- State of nature versus state of mind	
- A call for representations and images that emphasize comprehensibility over formalism and rigor	- Visualizing emergent understanding of problems and solutions
	- Knowledge creation and validation through assumption
- Representation of the activities and their dependencies in order to act and learn rather than to plan	identification and testing
Emergent prototypes of incomplete knowledge	Visualization in synthesis work, rapid prototyping
Processual perspective	
Boundedly planned	Experimental process rather than a planning process
Coordinating the combination and the creation of knowledge	- Iterations between divergent and convergent phases in multiple short cycles
	- Using tools and methods that encourage collaboration and integration
	- Non-linear perspective
Organizational perspective	
High-order principles (flexibility, agility, autonomy)	Iteration, motivation to learn, motivation to change the world
- Sharing the experience of collective action rather than having a shared collective meaning upfront	- Specific culture of innovation
	- Sense of purpose
- Community of learners	- Autonomy
Specific role of top management (framing problems rather than control)	Top managers ensure safety and support conducive to creativity and risk taking
- Evolving team and stakeholders	Collaboration and inclusion
- Shaping the organization (separating-allocating and integrating-collaborating)	

REFERENCES

Ahern, T., Leavy, B. & Byrne, P. J. (2014). Complex project management as complex problem solving: A distributed knowledge management perspective. *International Journal of Project Management*, 32(8), 1371–1381.

Auernhammer, J. & Roth, B. (2021). The origin and evolution of Stanford University's design thinking: From product design to design thinking in innovation management. *Journal of Product Innovation Management*, 38(6), 623–644.

Bakhshi, J., Ireland, V. & Gorod, A. (2016). Clarifying the project complexity construct: Past, present and future. *International Journal of Project Management*, 34(7), 1199–1213.

Beckman, S. L. S. & Barry, M. (2007). Innovation as a learning process: Embedding design thinking. *California Management Review*, 50(1), 25–56.

BenMahmoud-Jouini, S., Midler, C. & Silberzahn, P. (2016). Contributions of design thinking to project management in an innovation context. *Project Management Journal*, 47(2), 144–156.

Brown, T. (2008). Design thinking. *Harvard Business Review*, 86(6), 84–92.

Brown T. (2009). *Change by design: How design thinking transforms organizations and inspires innovation*. HarperBusiness.

Buchanan, R. (1992). Wicked problems in design thinking. *Design Issues*, 8(2), 5–21.

Buchanan, R. (2015). Worlds in the making: Design, management, and the reform of organizational culture. *She Ji: The Journal of Design, Economics, and Innovation*, 1(1), 5–21.

Carlgren, L. & BenMahmoud-Jouini, S. (2021). When cultures collide: What can we learn from frictions in the implementation of design thinking? *Journal of Product Innovation Management*, 39(1), 44–65.

Carlgren, L., Rauth, I. & Elmquist, M. (2016). Framing design thinking: The concept in idea and enactment. *Journal for Creativity and Innovation Management*, 25(1), 38–57.

Design Council (2005). *Eleven lessons: Managing design in eleven global brands. A study of the design process*. www.designcouncil.org.uk/sites/default/files/asset/document/ElevenLessons_Design _Council%20%282%29.pdf.

Elsbach, K. D. & Stigliani, I. (2018). Design thinking and organizational culture: A review and framework for future research. *Journal of Management*, 44(6), 2274–2306.

Engwall, M. (2003). No project is an island: Linking projects to history and context. *Research Policy*, 32(5), 789–808.

Floricel, S., Michela, J. L. & Piperca, S. (2016). Complexity, uncertainty-reduction strategies, and project performance. *International Journal of Project Management*, 34(7), 1360–1383.

Galbraith, J. R. (2008). Organization design. In T. G. Cummings (Ed.), *Handbook of organization development* (pp. 325–352). Sage Publications.

Hatch, M. J. & Cunliffe, A. L. (2012). *Organization theory: Modern, symbolic and postmodern perspectives* (3rd Ed.). Oxford University Press.

Ireland, V., Gorod, A., White, B. E., Gandhi, S. J. & Sauser, B. (2013). A contribution to developing a complex project management BOK. *Project Perspectives*, 35, 16–25.

Johansson-Sköldberg, U., Woodilla, J. & Çetinkaya, M. (2013). Design thinking: Past, present and possible futures. *Creativity and Innovation Management*, 22(2), 121–146.

Klenner, N. F., Gemser, G. & Karpen, I. O. (2021). Entrepreneurial ways of designing and designerly ways of entrepreneuring: Exploring the relationship between design thinking and effectuation theory. *Journal of Product Innovation Management*, 39(1), 66–94.

Kogut, B. & Zander, U. (1992). Knowledge of the firm, combinative capabilities, and the replication of technology. *Organization Science*, 3(3), 383–397.

Kolb, D. A. (1984). *Experiential learning: Experience as the source of learning and development*. Prentice-Hall.

Krippendorff, K. (1989). On the essential contexts of artifacts or on the proposition that 'design is making sense (of things)'. *Design Issues*, 5(2), 9–39.

Krippendorff, K. (2011). Principles of design and a trajectory of artificiality. *Journal of Product Innovation Management*, 28(3), 411–418.

Lenfle, S. (2008). Exploration and project management. *International Journal of Project Management*, 26(5), 469–478.

Liedtka, J. (2015). Perspective: linking design thinking with innovation outcomes through cognitive bias reduction. *Journal of Product Innovation Management*, 32(6), 925–938.

Liedtka, J. (2020). Putting technology in its place: Design thinking's social technology at work. *California Management Review*, 62(2), 53–83.

Loch, C. H., Solt, M. E. & Bailey, E. M. (2008). Diagnosing unforeseeable uncertainty in a new venture. *Journal of Product Innovation Management*, 25(1), 28–46.

Lockwood, T. (2009). Transition: How to become a more design-minded organization. *Design Management Review*, 20(3), 28–37.

Magadley, W. & Birdi, K. (2009). Innovation labs: an examination into the use of physical spaces to enhance organizational creativity. *Creativity and Innovation Management*, 18(4), 315–325.

Magistretti, S., Ardito, L. & Petruzzelli, A. M. (2021). Framing the microfoundations of design think-ing as a dynamic capability for innovation: Reconciling theory and practice. *Journal of Product Innovation Management*, 38(6), 645–667.

Martin, R. L. (2009). *The opposable mind: How successful leaders win through integrative thinking*. Harvard Business Press.

Martin, R. L. (2011). The innovation catalysts. *Harvard Business Review*, 89(6), 82–87.

Micheli, P., Wilner, S. J., Bhatti, S. H., Mura, M. & Beverland, M. B. (2019). Doing design thinking: Conceptual review, synthesis, and research agenda. *Journal of Product Innovation Management*, 36(2), 124–148.

Morris, P. W. G. (2013). *Reconstructing project management*. Wiley-Blackwell.

Owen, C. (1993). Considering design fundamentally. *Design Processes Newsletter*, 5(3).

Rittel, H. W. J. (1972). On the planning crisis: System analysis of the 'First and Second Generations'. *Bedriftsøkonomen*, 8, 390–396.

Sahakian, J. & BenMahmoud-Jouini, S. (2021). Design as a dynamic capability: A building capability framework. HEC Paris Research Paper. http://ssrn.com/abstract=3894466.

Schön, D. A. (1983). *The reflective practitioner: How professionals think in action*. Basic Books.

Schweitzer, J., Groeger, L. & Sobel, L. (2016). The design thinking mindset: An assessment of what we know and what we see in practice. *Journal of Design, Business and Society*, 2(1), 71–94.

Seidel, V. & Fixson, S. (2013). Adopting design thinking in novice multidisciplinary teams: The applica-tion and limits of design methods and reflexive practices. *Journal of Product Innovation Management*, 30(S1), 19–33.

Shenhar, A. J. (2001). One size does not fit all projects: Exploring classical contingency domains. *Management Science*, 47(3), 394–414.

Shenhar, A. J. & Dvir, D. (2004). How projects differ, and what to do about it. In P. W. G. Morris & J. K. Pinto (Eds), *The Wiley guide to project, program and portfolio management* (pp. 1265–1286). John Wiley & Sons.

Simon, H. A. (1969). *The sciences of the artificial*. MIT Press.

Snowden, D. J. & Boone, M. E. (2007). A leader's framework for decision making. *Harvard Business Review*, 85(11), 68–76.

Taxen, L. & Lillieskold, J. (2008). Images as action instruments in complex projects. *International Journal of Project Management*, 26(5), 527–536.

Verganti, R. (2008). Design, meanings, and radical innovation: A meta-model and a research agenda. *Journal of Product Innovation Management*, 25(5), 436–456.

Verganti, R., Dell'Era, C. & Swan, K. S. (2021). Design thinking: Critical analysis and future evolution. *Journal of Product Innovation Management*, 38(6), 603–622.

Weick, K. E. (1979). The social psychology of organizing (2nd Ed.). Addison-Wesley.

PART III

CHALLENGES OF COMPLEX PROJECT ORGANIZING

INTRODUCTION TO PART III

Maude Brunet

Part III provides authoritative reviews of particular research questions in the field of complex project organizing. Challenges in project organizing are numerous, bearing important theoretical and practical implications. As Geraldi et al. (2021) suggest, emphasizing complexity in project organizing research can yield important insights and so is an important line of research enquiry. As we have been arguing throughout this book, there are all sorts of 'complexities'. Shenhar and Dvir (2007) developed the diamond model consisting of four dimensions: system complexity; technological complexity; novelty; and pace. While the first two dimensions relate to static complexity (Chapter 3), the other two are more dynamic in essence (Chapter 14). Building on that initial model, Winch et al. (2022) distinguished organizational from technological complexity. This relates to a fundamental distinction between technical complexity (inherent in the artefact being delivered) and social complexity (inherent in the stakeholder environment). Geraldi et al. (2011) introduced this concept as socio-political complexity. Schoper (2021) referred to it as stakeholder complexity. A third distinction can be made between complexity as a state of mind (Snowden & Boone, 2007) and as a state of nature (e.g., Weaver, 1948). Additionally, uncertainty and complexity are at different levels of analysis – complexity at the organizational level and uncertainty at the decision-making level (Chapter 14).

While we could have developed many other interesting topics, we have focused on four overarching themes to address challenges of complex project organizing: organizational structures; inter-organizational relationships; stakeholders; and project value creation. While each topic gathers several chapters which may address distinctive facets of complexity, those topics are presented in a continuum, from the more static, system complexity (organizational structures), then socio-political complexity (inter-organizational relationships and stakeholders), to finish with a more subjective complexity (project value creation, as a state of mind).

The first theme tackles organizational structures and is based mainly on structural complexity (Floricel et al., 2018). Yet, organizational structures also carry important dynamic interrelations and interdependencies. Chapter 17 presents the project-based firm with its core operational capability being project organizing. While project-based firms can be found in many distinctive sectors, they organize their operations to deliver to their clients on a project basis, which brings specific challenges. Chapter 18 addresses the challenge around project governance, as a way to ensure that the organizational portfolio is in accordance with its strategic priorities, but more narrowly to ensure that each project is delivered efficiently (Ahola et al., 2014). Chapter 19 turns to challenges of new product development, as a key source of competitive advantage in a firm's innovation capability. Strategies suggested to boost performance in a dynamic environment are ambidexterity, agility, and adaptiveness. Chapter 20 sheds light on organizational project management (Sankaran et al., 2017). Four research strategies are presented, whether the focus is *in* or *around* the organization, and depending on whether organizational project management is considered as a *thing* or as a *process*.

The second theme focuses on inter-organizational relationships, which generate much dynamic and network complexity (Gorod et al., 2018). Chapter 21 uncovers governing inter-organizational relationships in large projects, as tensions arise around control and coordination needs. Whereas control protects an organization from potential opportunism, coordination allows adjusting partners' actions to achieve jointly determined goals. Chapter 22 presents public–private partnerships as vectors of complexity. As complex public projects always rely on private-sector firms, addressing the different inherent values and institutional logics of the private firms versus the public owner is highly relevant (Matinheikki et al., 2021). Chapter 23 exposes the main challenges around megaprojects, which revolve around their performance, their collaboration mechanisms including the need to consider multiple cultures, along with their leadership (Drouin et al., 2021).

The third theme brings many challenges for complex project organizing relating to stakeholders, their engagement, and their management (McGrath & Whitty, 2017). Chapter 24 proposes a framework based on structural, socio-political, and emergent complexity to discuss how project complexity influences stakeholder management. Challenges revolve around adopting a managing *of* stakeholders approach while opportunities are greater if the project owner chooses a managing *for* stakeholders approach (Eskerod et al., 2015). Chapter 25 turns to dynamics within the project teams, as project teaming is proposed as a perspective building on four pillars of psychological safety, experimentation, collaboration, and reflection (Edmondson, 2012). Teaming can be a real asset for complex project organizing, yet requires investment in leadership qualities, learning orientation, and collaborative mindset. Chapter 26 presents causal mapping as a technique to integrate risk, uncertainty, and stakeholders. By exploring several complexity factors such as heterogeneous stakeholder project objectives, effective negotiation and engagement can be developed along with strategies to address anticipated difficulties. Chapter 27 gives insights into research on project narratives, and how they shape the project vision, identity, and image to improve the project management practice (Sergeeva & Winch, 2021). Directions for research are suggested, including using theoretical lenses such as sensemaking, social identity theory, and organizational power to help understand narrative practices in project settings and their effects.

The last theme of this part is about project value creation (Martinsuo et al., 2019), and can broadly relate to complexity as a state of mind, also referred to as complicatedness (Chapter 3). Chapter 28 tackles project value creation in a project network. As value creation in projects is especially challenging when dealing with multiple stakeholders, several avenues are proposed, such as sensemaking and negotiation, shaping and co-creation, and monitoring and control. Chapter 29 offers a reconceptualization of project success. As this concept is rather vague, it is suggested that this notion be further 'complexified' by including efficiency, sustainability, uncertainty, and stakeholder views within. As such, it is suggested that project success be considered as multidimensional, contingent, and dynamic in nature. Chapter 30 suggests that we should uncover the fundamental role of the project owner, its function, and responsibilities, as the owner is ultimately responsible for achieving value and realizing the project benefits. Thus, project owners should develop a set of capabilities to capture project value, such as strategic, commercial, and governance capabilities. Chapter 31 argues that addressing sustainability creates complexity. Yet it is suggested that we embrace complexity to achieve sustainable projects, embedding sustainable objectives within project organizing.

REFERENCES

Ahola, T., Ruuska, I., Artto, K., & Kujala, J. (2014). What is project governance and what are its origins? *International Journal of Project Management*, 32(8), 1321–1332.

Drouin, N., Sankaran, S., Van Marrewijk, A., & Müller, R. E. (2021). *Megaproject leaders: Reflections on personal life stories*. Edward Elgar Publishing.

Edmondson, A. C. (2012). *Teaming: How organizations learn, innovate, and compete in the knowledge economy*. John Wiley and Sons.

Eskerod, P., Huemann, M., & Savage, G. (2015). Project stakeholder management – past and present. *Project Management Journal*, 46(6), 6–14.

Floricel, S., Piperca, S., & Tee, R. (2018). Strategies for managing the structural and dynamic consequences of project complexity. *Complexity*, 3190251.

Geraldi, J., Maylor, H., & Williams, T. (2011). Now, let's make it really complex (complicated). *International Journal of Operations and Production Management*, 31(9), 966–990.

Geraldi, J., Söderlund, J., & van Marrewijk, A. (2021). Bright and dark spots in project studies: Continuing efforts to advance theory development and debate. *Project Management Journal*, 52(3), 227–236.

Gorod, A., Hallo, L., & Nguyen, T. (2018). A systemic approach to complex project management: Integration of command-and-control and network governance. *Systems Research and Behavioral Science*, 35(6), 811–837.

Martinsuo, M., Klakegg, O. J., & van Marrewijk, A. (2019). Editorial: Delivering value in projects and project-based business. *International Journal of Project Management*, 37(5), 631–635.

Matinheikki, J., Naderpajouh, N., Aranda-Mena, G., Jayasuriya, S., & Teo, P. (2021). Befriending aliens: Institutional complexity and organizational responses in infrastructure public–private partnerships. *Project Management Journal*, 52(5), 453–470.

McGrath, S. K., & Whitty, S. J. (2017). Stakeholder defined. *International Journal of Managing Projects in Business*, 10(4), 721–748.

Sankaran, S., Müller, R., & Drouin, N. (2017). *Cambridge handbook of organizational project management*. Cambridge University Press.

Schoper, Y. (2021). 3 instead of 24 – complete closure of the A40 motorway. In N. Drouin, S. Sankaran, A. van Marrewijk, & R. E. Müller (Eds), *Megaproject leaders: Reflections on personal life stories*. Edward Elgar Publishing.

Sergeeva, N., & Winch, G. M. (2021). Project narratives that potentially perform and change the future. *Project Management Journal*, 52(3), 264–277.

Shenhar, A. J., & Dvir, D. (2007). *Reinventing project management: The Diamond Approach to successful growth and innovation*. Harvard Business School Press.

Snowden, D. J., & Boone, M. E. (2007). A leader's framework for decision making. *Harvard Business Review*, 85(11), 68–78.

Weaver, W. (1948). Science and complexity. *American Scientist*, 36(4), 536–544.

Winch, G. M., Maytorena-Sanchez, E., & Sergeeva, N. (2022). *Strategic project organizing*. Oxford University Press.

17. Project-based organizations: an overview of an emerging field of research

Jonas Söderlund

17.1 INTRODUCTION

Project-based organizations (PBO) have for decades been a popular organizational solution in a number of industries and sectors, such as construction and complex machinery (Scranton, 2014). The PBO is typically associated with firms assuming the responsibility to deliver capital goods and complex solutions, infrastructure and machinery to external clients (Acha et al., 2004).

However, we also find PBOs in various kinds of creative and knowledge-intensive industries, such as management consulting, advertising and design (DeFillippi, 2016). In these settings, project-based collaboration with external clients and financiers stands at the fore to ensure creative knowledge integration across several knowledge bases (DeFillippi, 2016). In these settings, the PBO becomes an organizational design that seeks to activate the creative and innovative spirit among the participants involved (Lindkvist, 2004), and where they are given the freedom to work within the limits set for the organization. In these settings, the idea of 'temporary decentralization' (Siggelkow & Levinthal, 2003) goes beyond solving the integration problem, but adds a mechanism that improves the creative and innovative potential of the organization and its members.

We define PBOs as those organizations that carry out their main value creation activities and deliveries through projects (Hobday, 2000). Managers turn to PBO as a solution to their problems related to integration and creativity – to make sure that the uniqueness of the clients' demands (Chapter 30) are taken care of, and that the integration of expertise from various domains is done efficiently.

The rise of the PBO in industries beyond construction spurred interest in researching the PBO from a number of scholarly disciplines, including organizational design, strategy, innovation and human resource management (Lundin et al., 2015; Sydow et al., 2004). To account for this development, this chapter provides an overview of research on PBOs and reviews the current state of the art. It demonstrates how research has contributed to our understanding of the nature and design of PBOs, as well as the strategy, capabilities and management challenges associated with them. Based on a review of the literature published in the past 20 years, I give an overview of research on PBOs, beyond the traditional focus on the nature and design of such organizations, to present what I believe is a more adequate and contemporary view that also showcases research on PBOs from perspectives such as strategy, innovation and human resource management, thus demonstrating what we can learn from these separate fields of inquiry about the preconditions and potentials of the PBO. I use Table 17.1 as a map for the overview that highlights some of the main streams of research on PBOs together with examples of core contributions within each of these streams.

Table 17.1   *Project-based organizations: an overview of the literature*

Research stream	Topics and questions	Contributions (examples)
Design of PBOs	Design alternatives for the PBO. Different types of PBOs. Advantages and disadvantages of PBOs.	Hobday (2000); Midler (1995); Miterev et al. (2017); Turner and Miterev (2019); Wheelwright and Clark (1992); Whitley (2006)
Strategy of PBOs	Strategy alternatives for the PBO. Project epochs in the evolution of the PBO. Strategy practices in the PBO. Project-based view on strategy.	Bresnen et al. (2005); Cattani et al. (2011); Lampel (2001); Löwstedt et al. (2018); Söderlund and Tell (2011); Winch and Schneider (1993)
Capabilities and routines of PBOs	The nature significance of project capabilities. The role of project capabilities for growth and innovation. How do PBOs develop project capabilities? What are the critical project capabilities that they need to stay competitive?	Cacciatori and Prencipe (2021); Davies and Brady (2000); Lampel (2001)
Learning and knowledge processes in PBOs	Learning processes in PBOs. Nature of learning in PBOs. Learning landscapes in PBOs. What problems of learning do PBOs experience? How do they transfer knowledge across projects?	Grabher (2004); Newell et al. (2006); Prencipe and Tell (2001); Scarbrough et al. (2004); Sydow et al. (2004); Wiewiora et al. (2020)
Managing PBOs	Governance in PBOs. Managing human resources in PBOs. Managing innovation in PBOs. Management control in PBOs.	Arvidsson (2009); Engwall and Jerbrant (2003); Keegan and Turner (2002); Keegan et al. (2018); Lindkvist (2004); Müller et al. (2015); Samimi and Sydow (2021)

17.2   THE DESIGN OF PROJECT-BASED ORGANIZATIONS

The PBO is called for in situations where there is a strong need for problem-solving across functional departments and experts with different backgrounds, for instance across mechanical and electrical engineering in the automotive industry. However, where there are limited interdependencies and rates of change within disciplines, then functional organization would be more advantageous. This line of thinking dominates classic organizational theory (Chapter 6), beginning with Lawrence and Lorsch (1967) and their work on projects as integration and Galbraith's (1973) continuation on the matrix architecture of the corporation. This is also the kind of contingency theory argument we find in some research on PBOs, such as Wheelwright and Clark (1992). This has been, and still very much is, the story of PBOs, and even today is very much the dominant line of reasoning when practitioners address the underlying motives for adopting a project-based organizational structure. However, this is not the complete story. There is a number of indications that projects are used purposefully to drive innovation, to create a more dynamic organization, to shake up traditional rigid structures, to create improved preconditions for learning and knowledge integration and to better govern the organization, to name a few of the diverse and many underlying reasons (Morris, 1994; Pettigrew et al., 2003). Traditional literature on PBOs (and matrix organizations) does not always reflect this broadening spectrum of PBO where the move towards the PBO is seen predominantly as a way to improve coordination and communication across functional units (Ford & Randolph, 1992).

In that respect, one might argue that conventional literature on PBOs has circled very much around that so-called 'integration problem' and less so around the 'creativity problem'.

Moreover, the PBO has a number of other salient characteristics (Söderlund & Tell, 2011), which are called for in specific situations. It is typically observed in situations where market conditions are differentiated and dynamic and where the output type produced by the organization is customized and involves a large number of subsystems and a bundle of services and products. The user involvement is typically high in the PBO, due to the extreme degree of customization, having normally many people from the client organization involved in the project. The production logic is unit- and deadline-centred. The output is one-off in this context. Moreover, the economic rationale of the organization, contrary to the mass production logic of scale and scope (Scranton, 2014), rests with economies of system (Nightingale et al., 2003) – that is, to be able to integrate and reap the benefits of the interaction between multiple subsystems. Furthermore, and in line with conventional structural contingency theory, PBOs typically deal with non-routine technology and reciprocal interdependencies between activities and tasks (Thompson, 1967).

The nature of tasks of the PBO can also be described as heterogeneous, infrequent and causally ambiguous (Prencipe & Tell, 2001). Looking at the structure of organizations, one might say that the problem typically associated with PBOs is nearly decomposable or even non-decomposable. The unit of production is the project – often involving multiple teams who bring the project to fruition. Team logic and coordination among teams within the PBO call for horizontal communication (Mintzberg, 1979). The decision structure, as mentioned earlier, can be viewed as one of 'temporary decentralization' – in that the responsibility for a project is decentralized to a separate management structure, though only temporarily; when the project is completed, the responsibility is returned to the upper management echelon.

There is an increasing interest in the variation among PBOs, and several studies have identified differences among them. Some might be working with tasks that are more or less singular – that the output might be highly unique or somewhat more routine. Another important characteristic concerns the separation of work roles. Whitley (2006) points out that in situations where there is a high degree of stability among work roles, then the role of the organization might be less prominent. From these two parameters, Whitley (2006) distinguished four kinds of PBO: organizational, craft, precarious and hollow. The organizational PBO produces multiple and varied outputs with different and changeable skills and roles, for instance, the typical management consulting firm. The craft PBO produces multiple incrementally related outputs with distinct and stable roles and skills. This kind of PBO is common in the advertising industry and some information technology consulting firms. The precarious and hollow types are different in that they operate to a much greater extent with a high degree of singularity in their output. The precarious PBO produces risky and unusual projects with varied and changeable skills and roles. This would be rather common in some biotechnology and software firms. The hollow PBO produces highly unique projects in contexts where work roles are relatively stable. In such situations, one might expect the organization as such to be rather weak, running the risk of providing little value and knowledge accumulation. This could, according to Whitley, be the case in film making and even one-off construction. Indeed, the organization may serve other purposes from financial and marketing viewpoints, but from a strictly organizational viewpoint, the organization might run the risk of becoming merely an administrative apparatus, as discussed by DeFillippi and Arthur (1998) in their analysis of the film-making industry.

More recent research has suggested several approaches for how to make distinctions among PBOs with regards to a range of other variables as well. In that regard, research has moved beyond the interdependence, complexity, uncertainty, singularity, role separation and knowledge development variables that have dominated so far in much research on the design of PBOs.

17.3 STRATEGY IN PROJECT-BASED ORGANIZATIONS

Within much of the project management literature and some of the more conventional strategy literature, projects have largely been seen as vehicles for strategy implementation. In that respect, much of the research on PBOs has addressed how these organizations implement strategy through projects. However, research into strategy and PBOs has detected some unique elements inherent in them when it comes to strategy formation (Mintzberg, 1979; Mintzberg & McHugh, 1985; Winch & Schneider, 1993). Researchers have pointed out the role of individual projects in driving and changing the strategy of the firm; the way projects create a stream of actions that constitutes the strategy of the firm; the unique character of business models within PBO (Kujala et al., 2010), which underlines that strategy, looks somewhat different in contexts of complex and dynamic environments.

Lampel (2001) identified three primary strategies that PBOs adopt for the delivery of complex projects: focusing, switching and combining. They differ primarily with regards to how the PBO relates to its current competencies and capabilities. The focusing strategy is associated with firms that are concentrating on conducting similar kinds of projects, within established areas of technology and knowledge. It is principally oriented towards maintaining existing capabilities and competencies. The switching strategy centres more on business opportunities with fewer restrictions by current competencies and capabilities; it also centres on a greater acknowledgement of business as well as technical risks. The combining strategy is a combination of the focusing and switching strategies. This framework was further developed by Söderlund and Tell (2011), who elaborated two primary distinctions between PBOs primarily giving emphasis to exploitation (building on current capabilities) or firms engaging in projects that were more exploratory. They also drew on project marketing researchers capturing the entrepreneurial element of strategy as either being primarily deterministic or predominantly voluntaristic. The latter centres on firms that to a greater extent seek to challenge the status quo, that are more entrepreneurial in their orientation, and focus to a greater extent on shaping strategy options and creating project opportunities. This distinction paved the way for four strategy archetypes among PBOs: focusing, shifting, combining and switching (see Table 17.2).

Within the project management literature, there has developed a strong interest beyond that of doing projects right. This research has generally addressed the question of how firms can do better projects, for instance through shaping better projects and selecting the best projects (Morgan et al., 2008). This stream of research has marked the close bond between strategy and project management, and generally highlighted the importance of project selection for strategy implementation, which has also emerged into a more articulate address of project-based view of strategy that extends beyond the context of the PBO (Cattani et al., 2011).

Several studies have underscored the importance of understanding strategy in PBOs from a comprehensive and evolutionary point of view. These studies suggest that there is a par-

Table 17.2   *Strategies in project-based organizations*

	Focusing	Shifting	Combining	Switching
Main characteristics	Strategy builds on current core competencies and seeks to comply with client needs and select those projects that are in line with current core competencies	The strategy capitalizes on new opportunities and to a lesser extent on core competencies. The strategy seeks to comply with client needs, but is deliberately seeking new clients or type of clients	The strategy departs from current core competencies, but it seeks to address the formulation and development of projects in order to affect client preferences and thereby ensure that projects are in line with current core competencies	The strategy departs from opportunities and to a lesser extent from current core competencies. The strategy is intended to affect client needs, or search actively for new clients by redefining projects
Key processes	Anticipation, project identification and screening	Anticipation, project identification and screening	Definition and redefinition, network construction, project creation	Definition and redefinition, network construction, project creation
Strategic risks	Willing to take technological risks but not business risks	Willing to take both technological and business risks	Willing to take technological risks but not business risks	Willing to take both technological and business risks
Core competencies	Evaluative, technical	Evaluative, technical	Entrepreneurial, relational	Entrepreneurial, relational
Capability formation	Focus on related set of competencies, competencies select project opportunities, project learning increase inter-competency integration	Focus on search for lucrative opportunities, stretch competencies to serve opportunities, maintain a loose relationship among competencies	Focus on related set of competencies, competencies select project opportunities, project learning increase inter-competency integration	Focus on search for lucrative opportunities, stretch competencies to serve opportunities, maintain a loose relationship among competencies

Source: Based on Lampel (2001); Söderlund and Tell (2011).

ticular dynamic associated with strategy formation in the PBO. For instance, Mintzberg and McHugh (1985) elicit a number of strategic periods in the history of the National Film Board in Canada. Whittington et al. (2006) continued along these lines and emphasized the central-ity of linking strategizing with organizing to understand strategy processes in PBOs. More recently, Söderlund and Tell (2009) analysed four primary 'project epochs' in the history of Asea Brown Boveri between 1950 and 2000. During each of these project epochs, a particular kind of project dominated that called for particular approaches to project shaping and project implementation. Löwstedt et al. (2018) presented a strategy-as-practice perspective on PBOs, emphasizing how strategy practices intermingle with project practices to shape strategy. In particular, this study demonstrated the role of projects and project practices in shaping strategy while maintaining the evolutionary understanding of strategy development in the PBO.

17.4   CAPABILITIES AND ROUTINES OF PROJECT-BASED ORGANIZATIONS

Organizational capabilities have been singled out as critical for the understanding of the nature and functions of organizations and firms; it is no surprise therefore that organizational capabilities have also been investigated in the context of PBOs. Davies and Brady (2000) observed that the growth of firms seems to depend upon the ability to transfer solutions from one type of project to the next and to create new organizational units that can take on new projects and repeat the solutions from prior projects. Project capabilities refer to key activities, including bidding, project setup and project organization, that are fundamental to delivering complex projects to external clients. There seems to be less scope for routinized learning in such low-volume contexts, but still 'economies of repetition', they argue, play a decisive role in the ability of firms to carry out a growing number of similar projects at lower costs with higher efficiency: Davies and Brady (2000, p. 932) pointed out that rather than embarking on one-off projects, firms can offer 'repeatable solutions' by transferring experience from one bid or project for others in the same line of business.

Besides investigating project capabilities essential for growth and diversification in project business, research has also explored the nature of core competence in PBOs. Lampel (2001) identified a set of core capabilities critical for the sustainability and success of PBOs under-scoring the importance of entrepreneurial competencies, technical competencies, evaluative competencies and relational competencies. The entrepreneurial competencies concern the cre-ation and shaping of projects, and the evaluative competencies relate to the activities needed to determine the business value and risks involved in particular projects. The technical risks and relationship competencies revolve largely around the implementation of projects and the linkages between technical and organizational problem-solving. Other research (Söderlund, 2005, 2008) developed a more fine-grained framework of project capabilities in PBOs by pointing out the dynamic relationship between project generation (project shaping and selec-tion), project organizing (organization and orchestration), project leadership (leadership con-stellation and capacities) and project teamwork (project teaming and knowledge integration) as four distinct building blocks of project competence needed to build successful PBOs. In particular, these empirical studies underlined how these four capabilities play a significant role in explaining the growth and success of PBOs.

Others have taken a more critical stance toward capability building in PBOs (DeFillippi & Arthur, 1998) and argued that many PBOs, in fact, represent a paradox for strategy. They claim that enterprises that display extreme features of projectification operate at odds with most conventional ideas of strategy and organization, and run the obvious risk of becoming little more than an administrative apparatus that adds little to value creation. The underlying point is that PBOs lack the long-term mechanisms that are needed to accumulate knowledge across projects.

17.5   KNOWLEDGE AND LEARNING IN THE PROJECT-BASED ORGANIZATION

Developing further the research on capabilities, research on PBOs has explored knowledge processes and learning to unveil the problems of learning across projects. This research clearly links with the earlier research on capabilities, although it goes into even more depth with various mechanisms of knowledge transfer and problems related to learning and knowledge transfer (Gann & Salter, 1998; Sydow et al., 2004). Several studies have highlighted the fundamental problems of learning and knowledge development in PBOs because of the unique mode of production and one-off character of their problem-solving (Ekstedt et al., 1999). Grabher (2004) pointed out the two learning processes typical among PBOs: cumulative learning and disruptive learning. In contexts of cumulative learning, the role of the firm is more oriented towards reusing tools, modules and products. In contexts of disruptive learning, the desire is rather to break away from such reuse and challenge existing knowledge. According to Grabher, the firm would have a much stronger role to facilitate such knowledge processes when operating with cumulative learning processes.

Other research has pointed out the different mechanism of learning and knowledge transfer that are common in PBOs. For instance, Prencipe and Tell (2001) distinguish between three learning processes: experience accumulation, knowledge articulation and knowledge codification. The authors suggest that the mechanisms for inter-project learning draw upon these learning processes and can be found at various levels of the PBO (individual, group, firm). From this distinction, they introduced various 'learning landscapes' within PBOs based on their focus on levels of analysis and types of knowledge process. They further argue that the choice between these learning processes largely depends on the frequency of projects, the heterogeneity of projects and the causal ambiguity of projects (cf. Zollo & Winter, 2002).

More detailed studies have explored the specific knowledge governance mechanisms operating in the PBO (Pemsel et al., 2016). Bresnen and colleagues presented a series of detailed studies of the problems that such organizations experience in transferring knowledge across projects (e.g. Newell et al., 2006; Scarbrough et al., 2004). Others have investigated the role of project management tools and boundary objects in ensuring knowledge integration and learning across projects and knowledge communities (Cacciatori, 2008; Sapsed & Salter, 2004). In many ways, these contributions point out the difficulty of learning and knowledge transfer in PBOs, yet they also detail how knowledge articulation, knowledge codification and experience accumulation may be implemented at various levels in the organization.

17.6 MANAGING THE PROJECT-BASED ORGANIZATION

Research on the nature of management has either focused on the more overarching elements addressing its governance (Lindkvist, 2004) and the various mechanisms of governance that are central for competitive PBOs (Müller et al., 2015), or on topics linked to the capabilities and knowledge processes mentioned earlier that focus on how firms seek to develop capabilities and establish learning processes in contexts where this seems particularly difficult. In addition, other important topics include more narrow topics associated with the management of human resources, the management of innovation and management control.

Human resources play a central role in many PBOs, as experts, key resources to work on advanced problem-solving and knowledge workers combing their uniquely held knowledge with experts from other fields. Several scholars have emphasized the rather unique preconditions for managing human resources, highlighting the specific work conditions of people working in PBOs (see Keegan et al., 2018) and team dynamics (Chapter 25). For instance, organizational psychologists have examined the problem of 'project overload' in PBOs that leaves much of the decision authority to the individual worker (Zika-Viktorsson et al., 2006). Bredin and Söderlund (2011) identified four different working conditions in PBOs based on two dimensions: team member intensity (project work as either focused or fragmented) and cross-functionality (project work as either intra-functional or inter-functional).

Others have investigated the unique challenges of innovation in PBOs. Keegan and Turner (2002) suggested that innovation in PBOs is often stifled by various management control systems that focus on project success rather than promoting innovation, identifying an innovation paradox in PBOs. Blindenbach-Driessen and Van den Ende (2006) specifically focused on innovation on new service development projects, developing hypotheses on the differences between success factors for development projects in PBOs and functionally organized firms. Some success factors were more important for PBOs compared to other firms: the application of contingent planning approaches, explicit project selection, senior management support, the availability of sufficient experts, making business cases and testing and launching new services.

Concerning the significance and nature of management control in PBOs, research has highlighted the critical role of management control to allow for integration in the PBO, and how to balance control with flexibility and innovation. De Rooij et al. (2019) suggested a configurational approach to performance management, emphasizing its central role to allow for integration within the PBO. Others have argued for a contingency approach highlighting the role of uncertainty and interdependence among projects in the design of management control systems in PBOs (Canonico & Söderlund, 2010; Engwall & Jerbrant, 2003).

17.7 CONCLUSIONS

As seen from this overview of research there is a rather interesting development of research on PBOs over the last 20 years or so. Research has moved from the classic matrix structure distinction highlighting the advantages and disadvantages of various project-based structures, particularly research focused on how organizations reap the benefits of these structures. It has now become a much more pluralistic field of research, yet still with a clear base relating to the unique characteristics of these distinctive organizations and how they work with their disadvantages and advantages. In particular, it seems that this stream of research has provided openings for interdisciplinarity and that scholars from strategy, innovation and human resource management have entered the field of project studies with the interest to investigate the specific advantages and disadvantages of PBOs. I certainly hope that this development will continue and that research will guide practice in the development of even stronger and better functioning PBOs that are performing well with regards to innovation, human resource management and value creation to clients.

REFERENCES

Acha, V., Davies, A., Hobday, M., & Salter, A. J. (2004). Exploring the capital goods economy: Complex product systems in the UK. *Industrial and Corporate Change*, 13(3), 505–529.

Arvidsson, N. (2009). Exploring tensions in projectified matrix organizations. *Scandinavian Journal of Management*, 25(1), 97–107.

Blindenbach-Driessen, F., & Van den Ende, J. (2006). Innovation in project-based firms: The context dependency of success factors. *Research Policy*, 35(4), 545–561.

Bredin, K., & Söderlund, J. (2011). The HR quadriad: A framework for the analysis of HRM in project-based organizations. *International Journal of Human Resource Management*, 22(10), 2202–2221.

Bresnen, M., Gousseveskaia, A., & Swan, J. (2005). Organizational routines, situated learning and processes of change in project-based organizations. Project Management Journal, 36(3), 27–41.

Cacciatori, E. (2008). Memory objects in project environments: Storing, retrieving and adapting learning in project-based firms. *Research Policy*, 37(9), 1591–1601.

Cacciatori, E., & Prencipe, A. (2021). Project-based organizing and temporary routine dynamics. In M. S. Feldman, B. T. Pentland, L. D'Adderio, K. Dittrich, C. Rerup & D. Seidl (Eds), *Cambridge handbook of routine dynamics* (pp. 407–420). Cambridge University Press.

Canonico, P., & Söderlund, J. (2010). Getting control of multi-project organizations: Combining contingent control mechanisms. *International Journal of Project Management*, 28(8), 796–806.

Cattani, G., Ferriani, S., Frederiksen, L., & Täube, F. (Eds) (2011). *Project-based organizing and strategic management: A long-term research agenda on temporary organizational forms*. Emerald Publishing.

Davies, A., & Brady, T. (2000). Organisational capabilities and learning in complex product systems: Towards repeatable solutions. *Research Policy*, 29, 931–953.

De Rooij, M., Janowicz-Panjaitan, M., & Mannak, R. (2019). A configurational explanation for performance management systems' design in project-based organizations. *International Journal of Project Management*, 37(5), 616–630.

DeFillippi, R. J. (2016). Managing project-based organization in the creative industries. In C. Jones, M. Lorenzen & J. Sapsed (Eds), *The Oxford handbook of creative industries* (pp. 268–273). Oxford University Press.

DeFillippi, R. J., & Arthur, M. B. (1998). Paradox in project-based enterprise: The case of film making. *California Management Review*, 40(2), 125–139.

Ekstedt, E., Lundin, R. A., Söderholm, A., & Wirdenius, H. (1999). *Neo-industrial organising: Renewal by action and knowledge formation in a project-intensive economy*. Routledge.

Engwall, M., & Jerbrant, A. (2003). The resource allocation syndrome in multi-project management. *International Journal of Project Management*, 21(6), 403–409.

Ford, R. C., & Randolph, W. A. (1992). Cross-functional structures: A review and integration of matrix management and project management. *Journal of Management*, 18(2), 267–294.

Galbraith, J. R. (1973). *Designing complex organizations*. Addison-Wesley.

Gann, D., & Salter, A. (1998). Learning and innovation management in project-based, service-enhanced firms. *International Journal of Innovation Management*, 2(4), 431–454.

Grabher, G. (2004). Temporary architectures of learning: Knowledge governance in project ecologies. *Organization Studies*, 25(9), 1491–1514.

Hobday, M. (2000). The project-based organization: An ideal form for management of complex products and systems? *Research Policy*, 29(7–8), 871–893.

Keegan, A., & Turner, J. R. (2002). The management of innovation in project-based firms. *Long Range Planning*, 35(4), 367–388.

Keegan, A., Ringhofer, C., & Huemann, M. (2018). Human resource management and project-based organizing: Fertile ground, missed opportunities and prospects for closer connections. *International Journal of Project Management*, 36(1), 121–133.

Kujala, S., Artto, K., Aaltonen, P., & Turkulainen, V. (2010). Business models in project-based firms: Towards a typology of solution-specific business models. *International Journal of Project Management*, 28(2), 96–106.

Lampel, J. (2001). The core competencies of effective project execution: The challenge of diversity. *International Journal of Project Management*, 19(8), 471–483.

Lawrence, P., & Lorsch, J. (1967). Differentiation and integration in complex organizations. *Administrative Science Quarterly*, 12(1), 1–47.

Lindkvist, L. (2004). Governing project-based firms: Promoting market-like processes within hierarchies. *Journal of Management and Governance*, 8(1), 3–25.

Löwstedt, M., Räisänen, C., & Leiringer, R. (2018). Doing strategy in project-based organizations: Actors and patterns of action. *International Journal of Project Management*, 36(6), 889–898.

Lundin, R. A., Arvidsson, N., Brady, T., Ekstedt, E., Midler, C., & Sydow, J. (2015). *Managing and working in project society: Institutional challenges of temporary organizations*. Cambridge University Press.

Midler, C. (1995). 'Projectification' of the firm: The Renault case. *Scandinavian Journal of Management*, 11(4), 363–375.

Mintzberg, H. (1979). *The structuring of organizations*. Prentice Hall.

Mintzberg, H., & McHugh, A. (1985). Strategy formation in an adhocracy. *Administrative Science Quarterly*, 30(2), 160–197.

Miterev, M., Mancini, M., & Turner, R. (2017). Towards a design for the project-based organization. *International Journal of Project Management*, 35(3), 479–491.

Morgan, M., Malek, W. A., & Levitt, R. E. (2008). *Executing your strategy: How to break it down and get it done*. Harvard Business Press.

Morris, P. W. G. (1994). *The management of projects*. Thomas Telford.

Müller, R., Pemsel, S., & Shao, J. (2015). Organizational enablers for project governance and governmentality in project-based organizations. *International Journal of Project Management*, 33(4), 839–851.

Newell, S., Bresnen, M., Edelman, L., Scarbrough, H., & Swan, J. (2006). Sharing knowledge across projects: Limits to ICT-led project review practices. *Management Learning*, 37(2), 167–185.

Nightingale, P., Brady, T., Davies, A., & Hall, J. (2003). Capacity utilization revisited: Software, control and the growth of large technical systems. *Industrial and Corporate Change*, 12(3), 477–451.

Pemsel, S., Müller, R., & Söderlund, J. (2016). Knowledge governance strategies in project-based organizations. *Long Range Planning*, 49(6), 648–660.

Pettigrew, A., Whittington, R., Melin, L., Sanchez-Runde, C., Van den Bosch, F. A., Ruigrok, W., & Numagami, T. (Eds) (2003). *Innovative forms of organizing*. Sage.

Prencipe, A., & Tell, F. (2001). Inter-project learning: Processes and outcomes of knowledge codification in project-based firms. *Research Policy*, 30, 1373–1394.

Samimi, E., & Sydow, J. (2021). Human resource management in project-based organizations: Revisiting the permanency assumption. *International Journal of Human Resource Management*, 32(1), 49–83.

Sapsed, J., & Salter, A. (2004). Postcards from the edges: Local communities, global programs and boundary objects. *Organization Studies*, 25(9), 1515–1534.

Scarbrough, H., Swan, J., Laurent, S., Bresnen, M., Edelman, L., & Newell, S. (2004). Project-based learning and the role of learning boundaries. *Organization Studies*, 25(9), 1579–1600.

Scranton, P. (2014). Projects as a focus for historical analysis: Surveying the landscape. *History and Technology*, 30(4), 354–373.

Siggelkow, N., & Levinthal, D. A. (2003). Temporarily divide to conquer: Centralized, decentralized, and reintegrated organizational approaches to exploration and adaptation. *Organization Science*, 14(6), 650–669.

Söderlund, J. (2005). Developing project competence: Empirical regularities in competitive project operations. *International Journal of Innovation Management*, 9(4), 451–480.

Söderlund, J. (2008). Competence dynamics and learning processes in project-based firms: Shifting, adapting and leveraging. *International Journal of Innovation Management*, 12(1), 41–67.

Söderlund, J., & Tell, F. (2009). The P-form organization and the dynamics of project competence: Project epochs in Asea/ABB, 1950–2000. *International Journal of Project Management*, 27(2), 101–112.

Söderlund, J., & Tell, F. (2011). Strategy and capabilities in the P-form corporation: Linking strategic direction with organizational capabilities. In G. Cattani, S. Ferriani, L. Frederiksen and F. Täube (Eds), *Project-based organizing and strategic management* (pp. 235–262). Emerald Publishing.

Sydow, J., Lindkvist, L., & DeFillippi, R. (2004). Project-based organizations, embeddedness and repositories of knowledge: Editorial. *Organization Studies, Special Issue*, 25(9), 1475–1489.

Thompson, J. D. (1967). *Organizations in action: Social science bases of administrative theory*. McGraw-Hill.

Turner, R., & Miterev, M. (2019). The organizational design of the project-based organization. *Project Management Journal*, 50(4), 487–498.

Wheelwright, S. C., & Clark, K. B. (1992). *Revolutionizing product development: Quantum leaps in speed, efficiency, and quality*. Free Press.

Whitley, R. (2006). Project-based firms: New organizational form or variations on a theme. *Industrial and Corporate Change*, 15(1), 77–99.

Whittington, R., Molloy, E., Mayer, M., & Smith, A. (2006). Strategising/organising: Broadening strategy work and skills. *Long Range Planning*, 39(6), 615–629.

Wiewiora, A., Chang, A., & Smidt, M. (2020). Individual, project and organizational learning flows within a global project-based organization: Exploring what, how and who. *International Journal of Project Management*, 38(4), 201–214.

Winch, G. M., & Schneider, E. (1993). Managing the knowledge-based organization: The case of architectural practice. *Journal of Management Studies*, 30(6), 923–937.

Zika-Viktorsson, A., Sundström, P., & Engwall, M. (2006). Project overload: An exploratory study of work and management in multi-project settings. *International Journal of Project Management*, 24(5), 385–394.

Zollo, M., & Winter, S. G. (2002). Deliberate learning and the evolution of dynamic capabilities. *Organization Science*, 13(3), 339–351.

18. Project governance: conceptual and practical challenges in complex project organizing

Ata Ul Musawir

18.1   INTRODUCTION

Project governance broadly refers to the framework within which major project decisions are made (Garland, 2009; Turner, 2020). Depending on how it is defined, it may span the breadth of project decisions from initiation to delivery (PMI, 2016), and/or the complete range of decisions from project conception to benefits realization (Bekker & Steyn, 2009; Thorp, 2007), including programme and portfolio management decisions. Unlike project management that tends to have an operational focus centred on the management of constraints, project governance has a strategic focus that is centred on realizing and optimizing the longer-term business or policy objectives of the key stakeholders (Müller, 2009), with primary emphasis on the investment objectives of the funding organization(s) (Zwikael & Smyrk, 2015).

A holistic approach to project governance comprises two distinct but intertwined objectives and related sets of decisions: (1) ensuring that the collection of projects selected and maintained in the organization's portfolio are in accordance with its strategic priorities, which is primarily accomplished through strategy translation and portfolio management; and (2) ensuring that individual projects are delivered efficiently and in accordance with their respective business cases, which is accomplished through a combination of assurance, oversight, and executive support. For the purpose of this book, project governance does not include the governance of inter-organizational relationships. Effective project governance is a key prerequisite for both project management success, in terms of efficient project delivery within defined constraints (Joslin & Müller, 2016; Musawir et al., 2017), as well as long-term project success, in terms of benefits realization and contribution to the achievement of organizational strategic objectives (APM, 2018; Turner et al., 2010).

The challenges of developing and implementing an effective governance system become more pronounced in the context of complex projects, wherein the traditional rigid and passive approach to governance is likely to be ineffective. Here, a system refers to 'a regularly interacting or interdependent group of items forming a unified whole' (as defined in the Merriam-Webster dictionary, 2019). In this case, the 'items' are governance elements such as policies, roles, responsibilities, structures, processes, etc. that altogether comprise the project governance system. The increasing size, uncertainty, and strategic significance of projects, as well as the accelerating pace of technological developments, serve to further compound this complexity. This chapter discusses the various conceptual and practical challenges pertaining project governance in the context of complex projects. It begins with an examination of the conceptual roots of project governance and describes the two main perspectives that have emerged in theory and literature. A holistic approach to project governance that integrates the two perspectives is subsequently proposed. Furthermore, some of the key practical challenges in the governance of complex projects are discussed and the relevant guidelines from the literature are summarized. Finally, future research directions for advancing project governance theory and practice are presented.

18.2   CONCEPTUAL FOUNDATIONS AND LINKS TO CORPORATE GOVERNANCE

The conceptual roots of governance can be traced back to the political science discipline, wherein it refers to the duties and actions of governments to achieve societal objectives (Volden & Samset, 2017). However, although the original use of the term was in the context of state-level affairs, governance has evolved to broadly refer to the 'modes and manner of governing' and has been applied to various contexts (Jessop, 1998). When governance is applied to the context of permanent organizations, it is referred to as corporate governance or organizational governance. In the context of projects, it is referred to as project governance.

The overarching dual aim of corporate governance is the creation and maintenance of sustainable value for the organization and its stakeholders while ensuring that the organization is being run in a responsible and ethical manner (OECD, 2015). Projects are an integral part of an organization's work and hence fall under the purview of corporate governance. Indeed, the general consensus in the literature is that project governance is a subset of corporate governance (Müller, 2009; Williams et al., 2010), i.e., the part of corporate governance that assumes delegated responsibility for the direction, oversight, and control of projects (APM, 2011). The alignment between project governance and corporate governance is necessary to ensure the alignment of an organization's projects with its strategic objectives (Hazard & Crawford, 2004).

The roots of the project governance literature lie predominantly in corporate governance research and theories, such as principal agent theory, stakeholder theory, and resource dependence theory, being applied to the context of project management (Biesenthal & Wilden, 2014). However, the link between corporate governance and project governance has diminished significantly in subsequent theoretical developments in the project governance literature (Bekker, 2015; Marnewick & Labuschagne, 2011). Although some studies have attempted to re-establish this link by conceptualizing project governance based on corporate governance principles, there remains a lack of a tenable link between the two (Marnewick & Labuschagne, 2011).

According to Bekker (2015), one likely cause is that existing conceptualizations of project governance have been driven from a 'project management' perspective, which is narrow and limited in its ability to provide concise governance guidelines due to the wide array of project types and structures. Hence, there is a need to shift to a strategic perspective that takes a broader view of projects from the standpoint of the project sponsor and top management, which is described by Bekker (2015) as the 'corporate governance' perspective. The following section contrasts these two views and describes a holistic conceptualization of project governance.

18.3   A HOLISTIC APPROACH TO PROJECT GOVERNANCE: INTEGRATING THE TWO MAIN VIEWS

One of the most pressing and fundamental issues afflicting the project governance body of knowledge is the lack of a mainstream definition and conceptualization of project governance (Bekker & Steyn, 2009; Pitsis et al., 2014; PMI, 2016), which has persistently impeded theoretical and practical developments in the field (Musawir et al., 2020; Roe, 2015). Different authors ascribe a wide range of meanings to the term, often depending on the respective backgrounds, perspectives, and interpretations of the authors (Bekker & Steyn, 2009). Furthermore, there are inconsistencies in how the scope of the term 'project governance' is delineated. It is sometimes used in a broad sense to refer to the governance of portfolios, programmes, projects, and project management (Müller, 2009), while in other cases it is used in a narrow sense to refer to the governance of individual projects (PMI, 2016). The tension between these two views may explain why the literature is bifurcated into two streams, as identified by Ahola et al. (2014). The first stream corresponds to a 'big picture' view of project governance that focuses on the collective strategic implications of an organization's projects, whereas the second stream corresponds to a 'narrow' view of project governance that focuses on the outcomes of individual projects.

   This dichotomy is a recurring theme in the literature and can be observed in the distinctions between the 'corporate governance' versus 'project management' perspectives of project governance proposed by Bekker (2015); between portfolio management and assurance aspects of governance described by Winch (2014); between organizational and project management office-level governance versus project-level governance described by Biesenthal and Wilden (2014); between the governance of complex change across the enterprise versus governance of individual change initiatives proposed by APM (2018); and between organizational project management, portfolio, and programme governance versus project governance proposed by PMI (2016). However, it is most effectively and rigorously captured in the distinction between governance of projects and project governance proposed by Müller and colleagues (Müller et al., 2014, 2015, 2016, 2017). The former refers to the governance of groups of projects that takes place at the programme, portfolio, and corporate or board levels. The aim of governance at these levels is to ensure that project outputs and outcomes support the realization of required benefits and the creation of long-term business value (Müller et al., 2014). The latter refers to the governance of individual projects. It occurs at the interface of an individual project with its funding organization and other stakeholders (Müller et al., 2014). The aim of governance at this level is to support project decision making and providing oversight and control to ensure successful project delivery.

   In sum, these studies are indicative of the bidimensional nature of the broader project governance construct, i.e., governance in the realm of projects (Müller et al., 2014, 2015, 2016). Both 'big picture' and 'narrow' views of project governance serve different but complementary purposes. Hence, they should not be viewed as competing perspectives but rather should be integrated into a holistic project governance system that seeks to simultaneously ensure the efficient delivery of individual projects as well as collectively optimizing the realization of benefits and strategic objectives through investments in projects. An important contribution in this regard is the model of organizational project management developed by Müller et al. (2019) that integrates the two views of governance in the context of projects.

18.4   CHALLENGES OF GOVERNING PROJECTS UNDER COMPLEXITY

The project management discipline has undergone rapid transformation over the past few years (Morris, 2016; Turner et al., 2011). Projects are increasingly becoming larger and more complex, with the involvement of a multitude of diverse stakeholders and participating organizations (Klakegg et al., 2016; Pitsis et al., 2014). Additionally, with the widespread adoption of project management techniques, projects are being conducted in a diverse range of industries with their own idiosyncratic practices and contextual factors. Furthermore, projects are increasingly assuming greater strategic significance as drivers of organizational transformation (APM, 2018; Pitsis et al., 2014), and are simultaneously coming under greater scrutiny to demonstrate their contribution to organizational strategic objectives (Mir & Pinnington, 2014). The resulting complexity is compounded by the fact that projects are increasingly required to operate in conditions of considerable uncertainty (Klakegg et al., 2016; Pitsis et al., 2014). These trends represent major challenges for developing and implementing an effective project governance system.

18.4.1   From Static to Dynamic Strategy

The accelerating pace of technological development and dynamic nature of markets has led to uncertainty not only in projects but also in permanent organizations. The traditional static model of organizational strategy has been replaced with the dynamic model that views strategy as an evolving process (Thiry & Deguire, 2007; Young et al., 2012). Mintzberg and Waters (1985) explained that in addition to 'deliberate' strategies, which are stable over a long period of time, organizations must also contend with 'emergent' strategies, which evolve in response to changes in the organization's internal and external environment. Furthermore, strategies are also past path dependent, i.e., they are, at least in part, a legacy of past decisions (Barnes et al., 2004). For example, previous decisions may determine whether an organization possesses the required capabilities to pursue a particular strategic direction, or may cause an organization to become 'locked in' to a suboptimal direction (Arthur, 1989).

Since projects essentially drive strategy implementation (Serra & Kunc, 2015), the project governance system must likewise adapt to the increasingly dynamic nature of organizational strategy. This entails an adaptive and responsive approach to governance (Dewulf & Garvin, 2020) and greater engagement with strategy decision makers (Morris & Jamieson, 2005) to ensure that the expected benefits of project investments are achieved, and that strategic projects help to create the capabilities necessary to unlock new directions for strategy, thus enabling organizations to cope with the increasingly complex and dynamic business environment. To develop such an approach, it is important to first examine, using a processual perspective, how abstract project governance frameworks and policies are translated into actual governance practices as well as how these practices evolve over time (Brunet, 2019; Brunet & Aubry, 2018).

18.4.2   Varying Governance Needs of Different Projects

The optimal form of governance for a project may vary based on a number of factors such as the level of complexity (Miller & Hobbs, 2005; Pitsis et al., 2014) and level of risk (Zwikael

& Smyrk, 2015). Standardized governance policies tend to stifle innovative projects that require greater autonomy (Du & Yin, 2009) and isolation from the disturbances from the permanent organization (DeFillippi & Sydow, 2016) in order to succeed. On the other hand, projects that are highly risky or strategically critical may require comprehensive direction and vigilant oversight as failure may lead to catastrophic damage to organizational performance and reputation.

The project delivery approach is another important factor that determines the appropriate project-level governance arrangements. Although the fundamental principles of governance apply equally to both predictive and agile approaches, some additional considerations are required for the latter (APM, 2016). For example, the governance of agile projects should be geared towards multiple incremental deliveries, where planning horizons are short and the full scope of the project investment cannot be defined at the start (Lappi et al., 2018). Under such circumstances, the governance system needs to be less rigid and more conducive to frequent changes, so long as they result in the greatest value delivered (APM, 2016). Furthermore, the governance system should adopt a facilitative stance towards self-organizing project teams by empowering them to take decisions with minimal bureaucratic burden (APM, 2016).

Therefore, a pluralistic approach to project governance is required to accommodate the increasing diversity of projects and their respective governance needs (Aubry, 2016). Indeed, Klakegg et al. (2016) warn that a governance framework relying purely on formal mechanisms such as stage gates may not be adequate for complex projects. These need to be supplemented with informal mechanisms based on decision makers' intuitive and instinctive judgements to create a more balanced and flexible approach to governance (Klakegg et al., 2016).

18.4.3   Public Infrastructure and Megaproject Governance

The largest and most complex projects are typically undertaken by the public sector or through public–private partnership (PPP) arrangements. A substantial body of knowledge in the literature is dedicated to exploring the governance challenges in this context. These projects are embedded in various institutional, political, legal, and social contexts that add several layers of complexity (Van den Hurk & Verhoest, 2015; Zhang et al., 2015). Furthermore, the decision-making process in these projects is substantially more complex due to the various stakeholders involved, many of whom are from the political sphere, who have different and sometimes competing interests (Van den Hurk & Verhoest, 2015) This leads to tensions between the individual goals of the stakeholders and the overall goals of the project (DeFillippi & Sydow, 2016). Furthermore, projects conducted in the public sector are also prone to perverse incentives, which refers to a situation where stakeholders may take, or push for, decisions out of self-interest with little oversight and accountability for financial and strategic performance (Samset & Volden, 2016). These challenges tend to be more pronounced in the case of megaprojects (Brunet, 2021; Flyvbjerg, 2014; Vukomanović et al., 2021).

18.4.4   Human Factors Contributing to Complexity

While project governance focuses on decision making, scant attention is given in the literature to the decision makers themselves. Research on optimism bias in the project context indicates that human biases have a sizable effect on project planning and estimation which, consequently, also influence actual and perceived performance (Flyvbjerg, 2008; Klakegg et al., 2016). Likewise, strategic misrepresentation may be used by some project participants to distort the facts and exaggerate capabilities to further their personal or organizational interests (Flyvbjerg, 2008). Furthermore, due to institutional and organizational politics in both the public and private sectors, project decisions are often made based on political interests (Williams et al., 2010) and not necessarily on what is objectively in the best interests of the project and key stakeholders. Similarly, at the executive level, dysfunctional advocacy may cause some projects to be favoured over others, leading to suboptimal investments in projects (Lechler & Thomas, 2015). Due to issues like normalization of deviance (Pinto, 2014), governance processes as stated in policies may also be carried out differently in practice. Finally, individual-level political and self-interested behaviour can affect governance outcomes. For example, Thiry and Deguire (2007) note that employees have a tendency to support the status quo as it provides stability and order, which can make it difficult to enact meaningful change in projects.

While the influence of human factors is pervasive, it is not always negative. For example, the literature indicates that a strong and highly engaged project owner is a key determinant of effective governance (Winch & Leiringer, 2016). These individuals play an essential role in identifying warning signs of deteriorating project performance as well as creating the political will at the senior management level to have difficult conversations about project progress and expected outcomes (Winch, 2014).

Despite the critical role of human factors in design, implementation, and outcomes of governance processes, research in this area is severely lacking. Müller and colleagues have once again led the research efforts in this direction by applying governmentality theory to the context of projects and empirically examining the governmentality profiles of projects in various contexts (Müller et al., 2014, 2015, 2016, 2017).

18.5   AN AGENDA FOR FUTURE RESEARCH

Project governance is a field that is ripe with opportunities for meaningful research that can have a substantial positive impact on the wider project management discipline. There has been increasing interest in project governance in not just project management journals but also journals in a wide range of disciplines such as organization studies, engineering management, information technology, and sustainable development (Musawir et al., 2020). However, given the criticality of project governance for ensuring that projects are conducted and delivered efficiently, and that they meet their intended investment objectives, the subject deserves much greater attention.

First and foremost, there is a need to develop an internally consistent and theoretically grounded conceptualization of project governance that represents a holistic approach combining both project-level governance and the governance of projects at the programme and portfolio levels (Müller et al., 2016). Additionally, research on project governance needs to engage with the concept at a more fundamental level to more adequately address the foundational questions such as what it means and what constitutes an effective project governance system, as these questions continue to confound both researchers and practitioners (Roe, 2015; Sergeeva, 2019). Furthermore, by adopting 'as-practice' and processual perspectives, there is a need to develop a greater understanding of how project governance is actually conducted in practice (Brunet, 2019; Brunet & Aubry, 2018).

Much of the existing literature employs qualitative methodologies to describe and evaluate governance arrangements and best practices in their respective fields. There is a need to consolidate and synthesize these insights to formulate middle-range theories of project governance that extend beyond the traditional perspectives of agency theory and transaction cost economics and explain the emergence and effectiveness of the varied governance arrangements observed in practice. This is vital for meaningful theoretical advancements in the field, and would additionally enable a wider use of quantitative methodologies that would contribute towards developing an empirically validated mainstream body of knowledge of project governance.

Second, in the context of large and megaprojects, additional research is needed on governance approaches that emphasize multi-party collaboration such as alliance governance (Hoetker & Mellewigt, 2009) and new public governance (Noone et al., 2021). Furthermore, owing to the urgency of the impending climate crisis, greater attention is required in examining green governance approaches in development projects for supporting sustainability goals (Ibrahim et al., 2020).

Third, given the ever accelerating pace of technological advancement and the emergence of 'black swan' events such as the COVID-19 pandemic, there is a need to explore alternative approaches to governance through the lens of complexity theory. In particular, the complex adaptive systems approach (Duit & Galaz, 2008) may be applied to study the development of robust governance systems that help to build resilience in projects. This approach may also be particularly suitable for studying governance in the context of agile projects (Sweetman & Conboy, 2018).

Fourth, there is a need to recognize that projects are inherently unique and can have widely varying governance needs depending on their characteristics, such as level of complexity and risk involved as well as the broader organizational context within which they exist (DeFillippi & Sydow, 2016; Sydow & Braun, 2018). Therefore, further research is needed to develop detailed guidelines on how the project governance system can be tailored to suit the needs of individual projects (PMI, 2016), as well as how a pluralistic approach to project governance can be developed to accommodate this (Aubry, 2016).

Finally, there is a need to address the gap in the literature on the human side of project governance. The existing process-centric approach employed in much of the extant literature largely neglects the influence of individual, social, political, and cultural factors. Potential avenues for research include examining the impact of political motivations and individual biases on governance decisions as well as how these can be mitigated (Lechler & Thomas, 2015), the influence of personality types on the preferred governmentality approach and the resulting governance outcomes, and competency models for identifying and developing qualified individuals to take on project governance roles and responsibilities.

REFERENCES

Ahola, T., Ruuska, I., Artto, K. & Kujala, J. (2014). What is project governance and what are its origins? *International Journal of Project Management*, 32(8), 1321–1332.

APM (2011). *Directing change: A guide to governance of project management* (2nd ed.). Association for Project Management.

APM (2016). *Directing agile change*. Association for Project Management.

APM (2018). *Directing change: A guide to governance of project management* (3rd ed.). Association for Project Management.

Arthur, W. B. (1989). Competing technologies, increasing returns, and lock-in by historical events. *The Economic Journal*, 99(394), 116–131.

Aubry, M. (2016). Simply, pluralism! *Project Management Journal*, 47(1), 3–6.

Barnes, W., Gartland, M. & Stack, M. (2004). Old habits die hard: Path dependency and behavioral lock-in. *Journal of Economic Issues*, 38(2), 371–377.

Bekker, M. C. (2015). Project governance: The definition and leadership dilemma. In B. Pasian & P. Storm (Eds), *Proceedings of the 2014 IPMA World Congress. Procedia – Social and Behavioral Sciences*, 194, 33–43.

Bekker, M. C. & Steyn, H. (2009). Project governance: Definition and framework. *Journal of Contemporary Management*, 6, 214–228.

Biesenthal, C. & Wilden, R. (2014). Multi-level project governance: Trends and opportunities. *International Journal of Project Management*, 32(8), 1291–1308.

Brunet, M. (2019). Governance-as-practice for major public infrastructure projects: A case of multilevel project governing. *International Journal of Project Management*, 37(2), 283–297.

Brunet, M. (2021). Making sense of a governance framework for megaprojects: The challenge of finding equilibrium. *International Journal of Project Management*, 39(4), 406–416.

Brunet, M. & Aubry, M. (2018). The governance of major public infrastructure projects: The process of translation. *International Journal of Managing Projects in Business*, 11(1), 80–103.

DeFillippi, R. & Sydow, J. (2016). Project networks: Governance choices and paradoxical tensions. *Project Management Journal*, 47(5), 6–17.

Dewulf, G. & Garvin, M. J. (2020). Responsive governance in PPP projects to manage uncertainty. *Construction Management and Economics*, 38(4), 383–397.

Du, Y. L. & Yin, Y. L. (2009). Study on the necessity for establishing the theory of public project governance. In *Proceedings of the 2009 International Conference on Information Management, Innovation Management and Industrial Engineering* (Vol. 3, pp. 599–602). IEEE.

Duit, A. & Galaz, V. (2008). Governance and complexity: Emerging issues for governance theory. *Governance: An International Journal of Policy, Administrations, and Institutions*, 21(3), 311–335.

Flyvbjerg, B. (2008). Curbing optimism bias and strategic misrepresentation in planning: Reference class forecasting in practice. *European Planning Studies*, 16(1), 3–21.

Flyvbjerg, B. (2014). What you should know about megaprojects and why: An overview. *Project Management Journal*, 45(2), 6–19.

Garland, R. (2009). *Project governance: A practical guide to effective project decision making*. Kogan Page Publishers.

Hazard, V. & Crawford, L. H. (2004). Defining project governance. In *Proceedings of ProMAC Research Conference*. Society of Project Management, Nanyang Technological University and Tsinghua University, Japan.

Hoetker, G. & Mellewigt, T. (2009). Choice and performance of governance mechanisms: Matching alliance governance to asset type. *Strategic Management Journal*, 30(10), 1025–1044.

Ibrahim, A., Bartsch, K. & Sharifi, E. (2020). Green infrastructure needs green governance: Lessons from Australia's largest integrated stormwater management project, the River Torrens Linear Park. *Journal of Cleaner Production*, 261, 121202.

Jessop, B. (1998). The rise of governance and the risks of failure: The case of economic development. *International Social Science Journal*, 50(155), 29–45.

Joslin, R. & Müller, R. (2016). The relationship between project governance and project success. *International Journal of Project Management*, 34(4), 613–626.

Klakegg, O. J., Williams, T. & Shiferaw, A. T. (2016). Taming the 'trolls': Major public projects in the making. *International Journal of Project Management*, 34(2), 282–296.

Lappi, T., Karvonen, T., Lwakatare, L. E., Aaltonen, K. & Kuvaja, P. (2018). Toward an improved understanding of agile project governance: A systematic literature review. *Project Management Journal*, 49(6), 39–63.

Lechler, T. G. & Thomas, J. L. (2015). Examining new product development project termination decision quality at the portfolio level: Consequences of dysfunctional executive advocacy. *International Journal of Project Management*, 33(7), 1452–1463.

Marnewick, C. & Labuschagne, L. (2011). An investigation into the governance of information technology projects in South Africa. *International Journal of Project Management*, 29(6), 661–670.

Miller, R. & Hobbs, J. B. (2005). Governance regimes for large complex projects. *Project Management Journal*, 36(3), 42–50.

Mintzberg, H. & Waters, J. A. (1985). Of strategies, deliberate and emergent. *Strategic Management Journal*, 6(3), 257–272.

Mir, F. A. & Pinnington, A. H. (2014). Exploring the value of project management: Linking project management performance and project success. *International Journal of Project Management*, 32(2), 202–217.

Morris, P. (2016). Reflections. *International Journal of Project Management*, 34(2), 365–370.

Morris, P. & Jamieson, A. (2005). Moving from corporate strategy to project strategy. *Project Management Journal*, 36(4), 5–18.

Müller, R. (2009). *Project governance*. Gower Publishing.

Müller, R., Pemsel, S. & Shao, J. (2014). Organizational enablers for governance and governmentality of projects: A literature review. *International Journal of Project Management*, 32(8), 1309–1320.

Müller, R., Pemsel, S. & Shao, J. (2015). Organizational enablers for project governance and governmentality in project-based organizations. *International Journal of Project Management*, 33(4), 839–851.

Müller, R., Zhai, L., Wang, A. & Shao, J. (2016). A framework for governance of projects: Governmentality, governance structure and projectification. *International Journal of Project Management*, 34(6), 957–969.

Müller, R., Zhai, L. & Wang, A. (2017). Governance and governmentality in projects: Profiles and relationships with success. *International Journal of Project Management*, 35(3), 378–392.

Müller, R., Drouin, N. & Sankaran, S. (2019). *Organizational project management: Theory and implementation*. Edward Elgar Publishing.

Musawir, A. u., Serra, C. E. M., Zwikael, O. & Ali, I. (2017). Project governance, benefit management, and project success: Towards a framework for supporting organizational strategy implementation. *International Journal of Project Management*, 35(8), 1658–1672.

Musawir, A. u., Abd-Karim, S. B. & Mohd-Danuri, M. S. (2020). Project governance and its role in enabling organizational strategy implementation: A systematic literature review. *International Journal of Project Management*, 38(1), 1–16.

Noone, J., Salignac, F. & Saunders, I. (2021). How can collaborative practices be supported in an era of new public governance? Lessons from an education initiative. *Australian Journal of Public Administration*, 80(3), 624–637.

OECD (2015). *G20/OECD principles of corporate governance*. Organisation for Economic Co-operation and Development.

Pinto, J. K. (2014). Project management, governance, and the normalization of deviance. *International Journal of Project Management*, 32(3), 376–387.

Pitsis, T. S., Sankaran, S., Gudergan, S. & Clegg, S. R. (2014). Governing projects under complexity: Theory and practice in project management. *International Journal of Project Management*, 32(8), 1285–1290.

PMI (2016). *Governance of portfolios, programs, and projects: A practice guide*. Project Management Institute.

Roe, P. (2015). *The factors which contribute to successful projects*. Bostock Marketing Group.

Samset, K. & Volden, G. H. (2016). Front-end definition of projects: Ten paradoxes and some reflections regarding project management and project governance. *International Journal of Project Management*, 34(2), 297–313.

Sergeeva, N. (2019). Towards more flexible approach to governance to allow innovation: The case of UK infrastructure. *International Journal of Managing Projects in Business*, 13(1), 1–19.

Serra, C. E. M. & Kunc, M. (2015). Benefits realisation management and its influence on project success and on the execution of business strategies. *International Journal of Project Management*, 33(1), 53–66.

Sweetman, R. & Conboy, K. (2018). Portfolios of agile projects: A complex adaptive systems' agent perspective. *Project Management Journal*, 49(6), 18–38.

Sydow, J. & Braun, T. (2018). Projects as temporary organizations: An agenda for further theorizing the interorganizational dimension. *International Journal of Project Management*, 36(1), 4–11.

Thiry, M. & Deguire, M. (2007). Recent developments in project-based organisations. *International Journal of Project Management*, 25(7), 649–658.

Thorp, J. (2007). *The information paradox: Realizing the business benefits of information technology.* Fujitsu Consulting.

Turner, R. (2020). Investigating how governmentality and governance influence decision making on projects. *Project Leadership and Society*, 1, 1–11.

Turner, R., Huemann, M., Anbari, F. T. & Bredillet, C. N. (2010). *Perspectives on projects.* Routledge.

Turner, R., Pinto, J. & Bredillet, C. (2011). The evolution of project management research: The evidence from the journals. In P. W. G. Morris, J. Pinto & J. Söderlund (Eds), *The Oxford handbook of project management* (pp. 65–106). Oxford University Press.

Van den Hurk, M. & Verhoest, K. (2015). The governance of public–private partnerships in sports infrastructure: Interfering complexities in Belgium. *International Journal of Project Management*, 33(1), 201–211.

Volden, G. H. & Samset, K. (2017). Governance of major public investment projects: Principles and practices in six countries. *Project Management Journal*, 48(3), 90–108.

Vukomanović, M., Cerić, A., Brunet, M., Locatelli, G. & Davies, A. (2021). Trust and governance in megaprojects. *International Journal of Project Management*, 39(4), 321–324.

Williams, T., Klakegg, O. J., Magnussen, O. M. & Glasspool, H. (2010). An investigation of governance frameworks for public projects in Norway and the UK. *International Journal of Project Management*, 28(1), 40–50.

Winch, G. M. (2014). Three domains of project organising. *International Journal of Project Management*, 32(5), 721–731.

Winch, G. M. & Leiringer, R. (2016). Owner project capabilities for infrastructure development: A review and development of the 'strong owner' concept. *International Journal of Project Management*, 34(2), 271–281.

Young, R., Young, M., Jordan, E. & O'Connor, P. (2012). Is strategy being implemented through projects? Contrary evidence from a leader in new public management. *International Journal of Project Management*, 30(8), 887–900.

Zhang, S., Gao, Y., Feng, Z. & Sun, W. (2015). PPP application in infrastructure development in China: Institutional analysis and implications. *International Journal of Project Management*, 33(3), 497–509.

Zwikael, O. & Smyrk, J. (2015). Project governance: Balancing control and trust in dealing with risk. *International Journal of Project Management*, 33(4), 852–862.

19. Addressing the challenges of new product development by Triple-A project management

Alexander Kock and Hans Georg Gemünden

19.1 INTRODUCTION

A key source of competitive advantage is a firm's capability to attract, create, and select innovative ideas and concepts for new products, services, and business models and effectively develop and diffuse them. Firms use projects as temporary organisations to manage these tasks effectively and efficiently. Consequently, they professionalised and projectified New Product Development (NPD) (Evanschitzky et al., 2012). First, they used single NPD projects to better integrate the involved corporate functions (e.g., marketing, research and development (R&D), operations) by implementing stage and gate approaches (Cooper & Kleinschmidt, 1995) and heavyweight project management (Clark & Wheelwright, 1992). Second, they used project portfolio management to align their NPD projects to strategic corporate goals, allocate scarce resources according to strategic priorities, leverage synergies between projects, and reduce the overall risk of the NPD portfolio (Cooper et al., 2001; Kester et al., 2014). Third, they used road-mapping, scenario tools, and platform strategies to manage sequences of projects that build on each other to create innovation paths (Midler, 2013). Using a project management lens, we will review these developments, discuss the resulting challenges, and describe how foci shifted over time. For example, for single projects, the focus went to the front end of the process to improve ideation and creativity and to external actors to better utilise external knowledge through open innovation. More recently, new paradigms evolved in dynamic environments comprising agile, ambidextrous, and strategically adaptive NPD.

19.2 MANAGING SINGLE NPD PROJECTS

NPD is a critical function for the competitiveness and growth of firms. It usually requires closely integrating different functions, such as marketing, R&D, operations, procurement, and controlling. To fulfil these requirements, firms delegate NPD to projects with cross-functional teams that should work together closely, share relevant information, and co-create new market–technology combinations that outperform existing products (Sivasubramaniam et al., 2012). Teamwork quality depends on team size, team composition, and leadership (Högl & Gemünden, 2001; Hülsheger et al., 2009). Ideally, a senior executive acts as a project manager with substantial expertise and primary influence over the project team members (Clark & Wheelwright, 1992; Patanakul et al., 2012). These 'heavyweight' NPD managers perform better in securing strategic alignment and creating a shared vision with clear targets (Rauniar et al., 2008). Although practitioners favour autonomous teams, the empirical evidence is mixed. Gemünden et al. (2005) find that organisational autonomy does not necessarily increase NPD performance, and the findings from Patanakul et al. (2012) are also not significant regarding overall performance. Moreover, the study from Szatmari et al. (2020) shows that project managers with a mid-level status perform best on average, whereas project managers with a high-level status produce more extreme results (i.e., they deliver high successes but also severe failures). Thus, we should be more careful in relying on informal status and granting excessive scope to high-level status managers.

Fundamental challenges in NPD mostly derive from innovation's inherent paradox of simultaneously achieving contradicting objectives: on the one hand, organisations want to create divergence and variety to increase creativity, but, on the other hand, they need convergence and alignment to maintain managerial control. NPD project management should therefore contain both open and closed action strategies (Gebert et al., 2010; Kock et al., 2015). Open action strategies such as creative encouragement (Kock et al., 2015), delegated leadership (Gebert et al., 2010), or team diversity (Hülsheger et al., 2009) promote knowledge and idea generation. Closed action strategies such as providing strategic clarity (Salomo et al., 2008), process formalisation (Kock et al., 2015), or directive leadership (Gebert et al., 2010) enhance knowledge integration. Other authors call these tensions and paradoxes *centrifugal and centripetal forces* (Sheremata, 2000) or *hybrid structures* (Brown & Eisenhardt, 1997).

NPD processes typically consist of ideation, development, and commercialisation phases organised by several stages and gates (Cooper & Kleinschmidt, 1995). In each stage, various tasks are fulfilled cross-functionally and assessed in the gates. Cost and risk are typically low in the early stages, with many degrees of freedom for potential solutions. As the cumulative cost and risk increase, the gates become more selective and rigid. Since the earlier study by Cooper and Kleinschmidt (1995), researchers have revised concepts considerably. The focus shifted to the front end of the process to improve ideation and creativity (Elling & Herstatt, 2017; Park et al., 2021; Williams et al., 2019) and to external actors to better utilise external knowledge through open innovation approaches (West & Bogers, 2014). The relative importance of the above-mentioned opposing forces also shifts during the development process's phases. Open action strategies are more important in the early stages than in the later stages. These contradictory requirements for their management make integrating the NPD project's front end with its back end so tricky. Discovering unfulfilled needs and superior technologies that better fulfil needs and formulating new product concepts requires creativity, openness, flexibility, autonomy, and a supportive climate of psychological safety. The development, detailed engineering, testing of concepts, and, finally, the delivery and implementation of user solutions require more formalisation. The front end is essential because this initial design phase determines more than 60 per cent of NPD-related parameters (Talke et al., 2006). Companies should create validated product concepts in the front end through continuous idea refinement and screening, idea alignment, and concept legitimisation (Florén & Frishammar, 2012). Managers can support these front-end activities, for example, using design thinking approaches (Carlgren et al., 2016) and idea crowdsourcing (Zhu et al., 2019).

Similarly, challenges arise because, for NPD projects, 'one size does not fit all'. NPD projects differ in size, complexity, and innovativeness. Regarding size, an increasing number of NPD projects are multi-team systems. Integrating several teams poses additional challenges and follows other mechanisms than within-team integration (Högl et al., 2004). Innovation of complex product systems (Hobday, 1998) delivered by a network of supplier organisations based on a web of coordinated contracts requires specific project management instruments going beyond typical NPD projects. Davies et al. (2014) developed a model derived from London's Crossrail on how to increase innovation in such projects. Roehrich et al. (2019)

address how different organisational structures in a complex-product-system setting change over time to support the process of management innovation.

However, the most substantial contingency factor is innovativeness, a project's novelty regarding technology, market, organisation, and environment, ranging from incremental to radical (Salomo et al., 2007). Innovativeness poses a double challenge. First, companies typically focus too much on incremental innovation and neglect radical innovation. Second, radical innovation requires entirely different management than incremental innovation. For example, Salomo et al. (2007) find that process formalisation and goal clarity are beneficial for incremental NPD projects, but the positive influence diminishes with increasing innovativeness until it becomes negative for radical NPD projects. If managers do not yet know how to reach the goals, traditional gates do not help, and goals do not motivate. Instead, they need extensive exploration of reaching a goal and discovering alternatives that may lead to replacing visions with more realistic goals. Specific success factors of very innovative NPD projects are interventions to open innovation processes and strengthen knowledge creation, exchange, and (re)combination. Teamwork quality (Högl et al., 2003), team co-location (Gemünden et al., 2005), or identifying latent needs through customer ethnography (Salzmann & Kock, 2020) are particularly relevant with higher innovativeness.

Integrating external actors through open innovation poses additional challenges and tension (West & Bogers, 2014). On the one hand, firms have to openly share knowledge to leverage the involved actors' expertise and create new knowledge combinations. On the other hand, participants need to protect themselves from unwanted outcomes such as misappropriation and knowledge leakage. Suggested measures like patents, contracts, selective revealing, or prespecified goals and behaviours may help overcome the tensions but also create additional challenges (Ahlfänger et al., 2022; Gretsch et al., 2020). Finally, lessons from the Covid pandemic show the challenge and importance of accelerating NPD processes (Cooper, 2021). Despite possible hidden costs of acceleration, companies try to reduce cycle time and increase responsiveness in NPD through focused teams (Cooper, 2021), combining stage gate with agile approaches (Bianchi et al., 2020), or establishing agile organisational structures (Meier & Kock, 2022).

19.3   MANAGING NPD PROJECT PORTFOLIOS

Innovation's uncertainty and the high likelihood of project failure require a portfolio perspective on NPD. The NPD portfolio comprises a firm's currently running NPD projects that share the same resources (Cooper et al., 2001; Kester et al., 2014). NPD portfolio management aims to foster conditions that facilitate the generation of creative ideas, establish processes to evaluate these ideas further, and align new idea initiatives with a firm's strategic future business (Kock et al., 2015). It focuses on assessing, prioritising, and selecting a portfolio's (potential) NPD projects and allocating available resources according to strategic priorities (Jonas et al., 2013). NPD portfolio success is multidimensional and aims to (1) maximise the portfolio's value and the project outcomes' commercial success, (2) balance the portfolio, (3) align the portfolio with the firm's strategic objectives, and (4) prepare the company for the future by building new competencies (Kester et al., 2014; Kock et al., 2015).

NPD portfolio management faces several challenges. First, NPD projects themselves are uncertain and difficult to predict because they apply new and uncertain technologies and address uncertain markets (Salomo et al., 2007). The higher the individual project's degree of innovativeness, the higher is the likelihood it will fail. Second, projects are highly interdependent because they share resources, risks, and benefits. This interdependency makes portfolio decisions inherently complex (Teller et al., 2012). Third, the decision process is very political because it involves the company's future and conflicting interests from influential stakeholders, resulting in negotiations, compromises, and decision-making biases (Martinsuo, 2013).

Several practices can help deal with these challenges and lead to more successful portfolios (Martinsuo, 2013; Meifort, 2016). First, it is essential that portfolio stakeholders communicate openly, share common goals, and support and trust each other (Jonas et al., 2013; Kock & Gemünden, 2021). This can be supported by clearly defined processes for portfolio and single project decisions (Schultz et al., 2013; Teller et al., 2012). Furthermore, the innovation strategy should be clearly formulated and communicated, and corporate and portfolio strategic planning should be closely linked so that the strategy is operationalised to the single project level (Kopmann et al., 2017; Salomo et al., 2008). High involvement of senior managers can be beneficial if they follow their own rules and do not regulate every detail (Unger et al., 2012).

To improve NPD portfolios' front end, ideation management can increase the value and feasibility of project candidates (Kock et al., 2015). Ideation management includes a supportive ideation strategy (providing a vision and guardrails aligned with corporate goals), a formalised ideation process (improving idea selection), and creative encouragement (giving employees autonomy, resources, and support for ideas' further development). The front end's positive effect on portfolio success is significantly stronger when companies are willing to take risks and when their NPD portfolios are larger and more complex (Kock et al., 2016). Thus, ideation pays back for large and complex NPD portfolios if the will to take risks is reasonably high. Furthermore, high customer involvement in portfolio boards is important. In their analysis of customer influence, Voss and Kock (2013) found that 'value *for* the customer' and 'value *from* the customer' increased NPD portfolio success.

Finally, decision-makers' fundamental strategic orientations guide their attitude and behaviour. These orientations are critical because they drive the application of other success factors, and more importantly, they can leverage their effects (Kock & Gemünden, 2021). Every managerial measure (e.g., formalisation or monitoring) can have negative side effects requiring an optimal dose to prevent overapplication. Leveraging success factors' effect through the proper strategic orientation can strengthen their impact without further increasing them and deviating from the optimal dose. A particularly important orientation is the entrepreneurial orientation, which is a widely used construct in the strategy and entrepreneurship literature comprising proactiveness, innovativeness, and risk-taking. Kock and Gemünden (2021) show that this mindset leverages the positive influence of several other success factors, such as stakeholder involvement and business case monitoring. This orientation also implies a *willingness to cannibalise* existing products, investments, and capabilities. Tellis et al. (2009) found that willingness to cannibalise is one of the strongest predictors of successful radical new product innovation. Rank et al. (2015) showed that stakeholder cooperation quality, willingness to cannibalise, and willingness to take risks contributed significantly to future preparedness.

19.4   TRIPLE-A PROJECT AND PORTFOLIO MANAGEMENT IN TURBULENT ENVIRONMENTS

Managing projects and portfolios in an increasingly turbulent environment may require new management principles. We call these principles Triple-A because project and portfolio management apply ambidexterity, agility, and strategic adaptiveness.

Ambidexterity means simultaneously performing projects that improve and exploit existing innovations (exploitation) and projects that develop new competencies and create new options (exploration). This balance is challenging because with increasing proficiency in one type of project, the ability in the other type wanes. And in portfolio decisions, exploitation projects tend to look more favourable. Companies can support this through an innovation-supporting culture (Kaufmann et al., 2021a), the use of strategic buckets that ensure balanced investment in radical and incremental innovation projects, or the definition of strategic innovation fields (Salomo et al., 2008). Furthermore, ambidextrous companies know that radical and incremental projects need different management principles (Gemünden et al., 2005; Salomo et al., 2007), which we discussed above. A challenge here is correctly assessing the degree of innovativeness because inappropriately applying practices suitable for the other kind of project may lead to inefficiency or ineffectiveness (Kock et al., 2011). Therefore, it is necessary to assess a project's innovativeness before project selection and continuously until after its completion.

Agility means to apply a set of principles and practices at the level of single innovative projects and at the level of innovation portfolios that increase and accelerate the recognition and implementation of critical benefits. The increased use of agile principles at the project level can be beneficial (Kaufmann et al., 2020) but also leads to complexity for the overall portfolio (Sweetman & Conboy, 2018). At the level of NPD portfolios, agility means flexibly adjusting the portfolio to changing conditions (Kester et al., 2014) and installing iterative portfolio decision-making processes that are continuously adjusted (Kock & Gemünden, 2016). Agility at the portfolio level strongly relates to portfolio success (Kester et al., 2014), however, it requires high decision-making quality and transparency (Kock & Gemünden, 2016). The challenge lies in achieving strategic and operational clarity and establishing a supporting culture to support this decision-making (Kock & Gemünden, 2016; Meier & Kock, 2022).

Adaptiveness means to recognise that, also in NPD, 'Rome was not built in a day'. Successful new products usually build on previous successful (and failed) products to improve functionality, usability, reliability, safety, etc. Therefore, firms develop products like the iPhone, Volkswagen Golf, the Star Wars movies, or the Civilisation strategy game in sequences of projects that describe successful innovation paths. Decision-makers need to think in project sequences, react flexibly to internal and external opportunities, and proactively open up long-term options. In contrast to single projects, which are temporary organisations with a predetermined time horizon, a project sequence building a long-term innovation path is not a temporary organisation because it is uncertain how many elements the sequence will have. Clark and Wheelwright (1992) already acknowledged the importance of project sequencing for building development capabilities. Midler (2013) studied Renault's successful Logan, designed as a low-cost car. Accompanied by aggressive marketing in price-sensitive markets, it established a new brand and product family. He coined the term project lineage for the management of such project sequences. Later Maniak and Midler (2014) extended the concept to multi-project environments. Koch-Ørvad et al. (2019) analysed how a sequence of exploratory projects helped to transform an ecosystem. Davies and Brady (2000) proposed an organisational learning cycle for the innovation of complex product systems, modelling capability building via lessons learned from initial projects and leading to improved project management procedures and higher performance of follow-up projects. Kock and Gemünden (2019) provide quantitative evidence that two principles of project sequence management, proactive and reactive lineage, positively relate to project portfolio success. Reactive lineage means learning from past projects by applying lessons-learned approaches (Ekrot et al., 2016); proactive lineage means recognising options of follow-up projects by planning generations of projects in advance, using tools like road-mapping or scenario analysis (Bengtsson & Lindkvist, 2017). Successful firms *consciously* manage project sequences rather than isolated projects and use established planning and knowledge management practices for their sequence management. Managing project sequences also has a behavioural side. Kaufmann et al. (2021b) found that *team continuity* positively affects the commercial success of movie projects, but with decreasing returns. In the case of innovative projects, the initial effect was higher, but the decreasing effect was stronger so that the two performance impact curves intersect at a medium level of team continuity. Buengeler at al. (2021) find in a study of 5,370 video games development projects several inverted u-shaped relationships between *team continuity* and different market-related measures of business success. So, team continuity pays back in sequences of NPD projects.

High-performing companies achieve strategic adaptiveness in NPD. They better implement deliberate and emergent strategies because they scrutinise their portfolio strategy through strategic monitoring (Kopmann et al., 2017) and incorporate real options reasoning (ROR) in their decision-making. Klingebiel and Adner (2015) define ROR with three elements. First, instead of deciding whether or not to fully finance an option at a certain point in time, the decision-makers distribute the investment sequentially over a period of time. Such distribution enables the option owner to decide on further investment, depending on the asset's development. Second, when applying ROR, only a low investment is initially made in selected options, increasing the autonomy of future decisions. Third, all available options, independent of their current phase, compete against one another for further investment. Investments can, therefore, efficiently shift from low-potential options to more promising ones. Kaufmann et al. (2021a) show that ROR positively relates to NPD portfolio innovativeness and success, especially when executives have a mindset favouring risk-taking, proactiveness, and innovativeness and when the environment is turbulent. Surprisingly, a firm's innovation climate did not further increase ROR's benefits but it did directly increase NPD portfolio innovativeness. These findings matter for the management of NPD project sequences. Securing a firm's survival requires not only investing in follow-up products but also creating innovation paths, and it seems particularly promising if there is high technological turbulence driving new products, but there is also high uncertainty. Therefore, investing in exploratory projects, possibly followed by more focused exploratory projects, makes sense. When they have matured and created value for attractive target groups, it is time to exploit the options delivered by exploratory projects.

19.5 CONCLUSION

Managing NPD projects, portfolios, and project sequences requires that companies combine the principles of ambidexterity, agility, and strategic adaptiveness. It is useful to follow ambidexterity and engage in a higher share of exploratory projects, manage them differently than exploitative projects, and reserve strategic buckets for the different categories of projects. But this is only necessary and not sufficient. If there is no overall strategy to seize the options gained from the projects in the exploratory buckets, if there is no entrepreneurial orientation to take risks and invest in them, if there is no agility in NPD portfolio management to seize these options as long as the window of opportunity is open, and if there is no strategic adaptiveness to recognise new innovation paths, then too many of the promising exploratory candidates will become *lost* opportunities. We think that NPD portfolio management is still considered too much an execution tool of strategy. However, it is the locus with the best information supply to make decisions about emerging strategies (Kopmann et al., 2017), and senior managers at the corporate level should sense and seize these impulses when they decide about the portfolio of future innovation paths. We know that emerging strategies are triggered by agile principles, ambidextrous NPD portfolio management, strategic control, and listening to the voice of experienced project managers. But is this enough for a viable and sustainable future-oriented leadership of an organisation?

REFERENCES

Ahlfänger, M., Gemünden, H. G. & Leker, J. (2022). Balancing value creation and capture: The efficacy of formal control in open innovation projects. *International Journal of Project Management*, 40(2), 105–119.

Bengtsson, M. & Lindkvist, L. (2017). Mapping the road to future projects: Roadmapping as a balancing and transformation process. *Project Management Journal*, 48(2), 39–54.

Bianchi, M., Marzi, G. & Guerini, M. (2020). Agile, stage-gate and their combination: Exploring how they relate to performance in software development. *Journal of Business Research*, 110, 538–553.

Brown, S. L. & Eisenhardt, K. M. (1997). The art of continuous change: Linking complexity theory and time-paced evolution in relentlessly shifting organisations. *Administrative Science Quarterly*, 42(1), 1–35.

Buengeler, C., Situmeang, F. B. I., van Eerde, W. & Wijnberg, N. M. (2021). Fluidity in project management teams across projects. *International Journal of Project Management*, 39(3), 282–294.

Carlgren, L., Rauth, I. & Elmquist, M. (2016). Framing design thinking: The concept in idea and enactment. *Creativity and Innovation Management*, 25(1), 38–57.

Clark, K. B. & Wheelwright, S. C. (1992). Organising and leading 'heavyweight' development teams. *California Management Review*, 34, 9–28.

Cooper, R. G. (2021). Accelerating innovation: Some lessons from the pandemic. *Journal of Product Innovation Management*, 38(2), 221–232.

Cooper, R. G. & Kleinschmidt, E. J. (1995). Benchmarking the critical success factors in new product development. *Journal of Product Innovation Management*, 12, 374–391.

Cooper, R. G., Edgett, S. J. & Kleinschmidt, E. J. (2001). *Portfolio management for new products*. Perseus Publications.

Davies, A. & Brady, T. (2000). Organisational capabilities and learning in complex product systems: Towards repeatable solutions. *Research Policy*, 29(7), 931–953.

Davies, A., MacAulay, S., DeBarro, T. & Thurston, M. (2014). Making innovation happen in a megaproject: London's Crossrail suburban railway system. *Project Management Journal*, 45(6), 25–37.

Ekrot, B., Kock, A. & Gemünden, H. G. (2016). Retaining project management competence: Antecedents and consequences. *International Journal of Project Management*, 34(2), 145–157.

Elling, K. & Herstatt, C. (2017). Managing the front end of innovation: Less fuzzy, yet still not fully understood. *Journal of Product Innovation Management*, 34(6), 864–874.

Evanschitzky, H., Eisend, M., Calantone, R. J. & Jiang, Y. Y. (2012). Success factors of product innovation: An updated meta-analysis. *Journal of Product Innovation Management*, 29(S1), 21–37.

Florén, H. & Frishammar, J. (2012). From preliminary ideas to corroborated product definitions: Managing the front end of new product development. *California Management Review*, 54(4), 20–43.

Gebert, D., Boerner, S. & Kearney, E. (2010). Fostering team innovation: Why is it important to combine opposing action strategies? *Organization Science*, 21(3), 593–608.

Gemünden, H. G., Salomo, S. & Krieger, A. (2005). The influence of project autonomy on project success. *International Journal of Project Management*, 23(5), 366–373.

Gretsch, O., Tietze, F. & Kock, A. (2020). Firms' IP ownership aggressiveness in university–industry collaboration projects: Choosing the right governance mode. *Creativity and Innovation Management*, 29(2), 359–370.

Hobday, M. (1998). Product complexity, innovation and industrial organisation. *Research Policy*, 26(6), 689–710.

Högl, M. & Gemünden, H. G. (2001). Teamwork quality and the success of innovative projects: A theoretical concept and empirical evidence. *Organization Science*, 12(4), 435–449.

Högl, M., Parboteeah, K. P. & Gemünden, H. G. (2003). When teamwork really matters: Task innovativeness as a moderator of the teamwork-performance relationship in software development projects. *Journal of Engineering Technology Management*, 20(4), 281–302.

Högl, M., Weinkauf, K. & Gemünden, H. G. (2004). Inter-team coordination, project commitment, and teamwork: A longitudinal study. *Organisation Science*, 15(1), 38–55.

Hülsheger, U. R., Anderson, N. & Salgado, J. F. (2009). Team-level predictors of innovation at work: A comprehensive meta-analysis spanning three decades of research. *Journal of Applied Psychology*, 94(5), 1128–1145.

Jonas, D., Kock, A. & Gemünden, H. G. (2013). Predicting project portfolio success by measuring management quality: A longitudinal study. *IEEE Transactions on Engineering Management*, 60(2), 215–226.

Kaufmann, C., Kock, A. & Gemünden, H. G. (2020). Emerging strategy recognition in agile portfolios. *International Journal of Project Management*, 38(7), 429–440.

Kaufmann, C., Kock, A. & Gemünden, H. G. (2021a). Strategic and cultural context of real option reasoning in innovation portfolios. *Journal of Product Innovation Management*, 38(3), 334–354.

Kaufmann, C., Resch, C. & Kock, A. (2021b, June). *Novelty in innovative project sequences: The effect of team continuity and domain experience*. Conference presentation, 20th EURAM Conference, Montreal.

Kester, L., Hultink, E. J. & Griffin, A. (2014). An empirical investigation of the antecedents and outcomes of NPD portfolio success. *Journal of Product Innovation Management*, 31(6), 1199–1213.

Klingebiel, R. & Adner, R. (2015). Real options logic revisited: The performance effects of alternative resource allocation regimes. *Academy of Management Journal*, 58(1), 221–241.

Koch-Ørvad, N., Thuese, Ch., Koch, Ch. & Berker, T. (2019). Transforming ecosystems: facilitating sustainable innovations through the lineage of exploratory projects. *Project Management Journal*, 50(5), 602–616.

Kock, A. & Gemünden, H. G. (2016). Antecedents to decision-making quality and agility in innovation portfolio management. *Journal of Product Innovation Management*, 33(6), 670–686.

Kock, A. & Gemünden, H. G. (2019). Project lineage management and project portfolio success. *Project Management Journal*, 50(5) 587–601.

Kock, A. & Gemünden, H. G. (2021). How entrepreneurial orientation can leverage innovation project portfolio management. *R&D Management*, 51(1), 40–51.

Kock, A., Gemünden, H. G., Salomo, S. & Schultz, C. (2011). The mixed blessings of technological innovativeness for the commercial success of new products. *Journal of Product Innovation Management*, 28(S1), 28–43.

Kock, A., Heising, W. & Gemünden, H. G. (2015). How ideation portfolio management influences front-end success. *Journal of Product Innovation Management*, 32(4), 539–555.

Kock, A., Heising, W. & Gemünden, H. G. (2016). A contingency approach on the impact of front-end success on project portfolio success. *Project Management Journal*, 47(2), 115–129.

Kopmann, J., Kock, A., Killen, C. & Gemünden, H. G. (2017). The role of project portfolio management in fostering both deliberate and emerging strategies. *International Journal of Project Management*, 35(4), 557–570.

Maniak, R. & Midler, C. (2014). Multiproject lineage management: Bridging project management and design-based innovation strategy. *International Journal of Project Management*, 32(7), 1146–1156.

Martinsuo, M. (2013). Project portfolio management in practice and in context. *International Journal of Project Management*, 31(6), 794–803.

Meier, A. & Kock, A. (2022). Agile R&D units' organisation beyond software: Developing and validating a multidimensional scale in an engineering context. *IEEE Transactions on Engineering Management*. doi: 10.1109/TEM.2021.3108343.

Meifort, A. (2016). Innovation portfolio management: A synthesis and research agenda. *Creativity and Innovation Management*, 25(2), 251–269.

Midler, C. (2013). Implementing a low-end disruption strategy through multiproject lineage management: The Logan case. *Project Management Journal*, 44(5), 24–35.

Park, D., Han, J. & Childs, P. R. N. (2021). 266 fuzzy front-end studies: Current state and future directions for new product development. *Research in Engineering Design*, 32(3), 77–409.

Patanakul, P., Chen, J. & Lynn, G. S. (2012). Autonomous teams and new product development. *Journal of Product Innovation Management*, 29(5), 734–750.

Rank, J., Unger, B. N. & Gemünden, H. G. (2015). Preparedness for the future in project portfolio management: The roles of proactiveness, riskiness and willingness to cannibalise. *International Journal of Project Management*, 33(8) 1730–1743.

Rauniar, R., Doll, W., Rawski, G. & Hong, P. (2008). The role of heavyweight product manager in new product development. *International Journal of Operations and Production Management*, 28(2), 130–154.

Roehrich, J. K, Davies, A., Frederiksen, L. & Sergeeeva, N. (2019). Management innovation in complex products systems: The case of integrated project teams. *Industrial Marketing Management*, 79, 84–93.

Salomo, S., Weise, J. & Gemünden, H. G. (2007). NPD planning activities and innovation performance: The mediating role of process management and the moderating effect of product innovativeness. *Journal of Product Innovation Management*, 24(4), 285–302.

Salomo, S., Talke, K. & Strecker, N. (2008). Innovation field orientation and its effect on innovativeness and firm performance. *Journal of Product Innovation Management*, 25(6), 560–576.

Salzmann, E. & Kock, A. (2020). When customer ethnography is good for you: A contingency perspective. *Industrial Marketing Management*, 88, 366–377.

Schultz, C., Salomo, S., de Brentani, U. & Kleinschmidt, E. J. (2013). How formal control influences decision-making clarity and innovation performance. *Journal of Product Innovation Management*, 30(3), 430–447.

Sheremata, W. A. (2000). Centrifugal and centripetal forces in radical new product development under time pressure. *Academy of Management Review*, 25(2), 389–408.

Sivasubramaniam, N., Liebowitz, S. J. & Lackman, C. L. (2012). Determinants of new product development team performance: A meta-analytic review. *Journal of Product Innovation Management*, 29(5), 803–820.

Sweetman, R. & Conboy, K. (2018). Portfolios of agile projects. *Project Management Journal*, 49(6), 18–38.

Szatmari, B., Deichmann, D., van den Ende, J. & King, B. G. (2020). Great successes and great failures: The impact of project leader status on project performance and performance extremeness. *Journal of Management Studies*, 58(5), 1267–1293.

Talke, K., Salomo, S. & Mensel, N. (2006). A competence-based model of initiatives for innovations. *Creativity and Innovation Management*, 15(4), 373–384.

Teller, J., Unger, B., Kock, A. & Gemünden, H. G. (2012). Formalisation of project portfolio management: The moderating role of project portfolio complexity. *International Journal of Project Management*, 30(5), 596–607.

Tellis, G. J., Prabhu, J. C. & Chandy, R. K. (2009). Radical innovation across nations: The preeminence of corporate culture. *Journal of Marketing*, 73(1), 3–23.

Unger, B. N., Kock, A., Gemünden, H. G. & Jonas, D. (2012). Enforcing strategic fit of project portfolios by project termination: An empirical study on senior management involvement. *International Journal of Project Management*, 30(6), 675–685.

Voss, M. & Kock, A. (2013). Impact of relationship value on project portfolio success: Investigating the moderating effects of portfolio characteristics and external turbulence. *International Journal of Project Management*, 31(6), 847–861.

West, J. & Bogers, M. (2014). Leveraging external sources of innovation: A review of research on open innovation. *Journal of Product Innovation Management*, 31(4), 814–831.

Williams, T., Vo, H., Samset, K. & Edkins, A. (2019). The front-end of projects: A systematic literature review and structuring. *Production Planning and Control*, 30(14), 1137–1169.

Zhu, H. Z., Kock, A., Wentker, M. & Leker, J. (2019). How does online interaction affect idea quality? The effect of feedback in firm-internal idea competitions. *Journal of Product Innovation Management*, 36(1), 24–40.

20. Four research strategies for studying organizational project management
Monique Aubry

When addressed in this way [a future-becoming], "organization" is not a thing but, rather, the names of a multiplicity of practices by which we invent and reinvent ourselves by *giving form* to ourselves as well as to others. (Weiskopf & Willmott, 2014, p. 516; emphasis in original)

20.1 INTRODUCTION

The citation above introduces well the emergent aspect of organizations and, more importantly, the coexistence of a diversity of practices shaping the organization as well as shaping individuals in and around the organization (Langley, 2009). The aim of this chapter is to identify challenges in studying organizational project management (OPM) due to the complexity of project organizing. In this chapter, we intend to bring attention to two paradoxical dimensions of OPM: (1) as a thing and as a process; and (2) its focus as *internal to* and *external to* the organization.

The term OPM emerged in the early 2000s, with the recognition that managing projects and programs has a strong relation to organizational strategy, specifically with respect to strategy implementation (Jamieson & Morris, 2004). Interest of the project management community moved from projects and programs to the organization for professional associations (e.g., Office of Government Commerce, 2008; Project Management Institute, 2003) as well as for scholars (Cooke-Davies et al., 2001). At the same time, some scholars engaged in project studies adopted by the organization as their level of analysis studying, among many subjects, OPM capabilities (Crawford, 2006), project portfolio (Cooper et al., 1997), project business (Artto & Wikstrom, 2005), and project management offices (Aubry et al., 2007).

The initial definition of OPM mainly focused on the dynamic structure articulated to maximize value (Aubry et al., 2007). The focus later turned towards mechanisms of coordination. We adopt the definition given by Müller, Drouin, and Sankaran (2019, p. 1): "OPM is the integration of the primarily project (management) – related activities of an organization into a cohesive network of activities which, by themselves and their interactions, can be understood, planned and managed for the benefit of the organization and its stakeholders." Therefore, OPM is understood largely to cover topics related to coordination mechanisms dedicated to project organizing, in different temporalities (temporary or permanent) such as project-based organizations, project-oriented organizations, project management offices, project portfolios, and project networks.

Currently, there is renewed interest to understand those mechanisms of coordination at work in complex project organizing (CPO) that is crossing organizational levels. This is in line with the call to open research to different levels of analysis in project studies (Geraldi & Söderlund, 2018). In other words, there is a preoccupation with how OPM evolves and develops in CPO.

In this chapter, we open with a review of the current scholarly literature, examining basic assumptions, and we suggest a renewal of those assumptions for scholars to study OPM. Then, we develop a proposal for the study of the complexity within OPM. This proposal addresses two dimensions to capture inherent paradoxes or tensions within organizations. Finally, four strategies are proposed towards a possible agenda for research in OPM.

20.2 FROM CURRENT TO RENEWED ASSUMPTIONS: REVEALING THE PARADOXES

In project studies, the term OPM intends mainly to describe the components and the scope of all activities in managing multiple projects within the organization: for example, the structure of the organization (Hobday, 2000; Miterev et al., 2017b), the roles and functions (Hobbs & Aubry, 2010), the temporary nature of projects (Bakker et al., 2016), and the governance (Müller, 2017). While research provides a wealth of answers to questions related to descriptive OPM within organizations, we know very little about the dynamic relationships of OPM *internal to* and *external to* the organization. First, with regard to the internal elements of the organization, the design of OPM is often treated as a top-down and scaffolded arrangement to provide a clear path through multiple layers of the project (e.g., Müller et al., 2019). With few exceptions, there is no inclusion of social and informal aspects in the concept of organizational design (Simard et al., 2018; Van Marrewijk et al., 2016) and very few references to governmentality that really take into account the internal power system (including lateral relations crossing internal boundaries) in an organization or the individuals, physically and emotionally (Clegg et al., 2002; Sergeeva & Ali, 2020). Second, organizations are part of a larger system (Hughes, 1998). Changes in the external environment shapes the approach to the OPM design such as abrupt economic change, political election, disruptive technology opportunities, or change in the regulation system (Aubry et al., 2008). However, in project studies, external aspects of the organization are usually either taken for granted or simply considered globally as context or environment (e.g., Morris & Geraldi, 2011) without considering the external relations and their role shaping the design and being shaped by them.

However, important research questions remain unanswered, such as *how* OPM happens the way it does and *why* changes happen so frequently. Answering these questions leads to revisiting some assumptions found in the current literature on OPM, such as stability, internal organization focus, and decision-making rationality. New assumptions build on acknowledging the existence of tensions or paradoxes within the organization (Smith & Lewis, 2011). With the recognition of these tensions and paradoxes, we also recognize that current assumptions can co-exist with new ones, forming renewed paradoxical assumptions (Clegg et al., 2022). For example, even if we adopt the assumption of emergent organization, there is still a need to study OPM as such, to be able to describe it at a specific point in time and space, and to "capture" it as if it were in a stable environment.

There is a need, in our view, to adopt theoretical assumptions that capture the areas of complexity in OPM. New paradoxical assumptions should contribute to a better understanding of such complexities. Table 20.1 provides a synthesis of current accepted assumptions and renewed paradoxical assumptions.

Table 20.1 Synthesis of the current and renewed paradoxical assumptions

	Current assumption		Renewed assumption		
Stability/dynamics	Organizational project management is designed to last in a stable environment. *Limitation:* Little attention given to changes	Hobbs and Aubry (2010); Miterev et al. (2017b)	Organizations are as dynamic as the world around them; this emphasizes the "design" activity of OPM	Process approach: studying changes as they unfold. Enlightening OPM in paradox view: both stable and moving	Aubry et al. (2022)
Focus internal/internal and external/external	OPM can be described as a set of roles and functions within the organization. *Limitation:* Little recognition of the interplay between the internal OPM and the external world	Hobday (2000)	Internal and external: not only are top-down relations considered as part of OPM, but lateral as well as informal relations are considered	To open the study of OPM to more complex internal dynamics and to external relations	Brunet (2021); Simard et al. (2018)
Rationality given/socially constructed	OPM is a decision-making process, in the hands of decision makers who act in a rational and reasoned manner. *Limitation:* Difficulty to understand and account for the complexity in real-life situations	Morris and Geraldi (2011); Jamieson and Morris (2004); Müller et al. (2019)	OPM is socially constructed with a multiple set of stakeholders who constantly transform the organization and, in turn, are transformed	Study complex situations as socially constructed. Time and temporalities are crucial to OPM studies	Clegg et al. (2002); Sergeeva and Ali (2020)

20.3   A PROPOSAL FOR THE STUDY OF COMPLEXITY IN OPM

Inspired by Van de Ven and Poole (2005) and our own previous work, we develop a proposal to identify certain aspects of complexity specific to OPM: (1) tackling OPM as both a thing and as a process; and (2) crossing the boundaries of the organization, that is, taking into account together the OPM relations internal to the organization and external to the organization (see Figure 20.1).

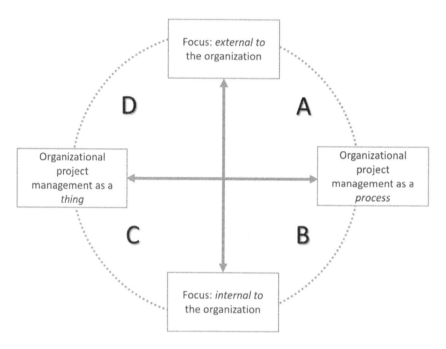

Figure 20.1   Framework for the study of OPM

20.3.1   OPM as a Stable Thing as well as an Organizing Process

This idea of considering an organization as a thing or as an organizing process emerged in management and organization studies mainly from the research on organizational change (Tsoukas & Chia, 2002; Van de Ven & Poole, 2005). Briefly, this trend of research emphasizes change as a normal way of life rather than an exceptional event.

Process research in project studies has recently been gaining ground (Brunet et al., 2021; Sergi et al., 2020). Brunet et al. (2021) suggest that research on process implies the presence of process data, such as ongoing flows of activity and contributions to process theory. The main arguments for a process approach in research rely mainly on the will to emphasize temporality and movement, in opposition to fixed objects that can be studied as variance in a statistical model (Langley, 1999).

We argue that OPM should be studied in tension, both as a thing (structure) and as a process (flows of activities, in flux), to produce together relevant knowledge within an arena of complexity. However, there is a predominance of process ontology in order to maintain ontological coherence that is to see the world in movement and organization as composed of organizing processes. In this approach, stable objects or things can be captured at certain times to study them in tension. For example, OPM may be described in terms of structure, roles, and functions, while taking into account the existence of tensions, conflicts, or issues among stakeholders that lead to reconstituting the project's organization. In this approach, OPM is considered a thing but including the inevitability for change.

20.3.2   The Focus on *Internal to* and *External to* in OPM

There is a second dimension to OPM where tensions should be explored: that is, scholars can expand their focus to include concepts of *internal to* and *external to* the organization. In *internal to* organizations, the coordination of project delivery activities is *per se* multidisciplinary; in terms of each individual project, there is a longstanding recognition of a multidisciplinary approach in the management of the project (Midler, 1993) and the need for integration of different domains (Winch, 2014). At the level of organization, coordination mechanisms should support and sustain the increased need for internal integration. In this line of thought, Müller et al. (2019) developed a multi-layer model, the onion model, where they identified seven layers interacting within the realm of OPM. Indeed, OPM involves numerous relations within and among layers. Some research in this area has emphasized the need for integration at the organizational level, such as in innovation (Sergeeva & Ali, 2020) or the PMO in the overall project control processes (Artto et al., 2011).

Moreover, there are also diverse interests to be considered *external to* the organization in OPM. While most of the research on OPM focuses on the aspect of *internal to* the organization (Müller et al., 2019), and while we still have much to learn in this area, we are facing more and more of a need to expand our studies to include relations in an external context. Morris and Geraldi (2011, p. 23) insisted on the importance of the external context in the management of projects: "The institutional context: management here is concerned with ensuring the long-term project management health of the organization." This call for an expansion into an examination of the external forces is very much in line with the call for expanding multi-level research in project studies (Geraldi & Söderlund, 2018). For example, Miterev et al. (2017a) adopted an institutional perspective in their research on project-based organizations.

Other research focusing on organizational design in major transformation projects found that institutional constraints contribute to shape the design in addition to equifinality in organizations (Aubry et al., 2022).

20.4   TOWARDS A FRAMEWORK FOR STUDYING OPM: FOUR RESEARCH STRATEGIES

The two dimensions described above, thing/process and internal/external focus, are not isolated from one other; they work in tandem, interacting with one another. Figure 20.1 illustrates the proposed framework for studying OPM and four possible research strategies. Each quadrant corresponds to a particular research strategy identified in bold uppercase letters A to D. Behind this representation is the idea to highlight the wide diversity of potential research of different intensities regarding the two dimensions while maintaining the integrity of the overall framework.

20.4.1   Research Strategy A: OPM as a *Process* with a Focus *External to* the Organization

The research in this quadrant tends to focus on the relation between OPM and the institutional field, exterior to the organization. This research considers the temporal aspect as central to the problem. The notion of a dynamic dyad of strategizing–structuring, as defined by Pettigrew and Fenton (2000), nicely demonstrates the relationship between the market dimensions of an organization and its internal structure, and this within a perspective of change and development (Pettigrew et al., 2001). Among six challenges Pettigrew et al. (2001) identified in their research on organizational change, they advocated the examination of multiple contexts and levels of analysis and the inclusion of time, history, process, and action. More specific to project management literature, Söderlund and Tell (2009) characterize what they call "P-form organization," that is project-based. This in-depth case study shows a connection between external changes in market, technology, product/service, and organization, and internal adaptation in the pursuit of business development and project competences. The same interplay is shown in the public sector in Brunet (2021). She studied the relations between the governance framework adopted by the government for the management of major projects in public infrastructure and the practices found in the operational management of these projects in the project's lifecycle. Adopting this research strategy provides a window into how the OPM is shaped by external opportunities and constraints; this research strategy could also offer the potential of learning how OPM is shaping components of its external environment.

20.4.2   Research Strategy B: OPM as a *Process* with a Focus *Internal to* the Organization

This research strategy takes time as a crucial perspective but limits the focus to within the organization. For example, Aubry et al. (2012) draw on the notion of function within the organization, to provide an understanding of the OPM activities. However, unlike usual organizational functions, the project function is generally not centralized in a unique organizational entity but rather network-based and spread out throughout the organization. From strategy implementation to project delivery and implementation, several entities will engage at different moments and with different interests in OPM. With a processual approach, this research strategy offers great opportunities to scrutinize the dynamic life of OPM, as experienced at different loci and with a variety of trajectories. Furthermore, it might highlight the "invisible" side of OPM: opening the black box, so to speak.

20.4.3   Research Strategy C: OPM as a *Thing* with a Focus *Internal to* the Organization

The general idea of this strategy is to capture OPM at a specific time and place; it is like stopping time and movement to understand and describe the object as carefully and in as much detail as possible. This research strategy offers the potential for researchers to learn about what OPM in the organization looks like at a specific time/space and gain a more detailed description and understanding of the context. A good description of this strategy is a description and definition of a variety of forms that may compose a project-based organization, all within consideration of the context (Hobday, 2000). This strategy provided Hobday (2000) with the opportunity to question the idealization of project-based organization and has served research, overall, by offering a scrutiny of the components involved, their relations to each other, and their complexity. This strategy may also offer great research opportunities to explore specific OPM facets such as innovation (Gemünden et al., 2018) or relations with strategy (Winch et al., 2022).

20.4.4 Research Strategy D: OPM as a *Thing* with a Focus *External to* the Organization

In this last quadrant, the research strategy deals with OPM as a rather fixed object, as above, but, here, includes the external environment. Few examples come in mind in relation with this research strategy such as interorganizational projects (Stjerne et al., 2019), institutions and projects (Söderlund & Sydow, 2019), and project networks (DeFillippi & Sydow, 2016). Following Söderlund and Sydow (2019), the study of interlinkages between OPM and institutions may highlight how OPM is shaped by institutions as well as institutions are shaped by the interaction with OPM. Aubry et al. (2022) offer a good illustration of this in the healthcare sector. Project networks, as studied by DeFillippi and Sydow (2016), refers to either a single inter-organizational project or to a series of interconnected projects. However, in both cases, challenges arise for OPM where different organizations with different roles form a coalition and, together with their interfaces, they contribute in different ways to the overall management of projects (Pinto & Winch, 2016).

20.5 DISCUSSION

In this chapter, we have proposed a framework for the study of OPM, bridging two dimensions that, together, can capture the dynamics inherent in the project's context (Söderlund & Tell, 2009). Our point of departure was the limitations found in the current research on OPM for addressing complex and pluralistic situations in research. The main contribution of this framework is its potential to address the core concepts in CPO, as identified in this book: uncertainty, complexity, temporality, and projectivity.

A diversity of levels of analysis is included in the definition of OPM (Müller et al., 2019), such as project, program, portfolio, and governance. One main problem with this definition by Müller et al. (2019) is the difficulty in undertaking research in which the overall integrity of OPM is preserved. The current trend is rather to study one component at a time: this can be seen, for example, with respect to project portfolio (Bredillet et al., 2018), governance (Brunet & Aubry, 2018), or PMO (Sergeeva & Ali, 2020), with a resulting fragmentation of knowledge in OPM (Söderlund, 2011). While our proposed research framework is still partial and incomplete, it offers the possibility of tackling two dimensions of complexity, which operates under the dynamics of paradoxes and tensions. A research agenda on OPM can, therefore, address complexity in terms of organizational flexibility and preparation for change, enlarging the scope to include external relations, and in a socially constructed rationality. The four research strategies proposed above take support from the existence of paradoxes and tensions in the study of OPM. Future research should work on OPM situations over time crossing both paradoxical dimensions.

Professionals are often left without resources when it comes to understanding or designing the OPM. Prescriptions available from professional publications provide rather fragmented knowledge that seem to be difficult to implement. In this proposed research agenda based on paradoxical situations, findings should inform professionals on OPM complexity and on the need for them to make sense of these findings in their own environment.

20.6   CONCLUSION

This chapter aims to expand the research approaches on OPM in context of complexity. Renewal of assumptions opens opportunities to study this topic with different research strategies where the emphasis is on the integration of two paradoxical dimensions into a framework for the study of OPM. While this framework may offer new potentialities in project studies, it also contains some challenges. The first concerns the potential difficulty of problematizing in elaborating the research question (Alvesson & Sandberg, 2011). Indeed, a research question should focus on a situation encompassing paradoxical dimensions instead of a focus on a specific organizational level or limitation to a "thing." The second challenge is related to the research methodology, which might be demanding in terms of preparation. It supposes access to multi-level data from various sources, which requires a considerable expenditure of effort for the application of multiple strategies in the data analysis (Langley, 1999).

In conclusion, there are probably more than two dimensions of study in complex OPM. However, in this field or in any project organizing research, serious effort must be taken when working through these complexities, to facilitate the management of projects, proactively, and to help better manage the burning challenges we are facing with our planet.

REFERENCES

Alvesson, M. & Sandberg, J. (2011). Generating research questions through problematization. *Academy of Management Review*, 36(2), 247–271.

Artto, K. A. & Wikstrom, K. (2005). What is project business? *International Journal of Project Management*, 23(5), 343–353.

Artto, K. A., Kulvik, I., Poskela, J. & Turkulainen, V. (2011). The integrative role of the project management office in the front end of innovation. *International Journal of Project Management*, 29(4), 408–421.

Aubry, M., Hobbs, B. & Thuillier, D. (2007). A new framework for understanding organisational project management through the PMO. *International Journal of Project Management*, 25(4), 328–336.

Aubry, M., Hobbs, B. & Thuillier, D. (2008). Organisational project management: An historical approach to the study of PMOs. *International Journal of Project Management*, 26(1), 38–43.

Aubry, M., Sicotte, H., Drouin, N., Vidot-Delerue, H. & Besner, C. (2012). Organisational project management as a function within the organisation. *International Journal of Managing Projects in Business*, 5(2), 180–194.

Aubry, M., Richer, M.-C., Lavoie-Tremblay, M., Fortin, C. & Fortin Verreault, J.-F. (2022). Revisiting organizational design in the light of isomorphism and equifinality: Insights from the study of three major transformation projects. *Project Management Journal*, 53(2), 161–180.

Bakker, R. M., DeFillippi, R. J., Schwab, A. & Sydow, J. (2016). Temporary organizing: Promises, processes, problems. *Organization Studies*, 37(12), 1703–1719.

Bredillet, C., Tywoniak, S. & Tootoonchy, M. (2018). Exploring the dynamics of project management office and portfolio management co-evolution: A routine lens. *International Journal of Project Management*, 36(1), 27–42.

Brunet, M. (2021). Making sense of a governance framework for megaprojects: The challenge of finding equilibrium. *International Journal of Project Management*, 39(4), 406–416.

Brunet, M. & Aubry, M. (2018). The governance of major public infrastructure projects: The process of translation. *International Journal of Managing Projects in Business*, 11(1), 80–103.

Brunet, M., Fachin, F. & Langley, A. (2021). Studying projects processually. *International Journal of Project Management*, 39(8), 834–848.

Clegg, S. R., Pitsis, T. S., Rura-Polley, T. & Marosszeky, M. (2002). Governmentality matters: Designing an alliance culture of inter-organizational collaboration for managing projects. *Organization Studies*, 23(3), 317.

Clegg, S. R., Pina e Cunha, M. & Berti, M. (2022). Research movements and theorizing dynamics in management and organization studies. *Academy of Management Review*, 47(3), 382–401. DOI: 10.5465/amr.2018.0466.

Cooke-Davies, T. J., Schlichter, J. & Bredillet, C. (2001). *Beyond the PMBOK® Guide*. Conference presentation, PMI North America Congress, Nashville.

Cooper, R. G., Scott, J. E. & Kleinschmidt, E. J. (1997). Portfolio management in new product development: Lessons from the leaders – II. *Research Technology Management*, 40(6), 43–52.

Crawford, L. (2006). Developing organizational project management capability: Theory and practice. *Project Management Journal*, 37(3), 74–86.

DeFillippi, R. & Sydow, J. (2016). Project networks: Governance choices and paradoxical tensions. *Project Management Journal*, 47(5), 6–17.

Geraldi, J. & Söderlund, J. (2018). Project studies: What it is, where it is going. *International Journal of Project Management*, 36(1), 55–70.

Gemünden, H. G., Lehner, P. & Kock, A. (2018). The project-oriented organization and its contribution to innovation. *International Journal of Project Management*, 36(1), 147–160.

Hobbs, B. & Aubry, M. (2010). *The project management office: A quest for understanding*. Project Management Institute.

Hobday, M. (2000). The project-based organisation: An ideal form for managing complex products and systems? *Research Policy*, 29(7–8), 871–893.

Hughes, T. P. (1998). *Rescuing Prometheus: Four monumental projects that changed the modern world*. Vintage.

Jamieson, A. & Morris, P. W. G. (2004). Moving from corporate strategy to project strategy. In P. W. G. Morris & J. K. Pinto (Eds), *The Wiley guide to managing projects* (pp. 177–205). John Wiley & Sons.

Langley, A. (1999). Strategies for theorizing from process data. *Academy of Management Review*, 24(4), 691–710.

Langley, A. (2009). Studying processes in and around organizations. In D. A. Buchanan & B. Alan (Eds), *The SAGE handbook of organizational research methods* (pp. 409–429). Sage.

Midler, C. (1993). *L'auto qui n'existait pas*. InterÉditions.

Miterev, M., Engwall, M. & Jerbrant, A. (2017a). Mechanisms of isomorphism in project-based organizations. *Project Management Journal*, 48(5), 9–24.

Miterev, M., Mancini, M. & Turner, R. (2017b). Towards a design for the project-based organization. *International Journal of Project Management*, 35(3), 479–491.

Morris, P. W. G. & Geraldi, J. (2011). Managing the institutional context for projects. *Project Management Journal*, 42(6), 20–32.

Müller, R. (2017). *Governance and governmentality for projects: Enablers, practices, and consequences*. Routledge.

Müller, R., Drouin, N. & Sankaran, S. (2019). *Organizational project management: Theory and implementation*. Edward Edgar Publishing.

Office of Government Commerce (2008). *Portfolio, programme and project offices (P3O)*. The Stationary Office.

Pettigrew, A. M. & Fenton, E. (Eds) (2000). *The innovating organization*. Sage.

Pettigrew, A. M., Woodman, R. W. & Cameron, K. S. (2001). Studying organizational change and development: Challenges for future research. *Academy of Management Journal*, 44(4), 697–713.

Pinto, J. K. & Winch, G. (2016). The unsettling of "settled science": The past and future of the management of projects. *International Journal of Project Management*, 34(2), 237–245.

Project Management Institute (2003). *Organizational project management maturity model: OPM3 knowledge foundation*. Project Management Institute.

Sergeeva, N. & Ali, S. (2020). The role of the project management office (PMO) in stimulating innovation in projects initiated by owner and operator organizations. *Project Management Journal*, 51(4), 440–451.

Sergi, V., Crevani, L. & Aubry, M. (2020). Process studies of project organizing. *Project Management Journal*, 51(1), 3–10.

Simard, M., Aubry, M. & Laberge, D. (2018). The utopia of order versus chaos: A conceptual framework for governance, organizational design and governmentality in projects. *International Journal of Project Management*, 36(3), 460–473.

Smith, W. K. & Lewis, M. W. (2011). Toward a theory of paradox: A dynamic equilibrium of organizing. *Academy of Management Review*, 36(2), 381–403.

Söderlund, J. (2011). Pluralism in project management: Navigating the crossroads of specialization and fragmentation. *International Journal of Management Reviews*, 13(2), 153–176.

Söderlund, J. & Sydow, J. (2019). Projects and institutions: Towards understanding their mutual constitution and dynamics. *International Journal of Project Management*, 37(2), 259–268.

Söderlund, J. & Tell, F. (2009). The P-form organization and the dynamics of project competence: Project epochs in Asea/ABB, 1950–2000. *International Journal of Project Management*, 27(2), 101–112.

Stjerne, I. S., Söderlund, J. & Minbaeva, D. (2019). Crossing times: Temporal boundary-spanning practices in interorganizational projects. *International Journal of Project Management*, 37(2), 347–365.

Tsoukas, H. & Chia, R. (2002). On organizational becoming: Rethinking organizational change. *Organization Science*, 13(5), 567–582.

Van de Ven, A. H. & Poole, M. S. (2005). Alternative approaches for studying organizational change. *Organization Studies*, 26, 1377–1404.

Van Marrewijk, A., Ybema, S., Smits, K., Clegg, S. & Pitsis, T. (2016). Clash of the titans: Temporal organizing and collaborative dynamics in the Panama canal megaproject. *Organization Studies*, 37(12), 1745–1769.

Weiskopf, R. & Willmott, H. (2014). Michel Foucault (1926–1984). In J. Helin, T. Hernes, D. Hjorth & R. Holt (Eds), *The Oxford handbook of process philosophy and organization studies* (pp. 515–533). Oxford University Press.

Winch, G. M. (2014). Three domains of project organising. *International Journal of Project Management*, 32(5), 721–731.

Winch, G. M., Maytorena, E. & Sergeeva, N. (Eds) (2022). *Strategic project organizing*. Oxford University Press.

21. Governing inter-organisational relationships in large projects: a review and future research agenda

Juliette Engelhart, Jens K. Roehrich and Brian Squire

21.1 INTRODUCTION

Large projects, in which multiple independent, public and private organisations engage in the pursuit of shared objectives for a predefined time period, are increasingly used to coordinate the delivery of complex products and services (Jones & Lichtenstein, 2008; Denicol et al., 2020). Indeed, large projects have gained much attention as governments and firms seek to address challenges such as climate change, energy and transportation through the construction of new, and refurbishment of existing, infrastructure (Matinheikki et al., 2019). To deliver these projects, the design and use of governance mechanisms are essential to manage the tensions of uncertainty, complexity and temporality across a diverse set of inter-organisational relationships (IORs) (Flyvbjerg, 2017).

The IOR governance literature defines governance mechanisms as the formal and informal rules of exchange between organisations (Vandaele et al., 2007). While formal rules refer to contractual governance mechanisms involving the use of (mainly written and detailed) contracts to manage relationships, informal rules refer to relational governance mechanisms such as trust and social norms (Poppo & Zenger, 2002). These governance mechanisms can be used individually or in combination to govern relationships in large projects (Cao & Lumineau, 2015), but prior governance and project (management) studies have largely developed in parallel with limited cross-fertilisation (Winch, 2014). Thus, this chapter brings together findings from the IOR governance literature to inform the management of the various IORs in large projects.

Two strands of research can be applied to governing large projects, the project governance literature (e.g. Ahola & Davies, 2012) and the IOR governance literature (e.g. Cao & Lumineau, 2015). The majority of project governance literature focuses on the relationship between the owners and project(s) by either taking an external view of a project, that is a project-based firm governing multiple projects with unidirectional governance relations, or an internal view, where a project-based firm has bidirectional governance relations with stakeholders (Ahola et al., 2014). In contrast, the IOR governance literature, which is largely based in strategy (e.g. Poppo & Zenger, 2002), as well as operations and supply chain management (e.g. Roehrich & Lewis, 2014), investigates how prevailing conditions are linked to the use of governance mechanisms in IORs with a particular focus on buyer–supplier relationships (e.g. Zheng et al., 2008) or alliance and joint ventures (e.g. Reuer & Ariño, 2007). These studies have provided valuable insights into contractual and relational governance mechanisms and their individual or combined impact on performance (Cao & Lumineau, 2015), and more recently they have shown that governance mechanisms have inherent functions of control and coordination (e.g. Schilke & Lumineau, 2018). In this chapter, we focus on the latter view, as it has received little consideration in the project governance literature despite its importance in projects (Winch, 2014).

This chapter lines out tensions in controlling and coordinating IORs through contractual and relational governance mechanisms in large projects. In particular, we position that large projects' inherent characteristics of complexity, uncertainty and temporality introduce tensions to control and coordinate IORs effectively. In this chapter, we elaborate on the control and coordination tensions, show ways to overcome these tensions and establish future research avenues for project scholars.

21.2   GOVERNING LARGE PROJECTS

21.2.1   Governance Mechanisms

This chapter focuses on governance mechanisms to control and coordinate large projects. While the chapter focuses on large projects, we acknowledge that some of our findings might also apply to smaller projects. Large projects, such as megaprojects, typically entail high complexity that increases with project scale, high uncertainty that rises with complexity and a long-time duration from initiation to finish (Davies et al., 2017; Denicol et al., 2020). To manage large projects effectively, it is essential to employ adequate contracts and build trusting relationships to overcome the negative consequences of complexity, uncertainty and time.

Considering the individual roles and limitations of both governance mechanisms, researchers have investigated their interplay (e.g. Cao & Lumineau, 2015). While early governance research indicates a substitutive relationship (where one type of governance mechanism replaces the other or reduces the other's effectiveness), recent evidence suggests a complementary relationship (where one type of governance mechanism is improved by the presence of the other) (Caniëls et al., 2012). As a result, researchers started to investigate the underlying functions of contractual and relational governancemechanisms that may contribute to these contradictory findings (Schepker et al., 2014).

One reason for these opposing views is the possible roles that control and coordination functions play within both governance mechanisms (e.g. Lumineau & Henderson, 2012). Control is concerned with safeguarding an organisation from potential opportunism (Schilke & Lumineau, 2018) and can be found in contract clauses, such as the right to terminate an agreement, applying penalties for non-performance and assigning rights (Roehrich & Lewis, 2014). On the other hand, coordination is defined as 'the deliberate and orderly alignment or adjustment of partners' actions to achieve jointly determined goals' (Gulati et al., 2012, p. 12). Coordination may be achieved through clauses that specify information sharing routines and clarify partners' contributions in terms of resources (Gulati et al., 2012). Control and coordination are important as they can drive or impede project performance (Schilke & Lumineau, 2018) and social value creation (Caniëls et al., 2012; Caldwell et al., 2017).

While the vast majority of prior IOR governance studies have focused on the role of control (e.g. Li et al., 2010), recent research has started to investigate the coordination function (e.g. Oliveira & Lumineau, 2017) and the interplay between both functions. For instance, Schilke and Lumineau (2018) demonstrate the roles of contractual control and coordination to resolve conflicts and their impact on performance.

21.2.2   Positioning and Tackling Control and Coordination Tensions in Large Projects

Large projects are characterised by complexity (Brady & Davies, 2014), uncertainty (Davies et al., 2017) and temporality (Davies & Hobday, 2005), which introduces a variety of control and coordination tensions. Figure 21.1 illustrates the tensions and solutions proposed in this section.

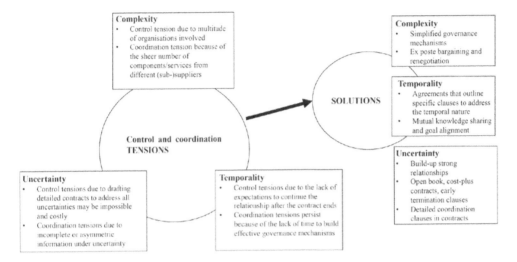

Figure 21.1   A framework of control and coordination tensions in large projects

First, complexity in projects is often split into: (1) structural complexity – 'arrangement of components and subsystems into an overall system architecture'; and (2) dynamic complexity – 'changing relationships among components within a system and between the system and its environment over time' (Brady & Davies, 2014, p. 24). Both complexity types introduce control and coordination tensions, such as drafting contracts that address all contingencies *ex ante* (Kapsali et al., 2019) and governing multiple stakeholders (Vukomanović et al., 2021). Control and coordination tensions arise due to complexity in projects that introduce limitations in foreseeing fully the relationship due to bounded rationality (Williamson, 1985). Thus, organisations cannot deploy contract clauses that address all possible contingencies to safeguard from opportunistic behaviour (Kapsali et al., 2019). This can result in inefficiencies and possible coordination failures, for instance, through unstructured communication and mis-allocation of resources (Kalra et al., 2021). Further, control tensions arise through a multitude of organisations working together on a large project (Chakkol et al., 2018), which introduces difficulties in detecting and preventing opportunism due to the sheer multitude of various actors. Coordination tension arises because of the sheer number of components and services that need to be delivered by different (sub)suppliers that require extensive coordination (Davies & Mackenzie, 2014).

To handle these tensions, prior studies suggest that contractual and relational governance mechanisms can address the control and coordination tensions manifested through complexity, but they require both *ex ante* and *ex post* management. For example, the study by Roehrich and

Lewis (2014) shows that while most organisations seek to reduce complexity by increasing the number of contractual clauses, more effective arrangements use more simplified governance mechanisms. Roehrich et al. (2020a) argue that if contracts are incomplete and unspecified *ex ante*, contracting parties might consider in *ex post* bargaining and renegotiation to increase contractual safeguards and/or coordination clauses. This suggests that it might be necessary to take a dynamic approach to updating governance mechanisms as the relationship evolves.

Second, uncertainty arises from unforeseeable events with unpredictable consequences (Davies & Mackenzie, 2014). Control tension persists in rapidly changing environments (e.g. new technologies), such as the early phase of a project (e.g. during the construction phase) when requirements of products and services change due to unforeseen circumstances, which then limits the ability to measure the performance against the *ex ante* defined contractual performance measures (Poppo & Zenger, 2002). However, drafting detailed contracts to reduce uncertainty is costly, time consuming and these clauses are often difficult to enforce and monitor due to asymmetric information between partnering organisations (Artz & Brush, 2000; Aben et al., 2021). In order to address gaps in contracts, parties could seek to build up relational governance mechanisms (Zheng et al., 2008), but this might also be resource/time consuming (Larson, 1992) and is often hindered by a lack of prior experience. Coordination tensions arise as uncertainty requires organisations to adapt with incomplete and sometimes asymmetric information (Zhou & Poppo, 2010). To counteract uncertainty, personal connections and ties among organisations can foster stability in uncertain times (Zhou & Poppo, 2010) but this might be challenging due to the limited shadow of the past or future, or procurement regulation/legislation.

To address uncertainty tensions, the IOR governance mechanisms literature provides several insights. Selviaridis (2016) provides a detailed understanding of uncertainty and control mechanisms suggesting the use of open book and cost-plus contracts to safeguard from environmental uncertainty, and early termination clauses to hedge against potential opportunism and financial losses. In a more nuanced analysis, Carson et al. (2006) suggest that volatility (rate and unpredictability of changes in an environment) renders contracts to be less useful and that organisations would be better served by relational governance mechanisms. However, their study shows that this relationship is reversed under conditions of ambiguity (uncertainty about the present and past experience). Thus, coordination mechanisms within contracts are essential under high uncertainty with a limited shadow of the past or future.

Third, control and coordination tensions in governing IORs arise through the temporal characteristics of large projects. Temporality arises as '(e)ach project is temporally limited and dynamically changing and (partially) reconstructed from one project to the next' (DeFillippi & Sydow, 2016, p. 8). Control tensions may arise because of deviant behaviour in IORs created by the lack of expectations to continue (i.e. lack of a shadow of the future) in the relationship after the contract ends (Poppo et al., 2008). With limited, and often no, shadow of the future to control behaviour (Das & Rahman, 2010), organisations require extensive control to detect and mitigate possible opportunistic behaviour. Coordination tensions arise to the extent that the temporary nature of the project might impact building effective contracts and trusting relationships (Kapsali et al., 2019). This can lead to coordination failures, especially when extensive coordination is required between project phases and among (sub)contractors (Olsen et al., 2005).

Prior IOR governance studies offer some guidance in how to control and coordinate temporality-induced tensions. In terms of control tension, Reuer and Ariño (2007) argue that organisations may craft agreements that include contractual provisions (e.g. termination, dispute resolution, confidentiality information and proprietary technology clauses) when a lack of the shadow of the future is present. Coordination tensions can be addressed through mutual knowledge and goal alignment which needs to be present for relational coordination to be effective when seeking to create (social) value (Caldwell et al., 2017).

While this section provided insights into the control and coordination tensions in large projects, there are still ample research opportunities to advance our understanding of the potential role of governance mechanisms. The following section outlines possible future research avenues.

21.3   FUTURE RESEARCH AGENDA

Our proposed research agenda includes governance constructs and dimensions (what?), actors (who?), contextual factors (where?), temporal factors (when?) and processes and dynamics (how?). Addressing these different questions will further advance our understanding and provide practical insights of governing IOR tensions in large projects. Table 21.1 provides an overview of the identified research opportunities.

We hope that further studies will conceptually extend and empirically investigate different types and functions of governance mechanisms in large projects' characteristics including the interwoven characteristics of complexity, uncertainty and temporality. We encourage future researchers to consider these characteristics when examining IOR governance mechanisms' effectiveness. For instance, researchers should examine how project characteristics may influence individuals' choices in governing IORs in large projects and project outcomes. This could extend Bercovitz and Tyler's (2014) study on job role preferences on governance mechanisms by focusing on how project characteristics influence individuals/teams developing and using contractual and relational governance mechanisms to control and coordinate IORs.

In terms of complexity, there are several avenues that researchers can address. Future studies should extend Olsen et al.'s (2005) study on complexity and its impact on governance mechanisms by integrating the different functions of governance mechanisms and how these might in/decrease project performance. Further, researchers should consider different forms of complexity (e.g. technological or services) and their impact on governance mechanisms in large projects to identify best practices. Moreover, future studies may address key research areas of the influence of complexity on *ex ante* versus *ex post* governance mechanisms in large projects. This can provide further insight into the dynamics of governance mechanisms to control and coordinate unknown complexities.

There are several key research areas to be studied around uncertainty. For instance, future research could extend Selviaridis's (2016) framework of uncertainty types (e.g. task uncertainty (internal), environmental uncertainty (external)) by studying how IORs use contractual and relational coordination to manage various types of uncertainty in large projects *ex ante* over time. Moreover, as behavioural and environmental uncertainty influence contract design and efficacy of contractual and relational governance mechanisms, future research might explore different actors' risk attitudes when drafting contracts to address different uncertainties in IOR *ex poste* (Roehrich et al., 2020b). This view could provide key insights into organisational-level factors or individual factors that contribute to aversion or risk-taking behaviour influencing the design of contracts and *ex post* management practices in IORs.

Table 21.1   *A research agenda for governing (controlling and coordinating) large projects*

	What?	Who?	Where?	When?	How?
Key concepts	Functions, dimensions and characteristics of contractual and relational governance mechanisms to manage complexity, uncertainty and time, such as:	Factors that influence individuals', teams', stakeholders' and organisations' ability/preference to control and coordinate complexity, uncertainty and time in large projects, such as:	Contextual factors that may impact the effectiveness of governance mechanisms to control and coordinate large projects, such as:	Temporal considerations impact on governance mechanisms to control and coordinate large projects, such as:	Strategies to develop, implement and use functions of governance mechanisms, such as:
	• Impact of governance mechanisms and their control and coordination functions on organisational and social processes (e.g. legitimacy, embeddedness, fairness) • The role of governance mechanisms to realise economic and social value creation in projects • Project boundaries (i.e. what should be controlled/coordinated) • Different types of relationships (e.g. public-private, non-governmental organisations)	• Individual (e.g. job role/experience/seniority, national culture, socio-psychological profile) • Team (e.g. leadership style, team dynamics) • Organisation (e.g. scale, scope, capital, culture) • Inter-organisational factors (e.g. direct or indirect relationship, prior history, dependency)	• Impact of diverse forms of uncertainty (i.e. technological, industry dynamics) • Impact of complexity (e.g. cultural dimensions) • Dynamics (industry, environment, political election cycle) • Influence of different legal systems	• Project life cycle/project stages and their specific requirements for coordination and control • Control and coordination tensions of critical events (operational events, i.e. time, cost, quality) • Speed and timing of tasks and their impact on control and coordination • (Lack of) shadow of the future/ shadow of the past	• Impact of complexity, uncertainty and time on path dependency of governance mechanisms to control and coordinate large projects • Impact of valence (degree of attraction/aversion that a party feels toward an entity/object) • Impact of complexity, uncertainty and time on (dys)functional governance mechanisms in large projects • Influence of different types of contracts to address complexity, uncertainty and time in large projects

	What?	Who?	Where?	When?	How?
Potential research questions	• How do different functions of contractual and relational governance mechanisms impact the (dys)function of large projects? • How do different functions of contractual and relational governance mechanisms (i.e. control versus coordination) differ in realising economic and social value creation in large projects? • How do different types of relationships (e.g. public-private, non-governmental organisations) and their boundaries impact the use of governance mechanisms to control and coordinate large projects?	• How does actors' national culture influence the prevalence of governance mechanisms to control or coordination in large projects? • How does an organisation's bargaining power influence the use of governance mechanisms to control or coordinate large projects? • How does the involvement of specific actors (e.g. internal legal representatives, external employees) impact the enactment of governance mechanisms to control or coordinate IORs in large projects?	• How do different types of uncertainty influence the effectiveness of contractual and relational control and coordination in large projects? • How does contractual and relational coordination effectively address high complexity in large projects? • How does the industry culture/standards influence the use of governance mechanisms to control and coordinate relationships? • How does the industry culture influence the choice of governance mechanisms in large projects?	• How do different project phases influence the interplay of contractual and relational governance mechanisms? • How do different project phases influence contractual and relational governance mechanisms' ability to control and coordinate large projects? • How does the speed and timing of tasks affect coordination and control of IORs in large projects? • When does asymmetry of socially constructed time (e.g. differences in urgency) between key project partners influence the use of governance mechanisms to control and coordinate large projects?	• How do project organisations develop control and coordination capabilities to govern relationships in projects? • How do an organisation's capabilities to use relational control and coordination develop over time? • How does prior relationship history influence the use of control and coordination in large projects? • How do (dysfunctional governance mechanisms influence the ability to control/coordinate IORs in large projects? • How does path dependency influence the use of contractual and relational governance mechanisms in large projects?
Extant governance literature examples	Malhotra and Lumineau (2011); Kapsali et al. (2019)	Bercovitz and Tyler (2014); Zheng et al. (2008)	Zhou and Poppo (2010); Brunet (2019)	Ancona et al. (2001); Van der Valk et al. (2020)	Kreye et al. (2015); Howard et al. (2019)

Lastly, there are ample opportunities to study temporal characteristics and how they influence governance mechanisms in large projects. Studies should address the potential differences in conceptualisation of temporality between organisations. For instance, Oliveira and Lumineau (2017) illustrate the impact of project phases on coordination effectiveness by showing that the fit between specific coordination mechanisms and project phases either hampers or enables performance. Thus, future studies should examine different temporalities that are common in large projects and how they influence governance mechanisms' effectiveness in managing IOR performance. A temporal lens might include the perception in event time duration, the tempo of changes in events, event speed, timing, clock time versus phase time (Van der Valk et al., 2020) and time pressure (Das & Rahman, 2010) that may influence governance mechanisms' effectiveness and performance outcomes.

21.4   CONCLUSIONS

In summary, we hope that this chapter will encourage future research to examine governance mechanisms in large projects and inform (project) management practices. We illuminate control and coordination tensions in governing IORs in large projects caused by complexity, uncertainty and temporality. Further, we position a future research agenda to guide research efforts and managerial practices. We encourage scholars to tie project governance and IOR governance literature together to advance our thinking in both research streams.

REFERENCES

Aben, T. A. E, Van der Valk, W., Roehrich, J. K. & Selviaridis, K. (2021). Digital transformation in public-private relationships: The role of inter-organisational governance in managing information asymmetry. *International Journal of Operations and Production Management*, 41(7), 1145–1191.

Ahola, T. & Davies, A. (2012). Insights for the governance of large projects. *International Journal of Managing Projects in Business*, 5(4), 661–679.

Ahola, T., Ruuska, I., Artto, K. & Kujala, J. (2014). What is project governance and what are its origins? *International Journal of Project Management*, 32(8), 1321–1332.

Ancona, D. G., Goodman, P. S., Lawrence, B. S. & Tushman, M. L. (2001). Time: A new research lens. *Academy of Management Review*, 26(4), 645–663.

Artz, K. W. & Brush, T. H. (2000). Asset specificity, uncertainty and relational norms: An examination of coordination costs in collaborative strategic alliances. *Journal of Economic Behavior and Organization*, 41(4), 337–362.

Bercovitz, J. E. L. & Tyler, B. B. (2014). Who I am and how I contract: The effect of contractors' roles on the evolution of contract structure in university–industry research agreements. *Organization Science*, 25(6), 1840–1859.

Brady, T. & Davies, A. (2014). Managing structural and dynamic complexity: A tale of two projects. *Project Management Journal*, 45(4), 21–38.

Brunet, M. (2019). Governance-as-practice for major public infrastructure projects: A case of multilevel project governing. *International Journal of Project Management*, 37(2), 283–297.

Caldwell, N. D., Roehrich, J. K. & George, G. (2017). Social value creation and relational coordination in public-private collaborations. *Journal of Management Studies*, 54(6), 906–928.

Caniëls, M., Gelderman, C. & Vermeulen, N. (2012). The interplay of governance mechanisms in complex procurement projects. *Journal of Purchasing and Supply Management*, 18(2), 113–121.

Cao, Z. & Lumineau, F. (2015). Revisiting the interplay between contractual and relational governance: A qualitative and meta-analytic investigation. *Journal of Operations Management*, 33–34(1), 15–42.

Carson, S. J., Madhok, A. & Wu, T. (2006). Uncertainty, opportunism, and governance: The effects of volatility and ambiguity on formal and relational contracting. *Academy of Management Journal*, 49(5), 1058–1077.

Chakkol, M., Selviaridis, K. & Finne, M. (2018). The governance of collaboration in complex projects. *International Journal of Operations & Production Management*, 38(4), 997–1019.

Das, T. K. & Rahman, N. (2010). Determinants of partner opportunism in strategic alliances: A conceptual framework. *Journal of Business and Psychology*, 25(1), 55–74.

Davies, A., Dodgson, M., Gann, D. M. & MacAulay, S. C. (2017). Five rules for managing large, complex projects. *MIT Sloan Management Review*, 59(1), 73–78.

Davies, A. & Hobday, M. (2005). *The business of projects*. Cambridge University Press.

Davies, A. & Mackenzie, I. (2014). Project complexity and systems integration: Constructing the London 2012 Olympics and Paralympics games. *International Journal of Project Management*, 32(5), 773–790.

DeFillippi, R. & Sydow, J. (2016). Project networks: Governance choices and paradoxical tensions. *Project Management Journal*, 47(5), 6–17.

Denicol, J., Davies, A. & Krystallis, I. (2020). What are the causes and cures of poor megaproject performance? A systematic literature review and research agenda. *Project Management Journal*, 51(3), 328–345.

Flyvbjerg, B. (2017). Introduction: The iron law of megaproject management. In B. Flyvbjerg (Ed.), *The Oxford handbook of megaproject management* (pp. 1–22). Oxford University Press.

Gulati, R., Wohlgezogen, F. & Zhelyazkov, P. (2012). The two facets of collaboration: Cooperation and coordination in strategic alliances. *Academy of Management Annals*, 6(1), 531–583.

Howard, M., Roehrich, J. K., Lewis, M. A. & Squire, B. (2019). Converging and diverging governance mechanisms: The role of (dys)function in long-term inter-organizational relationships. *British Journal of Management*, 30(3), 624–644.

Jones, C. & Lichtenstein, B. B. (2008). Temporary inter-organizational projects: How temporal and social embeddedness enhance coordination and manage uncertainty. In S. Cropper, C. Huxham, M. Ebers & P. Smith Ring (Eds), *The Oxford handbook of inter-organizational relations* (pp. 1–27). Oxford University Press.

Kalra, J., Lewis, M. & Roehrich, J. K. (2021). The manifestation of coordination failures in service triads. *Supply Chain Management*, 26(3), 341–358.

Kapsali, M., Roehrich, J. K. & Akhtar, P. (2019). Effective contracting for high operational performance in projects. *International Journal of Operations and Production Management*, 39(2), 294–325.

Kreye, M. E., Roehrich, J. K. & Lewis, M. A. (2015). Servitising manufacturers: The impact of service complexity and contractual and relational capabilities. *Production Planning and Control*, 26(14–15), 1233–1246.

Larson, A. (1992). Network dyads in entrepreneurial settings: A study of the governance of exchange relationships. *Administrative Science Quarterly*, 37(1), 76–104.

Li, Y., Xie, E., Teo, H.-H. & Peng, M. W. (2010). Formal control and social control in domestic and international buyer–supplier relationships. *Journal of Operations Management*, 28(4), 333–344.

Lumineau, F. & Henderson, J. E. (2012). The influence of relational experience and contractual governance on the negotiation strategy in buyer–supplier disputes. *Journal of Operations Management*, 30(5), 382–395.

Malhotra, D. & Lumineau, F. (2011). Trust and collaboration in the aftermath of conflict: The effects of contract structure. *Academy of Management Journal*, 54(5), 981–998.

Matinheikki, J., Aaltonen, K. & Walker, D. (2019). Politics, public servants, and profits: Institutional complexity and temporary hybridization in a public infrastructure alliance project. *International Journal of Project Management*, 37(2), 298–317.

Oliveira, N. & Lumineau, F. (2017). How coordination trajectories influence the performance of interorganizational project networks. *Organization Science*, 28(6), 1029–1060.

Olsen, E. B., Haugland, S. A., Karlsen, E. & Husøy, J. G. (2005). Governance of complex procurements in the oil and gas industry. *Journal of Purchasing and Supply Management*, 11(1), 1–13.

Poppo, L. & Zenger, T. (2002). Do formal contracts and relational governance function as substitutes or complements? *Strategic Management Journal*, 23(8), 707–725.

Poppo, L., Zhou, K. Z. & Ryu, S. (2008). Alternative origins to interorganizational trust: An interdependence perspective on the shadow of the past and the shadow of the future. *Organization Science*, 19(1), 38–55.

Reuer, J. J. & Ariño, A. (2007). Strategic alliance contracts: Dimensions and determinants of contractual complexity. *Strategic Management Journal*, 28(3), 313–330.

Roehrich, J. K. & Lewis, M. (2014). Procuring complex performance: Implications for exchange governance complexity. *International Journal of Operations and Production Management*, 34(2), 221–241.

Roehrich, J. K., Tyler, B. T., Kalra, J. & Squire, B. (2020a). The decision process of contracting in supply chain management. In T. Y. Choi, J. J. Li, D. S. Rogers, T. Schoenherr & S. M. Wagner (Eds), *The Oxford handbook of supply chain management*. Oxford University Press.

Roehrich, J. K., Selviaridis, K., Karla, J., Van der Valk, W. & Fang, F. (2020b). Inter-organizational governance: A review, conceptualisation and extension. *Production Planning and Control*, 31(6), 453–469.

Schepker, D. J., Oh, W. Y. & Poppo, L. (2014). The many futures of contracts: Moving beyond structure and safeguarding to coordination and adaptation. *Journal of Management*, 40(1), 193–225.

Schilke, O. & Lumineau, F. (2018). The double-edged effect of contracts on alliance performance. *Journal of Management*, 44(7), 2827–2858.

Selviaridis, K. (2016). Contract functions in service exchange governance: Evidence from logistics outsourcing. *Production Planning and Control*, 27(16), 1373–1388.

Van der Valk, W., Lumineau, F. & Wang, W. (2020). Research on contracting in supply chain management and related disciplines. In T. Y. Choi, J. J. Li, D. S. Rogers, T. Schoenherr & S. M. Wagner (Eds), *The Oxford handbook of supply chain management*. Oxford University Press.

Vandaele, D., Rangarajan, D., Gemmel, P. & Lievens, A. (2007). How to govern business services exchanges: Contractual and relational issues. *International Journal of Management Reviews*, 9(3), 237–258.

Vukomanović, M., Ceric, A., Brunet, M., Locatelli, G. & Davies, A. (2021). Editorial: Trust and governance in megaprojects. *International Journal of Project Management*, 39(4), 321–324.

Williamson, O. E. (1985). *The economic institutions of capitalism*. Free Press.

Winch, G. M. (2014). Three domains of project organising. *International Journal of Project Management*, 32(5), 721–731.

Zheng, J., Roehrich, J. K. & Lewis, M. A. (2008). The dynamics of contractual and relational governance: Evidence from long-term public-private procurement arrangements. *Journal of Purchasing and Supply Management*, 14(1), 43–54.

Zhou, K. Z. & Poppo, L. (2010). Exchange hazards, relational reliability, and contracts in China: The contingent role of legal enforceability. *Journal of International Business Studies*, 41(5), 861–881.

22. Public-private partnerships as vectors of complexity

Pierre-André Hudon, Maude Brunet and Nicolas Paquet

22.1 INTRODUCTION

Public-private partnerships (P3s, also often referred to as PPPs) have gained in popularity in the last decades for many reasons: the inability of the state to borrow money for major projects; the desire to leverage the so-called greater efficiency of integrated projects; the wish to foster innovation; the streamlining of management through outsourcing of responsibilities; better ability to manage risk; the desire to speed up project delivery; or even the explicit objective to reduce the size of the state by privatizing the delivery of services traditionally delivered by the public sector (Hodge & Greve, 2005).

Several authors point out the main advantages of P3s, such as attracting and mobilizing private finance to infrastructure projects; reducing financial risks (by transferring them to the private sector); avoiding capital costs; lowering procurement costs; helping to stabilize public spending and debt; giving the momentary appearance of budgetary control (as P3 projects would not/only partially enter the government's balance sheet); ensuring spending power without using money directly or indirectly taken from citizens; reducing the fiscal burden on governments and citizens; doing differently and better what the public sector cannot do or does less well; strategically combining public- and private-sector strengths; motivating the private partner to reduce costs throughout the infrastructure life cycle (design, construction, operation, maintenance); and gaining efficiency in performance, economies of scale, synergy and mutual learning opportunities (Boardman et al., 2015; Engel et al., 2020; Vining et al., 2005; Wettenhall, 2003).

If many researchers highlight potential benefits from using P3, many also raise a number of issues and criticisms. Some of the main concerns are: information asymmetry during the infrastructure life cycle; conservative project design; difficulty to benchmark against other projects; complex, energy-intensive, politicized and uncertain contracting processes requiring a variety of expertise; disagreements and tensions between actors; frequent renegotiations; frequent conflicts of interest (lobbying); corruption and opportunism; user fees for infrastructure or services and marginalization of certain categories of users; loss of decision-making autonomy and ability to set priorities; danger of foreign takeovers of critical infrastructure (e.g. ports, refineries); and the quality and overall coherence of infrastructure systems (Boardman et al., 2015; Levy, 2011; Siemiatyki, 2013; Wettenhall, 2003).

Prior research on P3s has adopted many theoretical perspectives, including political economy, public economics and public administration (Levitt et al., 2019). Others have mobilized urban studies, governance theory, sustainability and decision-making theory (Cui et al., 2018).

Whatever the reason for the usage of P3s, the sheer size of infrastructure projects and the intricate contractual structures that they require lead to greater complexity in terms of design, coordination processes, organizational structures and administrative tools used. They are institutional arrangements and may generate much uncertainty and unpredictability requiring renegotiations through time (Wang et al., 2018). In this chapter, we show that P3s act as vectors of complexity, building on the four facets presented in Chapter 3. We also highlight avenues for future research.

22.2 THE FUNCTIONING OF P3S

Although P3s have gained increased attention in the mainstream, they are still loosely defined and mischaracterized (Martin, 2016). Levitt et al. (2019, pp. 21–22) propose the following definition:

> A public-private partnership (PPP) is created when a government agency enters into a long-term (typically 25- to 50-year) concession agreement with a project-based legal entity called a special purpose vehicle (SPV), under which the SPV has the right and obligation to finance, design, build, operate and maintain a facility (or some subset of these roles) in accordance with contractually specified performance standards. The government generally retains ownership of the infrastructure asset and the land on which it is built, conceding only the rights associated with the asset to the SPV for a defined term. General characteristics of PPPs include:
> * A long-term contract(s) between the public sponsor and the private sector participant(s);
> * A private, or joint private and public, commitment to provide 'bundled' development and operational services;
> * Funding derived from user charges and/or governmental budgetary or borrowed resources over the lifetime of the asset. (Levitt et al., 2019, pp. 21–22)

In the media, the term P3 has been used in several ways: joint policy coordination such as industry roundtables, joint policy delivery such as private foundations providing 'public' services in line with government priorities or even private delivery of publicly funded policies. Nevertheless, in this chapter, we use a much narrower definition of P3s, which corresponds to the way they are generally understood in CPO research.

For our purposes, a P3 agreement corresponds to a contractual agreement through which the state delegates to a private entity the obligations to *design, build, operate, finance* and *maintain* a traditionally publicly financed and operated infrastructure. A single contract that delegates all or most of these obligations to a private provider can be considered a P3.

22.2.1 Standard P3 Contractual Structure

As shown in Figure 22.1, P3s are based on intricate contractual structures through which the aforementioned obligations are delegated by a public entity (1) to private company (2), named SPV, which then subcontracts the designing and building obligations to a builder (3) via the design-build subcontract (B) and the operation and maintenance obligations to an operator (4) via the operation and maintenance subcontract (C) (Hudon, 2016).

The builder and operator work in sequence, one after the other. The builder's obligations end when the infrastructure is commissioned, while the operator's obligations begin at that very moment. To avoid conflicts between both subcontractors, an interface contract (D) is signed, which serves as a dispute resolution mechanism. If an agreement cannot be reached, the interface agreement serves as a dispute resolution mechanism that usually involves arbi-

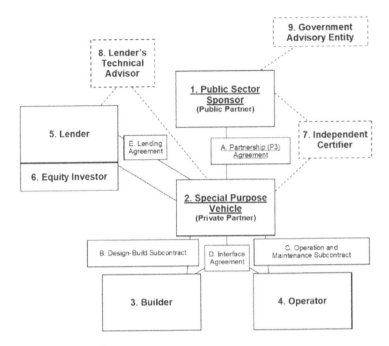

Source: Adapted from Hudon (2016).

Figure 22.1   Standard P3 contractual structure

tration. Nevertheless, the risk for conflict between the builder and the operator is mitigated by the fact that these two subcontractors are often subsidiaries of a large integrated construction group that ac as equity holder in the SPV.

To finance the construction of the infrastructure, the SPV needs to receive cash inflows which it can use to pay the builder. Like any other private entity, the SPV is financed using a mix of debt and equity, coming respectively from a lender (5) and an equity investor (6). Financing is usually done with a high leverage rate, at least during the capital-intensive construction period. The infrastructure only begins generating a revenue at commissioning, once it starts being operated. The lender's power and obligations are laid out in the lender's agreement (E).

Three other organizations are also linked to the contractual structure, in various ways. The independent certifier (7) is an entity (usually an engineering firm) whose role is to certify that the construction period is done, that the infrastructure performs as planned and that consequently it can be commissioned and start generating revenues. The lender's technical advisor (LTA) (8) has a similar role: on behalf of the lender, the LTA makes sure that the building is going according to plan and that capital transfers (from the lender to the SPV) can be done to finance the next step of the construction. Finally, since the public sponsors often have very little experience with P3s – much less, in fact, than private bidders – it will often require the services of a government advisory entity (9), whose role consists of oversight, assistance or advice.

Manoeuvring in such an intricate contractual and organizational environment requires a great deal of coordination, negotiation and competence. The contractual structure in and of itself, combined with the fact that P3s are mostly used in very big projects, constitutes an important factor of complexity.

22.2.2   Characteristics of P3s

Standard P3 processes also exhibit several characteristics that speak to their complexity. First, P3s are performance-based contracts, which means that they are less prescriptive than traditional contracts with regards to the expected scope of the work (Hartmann et al., 2014). Instead, they tend to specify performance criteria that need to be met for the infrastructure to be deemed 'available', i.e. for the infrastructure to be operational to a satisfactory degree. The issue of measuring the operational performance of the project is of utmost importance since availability is generally a condition for payment (Benítez-Ávila et al., 2018).

Second, P3 projects are generally financed through a two-stage scheme (Daube et al., 2008), whereby the capital necessary during the construction period is provided by private lenders and investors, and the operational revenues that begin after commissioning of the infrastructure come from a mix of user fees (for example, tolls), 'availability' payments from the public partner (i.e. rent), subsidies or autonomous revenues from commercial operations (for example, renting out concessions). Because in a P3, the infrastructure starts generating revenues only during the operational phase, private lenders are very exposed during the construction phase and, consequently, tend to demand important oversight powers (Madykov, 2014). This puts the SPV in a situation where it needs to answer to two different masters: the public partner, but also the lender. For accountability, transparency and overall democratic governance, this can become problematic, especially if the public partner is comparatively weak (Hodge & Greve, 2005).

Third, P3 projects generally emphasize a strict risk management strategy whereby each project risk is contractually transferred to the partner best able to bear it (Bing et al., 2005). This involves an explicit identification and definition of all project risks. However, since P3 projects often emphasize high levels of innovation, risk identification and a clear definition of performance criteria becomes more difficult. Paradoxically, P3 projects tend to be favoured in high innovation settings – usually to take advantage of the potential cost savings – though this very choice adds to their complexity by making their risk and performance management more challenging (Levitt et al., 2019).

Fourth, in most jurisdictions where they have been adopted, P3s have used novel public procurement methods that often clashed with tendering regulations and best practices (Burger & Hawkesworth, 2011). Perhaps the most important one of these is bilateral workshops, during which bidders can interact confidentially with the public sponsors to better understand its needs and to tailor the bid. Much has also been written about the public sector comparator, a tool that is used to justify the use of P3 procurement (as opposed to traditional procurement), by comparing the project's cashflows in P3s to what they would have been had the project been done with traditional procurement (for example, Bain, 2010; Khadaroo, 2008). However, this proved to be a highly complex and speculative exercise because of the high level of uncertainty, the ambiguity of financial discount rates and the unknown nature of bidding patterns and behaviours.

22.3 COMPLEXITY

To present an analysis of P3 complexity, we first dissect its meaning. To this end, we use the definition of system complexity (Chapter 3) which is comprised of four facets:

1. *Element complexity*: The number and variety of elements that constitute a system affect complexity. Consequently, the sheer quantity of elements at hand, coupled with their heterogeneity, contribute to make a system more complex. For the purpose of studying P3s, the elements of a project can be defined as:
   a. Results, including project specifications, expected performance, etc.
   b. Processes, such as procurement activities, managerial and accountability practices.
   c. Organizations that are linked by the contractual structure, as well as oversight and advisory entities.
   d. Tools, both analytical and managerial, that are used during the planning and management phases of the project.
   e. Goals. Because P3s tend to be traditionally public major infrastructure projects, goals are often akin to public policy outcomes.
2. *Relationship complexity*: Here again, both the number and the variety of relationships affect complexity, but so does their *criticality*. Criticality is defined as the need for a relationship to be managed in a specific, sophisticated way.
3. *Complicatedness*: Observer-dependent cognitive complexity brings a subjective dimension to the study of system complexity. Complicatedness can be linked, amongst others, to the perceived simplicity of a system, to its intuitiveness or to its novelty.
4. *Context complexity*: Though not directly linked to the inner workings of a system, context complexity, especially in public projects, can affect the project's goals and relationships.

These four facets constitute a working yet static framework for understanding project complexity. The next section links those facets to the specificities of P3 projects.

22.4 P3 AND THE FOUR FACETS OF COMPLEXITY

P3 projects exist at the interface between the public sector's concern for delivering services to the population and the private sector's interest in commercially viable endeavours. As such, they operate in an environment with competing institutional logics (Matinheikki et al., 2021), that is both concerned with traditional public values such as accountability, transparency and effectiveness and with private-sector concerns such as efficiency and profitability. These paradoxical, often discordant, concerns are the reasons for P3s' elaborate structures full of counterpowers, performance specifications and dispersed responsibilities.

22.4.1 Element Complexity

The first facet of complexity, element complexity, can be observed in P3s in several ways.

First, results complexity can be seen in the sheer number and variety of contractual requirements, which can be either specification-based or performance-based. This stems mostly from the sheer size of P3 projects, which tend to be used in major infrastructure projects. When requirements are performance-based, a second layer of complexity is added, because performance criteria need to be converted into measurable and objective performance indicators.

Second, process complexity can be observed at various moments in the P3 project's life cycle (Liu et al., 2015). Before the contract is even signed, the procurement process is both long and singular compared to traditional procurement. The integrated (construction and operation) and long-term nature of the contract also means that coordination and negotiation must happen continuously and that decisions made early on may impact the contractual process for many decades.

Third, organizational complexity is perhaps the most self-evident and can be noticed by looking at the number of entities involved in the contractual structure (see Figure 22.1) and in their variety (Levitt et al., 2019; Sainati et al., 2020).

Fourth, standard practices involve using several innovative tools that are specific to P3 procurement and management. For instance, the use of the public sector comparator, of bilateral workshops or of risk allocation registries all constitute P3-specific tools that add to managerial complexity.

Fifth, complexity in goals is linked to the multidimensional nature of major public infrastructure projects, which can often be seen as public policies 'incarnate'. They are also geographically anchored and bring irreversibility (Siemiatyki, 2013). Concretely, this means that, like other infrastructure projects, P3s are often much more than brick-and-mortar projects and can shape, or at least strongly influence, development strategies. The fact that P3 procurement is done using performance-based contracts also has the effect of shifting some responsibilities of policy development to the private sector, making policy coordination more difficult. Indeed, project goals are analogous to public policy outcomes and, by definition, those can be varied, politicized and associated with heterogeneous values and visions.

22.4.2 Relationship Complexity

Perhaps the most important aspect of P3 complexity is relationship complexity (Benítez-Ávila et al., 2018; South et al., 2019). Contractual relationships are numerous, but they also exhibit a high degree of 'criticality', i.e. of needing to be managed in a sophisticated and skilled way. Managing P3 projects requires technical, legal and financial competences (Umar et al., 2018), as well as specific collaborative and managerial skills (Feng et al., 2019; Préfontaine et al., 2009; Ramonjavelo et al., 2006).

We contend that this relationship complexity affects the conduct of P3 projects in three ways.

First, relationship management becomes a primary concern for the success of P3s (Zou et al., 2014), both in the front end and in the operating phase (McCann et al., 2015). Benítez-Ávila et al. (2018) have found that economic incentives and hierarchical relationships formalized in contract agreements require being internalized in working practices by means of informal and socially based mechanisms.

Second, control, monitoring and audit tools need to be adapted to account for this increased complexity (English et al., 2010; Jooste & Levitt, 2012). This also raises the question of the capability of the state to undertake these specific yet critical tasks (Sanderson & Winch, 2017).

Third, P3 relationship complexity generates concerns for democratic accountability and transparency, especially because of the ineffectiveness of public audit tools at investigating hybrid public-private structures (Broadbent & Laughlin, 2003).

22.4.3 Complicatedness

Complicatedness, which refers to the *perceived* complexity, is also a major issue in P3 management. Though P3s are less novel than they once were, many jurisdictions, especially ones with less public-sector capacity such as developing countries, municipalities or smaller front-line public organizations, do not use them frequently (Olojede et al., 2020; Siemiatyki, 2013). As such, they remain unusual – if not intimidating – for many less experienced public-sector organizations.

This complicatedness can partially be mitigated by relying upon an internal or external government advisory entity and by providing training to public-sector employees in charge of managing P3 projects (Olojede et al., 2020). This capacity building must include strategic abilities (deciding in which cases to use P3s), executive abilities (managing private partners) and political abilities (Jooste & Levitt, 2012).

22.4.4 Context Complexity

Finally, P3s exist in an institutional and political context that can be analysed at two levels.

The first level is not linked to the P3 model *per se*, but rather to the inherent politicization of most major infrastructure projects. This is extremely well documented (for example, Flyvbjerg, 1998; Olesen, 2020) and highlights the need for P3 practitioners to be able to deal with the thorny problem of large project stakeholder management (Henjewele et al., 2013).

The second level of institutional and political complexity is the *usage* of P3s as procurement and development instruments (Scott et al., 2011). Indeed, P3s have often been depicted as the by-product of neoliberal policies (for example, Flinders, 2005; Miraftab, 2004) and, as such, have attracted their fair share of controversy. Practitioners, especially those evolving at the strategic level of decision-making, must then be prepared for decisions to use P3 procurement to be called into question almost systematically by civil society groups, labour unions and opposition parties (Siemiatyki, 2013).

22.5 CONCLUSION

Although P3s generate much complexity in all their aspects, they are still very much alive, and increasing in number, especially in certain areas of the world (Osei-Kyei & Chan, 2015). Thus, research will likely continue and enrich our knowledge through an interdisciplinary lens of project management, public administration and public policy. In this line, we encourage researchers to delve into the three dimensions at the intersection of public policy and projects, which are efficiency (performance and value for money), legitimacy (public acceptability) and accountability (transparency of processes) (Brunet & Aubry, 2016).

To address further the notions of complexity and P3s, we suggest the following research avenues (Casady & Geddes, 2016; Cui et al., 2018; Hodge & Greve, 2007; Siemiatyki, 2013; Wang et al., 2018):

1. P3s and complex forms of cooperation or collaboration during the project life cycle.
2. P3s and collective decision-making.
3. P3s and resilience/vulnerability towards uncertainty.

4. Global production of P3s, forces at work, factors of adoption and organizational pressures.
5. Performance of P3s and performance of governance networks.
6. P3s and public accountability mechanisms.
7. P3s and the problem of value appropriation (collective/private; in line with common good/ business interests) and the sharing of project benefits.
8. P3s and actors' behaviour (motivation, negotiation, opportunism).
9. Institutions and success/failure of P3s (culture, politics, customs, economic institutions, legal framework, innovation).
10. P3 units and their actual/potential role in reducing complexity at multiple jurisdictional levels (unitary state, federal states, etc.).
11. The gap between rhetoric and reality (at a meta-analytical level; this gap adds to the intrinsic complexity of PPPs and confuses the discussion on public policy).

And though P3s have shown several advantages and disadvantages, they remain a tool that is frequently used by public administrations. Tackling their main complexities regarding elements, relationships, context and complicatedness will allow for a deeper understanding and refined solutions in the long term.

REFERENCES

Bain, R. (2010). Public sector comparators for UK PFI roads: Inside the black box. *Transportation*, 37(3), 447–471.
Benítez-Ávila, C., Hartmann, A., Dewulf, G. & Henseler, J. (2018). Interplay of relational and contractual governance in public-private partnerships: The mediating role of relational norms, trust and partners' contribution. *International Journal of Project Management*, 36(3), 429–443.
Bing, B., Akintoye, A., Edwards, P. J. & Hardcastle, C. (2005). The allocation of risk in PPP/PFI construction projects in the UK. *International Journal of Project Management*, 23(1), 25–35.
Boardman, A. E., Greve, C. & Hodge, G. A. (2015). Comparative analyses of infrastructure public-private partnerships. *Journal of Comparative Policy Analysis: Research and Practice*, 17(5), 441–447.
Broadbent, J. & Laughlin, R. (2003). Control and legitimation in government accountability processes: The private finance initiative in the UK. *Critical Perspectives on Accounting*, 14(1–2), 23–48.
Brunet, M. & Aubry, M. (2016). The three dimensions of a governance framework for major public projects. *International Journal of Project Management*, 34(8), 1596–1607.
Burger, P. & Hawkesworth, I. (2011). How to attain value for money: Comparing PPP and traditional infrastructure public procurement. *OECD Journal on Budgeting*, 11(1), 91–146.
Casady, C. R. & Geddes, R. R. (2016). *Private participation in US infrastructure: The role of PPP units*. American Enterprise Institute.
Cui, C., Liu, Y., Hope, A. & Wang, J. (2018). Review of studies on the public-private partnerships (PPP) for infrastructure projects. *International Journal of Project Management*, 36(5), 773–794.
Daube, D., Vollrath, S. & Alfen, H. W. (2008). A comparison of project finance and the forfeiting model as financing forms for PPP projects in Germany. *International Journal of Project Management*, 26(4), 376–387.
Engel, E., Fischer, R. & Galetovic, A. (2020). Public-private partnerships: Some lessons after 30 years. *Regulation*, 43, 30–35.
English, L. M., Guthrie, J., Broadbent, J. & Laughlin, R. (2010). Performance audit of the operational stage of long-term partnerships for the private sector provision of public services. *Australian Accounting Review*, 20(1), 64–75.
Feng, W., Lessard, D. R., Cameron, B. G. & Crawley, E. F. (2019). Stakeholders, issues and the shaping of large engineering projects. In R. E. Levitt, W. R. Scott & M. J. Garvin (Eds), *Public-private partnerships for infrastructure development: Finance, stakeholder alignment, governance* (pp. 87–101). Edward Elgar Publishing.

Flinders, M. (2005). The politics of public-private partnerships. *British Journal of Politics and International Relations*, 7(2), 215–239.

Flyvbjerg, B. (1998). *Rationality and power: Democracy in practice*. University of Chicago Press.

Hartmann, A., Roehrich, J., Frederiksen, L. & Davies, A. (2014). Procuring complex performance: The transition process in public infrastructure. *International Journal of Operations & Production Management*, 34(2), 174–194.

Henjewele, C., Fewings, P. & Rwelamila, P. D. (2013). De-marginalising the public in PPP projects through multi-stakeholders management. *Journal of Financial Management of Property and Construction*, 18(3), 210–230.

Hodge, G. A. & Greve, C. (2005). *The challenge of public-private partnerships: Learning from international experience*. Edward Elgar Publishing.

Hodge, G. A. & Greve, C. (2007). Public-private partnerships: An international performance review. *Public Administration Review*, 67(3), 545–558.

Hudon, P.-A. (2016). La dynamique des relations dans les partenariats public-privé: Le cas du modèle anglo-saxon. *Revue française d'administration publique*, 160(4), 1271–1288.

Jooste, S. F. & Levitt, R. E. (2012). *The impacts of infrastructure PPPs on public sector capacity*. American Society of Civil Engineers. DOI:10.1061/41020(339)120.

Khadaroo, I. (2008). The actual evaluation of school PFI bids for value for money in the UK public sector. *Critical Perspectives on Accounting*, 19(8), 1321–1345.

Levitt, R. E., Scott, W. R. & Garvin, M. J. (Eds) (2019). *Public-private partnerships for infrastructure development: Finance, stakeholder alignment, governance*. Edward Elgar Publishing.

Levy, S. M. (2011). *Public-private partnerships: Case studies on infrastructure development*. ACSE Press.

Liu, J., Love, P. E. D., Smith, J., Regan, M. & Davis, P. R. (2015). Life cycle critical success factors for public-private partnerships infrastructure projects. *Journal of Management Engineering*, 31(5), 04014073.

Madykov, M. (2014). Step-in right as a lender protection mechanism in project financed transactions. *DePaul Business and Commercial Law Journal*, 13(2), 273–300.

Martin, L. (2016). Making sense of public-private partnerships (P3s). *Journal of Public Procurement*, 16(2), 191–207.

Matinheikki, J., Naderpajouh, N., Aranda-Mena, G., Jayasuriya, S. & Teo, P. (2021). Befriending aliens: Institutional complexity and organizational responses in infrastructure public-private partnerships. *Project Management Journal*, 52(5), 453–470.

McCann, S., Aranda-Mena, G. & Edwards, P. J. (2015). Public private partnership projects in the operating phase: Three Australian case studies. *Journal of Strategic Contracting and Negotiation*, 1(4), 268–287.

Miraftab, F. (2004). Public-private partnerships: The Trojan horse of neoliberal development? *Journal of Planning Education and Research*, 24(1), 89–101.

Olesen, K. (2020). Infrastructure imaginaries: The politics of light rail projects in the age of neoliberalism. *Urban Studies*, 57(9), 1811–1826.

Olojede, B. O., Opawole, A. & Jagboro, G. O. (2020). Capability development measures adopted by public sector organizations in PPP projects delivery in developing countries. *Journal of Public Procurement*, 20(2), 145–161.

Osei-Kyei, R. & Chan, A. P. C. (2015). Review of studies on the critical success factors for public-private partnership (PPP) projects from 1990 to 2013. *International Journal of Project Management*, 33(6), 1335–1346.

Préfontaine, L., Skander, D. & Ramonjavelo, V. (2009). La capacité partenariale, pilier de la réussite d'un partenariat public-privé. *Revue francaise d'administration publique*, 130(2), 323–336.

Ramonjavelo, V., Préfontaine, L., Skander, D. & Ricard, L. (2006). Une assise au développement des PPP: La confiance institutionnelle, interorganisationnelle et interpersonnelle. *Canadian Public Administration/Administration Publique du Canada*, 49(3), 350–374.

Sainati, T., Locatelli, G., Smith, N., Brookes, N. & Olver, G. (2020). Types and functions of special purpose vehicles in infrastructure megaprojects. *International Journal of Project Management*, 38(5), 243–255.

Sanderson, J. & Winch, G. (2017). Public policy and projects: Making connections and starting conversations. *International Journal of Project Management*, 35(3), 221–223.

Scott, R. W., Levitt, R. E. & Or, R. J. (Eds) (2011). *Global projects: Institutional and political challenges*. Cambridge University Press.

Siemiatyki, M. (2013). The global production of transportation public-private partnerships. *International Journal of Urban and Regional Research*, 37(4), 1254–1272.

South, A. J., Levitt, R. E. & Dewulf, G. P. M. R. (2019). Stakeholder network dynamics in public-private partnerships. In R. E. Levitt, W. R. Scott & M. J. Garvin (Eds), *Public-private partnerships for infrastructure development: Finance, stakeholder alignment, governance*. Edward Elgar Publishing.

Umar, A. A., Zawawi, N. A. W. A. & Abdul-Aziz, A.-R. (2018). Exploratory factor analysis of skills requirement for PPP contract governance. *Built Environment Project and Asset Management*, 9(2), 277–290.

Vining, A. R., Boardman, A. E. & Poschmann, F. (2005). Public-private partnerships in the US and Canada: 'There are no free lunches'. *Journal of Comparative Policy Analysis: Research and Practice*, 7(3), 199–220.

Wang, H., Xiong, W. & Zhu, D. (2018). Public-private partnership in public administration discipline: A literature review. *Public Management Review*, 20(2), 293–316.

Wettenhall, R. (2003). The rhetoric and reality of public-private partnerships. *Public Organization Review*, 3(1), 77–107.

Zou, W., Kumaraswamy, M., Chung, J. & Wong, J. (2014). Identifying the critical success factors for relationship management in PPP projects. *International Journal of Project Management*, 32(2), 265–274.

23. Megaprojects: XL challenges in project organizing

Alfons van Marrewijk

23.1 INTRODUCTION: WHAT ARE INFRASTRUCTURE MEGAPROJECTS?

Although megaprojects have been executed ever since the construction of the Egyptian pyramids, the Canadian government and the American contractor Bechtel were among the first to conceptualize the notion of megaprojects in the early 1970s (Merrow et al., 1988). In the Oxford Advanced Learners Dictionary (1990) the word 'mega' is connected to the number of 1 million, to indicate something very large, great or extraordinary. 'Megaproject' thus emphasizes a project's greatness, large size, huge impact and enormous budget. Megaprojects are generally perceived as non-routine endeavours, requiring special authorizing, funding, revenues, land acquisition and regulatory actions by two or more levels of government, while they are initially controversial, proceeding slowly and passing through different electoral and business cycles in which public-private cooperation is needed (Altshuler & Luberoff, 2003). Furthermore, megaprojects require complex integration of tasks and technical expertise, resource and materials management, long time frames and numerous interfaces among multiple contractors and third parties (Greiman, 2013).

In recent decades there has been a clear increase in the magnitude and frequency of construction megaprojects (Flyvbjerg, 2017; Gemünden, 2014). According to Flyvbjerg (2014), megaprojects are attractive to decision-makers and investors due to the tendency to build larger, more complex and aesthetically interesting infrastructures. Such projects have become symbols of great engineering (van Marrewijk, 2017). Furthermore, megaprojects have become popular with public politicians and local officials as a way of creating attractive, sustainable and economically viable urban areas for citizens (Diaz Orueta & Fainstein, 2008; Lehrer & Laidley, 2008). Construction megaprojects thus serve as an important political legacy; as highly visible, material results of public policy and officials at the local and national levels (Trapenberger Fick, 2008). For example, the construction of the Øresund bridge and tunnel facilitated political, economic and cultural integration of the Copenhagen and Malmö region (Löfgren, 2015).

For a long time, academic attention to the organizing of megaprojects was reserved to the engineering discipline (Cicmil & Hodgson, 2006; Morris, 2012) and urban development discipline (Altshuler & Luberoff, 2003). In these disciplines, megaprojects were perceived as monolithic constructions. This type of megaproject, called 'old' megaprojects by Lehrer and Laidley (2008), received strong criticism for their dominant perception of organizing megaprojects as technically defined matters occurring in demarcated spatial settings with a particular set of complex tasks (Merrow et al., 1988). To counter the megaproject as a monolith view, scholars introduced critical perspectives of understanding the organizing of megaprojects as temporal, organizational and social arrangements that should be studied in their context, culture, conceptions and relevance (Kreiner, 1995; Lundin & Söderlund, 1995; Packendorff, 1995). Frequently, work-related goals and activities in megaprojects are not completely clear, nor can be fully predicted in advance as they have their own internal dynamics (van Marrewijk et al., 2008). Therefore, Flyvbjerg et al. (2003) call megaprojects 'political and physical animals'. This new and critical attention to megaprojects has resulted in a growing number of megaproject studies over the last two decades (Clegg et al., 2002; van Marrewijk et al., 2016; Winch, 2013).

23.2   THE CHARACTERISTICS OF A MEGAPROJECT

Do construction megaprojects differ enough from 'regular' construction projects to justify separate academic attention? Generally, a distinction between regular and megaprojects is made based upon the large financial capital needed for megaprojects; over $100 million (Flyvbjerg, 2012) or $1 billion (Merrow et al., 1988). Greiman (2013) suggests relating the labelling of an endeavour as a megaproject to a country's gross domestic product. Furthermore, megaprojects distinguish themselves from other projects by their characteristics: large-scale development projects with iconic design components, aimed to transform urban areas, and promoted and perceived as crucial catalysts for economic growth (Del Cerro Santamaria, 2013). Not surprisingly, megaprojects rarely remain uncontested, especially within a democratic political context, as they are perceived not only as costly, but also as significant threats to the local quality of life; 'a megaproject is not only big, in terms of scope and scale and costs, it is also big in its potential for politics in and around the project' (Pitsis et al., 2018, p. 9). Finally, complex megaprojects distinguish themselves from other projects in their structural complexity (Sykes, 1998), which is the interaction and interdependency of elements in a project, and their uncertainty, resulting from a lack of clearness and agreement over project goals and the way these goals have to be researched (Williams, 2002).

Based upon a brief analysis of megaproject literature, van Marrewijk (2015, p. 16) mentions a few additional characteristics of megaprojects. They have long, complex and critical front-end processes with new and unproven technologies and legislation with related risks of overcommitment. Furthermore, megaprojects have a non-linear project life cycle with high levels of ambiguity and uncertainty resulting in changing project scope over time. Finally, megaprojects are often unique at the national level, involving decision-making of many stakeholders with conflicting interests, with a mixture of joint organization and sub-contracting to legally separate partners.

These characteristics spell out that construction megaprojects differ enough from 'regular' construction projects to justify separate academic attention. Furthermore, megaprojects bring along challenges in organizing of which I have selected four key themes to discuss in this chapter: (1) (under)performance of megaprojects; (2) governance of megaprojects; (3) cross-cultural differences; and (4) leading a megaproject. The first two themes are well-known challenges and frequently discussed in megaproject literature (Brunet & Aubry, 2016; Flyvbjerg, 2017; Priemus & van Wee, 2013; Qiu et al., 2019), while the latter two are less developed but interesting. Megaprojects include project actors from a multitude of (international) organizations that have to work together and someone has to lead this extremely complex project organization. In the paragraphs below I will discuss the four key challenges and how researchers have dealt with these so far.

23.3 (UNDER)PERFORMANCE OF MEGAPROJECTS

Most visible and very frequently mentioned is the (under)performance of megaprojects, which manifests itself in exceeding budgets, falling behind in time schedules and failing to deliver project goals (e.g. Cantarelli & Flyvbjerg, 2013; Flyvbjerg et al., 2003; Merrow et al., 1988). Many evaluations of megaprojects, measured from the moment of ratification by national governments to delivery, show that the final costs of megaprojects exceed initial cost estimations by 50–200 per cent (Flyvbjerg, 2012; Flyvbjerg et al., 2003). Also, the length and scale of time delays are very visible and discussed in national media, with the ten-year delay of the delivery of the Berlin Brandenburg airport as an iconic example. Finally, changes in project specifications and scope, resulting in failing to meet project goals, are frequently mentioned in evaluations (e.g. van Marrewijk, 2017). In short, megaprojects don't seem to be the best way of infrastructure development (Flyvbjerg, 2021).

Scholars have come up with diverse explanations for the underperformance of megaprojects (see Sanderson, 2012). Flyvbjerg et al. (2003) introduced the concept of 'strategic misrepresentation', which is the practice of underestimating costs and overestimating benefits by project promotors to strategically influence the decision-making process. Their solution was to not trust the cost estimates presented by infrastructure promotors and forecasters but to develop institutional checks and balances with penalties. Some scholars explain the underperformance due to bad ex ante cost-benefit analysis, which is the capturing of as many pros and cons of a project (Priemus & van Wee, 2013). This may work well with clear preferences of users or consumers valuing the outcomes of a project, but is of little help when political preferences are involved. Therefore, Scott et al. (2011) see institutional and political challenges of megaprojects as the root of underperformance. Other scholars, for example Cantarelli and Flyvbjerg (2013) and Hetemi et al. (2020), see underperformance resulting from lock-ins, which is 'the over-commitment of decision makers to an ineffective course of action' (Cantarelli & Flyvbjerg, 2013, p. 340). Such overcommitment starts at an early stage, with weak alternative analysis, resulting in the continuous investing of large budgets, even when project goals are not met (Flyvbjerg, 2009). The phenomenon of lock-in is typically connected to the escalation of commitment and the sunk cost fallacy, with investments already made in the form of money, time and self-identities (Brockner, 1992).

Instead of seeing the inflated forecasts, delays, budget overruns and public disbenefit as occurring by malevolent design, some scholars see these as resulting from normal operating practices (e.g. Ruijter et al., 2020; van Marrewijk et al., 2008). Well-intentioned professionals, with fragmented focus and limited overview, are influenced dramatically by a range of ambiguous and uncertain external and internal forces. For example, Lundrigan et al. (2015) see the disappointing performance resulting from organizational structure developments, with new management renegotiating design choices and slippages in performance targets. Also, political tensions, role interpretations, management approaches and organizational cultures can influence the performance of a megaproject (van Marrewijk et al., 2016). Therefore, van Marrewijk et al. (2008) argue that an emic or internally focused, contextually grounded view of actual practice and sensemaking should be taken rather than an etic or outsider's, preordained view of megaprojects being condemned because they do not match an ideal where project objectives are achieved faultlessly and effortlessly.

23.4 GOVERNING THE LABORIOUS COLLABORATION BETWEEN PUBLIC AND PRIVATE PARTNERS

The second key challenge in the organizing of megaprojects is the collaboration between public and private partners. With the earlier discussed evolvement of 'old' into 'new' megaprojects (Fainstein, 2008), this collaboration has become increasingly important (Ruijter et al., 2020). 'New' megaprojects take the form of complex networks, characterized by a mix of uses, a variety of financing techniques and innovative contracting between public- and private-sector initiators (Klijn & Koppenjan, 2016). The construction of the Øresund bridge and tunnel (Löfgren, 2015), the Incheon bridge (Brunet, 2021) and the London Olympics (Davies & Mackenzie, 2014) are all examples of new megaprojects. In these projects, collaboration between the public client as commissioner and the private contractors executing the project is of crucial importance. However, in many countries this is an adversarial relationship, with confrontational attitudes, troubled cooperation, poor tendering practices and a lack of trust, based upon fundamental differences in interest between clients and contractors (Priemus, 2004). How to organize this troublesome relationship?

To ensure smooth collaboration of public and private partners in megaprojects, governance arrangements are required (Brunet & Aubry, 2016; Clegg et al., 2002; Miller & Hobbs, 2005; Qiu et al., 2019). In the academic debate on project governance two streams of literature can be distinguished (Ahola et al., 2014). In the first stream, project governance is understood as externally imposed systems to define and monitor standards, procedures and rules. Governance is then defined in contractual terms to ensure a consistent and predictable delivery by contractors within contractual limitations (Müller, 2012). Such an approach is expected to provide a blueprint for collaborative behaviour, and encourages actors to specify all the obligations of each party in advance, in preparation for possible future events (Benitez-Avila et al., 2018). These contractual pre-arrangements seek to address the many interests that are at stake (Müller, 2012).

In the second stream, project governance is tailored through arrangements defining shared sets of coordination, procedures, norms and rules, which together have to align the conflicting goals of participating organizations towards a joint goal (Ahola et al., 2014). Although contracts should provide a blueprint for collaborative behaviour for project partners (Benitez-Avila et al., 2018), relations between these partners can become complex and challenging when working together and conflict can arise. In this stream it is assumed that actors cannot mitigate or anticipate all such conflicts, but nonetheless maintain collaborative relationships (Latusk & Vlaar, 2018). As the relationship develops over time, assumptions about shared goals, responsibilities and actions can become increasingly vexing (Sanderson, 2012; van Marrewijk et al., 2016). Therefore, relational aspects mediate the effect of contracts (Benitez-Avila et al., 2018).

In particular, the development of trust is a major challenge for the governance of public-private collaboration in megaprojects (Maurer, 2010; Ruijter et al., 2020; Vukomanović et al., 2021). Trust in a megaproject context can be defined as 'the willingness of a party to be vulnerable to the actions of another party based on the expectations that the other will perform a particular action important to the trustor, irrespective of the ability to monitor or control the other party' (Mayer et al., 1995, p. 712). When trust is present, project actors are willing to proceed without defending, buffering or protecting themselves against risks (Latusk & Vlaar, 2018). Acting on trust thus becomes an 'organizing principle' of governing the interactions between organizations, which is constituted by a set of practices that (re)produce trust as a meaningful pattern of interaction (Sydow, 1998). In their study, Ruijter et al. (2020) show that trust building between public and private partners, which was done through reflective workshops, is a laborious process. In this process, reciprocity was negotiated in practice, thus buffering the potential loss of trust through conflicts between partners. When seriously organized, trust building has the transformational potential to improve the collaborative behaviour of project partners.

23.5 THE SOCIAL CONSTRUCTION OF CULTURAL DIFFERENCES IN MEGAPROJECTS

A third challenge for organizing megaprojects is the wide diversity of organizations involved, all with their own professional, organizational and national cultural backgrounds. Consequently, megaprojects 'may expect to encounter substantial differences in cultural-cognitive belief systems carried by varying types of participants' (Scott et al., 2011, p. 58). For example, if employees are unable to cope with diverse management styles and national cultures, decision-making processes in megaprojects may slow down and tensions may emerge (Smits, 2014). Therefore, it is now widely acknowledged that cultural differences are a challenge for international construction megaprojects (Orr & Scott, 2008).

Unfortunately, project studies on cross-cultural collaboration (see for example Staples & Zhao, 2006; Zwikael et al., 2005) are dominated by cultural value models, for example the cultural dimensions of Hofstede (1980). The basic argument of scholars using a cultural value model is that national cultures can be measured and typified by means of a set of predefined dimensions, such as power distance, masculinity, temporality and uncertainty. The national scores on these indicators define the 'fit' between organizations. These cultural value models have received critics over time (Jacob, 2005; Smits, 2014). Scholars claim that cultural heterogeneity, local management concepts and cultural imperialism make cross-cultural collaboration too complex to be understood with the help of cultural value models (Smits, 2014).

Indeed, cultural differences in megaprojects are not entirely fixed and determined but can be negotiated by project partners (Brannen & Salk, 2000). For example, in their study of cross-cultural collaboration in the Sakhalin megaproject, Van den Ende and van Marrewijk (2015) found that Gazprom's entry accelerated the strategic emphasizing of Russian culture, which impelled particularly Shell to strategically emphasize 'western' culture practices to secure their influence. Therefore, it is particularly relevant to adopting a power-sensitive understanding of managing cross-cultural differences in megaprojects (van Marrewijk et al., 2016). For example, in her study of the Panama Canal expansion programme, Smits (2014) found employees working in the Spanish, Italian and Belgian partner organizations were labelled as 'southerners', while the American consultancy firm were labelled as 'northerners'. In sum, differences in professional, organizational and national cultural backgrounds are manifested in megaprojects as socially constructed.

23.6 MEGAPROJECT LEADERS

The fourth and final challenge is the leading of a megaproject, as a great deal of responsibility lies on the shoulders of leaders of this type of project (Müller & Turner, 2010). Recently, the attention of megaproject scholars has turned to the topic of leading megaprojects (Drouin et al., 2021; Söderlund et al., 2017). Söderlund et al. (2017, p. 9) ask for research 'on the ongoing practices of managers getting the megaproject in place'. The requirements for such leaders are challenging. Megaprojects ask for leaders who are in control, are able to make decisions, have the ability to integrate diverse disciplines, engage with various stakeholders and adhere to decision-making processes (Greiman, 2013). Furthermore, leaders have to be team players; able to create, lead and inspire a team that fosters the autonomy of the project but, at the same time, strengthens the relationship with stakeholders and thus prevents the project's isolation (Willems et al., 2020). In sum, leadership in megaprojects can be understood as a complex interactive dynamic from which adaptive outcomes emerge (Uhl-Bien et al., 2007).

Müller and Turner (2010) identified critical thinking, influence, motivation and conscientiousness as four important capabilities for leaders of complex projects. Carlsen and Pitsis (2020) add the ability of leaders to reflect upon their personal styles of leading and managing (mega)projects as they attribute narrative elements from their projects to enrich their own professional life story. This capability helps leaders to construct meaningful narratives on behalf of their megaprojects, which help project members to engage in and make sense of the complex endeavour. For example, the leader of the Korean Incheon bridge megaproject explained that the project fulfilled the dreams of his father and grandfather (Brunet, 2021). In another example, the leader of the Panama Canal expansion megaproject used the historical narrative of 'One team – one mission' to revitalize the century-old Panamanian–American collaboration (van Marrewijk et al., 2016). The creation of a narrative that makes sense to project employees, stakeholders, but also to citizens helps the legitimation of megaprojects (Van den Ende & van Marrewijk, 2019).

To better understand the persons leading the multifaceted aspects and social dimensions of megaprojects, Drouin et al. (2021) focused upon the personal biographies of leaders of infrastructure megaprojects. They collected the life histories of 16 megaproject leaders from ten different countries and found them to be shaped by values in their families, by important turning points and by significant others. The biographical findings draw the focus away from administrative authority and technological expertise, showing that leaders of megaprojects are no 'super engineers', but people that have acquired a wide set of skills, capabilities and experiences (Drouin et al., 2021).

23.7   CONCLUSIONS

In this chapter I have discussed four key challenges of managing megaprojects and how researchers have dealt with these so far: (1) the performance of megaprojects; (2) the governance of megaprojects; (3) cross-cultural differences; and (4) leading a megaproject. A cultural perspective on construction megaprojects emerged from this discussion, which positions megaprojects to be as much the object and outcome of social interactions as any other form of organizing that occurs within a multiple context of socially interdependent networks. Such a perspective takes an emic or internally focused, contextually grounded view of actual practices and sensemaking of project actors. Consequently, with such a lens, less obvious challenges of managing megaprojects are found, such as rituals to guide the transition between megaproject phases (Van den Ende & van Marrewijk, 2014), or the symbolic value of megaprojects (van Marrewijk, 2017).

Future avenues for research using a cultural perspective on megaprojects are diverse and include interesting topics of which a few will be discussed here. First, such a perspective can help to better understand the dynamic organizing of megaprojects. Increasingly, megaprojects are being selected as change interventions to stimulate, for example, energy transition (Priemus & van Wee, 2013). The planning of renewable energy megaprojects, such as solar power plants, wind parks and mega-dams, has become a worldwide phenomenon (Schindler et al., 2019). Given their long time frame from planning to execution, renewable energy megaprojects have high risks of technological, social and political lock-ins. Consequently, megaprojects often continue to be developed with limited changes, despite the emergence of better technologic alternatives during their planning and establishment processes. The question is how the internal dynamics of megaprojects influence megaprojects' role in the transition towards a sustainable urban world.

A second avenue of the cultural perspective is the theoretical exploration of values in and of megaprojects. This perspective views megaprojects as vehicles for defining, creating and delivering value (Martinsuo et al., 2019). Project success, thereby, cannot merely be assessed in terms of reaching goals at the time of project completion, but also in terms of benefits compared to costs and the value achieved over the project life cycle compared to the original value expectations of various stakeholders (Martinsuo et al., 2019). The question of how we can measure the value of megaprojects is therefore also relevant.

Finally, I hope that the closer collaboration of academics and megaproject professionals results in a better understanding of the 'inside' of megaprojects, their multilevel dynamics, tensions, practices, values, trust, change and power. By reflecting on these issues, both academics and practitioners together can help to improve the performance of megaprojects.

REFERENCES

Ahola, T., Russka, I., Artto, K. & Kujala, J. (2014). What is project governance and what are its origins? *International Journal of Project Management*, 32(8), 1321–1332.

Altshuler, A. & Luberoff, D. (2003). *Megaprojects: The changing politics of urban public investments*. Brookings Institutions.

Benitez-Avila, C., Hartmann, A., Dewulf, G. & Henseler, J. (2018). Interplay of relational and contractual governance in public-private partnerships: The mediating role of relational norms, trust and partners' contribution. *International Journal of Project Management*, 36(3), 429–443.

Brannen, J. V. & Salk, J. E. (2000). Partnering across borders: Negotiating organizational culture in a German–Japan joint venture. *Human Relations*, 53(4), 451–487.

Brockner, J. (1992). The escalation of commitment to a failing course of action: Toward theoretical progress. *Academy of Management Review*, 17(1), 39–61.

Brunet, M. (2021). Incheon Bridge, South Korea: The actualization of a landmark envisioned a century ago. In N. Drouin, S. Shankaran, A. H. van Marrewijk & R. Müller (Eds), *Megaproject leaders: Reflections on personal life stories* (pp. 166–180). Edward Elgar Publishing.

Brunet, M. & Aubry, M. (2016). The three dimensions of a governance framework for major public projects. *International Journal of Project Management*, 34(8), 1596–1607.

Cantarelli, C. C. & Flyvbjerg, B. (2013). Mega-projects' cost performance and lock-in: Problems and solutions. In H. Priemus & B. van Wee (Eds), *International handbook on mega-projects* (pp. 333–355). Edward Elgar Publishing.

Carlsen, A. & Pitsis, T. (2020). We are projects: Narrative capital and meaning making in projects. *Project Management Journal*, 51(4), 351–356.

Cicmil, S. & Hodgson, D. (2006). New possibilities of project management theory: A critical engagement. *Project Management Journal*, 37(3), 111–122.

Clegg, S. R., Pitsis, T. S., Rura-Polley, T. & Marosszeky, M. (2002). Governmentality matters: Designing an alliance culture of interorganizational collaboration for managing projects. *Organization Studies*, 23(3), 317–337.

Davies, A. & Mackenzie, I. (2014). Project complexity and systems integration: Constructing the London 2012 Olympics and Paralympics Games. *International Journal of Project Management*, 32(5), 773–790.

Del Cerro Santamaria, G. (2013). Introduction. In G. Del Cerro Santamaria (Ed.), *Urban megaprojects: A worldwide view* (pp. xix–xlix). Emerald Publishing.

Diaz Orueta, F. & Fainstein, S. S. (2008). The new mega-projects: Genesis and impacts. *International Journal of Urban and Regional Research*, 32(4), 759–767.

Drouin, N., Shankaran, S., van Marrewijk, A. H. & Müller, R. (2021). *Megaproject leaders: Reflections on personal life stories*. Edward Elgar Publishing.

Fainstein, S. S. (2008). Mega-projects in New York, London and Amsterdam. *International Journal of Urban and Regional Research*, 32(4), 768–785.

Flyvbjerg, B. (2009). Survival of the unfittest: Why the worst infrastructure gets built – and what we can do about it. *Oxford Review of Economic Policy*, 25(3), 344–367.

Flyvbjerg, B. (2012). Over budget, over time, over and over again. Managing major projects. In P. W. G. Morris, J. K. Pinto & J. Söderlund (Eds), *The Oxford handbook of project management* (pp. 321–344). Oxford University Press.

Flyvbjerg, B. (2014). What you should know about megaprojects and why: An overview. *Project Management Journal*, 45(2), 6–19.

Flyvbjerg, B. (2017). *The Oxford handbook of megaproject management*. Oxford University Press.

Flyvbjerg, B. (2021). Make megaprojects more modular. *Harvard Business Review*, November–December, 58–63.

Flyvbjerg, B., Bruzelius, N. & Rothengatter, W. (2003). *Megaprojects and risk: An anatomy of ambition*. Cambridge University Press.

Gemünden, H. G. (2014). The fascinating world of megaprojects. *Project Management Journal*, 46(5), 3–8.

Greiman, V. A. (2013). *Mega project management: Lessons on risk and project management from the Big Dig*. Wiley.

Hetemi, E., Jerbrant, A. & Ordieres Mere, J. (2020). Exploring the emergence of lock-in in large-scale projects: A process view. *International Journal of Project Management*, 38(1), 47–63.

Hofstede, G. (1980). *Culture's consequences: International differences in work-related values*. Sage Publications.

Jacob, N. (2005). Cross-cultural investigations: emerging concepts. *Journal of Organisational Change Management*, 18(5), 514–528.

Klijn, E. H. & Koppenjan, J. (2016). *Governance networks in the public sector*. Routledge.

Kreiner, K. (1995). In search of relevance: Project management in drifting environments. *Scandinavian Journal of Management*, 11(4), 335–346.

Latusk, D. & Vlaar, P. (2018). Uncertainty in interorganizational collaboration and the dynamics of trust: A qualitative study. *European Management Journal*, 36(1), 12–27.

Lehrer, U. & Laidley, J. (2008). Old mega-projects newly packaged? Waterfront redevelopment in Toronto. *International Journal of Urban and Regional Research*, 32(4), 786–803.

Löfgren, O. (2015). Catwalking a bridge. A longitudinal study of a transnational project and its ritual life. In A. H. van Marrewijk (Ed.), *Inside mega-projects: Understanding cultural practices in project management*. Liber & Copenhagen Business School Press.

Lundin, R. A. & Söderlund, J. (1995). A theory of the temporary organization. *Scandinavian Journal of Management*, 11(4), 437–455.

Lundrigan, C. P., Gil, N. A. & Puranam, P. (2015). The (under)performance of mega-projects: A meta-organizational perspective. *Academy of Management Proceedings*, 1, 11299.

Martinsuo, M., Klakegg, O. J. & van Marrewijk, A. H. (2019). Introduction: Delivering value in projects and project-based business. *International Journal of Project Management*, 37(5), 631–635.

Maurer, I. (2010). How to build trust in inter-organizational projects: The impact of project staffing and project rewards on the formation of trust, knowledge acquisition and product innovation. *International Journal of Project Management*, 28(7), 629–637.

Mayer, R. C., Davis, J. H. & Schoorman, F. D. (1995). An integrative model of organizational trust. *Academy of Management Review*, 20(3), 709–734.

Merrow, E. W., McDonnell, L. M. & Arguden, R. Y. (1988). *Understanding the outcome of mega-projects: A quantitative analysis of very large civilian projects.* Rand Reports.

Miller, R. & Hobbs, B. (2005). Governance regimes for large complex projects. *Project Management Journal*, 36(3), 42–50.

Morris, P. W. G. (2012). A brief history of project management. In P. W. G. Morris, J. K. Pinto & J. Söderlund (Eds), *The Oxford handbook of project management* (pp. 15–36). Oxford University Press.

Müller, R. (2012). Project governance. In P. W. G. Morris, J. K. Pinto & J. Söderlund (Eds), *The Oxford handbook of project management* (pp. 297–320). Oxford University Press.

Müller, R. & Turner, R. (2010). *Project-oriented leadership.* Routledge.

Orr, R. J. & Scott, W. R. (2008). Institutional exceptions on global projects: A process model. *Journal of International Business Studies*, 39(4), 562–588.

Packendorff, J. (1995). Inquiring into the temporary organization: New directions for project management research. *Scandinavian Journal of Management*, 11(4), 319–333.

Pitsis, A., Clegg, S., Freeder, D., Sankaran, S. & Burdon, S. (2018). Megaprojects redefined – complexity vs cost and social imperatives. *International Journal of Managing Projects in Business*, 11(1), 7–34.

Priemus, H. (2004). Dutch contracting fraud and governance issues. *Building Research and Information*, 32(4), 306–312.

Priemus, H. & van Wee, B. (2013). *International handbook on mega-projects.* Edward Elgar Publishing.

Qiu, Y., Chen, H., Sheng, Z. & Cheng, S. (2019). Governance of institutional complexity in megaproject organizations. *International Journal of Project Management*, 37(4), 425–443.

Ruijter, H., van Marrewijk, A. H., Veenswijk, M. & Merkus, S. (2020). Filling the mattress. Trust development practices in the Schiphol-Amsterdam-Almere megaproject. *International Journal of Project Management*, 39(4), 351–364.

Sanderson, J. (2012). Risk, uncertainty and governance in megaprojects: A critical discussion of alternative explanations. *International Journal of Project Management*, 30(4), 432–443.

Schindler, S., Fadaee, S. & Brockington, D. (2019). Contemporary megaprojects: An introduction. *Environment and Society*, 10(1), 1–8.

Scott, W. R., Levitt, R. E. & Orr, R. J. (2011). *Global projects. Institutional and political challenges.* Cambridge University Press.

Smits, K. (2014). *Cross culture work: Practices of collaboration in the Panama Canal expansion program.* Gildeprint Drukkerijen.

Söderlund, J., Shankaran, S. & Biesenthal, C. (2017). The past and present of megaprojects. *Project Management Journal*, 48(6), 5–15.

Staples, D. S. & Zhao, L. (2006). The effects of cultural diversity in virtual teams versus face-to-face teams. *Group Decision and Negotiation*, 15(4), 389–406.

Sydow, J. (1998). Understanding the constitution of inter-organizational trust. In C. Lane & R. Bachmann (Eds), *Trust within and between organizations, conceptual issues and empirical applications* (pp. 31–63). Oxford University Press.

Sykes, A. (1998). Megaprojects: Grand schemes need oversight, ample funding. *Forum for Applied Research and Public Policy*, 13(1), 6–47.

Trapenberger Fick, K. (2008). The cost of the technological sublime: Daring ingenuity and the new San Francisco-Oakland Bay Bridge. In H. Priemus, B. Flyvbjerg & B. van Wee (Eds), *Decision-making on mega projects: Cost-benefit analysis, planning and innovation* (pp. 239–262). Edward Elgar Publishing.

Uhl-Bien, M., Marion, R. & McKelvey, B. (2007). Complexity leadership theory: Shifting leadership from the industrial age to the knowledge era. *The Leadership Quarterly*, 18(4), 298–318.

Van den Ende, L. & van Marrewijk, A. H. (2014). The ritualization of transitions in the project life cycle: A study of transition rituals in construction projects. *International Journal of Project Management*, 32(7), 1134–1145.

Van den Ende, L. & van Marrewijk, A. H. (2015). The social construction of cultural differences in a Siberian joint-venture megaproject. *Journal of Strategic Contracting and Negotiation*, 1(2), 168–185.

Van den Ende, L. & van Marrewijk, A. H. (2019). Teargas, taboo and transformation: A neo-institutional study of public resistance and the struggle for legitimacy in an Amsterdam subway project. *International Journal of Project Management*, 37(3), 331–346.

van Marrewijk, A. H. (Ed.) (2015). Inside megaprojects: Understanding cultural practices in project management. Liber & Copenhagen Business School Press.

van Marrewijk, A. H. (2017). The multivocality of symbols: A longitudinal study of the symbolic dimensions of the high-speed train megaproject (1995–2015). *Project Management Journal*, 48(6), 1–13.

van Marrewijk, A. H., Clegg, S., Pitsis, T. & Veenswijk, M. (2008). Managing public-private megaprojects: Paradoxes, complexity and project design. *International Journal of Project Management*, 26(6), 591–600.

van Marrewijk, A. H., Ybema, S., Smits, K., Clegg, S. & Pitsis, T. (2016). Clash of the titans: Temporal organizing and collaborative dynamics in the Panama Canal megaproject. *Organization Studies*, 37(12), 1745–1769.

Vukomanović, M., Cerić, A., Brunet, M., Locatelli, G. & Davies, A. (2021). Editorial: Trust and governance in megaprojects. *International Journal of Project Management*, 39(4), 321–324.

Willems, T., van Marrewijk, A. H., Kuitert, L., Volker, L. & Hermans, M. (2020). Practices of isolation: The shaping of project autonomy in innovation projects. *International Journal of Project Management*, 38(4), 215–228.

Williams, T. (2002). *Modelling complex projects*. Blackwell.

Winch, G. M. (2013). Escalation in major projects: Lessons from the Channel Fixed Link. *International Journal of Project Management*, 31(5), 724–734.

Zwikael, O., Shimuzu, K. & Globerson, S. (2005). Cultural differences in project management capabilities: A field study. *International Journal of Project Management*, 23(6), 454–462.

24. A complexity perspective on project stakeholder management

Jere Lehtinen, Christof Kier, Kirsi Aaltonen and Martina Huemann

24.1 INTRODUCTION

Managing project stakeholders, meaning organizations, groups and individuals who can influence projects' activities or be influenced by them, is the key for ensuring projects' value creation and performance (Winch, 2017). However, stakeholder management is challenging in complex projects (Ramasesh & Browning, 2014). For example, project stakeholders often have conflicting interests and diverging views about complex projects' value-creating activities and project managers find it difficult to include, balance and act upon the stakeholders' diverse views, needs and requirements to ensure that complex projects create value to stakeholders without compromising projects' performance (Davis, 2014). In addition to practical experiences, research has shown that managing project stakeholders in a value-adding manner is very challenging, due to, e.g., frequent stakeholder conflicts (Winch, 2004).

While researchers and practitioners have identified that project complexity influences stakeholder management activities, there is less understanding on how project complexity influences stakeholder management. To this end, this chapter reviews previous project stakeholder research from a complexity perspective and enriches complex project research by discussing how complexity influences stakeholder management. Acknowledging that complexity has been defined in various ways (see e.g., Whitty & Maylor, 2009). We adopt the complexity of projects perspective (Geraldi et al., 2011) and empirically validated framework by Maylor and Turner (2017), which divides complexity into three dimensions: structural, emergent and socio-political. Structural complexity means the complexity associated with the many different interdependent and interacting parts, organizations, systems and components that make up a project (Hobday, 2000). In turn, emergent complexity relates to the complexity stemming from a project's uncertainty and dynamism (Maylor & Turner, 2017). Lastly, socio-political complexity deals with the complexity stemming from the social and political aspects of the organizational environment (Maylor et al., 2013).

The next section briefly introduces stakeholder theory and stakeholder management in complex projects. After that, we analyze stakeholder management from the complexity of projects perspective by engaging in a narrative review and focusing on how the three dimensions influence stakeholder management in complex projects. We then discuss the findings and develop future research ideas including suggestions for research questions and theoretical perspectives to be mobilized forward.

24.2   STAKEHOLDER MANAGEMENT IN COMPLEX PROJECTS

Stakeholder management is rooted in strategic management and stakeholder theory, stemming from Freeman's (1984) seminal work *Strategic management: A stakeholder approach*. But the principle of stakeholder management has also a long tradition in project management (Cleland, 1986). For example, the task of liaising with groups outside of project organization can be traced back to the late 1950s, where stakeholder management is considered as a project manager's task and responsibility (Gaddis, 1959). Stakeholder theory argues that the primary purpose of any organization is to create value for its stakeholders (Phillips et al., 2019, p. 3). There exists a plethora of stakeholders subject to empirical and contextual considerations (Miles, 2017), for example, classification to internal-external stakeholders (Parmar et al., 2010), which is often used in the context of complex projects due to the organizational design that allows distinguishing those actors external and internal to a project organization. Internal stakeholders are considered those who have a formal, official or contractual link to an organization (Savage et al., 1991), such as contractors and clients in complex projects. In turn, external stakeholders are those who do not have a formal, official or contractual link to an organization but may affect or be affected by it (Eesley & Lenox, 2006), like non-governmental organizations and communities in complex projects.

There are two main approaches to stakeholder management: the managing of and managing for stakeholders (Freeman et al., 2007). These two represent the opposite ends of a continuum, being differentiated by the way they perceive and consider stakeholders, their value orientation and the challenges that come with adopting the approach. The two approaches are summarized in Table 24.1.

The "managing for stakeholders" approach is considered more challenging to implement than "managing of stakeholders" because increasing the number of stakeholders in project activities complicates decision-making and, following Ashby's law on variety (1961) that only variety can be absorbed by variety, it also reflects on project complexity itself. This means that project managers must understand the project complexity they have to deal with (Huemann et al., 2016), as well as the impacts that their stakeholder management decisions might carry. Successful stakeholder management therefore calls for a transparent understanding of the complexity of a project and its environment as well as the adequate structures to deal with them. The "managing for stakeholders" approach can be crystallized in the concept of stakeholder engagement that focuses on value creation with stakeholders and the inclusion of stakeholders in organizational activities in a positive manner (Greenwood, 2007).

Stakeholder management has been studied extensively in complex project literature (see e.g., Winch, 2004, 2017). Although single studies often focus on specific issues of stakeholder management, a generic, continuous management process consisting of four main phases can be defined. The first phase includes identifying project stakeholders, collecting relevant data of them and analyzing the data and stakeholders, for example, by using different stakeholder management tools and frameworks (Aaltonen, 2011). The second phase focuses on planning different stakeholder management activities (Eskerod & Huemann, 2014) and dividing appropriate roles and responsibilities for stakeholder management based on the first-phase analysis (Lehtinen & Aaltonen, 2020). In the third phase, the different stakeholder management activities, including higher-level strategies like persuasion strategy (Ninan et al., 2019) and concrete practices like seminars and workshops (Eskerod et al., 2015), are implemented. The fourth phase includes monitoring the implemented activities and their impact on stakeholders,

Table 24.1   *Two approaches to stakeholder management*

	Managing *of* project stakeholders	Managing *for* project stakeholders
Attitude towards stakeholders	Stakeholders are considered as obstacles or mere instruments for achieving project outcomes	Stakeholders are seen as a source of value creation and ideas that are required to complete the project successfully
Value orientation	Economic value drives stakeholder management Focus on short-term benefits Focus on reducing complexity Lack of ethical consideration (manipulative orientation)	Balancing social, environmental and economic interests of different stakeholders Balancing both short- and long-term benefits Balancing building up and increasing complexity Includes ethical consideration, fairness, transparency and participation
Perception of stakeholder conflicts	Conflicts are inherently a negative issue and should be avoided completely to safeguard project from disturbances	Conflicts are natural, unavoidable and enable negotiations with stakeholders to improve project's value creation
Breadth of stakeholder management	Only the most relevant project stakeholders are considered, often meaning internal stakeholders that have decision rights in a project Stakeholders (especially external) are ignored and excluded from the project whenever possible	All possible project stakeholders and their interests are acknowledged Stakeholders are engaged in projects and enfranchised as co-creators to develop project outcomes that yield value to a plethora of stakeholders
Challenges related to project organizing	Can lead to under-ambitious project outcomes: may fulfil project performance indicators but does not maximize value creation to stakeholders in a sustainable manner	Including a wide range of stakeholders can overload projects, may lead to slow decision-making processes, too ambitious scope, cul-de-sacs and even project cancellation

Source: After Huemann et al. (2016, pp. 189–190).

gathering feedback and additional data on stakeholders and then adjusting the management activities to better fit the prevalent context and purposes (De Schepper et al., 2014).

24.3   COMPLEXITY PERSPECTIVE ON PROJECT STAKEHOLDER MANAGEMENT

24.3.1   Structural Complexity and Stakeholder Management

Structural complexity covers the broad organization consisting of several interacting and specialized stakeholders located within different places (Maylor et al., 2008). This dimension also draws attention to the many interconnected project activities that stakeholders must complete to develop projects' end product (Chapman & Hyland, 2004), and the urgency and time criticality of such project activities (Geraldi et al., 2011). Regarding structural complexity, we identified two key issues that influence stakeholder management.

The first issue in this dimension relates to the fact that complex projects involve many interdependent stakeholders whose involvement intensity fluctuates (Maylor et al., 2008). The more there are diverse stakeholders with different and even conflicting requirements and interests, the more challenging it typically becomes for complex projects' managers to include, balance and act upon the differing needs and claims (Eskerod & Vaagaasar, 2014). On the other hand, however, there can exist opportunities in the diversity of stakeholders and their valuable inputs. For example, different inputs can facilitate co-creating innovative ideas and solutions that would not be possible otherwise (Lehtinen et al., 2019b). Hence, having a project constellation with aligned stakeholders can facilitate stakeholder management but may require sacrifices regarding innovation outcomes.

The second issue relates to high-paced coordination of tasks and activities that complicates stakeholder management (Müller & Turner, 2007). For example, the project organization of a complex project consists of multiple autonomous internal stakeholders that are required to work together toward a shared project goal for a limited time (Jones & Lichtenstein, 2008), but these internal stakeholders can respond very differently to each other's and external stakeholders' interests because they can have competing priorities and different views about the project (Aaltonen et al., 2015). This means that project organizations may have trouble in planning appropriate stakeholder management activities and dividing appropriate roles and responsibilities for stakeholder management.

24.3.2   Emergent Complexity and Stakeholder Management

Emergent complexity covers the dynamism and uncertainty of project activities (Maylor & Turner, 2017). Dynamism grasps changes in the stakeholder landscape and amendments in the coordination of project activities (Geraldi et al., 2011). In turn, uncertainty means the lack of knowledge related to the current and future states of the project and its stakeholders, and (un) availability of information needed for implementing project activities (Maylor et al., 2008). Regarding emergent complexity, we identified two key issues that influence stakeholder management.

The first issue relates to the uncertainty of stakeholders' goals and behaviors and, particularly, stakeholders' unclear, emergent and changing expectations and needs that have been associated with the unpredictability of projects in prior research (Ramasesh & Browning, 2014). This holds especially in the early stages of complex projects where projects are typically characterized by ambiguous, contrasting, fluctuating and unexpected stakeholder requirements as the overall project goals are yet to be formulated and negotiated with stakeholders (Martinsuo et al., 2019b). Embracing this uncertainty and addressing the changing needs well and in an agile manner can, however, improve the value creation of complex projects as more of the stakeholder demands can be incorporated into the project's value proposition, meaning that the project has the potential to create more value for stakeholders once completed (Lehtinen et al., 2019a). However, there can be a lack or ambiguity of knowledge regarding stakeholders which indicates that a project organization can have real difficulty in identifying relevant stakeholders or understanding their interests, expectations and claims (Missonier & Loufrani-Fedida, 2014). This also means that a project organization may not know all stakeholders' previous experiences with complex projects or whether some stakeholders even understand the implications of the project (Maylor et al., 2008). The lack of knowledge regarding stakeholders might make the project organization devise and implement inappropriate stakeholder management activities leading to stakeholder conflict.

The second issue relates to the dynamic organizational boundaries of complex projects (Bakker et al., 2016), which indicates that stakeholders unexpectedly and autonomously come and go during the project's lifecycle (Maylor et al., 2013), complicating timely stakeholder management activities. The dynamism also implies that stakeholders' attributes may change during the project. For example, a previously unidentified stakeholder may become unexpectedly prominent (Maylor & Turner, 2017), complicating timely stakeholder management activities.

24.3.3   Socio-Political Complexity and Stakeholder Management

Socio-political complexity deals with the challenging and unpredictable issues related to the social and political aspects of projects' stakeholder landscape and organizational setting (Maylor & Turner, 2017). This complexity calls for sensitiveness from the complex project organization to be able to interpret the signals and potential warning signs from the stakeholder environment. Regarding socio-political complexity, we identified one main issue that influences stakeholder management.

The issue relates to stakeholders' heterogeneity: stakeholders' different interests, expectations, planning horizons, goals, objectives and claims that may be in conflict or aligned (Geraldi et al., 2011). The heterogeneity of stakeholders complicates project organization's stakeholder management (Whitty & Maylor, 2009) because project organization and stakeholders must work together toward the shared project objective for a limited time with scarce resources, regardless of their different interests and goals (Jones & Lichtenstein, 2008). For example, project organization and stakeholders can react in very different ways to other actors' needs and claims because of their divergent goals and priorities (Aaltonen et al., 2015). Socio-political complexity is especially a relevant challenge for stakeholder management in projects with strong public-sector involvement (Samset & Volden, 2016). Public-sector involvement and related politics can increase the heterogeneity and even plurality of the stakeholder landscape (e.g., conflicting and even arbitrary interests from governmental actors and authorities who also often possess power to influence projects), leading to difficulty in managing different stakeholders (Flyvbjerg, 2014).

Despite the challenges imposed by socio-political complexity, it can also provide opportunities for stakeholder management. For example, successfully including various stakeholders' perspectives and institutional logics can equip the project organization with diverse knowledge bases that can positively contribute to a project's value creation and performance (Morris & Geraldi, 2011). This also indicates that a project organization can develop capabilities to manage various institutional environments, facilitating stakeholder management and the project's value creation activities. Adopting the above "pluralistic view" to stakeholder management that encourages participation from divergent stakeholders can be very challenging, but it may enhance the social acceptability of a project.

24.4 DISCUSSION AND FUTURE RESEARCH

The analysis indicated that the three types of complexity impose mainly challenges but also some opportunities for managing complex projects' stakeholders. The identified challenges are potential reasons for which project organizations tend to favor the "managing of stakeholders" approach. This approach is very limited in how it includes different stakeholders, helping to avoid several challenges. But, this approach cannot really enable the opportunities. In turn, the identified opportunities suggest reasons for which project organizations may adopt the "managing for stakeholders" approach. However, concurrently a project organization cannot avoid the challenges but must deal with them. Thus, it seems that there is a dilemma in adopting either one of the two approaches. We have summarized the findings in Table 24.2.

24.4.1 Challenges and Opportunities Imposed by Project Complexity on Stakeholder Management

Table 24.2 shows that the three complexity dimensions pose several challenges for stakeholder management. The challenges for stakeholder management emerging from project complexity have been documented rather well in prior literature, even though they have maybe not been synthesized according to the three dimensions systematically. There are also some studies that have examined, at least implicitly, how to deal with and respond to these challenges and create value for stakeholders (see, e.g., Maylor & Turner, 2017). For instance, the developed stakeholder management tools and understanding related to, e.g., dynamic stakeholder identification, dynamic stakeholder management practices and strategies and joint organizing solutions among stakeholders likely account well for the identified challenges that require dynamic stakeholder management over a project lifecycle. So, there might be potential in engaging in a systematic literature review to develop more structured theory around the solutions related to the complexity challenges that could then be elaborated via empirical research. We consider that it might be beneficial to bridge value (co-)creation research (Martinsuo et al., 2019a) with project complexity and stakeholder management literature to better understand the management implications of the complexity dimensions for value creation with stakeholders.

Based on the above, we suggest future researchers examine how to tackle complexity, and the three dimensions, to ensure successful stakeholder management and value creation. Potential research questions include: What do we know about complexity management related to stakeholders in complex projects? How do project organizations manage complexity for successful stakeholder management? How does project complexity influence value creation?

Table 24.2   *Summary of how structural, emergent and socio-political complexity influence stakeholder management in complex projects*

	Structural complexity	Emergent complexity	Socio-political complexity
Challenges: reasons for adopting *managing of stakeholders* approach	Several heterogeneous and autonomous stakeholders The involvement intensity of stakeholders fluctuates over time High-paced coordination of project activities among heterogeneous stakeholders	Unavailability of knowledge concerning stakeholders and their attributes Problems in identifying relevant stakeholders Dynamic organizational boundaries Stakeholders change over time	Heterogeneous and even pluralistic stakeholders required to work together toward the shared project goal, despite divergent attributes Project organization and stakeholders can respond very differently to each other's requirements because of competing priorities Unpredictable, heterogeneous and even pluralistic stakeholder landscape and organizational setting
Opportunities: reasons for adopting *managing for stakeholders* approach	Engaging heterogeneous stakeholders can facilitate co-creating innovations, solutions and value	Embracing dynamic and uncertain stakeholder landscape ensures the agility of project organization in responding to changing stakeholder needs, facilitating value creation	Utilizing stakeholders' different perspectives and institutional logics equips project with diverse knowledge bases and the capability to manage various institutional environments better Adopting a pluralistic view to stakeholder management can be very challenging but it may enhance the social acceptability of a project

Our analysis also identified that complexity does not only have negative influences for stakeholder management, but it can also offer opportunities that benefit stakeholder management of a project. For example, embracing the three complexities through the "managing for stakeholders" approach may offer opportunities such as new innovations and solutions, agility to respond to changing needs in projects and development of knowledge base and capabilities for various institutional environments that can yield benefits related to a project's value creation and performance. In the "managing for stakeholders" approach, a project organization's attitude towards stakeholders, value orientation, perception of stakeholder conflict and breadth of stakeholder engagement (see Table 24.1) seem well equipped for achieving such benefits. For instance, relying on the "managing for stakeholders" approach could facilitate unifying conflicting stakeholder interests through the inclusion of different stakeholders' perspectives from the early stages of a project and ensure the realization of benefits. Adopting the "managing for stakeholders" approach has an impact on designing a project organization and including plenty of stakeholders' representatives, thus increasing the project's complexity to unlock its benefits. The result is thus paradoxical in the sense that a project organization would increase complexity to deal with complexity. But there may also be compromises or sacrifices, because the "managing for stakeholders" approach requires a lot of resources (e.g., specific organizational roles to address stakeholder-related issues) and is time-consuming. In practice, project organizations often underestimate the time and resources the "managing for stakeholders" approach will take, and there may be losses/sacrifices that even outweigh the benefits. Also, there might be first the need to make the complexity visible and embrace it, and then define the project organization diverse enough to be able to handle the challenges and opportunities arising.

On the other hand, the "managing of stakeholders" approach may be more suited to avoid complexities, because a project organization's attitude towards stakeholders, value orientation, perception of stakeholder conflict and breadth of stakeholder engagement in this approach (see Table 24.1) focus on reducing complexity. However, adopting this approach comes with the cost of not being able to harness the opportunities imposed by complexity, meaning that it can be difficult to create value with stakeholders. Thus, in order to avoid many of the challenges and utilize the opportunities, a trade-off emerges where a project organization must continuously balance between managing of and for stakeholder approaches to decrease and increase complexity timely (Lehtinen et al., 2019a). The trade-off implies a vicious cycle where the choice of stakeholder management approach influences project complexity that in turn influences subsequent stakeholder management activities.

Our analysis and above discussion imply that the previous literature seems to be more focused on the challenges than the benefits or opportunities imposed by the complexity dimensions. Hence, we suggest future research focuses on how complexity, and the three complexity dimensions, can be harnessed for opportunities and benefits in stakeholder management to enable improved project performance and value creation. Research on benefit management (Zwikael et al., 2018) could be useful in understanding and studying this phenomenon. Potential research questions include: What kinds of opportunities and benefits does complexity pose for stakeholder management in complex projects? What kinds of organizational designs are required for embracing the opportunities and benefits of complexity for stakeholder management? How does complexity facilitate successful/effective stakeholder management in complex projects?

24.4.2   Theories to Study the Influence of Project Complexity on Stakeholder Management

We observed that the three complexity dimensions pose different requirements for stakeholder management. For example, emergent complexity can demand dynamic and flexible stakeholder management, structural complexity may require a decentralized structure such as a network or a heterarchy and socio-political complexity can necessitate understanding the institutional context of stakeholder management. Therefore, the following theoretical perspectives may be useful to better understand stakeholder management and how to deal with the three complexities.

Regarding emergent complexity, dynamic systems theories (see Chapter 14) could offer concepts and understanding to study project organizations as non-linear dynamic systems and thus better understand requirements for dynamic stakeholder management. Regarding structural complexity, research on inter-organizational relationships and governance (Zheng et al., 2008), organizational design (Puranam, 2018) and transaction cost economics could provide a variety of perspectives for understanding the required network/heterarchy structures that facilitate dealing with structural complexity. Regarding socio-political complexity, institutional theory, institutional logics and institutional complexity (Winch & Maytorena-Sanchez, 2020) could help understand the divergent attributes of stakeholders and thus better deal with socio-political complexity.

24.4.3   Research Limitations

There are at least the three following limitations to our analysis that provide additional ideas for future research. First, we addressed the relationship of each complexity dimension to stakeholder management separately. However, the implications of the different complexity dimensions are, assumably, not straightforward but there may be tensions or synergies that need to be understood to be able to devise and enact the most suitable managerial responses. Therefore, we propose researchers study the interdependencies and relationships of the three complexity dimensions and how such relationships need to be understood and managed for better stakeholder management. Potential research questions include: What kinds of relationships do the three complexity dimensions have and how do these contribute to stakeholder management in complex projects?

Second, we approached stakeholder management as an activity. To develop a more fine-grained understanding, we suggest approaching stakeholder management as a process and study how the complexity dimensions influence each process phase of stakeholder management as described in Section 24.2. Also, we did not specify the complex project context or stakeholders in the relationships between complexity dimensions and stakeholder management, which are required to be defined especially in empirical research for developing more accurate understanding.

Third, the three dimensions represent one school of thought and there exist many other perspectives on complexity (see Chapter 3). Taking use of other views on complexity can provide additional insights that help draw a more complete picture of how complexity influences stakeholder management. Thus, future researchers could approach complexity from other perspectives and schools of thought and investigate how complexity from these other perspectives influence stakeholder management.

REFERENCES

Aaltonen, K. (2011). Project stakeholder analysis as an environmental interpretation process. *International Journal of Project Management*, 29(2), 165–183.

Aaltonen, K., Kujala, J., Havela, L. & Savage, G. (2015). Stakeholder dynamics during the project front-end: The case of nuclear waste repository projects. *Project Management Journal* 46(6), 15–41.

Ashby, W. R. (1961). *An introduction to cybernetics*. Chapman and Hall.

Bakker, R. M., DeFillippi, R. J., Schwab, A. & Sydow, J. (2016). Temporary organizing: Promises, processes, problems. *Organization Studies*, 37(12), 1703–1719.

Chapman, R. & Hyland, P. (2004). Complexity and learning behaviors in product innovation. *Technovation*, 24(7), 553–561.

Cleland, D. I. (1986). Project stakeholder management. In D. I. Cleland & W. R. King (Eds), *Project management handbook* (pp. 275–301). John Wiley & Sons.

Davis, K. (2014). Different stakeholder groups and their perceptions of project success. *International Journal of Project Management*, 32(2), 189–201.

De Schepper, S., Dooms, M. & Haezendonck, E. (2014). Stakeholder dynamics and responsibilities in public-private partnerships: A mixed experience. *International Journal of Project Management*, 32(7), 1210–1222.

Eesley, C. & Lenox, M. J. (2006). Firm responses to secondary stakeholder action. *Strategic Management Journal*, 27(8), 765–781.

Eskerod, P. & Huemann, M. (2014). Managing for stakeholders. In R. Turner (Ed.), *Gower handbook of project management* (pp. 217–232). Gower Publishing Company.

Eskerod, P. & Vaagaasar, A. L. (2014). Stakeholder management strategies and practices during a project course. *Project Management Journal*, 45, 71–85.

Eskerod, P., Huemann, M. & Ringhofer, C. (2015). Stakeholder inclusiveness: Enriching project management with general stakeholder theory. *Project Management Journal*, 46(6), 42–53.

Flyvbjerg, B. (2014). What you should know about megaprojects and why: An overview. *Project Management Journal*, 45(5), 6–19.

Freeman, R. E. (1984). *Strategic management: A stakeholder approach*. Pitman.

Freeman, R. E., Harrison, J. S. & Wicks, A. C. (2007). *Managing for stakeholders: Survival, reputation, and success*. Yale University Press.

Gaddis, P. O. (1959). The project manager. *Harvard Business Review*, May–June, 89–97.

Geraldi, J., Maylor, H. & Williams, T. (2011). Now, let's make it really complex (complicated): A systematic review of the complexities of projects. *International Journal of Operations and Production Management*, 31(9), 966–990.

Greenwood, M. (2007). Stakeholder engagement: Beyond the myth of corporate responsibility. *Journal of Business Ethics*, 74(4), 315–327.

Hobday, M. (2000). The project-based organisation: An ideal form for managing complex products and systems? *Research Policy*, 29(7–8), 871–893.

Huemann, M., Eskerod, P. & Ringhofer, C. (2016). *Rethink ! Project stakeholder management*. Project Management Institute.

Jones, C. & Lichtenstein, B. B. (2008). Temporary inter-organizational projects: How temporal and social embeddedness enhance coordination and manage uncertainty. In S. Cropper, C. Huxham, M. Ebers & P. Smith Ring (Eds), *The Oxford handbook of inter-organizational relations* (pp. 231–255). Oxford University Press.

Lehtinen, J. & Aaltonen, K. (2020). Organizing external stakeholder engagement in inter-organizational projects: Opening the black box. *International Journal of Project Management*, 38(2), 85–98.

Lehtinen, J., Aaltonen, K. & Rajala, R. (2019a). Stakeholder management in complex product systems: Practices and rationales for engagement and disengagement. *Industrial Marketing Management*, 79(May), 58–70.

Lehtinen, J., Peltokorpi, A. & Artto, K. (2019b). Megaprojects as organizational platforms and technology platforms for value creation. *International Journal of Project Management*, 37(1), 43–58.

Martinsuo, M., Klakegg, O. J. & van Marrewijk, A. (2019a). Editorial: Delivering value in projects and project-based business. *International Journal of Project Management*, 37(5), 631–635.

Martinsuo, M., Vuorinen, L. & Killen, C. (2019b). Lifecycle-oriented framing of value at the front end of infrastructure projects. *International Journal of Managing Projects in Business*, 12(3), 617–643.

Maylor, H. & Turner, N. (2017). Understand, reduce, respond: Project complexity management theory and practice. *International Journal of Operations and Production Management*, 37(8), 1076–1093.

Maylor, H., Vidgen, R. & Carver, S. (2008). Managerial complexity in project-based operations: A grounded model and its implications for practice. *Project Management Journal*, 39(3), S15–S26.

Maylor, H. R., Turner, N. W. & Murray-Webster, R. (2013). How hard can it be? Actively managing complexity in technology projects: The complexity assessment tool offers a framework for articulating, assessing, and managing sources of complexity in technology projects. *Research Technology Management*, 56(4), 45–51.

Miles, S. (2017). Stakeholder theory classification: A theoretical and empirical evaluation of definitions. *Journal of Business Ethics*, 142(3), 437–459.

Missonier, S. & Loufrani-Fedida, S. (2014). Stakeholder analysis and engagement in projects: From stakeholder relational perspective to stakeholder relational ontology. *International Journal of Project Management*, 32(7), 1108–1122.

Morris, P. W. G. & Geraldi, J. (2011). Managing the institutional context for projects. *Project Management Journal*, 42(6), 20–32.

Müller, R. & Turner, J. R. (2007). Matching the project manager's leadership style to project type. *International Journal of Project Management*, 25(1), 21–32.

Ninan, J., Mahalingam, A. & Clegg, S. (2019). External stakeholder management strategies and resources in megaprojects: An organizational power perspective. *Project Management Journal*, 50(6), 625–640.

Parmar, B., Freeman, R., Harrison, J., Wicks, A., Purnell, L. & De Colle, S. (2010). Stakeholder theory: The state of the art. *Academy of Management Annals*, 3(1), 403–445.

Phillips, R. A., Barney, J. B., Freeman, R. E. & Harrison, J. S. (2019). Stakeholder theory. In J. S. Harrison, J. B. Barney, R. E. Freeman & R. A. Phillips (Eds), *The Cambridge handbook of stakeholder theory* (pp. 3–18). Cambridge University Press.

Puranam, P. (2018). *The microstructure of organizations*. Oxford University Press.

Ramasesh, R. V. & Browning, T. R. (2014). A conceptual framework for tackling knowable unknown unknowns in project management. *Journal of Operations Management*, 32(4), 190–204.

Samset, K. & Volden, G. (2016). Front-end definition of projects: Ten paradoxes and some reflections regarding project management and project governance. *International Journal of Project Management*, 34(2), 297–313.

Savage, G. T., Nix, T. W., Whitehead, C. J. & Blair, J. D. (1991). Strategies for assessing and managing organizational stakeholders. *Academy of Management Perspectives*, 5(2), 61–75.

Whitty, S. J. & Maylor, H. (2009). And then came complex project management (revised). *International Journal of Project Management*, 27(3), 304–310.

Winch, G. M. (2004). Managing project stakeholders. In: P. W. G. Morris & J. K. Pinto (Eds), *The Wiley guide to managing projects* (pp. 321–339). John Wiley & Sons.

Winch, G. M. (2017). Megaproject stakeholder management. In B. Flyvbjerg (Ed.), *The Oxford handbook of mega-project management* (pp. 339–361). Oxford University Press.

Winch, G. M. & Maytorena-Sanchez, E. (2020). Institutional projects and contradictory logics: Responding to complexity in institutional field change. *International Journal of Project Management*, 38(6), 368–378.

Zheng, J., Roehrich, J. K. & Lewis, M. A. (2008). The dynamics of contractual and relational governance: Evidence from long-term public-private procurement arrangements. *Journal of Purchasing and Supply Management*, 14(1), 43–54.

Zwikael, O., Chih, Y.-Y. & Meredith, J. R. (2018). Project benefit management: Setting effective target benefits. *International Journal of Project Management*, 36(4), 650–658.

25. Teaming for complex project organizing: a review of key concepts, project teaming studies and questions for future research

Anne Keegan

25.1 INTRODUCTION

The dynamic and competitive context facing many project-based organizations elevates concerns of how to promote learning, collaboration and experimentation by project teams. This is nowhere more evident than in the case of complex project organizations where traditional, control-focused project management approaches fall short as project teams seek solutions to emergent problems for which there is inadequate information (Geraldi et al., 2011; Shenhar & Dvir, 2007; Shenhar et al., 2016). The issues that emerge throughout dynamically complex projects means team members need to pool expertise in a flexible manner (Hansen et al., 2020; Kock & Gemünden, 2016; Pich et al., 2002).

What insights can be gleaned about how project teams should approach complex projects? We introduce the concept of teaming and discuss its relevance for complex project organizing. Teaming refers to "a new, more flexible way for organizations to carry out interdependent tasks. Unlike the traditional concept of a team, *teaming* is an active process, not a static entity" (Edmondson, 2012a, p. 2). Teaming has not featured extensively in studies of complex project organizing. However, where mobilized (Brady & Davies, 2014; Hansen et al., 2020), it has proven useful in foregrounding key behavioral challenges facing project teams responding to complex problems by drawing on groups of interdependent experts in a flexible and dynamic way.

The aim of the chapter is to introduce teaming and its constituent pillars, and to define key concepts used in the literature; the (few) project studies that draw explicitly on teaming are discussed while studies mobilizing the constituent pillars of teaming are also reviewed. Overlaps between the way complexity is seen within teaming studies and categories of project complexity in the literature are discussed. Finally, questions for future research on teaming for complex project organizing are presented.

25.2 TEAMING

Teaming is associated most with the work of Edmondson (2012a, 2012b) building on four pillars: (1) psychological safety; (2) experimentation; (3) collaboration; and (4) reflection. Years of research into how teams solve complex problems in product development, complex healthcare and government settings underpin the idea that fluid cross-boundary teaming is increasingly important for solving complex projects (Edmondson & Harvey, 2018). Teaming conveys both the importance of teams to innovation as well as the emergent, ad hoc process of collaboration needed to tackle complex projects. Edmondson (2012b, p. 75) calls it "team-work on the fly" and highlights the verb-like character of the term dovetailing with trends in rethinking project management that emphasize "process, verbs, activity" (Winter et al., 2006, p. 643). This departs from traditional characterizations of stable teams with careful selection of team members, time to learn to work together and clear goal definition (Hackman, 2002). Contexts where teaming has been deployed are summarized in Table 25.1.

Table 25.1   Studies on teaming in different contexts

Context	Study details
Operating rooms in hospitals	Edmondson, 2003
Development projects	Edmondson and Harvey, 2016a
New product development	Edmondson, 2012a; Edmondson and Harvey, 2016b
Urban regeneration	Edmondson et al., 2016; Edmondson and Harvey, 2018

With minimal formal structures (Valentine et al., 2015) teaming is very challenging for individuals and relies on broad learning rooted in the assumption that members work to the *current best definition* but are open to changes. Some light structuring may be helpful but any structuring is temporary scaffolding providing initial boundaries. Teaming can be inter-personally challenging for individual team members who must work interdependently and rely on each other's insights when organizing for complex problems with little time to get to know and trust each other.

Teaming is also challenging for project leaders who need to frame complex projects as learning endeavors (Edmondson & Harvey, 2016b) where experimenting, and failing, are inevitable due to the emergence of new issues over time. Team members need to take risks, and feel safe doing so, meaning leaders need to adopt more distributed leadership styles (Edmondson, 2012a). For teaming to work, team members should be framed as valuable collaborators rather than subordinates. Their ideas must be elicited openly, which means overcoming many of the barriers inherent in organizations that prevent people speaking up. Coordination between team members has a recursive character premised on interdependence in solving problems. Team members are tasked to tolerate ambiguity and adopt a collaborative orientation. Teaming means combining execution and learning based on reflection in iterative cycles while team members come and go as expertise demands. Newcomers need to learn quickly and the appropriate configuration of experts coming together is always a shifting target, based on a distributed network, who must collaborate to address complex problems.

25.2.1   The Pillars of Teaming

Psychological safety
The first and arguably most important pillar for teaming, psychological safety has been discussed for more than half a century (Kahn, 1990; Schein & Bennis, 1965). It is a bedrock of collaborative learning, allowing people to be open about their challenges without fear of rebuke, humiliation or punishment. It is associated with change readiness as related to "unfreezing" during change processes (Schein & Bennis, 1965). Kahn (1990, p. 708) defined psychological safety as "feeling able to show and employ one's self without fear of negative consequences of self-image, status, or career." Edmondson (1999, p. 350) defines team psychological safety as "a shared belief that the team is safe for interpersonal risk taking." As a team-level construct, psychological safety supports team members and promotes voice

behavior (Van Dyne & LePine, 1998), defined as "discretionary communication of ideas, suggestions, concerns, or opinions about work-related issues with the intent to improve organizational or unit functioning" (Morrison, 2011, p. 375).

Experimentation

Teaming is premised on a willingness and openness to experimentation and the failures that accompany it. Failures are framed as expected, conveying new and valuable information. It is however naïve to assume experimentation can be easily stimulated, as failure is stigmatized in many organizations. Experiments can and do fail, creating fear and anxiety for project team members about status, reputation and careers. The challenges facing project leaders to nurture and reward experimentation and failure are therefore significant.

Collaboration

Teaming relies on collaboration because of the requirement to combine insights from diverse team members – in real time – in generating solutions to complex problems. Collaboration is premised on reciprocal interdependence and mutual adjustment and asks team members to move beyond their comfort zones and consider problems from diverse perspectives. Edmondson (1999, 2012a) discussed the barriers that people face when asked to consider problems from different viewpoints. Her research reinforces the sustained effort needed to support people to engage collaboratively, particularly when they face time pressure or threats to their career or status. Teaming remains a valuable perspective for cases where specialists from individual disciplines cannot generate solutions on their own, and hand these off to others, because of the dynamic and ambiguous demands linked with complex projects.

Reflection

Edmondson (2012a) argues that reflection is a critical pillar for teaming but should not be seen as a formal process as much as a behavioral tendency. Her studies found different approaches to reflection including as after-action reviews and mid-term or half-time exercises. The habit of reflecting appeared to make more of a difference than any one best practice (Edmondson, 2012a). In fast-paced projects, reflection may happen at the same time as execution as team members combine dual foci of exploring and exploiting. Finally, teaming is also a complex endeavor because of the interdependence between the four pillars – without one or the other, it is unlikely to work (Edmondson, 2012a).

25.3   RESEARCH ON TEAMING IN PROJECT STUDIES LITERATURE

25.3.1   Teaming and Project Studies

Teaming is not extensively mobilized in project studies. However, two notable studies draw on teaming for managing complex projects. Teaming is examined in a study of the construction of Heathrow Terminal 5 and the London 2012 Olympics. It considers how teaming was adopted in a similar way in both projects "to support and encourage collaborative working and innovation" (Brady & Davies, 2014, p. 25).

Research in shipbuilding identifies concrete practices pertaining to collaboration: "at meetings, the chair habitually stressed that everybody continued to collaborate effectively" (Hansen et al., 2020, p. 639). In turn, "processes of collective problem solving" were identified that enabled "the project team to better absorb higher levels of emergent pressure on time and performance" (2020, p. 641). They provide a valuable reference for others interested in how teaming allows for both minimal structuring and maximum flexibility for complex project teams, highlighting that teaming's recursive, cyclical processes have profound behavioral implications for project leaders and members.

Teaming offers a behavioral view of projects that aligns with existing ideas on how to characterize project complexity (see Chapter 2). Where teaming is explicitly mobilized as a concept (Brady & Davies, 2014; Hansen et al., 2020), dynamic complexity (Geraldi et al., 2011) appears most evident. Responding to dynamic complexity is challenging due to a lack of clear and adequate information available to frame the problem at the outset. Emergent and unforeseen issues require teams to collaborate and experiment while also learning from their efforts and failures, recursively, and trying new things by encouraging teams "to be watchful, and to ensure rare events should be experienced 'richly' (from multiple angles)" (Pich et al., 2002, p. 1021). So, "there is little benefit in detailed planning of the entire project, because the unforeseen might alter its course and force the team to learn and continuously adjust the plan" (Shenhar et al., 2016, p. 68). Recent work highlights the difficulty faced by project leaders in responding to emergent changes in complex projects (Maylor & Turner, 2017), which links with the emphasis in teaming on providing safety for team members to respond flexibly and embrace emergent changes.

Teaming is not straightforward. It prioritizes a learning orientation consistent with the complex nature of problems. Uncertainty is accepted, and experimentation is seen as normal. Teaming facilitates an orientation by project teams on "new-to-the-world"-type projects (Shenhar et al., 2016). These have high levels of dynamic complexity where both goals and methods (Turner & Cochrane, 1993) are not well known from the outset. These are the teams that Edmondson (2012a, 2012b) targets in her studies, where teaming appears both necessary and worth the considerable investment required.

Project managers influence how project teams experience uncertainty by how they frame projects (Geraldi et al., 2011). This is a crucial point in teaming that is reinforced in other complex project studies (Havermans et al., 2015a; Pich et al., 2002). Project managers convey powerful messages about how teams should approach experimentation and failure.

25.3.2 Pillars of Teaming and Project Studies

While few project studies papers explicitly mobilize the concept of teaming, many focus on one or more pillars, particularly psychological safety.

Research on "mastery climate" suggests that psychological safety underpins collaboration and that "with a focus on cooperation, shared learning and psychological safety, a mastery climate is likely to stimulate and facilitate collaboration in teams" (Caniëls et al., 2019, p. 4). This expands understanding of why positive collaboration effects are found because of psychological safety by citing its importance in team members' pro-social behavior which encourages investment in the team (as opposed to in oneself) resulting in better collective performance.

Bolstering psychological safety supports voice behaviors of project managers (Ekrot et al., 2016). Many factors dissuade project managers and teams from speaking up with potentially important information. Project managers observe their context in similar ways and might block improvement information in teams from being communicated upward for fear of risks linked with negative project information. These insights from teaming are likely to build further on research on voice in project studies mobilizing insights on both contextual and individual voice predictors and highlighting beliefs about the risky nature of voice. This reinforces Edmondson's (1999, 2012a) arguments that perceptions of psychological safety are often implicitly held, and efforts to nurture a psychologically safe climate are essential when voice is important for project outcomes like innovation. Their work is a general reminder of the value of combining studies of (complex) projects with insights from organizational behavior and psychology which "have been very rarely combined" (Ekrot et al., 2016, p. 1040).

Bredin and Söderlund identify a trend towards increasingly complex projects, with more interdependencies where "a lot of coordination occurs across expertise boundaries" (2011, p. 77). One of the key issues they raise is the challenge of swift trust (Meyerson et al., 1996). While not discussing teaming or psychological safety, Bredin and Söderlund (2011) raise questions that similarly touch on the functioning of teams in complex, interdependent project settings and especially how they quickly learn together. Swift trust addresses these concerns from one angle – how team members think about their team colleagues and leaders, and the basis on which they think they can be vulnerable in these settings, and trust others. This complements Edmondson (1999, 2012a), who addresses not how team members *give trust*, but whether the team, and the broader climate, will *offer them safety* when they are open, when they experiment and fail and when they voice their concerns. Swift trust is "Can I be vulnerable to this team?" Psychological safety is "Does this team allow me to take risks, be vulnerable, be open?" Frazier at al. suggest that psychological safety differs from trust and is "conceptually unique in capturing perceptions of risk taking in the workplace" … [while] "trust is defined as the willingness to be vulnerable to the actions of others" … psychological safety captures "elements of vulnerability and risk one perceives in the workplace" (Frazier et al., 2017, p. 117). Further studies on how trust and psychological safety work together to support complex project organizing are highly worthwhile.

Collaboration is a pillar of effective teaming as it underpins capacity for learning quickly and adapting together to emerging but unknown issues in complex projects. In New Product Development (NPD): "the cost savings of NPD projects usually stem from cross functional cooperation, which enables teams to foresee potential problems at hand and put forward timely solutions" (Zhang & Min, 2019, p. 227). Explicit attention to collaboration is important for teaming because complex project teams will encounter reciprocal interdependence when completing tasks. Effective collaboration depends on team members being able to share opinions and work through conflict. Offering a socio-cognitive approach to learning in project teams, Chang et al. (2021, p. 3, emphasis added) highlight the dangers to collaboration when "project leaders actively discourage sharing different opinions, they make it difficult for the team to engage in effective conflict resolution. This, in turn, limits opportunities for team learning, *precluding true collaboration* and synergy from blending different members' ideas."

Project scholars have long highlighted the importance of experimentation in the explorative phases of complex projects that aim for innovation in areas such as research and development (Kock & Gemünden, 2016) and teaming suggests a behavioral focus on enablers and constraints of experimentation can be valuable. The stigmatization of failures in organizations frequently damages efforts to experiment (Turner & Keegan, 2007). This reinforces the importance of a deliberate learning orientation so creative projects can be successfully undertaken and suggests why project teams might fail to develop creative outcomes due to low learning orientation (Khedhaouria et al., 2017).

An orientation towards experimentation can also be stimulated by project leaders in their framing of the situation through language. The role of language has been a topic of interest in project studies for many years. Language shapes and constitutes rather than simply reflecting what happens in projects (Havermans et al., 2015b) and a focus on leadership practices should include linguistic practices which create everyday project realities shaping what people do in projects (Cicmil et al., 2006; Lindgren & Packendorff, 2009). How project managers frame complex problems is critical for successful experimentation and collaboration.

Reflection is the final core pillar of teaming and is important in project studies (Keegan & Turner, 2001; Turner & Keegan, 2007). Learning challenges confront project professionals working in high-paced teams: "Projects operate under extreme time pressures to deliver products or services. This often leaves *few resources or little time to reflect* on collective learnings that could promote innovative ideas and contribute to long-term organizational success" (Chang et al., 2021, p. 1). Reflection on trials and experiments is crucial in teaming which makes it important to distinguish between the adoption of superficial reflective practices and a strongly institutionalized orientation towards reflection in project teams (Keegan & Turner, 2001).

25.4   FUTURE RESEARCH QUESTIONS ON TEAMING FOR COMPLEX PROJECT ORGANIZATIONS

We have demonstrated that there is work emerging where the concept of teaming is mobilized, as well as work which relies on pillars of teaming. We have seen that there are many overlaps in how project complexity is seen in both project studies and teaming studies. Future research on the following topics will support complex project teams and their leaders by combining insights from these still rather separate domains.

25.4.1   When is Teaming Most Valuable?

Teaming can be successful when projects are complex and high levels of collaboration, experimentation and reflection are needed (Edmondson, 2012a). Teaming requires investment in leadership qualities, learning orientation and collaborative mindsets that are likely to be challenging and costly in many contexts. It requires sustained investment and effort to get employees to speak up, share ideas and discuss problems and errors (Edmondson, 1999). Where failure is stigmatized rather than seen as a source of learning, teaming is likely to be even more difficult to embed as a default way of working. Overcoming some of the widely known barriers to people speaking up, taking risks and offering new insights is therefore essential.

Edmondson's work suggests that a learning orientation anchored in psychological safety is likely to help all organizations with innovation. However, not all project contexts need teaming and complex projects will not all apply teaming in the same way. The idea that projects should be led differently depending on key contingencies is by now well accepted (Shenhar & Dvir, 2007). This sensibility remains important for any future studies of teaming in the context of (complex) project organizing. Projects characterized by complexity and interdependence are more suitable for teaming approaches than projects with low levels of structural and dynamic complexity (Geraldi et al., 2011) or where there is good information for the improvements needed (Shenhar et al., 2016). Future research on the relative importance of teaming in one project context over another, as well as the relative success of teaming depending on key contingencies, would make a valuable contribution to complex project studies.

25.4.2   Teaming and Voice

Perhaps above all other issues, the success of teaming relies on project professionals being willing and able to speak up and voice their concerns during the development and execution of complex projects. The nascent research on voice in project studies is ripe for connection with teaming studies, and vice versa (Ekrot et al., 2016). Voice influences all the main pillars of teaming, while the pillars of teaming are riven with voice-related implications. This work could be fruitfully extended to consider if and how complex projects can be developed into psychologically safe climates. Links between the institutional context of voice for workers, and psychological safety, should be given more emphasis. Voice has important employee-related implications in terms of perceived quality of work and well-being and is not solely an organizational issue. Considering the multi-level nature and effects of employment-related human resource management practices may shed light on how voice is supported (or not) in project-based organizations (Keegan et al., 2018). Two research questions are (1) whether the discourse of teaming might encourage more project managers to pay attention to voice behavior and (2) whether the institutional context of voice, including the presence of direct and indirect voice channels, including trade unions, enables psychological safety and speaking up in complex projects.

25.4.3   Teaming and Swift Trust

Swift trust has also been explored in project studies (Bredin & Söderlund, 2011), overlapping with studies on both voice and psychological safety in highlighting the importance of high-quality relationships that encourage teams to deal with failure in a constructive manner (Carmeli & Gittell, 2009). It would be fruitful for studies to tease out empirically how trust and psychological safety influence collaboration, experimentation and reflection in complex project organizing. Does psychological safety give more assurance to people than efforts to create trust between team members? Is trust a more dyadic concept, or do the ideas of Bredin and Söderlund (2011) on swift trust suggest a coming together of these ideas due to swift trust being less about the person than the role? Given psychological safety's importance to effective teaming, richer insights on these issues are likely to be valuable.

25.4.4   What Does Teaming Mean for Project Leaders?

Finally, what does teaming mean for those leading projects? Teaming asks a lot of leaders as it thrives in flattened hierarchies and in the context of distributed leadership. Leaders need to be accessible, approachable and open to admitting when they do not have the answers. Such humility is critical, though difficult, in contexts where hierarchy is still valued and upward voice is blocked by time pressures, bottom-line mentality and other aspects of project culture that silence people (Zhu et al., 2019). Fortunately, there is an expanding body of research on project leadership (Drouin et al., 2021; Keegan & Den Hartog, 2004; Turner & Müller, 2005) and potential overlaps between this and research on teaming appear numerous. Zhu et al. (2019) studied how transformational leadership impacts on silencing behavior of project team members, which they argue threatens project results. While they highlight the role of feeling trusted, it begs the question of how leaders can ensure people feel safe to speak up. Studies of different leadership styles are of value for studies of teaming. We know from research by Chang et al. (2021) that when project leaders actively discourage speaking up, this reinforces passivity among followers. The potential for cross-fertilization between studies on project leadership and on teaming is likely to be valuable. It is also worth studying if teaming is a concept that is practical for leaders and resonates with them in terms of emphasizing the more dynamic aspects of leading others to experiment, to collaborate and to reflect when faced with complex issues.

25.5   CONCLUSION

Although a relatively recent concept, teaming has become widely known in organizational and management studies literature. It has the potential to offer new behavioral insights and valuable research questions for the field of complex project organizing which is not fully realized. There are numerous areas of project scholarship that overlap with teaming issues, and many fruitful avenues where current studies of project complexity can enhance our understanding of teaming. This chapter has introduced teaming and its constituent pillars and offered suggestions for future research to support the cross-fertilization of insights on complex project organizing from both the project studies and broader management and organizational studies domains.

REFERENCES

Brady, T. & Davies, A. (2014). Managing structural and dynamic complexity: A tale of two projects. *Project Management Journal*, 45(4), 21–38.

Bredin, K. & Söderlund, J. (2011). *Human resource management in project-based organizations: The HR quadriad framework*. Springer.

Caniëls, M. C., Chiocchio, F. & van Loon, N. P. (2019). Collaboration in project teams: The role of mastery and performance climates. *International Journal of Project Management*, 37(1), 1–13.

Carmeli, A. & Gittell, J. H. (2009). High-quality relationships, psychological safety, and learning from failures in work organizations. *Journal of Organizational Behavior*, 30(6), 709–729.

Chang, A., Wiewiora, A. & Liu, Y. (2021). A socio-cognitive approach to leading a learning project team: A proposed model and scale development. *International Journal of Project Management*, 39(6), 646–657.

Cicmil, S., Williams, T., Thomas, J. & Hodgson, D. (2006). Rethinking project management: Researching the actuality of projects. *International Journal of Project Management*, 24(8), 675–686.

Drouin, N., Sankaran, S., van Marrewijk, A. & Müller, R. (2021). *Megaproject leaders: Reflections on personal life stories*. Edward Elgar Publishing.

Edmondson, A. C. (1999). Psychological safety and learning behavior in work teams. *Administrative Science Quarterly*, 44(2), 350–383.

Edmondson, A. C. (2003). Speaking up in the operating room: How team leaders promote learning in interdisciplinary action teams. *Journal of Management Studies*, 40(6), 1419–1452.

Edmondson, A. C. (2012a). *Teaming: How organizations learn, innovate, and compete in the knowledge economy*. John Wiley & Sons.

Edmondson, A. C. (2012b). Teamwork on the fly. *Harvard Business Review*, 90(4).

Edmondson, A. C. & Harvey, J. F. (2018). Cross-boundary teaming for innovation: Integrating research on teams and knowledge in organizations. *Human Resource Management Review*, 28(4), 347–360.

Edmondson, A. C. & Harvey, J. F. (2016a). Haiti hope: Innovating the mango value chain. *Harvard Business School Case*, 616-040.

Edmondson, A. C. & Harvey, J. F. (2016b). Open innovation at Fujitsu (A). *Harvard Business School Case*, 616-034.

Edmondson, A. C., Moingeon, B., Bai, G. & Harvey, J. F. (2016). Building smart neighborhoods at Bouygues. *Harvard Business School Case*, 617-007.

Ekrot, B., Rank, J. & Gemünden, H. G. (2016). Antecedents of project managers' voice behavior: The moderating effect of organization-based self-esteem and affective organizational commitment. *International Journal of Project Management*, 34(6), 1028–1042.

Frazier, M. L., Fainshmidt, S., Klinger, R. L., Pezeshkan, A. & Vracheva, V. (2017). Psychological safety: A meta-analytic review and extension. *Personnel Psychology*, 70(1), 113–165.

Geraldi, J., Maylor, H. & Williams, T. (2011). Now, let's make it really complex (complicated): A systematic review of the complexities of projects. *International Journal of Operations & Production Management*, 31(9).

Hackman, J. R. (2002). Why teams don't work. In R. S. Tindale, L. Heath, J. Edwards, E. J. Posavac, F. B. Bryant, Y. Suarez-Balcazar, E. Henderson-King & J. Myers (Eds), *Theory and research on small groups* (pp. 245–267). Springer.

Hansen, M. J., Vaagen, H. & van Oorschot, K. (2020). Team collective intelligence in dynamically complex projects: A shipbuilding case. *Project Management Journal*, 51(6), 33–655.

Havermans, L. A., Den Hartog, D. N., Keegan, A. & Uhl-Bien, M. (2015a). Exploring the role of leadership in enabling contextual ambidexterity. *Human Resource Management*, 54(1), 179–200.

Havermans, L. A., Keegan, A. & Den Hartog, D. N. (2015b). Choosing your words carefully: Leaders' narratives of complex emergent problem resolution. *International Journal of Project Management*, 33(5), 973–984.

Kahn, W. A. (1990). Psychological conditions of personal engagement and disengagement at work. *Academy of Management Journal*, 33(4), 692–724.

Keegan, A. E. & Den Hartog, D. N. (2004). Transformational leadership in a project-based environment: A comparative study of the leadership styles of project managers and line managers. *International Journal of Project Management*, 22(8), 609–617.

Keegan, A. & Turner, J. R. (2001). Quantity versus quality in project-based learning practices. *Management Learning*, 32(1), 77–98.

Keegan, A., Ringhofer, C. & Huemann, M. (2018). Human resource management and project based organizing: Fertile ground, missed opportunities and prospects for closer connections. *International Journal of Project Management*, 36(1), 121–133.

Khedhaouria, A., Montani, F. & Thurik, R. (2017). Time pressure and team member creativity within R&D projects: The role of learning orientation and knowledge sourcing. *International Journal of Project Management*, 35(6), 942–954.

Kock, A. & Gemünden, H. (2016). Antecedents to decision-making quality and agility in innovation portfolio management. *Journal of Product Innovation Management*, 33(6), 670–686.

Lindgren, M. & Packendorff, J. (2009). Project leadership revisited: Towards distributed leadership perspectives in project research. *International Journal of Project Organisation and Management*, 1(3), 285–308.

Maylor, H. & Turner, N. (2017). Understand, reduce, respond: Project complexity management theory and practice. *International Journal of Operations and Production Management*, 37, 1076–1093.

Meyerson, D., Weick, K. E. & Kramer, R. M. (1996). Swift trust and temporary groups. In R. M. Kramer & T. R. Tyler (Eds), *Trust in organizations: Frontiers of theory and research* (pp. 166–195). Sage.

Morrison, E. W. (2011). Employee voice behaviour: Integration and directions for future research. *Academy of Management Annals*, 5(1), 373–412.

Pich, M. T., Loch, C. H. & Meyer, A. D. (2002). On uncertainty, ambiguity, and complexity in project management. *Management Science*, 48(8), 1008–1023.

Schein, E. H. & Bennis, W. G. (1965). *Personal and organizational change through group methods: The laboratory approach*. John Wiley & Sons.

Shenhar, A. J. & Dvir, D. (2007). *Reinventing project management: The diamond approach to successful growth and innovation*. Harvard Business School Press.

Shenhar, A. J., Holzmann, V., Melamed, B. & Zhao, Y. (2016). The challenge of innovation in highly complex projects: What can we learn from Boeing's Dreamliner experience? *Project Management Journal*, 47(2), 62–78.

Turner, J. R. & Cochrane, R. A. (1993). Goals-and-methods matrix: Coping with projects with ill defined goals and/or methods of achieving them. *International Journal of Project Management*, 11(2), 93–102.

Turner, J. R. & Müller, R. (2005). The project manager's leadership style as a success factor on projects: A literature review. *Project Management Journal*, 36(2), 49–61.

Turner, R. & Keegan, A. (2007). Managing technology: Innovation, learning and maturity. In P. W. G. Morris & J. K. Pinto (Eds), *The Wiley guide to project technology, supply chain and procurement management* (pp. 177–200). John Wiley & Sons.

Valentine, M. A., Nembhard, I. M. & Edmondson, A. C. (2015). Measuring teamwork in health care settings: A review of survey instruments. *Medical Care*, 53(4), e16–e30.

Van Dyne, L. & LePine, J. A. (1998). Helping and voice extra-role behaviors: Evidence of construct and predictive validity. *Academy of Management Journal*, 41(1), 108–119.

Winter, M., Smith, C., Morris, P. W. G. & Cicmil, S. (2006). Directions for future research in project management: The main findings of a UK government-funded research network. *International Journal of Project Management*, 24(8), 638–649.

Zhang, Z. & Min, M. (2019). The negative consequences of knowledge hiding in NPD project teams: The roles of project work attributes. *International Journal of Project Management*, 37(2), 225–238.

Zhu, F., Wang, L., Yu, M., Müller, R. & Sun, X. (2019). Transformational leadership and project team members' silence: The mediating role of feeling trusted. *International Journal of Managing Projects in Business*, 12(4), 845–868.

26. Increasing the effectiveness of project management: using causal mapping to integrate risk, uncertainty, and stakeholders

Fran Ackermann and Eunice Maytorena-Sanchez

26.1 INTRODUCTION

Managing uncertainty and stakeholders are significant challenges when organising complex projects (Lenfle & Loch, 2017). Project managers need 'to be more *collaborative and engaging* rather than process bound and able to *respond to uncertainty and handle complexity*' (Sexton et al., 2019, p. 1). However, current literature and practice guides tend to treat uncertainty and stakeholder management as separate entities with the advantages of a more 'joined-up' synergistic approach being lost.

This chapter illustrates how causal mapping can provide the project practitioner a more integrated perspective, enabling a 'joined-up' approach to the management of stakeholders and uncertainty. It also acknowledges the intimate connection between managing uncertainty and managing risk. Causal mapping is a technique used extensively in the management of complexity (in strategy, project management and conflict). It supports project practitioners by enabling them to tap the wisdom and experience of staff in a structured and analysable format thus enabling them to manage complexity.

We begin by briefly outlining recent research in risk, uncertainty and stakeholders relating to project risk management (PRM) along with reviewing cause mapping. We next discuss three factors necessitating stakeholders, risk and uncertainty to be considered in an integrative fashion and illustrate how causal mapping can assist. Finally, we discuss the benefits and practical implications before concluding with some avenues for future research.

26.2 LITERATURE REVIEW

26.2.1 Stakeholders and Their Impact on Risk and Uncertainty

Risk management of complex projects has been of considerable interest over the past three decades (Williams, 2017; Winch & Maytorena, 2011). Practitioners recognise the importance of effective risk management and its impact on project performance.

The most recent research on PRM in complex projects tends to focus on two considerations: first, understanding the relationship of risk with uncertainty and complexity (Browning & Ramasesh, 2015; Daniel & Daniel, 2018); second, the need to go beyond risk management (aleatoric uncertainty) and consider uncertainty management (epistemic uncertainty) (Pich et al., 2002). See Chapter 2 for a discussion on analytic and cognitive perspectives on uncertainty.

This chapter identifies three challenges in current practice.

First, there is limited recognition and understanding of complexity and uncertainty. The world we face is uncertain rather than deterministic. Understanding the difference between risk and uncertainty in complex situations can help practitioners adapt their management approaches and develop more appropriate responses. Engaging in a process of inquiry enables an improved understanding of complex and uncertain situations (Kay & King, 2020).

Second, there is a narrow understanding of systemicity in current PRM approaches (Bloomfield et al., 2019). Project management bodies of knowledge mention the importance of considering risk interaction and dynamics; however, the focus tends to be on single risks. A more holistic perspective of risks and uncertainties, interdependencies, causes, consequences and options for actions can be acquired by visualising the systemicity and broader context (Ackermann, 2019). This provides an improved appreciation of the complex situation.

Third, there is inadequate attention to the behavioural aspects and their potential impact on the management of risks, uncertainties and project complexities. The diversity of stakeholders, their interests and power bases, the uncertainty in stakeholder deliberations, and potential conflicts, and their networks and dynamics all contribute to complexities in projects (Winch, 2017).

Thus, these project practices need to be integrated. The effective management of risk, uncertainty and complexity in projects is dependent on several elements: the timely analysis and engagement of a diverse range of stakeholders; capturing and understanding different perceptions of complex situations; and developing and agreeing mitigation strategies alongside their possible implications. Visual representations developed through a systematic form of inquiry which embraces a variety of perspectives can help furnish project practitioners with a holistic view of the project and its context.

26.2.2 Causal Mapping

Causal mapping is a technique for modelling subjective, qualitative data – predominantly individual perceptions of a particular situation. Causal maps, comprising chains of cause and effect, enable decision makers to 'make sense' of the complexity surrounding a situation through capturing issues, objectives, options and contextual detail. These components, along with their impacts on one another, help gain a *holistic* and *systemic* understanding of the situation, as the process facilitates teasing out tacit knowledge for deeper consideration. Maps contribute to ensuring procedural rationality (Simon, 1976) through enabling an exploration of the range of interacting issues and associated argument along with procedural justice (Kim & Mauborgne, 1995) through actively engaging with, and listening to, a range of stakeholders.

Research into cause maps has resulted in several forms emerging, each with different nuances in terms of their theoretical underpinnings and practical application. Huff and Jenkins (2002) provide a good overview of strategy mapping techniques. Cause maps are sometimes seen as synonymous with cognitive maps (Tegarden & Sheetz, 2003), often taking a nomothetic approach (Laukkanen, 1994). Other forms are more idiographic in nature and represent the range of perceptions in detail comprising hundreds of concepts (Eden & Ackermann, 1998). Causal mapping has been used widely when seeking to manage complex and messy situations, for example supporting individual or group decision making (Bryson et al., 2004), enabling shared understanding (Langfield-Smith, 1992) and developing strategy (Ackermann & Eden, 2011). One form of causal mapping, based on Personal Construct Theory (Kelly, 1957), is Eden's Cognitive Mapping (1988). The technique comprises a set of mapping formalisms (Bryson et al., 2004) and encompasses a range of analyses (Eden & Ackermann, 1998). Eden (1988) sees cognitive maps as comprising representations of individual cognition whereas cause maps comprise statements from many individuals and aim to enable the development of shared and wider understanding.

Mapping has also been used to model disruption and delay on projects (Eden et al., 2000), enabling those seeking redress to demonstrate how a range of triggers (e.g., change of mind, late approval) have significant consequences on a project's outcomes. The technique enables project personnel to understand the triggers, dynamic behaviour and multiple ramifications of actions (Ackermann & Eden, 2005; Williams, 2016). Causal mapping reveals the systemic impacts of risks and management behaviours on projects and helps explain overruns in costs (Ackermann, 2019). Causal mapping also can help enhance the risk and uncertainty of the management process by proactively involving stakeholders in risk workshops (Ackermann et al., 2014), enabling a wider range of risks to surfaced and be structured and subsequently analysed.

Causal mapping is an important technique which can support the cognitive perspective of uncertainty (see Chapter 2). Mapping can assist project practitioners in 'making sense' of the uncertainty surrounding them, and manage risks and stakeholders better, by visualising risks, uncertainties and consequences in a systemic manner allowing for reflection, and additionally attending to the potential impact of behavioural aspects.

26.3   FACTORS FOR INTEGRATION

An *integrative* approach to managing risk, uncertainty and stakeholders needs to consider at least three factors. The first centres on project context, that is, understanding the scope, purpose and project's strategic *objectives* against which success is to be measured. The second takes a processual perspective, reflecting the need for *negotiation* and *engagement* between internal and external stakeholders as a means of managing risks. The third factor centres upon *dynamics* – particularly pertinent when projects have lengthy durations (Alexander et al., 2019). Each factor is briefly explained with causal mapping examples to illustrate the techniques' ability to manage them.

26.3.1   Surfacing and Exploring Stakeholder Project Objectives

Risks and uncertainties are intimately related to the realisation of desired outcomes (project objectives, organisational goals, individual beliefs – regardless of the term being used, each relates to something that is 'good in its own right') albeit in a negative manner. For example, a risk such as *supplier unable to deliver a product* may negatively impact on the project objective of *delivering on time*. Furthermore, risks and uncertainties can affect many objectives and the number of adverse effects may influence whether the risk or uncertainty is prioritised for action. Returning to the example, the supplier's inability might also impact on the project objective of *keeping within budget* as alternative and potentially more expensive suppliers need to be sought. As such, project teams and their stakeholders are constantly navigating and negotiating a *system* of objectives (Bryson et al., 2016). This plurality of objectives is reflected to a degree in the 'iron triangle'. However, projects tend to have more than just three objectives reflecting the owner/operator's organisational strategies and markets.

A plurality of objectives is a challenge when organising projects as different perceptions (and associated objectives) impact on what is perceived as a successful project and thus how the project is executed. For example, when designing a new community power system, different objectives may influence the project's direction. These objectives might range from 'meeting renewable energy targets' to 'keeping the lights on' or even 'ensuring cost efficiencies'. Each objective influences the actions being taken by the project team resulting in potentially competing narratives. This may occur for example in transformation projects when there is a single organisation where competing demands on resources exist (e.g., expertise, cash) The potential tension is even greater in joint ventures and public private partnership projects.

Likewise, it is important to understand the array of risks and uncertainties as their identification and management helps minimise negative outcomes. Surfacing risks and uncertainties may reveal tacit objectives as understanding the nature of the threat reveals this knowledge is particularly useful as objectives are hard to fully identify (Keeney, 2013). Moreover, involving a wide range of stakeholders in the identification of risks and uncertainties can be beneficial (Ackermann, 2019) as they bring a diversity of perspectives to the discussion – accrued through their different discipline backgrounds and experiences. Incorporating mapping in a workshop environment, and ensuring diverse thinking, facilitates a comprehensive and systemic appreciation of the potential risks, uncertainties and associated objectives (Ackermann et al., 2014). Thus, attending to risks and uncertainties not only helps in the elicitation of objectives but also widens the threat of the identification lens.

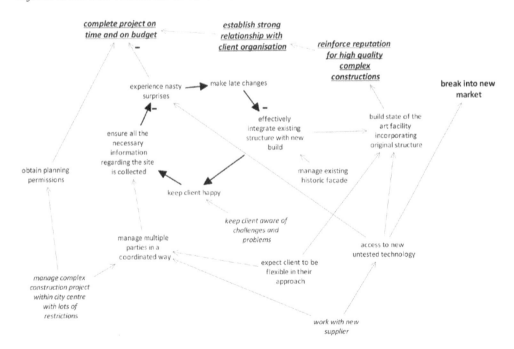

Figure 26.1   *A fragment of a larger map, revealing the systemic impacts of actions (displayed in italics), and project objectives (displayed in bold – where the client organisation's goals are underlined to distinguish them from the supplier's goals)*

Mapping enables each of the risks and uncertainties surfaced to be explored in terms of its consequences – which might exacerbate further risks (i.e., one risk compounds another) and/ or adversely affect objectives. For example, the map in Figure 26.1 shows that to *gain access to new untested technology* the construction company needs to *work with a new supplier*. This helps achieve the objective regarding *reinforce reputation* (through *building a state-of-the-art facility*) but may also trigger the risk of *experiencing nasty surprises* which may negatively impact the objective of *completing the project on time and on budget*. Thus, the map reveals risks, their interactions and their impact on project objectives in a coherent and systemic manner. Attending to the systemic impacts is important as any action taken to ameliorate one risk must be considered alongside the other risks and actions to maximise effective outcomes.

Mapping helps capture the breadth of views, gain a deeper understanding of their myriad ramifications and negotiate a shared understanding of both project objectives and risk uncertainty management. Where a negative link is shown (arrow with a negative symbol), this represents the reverse, i.e., experience nasty surprises may lead to not complete project on time and on budget. Bold arrows denote the presence of a feedback loop.

26.3.2   Ensuring Effective Negotiation and Engagement between Stakeholders

Effective stakeholder engagement requires the identification and management of stakeholders – essential activities for successful project delivery (Winch, 2017). Stakeholders can take different positions; they can support or actively work against the project (Ackermann & Eden, 2011) and mismanagement of stakeholders can have severe consequences on the project. For example, ignoring stakeholders and being oblivious to their objectives and associated actions can adversely affect the goals as illustrated in the Brent Spar project (Gordon et al., 2018), where Shell's original decommissioning project plan was affected by the actions of Greenpeace. Thus, stakeholder management and risk uncertainty management are closely aligned. Effectively integrating risk uncertainty management and stakeholder management by understanding the interests (objectives) and power (potential for action) of each stakeholder can be critical in ensuring project success (Ackermann & Eden, 2011).

Identifying and aligning project objectives can enable effective engagement with a range of project stakeholders for two reasons. First, structured conversations facilitate learning as stakeholders raise different risks, uncertainties and objectives ensuring a comprehensive, and therefore robust, understanding. Second, the process enables co-creation, engendering ownership and engagement. This procedural justice aspect is important in facilitating agreement as the set of possible stakeholder objectives may be greater than the resources available for the project, and objectives 'compete'. In these instances, negotiation towards an agreed set of objectives against which the project's success will be judged is important. Negotiation starts with actively listening to each stakeholder's views seeking to construct co-created outcomes.

Causal mapping can facilitate shared understanding of the stakeholder objectives through: (1) enabling each stakeholder to understand their own objectives (see above factor); (2) understanding the objectives of other stakeholders; and (3) identify actions that support both sets of objectives (Bryson et al., 2016). For example, a new nuclear power station project sought to ensure stakeholder alignment. Both parties had a reasonable understanding of their own objectives, but a weaker understanding of the other's objectives. Consequently, each spent time developing a causal map of their objectives for the project. The two maps were integrated providing the basis for exploration in a workshop. Each party was interested in seeing how their objectives interacted with those of the other. Two outcomes emerged. First, there was a negotiated agreement of shared objectives shaping the project's design and against which success would be determined. Second, each party gained a deeper appreciation of their counterpart's goals, enabling subsequent actions to support the shared goals be put in place without damaging either party's core goals. Mapping enabled them to see the range of objectives being considered and 'play' with the structure.

The same process is undertaken for managing risks and uncertainties. Involving stakeholders to risk workshops supported by causal mapping not only allows a wider consideration of risks and uncertainties, increasing the robustness of the management process, but also helps stakeholders gain a more holistic understanding of the project, appreciate the risks and uncertainties facing each stakeholder and thus ensure that actions taken to manage risks and uncertainties do not amplify another.

26.3.3   Recognising the Dynamics within and across Stakeholders and Uncertainty

The final factor relates to stakeholder and risk dynamics recognising that both change over the duration of a project. Industry has noted that 'the need to develop skills to *handle complex and dynamic project environments*' (Sexton et al., 2019, p. 12) is critical. Risks change salience as new information becomes available, and associated uncertainties are reduced (Winch & Maytorena, 2011). Likewise, project stakeholders change, with some stakeholders involved in a specific phase, e.g., estimators and suppliers or on lengthy projects (20–30 years), incorporating not only the design and build phases but operations, maintenance and sometimes decommissioning (Alexander et al., 2019). The shifting dynamics between stakeholders may result in a potential conflict of interest, not only between the project delivery team and its stakeholders (e.g., owners, suppliers, project-based firm), but also between project stakeholders more widely (Jepsen & Eskerod, 2009), with one stakeholder scrutinising the responses of another and adjusting their behaviour accordingly – illustrating why the behavioural challenge is important to address in practice.

Whilst it is important to attend to the dynamics associated with the changing stakeholder landscape and the changing risk and uncertainty profile, it is also important to consider the dynamics between the two. New stakeholders might have different objectives influencing their actions, and they may lack historical knowledge of what has been agreed, resulting in new risks to the project. Likewise, unforeseen events (e.g., a supplier being 'bought out' by another), may result in new stakeholders to be managed.

Causal mapping helps navigate this dynamic environment in several ways. Firstly, the maps created to surface, structure and manage risks, uncertainties and negotiate objectives, etc. can be used to help new stakeholders develop a nuanced understanding of the project. These new stakeholders can see the rationale between mitigating actions and risks and so focus energy effectively. They can add their knowledge to the map, helping to refine thinking. Secondly, mapping can facilitate the management of new risks and uncertainties, within the context of the entire risk map identifying where potential responses may negatively affect other risks in the network (to be avoided), and creatively design responses to manage other risks enabling the greatest 'bang for the buck'. Mapping can also enable reflection on potential actions, exploring how stakeholders watching the responses of other stakeholders may respond – an unfolding stakeholder dynamic (Eden & Ackermann, 2021).

Figure 26.1 illustrates how *working with a new supplier* may result in *experiencing nasty surprises* thus needing to *make late changes* which negatively impacts on *effectively integrating the existing structure* and subsequently has an impact on *keeping the client happy*, which is important as it *ensures all the necessary information* which aims to prevent *nasty surprises*. This reveals a vicious cycle (illustrated in bold arrows) – a particularly problematic risk dynamic.

We have presented three factors important to consider when integrating risk, uncertainty and stakeholder management practices. Whilst each factor has been presented individually, they impact one another – potentially causing more uncertainty. Objectives change, new social relationships are required if risks and uncertainties are to be managed and impacts of the external world are constantly navigated.

26.4 DISCUSSION

We began this chapter by identifying three challenges in current PRM practice: (1) limited recognition and understanding of complexity and uncertainty; (2) narrow understanding of systemicity in current PRM approaches; and (3) inadequate recognition of the behavioural aspects and their potential impact on project outcomes. We stressed the need to integrate risk management – extended to encompass uncertainty management – and stakeholder management particularly in the context of complex project organising. We then introduced causal mapping as a technique to help address these challenges and as a proposed 'joined-up' approach exploring three important interrelated factors. We now discuss some of the implications of this 'joined-up' approach in relation to the current literature and practice.

First, causal mapping enables a better understanding of project complexity and uncertainty to be gained. Mapping encourages dialogue within and across the project network, as it enables the stakeholders to engage in an important process of inquiry (Kay & King, 2020). It discourages a 'box-ticking' approach to the identification of risks and allows practitioners to recognise the context through surfacing and exploring stakeholder objectives (see Section 26.3.1). This helps stakeholders understand the difference between risk (aleatoric) and uncertainty (epistemic) and its relation to project complexities – important for developing more thoughtful management approaches and facilitating effective negotiation amongst stakeholders (see Section 26.3.2). In addition, mapping contributes towards the development of four uncertainty management strategies (Cleden, 2009, p. 1): (1) *knowledge strategies*, through the creation of 'knowledge maps' which capture what is known and what are the 'blind spots' in relation to a situation; (2) *anticipation strategies*, as mapping facilitates thinking forwards and backwards to generate possible future scenarios and create narratives (Kay & King, 2020) to help prepare for the unexpected; (3) *resilience strategies*, by understanding the inherent project conditions practitioners can identify triggers, learn and be more agile in their responses, which over time can contribute to enhanced organisational resilience (Nachbagauer et al., 2019); and (4) *learning strategies*, as mapping can encourage a learning process through which equivocality is reduced. It enables changes in mindset as there is a need to be open to new ways of thinking and adapt to changing circumstances.

Second, mapping enables the analysis of systemicity by visualising the interaction of risks, uncertainties and their dynamics within the project's context. This provides a holistic view of the project situation and enhances understanding of the impact of risk interactions on project objectives and a basis for effective stakeholder negotiation and engagement (see Section 26.3.2). Mapping enables stakeholders to capture their ideas (objectives, goals, interests) and relationships in a visual manner, and see these from different perspectives (see Section 26.3.1). Mapping can help communicate and clarify multiple interpretations, enable collaborations, define ideas, facilitate reasoning and learning, synthesise or elaborate thinking as well as understand and appreciate the complexity of a situation. The causal map conceived as a boundary object allows meaning to be co-created through dialogue and for action to be coordinated. Diverse thinking is increasingly important in the context of complex projects as the process of exploration and surfacing (Section 26.3.1) of negotiating and agreeing (Section 26.3.2) needs to be done from multiple perspectives. This is achieved by effectively engaging with the project stakeholders undertaken through a process of inquiry where relationships are built based on interests.

This leads to our final point, the need to attend to the behavioural aspects and their potential impact on the management of risks and uncertainties. The mapping process helps to capture the diversity of stakeholder interests and power bases, their actions (positive or negative), identify potential areas of conflict, their networks (see Ackermann & Eden, 2011) and develop options for action. Causal mapping contributes towards developing a shared understanding, it brings more coherence in group working and is conducive to building trust and collaboration, all essential parts of stakeholder engagement. Integrating risk uncertainty and stakeholder management with the aid of causal mapping can provide a synergistic approach which can help practitioners make *sense* of complex project situations, enhance abilities to *shape* situations through the exploration of goals, actions and their consequences and *adapt* to possible changes over time by recognising the dynamic nature of stakeholders and threats.

Awareness of these challenges has important implications for developing research which is discussed next.

26.5 FUTURE RESEARCH

As noted above there are three challenges and three factors. Understanding better how these can be integrated, both practically and conceptually, is an important direction to ensure successful project outcomes. To do this, we need a more intimate knowledge of how project practitioners perceive risk and uncertainty, particularly when considering the project's context which includes paying attention to stakeholders. We also need to find methods for encouraging project managers to think systemically rather than retaining a more linear and discrete mode of thought. Teasing out the barriers and enablers for taking systemic approaches encompassing stakeholders, uncertainty and risk is another important direction. Finally exploring further the role causal mapping can play, potentially acting as boundary objects, facilitating project narratives and enabling the management of complexity necessary to increase the likelihood of project outcome success.

REFERENCES

Ackermann, F. (2019). Systemic risk. In A. Gorod, L. Hallo, V. Ireland & I. Gunawan (Eds), *Another dimension in evolving toolbox for complex project management* (pp. 485–510). Taylor & Francis Group.

Ackermann, F. & Eden, C. (2005). Using causal mapping with group support systems to elicit an understanding of failure in complex projects: Some implications for organizational research. *Group Decision and Negotiation*, 14(5), 355–376.

Ackermann, F. & Eden, C. (2011). *Making strategy: Mapping out strategic success*. Sage.

Ackermann, F., Howick, S., Quigley, J., Walls, L. & Houghton, T. (2014). Systemic risk elicitation: Using causal maps to engage stakeholders and build a comprehensive view of risks. *European Journal of Operational Research*, 238(1), 290–299.

Alexander, J., Ackermann, F. & Love, P. E. D. (2019). Taking a holistic exploration of the project life cycle in public–private partnerships. *Project Management Journal*, 50(6), 673–685.

Bloomfield, K., Williams, T., Bovis, C. & Merali, Y. (2019). Systemic risk in major public contracts. *International Journal of Forecasting*, 35(2), 641–643.

Browning, T. R., & Ramasesh, R. V. (2015). Reducing unwelcome surprises in project management. *MIT Sloan Management Review*, 56(3), 53–62.

Bryson, J., Ackermann, F., Eden, C. & Finn C. (2004). *Visible thinking: Unlocking causal mapping for practical business results*. John Wiley & Sons.

Bryson, J., Ackermann, F. & Eden, C. (2016). Discovering collaborative advantage: The contributions of goal categories and visual strategy mapping. *Public Administration Review*, 76(6), 912–925.

Cleden, D. (2009). *Managing project uncertainty*. Gower.

Daniel, P. A. & Daniel, C. (2018). Complexity, uncertainty and mental models: From a paradigm of regulation to a paradigm of emergence in project management. *International Journal of Project Management*, 36(1), 184–197.

Eden, C. (1988). Cognitive mapping: A review. *European Journal of Operational Research*, 36(1), 1–13.

Eden, C. & Ackermann, F. (1998). Analyzing and comparing idiographic causal maps. In C. Eden & J. C. Spenders (Eds), *Managerial and organizational cognition: Theory, methods and research* (pp. 192–209). Sage.

Eden, C. & Ackermann, F. (2021). Modelling stakeholder dynamics for supporting group decision and negotiation: Theory to practice, group decision and negotiation. *Group Decision and Negotiation*, 30(5), 1001–1025.

Eden, C., Williams, T., Ackermann, F. & Howick, S. (2000). The role of feedback dynamics in disruption and delay on the nature of disruption and delay (D&D) in major projects. Journal of the Operational Research Society, 51(3), 291–300.

Gordon, G., Paterson, J. & Usenmez, E. (2018). *UK oil and gas law: Current issues and emerging trends, Volume I: Research Management and Regulatory Law* (3rd ed.). Edinburgh University Press.

Huff, A. S. & Jenkins, M. (2002). *Mapping strategic knowledge*. Sage.

Jepsen, A. L. & Eskerod, P. (2009). Stakeholder analysis in projects: Challenges in using current guidelines in the real world. *International Journal of Project Management*, 27(4), 335–343.

Kay, J. A. & King, M. A. (2020). *Radical uncertainty*. Bridge Street Press.

Keeney, R. (2013). Identifying, prioritizing, and using multiple objectives. *EURO Journal on Decision Processes*, 1(1–2), 45–67.

Kelly, G. (1957). *The psychology of personal constructs*. Norton.

Kim, W. C. & Mauborgne, R. A. (1995). A procedural justice model of strategic decision making: Strategy content implications in the multinational. *Organizational Science*, 6(1), 44–61.

Langfield-Smith, K. (1992). Exploring the need for a shared cognitive map. *Journal of Management Studies*, 29(3), 349–368.

Laukkanen, M. (1994). Comparative cause mapping of organizational cognitions. *Organization Science*, 5(3), 322–343.

Lenfle, S. & Loch, C. (2017). Has megaproject management lost its way? Lessons from history. In B. Flyvbjerg (Ed.), *The Oxford handbook of megaproject management* (pp. 21–38). Oxford University Press.

Nachbagauer, A., Andreas, G. M. & Schirl-Boeck, I. (2019). Managing the unexpected in megaprojects: Riding the waves of resilience. *International Journal of Managing Projects in Business*, 13(3), 694–715.

Pich, M. T., Loch, C. H. & De Meyer, A. (2002). On uncertainty, ambiguity and complexity in project management. *Management Science*, 48(8), 1008–1023.

Sexton, P., Foley, E. & Wagner, R. (Eds) (2019). *The future of project management: Global outlook 2019*. KPMG, Australian Institute of Project Management and IPMA.

Simon, H. A. (1976). From substantive to procedural rationality. In S. J. Latsis (Eds), *Method and appraisal in economics* (pp. 129–148). Cambridge University Press.

Tegarden, D. P. & Sheetz, S. D. (2003). Group cognitive mapping: A methodology and system for capturing and evaluating managerial and organizational cognition. *Omega*, 31(2), 113–125.

Williams, T. (2016). Identifying success factors in construction projects: A case study. *Project Management Journal*, 47(1), 97–112.

Williams, T. (2017). The nature of risk in complex projects. *Project Management Journal*, 48(4), 55–66.

Winch, G. M. (2017). Megaproject stakeholder management. In Flyvbjerg, B. (Ed.), *The Oxford handbook of megaproject management* (pp. 339–361). Oxford University Press.

Winch, G. M. & Maytorena, E. (2011). Managing risk and uncertainty on projects: A cognitive approach. In P. W. G. Morris, J. K. Pinto & J. Söderlund (Eds), *The Oxford handbook of project management* (pp. 345–364). Oxford University Press.

27. Project narratives: directions for research

Natalya Sergeeva and Johan Ninan

27.1 INTRODUCTION

Projects are peopled at all levels. Scholars have argued that project management is about people who make decisions that enable action (Morris & Pinto, 2010; Volker, 2019). Hence, the actions, practices and behaviours of the project management participants are to be explained by their motivations and human needs. After all, decision making is a social behaviour even when nobody else is present, as the decision maker can anticipate how others will react and factor it into their decision (Beach & Connolly, 2005). Constructs such as vision, identities and image at the individual and the collective levels are social constructions often created by discourses and narratives (Gioia et al., 2000; Humphreys & Brown, 2002). Projects can be better understood as continuously reconstructed entities with narratives driving experiences through dramatizing trajectories of practice (Carlsen, 2006; Tsoukas & Chia, 2002).

Organizational narratives as defined by Vaara et al. (2016) are the temporal and discursive constructions that provide a means for individual, social and organizational sensemaking and sensegiving. In a broad sense, a narrative is anything told or recounted by an individual, groups of individuals or an organization (Ninan & Sergeeva, 2021; Veenswijk & Berendse, 2008). Narratives are present everywhere and can be oral, written or filmed, fictional or non-fictional (Verduijn, 2007). Polkinghorne (1991) recorded that people make sense of their lives via narrative thought as the temporal and dramatic dimension of human existence is emphasized in them. He highlighted that the way people organize is dependent on the cues emanating from external perpetual senses and cognitive memories; and narratives are one of the main cognitive organizing processes which shape temporal events around people. Narratives can be treated as a 'cognitive instrument' as they impact subjects' thinking and emotional life (Rappaport, 2000). Strategically, policymakers employ plotted, plausible and repeated narratives to shape the reaction of people to the changes occurring around them (Abolafia, 2010).

Narratives help make sense of practices in project settings. For example, the change process in projects can be understood through narratives as a process of negotiated meaning and can enable researchers to comprehend different voices (Ninan & Sergeeva, 2021; Veenswijk & Berendse, 2008). The innovation process in projects can be understood through the ways in which project leaders speak, communicate and converse about innovation in the context of everyday practical activities (Sergeeva, 2017). Establishing an identity, brand positioning and packaging projects as innovative have become important strategies for many project-based organizations. Even the role of different actors in the evolution of projects can be studied by considering narratives as devices that capture, interpret, construct and change organizational time (Vaara et al., 2016). Narratives can make sense of the process of sustaining change in organizations by enhancing self-legitimization (Sergeeva, 2014).

This chapter is organized as follows. First, we provide a brief overview of narratives in project settings and record some project narratives from the High Speed 2 (HS2) megaproject in the United Kingdom (UK). In the next section, we highlight why narratives are important in project settings and record some organizational theories that can help make sense of narratives. Following this, we suggest some ways to craft and maintain project narratives. Finally, we suggest some directions for future research in project narratives by highlighting the data sources, methods of investigation and some additional suggestions of theories that can make sense of and provide insights to managing narratives in project settings.

27.2 PROJECT NARRATIVES

There are different narratives in project settings. For example, in the case of the HS2 rail megaproject in the UK there was the narrative of the need for the project, narrative of the consultation process, narrative of the sustainability of the project, etc. The HS2 megaproject was proposed in 2009 to connect London and Birmingham in 45 minutes through trains travelling at speeds of 225 mph. During the early stages of the project, the Transport Secretary created a narrative of the need for the project by highlighting that it would transform transport in the country and provide numerous benefits. The minister claimed, 'I am excited about the possibilities that HSR [High Speed Rail 2] has to transform transport in this country for the better – providing environmental benefits, encouraging investment and boosting business and jobs' (The Telegraph, 2009).

While there are narratives of the need for a project, there are also narratives that a project is not needed. For instance, projects are highlighted as a 'white elephant' (Winch, 2010) or as 'eye-wateringly expensive' (Ninan & Sergeeva, 2021) by protesters to create an alternative narrative.

Similarly, during the consultation phase of the HS2 project, a narrative of 'one of the largest consultations ever' was created by the spokesperson of the UK Department of Transport to show the inclusive nature of the consultation. The spokesperson claimed, '(t)his was one of the largest consultations ever undertaken by a government with over 30 events along the line of route attended by tens of thousands of people' (Mail Online, 2011). Additionally, a narrative of sustainability was also established, and the project was promoted as a low-carbon and environmentally sustainable transport solution. The Chief Executive of Network Rail recorded that the HS2 project 'is the low-carbon, sustainable transport of the future' (BBC News, 2010).

In project settings, there are other narratives such as the narrative of innovation in the project (Enninga & van der Lugt, 2016; Sergeeva & Winch, 2020), narrative of quality (Chinyamurindi, 2017), narrative of safety (Ninan, 2021), narrative of performance, etc. These narratives influence and shape actors' vision, identity, image and consequently their social practices (Heracleous, 2006). In the next section, we proceed to highlight how narratives influence and shape actors' interpretations and actions.

27.3 VISION, IDENTITY, IMAGE AND PROJECT NARRATIVES

Narratives can be applied in a project setting to shape the vision, identity and image of the project, which can result in an improved project performance.

A credible vision for the project can help address the blame culture, lack of trust and fragmentation in project settings. Globally, projects experience deficiencies due to segregation which result in adversarial relationships, confrontational attitudes, poor tendering practices, a blame culture and a lack of trust and cooperation (Bresnen & Marshall, 2000). The root cause of these problems in project settings is that not all actors have the same interests or interpretation of the proposed initiatives (Cicmil & Hodgson, 2006). Most of the challenges projects face are managerial often in the integration of different disciplines (Sergeeva & Winch, 2021). Narratives can organize people's lived experiences and create order out of random incidents and events. Such an order can help project participants understand the passage of events and even guide cooperative action. A vision is critical for temporary organizations as it seeks to bring all stakeholders together to achieve the common goal. Theories such as sensemaking can ascertain how project practitioners make sense of their daily routine (Weick et al., 2010). It is necessary to understand narratives emergent from retrospect, present experiences and presumptions about the future in order to make sense of the different practices throughout the project lifecycle (Sergeeva, 2014). Thus, effective project narratives need to be crafted for defining the project mission and vision, which in turn help the project get necessary approvals as well as improve cooperation and trust (Sergeeva & Winch, 2021).

Identity is a social and cultural phenomenon that encompasses macro-level categories, temporary and interactionally specific stances and cultural positions (Bucholtz & Hall, 2005). Organizational identity can commonly be understood as an organization's members' collective understanding of the features presumed to be central and relatively permanent, which distinguish the organization from other organizations (Gioia et al., 2000). For example, the stakeholders from whom land was acquired in the case of the HS2 project came together as they resonated with the identity of being against the project: 'In some ways the issue has brought the village closer together, as there's been this sort of "our backs are against the wall" situation, but there is also a higher level of depression and a lot less smiles' (Northampton Chronicle & Echo, 2012). 'Most of those worst affected by the HS2 line are not rich people in the Chilterns. They are ordinary people in inner London. We are talking about hundreds of council homes going when the waiting list in London is already 800,000' (The Telegraph, 2010).

Project identities at all levels, be it at industry level, organizational level, project level, group level or individual level, can be considered as a social construction and they are subject to multiple interpretations and crafted by narratives (Stets & Burke, 2000). Fiol (2002) theorizes that narratives reflect and produce processes of identification in discourse. Narratives help employees to dis-identify with the old and re-identify with the new identity. Theories such as social identity theory help to understand how narratives employed by practitioners are used to identify projects, for example, as innovative (Sergeeva, 2017). Project leaders consider it important to construct a coherent and consistent narrative, which in turn establishes a project identity which is instrumental for maintaining stability in the context of the ever dynamic project environment (Sergeeva & Winch, 2021).

Image is the perception of the organizational purpose, aims and values and the resulting general impression in the mind of all stakeholders (Gregory, 2004). A positive organizational image can create trust and commitment in the members and help achieve a sustainable structure for the organization (Kalkan et al., 2020). During the initial stages of the HS2 project, the Transport Secretary stated how the project's purpose was to develop the country, 'I want Britain to be a pioneer in low-cost, mass-market high-speed rail' (The Telegraph, 2009).

The image of the project as one meant to develop the country helps garner support from the wider community. Sergeeva and Winch (2021) note that image narratives are crafted during the shaping phase of a project to get approval and support from external stakeholders about

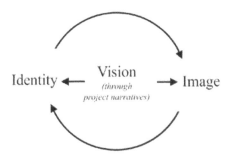

Figure 27.1   *Interaction between vision, identity and image through project narratives*

intended project outputs and outcomes, and in contrast, identity narratives are crafted during the delivery phase of a project to bring internal stakeholders together for achieving the project output. Narratives can be mobilized for creating a collective brand image at the levels of the firm and sector as a whole (Duman et al., 2018). Theories such as organizational power can help understand image narratives. For example, using Foucault's governmentality theory, Ninan et al. (2019) studied the branding practices of a megaproject. The megaproject used narratives through social media to create a brand image of the project as beneficial for the community resulting in support for the project. For example, the branding effect of narratives can lead to community support for construction activities and insensitivity towards traffic diversions and other inconveniences caused by the construction activities.

The interaction between vision, identity and image through project narratives is shown in Figure 27.1. Project narratives can shape the vision of a project, such as on sustainability or innovation. Sergeeva and Winch (2021) highlight that such a vision becomes formalized and communicated to different stakeholders thereby shaping the identity and image of the project organization. The vision can shape an individual's identity and affect the decisions internal stakeholders take regarding the project, helping the project achieve its objective. The vision can also shape the image of the project and can lead to community and external stakeholder support. Ninan et al. (2021) argue that a positive image of the project can not only affect the external stakeholders, but also shape the identity of the internal stakeholders such as the project team. For example, the authors note from the case of a metro rail project in India that an image narrative of the project as an 'urgent infrastructure asset' led the project team to take decisions prioritizing a reduction in the construction time of the project, sometimes at the expense of cost and quality. Thus, as Vaara et al. (2016) argue, a focus on narratives allows for understanding how even the seemingly personal growth of an individual is nonetheless deeply intertwined with broader organizational and even societal narratives that produce common, stable paths out of the unique experiences and choices people make.

27.4   MANAGING NARRATIVES

It should be noted that narratives are not one-sided. Narratives are interpreted, shared and challenged by various organizational actors in the 'game of managing meaning' (Granlund, 2002). It is important to consider the multi-authored process of narratives to understand practice (Buchanan & Dawson, 2007). For example, in the practice of the selection of a project, the promoters of a project, such as the government, contractors and financers, are interested in awarding the project, and the protesters of the project, such as project-affected parties and the opposition party of the government, campaign to stall the project (Ninan & Sergeeva, 2021). Both promoters and protesters draw on narratives for their vested interests. Hence, there is a need to manage narratives for the successful completion of the project.

Veenswijk and Berendse (2008), in their study of a Dutch infrastructure project, record how the project manager and local experts served as 'editing' actors by actively reshaping the narrative concerning the project. Narratives need to be crafted and maintained. Protesters' narratives may need to be converted into promoters' narratives. Riessman (2002) stresses the importance of tools and structures employed by the narrator and calls for research to uncover and track them. Stories, labels and comparisons help in crafting narratives, while repeating, endorsing, humourizing and actioning can help in maintaining the crafted narratives.

Stories are recorded as one of the main discourses used to craft narratives, particularly in the works of Boje (2008). He highlights that there is a 'story turn' before the 'narrative turn' demonstrating the role of stories in creating a narrative. Storytelling is defined as an activity of telling or sharing stories about personal experiences, life events and situations (Sergeeva & Trifilova, 2018). Stories are more than descriptions and can be an avenue for emotional engagement with the audience (Gabriel, 2000; Sergeeva & Green, 2019). Such an emotional engagement can result in support or empathy and can create a strong narrative for or against the project. Another way to craft a narrative is through the use of labels. Logue and Clegg (2015) record that a label can be used as a political tool or a resource as it can build or reinforce systems of meaning. When organizations claim the label of a well-established category, it triggers assumptions of its products and practices similar to the category it claimed (Pontikes, 2018). For example, the 'green' label was used in the case of the HS2 project: 'But virtually the whole of the developed world is now going ahead with high speed rail because it's the green solution to providing fast, high capacity connections between cities' (BBC News, 2011).

Ninan and Sergeeva (2021) note the use of labels of people, project and practice by the promoters and protesters to craft narratives. For example, the promoters called the project 'low carbon', the protesters were labelled as 'NIMBY' (not in my backyard activists) and the consultation practice 'transparent'. Another way to craft a narrative is through the use of comparisons. Comparisons involve comparing oneself or others with others (Suls et al., 2002). In an intra-organizational context, Roberson (2006) highlights that comparisons with peers in an organization can influence an individual's justice perception. Within the project context, Ninan et al. (2019) record how a megaproject using comparisons and claiming that another project in a different city looks up to them resulted in a positive community sentiment and a favourable narrative for the project.

One of the ways to maintain a crafted narrative is by repeating the narrative. Stories are repeated in organizations whether over the water cooler or in a formal quarterly meeting (Dailey & Browning, 2014). Garud and Turunen (2017) argue how retelling stories is a way of reinforcing cultural norms and values. Ideas sink in only after they have been heard many times (Kotter, 2012).

Another way to maintain a crafted narrative is by a prominent person endorsing the narrative. Lim et al. (2006) record how trust transference through associations with existing reputed people or organizations is instrumental in trust-building and stability. Thus, endorsing the stories, labels or comparisons by people who occupy eminent positions can enhance trust. Within megaprojects, publicizing the visit of regional leaders and celebrities to the construction site is discussed in Ninan et al. (2019) as a branding strategy effective in changing the project community to advocates of the project. Another way to maintain a crafted narrative is by humourizing the narrative. Humour can affirm an existing narrative in an organization (Jarzabkowski & Lê, 2017). Discourses that have a sense of humour in them are clearly memorable and rendered more (Sergeeva & Green, 2019). Additionally, actioning wherein an action is allotted to a narrative can stabilize the narrative. Individuals reconstitute narratives through their actions (Vaara et al., 2016). As Weick (1988) notes, actions test provisional understanding generated through prior sensemaking and thereby strengthen existing narratives.

27.5   FUTURE DIRECTIONS OF RESEARCH

The objective of this chapter is to emphasize the role of narratives in projects. Narratives are particularly important in project settings as they are temporary organizations, and it is critical to bring multiple diverse stakeholders together to achieve the common goal. Some narratives in project settings such as narratives of the need for the project, narratives of sustainability and narratives of the consultation process are discussed. We also highlight the interaction of vision, identity and image through project narratives as shown in Figure 27.1. Narratives of the vision of a project can create an identity for the internal stakeholders which helps in collaboration and can create a positive image for external stakeholders which helps in garnering support for the project, both of which increase the likelihood of project success. Some of the ways to craft narratives such as stories, labels and comparisons, and some ways to maintain project narratives such as repeating, endorsing, humourizing and actioning are also discussed. There is still more research work that needs to be done to understand the practice of managing and organizing projects through narratives. While some organizational theories such as sensemaking, social identity theory and organizational power theories are considered in project settings, other theories such as attribution theory (Vaara, 2002), institutional theory (Skoldberg, 1994) and practice theory (Carlsen, 2006) can be employed to make sense of narratives in projects.

Some research methodologies that can aid researchers in investigating narratives include semi-structured or unstructured open-ended interviews, participant observations and online naturalistic inquiry such as the study of social media, news articles and project newsletters. While narratives in project studies are usually associated with written texts or spoken words, other forms of communication such as visual, audio and even actions can be considered. A study on video narratives can significantly inform project management practice since they have a richer ability to account for emotions in the form of changes in tone, calmness and anxiety (Huy, 2002). Many projects, such as the Tideway project in the UK, upload short videos on YouTube to disperse their message to a wider audience. These short videos capture people's experiences of their everyday work. Future research can study the role of these videos in project organizing and narratives. Of further interest is how posted videos of current projects by project leaders enable them to win other projects. Other avenues such as micro-stories by the project members of the work they do (Fenton & Langley, 2011) can significantly improve our understanding of the project management career.

To understand project management in the twenty-first century, we also have to study the practice of projects in the online environment (Ninan, 2020). Many conversations relating to projects happen on Twitter, Facebook, LinkedIn, WhatsApp and news media articles. Social media provides an opportunity to the project community and empowers the marginalized by providing them with an audience for their stories (Vaara et al., 2016). In social media different forms of data such as text, picture and video are often interwoven (Ninan et al., 2019). The archive of digital media enables researchers to study narratives longitudinally. Even retrospective data relating to a project can be retrieved and analysed for the role of narratives. Additionally, narratives in real time can be studied to understand the convergence and divergence of meaning, such as in the case of project benefit realization (Mathur et al., 2021). Thus, to better understand the process of narrating in project organizing, more longitudinal, multi-method and multi-theoretical research is called upon, which will in turn help us to understand and improve project management practice.

ACKNOWLEDGEMENTS

This research was supported by Economic and Social Research Council Grant ES/R011567/1.

REFERENCES

Abolafia, M. Y. (2010). Narrative construction as sensemaking: How a central bank thinks. *Organization Studies*, 31(3), 349–367.
BBC News (2010, 11 March). *High-speed rail plans announced by government*. www.bbc.co.uk/news/1/hi/uk/8561286.stm.
BBC News (2011, 19 February). *High-speed rail campaigners gather for national meeting*. www.bbc.co.uk/news/uk-england-12514335.
Beach, L. R. & Connolly, T. (2005). *The psychology of decision making*. Sage.
Boje, D. M. (2008). *Storytelling organizations*. Sage.
Bresnen, M. & Marshall, N. (2000). Partnering in construction: A critical review of issues, problems and dilemmas. *Construction Management and Economics*, 18(2), 229–238.
Buchanan, D. & Dawson, P. (2007). Discourse and audience: Organizational change as multi-story process. *Journal of Management Studies*, 44(5), 669–686.
Bucholtz, M. & Hall, K. (2005). Identity and interaction: A sociocultural linguistic approach. *Discourse Studies*, 7(4–5), 585–614.
Carlsen, A. (2006). Organizational becoming as dialogic imagination of practice: The case of the indomitable Gauls. *Organization Science*, 17(1), 132–149.
Chinyamurindi, W. (2017). The role of information management in project management success: Narratives from entrepreneurs operating within the South African construction industry. *South African Journal of Information Management*, 19(1), 1–9.
Cicmil, S. & Hodgson, D. E. (2006). Critical research in project management: An introduction. In D. E. Hodgson & S. Cicmil (Eds), *Making projects critical* (pp. 1–28). Palgrave Macmillan.
Dailey, S. L. & Browning, L. (2014). Retelling stories in organizations: Understanding the functions of narrative repetition. *Academy of Management Review*, 39(1), 22–43.
Duman, D. U., Green, S. D. & Larsen, G. D. (2018). Historical narratives as strategic resources: Analysis of the Turkish international contracting sector. *Construction Management and Economics*, 36(1), 1–17.
Enninga, T. & van der Lugt, R. (2016). The innovation journey and the skipper of the raft: About the role of narratives in innovation project leadership. *Project Management Journal*, 47(2), 103–114.
Fenton, C. & Langley, A. (2011). Strategy as practice and the narrative turn. *Organization Studies*, 32(9), 1171–1196.
Fiol, C. (2002). Capitalizing on paradox: The role of language in transforming organizational identities. *Organization Science*, 13(6), 653–666.
Gabriel, Y. (2000). *Storytelling in organizations: Facts, fictions, and fantasies*. Oxford University Press.

Garud, R. & Turunen, M. (2017). The banality of organizational innovations: Embracing the substance-process duality. *Innovation*, 19(1), 31–38.

Gioia, D. A., Schultz, M. & Corley, K. G. (2000). Organizational identity, image, and adaptive instability. *Academy of Management Review*, 25(1), 63–81.

Granlund, M. (2002). Changing legitimate discourse: A case study. *Scandinavian Journal of Management*, 18(3), 365–392.

Gregory, J. R. (2004). *The best of branding: Best practices in corporate branding*. McGraw-Hill.

Heracleous, L. (2006). *Discourse, interpretation, organization*. Cambridge University Press.

Humphreys, M. & Brown, A. D. (2002). Narratives of organizational identity and identification: A case study of hegemony and resistance. *Organization Studies*, 23(3), 421–447.

Huy, Q. (2002). Emotional balancing of organizational continuity and radical change: The contribution of middle managers. *Administrative Science Quarterly*, 47(1), 31–69.

Jarzabkowski, P. A. & Lê, J. K. (2017). We have to do this and that? You must be joking: Constructing and responding to paradox through humor. *Organization Studies*, 38(3–4), 433–462.

Kalkan, Ü., Altınay Aksal, F., Altınay Gazi, Z., Atasoy, R. & Dağlı, G. (2020). The relationship between school administrators' leadership styles, school culture, and organizational image. *Sage Open*, 10(1). DOI: 2158244020902081.

Kotter, J. P. (2012). *Leading change*. Harvard Business Press.

Lim, K. H., Sia, C. L., Lee, M. K. & Benbasat, I. (2006). Do I trust you online, and if so, will I buy? An empirical study of two trust-building strategies. *Journal of Management Information Systems*, 23(2), 233–266.

Logue, D. M. & Clegg, S. R. (2015). Wikileaks and the news of the world: The political circuitry of labeling. *Journal of Management Inquiry*, 24(4), 394–404.

Mail Online (2011, 13 November). *Fury for home-owners booted out to make room for a high speed rail link*. www.dailymail.co.uk/news/article-2060575/Home-owners-booted-make-room-rail-link -Buckinghamshire.html.

Mathur, S., Ninan, J., Vuorinen, L., Ke, Y. & Sankaran, S. (2021). An exploratory study of the use of social media to assess benefits realization in transport infrastructure projects. *Project Leadership and Society*, 2, 100010.

Morris, P. W. G. & Pinto, J. K. (Eds) (2010). *The Wiley guide to project organization and project management competencies*. John Wiley & Sons.

Ninan, J. (2020). Online naturalistic inquiry in project management research: Directions for research. *Project Leadership and Society*, 1(1), 1–9.

Ninan, J. (2021). Construction safety in media: An overview of its interpretation and strategic use. *International Journal of Construction Management*. DOI: 10.1080/15623599.2021.1946898.

Ninan, J. & Sergeeva, N. (2021). Labyrinth of labels: Narrative constructions of promoters and protesters in megaprojects. *International Journal of Project Management*, 39(5), 496–506.

Ninan, J., Clegg, S. & Mahalingam, A. (2019). Branding and governmentality for infrastructure megaprojects: The role of social media. *International Journal of Project Management*, 37(1), 59–72.

Ninan, J., Mahalingam, A. & Clegg, S. (2021). Asset creation team rationalities and strategic discourses: Evidence from India. *Infrastructure Asset Management*, 8(2), 1–10.

Northampton Chronicle & Echo (2012, 16 January). *The Chronicle looks at what it will mean to Northamptonshire if the HS2 is created*. www.northamptonchron.co.uk/news/the-chron-looks-at -what-it-will-mean-to-northamptonshire-if-the-hs2-is-created-1-3423516.

Polkinghorne, D. E. (1991). Narrative and self-concept. *Journal of Narrative and Life History*, 1(2–3), 135–153.

Pontikes, E. G. (2018). Category strategy for firm advantage. *Strategy Science*, 3(4), 620–631.

Rappaport, J. (2000). Community narratives: Tales of terror and joy. *American Journal of Community Psychology*, 28(1), 1–24.

Riessman, C. K. (2002). Narrative analysis. In A. M. Huberman & M. B. Miles (Eds), *The qualitative researcher's companion* (pp. 17–70). Sage.

Roberson, Q. M. (2006). Justice in teams: The activation and role of sensemaking in the emergence of justice climates. *Organizational Behavior and Human Decision Processes*, 100(2), 177–192.

Sergeeva, N. (2014). Understanding of labelling and sustaining of innovation in construction: A sensemaking perspective. *Engineering Project Organization Journal*, 4(1), 31–43.

Sergeeva, N. (2017). Labeling projects as innovative: A social identity theory. *Project Management Journal*, 48(1), 51–64.

Sergeeva, N. & Green, S. D. (2019). Managerial identity work in action: Formalised narratives and anecdotal stories of innovation. *Construction Management and Economics*, 37(10), 604–623.

Sergeeva, N. & Trifilova, A. (2018). The role of storytelling in innovation process. *Creativity and Innovation Management*, 27(4), 1–10.

Sergeeva, N. & Winch, G. M. (2020). Narrative interactions: How project-based firms respond to government narratives of innovation. *International Journal of Project Management*, 38(6), 379–387.

Sergeeva, N. & Winch, G. M. (2021). Project narratives that potentially perform and change the future. *Project Management Journal*, 52(3), 264–277.

Skoldberg, K. (1994). Tales of change: Public administration reform and narrative mode. *Organization Science*, 5(2), 219–238.

Stets, J. E. & Burke, P. J. (2000). Identity theory and social identity theory. *Social Psychology Quarterly*, 63(3), 224–237.

Suls, J., Martin, R. & Wheeler, L. (2002). Social comparison: Why, with whom, and with what effect? *Current Directions in Psychological Science*, 11(5), 159–163.

The Telegraph (2009, 30 December). *High speed rail must have 'Easytrain' prices says Transport Secretary*. www.telegraph.co.uk/news/uknews/road-and-rail-transport/6911032/High-speed-rail -must-have-Easytrain-prices-says-Transport-Secretary.html.

The Telegraph (2010, 18 December). *High-speed line noise will affect 50000 people*. www.telegraph.co .uk/news/uknews/road-and-rail-transport/8212095/High-speed-line-noise-will-affect-50000-people .html.

Tsoukas, H. & Chia, R. (2002). On organizational becoming: Rethinking organizational change. *Organization Science*, 13(5), 567–582.

Vaara, E. (2002). On the discursive construction of success/failure in narratives of postmerger integration. *Organization Studies*, 23(2), 211–248.

Vaara, E., Sonenshein, S. & Boje, D. (2016). Narratives as sources of stability and change in organizations: Approaches and directions for future research. *Academy of Management Annals*, 10(1), 495–560.

Veenswijk, M. & Berendse, M. (2008). Constructing new working practices through project narratives. *International Journal of Project Organisation and Management*, 1(1), 65–85.

Verduijn, K. (2007). *Tales of entrepreneurship: Contributions to understanding entrepreneurial life*. PhD thesis, Vrije Universiteit Amsterdam.

Volker, L. (2019). Looking out to look in: Inspiration from social sciences for construction management research. *Construction Management and Economics*, 37(1), 13–23.

Weick, K. E. (1988). Enacted sensemaking in crisis situations. *Journal of Management Studies*, 25(4), 305–317.

Weick, K. E., Sutcliffe, K. M. & Obstfield, D. (2010). Organizing and the process of sensemaking. In P. C. Nutt & D. Wilson (Eds), *Handbook of decision making* (pp. 83–104). John Wiley & Sons.

Winch, G. M. (2010). *Managing construction projects*. John Wiley & Sons.

28. Project value creation: sensemaking, shaping, and monitoring in a project network

Miia Martinsuo

28.1   INTRODUCTION

Projects are considered as vehicles for value creation (Winter & Szczepanek, 2008), besides their role in solving a specific problem and fulfilling a customer need. While contractors typically may put resources and effort to creating value into a solution (for example, a building, an infrastructure, a technical process, or a piece of equipment), the solution owners as customers are interested in how the solution creates value in their business over time. Contractors and customers necessarily interact to co-create value over the project lifecycle, to fulfil both partners' expectations of value. This idea of key actors' different value expectations and their need for co-creation is already well understood and to some extent researched (Fuentes et al., 2019; Liu et al., 2019).

In complex projects, however, a complex system is delivered and requires versatile capabilities and resources, so this single-organizational or dyadic view to value creation is overly simplistic. Complex projects involve multiple organizations in a project network, the configuration of the network may evolve over time, and each stakeholder contributes to the project's value creation in some ways. The dispersion of knowledge and work tasks in this network creates challenges, both in terms of uncertainty and organizational complexity. Stakeholders also have different value priorities that need to be understood, negotiated, and coordinated, to establish a shared idea of what value is being created and how (Martinsuo, 2020), and to ensure value-oriented monitoring and control (Martinsuo et al., 2019a). Value is co-produced together, instead of added by one stakeholder (Ramirez, 1999). The starting point for this chapter is the need to understand project value creation and value-oriented control in complex projects, when multiple stakeholders are involved.

This chapter concentrates on project value creation within the project, i.e., the ways in which stakeholders create value in and during the design and delivery of a complex system in a project network. The project lifecycle from the front end to implementation and closure is covered, and the link to post-project operations is mentioned briefly. Thereby, the aspect of the customer creating value through and after the project and stakeholders' views to value capture are purposely excluded. The goal is to expand the concept of project value creation toward the project network level and specify value creation as network-level processes of sensemaking, shaping, and monitoring. As the focus is on complex project organizing, complexity, uncertainty, projectivity, and temporality are inherent features in the system to be delivered as well as the project network and its value creation processes. This chapter reviews previous research on the involvement of stakeholders in project value creation, maps three dominant modes of value creation during the project, and develops a conceptual framework on value creation in project networks. Future pathways for research are proposed, especially for theorizing project value creation from the perspectives of strategy and sensemaking, technology management and material aspects of actor-network theory, and organizational control and behavioral decision making.

28.2   VALUE FOR MULTIPLE STAKEHOLDERS IN A PROJECT NETWORK

When projects are seen as vehicles for value creation, we can immediately ask: what value, and for whom? The concept of project value is inherently multidimensional (Ahola et al., 2008; Eskerod & Ang, 2017; Flyvbjerg, 2017; Martinsuo & Killen, 2014; Martinsuo et al., 2019a; Vuorinen & Martinsuo, 2019), so the financial value of a project has to be considered in light of many other value dimensions such as technical, social, ecological, emotional, and aesthetic. Also, value may be observed on multiple levels; value experienced at the project level will appear differently for the firm, relationship, or business network level (Martinsuo, 2019), and regional, national, and user levels (Zerjav et al., 2021). Besides multidimensionality, previous research has increasingly acknowledged that different stakeholders may have different ideas of project value (Ahola et al., 2008; Eskerod & Ang, 2017), and the stakeholders' conceptions of value may evolve over the lifecycle of the project when they accumulate knowledge (Martinsuo, 2020). Laursen (2018) has specifically concentrated on value creation in project networks, and Martinsuo (2020) encouraged further research to look into different stakeholders' value priorities and related negotiation and decision making.

Project networks include multiple different organizations, each with their expectations toward the project. Different stakeholders may have their own idea of why they participate in projects and what they expect from the projects, potentially depending on their position in the project network, their strategies, and type of investment they make in the project. Zerjav (2021, building on the three domains of organizing by Winch, 2014) divides between owner, project-based organization as the core contractor, and the temporary project organization as the key value domains of project organizing and also acknowledges the possible involvement of other stakeholders in them. The project network may take shape in very different kinds of constellations of value creation, depending on who are the recipients of value (Laursen, 2018). Also, the timing of value creation may be crucial for some stakeholders (Svejvig et al., 2019).

Among the key challenges concerning value management in project networks are the emergence of value and the plurality of stakeholders' perspectives over the project lifecycle (Artto et al., 2016; Eskerod & Ang, 2017; Martinsuo, 2020). Each stakeholder invests in the project in some ways (through allocating money, materials and tools, work effort, and time), and these investments accumulate as costs over time. Similarly, each stakeholder receives various benefits from the projects (in terms of outputs, knowledge and learning, feelings of satisfaction, and income), and these benefits accumulate over time. Individuals and organizations each have their unique experiences both during and after the delivery of the complex system (Eskerod & Ang, 2017), potentially reflected in the reputation and brand image of the project in the institutional field (Ninan et al., 2019). In this way, each project can be considered to have multiple value streams (processes of creating value). However, one stakeholder's cost may not produce benefits to that stakeholder directly, but through another stakeholder's benefits or investments only. This implies that the stakeholders' value streams are linked and even interdependent.

Zerjav (2021) emphasizes that owner, project-based organization, and temporary project domains of project organizing each have a different approach to value creation and capture:

asset investment, service provision, and collaboration on joint outputs. While the dominant focus of research is often either on the owner's or contractor's project outcome-related value stream, the context of the project network may be much more complex due to the stakeholders' interconnected value streams. Therefore, there is a need to understand value creation specifically in project networks and identify episodes where multiple stakeholders' value priorities may clash.

28.3   VALUE CREATION THROUGH SENSEMAKING AND NEGOTIATION

Particularly in the early phases of the project, value creation takes place in the cognitive and social processes of involved stakeholders, as tacit thoughts and explicit expressions of what is important and valuable in the project. Even if each stakeholder has well-established strategies and espoused values, they always make sense of project-specific possibilities and circumstances, to specify project-specific value expectations. Stakeholders frame their lifecycle value expectations differently, for example based on uncertainty, timing of cost and benefit realization, project relations, and external sponsorship (Martinsuo et al., 2019b). These early value considerations are then the foundation for justifying the project (Zerjav et al., 2021) and later value generation (Kolltveit & Grønhaug, 2004). The project front-end activities typically concentrate on immaterial activities – thoughts, wishes, projections of the future – although the planning and negotiations are also documented in project-related artifacts such as project charters, plans, and contracts.

Each stakeholder in the project network may have its own idea of what is of value and what to expect from the project throughout its lifecycle (Martinsuo, 2020). While it is customary to concentrate on the customer's (owner's) requirements as guidance to what is done in the project and acknowledge the contractor's expectations and priorities, also the suppliers and subcontractors, end users, common public, and any third parties all have their value conceptions when joining a project. At the front end of complex projects only limited information is available and uncertainty prevails, so conceptions of value reflect opportunities and risks that need to be managed to achieve value (Kolltveit & Grønhaug, 2004). When complex projects are defined in conditions of risks and opportunities, managers use their accumulated previous understanding, intuition, and confidence when making decisions (Chenger & Woiceshyn, 2021).

When multiple stakeholders are involved, they need to negotiate how value will be created and delivered in the project, and build shared understanding and agree on goals (Edkins et al., 2013; Liu et al., 2019; Martinsuo, 2019; Matinheikki et al., 2016; Williams & Samset, 2010). The shared goal could be explicated in the project's value proposition or business case, not just in financial terms but more generally. Matinheikki et al. (2016) emphasize the relational and cognitive activities of early-phase project networks as mechanisms for building trust and devising a shared vision, which are necessary for creating relationship value. There is a need for stakeholders to share their views and align their different goals and expectations to help move the project forward (Artto et al., 2016; Matinheikki et al., 2016) and create a shared image and identity for the project (Artto et al., 2016). One of the key tasks then is the readiness for stakeholders to voice their value expectations and concerns early on in the project. The use of discursive and rhetorical tactics are central in the cognitive and social processes of value creation and deserve further research attention (Zerjav et al., 2021). Any implicit, unmentioned value expectations are likely to cause problems and errors later in the project as other stakeholders cannot guess and acknowledge them in their work.

Sensemaking and negotiation of value priorities continue throughout the project and influence the project activities also throughout its later lifecycle (Martinsuo, 2020). Artto et al. (2016) reported that project stakeholders' expectations evolve over time and they continue to create visions of the future and should continue to share them throughout the project, so that the evolving needs can be responded to in a flexible manner. They also emphasized the necessity to anticipate the operations phase in the project's lifecycle: operations will bring in new stakeholders to the project network later in the project with new value priorities and expectations that need to be acknowledged.

28.4   VALUE SHAPING AND CO-CREATION

During project implementation, value creation occurs through various behavioral and operational processes among the involved stakeholders, in the form of resource and material access, use, consumption, and transfer. Different stakeholders are involved in value creation by procuring, shaping, and consuming resources and materials – including human resources, technologies, raw materials, and components – in various ways. While these activities are at the center of all projects, the mechanisms of value creation in these activities are surprisingly little discussed in research. In value shaping and co-creation, material activities and processes dominate: resources and materials are purposely accessed, consumed, molded, and transferred. However, it is necessary to acknowledge both material-centric and knowledge-centric value creation processes, as they both are relevant in project networks.

In intra-organizational projects, the overall idea of value creation could be seen as streams of activities concerning resource allocation and material procurement and use. When a certain host organization has full control over the resources and materials, then it also has the possibility to optimize the processes of value creation for maximum efficiency. With project networks, however, the setting becomes more complex, as multiple stakeholders join forces to create value in the project (Fuentes et al., 2019; Laursen, 2018; Lehtinen et al., 2019). Various contracts and plans govern how each stakeholder consumes its resources and materials in the project. Even in project networks it is likely that the main contractor has a dominating role as they are responsible for value creation during project implementation (Martinsuo, 2020), but they do not possess perfect information about the resources, materials, and processes of all stakeholders and guarantee process efficiency.

The engineering and delivery processes in project business tend to be well known, but their logics of value creation deserves further attention, particularly in project networks. In fact, current research tends to cover value creation indirectly, through mechanisms and activities that bring stakeholders together in the complex project, instead of the mechanisms and activities of manipulating resources and materials used directly for value creation. For example, Artto et al. (2016) concentrated on value-enhancing integration mechanisms across the stakeholders. Laursen (2018) identified four value creation activities: developing infrastructure, creating knowledge, changing minds, and managing for value capture. Lehtinen et al. (2019) covered the design principles, operating mechanisms, joint activities, and relational positions in megaprojects as organizational platforms. Where all these studies emphasize the multi-stakeholder interactions in value creation, they do not cover the material value creation processes explicitly. Lehtinen et al. (2019), however, pointed out that partial products, technologies, and solutions during the project help stakeholders in understanding each other's value creation and joint value capture.

Recent research has clearly concentrated on value creation through immaterial knowledge processes, particularly following a service-dominant logic of business. In this view, stakeholders together co-create value by interactions that enhance the project outcomes over time (Fuentes et al., 2019). Building on the sensemaking, negotiation, and alignment activities at the front end and resulting in a shared value proposition, Fuentes et al. (2019) emphasize co-designing and co-developing services that produce customers' expected value outcomes. Particularly in creative projects value is managed by controlling the distance between new knowledge (or new product/service concepts) and the dominant design, which may occur, for example, through identifying a 'common unknown', learning, imagining, and building new evaluation criteria (Gillier et al., 2015). Green and Sergeeva (2019) emphasize that project value is a social construct that is ultimately shaped by narratives, i.e., in stakeholders' spoken language, whereby value creation through such narratives effectively represents continuous identity work in the project.

28.5   VALUE CREATION THROUGH MONITORING AND CONTROL

Especially in the later phases of projects, value creation happens through evaluation and decision-making processes of the stakeholders, when project outcomes are compared with expectations and goals and transferred to users. In reality, monitoring and control begin already at the project front end (Volden, 2019) and continue through the project implementation, but the outcome view becomes particularly central when nearing project closure and commissioning. Different stakeholders may have their own evaluation criteria for projects, but project plans and contracts feature mechanisms for the project's own monitoring and control (Kivilä et al., 2017). Value creation then occurs through the assessment and communication of benefit realization, detection and management of risks, deviances and errors, and problem solving. In monitoring and control, immaterial and material activities and processes are in constant interaction: tangible outcomes are reviewed and evaluated, and this information is used in making decisions about the next course of action.

Stakeholders in the project network each have their specific experiences of the different value dimensions (Eskerod & Ang, 2017), even if they are committed to the same project plan and contract with the others. Monitoring and control typically rely on measurable success criteria, but also more comprehensive value assessments are increasingly used. While it is quite typical to assess costs or sacrifices and benefits separately in the early phases of the project (Ahola et al., 2008; Volden, 2019), monitoring and controlling the resource and material consumption and assessing them in light of the actual benefits could also be useful later on. Besides the immediate outcome measures, there is a need to monitor and control other aspects of value. For example, public-private partnership projects will need to adhere to local, regional, national, and potentially also international regulations and laws and carry out related monitoring and control, in addition to following the project's plan and contract (Kivilä et al.,

2017). Failing to take relevant value dimensions and relevant stakeholders' views into account in monitoring and control may, again, result in later problems.

Stakeholders may differ in their power and influence when monitoring and controlling projects. In stakeholder management research, the attention is often directed at the salience or centrality of the stakeholder with regards to the project, and stakeholders' influence strategies in the project (Aaltonen & Kujala, 2010). Directly related to stakeholders' value-oriented influence, Vuorinen and Martinsuo (2019) mapped four stakeholder influence strategies: communicating, complaining and resolving disputes, setting rules and supervising the project, and using decision-making authority. Some research indicates that stakeholders may need to make tradeoffs concerning their value expectations and handle risks of value slippage when involved in project networks (Bos-de Vos et al., 2016, 2019). Also, risk management is considered an aspect of value creation in projects (Willumsen et al., 2019). Martinsuo (2020) has drawn attention to the incompleteness of the idea of project value and related tensions between stakeholders, and between goals and accumulated benefits, as key challenges in project value creation.

Monitoring and control may lead to actions and changes that can have very significant effects on the project outcomes. Fuentes et al. (2019) describe the inevitability of problems in projects and the consequent need to co-solve problems, jointly transfer the project outcomes to operations, and monitor and control the emerging value outcomes also after project completion to achieve the usefulness of the outcomes to stakeholders. Particularly during the project, monitoring and control are directly linked with value creation through sensemaking and shaping activities, as the identified deviances or problems may require renegotiation of project tasks and rearrangement of resources.

28.6 CONCEPTUAL FRAMEWORK

The above discussion portrays value creation in the project networks of complex projects in three modes: sensemaking and negotiation; shaping and co-creation; and monitoring and control. The conceptual framework, as summarized in Table 28.1, illustrates how the material and immaterial aspects of value creation are intertwined in cognitive, operational, and evaluative processes in the project network. The discussion highlighted that the processes include activities of single stakeholders as well as activities carried out jointly by multiple stakeholders in the project network. The connectedness of separate value streams is central in the value creation of complex projects, while also making value creation particularly complex and challenging to observe.

28.7 CONCLUSIONS

This chapter has expanded the concept of project value creation toward the project network level and introduced three modes of value creation in complex projects: sensemaking and negotiation, shaping and co-creation, and monitoring and control. The three modes purposely include both stakeholder-specific aspects (sensemaking, shaping, monitoring) and interactive aspects (negotiation, co-creation, control), as value creation in project networks occurs through the interplay of them both. Also, both the material and immaterial aspects of value

Table 28.1   *Three modes of value creation in the project networks of complex projects*

	Sensemaking and negotiation	Shaping and co-creation	Monitoring and control
Processes of value creation	Cognitive and social	Operational and behavioral	Evaluation and decision making
Nature of value creation	Dominantly immaterial	Dominantly material	Both material and immaterial
Key phase in the project lifecycle	Front end (extending to full lifecycle)	Project implementation (extending to full lifecycle)	Project control, closure and commissioning (extending to full lifecycle)
Purpose in a project network	Understanding stakeholders' priorities and adjusting them to achieve shared value goals	Designing a feasible project concept and using/modifying resources and materials to achieve the shared goal	Resolving problems and achieving maximized project value and continued value creation at the post-project operations phase
Challenges in a project network	Owner may dominate; all stakeholders' voices are not necessarily heard; peripheral stakeholders are often neglected	Contractor may dominate, but in line with owner's rules; stakeholders may have competing priorities or fail to voice their values	Owner may dominate; stakeholders' interests are not necessarily monitored or controlled as part of official project governance
Practices of value creation in a project network	Dreaming, thinking, visioning; speaking, listening, discussing	Investing and using resources (people, knowledge, time); using, consuming and molding material	Assessing benefit realization; communicating; detecting and managing risks, deviances; and errors Problem solving
Examples of previous studies	Kolltveit and Grønhaug (2004); Martinsuo et al. (2019b); Matinheikki et al. (2016); Williams and Samset (2010); Zerjav et al. (2021)	Artto et al. (2016); Fuentes et al. (2019); Laursen (2018); Lehtinen et al. (2019)	Aaltonen and Kujala (2010); Ahola et al. (2008); Fuentes et al. (2019); Kivilä et al. (2017); Volden (2019); Vuorinen and Martinsuo (2019)

creation have been emphasized, with the idea that also the material, tangible aspects of value creation could be considered more, besides the immaterial aspects. Particularly in complex projects, the material value creation becomes uncertain and requires attention. Future research is encouraged both concerning this overall framework and its three modes separately.

The conceptual framework as a whole offers a way to structure and categorize value-creating processes and practices in complex projects. It also enables adopting different viewpoints to value creation: that of certain stakeholders or the entire project network, that of immaterial or material value creation, or that of specific lifecycle phases or the entire project lifecycle. Selecting any of these viewpoints and combining them in creative ways in different complex projects and for specific project contexts could open up pathways for forthcoming research. Increasing interest in the connections between projects and their surrounding institutional field will create possibilities to explore value creation in complex projects in specific contexts and circumstances, including crises and other dramatic events.

Sensemaking and negotiation deal with the cognitive and social processes that are particularly active at the front end of the project. As the multidimensionality of value and the different value perceptions of stakeholders have been well covered in previous research, it will be relevant to investigate the events where their negotiation occurs and expected value from the project is specified. Also, it is important to understand how value conflicts and competition are resolved in project networks. Different types of project networks could be explored, for example, to reveal how dramatically single stakeholders can drive or restrain the accumulation of value, through their sensemaking and influence. Theoretically, the emerging sensemaking lens will open up relevant connections, for example, to strategy research.

Shaping and co-creation deal with the behavioral and operative processes, especially during project implementation. To complement the dominant knowledge-centric view of these processes, future research could map the material and resource-related value streams, to identify how the tangible aspects of value unfold in projects. There is a need to delve deeper into the micro-level mechanisms of value creation through resource and time investments into project tasks, to understand how project work adds material and immaterial value toward the project outcome, especially under conditions of uncertainty. In particular, as the value streams of multiple stakeholders interact, it is of interest to understand how their resource and material consumption is converted to added value and how the stakeholders transfer this value within their network. Theoretically, technology management and material aspects of actor-network theory could complement the knowledge and service-centric views in interesting ways.

Monitoring and control focus on value-oriented evaluation and decision making, which are particularly prevalent at the end of project. Even if this phase is crucial in bridging value creation and capture, its unique value-creating nature deserves further research attention. For example, there is a need to understand the mechanisms of value creation in the purposive deviation from goals and status quo as well as managing changes that preserve or add value in uncertain conditions. Also, the disputes and conflicts preceding decisions deserve further attention. Theoretically, the connection of project value and organizational control will be particularly interesting, in addition to behavioral decision making.

A core interest for any stakeholder in complex projects is value capture, i.e., how the created project value can be converted to the stakeholders' own use value, especially in financial terms (Bos-de Vos et al., 2016, 2019). The current research tends to emphasize the non-financial, strategic dimensions of project value, to emphasize that it is not only financial (in line with Martinsuo & Killen, 2014), and the tradeoffs that stakeholders need to make in their value priorities (Bos-de Vos et al., 2016). The logic concerning project value creation and stakeholder-specific value capture is particularly challenging in complex project networks and also deserves further research attention.

REFERENCES

Aaltonen, K. & Kujala, J. (2010). A project lifecycle perspective on stakeholder influence strategies in global projects. *Scandinavian Journal of Management*, 26(4), 381–397.

Ahola, T., Laitinen, E., Kujala, J. & Wikström, K. (2008). Purchasing strategies and value creation in industrial turnkey projects. *International Journal of Project Management*, 26(1), 87–94.

Artto, K., Ahola, T. & Vartiainen, V. (2016). From the front end of projects to the back end of operations: Managing projects for value creation throughout the system lifecycle. *International Journal of Project Management*, 34(2), 258–270.

Bos-de Vos, M., Wamelink, H. & Volker, L. (2016). Trade-offs in the value capture of architectural firms: The significance of professional value. *Construction Management and Economics*, 34(1), 21–34.

Bos-de Vos, M., Volker, L. & Wamelink, H. (2019). Enhancing value capture by managing risks of value slippage in and across projects. *International Journal of Project Management*, 37(5), 767–783.

Chenger, D. & Woiceshyn, J. (2021). Executives' decision processes at the front end of major projects: The role of context and experience in value creation. *Project Management Journal*, 52(2), 176–191.

Edkins, A., Geraldi, J., Morris, P. & Smith, A. (2013). Exploring the front-end of project management. *Engineering Project Organization Journal*, 3(2), 71–85.

Eskerod, P. & Ang, K. (2017). Stakeholder value constructs in megaprojects: A long-term assessment case study. *Project Management Journal*, 48(6), 60–75.

Flyvbjerg, B. (2017). Introduction: The iron law of megaproject management. In B. Flyvbjerg (Ed.), *The Oxford handbook of megaproject management* (pp. 1–18). Oxford University Press.

Fuentes, M., Smyth, H. & Davies, A. (2019). Co-creation of value outcomes: A client perspective on service provision in projects. *International Journal of Project Management*, 37(5), 696–715.

Gillier, T., Hooge, S. & Piat, G. (2015). Framing value management for creative projects: An expansive perspective. *International Journal of Project Management*, 33(4), 947–960.

Green, S. & Sergeeva, N. (2019). Value creation in projects: Towards a narrative perspective. *International Journal of Project Management*, 37(6), 636–651.

Kivilä, J., Martinsuo, M. & Vuorinen, L. (2017). Sustainable project management through project control in infrastructure projects. *International Journal of Project Management*, 35(6), 1167–1183.

Kolltveit, B. J. & Grønhaug, K. (2004). The importance of the early phase: The case of construction and building projects. *International Journal of Project Management*, 22(7), 545–551.

Laursen, M. (2018). Project networks as constellations for value creation. *Project Management Journal*, 49(2), 56–70.

Lehtinen, J., Peltokorpi, A. & Artto, K. (2019). Megaprojects as organizational platforms and technology platforms for value creation. *International Journal of Project Management*, 37(1), 43–58.

Liu, Y., van Marrewijk, A., Houwing, E.-J. & Hertogh, M. (2019). The co-creation of values-in-use at the front end of infrastructure development programs. *International Journal of Project Management*, 37(5), 684–695.

Martinsuo, M. (2019). Strategic value at the front end of a radical innovation program. *Project Management Journal*, 50(4), 431–446.

Martinsuo, M. (2020). The management of values in project business: Adjusting beliefs to transform project practices and outcomes. *Project Management Journal*, 51(4), 389–399.

Martinsuo, M. & Killen, C. P. (2014). Value management in project portfolios: Identifying and assessing strategic value. *Project Management Journal*, 45(5), 56–70.

Martinsuo, M., Klakegg, O. J. & van Marrewijk, A. (2019a). Editorial: Delivering value in projects and project-based business. *International Journal of Project Management*, 37(5), 631–630.

Martinsuo, M., Vuorinen, L. & Killen, C. (2019b). Lifecycle-oriented framing of value at the front end of infrastructure projects. *International Journal of Managing Projects in Business*, 12(3), 617–643.

Matinheikki, J., Artto, K., Peltokorpi, A. & Rajala, R. (2016). Managing inter-organizational networks for value creation in the front-end of projects. *International Journal of Project Management*, 34(7), 1226–1241.

Ninan, J., Clegg, S. & Mahalingam, A. (2019). Branding and governmentality for infrastructure megaprojects: The role of social media. *International Journal of Project Management*, 37(1), 59–72.

Ramirez, R. (1999). Value co-production: Intellectual origins and implications for practice and research. *Strategic Management Journal*, 20(1), 49–65.

Svejvig, P., Geraldi, J. & Grex, S. (2019). Accelerating time to impact: Deconstructing practices to achieve project value. *International Journal of Project Management*, 37(5), 784–801.

Volden, G. H. (2019). Assessing public projects' value for money: An empirical study of the usefulness of cost–benefit analyses in decision-making. *International Journal of Project Management*, 37(4), 549–564.

Vuorinen, L. & Martinsuo, M. (2019). Value-oriented stakeholder influence on infrastructure projects. *International Journal of Project Management*, 37(5), 750–766.

Williams, T. & Samset, K. (2010). Issues in front-end decision making on projects. *Project Management Journal*, 41(2), 38–49.

Willumsen, P., Oehmen, J., Stingl, V. & Geraldi, J. (2019). Value creation through project risk management. *International Journal of Project Management*, 37(5), 731–749.

Winch, G. M. (2014). Three domains of project organising. *International Journal of Project Management*, 32(5), 721–731.

Winter, M. & Szczepanek, T. (2008). Projects and programmes as value creation processes: A new perspective and some practical implications. *International Journal of Project Management*, 26(1), 95–103.

Zerjav, V. (2021). Why do business organizations participate in projects? Toward a typology of project value domains. *Project Management Journal*, 52(3), 287–297.

Zerjav, V., McArthur, J. & Edkins, A. (2021). The multiplicity of value in the front-end of projects: The case of London transportation infrastructure. *International Journal of Project Management*, 39(1), 507–519.

29. Nothing succeeds like success, but what is it anyway? Reconceptualizing project success

Lavagnon A. Ika and Jeffrey K. Pinto

29.1 INTRODUCTION

The concept of project success (what we seek to accomplish) lies at the heart of our understanding of the purpose behind projects – 'temporary endeavours undertaken to create a unique product, service, or result' (Project Management Institute, 2021). Seemingly, the very uniqueness and purpose of the project should dictate the way we assess its performance – the degree of success or failure actually reached during project execution or after project completion. Yet, simplicity lies a long way from the heart of our understanding of success. It is ironic that a discipline focused on the delivery of organizational value through the use of projects and project management techniques still appears mired in conceptual confusion around such basic principles as consistent, generally accepted definitions of 'success'. Indeed, practitioners seem to know success when they see it but apparently find the steps to achieving it difficult to replicate or allow for the establishment of clear linkages in their professional lives. Practitioners, however, recognize that 'success is, in fact, a dangerous guide to follow too closely' (Petroski, 2013, p. 23), as carbon-copy replication may not be a winning recipe, and success may derive from failure and vice versa. In particular, replicating the conditions that led to one successful project, whether they pertain to what happens 'in advance of the project' or 'in the wake of the project' (Hirschman, 1967, p. 146), might be impossible due notably to complexity and uncertainty (Ika & Donnelly, 2017).

Some 35 years of research on the topic demonstrates that project success and failure are not 'black and white' issues, and that the two concepts are still complex, ambiguous, and difficult to define and measure (De Wit, 1988; Pinto et al., 2021). Notably, there are shades of grey between success and failure. Success–failure and failure–success paradoxes are quite common; for example, an over-budget and poorly managed project can subsequently succeed only because creativity kicks in after completion. A project might be viewed a success yet drag other projects in the same program/portfolio into failure as complexity and uncertainty take hold (Ika et al., 2020).

Other complications arise when we consider that a successful project may well be a product of random chance (Barney, 1986; Ika, 2018). Success criteria or *ex-ante* decision-makers' calculations may fall short, shared feelings will prevail in the end, and deviations from plans and targets can lead to (biased) attributions of success or failure. Hence, setting success criteria *ex-ante* and assessing project performance *ex-post* may be far from objective (Kreiner, 2014; Ika et al., 2020), especially as stakeholders seldom hold the same point of view on project performance (Baker et al., 1974; Davis, 2018). Chronos (clock) and Kairos (event) time conceptions, both objective and subjective, chronological and non-chronological, matter a good deal in the appreciation of success, as the former is often associated with 'doing things right' (efficiency) and the latter with 'doing the right things right' (effectiveness) (Turner et al., 2020). Finally, a project that meets business expectations may have unintended negative consequences for broader society or the environment, making sustainability and the 'triple bottom line' of profit, people, and planet crucial (Maltzman & Shirley, 2015; Carvalho & Rabechini, 2017).

Due to these multiple and recurring challenges, practitioners and scholars may have only a vague notion of what success is and thus settle for conflicting or inaccurate attributions of project performance (Pinto & Slevin, 1988; Jugdev & Müller, 2005; Shenhar & Dvir, 2007; Ika, 2009; Pinto et al., 2021; Zwikael & Meredith, 2021). Indeed, these words written by Pinto and Slevin (1988, p. 67) still ring true after 35 years: 'There are few topics in the field of project management that are so frequently discussed and yet so rarely agreed upon as the notion of project success.'

Consequently, at a time when the question – what explains project underperformance – is fraught with contentious debates between researchers (Ika et al., 2020), the 'complex and often illusory construct' of success (Pinto & Slevin, 1988, p. 71) warrants a reconceptualization. The chapter seeks to update and reconceptualize the most significant literature on project success to account as much as possible for efficiency, effectiveness, and sustainability as well as complexity, uncertainty, and stakeholder views and attributions.

While it is customary to distinguish between critical success factors (conditions, events, and circumstances that contribute to project outcomes) and success criteria or dimensions (e.g., key performance indicators – principles/standards or groups of these used to measure or gauge project success) (Ika, 2009), this chapter emphasizes the latter. Put differently, the chapter focuses not on *what makes a given project successful* (e.g., getting a project's goal setting or top management support right) but instead *what constitutes success* in the project and how to know if it is successful (e.g., meeting business case or stakeholder expectations). In so doing, this chapter concentrates on individual project success (Griffin & Page, 1996), not the success or value of a project portfolio, program, or network, though the former will likely contribute to the latter (Martinsuo & Killen, 2014). Finally, a reasonable argument can be made that within the broader classes of projects (e.g., construction, pharmaceutical, aerospace and engineering, information technology and software, etc.) there exist some idiosyncratic or uniquely critical project elements that 'drive' success. Here, however, we opt to discuss projects in the more generic sense, in order to focus on what features and challenges they have in common, rather than their unique differences (Zwikael & Meredith, 2021).

The chapter first discusses the elusive, multidimensional, and complex notion of project success and highlights the importance of issues such as stakeholder views and attributions of success and sustainability. The chapter then builds on key existing evaluation models and offers a few insights for the development of a new and integrative model of success. We conclude with an agenda of research to further our understanding of the project success phenomenon.

29.2   THE ALL-IMPORTANT BUT ELUSIVE NOTION OF PROJECT SUCCESS

Project-based work is widespread as projects have become a kind of administrative commodity to fund, initiate, plan, deliver, and measure organizational work performance (value) in every sector of the world economy. As a result, the topics of project success and failure continue to garner interest from both practitioners and scholars in the project management domain of knowledge (Denicol et al., 2020; Zwikael & Meredith, 2021). This is testament to the sheer volume of work undertaken to better comprehend what project success entails and what it does not.

'The body of literature on project success also encompasses project failures' (Jugdev & Müller, 2005, p. 26). Notably, one can think about success as the stark opposite of failure. 'A success is just that – a success. It is something that works well for a variety of reasons, not the least of which may be luck. But a true success often works precisely because engineers thought first about failure. Indeed, 'one simple definition of success might be the obviation of failure', writes Petroski (2013, p. 24) about engineering design success. But success and failure are not themselves black and white notions, as the same project may present both elements of success and failure, and different stakeholders may have different views (Baker et al., 1974; Turner & Zolin, 2012; Davis, 2018). For example, the Airbus A-380 aircraft was a technical success yet a business failure. While Heathrow Terminal 5 appeared to be an overall success, it has been hailed a failure by customers and the public due to baggage-checking issues. As a result, there is often a suspicion that project success can be more directly framed as something that depends on who you ask and when.

Consequently, project success remains a complex, ambiguous, and non-consensual concept. Indeed, project success is often blurred with cognate concepts such as efficiency, effectiveness, and performance, which few authors attempt to define explicitly (Ika, 2009; Zidane & Olsson, 2017). Project success and performance include elements of both efficiency ('doing things right' or maximizing output for a given quantity of inputs or resources) and effectiveness ('doing the right things' or achieving the project's goals and objectives). Moreover, project *success* differs from project *performance*. Project success is the clear goal toward which all project management efforts are aimed; project performance measures the extent to which, at any point in time during project execution or after completion (that is, during operations), this goal is (being) reached or not, planned targets or key performance indicators are achieved or not, and stakeholder expectations are met or not. In sum, project performance is the degree of success or failure actually reached during project execution or after project completion (Ika, 2009).

29.3   THE MULTIDIMENSIONAL, CONTINGENT, AND DYNAMIC NATURE OF PROJECT SUCCESS

This conceptual ambiguity is not without consequences. Project success constitutes a multidimensional and multifaceted phenomenon that evolves with time according to the type of project, stakeholder, and broader context (Shenhar & Dvir, 2007; Ika & Donnelly, 2017; Davis, 2018; Turner et al., 2020). In accordance with contingency theory, different types of projects will have different measures of success. Short-term performance assessments may not work for those projects that need time for commercialization efforts to pan out (e.g., new product developments) or social impacts to turn up (e.g., social infrastructure, international development projects). Even the same type of project may have different measures of success; more than 75 separate measures of success for new product development projects exist and there is no consensus on which one works best (Griffin & Page, 1996). National culture may also impact how we assess success, especially long-term success (Turner et al., 2020).

Traditionally, project success has been equated to the 'iron triangle' of time, cost, and quality (Barnes, 1969). However, while conceptually and intuitively pleasing, the iron triangle has been the subject of serious rethinking for some time now. In 1988, Pinto and Slevin proposed a modification to Barnes' triple constraint by adding stakeholder satisfaction to the traditional iron triangle, arguing that a success measure absent external client validation was seriously compromised. Atkinson (1999) further remonstrated against the iron triangle, in a much cited paper, suggesting that time and cost represented two 'best guesses' with quality akin to a 'phenomenon'. In spite of pointed criticism, many have continued to refer to the time, cost, and quality dimensions as the 'golden triangle', the 'Holy Trinity', or the 'triangle of virtue' (Ika, 2009). Much current cost overrun research and Flyvbjerg's iron law – projects are 'over budget, over and over again' – essentially belong to this relatively narrow project success research tradition (Flyvbjerg, 2017; Love et al., 2019).

This trilogy, however, is just one component of project success. Based on contingency theory, Shenhar and Dvir (2007) proposed five overlapping success dimensions but with different time frames over the course of the project and product lifecycles: efficiency (during execution or at completion); impact on team (months after completion); impact on customer (months after completion); business and direct success (often one or two years after completion); and preparation for the future (likely three or five years after completion). Sustainability considerations may even take decades or centuries (Maltzman & Shirley, 2015). As Zwikael and Meredith (2021, p. 1746) suggest, '[r]eflection on project success can also change as time progresses, conditions change, and the project is viewed in longer retrospect'. Hence, there are shades of grey between success and failure along with success–failure and failure–success paradoxes in project management theory and practice (Ika et al., 2020).

Indeed, a 'percussion effect' seems to take place as projects that are hailed as a success in the short term can later become long-term, business, organizational, or strategic disasters, and others that are considered short-term failures may well turn into a resounding success over time (Ika, 2009; Pinto et al., 2021). For example, projects such as the Hoosac Tunnel, Rideau Canal, Ford Taurus 1, and Sydney Opera House ended up becoming a great success, though they were delivered late and over budget at their completion. In contrast, others such as the Ford Taurus 2, LA Red Line Metro, Sony Betamax, and New Coke were delivered within time and cost, yet turned over time (relatively quickly, in fact) into disaster (Maltzman & Shirley, 2015; Ika, 2018).

In line with such a paradox, De Wit (1988) distinguishes between project management success – the short-term delivery of the project within time, cost, and quality targets – and *project* success – the long-term achievement of project goals and objectives. Likewise, other scholars have made the distinction between project management success – that is, achieving the project plan – and 'deliverable' success (Ika, 2018) or 'project investment success' – that is, realizing the business case objectives at some point after completion (Zwikael & Meredith, 2021). Taking a cue from benefits realization theory, we will call project investment success in this chapter 'business case success'.

This customary distinction between project management success and business case success mirrors the common division between internal, objective (time, cost, and quality), and external, subjective (project impacts on different stakeholders) measures of success (Pinto & Slevin, 1988). In reality, project management success and business case success constitute two sides of the same coin, the first being 'tactical' and the second 'strategic' (Slevin & Pinto,

1987). However, though they are correlated, the former may not necessarily lead to the latter, perhaps due to such things as uncertainty, as complexity theory teaches us (Ika, 2018).

Such a contrast between short-term and long-term success is not trivial, as time theory suggests (Turner et al., 2020). For example, this separation is at the heart of the tensions surrounding the so-called 'planning fallacy debate' over the extent to which projects tend to overpromise (e.g., cost overrun) and underdeliver (e.g., benefit shortfall) (Ika et al., 2020). Champions of the planning fallacy assume that project performance is 'causally insulated' from the project management process (Kreiner 2020), and thus we already know what success is (e.g., meeting the success criteria established up-front in the project plan) and how to measure it (e.g., budget target) (Flyvbjerg, 2017). In contrast, critics of the planning fallacy take a broader notion of projects, rationality, and success, assume that the project management process is consequential, argue agency plays a key role in 'successfulness', and thus, we cannot presume we know in advance what success is going to be and how to measure it, especially in the face of changing circumstances (Ika et al., 2020).

We suggest that despite a lack of agreement on the nature of project performance dimensions, over the years, project success measurement has moved from a rather unidimensional, simplistic, and reductionist scale such as the iron triangle to more multidimensional, holistic, dynamic, and complex accounts (Pinto et al., 2021). For example, the most recent models of success incorporate such considerations as stakeholder views (e.g., Zwikael & Meredith, 2021) and sustainability aspects (e.g., Maltzman & Shirley, 2015).

29.4 THE SIGNIFICANCE OF STAKEHOLDER VIEWS AND ATTRIBUTIONS OF SUCCESS AND SUSTAINABILITY CONSIDERATIONS

Based on contingency and stakeholder theories, we know that different stakeholders may have different appreciations of the project outcomes for different projects (Davis, 2018). Noting that the project owner (a senior manager in charge of the project) may have a different perspective than the project funder or manager, Zwikael and Meredith (2021) propose yet another dimension of success: 'project ownership success' (delivering the business case some time after the benefits are secured). Thus, we can assess the performance of the project manager in achieving short-term project goals, and the performance of the project owner and the project funder in achieving the project's long-term benefits. Echoing this view, Davis (2018) has shown that there is a disparity between the views of success held by different stakeholder groups. They may include senior management, the project core team, and the project recipient.

Such a shared view of success between (internal and external) stakeholders is by nature a collective, intersubjective, and difficult-to-measure feeling about what the project has achieved and not necessarily the easy-to-measure and presumably objective, planned, and agreed success targets set by decision-makers (Kreiner, 2014). In this instance, these rhetorical and symbolic stakeholder evaluations of success may be seen as narratives where meaning and action are intertwined (Fincham, 2002). As Turner and Zolin (2012, p. 87) write: 'The perception of success by a project's stakeholders often has little to do with whether the project was completed on time, at cost, and with the desired quality.' Regrettably, however, a pervasive 'fundamental attribution error' tends to prevail where deviations from plans and targets lead to blaming such (internal) stakeholders as project team members, thus underestimating the role of complexity and uncertainty in projects and creating favorable conditions for the business case to fail (Kreiner, 2014; Ika et al., 2020).

'Even if such compliance is achieved, the costs of such achievement may be the costs of anomia, including the loss of meaning and a sense of community' (Kreiner, 2014, p. 28). Indeed, long ago, it was shown that projects may have unintended consequences that may be dire for their beneficiaries, the environment, the community, or the society as a whole (Hirschman, 1967). Project funders and managers may reach efficiency and yet sacrifice effectiveness or even worse sustainability (Carvalho & Rabechini, 2017).

29.5   FROM OLD MODELS TO A NEW MODEL OF SUCCESS?

The lessons from the longitudinal and historic reviews of project success (Jugdev & Müller, 2005; Ika, 2009) are instructive. There has been a gradual broadening in our understanding of project success since the 1960s. Table 29.1 lists some of the key existing models of success in the project management literature.

In the first period (1960s–1980s), the 'iron triangle' was the dominant success dimension and there was a lack of empirical studies as most reports centered on practitioners' accounts of their experience (Barnes, 1969). The second period (1980s–2000s) focused on empirical studies. For example, Pinto and Slevin's (1988) model of success includes time, cost, performance, perceived quality, and client satisfaction. The emphasis at the time moved from *project management* success to *business case* success, albeit with some consideration of internal stakeholders (see DeLone & McLean, 2003 and Shenhar & Dvir, 2007 for examples of such models).

The ongoing third period focuses not only on business case success but also on *multiple and diverse stakeholder, environmental, and societal impacts*, including competitive advantage for the organization (Zwikael & Meredith, 2021), added value for both internal and external stakeholders, and their individual or collective symbolic and rhetoric evaluations and attributions of success (e.g., Fincham, 2002; Ika, 2009; Kreiner, 2014; Davis, 2018). The impacts on the environment, the community, or the society as a whole become more important and there is more emphasis on sustainability or 'green success' and 'triple bottom line success' (e.g., Carvalho & Rabechini, 2017). Three models of success are worthy of attention in this period.

Turner and Zolin (2012), in their model of forecasting performance indicators for managers, propose nine scales for different stakeholder groups whose perceptions of project outcomes may change over months and years: stakeholder satisfaction, project executive satisfaction, product satisfaction, product efficiency, satisfaction with specifications, project manager satisfaction, contractor satisfaction, supplier profitability, and public stakeholder satisfaction. Ika (2018), in his success model for international development projects based on deliberate strategy theory, results-based management view, and the well-established Organisation for Economic Development and Co-operation evaluation criteria of efficiency, effectiveness, relevance, impact, and sustainability, draws a two-by-two matrix that, over time, relates project management success (time, budget, specific objectives) to deliverable success (relevance for country, relevance for beneficiaries, institutional impact, and sustainability). Zwikael and Meredith (2021) capture the performance of the project manager, the funder, and the owner separately. Inspired by sustainability theory, Maltzman and Shirley (2015) include 'green success' in the long-term effectiveness of projects alongside an efficiency-effectiveness map or a two-by-two matrix with two axes (project management success and project success).

The complexity associated with sampling multiple stakeholders with, assumedly, multiple perspectives and 'decision triggers' when evaluating project success (Davis, 2018) also factors into newer perspectives for evaluating a successful project; namely, the Anna Karenina Principle (AKP), first proposed by Diamond (1997), more recently applied to the challenges of maintaining positive public opinion in the face of developmental challenges faced by nearly all types of megaprojects (Kundu et al., 2021). The AKP idea derives from the famous opening line of *Anna Karenina* by Tolstoy: 'all happy families are alike; each unhappy family is unhappy in its own way'. Researchers have applied this idea to explain success (but more commonly, failure) in a variety of fields, most recently megaprojects. Thus, if it is true that a deficiency in any one of a number of factors dooms an endeavor to failure, the concomitant argument suggests that for a project to succeed, it requires that all of a set of performance metrics be achieved. While this idea represents an alternative new perspective for project researchers, its implications for our deeper understanding of success are intriguing, to say the least. That is, reflecting not simply on 'success' but on the factors that can drive 'failure' offers an obverse perspective that opens new perspectives. 'We tend to seek easy, single-factor explanations for success, but for most important things, success requires avoiding many possible causes of failure' (Diamond, 1994, p. 4).

Table 29.1 shows that the existing models focus on a specific type of project but they run from the generic to those catering to different types of projects (Zwikael & Meredith, 2021). Further, they seldom factor in the key influence of aspects such as stakeholder views (Davis, 2018), time conceptions (Turner et al., 2020), and sustainability considerations (Maltzman & Shirley, 2015). Although the latter authors integrate green success into their evaluation model, it remains unclear how green success relates specifically to each of the efficiency and effectiveness dimensions. Hence the need for a new and integrative success model.

29.6 CONCLUSIONS AND OUTLOOK

Project success remains a crucial yet complex, multidimensional, contingent, and dynamic concept for project management theory and practice. Our evolving understanding of success certainly matters for how project organizations operate, how they reward or sanction their employees, and how they strategically invest in projects (Pinto et al., 2021). This chapter, which focuses on success criteria and dimensions, takes stock of decades of research on project success, and updates and reconceptualizes the literature on project success. The chapter highlights the contrast between short-term *project management* success and long-term *business case* success and the tensions between 'objective' evaluation of project outcomes and 'subjective' stakeholder perceptions and attributions of success, not to mention the issue of 'green' or 'triple bottom success' (Maltzman & Shirley, 2015). Our goal is to chart the movement away from the reductionist iron triangle through an attempt to 'complexify' (Tywoniak et al., 2021) project success by taking into consideration efficiency, effectiveness, sustainability,

Table 29.1   Seven models of success

Barnes (1969)	Pinto and Slevin (1987)	DeLone and McLean (2003)	Shenhar and Dvir (2007)	Maltzman and Shirley (2015)	Ika (2018)	Zwikael and Meredith (2021)
Generic	Generic	Information systems	New product development	Generic	International development projects	Generic
Time, cost, and quality (iron triangle)	Time, cost, and performance Perceived quality Client satisfaction	Information quality System quality Service quality Intention to use User satisfaction Net benefits	Efficiency Impact on customer Impact on team Business and direct success Preparation for future	Project management success Project success Green success	Project management success (efficiency: time and cost; effectiveness: objectives) Deliverable success (relevance for country, relevance for beneficiaries, institutional impact; sustainability)	Project management success (time, budget, scope, no undesirable impacts by project manager) Project ownership success (target benefits; business case realized) Project investment success (satisfactory results; investment again by funder; overall success)

complexity, time, uncertainty, and stakeholder views and attributions. The chapter indicates the need for empirical research to tackle the following questions:

1. Based on emerging strategy and/or time theories, how does the issue of time shed light on success–failure and failure–success projects and other shades of grey between project success and failure?
2. How can paradox theory help us understand better success–failure and failure–success projects and other shades of grey between project success and failure?
3. How can contingency, complexity, and cultural theories help complexify our research on project success in different types of projects and different contexts?
4. Taking a cue from attribution theory, what explains the gap between planned success criteria and targets and stakeholder attributions of success?
5. What can we learn from the unintended impacts of projects on organizations, stakeholders, community, environment, and society as a whole?
6. Does the Anna Karenina principle apply to the study of success and failure in megaprojects; i.e., does it take only one metric shortcoming to label the entire venture as flawed? Are there certain classes of projects for which one element of a multi-attributional model of success can subvert the overall project?

REFERENCES

Atkinson, R. (1999). Project management: Cost, time and quality, two best guesses and a phenomenon, it's time to accept other success criteria. *International Journal of Project Management*, 17(6), 337–342.

Baker, B. N., Murphy, D. C. & Fisher, D. (1974). Factors affecting project success. In D. I. Cleland & W. R. King (Eds), *Project management handbook* (pp. 902–919). Van Nostrand Reinhold.

Barnes, M. (1969). Email dated 14/12/2005 and interview on January 2006. In P. Weaver (2007, April). *The origins of modern project management*. Conference presentation, Fourth Annual Project Management Institute College of Scheduling Conference, Vancouver.

Barney, J. B. (1986). Strategic factor markets: Expectations, luck, and business strategy. *Management Science*, 32(10), 1231–1241.

Carvalho, M. M. & Rabechini, R. (2017). Can project sustainability management impact project success? An empirical study applying a contingent approach. *International Journal of Project Management*, 35(6), 1120–1132.

Davis, K. (2018). An empirical investigation into different stakeholder groups perception of project success. *International Journal of Project Management*, 35(4), 604–617.

De Wit, A. (1988). Measurement of project success. *Project Management Journal*, 6(3), 164–170.

DeLone, W. H. & McLean, E. R. (2003). The DeLone and McLean model of information systems success: A ten year update. *Journal of Management Information Systems*, 19(4), 60–95.

Denicol, J., Davies, A. & Krystallis, I. (2020). What are the causes and cures of poor megaproject performance? A systematic literature review and research agenda. *Project Management Journal*, 51(3), 328–345.

Diamond, J. (1994). Zebras and the Anna Karenina principle. *Natural History*, 103(9), 4–11.

Diamond, J. (1997). *Guns, germs and steel: The fate of human societies*. W. W. Norton & Co.

Fincham, R. (2002). Narratives of success and failure in systems development. *British Journal of Management*, 13(1), 1–14.

Flyvbjerg, B. (2017). Introduction: The iron law of megaproject management. In B. Flyvbjerg (Ed.), *The Oxford handbook of megaproject management* (pp. 1–18). Oxford University Press.

Griffin, A. & Page, A. L. (1996). PDMA success measurement project: Recommended measures for product development success and failure. *Journal of Product Innovation Management*, 13(1), 478–496.

Hirschman, A. O. (1967). *Development projects observed*. The Brookings Institution.

Ika, L. (2009). Project success as a topic in project management journals. *Project Management Journal*, 40(4), 6–19.

Ika, L. A. (2018). Beneficial or detrimental ignorance: The straw man fallacy of Flyvbjerg's test of Hirschman's Hiding Hand. *World Development*, 103(1), 369–382.

Ika, L. A. & Donnelly, J. (2017). Success conditions for international development capacity building projects. *International Journal of Project Management*, 35(1), 44–63.

Ika, L. A., Love, P. E. D. & Pinto, J. K. (2020). Moving beyond the planning fallacy: The emergence of a new principle of project behavior. *IEEE Transactions on Engineering Management*. DOI: 10.1109/TEM.2020.3040526.

Jugdev, K. & Müller, R. (2005). A retrospective look at our evolving understanding of project success. *Project Management Journal*, 36(4), 19–31.

Kreiner, K. (2014). Restoring project success as phenomenon. In R. A. Lundin & M. Hällgreen (Eds), *Advancing research on projects and temporary organizations* (pp. 21–40). Copenhagen Business School Press and Liber.

Kreiner, K. (2020). Conflicting notions of a project: The battle between Albert O. Hirschman and Bent Flyvbjerg. *Project Management Journal*, 51(4), 400–410.

Kundu, O., James, A. D. & Rigby, J. (2021). Public opinion on megaprojects over time: Findings from four megaprojects in the UK. *Public Management Review*. DOI: 10.1080/14719037.2021.2003107.

Love, P. E. D., Sing, M. C. P., Ika, L. A. & Newton, S. (2019). The cost performance of transportation projects: The fallacy of the planning fallacy account. *Transportation Research Part A: Policy and Practice*, 122(C), 1–20.

Maltzman, R. & Shirley, D. (2015). *Driving project, program, and portfolio success: The sustainability wheel*. CRC Press.

Martinsuo, M. & Killen, C. P. (2014). Value management in project portfolios: Identifying and assessing strategic value. *Project Management Journal*, 45(5), 56–70.

Petroski, H. (2013). Success through failure. *Ask Magazine*, 23–25.

Pinto, J. K. & Slevin, D. P. (1987). Critical factors in successful project implementation. *IEEE Transactions on Engineering Management*, 34(1), 22–27.

Pinto, J. K. & Slevin, D. P. (1988). Project success: Definitions and measurement techniques. *Project Management Journal*, 19(1), 67–72.

Pinto, J. K., Davis, K., Ika, L.A., Jugdev, K. & Zwikael, O. (2021). Call for papers for special issue on project success. *International Journal of Project Management*, 39(2), 213–215.

Project Management Institute (2021). *A guide to the project management body of knowledge* (7th ed.). PMI.

Shenhar, A. J. & Dvir, D. (2007). *Reinventing project management: The diamond Approach to successful growth and innovations*. Harvard Business School Press.

Slevin, D. P. & Pinto, J. K. (1987). Balancing strategy and tactics in project implementation. *Sloan Management Review*, 29(1), 33–41.

Turner, R. & Zolin, R. (2012). Forecasting success on large projects: Developing reliable scales to predict multiple perspectives by multiple stakeholders over multiple time frames. *Project Management Journal*, 43(5), 87–99.

Turner, R., Crawford, L. & Pollack, J. (2020, December). *Perceptions of time on projects*. Conference presentation, European Academy of Management, Dublin.

Tywoniak, S., Ika, L. A. & Bredillet, C. (2021). A pragmatist approach to complexity theorizing in project studies: Orders and levels. *Project Management Journal*, 52(3), 298–313.

Zidane, Y. J.-T. & Olsson, N. O. (2017). Defining project efficiency, effectiveness and efficacy. *International Journal of Managing Projects in Business*, 10(3), 621–641.

Zwikael, O. & Meredith, J. (2021). Evaluating the success of a project and the performance of its leaders. *IEEE Transactions on Engineering Management*, 47(3), 127–134.

30. Owner project capabilities for complex project organising

Roine Leiringer

30.1 INTRODUCTION

Projects have become increasingly important forms of organisational economic activity across different sectors and are widely accepted as strategic vehicles to deliver strategic goals of an organisation. Following the work of Winch (2014), complex project organising (CPO) can usefully be divided up into three principal organisational domains. Each domain identifies a distinctive type of project organisation with different organisational structures and business models (Winch & Leiringer, 2016): (1) the supplier domain, which consists of project-based firms (cf. Chapter 17) that provide human and material resources to the project; (2) the domain of the project organisation, consisting of multiple parties, that delivers the project output; and (3) the owner domain of the investor organisation that charters the project and usually is charged with operating the completed asset to achieve project outcomes. Fundamental for the argument that will be progressed in this chapter is that whilst both owners and suppliers are relatively permanent organisations, which come together to resource a temporary project organisation, the suppliers are project-based and derive most of their business from projects. The owners' core operations are, on the other hand, commonly outside the project domain, and projects are undertaken because of ongoing business concerns, such as the need to grow, perceived inadequacies in existing infrastructure, or policy initiatives within parent organisations. In the public sector, for example, the key concern for the majority of the owner organisations is the operation and maintenance of the completed infrastructure assets, not their production.

Our point of departure is the observation that the literature on CPO is predominantly supplier-focused. Put somewhat differently, the research and associated literature that focuses on improving project delivery performance primarily targets the role of project-based suppliers and the processes that are used for project delivery (Flowers, 2007; Winch & Leiringer, 2016). While this is highly understandable given the historic development of project management as a research discipline, a case can be made that the causes of poor delivery performance, in many cases, lie in areas that are within the remit of the project owner. For example, after conducting research into 300+ major engineering projects over 30 years, Merrow (2011) drew the conclusion that factors contributing to unfavourable project outcomes are largely endogenous and the root cause can be found in the process of 'project shaping' by project owners. His findings in many ways echoed those of Miller and Lessard (2001), who a decade earlier had drawn similar conclusions in their study of 60 large engineering projects concluding that the 'front end' of the project, and the sponsor's ability to shape strategy and deal with suppliers, were by far the most important in terms of determining success and failure(s).

These broad arguments have found plenty of support from a wide variety of sources in the project-organising domain. Rowlinson (2014), for example, shows how most of the factors driving cost escalation in the Hong Kong construction sector at the time resided firmly within the remit of project owners. Similarly, studies drawing on content analysis of National Audit Office reports in the United Kingdom have shown that project delivery problems in large public-sector projects are overwhelmingly caused by internal client processes, rather than contractors' incompetence or external risk events (Winch & Cha, 2020). More generally, in their review of the megaproject literature, Denicol et al. (2020) suggest that two main reasons for poor project performance are early stage decision-making and an insufficient understanding of how firms organise themselves among partners and suppliers and how in-house and external capabilities are combined in the delivery of projects.

Whilst the above examples point to the importance of project owners, our understanding of the role, function and responsibilities of these organisations in programmes and projects remains patchy (cf. Winch & Cha, 2020). Where the literature devotes attention to project owners, they are commonly treated in CPO research as clients that are purchasing a service, rather than as strategic actors with important roles to perform on projects. There are no clear answers to questions such as 'what' makes up a strong and/or capable owner organisation, 'which' role(s) should project owners play, 'how' they play such roles, and 'which' kinds of organisational structures are suitable for owner organisations. In short, we do not know enough about the core skills, competencies, routines and processes that project owners need in order to increase the likelihood of 'successful' project delivery. In this chapter, I address these questions by drawing on the growing literature on project capabilities and the sub-set of 'owner project capabilities'.

30.2   THE PROJECT OWNER

Traditionally, the organisational entity that initiates and invests in the project has in project management research been referred to as the 'client'. This remains the most widespread term for the organisation (or individual) for whom the supplier(s) provides project services. It is, however, a relatively narrow concept in a project-organising sense, as it limits the role to a commercial/contractual one (Winch et al., 2022). Another term that is sometimes used is project 'sponsor', which also limits the role as this per definition is a 'person or group that provides financial resources, in cash or in kind, for the project' (PMI, 2008), i.e., the budget holder who controls the money flow within projects. Project owners, as conceptualised in this chapter, are not merely clients, sponsors, champions or contract givers, they also act as investors, innovators, operators and the voice of customers. Fundamentally, they retain overall accountability for projects. Hence, the project owner, whether public or private, is the entity that initiates a project, finances it, contracts with other parties for supply of goods and services, oversees delivery and operates it and/or ultimately benefits from the final outputs.

It goes without saying that the nature and amount of projects an owner organisation undertakes varies; from routinely undertaking multiple similar projects, through having some routine projects coupled with the odd one-off project, to only very rarely having to invest in new assets. Regardless of which, investment projects are, for the vast majority of owner organisations, inherently lumpy compared to managing operations. They therefore pose a number of challenges in terms of managing project portfolios, project programmes and individual projects. These challenges are further compounded by the fact that most owner organisations, out of commercial necessity, do not possess all the resources needed to fully take on their role in CPO. Thus, they are forced to rely on the supply side to undertake tasks for which they have no permanent in-house capacity, i.e., they rely on external advisors such as consultants and pay for the services of suppliers to undertake the actual project delivery.

For complex business projects, project owner organisations can usefully be categorised into two types: the relatively permanent owner organisation that initiates projects if and when there is a need, ranging from one-off large complex projects to numerous and frequent small-scale routine projects, and the temporary owner organisation (here conceptualised as the owner's delivery vehicle) established specifically to execute the project as a one-off venture. The former category of project owner is by far the most common, but also the most diverse and difficult to generalise. There are, for example, obvious differences between a manufacturer that wishes to build a brand new factory and a large real estate developer. The manufacturer is most likely an infrequent construction project owner and hence does not need to have expertise in the shaping and management of construction projects, nor does it serve any greater purpose for them to maintain long-term relationships with suppliers of construction work (perhaps with the exception of term contractors for maintenance work). The real estate developer would, on the other hand, given their business proposition, likely be a repetitive (experienced) project owner and expected to have accumulated some levels of construction experience and capacity in-house for delivering, more or less, routine projects. Such an owner organisation would have a relatively stable knowledge base and established processes to execute projects such as project definition, how to procure services and how to manage the supply chain. They are also more likely to have opportunities and incentives to establish formal mechanisms, procedures and routines to deliver what they are expected to and be able to adapt for subsequent projects (cf. Davies & Brady, 2016).

A temporary (one-off) project owner refers to an organisation that is established for the delivery of a particular project, commonly a single, large complex project. This type of owner organisation has over time received increasing research attention, mostly due to increased research focus on large-scale (mega)projects, and how and why they are fraught with cost and time overruns (e.g., Morris & Hough, 1987; Miller & Lessard, 2001; Denicol et al., 2020). There are, of course, many ways of organising large investment projects, encompassing arrangements from conventional arm's length works contracts to public-private partnerships that combine separate arrangements into one contract. Commonly, though, these projects are organised in the form of a programme of projects and/or sub-projects (Turner & Müller, 2003; Davies & Brady, 2016), and at the core of these arrangements is the establishment of the standalone, temporary owner organisation. This organisation is responsible for managing the overall programme and the interfaces between projects, as well as coordinating and integrating the efforts of the parties involved in the project activities (Davies & Mackenzie, 2014). Typically, the arrangement will involve several organisational entities and thus include inter-organisational collaborations in order to put together the necessary organisational capabilities. Ensuring alignment within the organisation is by no means an easy task, as the involved actors might be pursuing different strategic objectives and likely are operating on the basis of different rationales and value propositions (cf. Liu et al., 2019).

30.3   OWNER PROJECT CAPABILITIES

Organisational capabilities can be understood as the particular combination of skills, competencies, resources, routines and behaviours of an organisation that enables it to perform an activity in a reliable manner to achieve a (satisfactory) determined outcome (cf. Dosi et al., 2000). They are usually divided into two types: 'operational capabilities' which capture the day-to-day, month-by-month ability of the organisation to deliver on its mission; and 'dynamic capabilities' which capture the ability of the organisation to change and develop in order to meet new challenges (Helfat & Winter, 2011). There is a growing body of literature that seeks to apply the organisational capability concept to the project-based setting, coupled with an emerging literature on project capabilities (see Davies & Brady, 2016). The concept was originally developed in reference to the core knowledge, experience and skills located within an organisation to establish, coordinate and deliver projects, from the perspective of project-based firms (Davies & Brady, 2000). Subsequent research has distinguished between project capabilities at the operational level and dynamic capabilities at the strategic level of the organisation. It is suggested that the relationship between dynamic and project capabilities is reciprocal, recursive and mutually reinforcing (Davies & Brady, 2016). This work has started to gain traction (see Leiringer & Zhang, 2021), but in line with its origins, with a few notable exceptions (e.g., Davies et al., 2016; Winch & Leiringer, 2016; Zerjav et al., 2018), subsequent research has tended to focus on the supply side and operational-level capabilities. Of importance here is that, as Winter (2003) points out, what constitutes an operational capability for a supplying firm may well be a dynamic capability for a purchasing firm. The purchaser firm engages in projects due to a need to acquire assets, which allows it to conduct and develop its business (Flowers, 2007). These organisations' operational capabilities are not normally geared up for projects, and dynamic capabilities are essential to meet the requirements needed to engage in them. In other words, investment projects are fundamentally about change in the owner organisation – either extending in scope their operational capabilities or creating new ones to meet new challenges. It follows that project capabilities for a supplier firm usually are operational, but for an owner they are almost always dynamic.

Drawing on the project capabilities perspective described above, Winch and Leiringer (2016) sought to propose an owner project capability framework that captures the broad group of activities and roles that an owner organisation needs to perform in the delivery of infrastructure projects. In so doing, we sought to move the discussion of the owner role from the transaction-oriented client to focus instead on the sort of routines, skills, resources and organisational structures needed by project owner organisations. We suggested that the project owner needs to be able to perform a distinct set of roles in CPO both within their own organisation and at the interfaces with other organisations. These roles encompass the very origins of the project and its 'shaping', as well as its operation and 'benefits realisation'. The proposed conceptual framework can be summarised as follows (cf. Winch & Leiringer, 2016): *Strategic capabilities* is the set of activities that the owner organisation uses to successfully initiate its investment projects. These mainly relate to activities that define, conceptualise and outline the benefits of the project for formal approval. Broad activities include: project selection, project definition, raising capital, stakeholder management and project portfolio management. *Commercial capabilities* refers to activities the owner organisation undertakes to manage the interface between the owner organisation and the project-based firm. They include activities such as the clear definition and packaging of works to be undertaken by the supplier, selecting and motivating potential suppliers to undertake a task at an optimal cost and making use of appropriate contract mechanisms to engage suppliers. Here project owners have the challenge of identifying which supplier is best suited for an activity, what mechanisms may incentivise or motivate that supplier and how to manage the relationship. *Governance capabilities* is the capability set needed to manage the interface between the owner organisation and the temporary project organisation set up to deliver the project. Activities here focus on assuring relevant stakeholders of project progress, managing or coordinating the project during its execution and ensuring that completed projects are integrated into existing operations of the owner.

As acknowledged in the original work and evidenced in several publications drawing on the framework (e.g., Turner & Müller, 2017; Adam et al., 2020; Zerjav, 2021), there is no one ideal capability set applicable for all situations. History has shown that it is neither feasible nor desirable to establish owner organisations that are literally one-stop shops. Thus, it is not a matter of adding extra capabilities to the organisation just for the sake of it. It is how the capability sets can be developed, maintained and configured in different contexts that is important. In the paragraphs below I will discuss some key challenges and how the owner capability concept has been, and further could be, applied in meeting them.

30.4   RESEARCH CHALLENGES

30.4.1   Strategic Capabilities

As noted in the introduction to this chapter, the front end of the project in general and the owner's 'project shaping' in particular has been proven to be one of the root causes to why so many complex projects (seemingly) fail to deliver on expectations. There is, however, remarkably little research on how this shaping process actually works (cf. Winch & Cha, 2020) and the earliest phase of the project where it is formulated, shaped and initially developed has often fallen outside the remit of 'project management' research (an argument long championed by Peter Morris). The work of Flyvbjerg and colleagues on project escalation and the work that has followed on from this has done much to explain the 'why' and 'how' of cost and time overruns on large projects. Issues such as strategic misrepresentation and optimism bias in the investment appraisal and definition of the project mission have as such been highlighted. Questions remain, however, as to how the strategic capabilities necessary to select the most beneficial project, defining the project mission, aligning the project strategy with that of the organisation, i.e., the project value proposition, can be developed, and subsequently where they should reside. The latter is important not least for public-sector clients where many key decisions are taken outwith their direct organisational remit (Winch & Leiringer, 2016).

It follows that there are numerous areas within this capability set that are worthy of further research. To give but one example, a strong case can be made for broadening our understanding of investment appraisals and cost-benefit analysis. These activities are easily manipulated (strategic misrepresentation) and are also prone to be performative, i.e., the available tools do not merely objectively evaluate the proposed investment but they end up shaping it (Winch et al., 2022). However, bringing the issue to a more general level, a key area of concern is how the 'shaping' process can be elevated from the individual level to an organisational level and in turn how the developed capabilities can be reused on future projects. As noted by Morris (2022), 'the bigger project shapers [referring to senior project managers] will rarely need help with applying past learning to shape future work; however, scaling this up from the level of the individual is not simple'. This is clearly an organisational learning issue and it is here where research on developing organisational routines (e.g., Davies et al., 2018) has promise.

30.4.2   Commercial Capabilities

Project owners need commercial capabilities to manage the interfaces with the suppliers delivering the project. In general terms, these capabilities can be considered as dynamic in nature as they allow the project owner to extend its existing resource base through the acquisition and application of external capabilities from suppliers. Some of the activities and underlying capability sets are well understood, whilst others have received much less research attention. One such area, worthy of further research attention, is that of relational capabilities (cf. Caldwell & Howard 2010). These capabilities enable owners to interact effectively with their supply chain and to select and implement the appropriate mix of formal (contractual) and trust-based relations on the project. Relational capabilities are essentially outward facing, concerned with the relationship with suppliers of the services that allow the project to be developed and delivered. They expand beyond the buyer–supplier relationship to also take into consideration relationships with actors as diverse as regulators, present and future users, local and national authorities and objectors, i.e., stakeholder capabilities. The question then becomes how an owner organisation can develop relational capabilities (cf. Hartmann et al., 2010; Davies et al., 2018), in particular, how these capabilities can be embedded in the collective, learned and patterned routines for organisations to identify, establish, coordinate and maintain trust-based relationships within the project coalition.

30.5   GOVERNANCE CAPABILITIES

The importance of the above two sections notwithstanding, defining the project and procuring suppliers to undertake its delivery are not by themselves guarantees for project success. This is where project governance capabilities come in. Here, too, some areas are well researched, whilst others have only rarely been a research object in their own right. Areas worthy of further research interest include project assurance capabilities and issues such as how the project owners can forecast in advance issues that are likely to occur, monitor the progress of the project, report to relevant stakeholders the project progress and take corrective actions where necessary so as to ensure the project will proceed as planned. Useful areas for future research could be risk management and the further development of the project audit function. In order for assurance to function properly project suppliers need to be coordinated and control mechanisms put in place to monitor the project on a regular basis and implement corrective action where necessary, i.e., project coordination capabilities somehow need to be in place. An area of principal concern here is that of 'oversight' – that is the ability of the owner organisation to monitor project processes within its capability scope. A further area of concern is that of the 'line of visibility' into the project – that is the depth of oversight that the owner has into what the supply chain is actually doing during project execution, which will be a function of the contractual arrangements on the project. Quite naturally this has direct consequences for the size of the owner's project team. Finally, in order to derive the benefits from the project the completed asset needs to be integrated into existing operations. Where projects are delivered as part of a broader programme, benefits from the individual project can only be fully derived when it is integrated to the whole. This is by no means trivial and requires a set of asset integration capabilities deployed throughout the project in order to ensure operational readiness (see Zerjav et al., 2018). The importance of the above issues is of course not lost on the research community and a variety of studies have focused on governance frameworks and their under-pinning routines and capabilities (e.g., Klakegg et al., 2008). Yet, most of these tend to focus on a specific stage of the project, rather than taking a project lifecycle perspective.

30.6 CONCLUDING REMARKS

Hopefully this chapter has shown that applying the organisational capability construct to the study of project owners brings complementary angles of inquiry and sets of explanations to those of other popular perspectives, such as structural contingency and neo-institutionalism. While long being popular in the broader strategic management literature it has been slower in uptake in project management research (Leiringer & Zhang, 2021). As with many other theoretical perspectives there is still much to do in order to achieve the required convergence within the project management literature for research work to start to be cumulative and have practical purchase. However, as briefly outlined below there are several pockets in which this is happening for both broad types of owner organisations dealt with in this chapter.

The 'permanent' owner organisation, responsible for executing numerous routine projects and a few less frequent, complex projects, has the opportunity to build up and improve on their in-house project capabilities over many years (Davies & Brady, 2016). It is unsurprising, therefore, that an area that has received substantial attention is that of programme and port-folio capabilities at the organisational level (e.g., Killen & Hunt, 2013). These studies could usefully be complemented by extending the research onto the project level, in particular in terms of project governance and oversight. There lies, I suggest, a significant research agenda around what quantity and quality of project capabilities are required by the owner's in-house team (Adam et al., 2020), the extent to which these capabilities can be leveraged by using consultants (Flowers, 2007) and how they should be deployed in partnership with the supply side (Melkonian & Picq, 2011). A further question worth reflecting on is how these types of owners can develop the desired level of capabilities. The answer to this is not obvious given the lumpiness of investment projects. To further complicate things, capabilities are acquired in different ways and the process is heavily path dependent. This means that some capabil-ities can be developed rather quickly through specific human resource investments, such as employing new staff or hiring consultants. Certain types of coordination capabilities, such as the cost control function on a construction project, would fall into this category, while others can only feasibly be developed over time. Relational capabilities are, for example, the outcome of learning through repeated interactions and will follow different learning trajectories depending on whether they concern formal or trust-based relations.

For the 'temporary' owner organisation, established to execute a single project or pro-gramme, the project capabilities have to be identified, built, combined and developed specif-ically for the project (cf. Grabher & Thiel, 2015). A key challenge here lies in furthering our understanding of how project capabilities can be identified and assembled within a limited period of time and in extension how they might be successfully reused by one or several of the involved parties on subsequent projects (e.g., DeFillippi & Arthur, 1998; Grabher & Thiel, 2015; Zerjav et al., 2018). Indeed, there has so far been limited interest in external capability acquisition from the owner perspective (Leiringer & Zhang, 2021). This is somewhat surpris-ing given how project (and programme) organisations/coalitions/teams are formed, especially for large projects. At the project level, an example of a compelling question that has yet to receive any great attention is who deploys which capabilities in CPO (cf. Ruuska et al., 2013; Winch & Leiringer, 2016). Notwithstanding, some authors, e.g., Schüßler et al. (2012) and Lobo and Whyte (2017), have sought to examine how firms can leverage the capabilities of the project coalition, while others have investigated the capability base in project networks (e.g., DeFillippi & Arthur, 1998; Grabher & Thiel, 2015). Such research would, arguably, add both theoretically and practically to the burgeoning research agenda around megaprojects.

As a final remark, I cannot help but reflect on the contents of this last section. They deal almost exclusively with issues that could be deemed to come into play well into the project lifecycle. This is somewhat disconcerting given my arguments around the importance of 'project shaping' for the overall project outcomes. Hopefully others can pick up on this shortcoming, so that future chapters on this topic can better explain how project owners can deal with this very important part of CPO.

REFERENCES

Adam, A., Lindahl, G. & Leiringer, R. (2020). The dynamic capabilities of public construction clients in the healthcare sector. *International Journal of Managing Projects in Business*, 13(1), 153–171.

Caldwell, N. & Howard, M. (Eds) (2010). *Procuring complex performance: Studies of innovation in product-service management*. Routledge.

Davies, A. & Brady, T. (2000). Organisational capabilities and learning in complex product systems: Towards repeatable solutions. *Research Policy*, 29(7), 931–953.

Davies, A. & Brady, T. (2016). Explicating the dynamics of project capabilities. *International Journal of Project Management*, 34(2), 314–327.

Davies, A. & Mackenzie, I. (2014). Project complexity and systems integration: Constructing the London 2012 Olympics and Paralympics Games. *International Journal of Project Management*, 32(5), 773–790.

Davies, A., Dodgson, M. & Gann, D. (2016). Dynamic capabilities in complex projects: The case of London Heathrow Terminal 5. *Project Management Journal*, 47(2), 26–46.

Davies, A., Fredriksen, L., Cacciatori, E. & Hartmann, A. (2018). The long and winding road: Routine creation and replication in multi-site organizations. *Research Policy*, 47(8), 1403–1417.

DeFillippi, R. J. & Arthur, M. B. (1998). Paradox in project-based enterprise: The case of film making. *California Management Review*, 40(2), 125–139.

Denicol, J., Davies, A. & Krystallis, I. (2020). What Are the causes and cures of poor megaproject performance? A systematic literature review and research agenda. *Project Management Journal*, 51(3), 328–345.

Dosi, G., Nelson, R., & Winter, S. (2000). *The nature and dynamics of organizational capabilities*. Oxford University Press.

Flowers, S. (2007). Organizational capabilities and technology acquisition: Why firms know less than they buy. *Industrial and Corporate Change*, 16(3), 317–346.

Grabher, G. & Thiel, J. (2015). Projects, people, professions: Trajectories of learning through a mega-event (the London 2012 case). *Geoforum*, 65, 328–337.

Hartmann, A., Davies, A. & Frederiksen, L. (2010). Learning to deliver service-enhanced public infrastructure: Balancing contractual and relational capabilities. *Construction Management and Economics*, 28(11), 1165–1175.

Helfat, C. E. & Winter, S. G. (2011). Untangling dynamic and operational capabilities: Strategy for the (n)ever-changing world. *Strategic Management Journal*, 32(11), 1243–1250.

Killen, C. P. & Hunt, R. A. (2013). Robust project portfolio management: Capability evolution and maturity. *International Journal of Managing Projects in Business*, 6(1), 131–151.

Klakegg, O. J., Williams, T., Magnussen, O. M. & Glasspool, H. (2008). Governance frameworks for public project development and estimation. *Project Management Journal*, 39(1), S27–S42.

Leiringer, R. & Zhang, S. (2021). Organisational capabilities and project organising research. *International Journal of Project Management*, 39(5), 422–436.

Liu, Y., van Marrewijk, A., Houwing, E.-J. & Hertogh, M. (2019). The co-creation of values-in-use at the front end of infrastructure development programs. *International Journal of Project Management*, 37(5), 684–695.

Lobo, S. & Whyte, J. (2017). Aligning and reconciling: Building project capabilities for digital delivery. *Research Policy*, 46(1), 93–107.

Melkonian, T. & Picq, T. (2011). Building project capabilities in PBOs: Lessons from the French special forces. *International Journal of Project Management*, 29(4), 455–467.

Merrow, E. W. (2011). *Industrial megaprojects: concepts, strategies, and practices for success.* John Wiley & Sons.

Miller, R. & Lessard, D. R. (2001). *The strategic management of large engineering projects: shaping institutions, risks, and governance.* MIT Press.

Morris, P. W. G. (2022). A working account of the rise of project management. *International Journal of Project Management*, 40(2), 91–94.

Morris, P. W. G. & Hough, G. H. (1987). *The anatomy of major projects: A study of the reality of project management.* John Wiley & Sons.

PMI (2008). *A guide to the project management body of knowledge* (PMBOK® Guide 4th ed.). Project Management Institute.

Rowlinson, S. (2014). *Cost escalation in the Hong Kong construction industry report.* University of Hong Kong. https://s3.ap-southeast-1.amazonaws.com/hkca.com.hk/upload/doc/publication/Cos tEscalationintheHongKongConstructionIndustryReport%28EN%29-jw2CB.pdf.

Ruuska, I., Ahola, T., Martinsuo, M. & Westerholm, T. (2013). Supplier capabilities in large shipbuilding projects. *International Journal of Project Management*, 31(4), 542–553.

Schüßler, E., Wessel, L. & Gersch, M. (2012). Taking stock: Capability development in inter organizational projects. *Schmalenbach Business Review*, 64(3), 171–186.

Turner, J. R. & Müller, R. (2003). On the nature of the project as a temporary organization. *International Journal of Project Management*, 21(1), 1–8.

Turner, J. R. & Müller, R. (2017). The governance of organizational project management. In S. Sankaran, R. Muller & N. Drouin (Eds), *The Cambridge handbook of organizational project management* (pp. 75–91). Cambridge University Press.

Winch, G. M. (2014). Three domains of project organising. *International Journal of Project Management*, 32(5), 721–731.

Winch, G. M. & Cha, J. (2020). Owner challenges on major projects: The case of UK government. *International Journal of Project Management*, 38(3), 177–187.

Winch, G. M. & Leiringer, R. (2016). Owner project capabilities for infrastructure development: A review and development of the 'strong owner' concept. *International Journal of Project Management*, 34(2), 271–281.

Winch, G. M., Maytorena-Sanchez, E. & Sergeeva, N. (2022). *Strategic Project Organizing.* Oxford University Press.

Winter, S. G. (2003). Understanding dynamic capabilities. *Strategic Management Journal*, 24(10), 991–995.

Zerjav, V. (2021). Why Do business organizations participate in projects? Toward a typology of project value domains. *Project Management Journal*, 52(3), 287–297.

Zerjav, V., Edkins, A. & Davies, A. (2018). Project capabilities for operational outcomes in inter-organisational settings: The case of London Heathrow Terminal 2. *International Journal of Project Management*, 36(3), 444–459.

31. Embracing complexity in sustainable project management

Luca Sabini and Gilbert Silvius

31.1 INTRODUCTION

Academic literature on project management (PM) has paired the concepts of sustainability and PM for a more than quarter of a century (Sabini et al., 2019; Silvius & Schipper, 2014). In PM literature this stream has become a recognized new school of thought (Silvius, 2017), often referred to as sustainable project management or SPM (Sabini et al., 2019; Silvius & Schipper, 2014). In parallel with academia, the professional world is also experiencing a transformation of PM (Code of Ethics and Professional Conduct, 2015; PMI, 2010, 2016) where professional boundaries and duties have been widened to include social and environmental aspects in the development of the project (Huemann & Silvius, 2017; Sabini, 2016; Sabini et al., 2017).

A common sentiment among practitioners when asked to consider sustainability in their projects is opposition, since it is perceived to add complexity (Sabini & Alderman, 2021). In this chapter, drawing from this consideration, we discuss main PM research findings linked to the SPM and its relationship with project complexity. Indeed, we show how the inclusion of sustainability objectives in the management of projects generates a series of challenges to overcome (e.g., high number of elements to control and relationships to manage) and opportunities to exploit (e.g., opportunities for innovation and experimentation). The increase of number of elements to control and relationships to manage in a project essentially adds complexity which is seen as something to be reduced or simplified by traditional PM methods. This chapter contributes to SPM literature by showing how to embed sustainability in project-organizing settings, and reflect how to do so, and showing that complexity needs to be embraced rather than simplified.

In the rest of the chapter, we discuss the challenges coming from traditional the PM approach to simplify complexity, the opportunities that come from embracing complexity, and draw some conclusions with possible future research directions.

31.2 SUSTAINABILITY AND COMPLEXITY

Before examining the complexity in SPM, it is worth reflecting on how the abstract concept of sustainable development is itself intrinsically complex. Sustainability issues are by nature complex and wicked. From the 1987 Brundtland seminal definition of sustainable development, it is not clear how society and economies, set up to chase unlimited growth with a limited amount of resources, can ensure continuous development without jeopardizing the ability of future generations to do the same.

Sustainability requires, for instance, the consideration of all externalities produced by a business or individual action, e.g., carbon dioxide (CO_2) emitted, or pollution created. These objectives tend to be an addition to the number of other objectives already considered and managed when performing a specific action. The increase in number of elements that a given system displays is called element complexity. Moreover, when looking at the trade-off's relationship that inclusion of sustainability objectives will produce, for example, considering how pursuing short-term objectives will hinder/enhance long-term ones, there is a further increase of complexity. Again, this second point means that any business or individual action would need to navigate the increased number of existing connections and relationships which can often be competing for the same resources (i.e., long- versus short-term objectives). This is called relationship complexity. Hence the complexity connected with concepts of sustainability or sustainable development is associated with element and relationship complexity (see Chapter 3).

Further adding to this, very often (if not always), the consideration of sustainability relates to less objective characteristics of a system (i.e., subjective to who observes the system). The way we can assess how eco-friendly is an electric car can change due to its newness (e.g., in the same way asbestos was labelled the 'magic mineral' at the beginning of the twentieth century). Subject to the point of view, the benefit of incinerating waste to produce electricity is seen as controversial as it releases CO_2 in the atmosphere. Depending on the professional background and capabilities, sustainability objectives can be ranked differently (e.g., expert in biodiversity versus electric engineer). These are examples of how sustainability increases the cognitive complexity for decision makers which adds to the abovementioned objective system complexity. Although not necessarily increasing the objective characteristics of a system (element or relationship complexity), sustainability increases its complicatedness (or cognitive complexity) since it adds novelty, divergent viewpoints, and observer capability.

Therefore, when considering how to be more sustainable, all sectors of society face these increasing complexity issues, often labelled with the expression sustainability transitions. In line with the sentiment of wider society toward the importance of including sustainability considerations in our everyday life, PM literature has witnessed how the key challenges of the PM discipline have moved from consideration of the traditional triad of time, cost, and quality to a wider set of factors. Therefore, projects have become more ambitious and expensive, and as they 'have become more and more complex, there has been an increasing concern about the concept of project complexity' (Cristóbal et al., 2018, p. 1).

We use this traditional approach to complexity as a function of its elements and their relationships to discuss some explicative examples of the impact of sustainability on projects of both element complexity and relationship complexity. Indeed, we argue that the consideration of sustainability perspectives adds both element complexity and relationship complexity. For example, complexity can come from environmental and social sustainability objectives added to the project, since it increases the number of elements to consider (element complexity). A construction project would need to consider environmental sustainability objectives (e.g., assess and manage CO_2 embedded in construction activities) and social sustainability objectives (e.g., minimize nuisance around working site); a product development project would need to use low energy-consuming products – environmental sustainability – or for example maximize product usability for disabled people – social sustainability; an organizational change project would need to develop more efficient use of organizational resources and offices – environmental sustainability – or aim at a better work–life balance for its employees – social sustainability. These objectives tend to be added on top of traditional project objectives.

However, complexity is further increased by the number of interactions with a set of different stakeholders (relationship complexity). A construction project would need to interact with specialists in CO2 for environmental sustainability objectives and local councils for social sustainability objectives; a product development project would interact with specialists in low energy for environmental sustainability objectives and charities for social sustainability objectives; and an organizational change project would engage in talks with its employees to meet environmental and social sustainability objectives.

On another level, literature on complexity highlights another aspect, that of organicism and emergent properties (Gilbert & Sarkar, 2000). Organicism suggests that the total is more than the sum of its parts. The properties of a certain phenomenon cannot be ascribed directly to its component parts but arise only because of the interactions among the parts (Gilbert and Sarkar, 2000). Such properties, that are not those of any part but that arise through the interactions of parts, are called emergent properties. This is a relevant insight, as the usual approach to handling complexity in PM is to break down the task or object at hand into more manageable elements. For example, the Work Breakdown Structure is a PM method that embodies this approach. The concept of organicism implies that in this breakdown the emergent properties are overlooked, and that the breakdown therefore does not lead to a fruitful understanding and organization of the work in a project.

31.3   THE COMPLEXITY OF SUSTAINABLE PROJECT MANAGEMENT

Modern project management already involves several complex decisions, which normally require trade-offs, and the introduction of sustainability concepts in the PM profession has radically changed the overall approach to the management of the project (Sánchez, 2015), inevitably increasing 'the number of those trade-offs' (Sabini & Alderman, 2021, p. 2).

SPM, according to Silvius and Schipper (2014), consists of traditional PM activities with consideration of the sustainability aspects in the whole project life cycle to realize benefits for types of stakeholders. This literature categorized changes to traditional and established PM tools, techniques, and methodologies on three main levels: (1) micro – individual project manager; (2) meso – project; and (3) macro – entire project context. All the elements that are highlighted below add to the project's element, relationship, and cognitive complexity (or complicatedness, as Chapter 3).

On the micro level, when looking at the project manager individual sphere, the implementation of sustainable objectives requires specific competences, which Silvius (2017) identifies as systems thinking competences, anticipatory competences, normative competences, strategic competences, and interpersonal competences. These skills, not traditionally taught in project manager education processes, need therefore to be achieved on the field (with experience) or in the education process (e.g., at university level or with certifications). Unfortunately, this has not 'been part of conventional design education, and therefore, institutions providing design education need to start developing and implementing curriculums that will equip graduates with these new professional capacities' (Gaziulusoy & Ryan, 2017).

At the project level, the increasing complexity coming from the consideration of sustainability relies on the often conflicting objectives it poses, and the trade-offs arising. For example, the achievement of social sustainability will probably require some compromises on the environmental dimension of sustainability. Studying construction projects (Fernández-Sánchez & Rodríguez-López, 2010), propose to identify, classify, and prioritize sustainability indicators by working with the different project stakeholders. They underline how SPM poses fundamental problems of complexity when dealing with stakeholders, calling for the involvement of every participant in the project life cycle to find a proper balance between all actors. This difficulty is understandable since even in PM standards, where the management of stakeholders takes significant time, there are 'different understandings of project stakeholders and project stakeholder management' (Eskerod & Huemann, 2013, p. 45). In an attempt to support a holistic view of these issues Edum-Fotwe and Price (2009) propose a tool to provide a systematic assertion of sustainable dimensions in construction projects. In this way they hope to help in understanding 'the nature of the internal interaction between the issues that define social sustainability' (Edum-Fotwe & Price, 2009, p. 321).

Moreover, Talbot and Venkataraman (2011) give some guidelines on how PM practices can be amended to include sustainability. In their model of SPM, they suggest collecting information regarding stakeholder requirements, linking them with high-level sustainability indicators, assigning them an owner, and clarifying under which conditions the criteria are successful. In this way each actor holds responsibility for deploying their sustainability duties. A critique of Talbot and Venkataraman's (2011) approach relates to the project manager's level of authority. Control over some of the stages in their model could simply be beyond the project manager's authority (Turner et al., 2010). Indeed, control over the project may rest with the client or sponsor, which could reduce the project manager's ability to follow these sustainability models. This situation reflects the fact that making PM sustainable does not rest with any single stakeholder but is a collective duty requiring the collaboration of multiple actors with their distinct agendas, resources, and capabilities.

On the macro level, one of the main tensions arising from the introduction of sustainability objectives is the consideration about different time horizons characterizing sustainability and projects. The fundamental struggle to integrate these two concepts stems from how sustainability is oriented towards long-term objectives whilst projects traditionally operate in a much more short-term setting (although very recently this is changing in favour of a long-term view of projects). In this context, Brones et al. (2014) explicitly frame the knowledge gap between sustainability and PM around three areas: normative, professional, and academic. The first relates to the sphere of technical norms (International Organization for Standardization (ISO) norms). In ISO norms, the concept of PM is never mentioned in connection with sustainability, not even in the ecologically oriented ISO 14062 and ISO 14006 norms, which are considered to be the reference documents for the definition of eco-design. Even as far back as 1994, a Policy Brief journal article on sustainability in PM recognized that 'while its breadth of interpretation makes it politically appealing, it also makes the concept confusing as a point of reference for any concrete project activity' (Gregersen et al., 1994, p. 1). In terms of professional associations, Brones et al. (2014) found that 'current project management best practices … traditionally ignore environmental sustainability' (Brones et al., 2014, p. 116), and as a consequence of that project managers 'lack of awareness with regard to sustainability issues' (Al-Saleh & Taleb, 2010, p. 50). Finally, in the academic research context, Brones et al. (2014) find from a search for the term project management in conjunction with eco-design on the ISI Web of Science that in only 0.2 per cent of papers (42 out of 25,066 papers on PM) is there any sort of link between the two concepts.

A more prescriptive way to adapt PM practices would involve a change in all project phases (Robichaud & Anantatmula, 2010). This approach suggests specific activities should be carried out at every project step (i.e., feasibility, design, implementation, and closeout), including environmental and market needs, ecological benefits in budget analysis, and community input for site selection in the feasibility of the project (Robichaud & Anantatmula, 2010).

An analysis of how sustainability creates complexity in PM can also be done by looking at the project life cycle. Indeed, in the initiation phase, Labuschagne et al. (2005) and Shen et al. (2010) give clear examples of how important it is to implement SPM in the initial project phases. Shen et al. (2010) clarify how to correctly implement sustainable practices in the construction industry in China, in particular, recognizing that project feasibility studies take into account mainly economic performance. They suggest a way to shift the 'traditional approach of project feasibility study to a new approach that embraces the principles of sustainable development' (Shen et al., 2010, p. 254). Distinguishing between residential, public, private, and commercial construction projects, they recognize how, especially in residential construction projects, the constitution of social and environmental factors is very poor. To overcome this problem, they advocate, on the one hand, for more public policies and, on the other, for more explicit and rigorous professional guidelines in the PM discipline. Similarly, Labuschagne et al. underline how 'suitable environmental indicators are essential to provide designers and project managers with the necessary protocols to internally assess processes' (Labuschagne et al., 2005, p. 42) and therefore have to be considered at the earliest possible stage in a project.

Fernández-Sánchez and Rodríguez-López (2010), specifically on the execution phase of the project, highlight the importance of focusing on stakeholder relationships. The consideration of SPM poses fundamental problems of complexity when dealing with stakeholders, calling for the involvement of every participant in the project life cycle to find a proper balance between all actors. Eskerod and Huemann (2013) tried to answer the stakeholder issue by analysing how different PM standards have addressed the stakeholder management and sustainable development principles in their standards. The finding is that in PRINCE2 and in PMBOK the topic is just sketched, while in the ICB4 (International Project Management Association, 2015) there is some evidence that stakeholders are considered in deep. This analysis revealed that among the different standards there are 'different understandings of project stakeholders and project stakeholder management' (Eskerod & Huemann, 2013, p. 45). Therefore, a more uniform consideration of them is required.

Another subset of authors focuses on the closing part of the project (Fourie & Brent, 2006; Invernizzi et al., 2020). Even in the closing phases a project should take into account sustainability issues. Focusing on a Mine Closure Model for the correct management of mining industry projects, Fourie and Brent (2006) advise on some of the factors that need to be considered at the end of the project such as the maintenance of natural resources impacted by the project (i.e., water quality), the 'safe disposal of infrastructures', 'meeting community expectations', and the 'development of sustainable ecosystems'. The study of effects occurring after project closure, even if it is quite a sensitive theme, is somewhat underemphasized. As a matter of fact, projects are often blamed for abandoning the artefact that has been produced during the life of the project, raising significant sustainability issues (Keeys & Huemann, 2017).

In summary, it can be argued that consideration of sustainability in projects increases its complexity on two interconnected levels. On one level addressing sustainable objectives increases the project scope, e.g., going beyond the business case, return on investment, or other traditional financial measures. On another interconnected level it entails more activities, e.g., environmental and social impact assessments to be carried out and stakeholders to be heard.

31.4   EMBRACING COMPLEXITY TO ACHIEVE SUSTAINABILITY

PM evolved from the desire to have a specific group of people focus on a specific task for a limited amount of time (Andersen, 2010). This so-called task perspective aimed to reduce the complexity for the team members by allowing them to just focus on the task at hand, while paying less attention to developments in the project context that might interfere with this task. Of course, the task at hand can still be inherently complex, as projects consist of many interrelated processes needed to achieve a given outcome. The PM methods employed aim to manage this complexity as a deterministic system (Hitchins, 2003). Many well-known and most established PM methods reflect this view (e.g., Work Breakdown Structure – dividing the project deliverable into smaller components; Gantt chart – depicting graphically and temporally tasks to be done; and Critical Path Method – identifying critical project activities). According to this approach, the management of a complex system can be achieved by breaking down its component into smaller, more manageable pieces. This approach, i.e., systems management by Hertogh and Westerveld (2010), is not capable of absorbing the full complexity of a project, since it is not compatible with the pursuit of sustainability objectives, which, as discussed in the previous section, would increase the complexity of projects.

The consideration of sustainability in PM increases both the structural and dynamic types of complexity and will require the adoption of a more dynamic approach that also embeds a non-deterministic perspective on PM, i.e., addressing the variability in project phenomena and employing the appropriate theoretic and methodological approaches (Padalkar & Gopinath, 2016).

Even if the increase of project complexity is a natural effect of inclusion of sustainability considerations, SPM literature has not fully investigated this yet. Table 31.1 proposes the main differences between the simplifying versus embracing complexity approaches, applied to the planning, monitoring, and controlling of projects, which may need further analysis by academics.

In the planning phase of a project, a traditional approach appears through the careful preparation, with engagement of the right experts, of the best estimate plan. The task that the project implies is carefully analysed and broken down in great detail in order to be able to make a realistic estimation and schedule. Uncertainties are addressed as risks that potentially influence the realization of the project's deliverables. All this might be recognized as good, but traditional, PM, where sustainability objectives (needing more broad and blurred boundaries) cannot be contemplated.

Embedding sustainability in the planning phase of a project would put more effort into creating a shared understanding about, especially the goal of, the project (Luhmann, 1995). Sensemaking is key and ideas on how the desired goal can be realized are based on a participatory process of many stakeholders, expertise, and disciplines (Winkler, 2016). In planning, key uncertainties are identified, with explicit assumptions about their possible values or conditions, resulting in multiple anticipated scenarios (Miller, 2011). And although a most likely scenario may be adopted as a plan for the project, the project organization is well aware of the

Table 31.1   Necessary changes to be made to traditional PM in order to embed sustainability

Simplifying complexity	Embed sustainability (embrace complexity)
Project planning	
Focus on planning	Focus on sensemaking
Plan a single best estimate scenario	Anticipate multiple potential scenarios
Rely on expertise of a few	Co-production of knowledge by many
Implicit assumptions	Explicit assumptions
Considering parts	Considering the whole
Deliverable oriented	Goal oriented
Project monitoring and control	
Oriented on control	Oriented on interaction
Plan is the basis	Reality is the basis
Manage the output	Manage the process
Focused on output criteria	Focused on input factors

uncertainties and assumptions of this plan and will be monitoring these during the execution of the project, based on how the project unfolds in reality. Therefore, as Cristóbal et al. underline, project managers 'must begin to pay greater attention to the nonlinear and subtle influences in their planning and management styles' (Cristóbal et al., 2018, p. 8).

During project monitoring and control (i.e., the execution of the project), a traditional approach is oriented towards controlling the output of scheduled activities, with the plan as baseline. Deviations from the plan are considered exceptions and should be kept to a minimum. Embedding sustainability in the monitoring and controlling of the project is oriented towards interaction with stakeholders (Luhmann, 1995) in order to continue the sensemaking while the project unfolds in reality. The goal of the project provides the main orientation and control is oriented towards input factors that will influence the future reality of the project. The process of project execution includes frequent feedback loops that include reflection and recalibration of objectives and plans (Hatt, 2009).

In summary, the consideration of sustainability objectives in the planning, monitoring, and controlling of a project-organizing setting essentially implies the examination of a wider set of factors (e.g., long-term project effects, larger audience of stakeholders – and its implications with emerging conflicting interests, flexibility, and adaptation). These factors are perfectly aligned with the main traits of complex project organizing: uncertainty, complexity, and temporality.

31.5   CONCLUSIONS AND FUTURE RESEARCH DIRECTIONS

The consideration of economic, environmental, and social factors in project-organizing settings creates a number of challenges to overcome and opportunities to exploit. The inclusion of these considerations challenges the effectiveness of traditional PM approaches that treat projects as a deterministic system and tend to simplify complexity, in order to make the planning, execution, and closure of a project more manageable. This chapter offered a brief overview of why and how this happens and, based on the analysis that the consideration of sustainability requires PM to embrace the resulting complexity rather than dismissing or simplifying it, proposed an approach to the planning, monitoring, and controlling of projects that embraces complexity.

This is a necessary effort since society in general exerts institutional pressures over individuals and organizations to consider sustainability and sustainable objectives. The question over the precise means to pursue these objectives is, however, still unfolding. The translation of the abstract concept of sustainability in practice entails a process of trial and error that works for only that specific contextuality. PM professional associations started to pave the way with a code of ethics and professional standards (International Project Management Association, 2015; PMI, 2010), however, the key to move forward rests with all stakeholders in the project (project manager, project team, sponsors, owner, etc.).

Embedding sustainable objectives in project implementation involves changes in the traditional way in which activities are carried out. These changes will inevitably lead to tensions coming from the increase of trade-off situations, and the acceptance of such tensions can be the start of dealing with sustainable objectives.

An interesting future research direction can be in the study of project paradoxes and trade-offs caused by the contradicting nature of sustainability objectives (Sabini & Alderman, 2021). By acknowledging paradoxical situations originating from the contradictory nature of sustainability objectives it will be possible to develop alternative approaches and solutions to tackle these objectives. Future research could explore how project managers experience tension and paradoxical situations in project appraisal (e.g., energy from solar farm versus farm land), in project deliverables (e.g., installing sensors to monitor indoor air quality versus cutting electricity consumption by reducing electric appliances), or in day-to-day project decisions (e.g., considering local community in a construction site by working 24/7 to reduce project duration versus weekends to minimize hassle during the week).

This approach could reveal future research streams on ways that 'practitioners, professional bodies, and regulators make sense of these contradictions and deal with paradoxes in their everyday practices' (Sabini & Alderman, 2021, p. 12). A starting point for these research streams can be Table 31.1, in which we propose several approaches to the planning, monitoring, and controlling of projects that embrace complexity. In order to develop these approaches into actionable practices that can find their way into the practical reality and standards of PM, further studies will be necessary.

REFERENCES

Al-Saleh, Y. M. & Taleb, H. N. (2010). The integration of sustainability within value management practices: A study of experienced value managers in the GCC countries. *Project Management Journal*, 41(2), 50–59.

Andersen, E. S. (2010). Rethinking project management: An organisational perspective. In *Strategic Direction*, 26(3).

Brones, F., Carvalho, M. M. de & Zancul, E. de S. (2014). Ecodesign in project management: A missing link for the integration of sustainability in product development? *Journal of Cleaner Production*, 80, 106–118.

Cristóbal, J. R. S., Carral, L., Diaz, E., Fraguela, J. A. & Iglesias, G. (2018). Complexity and project management: A general overview. *Complexity*. DOI: 10.1155/2018/4891286.

Edum-Fotwe, F. T. & Price, A. D. F. (2009). A social ontology for appraising sustainability of construction projects and developments. *International Journal of Project Management*, 27(4), 313–322.

Eskerod, P. & Huemann, M. (2013). Sustainable development and project stakeholder management: What standards say. *International Journal of Managing Projects in Business*, 6(1), 36–50.

Fernández-Sánchez, G. & Rodríguez-López, F. (2010). A methodology to identify sustainability indicators in construction project management: Application to infrastructure projects in Spain. *Ecological Indicators*, 10(6), 1193–1201.

Fourie, A. & Brent, A. (2006). A project-based mine closure model (MCM) for sustainable asset life cycle management. *Journal of Cleaner Production*, 14, 12–13.

Gaziulusoy, A. İ. & Ryan, C. (2017). Roles of design in sustainability transitions projects: A case study of Visions and Pathways 2040 project from Australia. *Journal of Cleaner Production*, 162, 1297–1307.

Gilbert, S. F. & Sarkar, S. (2000). Embracing complexity: Organicism for the 21st century. *Developmental Dynamics*, 219(1), 1–9.

Gregersen, H., Lundgren, A. L. & White, T. A. (1994). *Improving project management for sustainable development*. Policy Brief 7. University of Wisconsin.

Hatt, K. (2009). Considering complexity: Toward a strategy for non-linear analysis. *Canadian Journal of Sociology*, 34(2), 313–347.

Hertogh, M. & Westerveld, E. (2010). *Playing with complexity: Management and organisation of large infrastructure projects*. Erasmus University Rotterdam.

Hitchins, D. K. (2003). *Advanced systems thinking, engineering, and management*. Artech House Publishers.

Huemann, M. & Silvius, G. (2017). Projects to create the future: Managing projects meets sustainable development. *International Journal of Project Management*, 35(6), 1066–1070.

International Project Management Association (2015). *IPMA Code of Ethics and Professional Conduct*. International Project Management Association.

Invernizzi, D. C., Locatelli, G. & Brookes, N. J. (2020). Characterising nuclear decommissioning projects: An investigation of the project characteristics that affect the project performance. *Journal Construction Management and Economics*, 38(10), 947–963.

Keeys, L. A. & Huemann, M. (2017). Project benefits co-creation: Shaping sustainable development benefits. *International Journal of Project Management*, 35(6), 1196–1212.

Labuschagne, C., Brent, A. C. & Van Erck, R. P. G. (2005). Assessing the sustainability performances of industries. *Journal of Cleaner Production*, 13(4), 373–385.

Luhmann, N. (1995). *Social systems*. Stanford University Press.

Miller, R. (2011). Futures literacy: Embracing complexity and using the future. *Ethos*, 10, 23–28.

Padalkar, M. & Gopinath, S. (2016). Six decades of project management research: Thematic trends and future opportunities. *International Journal of Project Management*, 34(7), 1305–1321.

PMI (2010). *White paper. The bottom line on sustainability*. Project Management Institute.

PMI. (2016). Sustainability. Project Management Institute. www.pmi.org/learning/featured-topics/sustainability.

Robichaud, L. & Anantatmula, V. (2010). Greening project management practices for sustainable construction. *Journal of Management in Engineering*, 27(1), 48–57.

Sabini, L. (2016). *Project management and sustainability*. Brief for Global Sustainable Development Report. https://sustainabledevelopment.un.org/content/documents/998449_Sabini_Project%20Management%20and%20Sustainability.pdf.

Sabini, L. & Alderman, N. (2021). The paradoxical profession: Project management and the contradictory nature of sustainable project objectives. *Project Management Journal*, 52(4), 379–393.

Sabini, L., Muzio, D. & Alderman, N. (2017, 1–17 April). *Integrating sustainability into project management practice: The perspective of professional institutions*. Conference presentation, International Research Network on Organizing by Projects, Boston, MA.

Sabini, L., Muzio, D. & Alderman, N. (2019). 25 years of 'sustainable projects'. What we know and what the literature says. *International Journal of Project Management*, 37(6), 820–838.

Sánchez, M. A. (2015). Integrating sustainability issues into project management. *Journal of Cleaner Production*, 96, 319–330.

Shen, L., Tam, V., Tam, L. & Ji, Y. (2010). Project feasibility study: The key to successful implementation of sustainable and socially responsible construction management practice. *Journal of Cleaner Production*, 18(3), 254–259.

Silvius, G. (2017). Sustainability as a new school of thought in project management. *Journal of Cleaner Production*, 166, 1479–1493.

Silvius, G. & Schipper, R. P. J. (2014). Sustainability in project management: A literature review and impact analysis. *Social Business*, 4(1), 63–96.

Talbot, J. & Venkataraman, R. (2011). Integration of sustainability principles into project baselines using a comprehensive indicator set. *International Business and Economics Research Journal*, 10(9), 29–40.

Turner, J. R., Huemann, M. & Bredillet, C. N. (2010). *Perspectives on projects*. Routledge.

Winkler, J. A. (2016). Embracing complexity and uncertainty. *Annals of the American Association of Geographers*, 106(6), 1418–1433.

PART IV

TOWARDS PROJECT ORGANIZING 4.0

INTRODUCTION TO PART IV

Dongping Cao

As an integral part of economic and social life, project activities have experienced substantial developments anchored by the three previous industrial revolutions of mechanization, electrification and automation during the past decades. These developments include not only the progress of project delivery technologies and tools but also the evolution of organizing practices for the 'management of projects' (Morris, 2013; Winch, 2022). Although project activities have been with us since the coming of humans on earth, during the pre-industrial era project-organizing practices, including those for complex projects such as the Giza Pyramids around 2600 BC and the Great Wall of China around 200 BC, were predominantly based on intuition and experience rather than professionalized science. With the occurrence of the three previous industrial revolutions that have significantly reshaped the operation paradigms of economic and social life, as illustrated in Figure IV.1, project organizing has gradually developed as a professionalized and formalized practice (Winch, 2022).

Triggered by the invention of steam engine technology, the first industrial revolution started in England around 1780 and ushered in the transition from hand production methods to mechanical production driven by steam power. While the transition to steam-based mechanical production stimulated and enabled the increase of large-scale infrastructure development projects such as railways and canals, this period also witnessed the emergence of contracting strategies by infrastructure investors to address their extended project development needs and the emergence of the contractor as a distinctive project-based firm. Following the revolution of mechanization, the second industrial revolution fostered by the advent of electricity took place in the second half of the nineteenth century to the early twentieth century. Mass production facilitated by electricity and assembly lines in this period also enabled the further

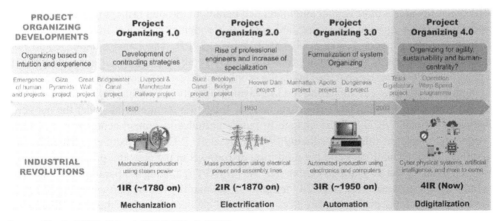

Source: Morris (2013); Schwab (2016); Winch (2022).

Figure IV.1   Developments of project organizing through industrial revolutions

developments of manufacturing technologies and accelerated the processes of urbanization and population movement, which were accompanied by the increase of complex development projects for urban transit systems, railroad networks and aircraft systems. In terms of project organizing, this period witnessed the rise of professions such as civil engineers as well as the increase of specialization, which strengthened the critical role of integration in project organizing. Catalyzed by the technological developments of electronics, computers and the internet, the third industrial revolution arose in the aftermath of the Second World War and led to the development of automated production. As some of its technological evolutions have origins in military works, this wave of industrial revolution was accompanied by not only the increase of complex industrial projects such as nuclear power plants but also the emergence of development projects for the military-industrial complex in the domains of the space race and weapon systems (Winch, 2022). In terms of project organizing, this period witnessed the formalization of system-organizing practices in the domains of, for instance, the project office, the project manager role and the matrix organization. This period also witnessed the foundation of globally influential project management associations including the International Project Management Association in 1965 and the Project Management Institute in 1969.

The term 'Industry 4.0' was first coined in Germany around 2011 to promote the idea that we are at the dawn of a new industrial revolution catalyzed by the advance and convergence of a range of emerging digital technologies that allow for an almost real-time and intelligent connection between physical and digital systems. The primary technologies underlying this new wave of industrial revolution, which was popularized as the fourth industrial revolution by Schwab (2016), include the internet of things, blockchain, cloud computing, advanced robotics, big data analytics and artificial intelligence that hold the promise to collectively blur the lines between the physical and digital worlds throughout a project lifecycle. It is asserted that these digital innovations are on the brink of fueling momentous and inevitable changes in the economic and social systems throughout the world that are fundamentally different from previous revolutions (Schwab, 2016).

Due to the inherently close relations of data/information processing with both these digital innovations (Tao et al., 2019) and project organizing (Winch, 2015), the emerging revolution in digitalization also has a great potential to enable the transformation of project-organizing approaches towards a more digital and integrated paradigm through reshaping data collecting, modeling, storing, sharing, analyzing and applying throughout a project lifecycle in the era of Industry 4.0 (Papadonikolaki et al., 2022; Whyte, 2019). The transformation could not only help to address the efficiency problems widely rooted in traditional complex project organizing (CPO) practices but also holds the promise of effectively coping with the emerging disruptions in the new era, including the increasing volatility and ambiguity of project delivery environments (Levitt, 2011), the sustainability transition requirements under the net-zero challenge (Winch, 2022) and the change in public attitudes to human-centered issues such as equality, mental health and wellbeing (Whitmore et al., 2020). Collectively shaped by the enabling digital technologies and the inhibiting disruptions in the new era, project-organizing practices hold a great potential to evolve into the Project Organizing 4.0 paradigm (in analogy to Industry 4.0) that are more targeted for agility, sustainability and human-centrality. Despite its great potential, the evolution also faces a variety of challenges such as the redistribution of benefits and risks at the inter-organizational level, the integration of multi-project resources at the organizational level and the governance of resistance behaviors at the individual level (Cao et al., 2017, 2022; Oraee et al., 2019; Whyte, 2019).

Figure IV.2   *Framework of chapters in Part IV*

Part IV focuses on discussing how emerging digital technologies underlying the fourth industrial revolution could be utilized to facilitate the evolution of traditional project-organizing approaches towards Project Organizing 4.0. As illustrated in Figure IV.2, Part IV comprises Chapters 32–38. Chapters 32–37 focus on discussing the integration of CPO practices with the following six technologies: model-based definition (also termed as building information modeling in some industries, Chapter 32), the internet of things (Chapter 33), artificial intelligence (Chapter 34), blockchain (Chapter 35), big data analytics (Chapter 36) and system simulation (Chapter 37).

Each of these chapters not only outlines the scenarios in which the technology could be integrated with CPO activities for higher value-adding processes but also discusses state-of-the-art practices, inherent challenges and future development trends of the integrations. The technologies cover the whole data-processing lifecycle including the stages of data collection, data modeling, data storage and sharing and data analysis and application. As Project Organizing 4.0 is not simply an umbrella term for a range of separate digital technologies but is primarily based on the synergies of different technology sets, Chapter 38 further discusses the impacts of the digital revolution on CPO from a comprehensive perspective. We hope this chapter will contribute to a deepened understanding of the implications of Project Organizing 4.0 on CPO as well as potential future research directions in this area.

REFERENCES

Cao, D., Li, H., Wang, G., & Huang, T. (2017). Identifying and contextualising the motivations for BIM implementation in construction projects: An empirical study in China. *International Journal of Project Management*, 35(4), 658–669.

Cao, D., Shao, S., Huang, B., & Wang, G. (2022). Multidimensional behavioral responses to the implementation of BIM in construction projects: An empirical study in China. *Engineering, Construction and Architectural Management*, 29(2), 819–841.

Levitt, R. E. (2011). Towards project management 2.0. *Engineering Project Organization Journal*, 1(3), 197–210.

Morris, P. W. (2013). *Reconstructing project management*. Wiley-Blackwell.

Oraee, M., Hosseini, M. R., Edwards, D. J., Li, H., Papadonikolaki, E., & Cao, D. (2019). Collaboration barriers in BIM-based construction networks: A conceptual model. *International Journal of Project Management*, 37(6), 839–854.

Papadonikolaki, E., Krystallis, I., & Morgan, B. (2022). Digital technologies in built environment projects: Review and future directions. *Project Management Journal*. DOI: 87569728211070225.

Schwab, K. (2016). *The fourth industrial revolution*. World Economic Forum.

Tao, F., Qi, Q., Wang, L., & Nee, A. Y. C. (2019). Digital twins and cyber–physical systems toward smart manufacturing and industry 4.0: Correlation and comparison. *Engineering*, 5(4), 653–661.

Winch, G. M. (2015). Project organizing as a problem in information. *Construction Management and Economics*, 33(2), 106–116.

Winch, G. M. (2022). Projecting for sustainability transitions: Advancing the contribution of Peter Morris. *Engineering Project Organization Journal*, 11(1).

Whitmore, D., Papadonikolaki, E., Krystallis, I. & Locatelli, G. (2020). Are megaprojects ready for the fourth industrial revolution? *Proceedings of the Institution of Civil Engineers-Management, Procurement and Law*, 174(2), 49–58.

Whyte, J. (2019). How digital information transforms project delivery models. *Project Management Journal*, 50(2), 177–194.

32. Model-based definition and project organising: towards digital and integrated project delivery

Dongping Cao, Shiting Shao and Guangbin Wang

32.1 INTRODUCTION

Project activities can not only be widely observed in typical project-based industries such as construction and software development but also increasingly identified in other industries like manufacturing, education and financial services (Schoper et al., 2018). Empirical investigations in Germany provide evidence that around 41 per cent of economic activities were carried out in the form of projects in 2019 (Nieto-Rodriguez, 2021). Despite being increasingly omnipresent and significant, project activities are largely plagued with a variety of performance problems such as cost overruns, schedule slippages and quality deficiency (Flyvbjerg et al., 2003; Love et al., 2019). For instance, Love et al. (2019) found that 47 per cent of transportation projects experience cost overruns in Hong Kong. The presence of these performance problems could be largely attributed to the fragmentation of information and processes in traditional project-organising approaches to manage the uncertainties of complex one-off project activities among different types of participants throughout a project lifecycle (Baiden et al., 2006; Winch, 2015).

During the past decades, model-based definition (MBD) as a fundamentally new way to model project lifecycle information and facilitate intensified process integration has been increasingly regarded by practitioners and researchers as a promising technology to reshape traditional project-organising paradigms and thus address project performance problems (Quintana et al., 2010; Sacks et al., 2018). This chapter aims to discuss why and how the emerging MBD technology could be comprehensively utilised to facilitate the transformation of traditionally fragmented project processes towards a digital and integrated project delivery (IPD) paradigm. The remainder of this chapter is organised as follows. Section 32.2 provides an overview of the history and the primary characteristics of MBD. Section 32.3 discusses how MBD can be integrated with different aspects of project-organising practices. The final section discusses the primary challenges and future research directions in this domain.

32.2 MODEL-BASED DEFINITION: EVOLUTION AND CHARACTERISTICS

The core concept embodied in MBD is that 3D object-based product models are the only authoritative and complete sources of information for all involving organisations to perform their portion of the product delivery cycle in a coordinated manner (Quintana et al., 2010; Ruemler et al., 2017). These can not only include basic 3D geometric data for physical components but can also be further annotated with associated parametric information for functional properties and manufacturing/building processes. With MBD, traditional 2D document-based workflows can be transformed to 3D model-based workflows with product lifecycle data integrated into one digital model in a parametric, visual, systematic and consistent manner rather than scattered in separate documents or computer applications (Alemanni et al., 2011). MBD enables objects to connect with each other and automatically update themselves since all objects are parametrically defined and controlled. In addition, MBD-enabled models can contain systematic product, performance and process information that is interoperable among different applications and is consistent at any stage of the product lifecycle. This facilitates data exchange and eliminates deviations among different models from different disciplines. MBD as a foundational technology is specifically expressed with different terms in different industries. For instance, while the term 'MBD' or digital product definition is commonly used in the automotive and aircraft manufacturing industries, 'building information modelling' (BIM) is the most widely used term in the construction industry to describe MBD (Sacks et al., 2018).

The advent of MBD technology is the outgrowth of past decades of research and development on computer-aided design (CAD) technology for 3D modelling and object-based parametric modelling. To better capture the characteristics of MBD and understand why MBD could facilitate the revolution of traditional project-organising approaches, the incremental evolution of CAD and MBD is briefly reviewed in Figure 32.1. The first CAD system was developed in 1957 as a 2D drafting design tool. However, 2D modelling could not meet the requirements of designing complex curves and surfaces, which led to the first revolutionary leap for CAD from 2D to 3D surface modelling in the late 1970s. In 1982, CAD underwent its second revolution with the introduction of solid modelling. Nonetheless, 3D models at that time only included detailed geometry data while not integrating any non-geometric information about product design intents, such as geometric dimensioning and tolerancing (GD&T) data, materials and colours, which led to practitioners using 3D models to visualise complex shapes of their products but using 2D drawings to express detailed design intents. This all changed in 1987 with the advent of Pro/Engineer based on object-based parametric solid modelling technology. The advent of this program made it possible to define clearly GD&T, relationships, notes and symbols in 3D models, which is a key characteristic of MBD technology, and to eliminate gradually the predominant dependency on 2D drawings.

As shown in Figure 32.1, the evolution of MBD technology is also closely related to its permeation in related industry practices and the development of related industry standards. The Boeing 777 project was one of the first in the aircraft manufacturing industry to have a 100 per cent digital design process in the 1990s. Due to the success of the Boeing 777 project, in 2003 the American Society of Mechanical Engineers (ASME) published the ASME Y14.41-2003 Digital Product Definition Data Practices, which provides the first comprehensive MBD standard for directly annotating 3D product models with GD&T data and notes. Boeing then fully used MBD in the Boeing 787 project from the design stage to the manufacturing stage in 2004. For the construction industry, the first commercial MBD software, ArchiCAD, was released about 13 years after the prototype of MBD for buildings was first proposed in 1974. With the development of related modelling technologies, industry standards and institutional environments during the past decades, MBD or BIM has been widely regarded as one of the most promising technologies to address the process problems deeply rooted in traditional construction project practices (Cao et al., 2017; Sacks et al., 2018).

Projects are inherently uncertain endeavours with the objective of achieving the desired future states of a specific product or service (Winch, 2010). While physical resources such

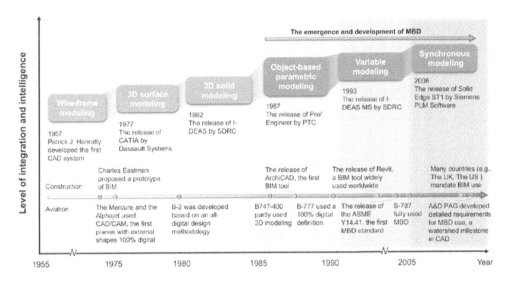

Figure 32.1   Evolution of CAD and MBD

as materials and equipment are the basis for most project activities, information also plays a critical role in complex project organising due to the continuous needs to effectively manage the uncertainty encountered when making the decisions required to advance the project through the project lifecycle (Winch, 2015). As projects in many industries are becoming more complex, tasks in a project tend to be more elaborately decomposed and assigned to different types of specialist participants, which poses further challenges to integrate different types of information for different tasks among different participants across different project stages. Through creating, sharing and utilising project lifecycle information in a parametric, visual, systematic and consistent manner, MBD could help to better manage the complexity of information in a project in terms of not only information concretisation but also information integration. Figure 32.2 compares the levels of information concretisation and integration among the four types of worlds involved in project practices: the actual real world of the project, the mental world that project participants build up in their own minds to understand the real-world project, the document/2D-based world and the MBD-based world which are used by project participants to transform their mental-world models to the real-world project.

Among the four identified worlds shown in Figure 32.2, the real-world project not only has fully concretised information but also holds the highest level of information integration as project components within the real world are inherently interdependent with each other (Froese, 2010). In order to achieve a desired state of the real-world project, project activities generally need to be decomposed into a variety of closely related tasks such as conceptual design, design development, component production and on-site assembling. To a large extent, each task can be undertaken by a specific participant and work with a type of information model that reflects the participant's unique view related to the task (Ruemler et al., 2017; Sacks et al., 2018). The mental models that project participants build up in their own minds to understand the real-world project are not only fully abstracted but also have a low degree of integration between the views for different tasks. Compared with mental models, models based on traditional 2D computer applications and documents can help to better concretise the

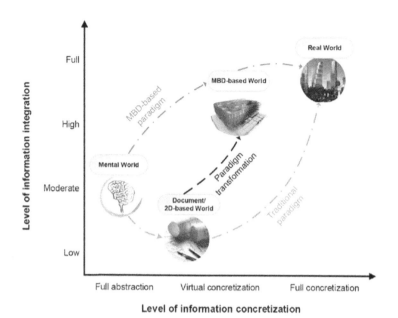

Figure 32.2   Value of MBD in project information concretisation and integration

project lifecycle information through providing, for example, more accurate product geometric data, more quantitative performance analysis results and more comprehensive manufacturing/building process specifications. However, document/2D-based models generally fail to integrate fully the information embodied in separate views/models and thus would be unlikely to reflect any of the interdependence of different project tasks until they were manually linked by the project participants (Froese, 2010). This could cause subsequent problems such as clashes, omissions, cost overruns, schedule slippages and quality deficiency. With its inherent characteristic in modelling project product, performance and process information that could be interoperable and automatically coordinated among different applications, MBD can help to substantially improve the integration level of project lifecycle information and comprehensively manage the interdependence of tasks among different participants.

32.3   MBD-ENABLED COMPLEX PROJECT ORGANISING: A FRAMEWORK

Through creating, sharing and utilising project lifecycle information with higher levels of concretisation and integration, MBD technology can not only provide a more integrated digital infrastructure to manage the interdependence of different project tasks but also further support process interaction and foster trust among different project participants. These impacts are critical to facilitate the evolution of traditional project-organising paradigms, which are characterised by high ambiguity and fragmentation, towards a more digital and integrated paradigm. A core concept to characterise this evolution tendency is IPD, an emerging project delivery method that not only emphasises the integrated project coalition governed by multi-party

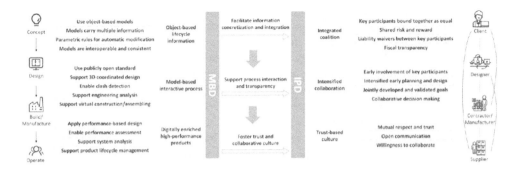

Figure 32.3   A framework of MBD-enabled integrated project delivery

agreements but also underlines intensified collaboration and a trust-based culture (Azhar et al., 2015; Hall & Scott, 2019). As shown in Figure 32.3, a framework is developed to illustrate how MBD can be integrated with different aspects of project lifecycle-organising practices to achieve the key principles of IPD.

First, IPD requires the formation of an integrated project coalition that emphasises equality, shared risk and reward, liability waivers and fiscal transparency among key participants (AIA National & AIA California Council, 2007). This can be realised with the use of MBD that facilitates the concretisation and integration of project lifecycle product, performance and process information among different participants. Specifically, through modelling information in an object-based parametric manner and enabling the interoperability and consistency of information models between different applications, MBD integrates information not only horizontally across all the disciplines but also vertically over the project lifecycle. This enhances ease of information sharing and enables project teams from various disciplines to effectively manage the dependencies of their tasks on other disciplines in different project stages (Fischer et al., 2017). When all participants openly share information in a parametric, visual, systematic and consistent manner, they can more clearly define the responsibility of each participant, more precisely measure the value of each activity, more reasonably allocate the benefits of collective efforts and, therefore, bind with each other as a more integrated coalition (Liu et al., 2017).

Second, MBD also has the potential to support interactive and transparent processes to intensify the collaboration among project participants. This is inherent in IPD that requires early involvement of key participants, intensified early planning and design, jointly developed and validated goals and collaborative innovation and decision making (AIA National & AIA California Council, 2007). Specifically, by implementing MBD in areas such as 3D coordination, system layouts optimisation (e.g., mechanical, heating, ventilation, air conditioning, electrical and piping) and facility operation performance simulation (Sacks et al., 2018), the expertise of key contractors/manufacturers and suppliers can be more appropriately incorporated into early planning and design processes. Project goals can also be developed jointly to consider the needs and resources of different participants, and key decisions can be more unanimously made through comprehensively and visually comparing different candidate solutions.

Third, IPD also underlines the importance of a trust-based collaborative culture which is composed of mutual respect and trust, open communication and willingness to collaborate (AIA National & AIA California Council, 2007). MBD technology can help to foster a more trust-based collaborative culture through improving project process efficiency and delivering digitally enriched high-performance products (Ahmad et al., 2018; Whyte, 2019). For instance, with its capability to conduct multi-stage process simulation and multi-dimensional performance analysis, MBD technology can not only help to automatically detect potential clashes among different tasks during the project delivery process but also substantially improve the quality and operational performance of the finally delivered facilities (Bynum et al., 2013; Quintana et al., 2010). These benefits can reduce potential project conflicts and also help to better illustrate the value of integration and thus encourage participants to be more extensively committed to collaborating as a team in the best interests of the whole project.

MBD has been integrated with the above aspects of organising practices for higher value-adding processes across many industries. For instance, the Boeing 787 project was one of the first in the aircraft manufacturing industry to comprehensively implement MBD throughout the project lifecycle, within which each participant was enabled to access the full product design and instantly retrieve information that could help to eliminate potential clashes and ensure that thousands of heterogenous components of the aircraft are at accurate positions with required functional properties (Quintana et al., 2010). Additionally, the MBD-enabled production process also allows efficient and less fault-prone coordination among thousands of design engineering groups around the world.

32.4 DISCUSSION

As a fundamentally new way of creating, sharing and utilising product lifecycle information in a parametric, visual, systematic and consistent manner, MBD has been increasingly regarded as one of the most promising technologies to address the process and performance problems rooted in many project-based industries. With its advantage in managing the project lifecycle with higher levels of concretisation and integration, MBD technology can provide integrated digital infrastructure to manage the interdependence of different project tasks, support process interaction and transparency throughout the project lifecycle and foster a trust-based collaboration culture among different project participants. It can therefore facilitate the evolution of traditional project-organising approaches towards a more digital and integrated delivery paradigm for complex projects.

Despite its great potential, the evolution towards an MBD-enabled IPD paradigm still faces a variety of challenges that need to be further investigated in future research. While MBD has the potential to be utilised comprehensively throughout a project lifecycle to reshape fundamentally traditional project-organising paradigms, its practical implementation in many industries is still in a relatively infant stage. In the construction industry, for example, MBD is frequently used as a visualisation tool in a manner separate from the principal project information flow, and its huge potential to integrate project lifecycle information, processes and organisations is still largely unfulfilled (Cao et al., 2015; Sacks et al., 2018).

With the development of MBD technology as well as its integrated implementation with other technologies such as the internet of things, artificial intelligence and blockchain (see Chapters 33, 34 and 35), it would be worthwhile to further explore how MBD can be more deeply integrated with complex project-organising practices to facilitate a more integrated and intelligent delivery paradigm. Moreover, as a basis to leverage its potential to integrate lifecycle processes and organisations, the implementation of MBD might require the substantial redistribution of workloads, responsibilities, risks and benefits among project participants. This might lead to new collaboration problems and resistance behaviours under specific institutional and cultural environments (Cao et al., 2014, 2022; Oraee et al., 2019). While the vast majority of extant studies on MBD have focused on technical issues such as data interoperability, more research efforts can be devoted to investigating related contractual, cultural and legal issues for the integration of MBD with project lifecycle practices to facilitate the evolution of traditional project-organising approaches towards a digital and integrated delivery paradigm for complex projects in the future.

REFERENCES

Ahmad, I., Azhar, N. & Chowdhury, A. (2018). Enhancement of IPD characteristics as impelled by information and communication technology. *Journal of Management in Engineering*, 35(1), 04018055.

AIA National & AIA California Council (2007). *Integrated project delivery: A guide*. American Institute of Architects.

Alemanni, M., Destefanis, F. & Vezzetti, E. (2011). Model-based definition design in the product lifecycle management scenario. *International Journal of Advanced Manufacturing Technology*, 52(1–4), 1–14.

Azhar, N., Kang, Y., Ahmad, I. & Asce, F. (2015). Critical look into the relationship between information and communication technology and integrated project delivery in public sector construction. *Journal of Management in Engineering*, 31(5), 04014091.

Baiden, B. K., Price, A. D. F. & Dainty, A. R. J. (2006). The extent of team integration within construction projects. *International Journal of Project Management*, 24(1), 13–23.

Bynum, P., Issa, R. R. & Olbina, S. (2013). Building information modeling in support of sustainable design and construction. *Journal of Construction Engineering and Management*, 139(1), 24–34.

Cao, D., Li, H. & Wang, G. (2014). Impacts of isomorphic pressures on BIM adoption in construction projects. *Journal of Construction Engineering and Management*, 140(12), 04014056.

Cao, D., Wang, G., Li, H., Skitmore, M., Huang, T. & Zhang, W. (2015). Practices and effectiveness of building information modelling in construction projects in China. *Automation in Construction*, 49(Part A), 113–122.

Cao, D., Li, H., Wang, G. & Huang, T. (2017). Identifying and contextualising the motivations for BIM implementation in construction projects: An empirical study in China. *International Journal of Project Management*, 35(4), 658–669.

Cao, D., Shao, S., Huang, B. & Wang, G. (2022). Multidimensional behavioral responses to the implementation of BIM in construction projects: An empirical study in China. *Engineering, Construction and Architectural Management*, 9(2), 819–841.

Fischer, M., Ashcraft, H. W., Reed, D. & Khanzode, A. (2017). *Integrating project delivery*. John Wiley & Sons.

Flyvbjerg, B., Bruzelius, N. & Rothengatter, W. (2003). *Megaprojects and risk: An anatomy of ambition*. Cambridge University Press.

Froese, T. M. (2010). The impact of emerging information technology on project management for construction. *Automation in Construction*, 19(5), 531–538.

Hall, D. M. & Scott, W. R. (2019). Early stages in the institutionalization of integrated project delivery. *Project Management Journal*, 50(2), 128–143.

Liu, Y., van Nederveen, S. & Hertogh, M. (2017). Understanding effects of BIM on collaborative design and construction: An empirical study in China. *International Journal of Project Management*, 35(4), 686–698.

Love, P. E. D., Sing, M. C. P., Ika, L. A. & Newton, S. (2019). The cost performance of transportation projects: The fallacy of the planning fallacy account. *Transportation Research Part A*, 122, 1–20.

Nieto-Rodriguez, A. (2021, November). The project economy has arrived. *Harvard Business Review*. https://hbsp.harvard.edu/product/S21061-PDF-ENG.

Oraee, M., Hosseini, M. R., Edwards, D. J., Li, H., Papadonikolaki, E. & Cao, D. (2019). Collaboration barriers in BIM-based construction networks: A conceptual model. *International Journal of Project Management*, 37(6), 839–854.

Quintana, V., Rivest, L., Pellerin, R., Venne, F. & Kheddouci, F. (2010). Will model-based definition replace engineering drawings throughout the product lifecycle? A global perspective from aerospace industry. *Computers in Industry*, 61(5), 497–508.

Ruemler, S. P., Zimmerman, K. E., Hartman, N. W., Hedberg, T. & Barnard Feeny, A. (2017). Promoting model-based definition to establish a complete product definition. *Journal of Manufacturing Science and Engineering*, 139(5), 051008.

Sacks, R., Eastman, C., Lee, G. & Teicholz, P. (2018). *BIM handbook: A guide to building information modeling for owners, designers, engineers, contractors, and facility managers* (3rd ed.). John Wiley and Sons.

Schoper, Y. G., Wald, A., Ingason, H. T. & Fridgeirsson, T. V. (2018). Projectification in Western economies: A comparative study of Germany, Norway and Iceland. *International Journal of Project Management*, 36(1), 71–82.

Whyte, J. (2019). How digital information transforms project delivery models. *Project Management Journal*, 50(2), 177–194.

Winch, G. M. (2010). *Managing construction projects: An information processing approach* (2nd ed.). Wiley-Blackwell.

Winch, G. M. (2015). Project organizing as a problem in information. *Construction Management and Economics*, 33(2), 106–116.

33. Has the Internet of Things made a real difference to the management of projects?

Igor Martek, M. Reza Hosseini, David John Edwards and Faris Elghaish

33.1 INTRODUCTION

The Internet of Things (IoT) is a wonderful development. That is the consensus. For engineers who love technical things, what could be more desirable than a technology that links together every other technology. The rationale, of course, is that IoT is useful, and will in time undoubtedly become essential. Here is how Parise and colleagues explain what we have all come to accept:

> In ordinary conditions and especially in critical conditions, a prompt availability of all the needed data is essential to decision making. Therefore, IoT is able to assist the solution of problems in real-time, offers opportunities to integrate the physical world into a computer-based system, producing efficient enhancements, welfares, and assisting human work. (Parise et al., 2018, p. 95)

Good business decisions, project management decisions, indeed all decisions, are predicated on effectively responding to the environment and the changes occurring within it. Decisions axiomatically require the pursuit of a goal or outcome – some adjustment between a current situation leading to a more optimal future sought-after status. While the goal may be defined, the current situation may be less transparent. Of course, in the past, when the world was less complex, the status of a situation may have been readily apparent. But given the multiple interdependencies of numerous factors that combine to generate a 'present status' in modern project management, an existing status quo may be both highly dynamic as well as opaque. Consequently, IoT offers a way forward in unmasking project situational opacity. If 'good' decisions are to be made, they must be informed by 'good' data. Three vectors figure in the quality of situational awareness informing decision response. These are the comprehensiveness of the range of environmental input sources, the quality of the data inputs from those sources, and timeliness (initial speed and refresh turn-around time) with which that data are received (Ghimire et al., 2017).

33.2 THE FOURTH INDUSTRIAL REVOLUTION AND THE INTERNET OF THINGS

Historically, project management proceeded through human monitoring of multiple data sources. Firstly, required information was identified. This has become an established protocol, codified through experience, entrenched in educational programs, and manifested in management practices. Those sources and their management have become disciplines in their own right, and include quantity surveying, procurement and sourcing, budgeting, supply management, logistics, scheduling, cash-flow management, and so on. Secondly, that data, such as they exist, have to be manually mined by search routines of printed materials or computer downloads, files, logs, reports, meeting notes, and other data repositories. And thirdly, even when all this is ostensibly computerized, its access, retrieval, and, most importantly, its interpretation have remained a human activity. The promise of IoT is that it will not only deliver a higher level of situational awareness of the environmental events impacting a project, but also integrate multiple realities into a holistic, unified 'truth' from which a singular, optimal course of action – one with the highest probability of apprehending the desired project outcome – can be defined (Hurtoi & Avadanei, 2020).

The question is, how close are we to IoT actually delivering such optimal outcomes?

There is a variety of technologies associated with the fourth industrial revolution (Schwab, 2018) amongst which Industry 4.0 (I4.0) is one of the most important, but nine key innovations represent the cornerstones of the 'revolution'. (1) Advanced robots: machines able to replicate human activities with greater speed, precision, durability, and reliability. (2) Cloud: open-access data storage systems allowing multi-party real-time communications. (3) Simulation: real-time high-speed data integration that projects present situations into the future, facilitating decision-making. (4) Vertical and horizontal integration: generating algorithms that optimize logistics, manufacturing, and knowledge flows in order to optimize complex activities under uncertainty. (5) Additive manufacturing: decentralization of manufacturing and elimination of transportation and inventory through 3D printing. (6) Cyber security: high-level networking between intelligent machines. (7) Industrial internet: multidirectional, real-time communication both up and down end-to-end manufacturing value chains that streamline and optimize end-user needs with supplier capabilities. (8) Augmented reality: integration of information displays in order to enhance conceptualization, understanding, and utility. (9) Big data analytics (Chapter 36): assimilation of vast and diverse data sources that generate 'big picture' understanding of underlying trends, with the view to policy and strategic decision-making (Win & Kham, 2018).

The feature that connects all of these is of course the internet; hence the Internet of Things. IoT has been very drily defined as: 'A dynamic global network infrastructure with self-configuring capabilities based on standard and interoperable communication protocols' (Vermesan et al., 2011, p. 12).

33.3   THE POTENTIAL OF THE INTERNET OF THINGS

With the history and background out of the way, it remains to be seen to what degree the vast potential of IoT has been realized by industries. Oil and gas (O&G) projects are high-risk, high-capital asset concerns. Consequently, O&G companies are prone to run digital twins (DT) of their assets in order to test and assess safety and efficiency in simulation before implementing in practice. Development in O&G DTs, however, remains in its infancy. DTs are used to provide insights on production rates, operational conditions, system bottlenecks, as well as to test structural integrity, control responsiveness, and potential failure points. Yet, to date, much of these routines remain grounded in Industry 3.0 (I3.0) computerizations. To the extent that I4.0 has been implemented, the greatest progress is reported to be in the area of asset risk assessment, where artificial intelligence is used to create learning algorithms to identify and remediate asset malfunctions. An emerging area is in virtual training, which on face value appears peripheral to the real business of O&G operations. However, the industry is forecasting an employee crisis, anticipating that around 50 percent of its workforce will retire in the near future, triggering a consequent loss of tacit knowledge and experience. In facing what the industry dubs the 'big-crew change', it is invoking a recruitment and training program to be run on a global scale over global platforms (Anderson, 2017; Wanasinghe et al., 2020).

Supply chain management (SCM) is similarly endeared to IoT. Surprisingly, perhaps, the majority of IoT research in this domain emphasizes the tracking and tracing of perishable foodstuffs. Lobster shipments, for example, are high-value items that need to move, say, from Nicaraguan wharfs to New York restaurant dining tables in a matter of hours. Not only are speed and location the issue, but so also are temperature, humidity, weather, etc., all of which can be remotely monitored (Affia et al., 2019). IoT is particularly suited to SCM in manufacturing, too, since it provides, in theory, a seamless monitoring of the movement of goods from supplier, through factories, distributors, and finally retailers and customers. The working paradigm is that IoT increases product lifespan, improves quality, and reduces waste, all for a lower cost. The elements that make up SCM IoT are fairly fundamental. Almeida and colleagues (2019) describe three components. First, sensing nodes, such as cameras, digital readers, and environmental scanners, identify current statuses. Second, wireless communications transfer status information to a central processing hub. Finally, the collective data are processed for holistic status evaluation. Mostafa and colleagues (2019) broadly concur, but describe SCM IoT as occurring in four steps. First, sensors, such as radio-frequency identification, actuators, and controllers provide 'perception'. Next, protocols, such as Zigbee and 6LoWPAN, effect data 'transmission'. Then a 'computational layer' processes the data through algorithms, and finally further software packages, such as MQTT, AMQP, and CoAP, respond (without the aid of human intervention) through an 'application layer' (Abdel-Basset et al., 2018).

33.4 THE VULNERABILITIES OF THE INTERNET OF THINGS

Further implementation of I4.0 initiatives have, however, run up against complications. For one, as has already been made plain, the vindication of IoT is founded squarely in its ability to deliver fast, accurate, and full data necessary to decision-making – data that are more reliable and more relevant and more complete than can be accumulated by human activity alone. Yet difficulties remain in interfacing between project functions, such as between designers, clients, the industry at large, and the various branches of operators. Data remain siloed, and to the extent walls are broken down, but not fully, risks of any single critical information not being shared where needed kill the erstwhile benefits of a greater cumulative information free-flow. Moreover, data have to be standardized and codified in order to be universally interpreted and appraised, and how this should be done remains unresolved. Similarly, storage, curation, and reuse are additional fully unanticipated further challenges. Indeed, the plethora of information bombarding decision-makers has been documented as counter-productive, having the effect of grey noise that must be washed out of systems in order for the limited meaningful data to be extracted (AlBar et al., 2019; Wanasinghe et al., 2020).

Then there is the problem of cyber security. In the United States (US), 75 percent of companies operating in the energy sector report having experienced cyber-related attacks. This can compromise operations by means unavailable to criminals prior to IoT implementations. The tampering of sensors and such like can also corrode operability, and this is a growing concern. Not only can facilities now be shut down from the other side of the world, when once this was impossible, but also designs can be stolen and intellectual property and innovations appropriated with apparent ease. The US, again, reports trillions of dollars' worth of technology being purloined by the Chinese alone, yearly, all by way of the internet. Critically, despite the potential, and despite progress made, IoT has not yet been able to deliver measurable benefits. It is reported that transition to IoT-dependent operations is extremely costly and disruptive, but has so far only added marginal operational improvements (Lu & Da Xu, 2018; Wanasinghe et al., 2020).

The vulnerabilities that capital assets and business operations are exposed to through hackings and other cyber attacks highlight a further weakness of IoT: network dependency. The functionality of I4.0-actualized projects is only as good as the network into which they are embedded. And networks are not always at the standard required in order to deliver full IoT functionality. A recent study by Saragih and colleagues (2021) points out that telecommunication network providers are not keeping up with the 5G upgrades and other demands that IoT relies on in order to operate optimally. In other words, companies and projects cannot put IoT-dependent capabilities into effect where network infrastructure is not state of the art; and that is almost everywhere. All that can be hoped for is a closed-loop system, but that is not true IoT. A stronger criticism, and one that interrogates the philosophical justification for IoT, is that while it serves to manage greater environmental complexity, that increased complexity is at least partially attributable to the emergence of IoT. That is, IoT is a self-serving solution to problems it is complicit in creating. As Ghimire et al. put it: 'With advances in technologies, the amount of information that has to be incorporated into decision-making … steadily increases. The resulting huge amount of information, if not harnessed properly, leads to an information overload' (Ghimire et al., 2017, p. 3).

As for SCM, once again, there are challenges. Security concerns remain unresolved. Some 70 percent of research on SCM IoT broaches this point (Ben-Daya et al., 2019). Reliance on third-party applications comes with suspicion, while firms rarely have the hardware or software resources to secure against hostile outsider intrusions. Then again, while firms 'cooperate' upstream and downstream with suppliers and customers, they remain shy about unnecessarily revealing aspects of their business process. For one, these may be considered proprietary advantage, for another, should things go wrong, this will be more apparent to the injured party and exposes firms to litigation. Blockchain models (Chapter 35) are an emerging remedy, however, in short, trust and desires for privacy have not kept pace with technology. Neither has interoperability been resolved. Firms within the value chain need to interface, and to some degree at least, that means synchronizing technological packages as well as data standards. This may lock firms into relationships, limiting their ability to remain agile and shift to other partners as competitive demands dictate. Ironically, the flexibility afforded by IoT would then have the counter-productive effect of ossifying supply chains into rigid systems. And here lies a further objection: IoT requires participating firms in a supply chain to align strategic objectives, which again may not be practical, let alone the ideal outcome, for anyone (Abdel-Basset et al., 2018; Hendrik Sebastian & Evi, 2019).

All this aside, the improved 'traceability' afforded by IoT remains merely a subservient company goal to that of profit, or even broader strategic objectives. This is far from assured under current conditions. A survey of 235 German companies, which are leaders in technological adoption, found that if IoT is to truly deliver, it would involve the installation of literally hundreds of components and devices, combined with massive organizational disruption and workforce reskilling. On average, the assessment was that in order to achieve a workable transformation to IoT SCM, some 50 percent of planned capital investment would have to go into a company's transition over a minimum of five years; and all without a firm indication of the tangible benefits to be extracted (Gerami & Sarihi, 2020; Wegener, 2015). What is interesting, however, and what presents as an emerging global competitive threat, is that the Chinese government is prepared to foot the bill for the exorbitant costs associated with initiating its own nationally grounded, fully integrated IoT business environment (Shah & Ververi, 2018).

And there is the issue with costs of establishing IoT. The cost of IoT lies not only in the technology, but in the collateral damage being caused. Smart devices rely on rare earth metals, such as cerium, neodymium, terbium, and holmium, which have magnetic properties; lithium is used in batteries; gallium is used in LEDs; tantalum in capacitors. Apart from the fact that China controls 80 percent of the world supply (and Afghanistan controls a further US$3 trillion in reserves), these materials pollute ground water when mined and pollute the earth when later dumped. Unlike radioactive materials, the toxicity of these metals does not decay. Recycling rates are as low as 4 percent, half of the world's nations have no adequate laws controlling disposal, while the annual current rate of e-waster generation is 44 trillion metric tons, or about 6 kilograms per person on earth (Nižetić et al., 2020; Penke, 2021).

Then there is the energy cost; a consideration often overlooked. Running 5G networks can consume four times the energy required for 4G. Fossil fuel usage will spike, not decrease, should there be full 5G implementation. Consider that China, which is a leader in 5G development through Huawei, has already had to revert to 4G networks in regions where energy supply could not service the 5G infrastructure it had installed (Morris, 2018). Businesses do see IoT as the way of the future, but not always with enthusiasm. In a survey of 34 project management firms across the US, not one single firm expressed confidence in their ability to navigate a transition to an IoT business model (Prasher, 2018). In fact, a study by Tang et al. showed that while IoT-configured businesses delivered productivity spikes of between 6.3 and 5.1 percent, it turned out that the debt taken on resulted in a negative impact of 14.9 percent (Tang et al., 2018).

33.5   THE ROLE OF RESEARCH IN PROGRESSING THE INTERNET OF THINGS UPTAKE

Despite the reservations and objections, there is no going back. IoT is here to stay. So, with the challenges identified, where to from here? Well, there is one more deficiency, and that lies in the nature of research being undertaken that would support a transition to IoT. The scope of research achieved to date can be gleaned from a range of literature reviews (Ben-Daya et al., 2019; Lu & Da Xu, 2018). These outline technological capabilities, industrial applications, benefits, as well as hindrances. However, what comes across as conspicuously under-represented is discussion of the means by which to effect transition to an IoT business model. Marnewick and Marnewick (2020) map a range of critical success factors that would be required to make the transition. For them, leadership roles would have to shift to become less authoritarian. Indeed, the whole organizational culture would have to change to embrace agility. People within the organization will need to be less risk averse while being more empowered. Project management routines will need to be less rigid and teamwork and collaboration will need to improve. What should strike the reader is how superficial such recommendations are. More to the point, assuming this really is the remedy needed, what would such vague prescriptions even mean in practice, and how should these recommendations be realized?

Hirman and colleagues (2019) outline an implementation framework for project management transition to I4.0 in a seven-phase model: (1) define the company vision for I4.0; (2) identify company processes; (3) implement a full data management system; (4) digitize all data; (5) implement horizontal integration across the organization; (6) install data analysis systems; and (7) initiate self-managed production and logistics. While this recipe appears more tangible, it falls far short on specifics and cannot be considered a workable template. What appears to be taking place is that academics are talking to other academics, and not to industry. Consider the simplicity of this recommendation: 'The whole implementation process can be realized in one step if the company is small but in most cases the implementation project is too large' (Hirman et al., 2019, p. 10). The advice from Whitmore et al.'s study reads like a self-help slogan: 'Think big; start small; learn fast' (Whitmore et al., 2020).

Turning to project managers, how should they ready themselves for I4.0? The advice is: (1) promote agility; (2) evolve intellectual capacity; (3) embrace resource dynamics; and (4) refine emotional intelligence (Bolick, 2019). Numerous researchers have suggested a range of transformational leadership, managerial, and even administrative styles that must accompany I4.0 integration. Thee and Nang (2018), however, see I4.0 simply piling more demands on project managers than they currently carry. They identify six roles that traditional project managers undertake; roles such as adhering to budgets, schedules, and scope. Under an I4.0 paradigm, traditional roles remain, but are expanded to encompass at least ten more – things like 'complex systems execution strategy formulation and delivery' and 'supporting the tracking and managing of a complex autonomous fleet', to name two.

None of this is said to gratuitously disparage the research being done, but only to highlight that the transition pathway to an IoT economy remains fraught with real and present unknowns.

33.6   INTO THE FUTURE WITH THE INTERNET OF THINGS

While IoT has been identified as a 'game changer' in project management, as argued by Prasher (2018) and Reja and Varghese (2019), the question once again remains, how is the game being changed? The TW Project Group, which is a leading European-based consultancy on project management, explains the benefits of I4.0 and IoT in this way:

> Let's take the example of a project manager working in the construction sector. He can use a tablet and write reports during site inspections. He can thus take pictures of a damaged or incorrectly labeled door or cable and then insert them directly into the report together with the relevant annotations. In this way, in essence, it is possible to generate a site inspection report in an extremely simple, fast and effective way ... Digitization therefore saves time and a large amount of telephone calls. (TW Project, n.d.)

This is progress; for sure. However, this is not I4.0 or IoT; it is merely the project management profession catching up with I3.0. At this point, project management enthusiasts will invoke model-based definition (MBD) as evidence of the advancements being achieved by the profession (Chapter 32). While a valid assertion, MBD, as utilized widely today, also remains in the realm of I3.0. To be clear, I4.0 is where machines talk to machines, while MBD is merely a real-time platform for assimilating project data that still relies on human interface (Cakmakci, 2019; López-Robles et al., 2020).

In short, IoT can be characterized as big, linked and open. Big in the sense that it will ultimately impact the whole world, requiring global integration from infrastructure architecture to legislative and regulatory alignments across nations. Linked in the sense that individuals, companies and even countries will become subject to network interdependencies never seen before in history, demanding cooperation and trust at a scale never yet achieved. And open in the sense that stakeholders will now become exposed to influences, both friendly as well as hostile, that cannot easily be kept at bay (Brous et al., 2020). In 2021 alone, US$120 trillion is being invested in IoT devices, while Forbes predicts expenditure will continue to grow at a rate of 7.3 percent per annum. Over the next ten years some 125 billion IoT devices are forecast to become globally interconnected. Yet, while the transition to I4.0 is set to improve lives, it may also well exacerbate the divide between rich and poor. Partly this is because investment in IoT is so uneven. Typical Wi-Fi speeds in Asia have shot up from 26.7 Mbps in 2017 to 54.2 Mbps currently. The US has gone from 37.1 to 83.8 over the same period. By contrast, today, much of Europe still hovers at about 32.8 Mbps, Latin America at 16.8 and Africa at 11.2 (Nižetić et al., 2020).

The value of IoT will ultimately be driven by its capacity to improve the value proposition of businesses, but also of its impact on society as a whole. A closing thought from Parise et al. sums up how we ought to proceed:

> It is generally recognized that human society was born based in the social contract for which the individuals consent to submit some of their freedoms to defend their remaining human rights. The achievement of an ethic globalization of advanced IoT and the progress of its security and safety are mandatory. (Parise et al., 2018, p. 2)

IoT is an inevitability, but the benefits and the costs will remain a matter for further research and discussion.

REFERENCES

Abdel-Basset, M., Manogaran, G. & Mohamed, M. (2018). Internet of Things (IoT) and its impact on supply chain: A framework for building smart, secure and efficient systems. *Future Generation Computer Systems*, 86, 614–628.

Affia, I., Yani, L. P. E. & Aamer, A. (2019). Factors affecting IoT adoption in food supply chain management. *Proceedings of the 9th International Conference on Operations and Supply Chain Management*, Ho Chi Minh City.

AlBar, A., Asfoor, H., Goz, A. & Ansari, N. (2019, March 26–28). Combining the power of IoT and big data to unleash the potential of digital oil field. 11th International Petroleum Technology Conference, Beijing.

Almeida, R. B., Junes, V. R. C., Machado, R. d. S., Rosa, D. Y. L. d., Donato, L. M., Yamin, A. C. & Pernas, A. M. (2019). A distributed event-driven architectural model based on situational awareness applied on Internet of Things. *Information and Software Technology*, 111, 144–158.

Anderson, R. N. (2017). 'Petroleum analytics learning machine' for optimizing the Internet of Things of today's digital oil field-to-refinery petroleum system. In J.-Y. Nie et al. (Eds), *Proceedings of the 2017 IEEE International Conference on Big Data*, Boston, MA.

Ben-Daya, M., Hassini, E. & Bahroun, Z. (2019). Internet of Things and supply chain management: A literature review. *International Journal of Production Research*, 57(15–16), 4719–4742.

Bolick, C. (2019). How can project managers prepare for the fourth industrial revolution? Northeastern University. www.northeastern.edu/graduate/blog/project-management-fourth-industrial-revolution/.

Brous, P., Janssen, M. & Herder, P. (2020). The dual effects of the Internet of Things (IoT): A systematic review of the benefits and risks of IoT adoption by organizations. *International Journal of Information Management*, 51, 101952.

Cakmakci, M. (2019). Interaction in project management approach within Industry 4.0. In J. Trojanowska, O. Ciszak, J. Machado & I. Pavlenko (Eds), *Advances in manufacturing, II: Manufacturing* 2019 (pp. 176–189). Springer.

Gerami, M., & Sarihi, S. (2020). The impacts of Internet of Things (IOT) in supply chain management. *Journal of Management and Accounting Studies*, 8(3), 31–37.

Ghimire, S., Luis-Ferreira, F., Nodehi, T. & Jardim-Goncalves, R. (2017). IoT based situational awareness framework for real-time project management. *International Journal of Computer Integrated Manufacturing*, 30(1), 74–83.

Hendrik Sebastian, B. & Evi, H. (2019). Impact of IoT challenges and risks for SCM. *Supply Chain Management: An International Journal*, 24(1), 39–61.

Hirman, M., Benesova, A., Steiner, F. & Tupa, J. (2019). Project management during the Industry 4.0 implementation with risk factor analysis. 29th International Conference on Flexible Automation and Intelligent Manufacturing, Limerick. *Procedia Manufacturing*, 38, 1181–1188.

Hurtoi, V. & Avadanei, D. (2020). IoT project management. *Informatica Economica*, 24(3), 75–80.

López-Robles, J.-R., Otegi-Olaso, J.-R., Cobo, M.-J., Bertolin-Furstenau, L., Kremer-Sott, M., López-Robles, L.-D. & Gamboa-Rosales, N.-K. (2020, February 20–21). *The relationship between project management and Industry 4.0: Bibliometric analysis of main research areas through Scopus*. 3rd International Conference on Research and Education in Project Management, Bilbao. http://eprints.rclis.org/40508/.

Lu, Y., & Da Xu, L. (2018). Internet of Things (IoT) cybersecurity research: A review of current research topics. *IEEE Internet of Things Journal*, 6(2), 2103–2115.

Marnewick, A. L. & Marnewick, C. (2020). The ability of project managers to implement Industry 4.0-related projects. *IEEE Access*, 8, 314–324.

Morris, I. (2018, November 26). Bill shock: Orange, China Telecom fret about 5G energy costs. *Light Reading*. www.lightreading.com/mobile/5g/bill-shock-orange-china-telecom-fret-about-5g-energy-costs/d/d-id/747781.

Mostafa, N., Hamdy, W. & Alawady, H. (2019). Impacts of Internet of Things on supply chains: A framework for warehousing. *Social Sciences*, 8(3), 84.

Nižetić, S., Šolić, P., González-de, D. L.-d.-I. & Patrono, L. (2020). Internet of Things (IoT): Opportunities, issues and challenges towards a smart and sustainable future. *Journal of Cleaner Production*, 274, 122877.

Parise, G., Parise, L. & Parise, M. (2018, November 13–14). *Evolution of human society and of things assisted by IoT*. Conference paper, 2018 IEEE International Symposium on Technology and Society (pp. 95–101). IEEE, George Washington University.

Penke, M. (2021, April 13). Toxic and radioactive: The damage from mining rare elements. *Deutsche Welle*. www.dw.com/en/toxic-and-radioactive-the-damage-from-mining-rare-elements/a-57148185.

Prasher, V. S. (2018). Internet of Things (IoT) and changing face of project management. Master of Science thesis, Harrisburg University of Science and Technology. https://digitalcommons.harrisburgu.edu/pmgt_dandt/49/.

Reja, V. K. & Varghese, K. (2019, May 21). *Impact of 5G technology on IoT applications in construction project management*. Proceedings of the 36th International Symposium on Automation and Robotics in Construction, International Association for Automation and Robotics in Construction, Banff.

Saragih, L. R., Dachyar, M. & Zagloel, T. Y. M. (2021). Implementation of telecommunications cross-industry collaboration through agile project management. *Heliyon*, 7(5), e07013.

Schwab, K. (2018). Shaping the future of the fourth industrial revolution: A guide to building a better world. Portfolio Penguin.

Shah, S. & Ververi, A. (2018). *Evaluation of Internet of Things (IoT) and its impacts on global supply chains*. IEEE International Conference on Technology Management, Operations and Decisions, Marrakech.

Tang, C.-P., Huang, T. C.-K. & Wang, S.-T. (2018). The impact of Internet of Things implementation on firm performance. *Telematics and Informatics*, 35(7), 2038–2053.

Thee, Z. W. & Nang, S. M. K. (2018). Transformation of project management in Industry 4.0. *Proceedings of the 12th International Conference on Project Management* (pp. 37–44). Society of Project Management.

TW Project. (n.d.). *Project management in Industry 4.0*. https://twproject.com/blog/project-management -industry-4-0/.

Vermesan, O., Friess, P., Guillemin, P., Gusmeroli, S., Sundmaeker, H., Bassi, A., Jubert, I. S., Mazura, M., Harrison, M., & EisePnhauer, M. (2011). Internet of Things strategic research roadmap. *Internet of Things: Global Technological and Societal Trends*, 1(2011), 9–52.

Wanasinghe, T. R., Wroblewski, L., Petersen, B. K., Gosine, R. G., James, L. A., De Silva, O., Mann, G. K., & Warrian, P. J. (2020). Digital twin for the oil and gas industry: Overview, research trends, opportunities, and challenges. *IEEE Access*, 8, 104175–104197.

Wegener, D. (2015). Industry 4.0–vision and mission at the same time. Industry 4.0 – opportunities and challenges of the industrial internet. In T. Bauernhansl, M. ten Hompel & B. Vogel-Heuser (Eds), *Industrie 4.0 in Produktion, Automatisierung und Logistik Anwendung, Technologien, Migration* (pp. 343–358). Springer.

Whitmore, D., Papadonikolaki, E., Krystallis, I. & Locatelli, G. (2020). Are megaprojects ready for the fourth industrial revolution? Proceedings of the Institution of Civil Engineers: Management and Law, 174(2), 49–58.

Win, T. Z. & Kham, N. S. M. (2018). Transformation of project management in Industry 4.0. *Proceedings of the 12th International Conference on Project Management*, Bangkok.

34. Artificial intelligence in project organizing

Chao Xiao, Qian Shi and Huijin Zhang

34.1 INTRODUCTION

In general, artificial intelligence (AI) is the ability of a digital computer or computer-controlled robot to perform tasks commonly associated with intelligent beings (Nilsson, 1998). The term is frequently applied to projects for developing systems endowed with the intellectual processes characteristic of humans, such as the ability to reason, discover meaning, generalize, or learn from past experience. It has two unique capabilities – automation and smartness – which are associated with physical machines or software that replace manual work through automated processes, or augment human work through smart decisions (Boute & van Mieghem, 2021).

Modern AI research came from a workshop offered by Dartmouth College in the summer of 1956. A machine with human-level intelligence was expected to be invented within no more than one generation. After several waves of optimism, AI experienced its first winter between the 1970s and 1980s primarily because of the poor estimation of its difficulty and the absence of capable computation power. With more powerful hardware being invented, more data being collected, and more sophisticated algorithms being proposed, investment and interest in AI have come back since the beginning of the twenty-first century as machine learning (ML) and deep learning (DL) techniques start to attract attention in different fields. AI is becoming the new operational foundation of business and has transformed the very nature of companies and organizations in terms of how they operate and how they compete (Iansiti & Lakhani, 2020).

AI contains a wide range of disciplines and techniques, as shown in Figure 34.1. ML as one approach to AI is popular because of its capability to extract and generate automatically knowledge using raw data and thus to solve problems intuitively just like human beings. The ML application is organized around three primary research focuses: task-oriented studies, cognitive simulation, and theoretical analysis. Although many research efforts strive primarily towards one of these objectives, progress towards these objectives is often related. Within the concept of ML, DL is a rapidly growing field. Conventional ML techniques were limited to processing natural data in their original form. DL is making major advances in solving this problem and allows computational models that are composed of multiple processing layers to learn representations of data with multiple levels of abstraction (LeCun et al., 2015).

With the adoption of digital technologies, the quantities of data available across various industries are expected to increase exponentially. With appropriate processing and analysis of these large amounts of data, known as Big Data (Chapter 36), operations and organizations in many industries could be revolutionized. Other than Big Data, Computer Vision (CV) is another important AI technology that has been widely adopted for object recognition and detection, where recognition refers to the process of classifying an image to a specific category, and detection refers to the process of not only detecting multiple objects belonging to different categories within a single image but also localizing the objects in the image.

AI has created new business opportunities and delivered value to organizations in numerous ways. However, we still lack a comprehensive understanding of how it affects specific

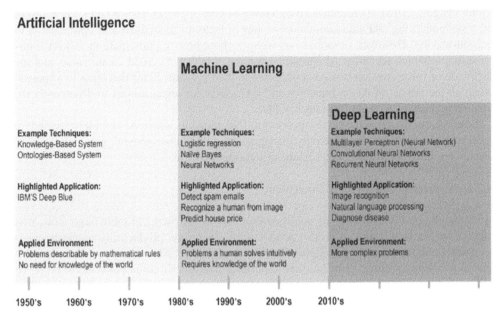

Source: Developed from Copeland (2016) and Goodfellow et al. (2016).

Figure 34.1   *Relationship among artificial intelligence, machine learning and deep learning*

activities in complex project organizing (CPO), how it interacts with different stakeholders and participants, and how humans perceive it in different settings. A comprehensive review in this chapter, therefore, can help us to tease out the current research status and to identify the novel and important research questions that will emerge from the advancement and adoption of AI in CPO.

It is difficult to accurately describe the applications in specific scenarios with the general concept of AI, since AI involves a wide range of methods and technologies and their development and application are uneven. Representative technologies of AI are often selected as examples of alternatives to AI. For instance, ML is a popular method of AI that is often used as an alternative concept to AI (Emmert-Streib et al., 2020). Therefore, we use ML as a typical example to describe its application in detail. This chapter not only discusses the application scenarios but also analyzes the process, effects, and bottlenecks of ML applications in various scenarios. The findings could help to advance the understanding of how ML techniques can be effectively applied to address inherent challenges rooted in traditional project practices and catalyze the evolution towards a new project-organizing paradigm.

34.2   THE APPLICATION OF AI IN PROJECT ORGANIZING

AI technologies are beginning to have a significant impact on project organizations and operations. For instance, the market size of chatbot and intelligent semantic analysis technology is expected to expand from $250 million in 2017 to an estimate of $1.34 billion in 2024 (Global

Market Insights, 2018). AI presents a progression of new opportunities for CPO starting from real-time monitoring and autonomous operations in factories to analysis and optimization in decision-making. However, organizations wonder about how to participate in this AI transformation, to which scenarios AI should be applied, whether AI could create value, and the magnitude of value creation that AI could bring to their projects. Since this leads to a societal debate on the impact of AI on human work, it is useful for organizations to disentangle the potential impacts of AI's applications in CPO.

Therefore, we organize the review process in five domains, where AI is widely applied, in project organizing, that is, productivity management, quality management, risk management, stakeholder integration, and project financial status assessment.

34.2.1   Project Productivity Management

To ensure the on-time delivery of qualified products to the owner at their target cost, it is essential to precisely estimate project productivity. Therefore, productivity management is a persistent popular subject in the field of project management. The majority of studies in this domain focus on applying AI techniques to perform analysis based on collected or recorded data, to perform real-time automated analysis of on-site productivity, or to predict the productivity of project teams, equipment, and machinery in use.

To overcome the drawbacks of extremely time-consuming manual on-site observation by project management personnel, (semi-)automatic and (near) real-time interpretation of imagery data collected from the job sites becomes an increasing trend. In early studies, Gong and Caldas (2011) designed and developed a semi-automatic video interpretation system combining CV and ML techniques. This system automatically recognized and tracked a variety of construction-related entities in videos collected from jobsites. Soltani et al. (2018) developed a process which determined the 2D skeleton of excavators on video frames. The contribution of this study was that it implemented synthetic images as the training images for the ML algorithm. It may inspire other researchers who have difficulties on obtaining enough training data.

Most of the productivity studies need to use large amounts of historical data in order to provide accurate forecasts. Oral and Oral (2010) introduced an unsupervised ML algorithm named Self Organizing Map (SOM). Their model was validated with data collected from 346 construction crews performing tasks on concrete pouring, formwork, and reinforcement. The results have shown that SOM was not only capable of predicting crew productivity, but also could be used to analyze and visualize the effects of various input variables on productivity.

Different from studies focusing on crew productivity predication and management, many other scholars have paid attention to predicting other productivity-relevant factors in specific projects, such as estimating the effectiveness ratios of earth-moving machinery (Schabowicz & Hola, 2008), production rates in tunneling projects (Lau et al., 2010), and productivity losses due to change orders (Cheng et al., 2015). Their study results have shown that AI techniques can not only be employed to predict crew productivity but also predict a wide range of project productivity-related values.

34.2.2   Project Quality Management

As a project proceeds, measuring its quality can help the project management team and project owner evaluate whether or not their objectives are met, which is critical to the success of the project. AI has been applied in this research field to monitor project quality dynamically (Kropp et al., 2018), to identify causes for project quality failure (Dissanayake & Fayek, 2008), and to measure the quality of different activities which may influence project success.

A good project quality management system should also be able to predict project quality dynamically. The ability of CV to (semi-)automatically analyze images and video has been noticed in the last five years, and there are also several researchers considering CV as a potential tool to monitor on-site project quality in real time. Kropp et al. (2018) proposed a novel video-based progress-monitoring model that recognized the actual state of construction activities from as-built video based on as-planned building information model (BIM) data using CV algorithms to increase the degree of automated project quality management, especially for indoor environments.

Many research activities focus on the influence of certain activities on project quality and project success. Palaneeswaran et al. (2008) implied ML algorithms with data obtained from 112 construction projects to examine the influence of rework causes. Wang and Gibson (2010) investigated the relationship between pre-project planning and project quality. They applied a Project Definition Rating Index score as the indicator to describe the level of pre-project planning. With this indicator, ML algorithms were applied to predict project cost and schedule.

34.2.3　Project Risk Management

Proper risk management is beneficial to the success of the project as current projects are characterized by various uncertainties and unsafe factors that can negatively impact the completion of the project. AI techniques have gradually been applied to risk factor identification, risk assessment, risk allocation among stakeholders, and early warning of unsafe behaviors during project progresses. Projects involve numbers of different participants with their own interests. For this reason, managing different interests and potential arguments is also an important content of project risk management.

One of the major research areas regarding AI applications in project claims and litigations is to predict their potential occurrence. Chen and Hsu (2007) applied a compound AI model that integrated Back-Propagation Neural Network and Case-Based Reasoning (CBR). This early study showed the feasibility of applying AI techniques to predict potential litigation. Chou and Lin (2013) compared various ML algorithms and ensemble learning systems to predict dispute occurrence. The effectiveness of applying AI to proactively predict potential occurrence of dispute was reconfirmed. Taking a step further, not only the potential occurrence, but also the severity of claims regarding time and cost in projects are also investigated by AI techniques (Yousefi et al., 2016).

Besides predicting the occurrence of potential claims and litigation, scholars also predicted their outcomes by taking advantage of AI techniques. Chau (2007) developed a hybrid AI system to predict litigation results in construction projects. Arditi and Pulket (2010) also compared the performance of various ML techniques including neural networks, CBR, and Boosted Decision Tree on predicting project litigation outcomes. With the help of AI techniques, we can now predict the potential occurrences of claims and litigation ahead and respond to them wisely with the support of analysis of previous experience.

To provide construction project stakeholders with efficient tools to support their decisions on risk allocation, various AI techniques have been studied. An AI approach was proposed by Jin (2011) to recommend the most appropriate risk allocation scheme for public-private partnership infrastructure projects. Because the establishment of risk allocation models were highly relying on qualitative expert knowledge that was represented in the format of natural language, AI techniques were adopted in their study for natural language quantification and reasoning.

34.2.4   Project Stakeholder Integration

Evaluating the suitability and qualification of project stakeholders, such as contractors and subcontractors, is one of the most important tasks in project organizing and is essential for achieving overall project success. However, precise mathematical evaluation models that take complex criteria into consideration have not yet been delivered. To overcome this situation, various AI techniques have been studied for stakeholder evaluation (Bendana et al., 2008) and knowledge management practice evaluation (Liu & Yeh, 2016).

Lam et al. (2009) developed a binary support vector machine model to evaluate whether a contractor was qualified for a job or not, while Bendana et al. (2008) employed a scoring system to evaluate contractors. Both of their studies established a dataset through collaboration with real construction projects to acquire project information and construction experts for input variable selection and evaluation. AI techniques have also been applied in project subcontractor and supplier selection and evaluation. Ko et al. (2007) employed a hybrid AI approach to score subcontractors based on evaluation factors like techniques, duration control ability, corporative manner, and material wastage. Ng and Luu (2008) developed a CBR-based construction subcontractor registration system to access companies with reliable standards and mechanisms.

34.2.5   Project Financial Status Assessment

The financial status of firms is usually of high concern for other stakeholders involved in the same project (Tserng et al., 2011), as a healthy financial status is essential for the business to survive and for a project to succeed. Many financial status forecasting models, especially for financial default and bankruptcy prediction, are studied for non-specific industries, however, the existing models can only be applied with difficulty to project-based organizations (PBO) (Chapter 17) due to their different capital structures. To address this situation, various AI techniques were tested to predict the default and bankruptcy of PBOs such as construction firms. For example, a hybrid approach optimizes the fuzzy expert system (FES) with adaptation techniques and applies data-based adaptive learning for contractor default prediction for surety bonding. It enables systematic tuning of the fuzzy membership function (MBF) and rules' degree of support (DoS), which are core knowledge bases in a FES as rule-based systems to simulate the human reasoning process (Awad & Favek, 2013). A default prediction model integrates the grey system theory for predicting the probability of construction firm default. The grey system theory deals with unascertained systems with partially unknown parameters and small samples by grey incidence analysis to reveal the critical factors affecting a selected object and the basic relationship between an influential factor and the selected object (Tserng et al., 2015). AdaBoost (adaptive boosting) judges the financial risk of Korean construction companies and proves its predictive power combining weak classifiers to build a learning algorithm with stronger classifiers (Heo & Yang, 2014).

Besides predicting the default and bankruptcy of PBOs, AI techniques have also shown great potential for predicting other financially related indicators. For example, automatic detection models that integrated multilayer perceptron, learning vector quantization, decision tree, and Hyper-Rectangular Composite Neural Network methods for discovering erroneous tax reports (Chen et al., 2011). In addition, Mohamad et al. (2014) presented a hybrid AI approach to predict the working capital, net profit, and annual work volume for an upcoming year.

34.3   DISCUSSION OF AI APPLICATION CHALLENGES

Not everything is perfect. The emergence of new AI-based technologies has sparked deep concerns that we have not carefully evaluated the risks associated with their use. Based on content analysis that discussed five major AI application fields to assist CPO, we raise further concerns by generalizing commonly encountered limitations and challenges when applying AI techniques to solve problems in the project management domain, and identify potential directions.

34.3.1   Lack of AI-Based Project Organizing Built on the Concept of Project Life-Cycle Data Integration

Most current AI applications focus on a certain phase of projects. However, each project phase is not isolated. It is a critical part of the entire life-cycle of a project. Furthermore, data from specific phases are highly related to the previous and subsequent phases. Effective integration of data could enhance the efficiency of AI models for CPO and project management more generally. In addition to the integration of similar data at different stages, the integration of different data types generated at different stages is also important. For example, in construction, BIM models used in the design and construction phases focus on the micro-level representation of buildings, and geographical information system results generated during surveys provide macro-level representations of the external environments of buildings. These two data sources could be integrated to improve the current performance of construction safety management (Wang et al., 2019). Traditional project management analysis models may not be capable of integrating different types of data effectively, but the performance of AI-based models has not been explored.

34.3.2   Inadequate Data and Limited Data Availability

The performance of AI systems relies heavily on both the quantity and quality of the training and validation datasets. Furthermore, project-relevant decisions are supported by various project influential factors derived directly or indirectly. An extensive and high-quality database is a prerequisite to ensuring successful AI application in project organizing. Previous studies lack adequately sized databases to ensure the accuracy of results derived from AI. Moreover, most project-relevant information is unstructured and is even recorded and stored in a paper-based format, which requires a considerable amount of time and effort to clean and label and then to extract useful information. Researchers reliant on small databases will need to use data augmentation techniques to increase their sample size, which may lead to potential losses of relevant data or outliers.

Although many advanced methods, such as unmanned aerial vehicles and wearable devices, have been used for experimental data collection, they have seldom been used for data collection in real projects. Hence, the next step in project management research is to study the feasibility and application strategy of these techniques as reliable data collection methods to extend the quality and quantity of real project datasets. In addition, the establishment of large datasets of imagery data, audio data, project documents, operations data, engineering data, and financial data has been suggested by multiple researchers (Zhong et al., 2019).

34.3.3 Need for Real-Time Project Organizing Decision Support for Smart Business

The latest advances in project management are leading the transition from activity-based to flow-based management, which imposes a set of flows to reach efficiency. This approach expects that all work progress must be regularly monitored, and decision-making models must be available to project managers to redirect the work plan during execution. Nonetheless, the majority of existing AI systems we discussed do not satisfy the requirements of immediate support. To accomplish real-time feedback and decision-making, interconnections of physical devices are required as a fundamental pillar to enable AI systems to read data from sensors and send actions to actuators during project execution. With collected data in various formats, the next and most crucial step is exploitation and exploration in the information space. ML, CV, and natural language processing methods have advantages in extracting and understanding meaningful information from raw data and then facilitating real-time decision-making. The current application of AI systems is primarily built upon the use of historical data to support decision-making. However, no two projects are executed and organized in the same way. Thus, the combination of historical and real-time monitoring data could guarantee predicted outcomes to adapt to the needs of real situations and offer great potential for improving project management performance.

34.4 CONCLUSION

The capability of AI in solving problems, such as data analyzation, heavily relies on human intuition and experience. In response to current academic and practical trends in AI, this chapter conducted a comprehensive review of the application of AI techniques to solve problems rooted in traditional project-organizing practices, principally the application of AI in productivity management, performance management, risk management, stakeholder integration, and project financial status assessment. These specific applications can reflect the realistic value and meaningful impacts of AI on project organizing. However, due to the development and innovation stage of AI technology, there are still many deficiencies in the application of AI in specific scenarios. Based on the above review, this chapter further discussed the challenges faced by AI applications, such as the difficulty of integrating datasets of different types and project stages, insufficient historical data and limited availability of data, and weak operability of dynamic real-time tracking data. These challenges will guide the development of future research, such as data collection and processing for AI applications.

This chapter aims to sort out the current research about AI from a micro perspective. Specifically, this chapter provides its readers with a broader picture illustrating (1) the trend of AI in CPO, (2) specific problems that can be solved with AI technology, and (3) commonly encountered challenges and limitations in related studies. We hope that the chapter is able to help newcomers who are interested in AI application and related research to have a preliminary understanding.

ACKNOWLEDGEMENTS

This material is based in part upon work supported by the National Natural Science Foundation of China under Grant #72072131, Shanghai Municipal Science and Technology Commission under Grant #19DZ1202803, Shanghai Pujiang Program under Grant # 2020PJC109, and the Fundamental Research Funds for the Central Universities under Grant #44202150002/006. Any opinions, findings, and conclusions or recommendations expressed in this material are those of the authors and do not necessarily reflect the views of any funding agencies.

REFERENCES

Arditi, D. & Pulket, T. (2010). Predicting the outcome of construction litigation using an integrated artificial intelligence model. *Journal of Computing in Civil Engineering*, 24(1), 73–80.

Awad, A. & Fayek, A. R. (2013). Adaptive learning of contractor default prediction model for surety bonding. *Journal of Construction Engineering and Management*, 139(6), 694–704.

Bendana, R., del Cano, A. & de la Cruz, M. P. (2008). Contractor selection: Fuzzy-control approach. *Canadian Journal of Civil Engineering*, 35(5), 473–486.

Boute, R. N. & van Mieghem, J. A. (2021). Digital operations: Autonomous automation and the smart execution of work. *Management and Business Review*, 1(1), 177–186.

Chau, K. W. (2007). Application of a PSO-based neural network in analysis of outcomes of construction claims. *Automation in Construction*, 16(5), 642–646.

Chen, J.-H. & Hsu, S. C. (2007). Hybrid ANN-CBR model for disputed change orders in construction projects. *Automation in Construction*, 17(1), 56–64.

Chen, J.-H., Su, M.-C., Chen, C.-Y., Hsu, F.-H. & Wu, C.-C. (2011). Application of neural networks for detecting erroneous tax reports from construction companies. *Automation in Construction*, 20(7), 935–939.

Cheng, M.-Y., Wibowo, D. K., Prayogo, D. & Roy, A. F. V. (2015). Predicting productivity loss caused by change orders using the evolutionary fuzzy support vector machine inference model. *Journal of Civil Engineering and Management*, 21(7), 881–892.

Chou, J.-S. & Lin, C. (2013). Predicting disputes in public-private partnership projects: Classification and ensemble models. *Journal of Computing in Civil Engineering*, 27(1), 51–60.

Copeland, M. (2016). *What's the difference between artificial intelligence, machine learning and deep learning?* https://blogs.nvidia.com/blog/2016/07/29/whats-difference-artificial-intelligence-machine -learning-deep-learning-ai/.

Dissanayake, M. & Fayek, A. R. (2008). Soft computing approach to construction performance prediction and diagnosis. *Canadian Journal of Civil Engineering*, 35(8), 764–776.

Emmert-Streib, F., Yli-Harja, O. & Dehmer, M. (2020). Explainable artificial intelligence and machine learning: A reality rooted perspective. *Wiley Interdisciplinary Reviews: Data Mining and Knowledge Discovery*, 10(6), e1368.

Global Market Insights (2018, June 13). *Chatbot Market to surpass $1.34bn by 2024: Global Market Insights, Inc.* www.globenewswire.com/news-release/2018/06/13/1520873/0/en/Chatbot-Market-to -surpass-1-34bn-by-2024-Global-Market-Insights-Inc.html.

Gong, J. & Caldas, C. H. (2011). An object recognition, tracking, and contextual reasoning-based video interpretation method for rapid productivity analysis of construction operations. *Automation in Construction*, 20(8), 1211–1226.

Goodfellow, I., Bengio, Y & Courville, A. (2016). *Deep learning*. MIT Press.

Heo, J. & Yang, J. Y. (2014). AdaBoost based bankruptcy forecasting of Korean construction companies. *Applied Soft Computing*, 24, 494–499.

Iansiti, M. & Lakhani, K. R. (2020). *Competing in the age of AI: Strategy and leadership when algorithms and networks run the world*. Harvard Business Press.

Jin, X.-H. (2011). Model for efficient risk allocation in privately financed public infrastructure projects using neuro-fuzzy techniques. *Journal of Construction Engineering and Management*, 137(11), 1003–1014.

Ko, C.-H., Cheng, M.-Y. & Wu, T.-K. (2007). Evaluating sub-contractors performance using EFNIM. *Automation in Construction*, 16(4), 525–530.

Kropp, C., Koch, C. & Koenig, M. (2018). Interior construction state recognition with 4D BIM registered image sequences. *Automation in Construction*, 86(2), 11–32.

Lam, K. C., Palaneeswaran, E., & Yu, C.-y. (2009). A support vector machine model for contractor prequalification. *Automation in Construction*, 18(3), 321–329.

Lau, S.-C., Lu, M., & Ariaratnam, S. T. (2010). Applying radial basis function neural networks to estimate next-cycle production rates in tunnelling construction. *Tunnelling and Underground Space Technology*, 25(4), 357–365.

LeCun, Y., Bengio, Y. & Hinton, G. (2015). Deep learning. *Nature*, 521, 436–444.

Liu, Y.-C. & Yeh, I. C. (2016). Building valuation model of enterprise values for construction enterprise with quantile neural networks. *Journal of Construction Engineering and Management*, 142(2), 04015075.

Mohamad, H. H., Ibrahim, A. H., & Massoud, H. H. (2014). Modelling the financial performance of construction companies using neural network via genetic algorithm. *Canadian Journal of Civil Engineering*, 41(11), 945–954.

Ng, S. T. & Luu, C. D. T. (2008). Modeling subcontractor registration decisions through case-based reasoning approach. *Automation in Construction*, 17(7), 873–881.

Nilsson, N. J. (1998). *Artificial intelligence: A new synthesis*. Morgan Kaufmann.

Oral, E. L. & Oral, M. (2010). Predicting construction crew productivity by using self organizing maps. *Automation in Construction*, 19(6), 791–797.

Palaneeswaran, E., Love, P. E. D., Kumaraswamy, M. M. & Ng, S. T. (2008). Mapping rework causes and effects using artificial neural networks. *Building Research and Information*, 36(5), 450–465.

Schabowicz, K. & Hola, B. (2008). Application of artificial neural networks in predicting earthmoving machinery effectiveness ratios. *Archives of Civil and Mechanical Engineering*, 8(4), 73–84.

Soltani, M. M., Zhu, Z. & Hammad, A. (2018). Framework for location data fusion and pose estimation of excavators using stereo vision. *Journal of Computing in Civil Engineering*, 32(6), 04018045.

Tserng, H. P., Lin, G.-F., Tsai, L. K. & Chen, P.-C. (2011). An enforced support vector machine model for construction contractor default prediction. *Automation in Construction*, 20(8), 1242–1249.

Tserng, H. P., Thanh Long, N., Chen, P. C. & Le Quyen, T. (2015). A grey system theory-based default prediction model for construction firms. *Computer-Aided Civil and Infrastructure Engineering*, 30(2), 120–134.

Wang, H., Pan, Y. & Luo, X. (2019). Integration of BIM and GIS in sustainable built environment: A review and bibliometric analysis. *Automation in Construction*, 103, 41–52.

Wang, Y.-R. & Gibson, G. E., Jr. (2010). A study of preproject planning and project success using ANNs and regression models. *Automation in Construction*, 19(3), 341–346.

Yousefi, V., Yakhchali, S. H., Khanzadi, M., Mehrabanfar, E. & Saparauskas, J. (2016). Proposing a neural network model to predict time and cost claims in construction projects. *Journal of Civil Engineering and Management*, 22(7), 967–978.

Zhong, B., Wu, H., Ding, L., Love, P. E. D., Li, H., Luo, H. & Jiao, L. (2019). Mapping computer vision research in construction: Developments, knowledge gaps and implications for research. *Automation in Construction*, 107, 102919.

35. Taming complexity in project organising through blockchain

Eleni Papadonikolaki and Klaudia Jaskula

35.1 INTRODUCTION: COMPLEX PROJECT ORGANISING AND INFORMATION

Complexity is a key challenge in project organising, caused by a high number of interdependences and relationships among components of a project system (see Chapters 3 and 14). Projects are complex systems with various interacting parts. Complexity has been primarily related to executing complex tasks in projects (Ramasesh & Browning, 2014). Although a project system with a few components is easy to manage and organise through traditional project management approaches and tools, more complex product systems require a network of collaborators coordinated by a large organisation reliant on formal, elaborate and bureaucratic processes of reporting and control (Shenhar & Dvir, 2007). Large and complex systems lead to complexity of management systems (Brady & Davies, 2014). Apart from a large number of components, in a complex project, these components must be mutually adjusted to each other, which creates the need for dynamic adjustments and interactions of the components (Morris, 2013). To this end, the more complex the system, the higher the likelihood of information uncertainty, making task coordination and project management more difficult (Hobday, 1998). Project organising can therefore be conceptualised as an information-processing system (Winch, 2014).

In our current digital economy, information processing becomes less human-centric and instead grows increasingly powerful due to digitalisation and innovative information systems. According to Whyte and Levitt (2011), 'information management has played a central, but under-recognised, role in the history of project management'. Having conceptualised the link between complex project organising and information, this chapter aims to look at what opportunities digital technologies, such as blockchain, can offer to address complexity in project organising.

35.2 BLOCKCHAIN AS A TRUSTED SOURCE OF INFORMATION

The origins of information management and digital technologies are intertwined (Whyte & Levitt, 2011). Digital technology relies on using microprocessors, computers and applications dependent on the Internet, and other devices such as video cameras, mobiles, headsets, etc. (Salmons & Wilson, 2008). With rapid increase in computational power and variety in input and output devices of all sizes, speeds, performance metrics and prices, digital technologies are advancing.

Yoo et al. (2010) identified three unique characteristics of digital technology: (1) reprogrammability of digital devices; (2) the homogenisation of data accessible by devices; and

(3) the self-referential nature of digital technology in a mutually reinforcing relation with the Internet, accelerating the creation and availability of digital devices, networks, services and content. Digital technologies become increasingly connected, open and interdependent (Papadonikolaki et al., 2020). Blockchain is such a disruptive digital solution addressing complexity (Tapscott & Tapscott, 2016).

Overall, blockchain is a distributed ledger technology (DLT), a database not centrally owned but instead existing across several locations – computer nodes – or among multiple participants (Li et al., 2019). Contrary to centralised databases on fixed locations, a distributed ledger is decentralised and eliminates the need for a central authority or intermediary to process, validate or authenticate transactions (Nawari & Ravindran, 2019; Hunhevicz & Hall, 2020). By removing intermediaries, blockchain allows transactional data recorded chronologically onto a 'chain' of data-blocks using cryptographic code (Wang et al., 2017; Perera et al., 2020). Such transactions can be validated by nodes or miners – computer nodes connected over a specific blockchain network – over a predefined consensus protocol.

35.2.1 Types of Blockchain

Different types of blockchain technology imply various governance mechanisms, depending on how governance rules are set and controlled. There exist various blockchain ecosystems, such as Ethereum (public) or Hyperledger (private), where blockchain applications, such as smart contracts (trusted code protocols), proof of provenance, payments and cryptocurrencies can be deployed. Blockchain platforms such as Ethereum or Hyperledger offer common architectures for various blockchain applications to be deployed on them. Blockchain enables direct peer-to-peer transactions of value across a distributed network and deployment of trusted code protocols or governance rules called 'smart contracts'. Smart contracts are sets of logical rules as coded scripts triggering transactions on a particular blockchain network automatically upon meeting conditions.

In a public blockchain, such as Bitcoin or Ethereum, parties are free to join and participate in activities of the network. In a private blockchain, however, such as Hyperledger Fabric, only selected parties can enter and the operator has rights to override, edit or delete entries on the blockchain. Public or private blockchains relate to access to the blockchain network. Another distinction is between permissionless and permissioned blockchains. Permissionless blockchains require no permission from parties to join and interact with and there is no authority on a network level. Permissioned blockchains, such as Hyperledger Fabric, allow parties to join after suitable verification that an operator or maintainer sets, to perform only certain activities. Therefore, permissionless or permissioned blockchain relates to governance mechanisms.

35.2.2 Organisational Implications of Blockchain Technology

Blockchain technology is a distributed database that maintains a continually growing list of immutable data records. It was first developed to enable purely peer-to-peer electronic cash (Bitcoin) transactions, without needing approving third parties, like banks (Nakamoto, 2008), and has numerous applications in cryptocurrencies. Due to blockchain's encrypted digital ledger, stored in a public or private network on numerous nodes (computers), transactions are validated through a decentralised consensus mechanism. This encrypted immutable chain of records (Swan, 2015) has found further applications than cryptocurrencies, for example in logistics, supply chain management, finance and healthcare sectors.

Because of its distributed nature, including accessors, participants, miners and regulators, blockchain technology relates to inter-organisational settings and ecosystems and, by using open-source code, allows for value creation by community members (Unalan & Ozcan, 2020). Blockchain has attracted a lot of interest in project organising due to its potential to reduce complexity by bypassing intermediaries (Catalini & Gans, 2016) and transferring trust from people to information (De la Pena & Papadonikolaki, 2019; Qian & Papadonikolaki, 2020). Because of its transparent, immutable and distributed nature, blockchain can solve the challenges of long, hierarchical and fragmented supply chains in capital project industries.

35.3   BLOCKCHAIN APPLICATIONS IN PROJECT ORGANISING

35.3.1   Blockchain Technology Use Cases across Key Sectors

The three domains of project organising are: (1) project-based firms (PBFs); (2) projects and programmes; and (3) owners and operators. The three interfaces of commercial, resources and governance (Winch, 2014) have interesting connections with blockchain technology. Both permanent commercial interfaces between PBFs and owners/operators and temporary interfaces of resourcing and governance with projects and programmes imply the existence of opportunities for streamlining data and information.

To identify current research trends and opportunities around the application of blockchain technology for project organising we conducted a Systematic Mapping Study (SMS), providing a broad review of primary studies in a specific topic area and identifying what evidence and in what quantity is available on the topic (Kitchenham & Charters, 2007). We used the Scopus database and sampling keywords related to the three domains of project organising and analysed 2674 publications. SMS are scoping studies providing an overview of a research area through classification and counting contributions across categories of that classification (Petersen et al., 2015). The key trends revealed in the SMS were that: (1) from the three interfaces of project-organising domains (commercial, resources and governance) the blockchain literature relates more to commercial interfaces, e.g. transactions, supply chains, payments and financing; and (2) research topics such as human resources are the least studied, revealing an overemphasis of blockchain applications on transactions and a socio-technical gap in the soft aspects of business models and people and behavioural aspects. We further refined our analysis by conducting a meta-review of studies on blockchain and project organising, which is what we report here. Blockchain applications have application across different industries, not only project-based sectors. For a better overview of current blockchain use cases we narrowed down the number of publications in our search results described in the previous sub-section by adding 'AND TITLE ('review')' to the combined search string which returned 107 results. The idea was to conduct a review of a review – a meta-review. Meta-reviews or 'overview of reviews' are a systematic way to elicit knowledge from other reviews (Higgins et al., 2019). Given that 2674 publications were extracted in our SMS, limiting scope further to review publications reduced the workload of reviewing literature (Sarrami-Foroushani et al., 2015). Overall, stages of meta-reviews are not very different from completing other systematic reviews (Higgins et al., 2019). We scanned the titles of all results and chose one paper per sector to understand the current state of the art there, presented in Table 35.1.

Due to a close relationship between blockchain and cryptocurrency developments, the financial sector is the first experiencing disruption from blockchain. Traditional financial services are strongly centralised as all transactions rely on financial institutions like banks. Due to blockchain, smart contracts and decentralised applications, a new trend called Decentralised Finance (DeFi) has emerged. DeFi applications allow automation of financial services without intermediaries, making them cheaper, more efficient and accessible and at the same time securing high levels of privacy, openness and transparency of the source code. DeFi platforms offer decentralised payments and transfers, decentralised loans and credits, decentralised exchanges, derivatives and asset management services (Stepanova & Eriņš, 2021).

Logistics and supply chain management is another sector with high potential for blockchain implementation. Blockchain, combined with Internet of Things (IoT) (see Chapter 33) and Radio Frequency Identification tags, provides immutable records of transactions across supply chains improving trust, traceability and transparency. Successful blockchain implementations in supply chain management include Walmart's food supply chain, allowing fast and reliable identification of contaminated food, and IBM's Hyperledger Fabric blockchain for vaccine cold chains, enabling tracking the conditions of vaccines during transportation (Pournader et al., 2020).

Blockchain becomes very useful in manufacturing sectors. Apart from improving transportation logistics, it can be used throughout automotive production. In pre-production it is used for coordination with suppliers in developing a supplier evaluation system for quality reports. During production phases, blockchain can enable preventive maintenance of machine tools, optimisation of inventory, coordination through authentication and effective disposal of parts after usage. Lastly, in distribution phase warranty claims could be dealt with more efficiently, recalling defect-driven product would be easier and business plans and demand analysis could be conducted based on the original equipment manufacturers' footprint (Raj Kumar Reddy et al., 2021).

Implementing blockchain in energy sectors attracts various stakeholders, utility companies and energy decision-makers. The largest number of use cases in energy is about decentralised energy trading such as wholesale, retail and peer-to-peer energy-trading platforms between consumers in blockchain-enabled microgrids. Cryptocurrencies or tokens for energy facilitate green energy investments and asset co-ownership or reward low-carbon and green energy production. Blockchain-based asset management through IoT and smart devices, billing and metering methods and grid management supports green certificates and carbon trading (Andoni et al., 2019).

In healthcare, blockchain can be used to manage and share secure, transparent and immutable audit trails with reduced systematic fraud. Simultaneously, it secures interoperability and authenticity of streamlined transactions and a patient-centric approach without a third controlling party can be implemented. Platforms like MedRec or Guardtime Healthcare from Estonia provide decentralised record management, authorisation and data sharing between patients and healthcare institutions securing confidentiality (Yaqoob et al., 2019).

Many countries investigate the potential of blockchain to improve government services, especially by introducing blockchain-based e-services for citizens like digital identity or online elections (Li et al., 2019). Estonia is pioneering this by introducing e-residency and online elections and aiming to introduce digital identity cards. Malaysia already uses photo

Table 35.1   *Summary of blockchain use cases across industries*

Industry	Use cases	Intended aim and benefits
Finance	- Payment and transfer platforms: Flexa, Lightning Network, xDai - Lending platforms: Maker, Compound, Aave - Decentralised exchange platforms: Uniswap, Curve Finance, Balancer - Derivatives platforms: Synthetix, Nexus Mutual, Erasure - Asset management platforms: WBTC, Harvest Finance, yearn finance (Stepanova & Eriņš, 2021)	Lower transaction fees, no control by large financial institutions (banks), improved accessibility, higher privacy, open-source software
Manufacturing	- Pre-production purchase and procurement - Transportation logistics - Production - Distribution and marketing for warranty claims, recalling actions or demand analysis (Raj Kumar Reddy et al., 2021)	Transparency, traceability, efficiency, trust, better control
Logistics	- Walmart's two supply chain initiatives powered by Hyperledger Fabric to track Chinese pork and Mexican mangoes from producer to consumer (Frizzo-Barker et al., 2020) - Vaccine cold chain (Pournader et al., 2020)	Higher efficiency, lower cost of logistics, faster tracking of contamination incidents
Energy	- Metering, billing and security - Cryptocurrencies, tokens and investments - Decentralised energy trading - Green certificates and carbon trading - Smart grid applications and data transfer – Internet of Things, smart devices, automation and asset management - Grid management - Electric e-mobility - General purpose initiatives and consortia (Andoni et al., 2019)	Enhanced use of renewable energy sources through transparent, immutable transactions

Industry	Use cases	Intended aim and benefits
Healthcare	- MedRec platform – provides decentralised record management, authorisation and data sharing among healthcare stakeholders - Gem Health Network – addresses operational costs - Guardtime healthcare platform – creates a non-intermediated relationship between patient and provider in Estonia - Healthbank platform – allows patients to save and share their health data with research organisations (Yaqoob et al., 2019)	Record management, data exchange, security and privacy, data provenance, financial rewards
Government	- Estonia Digital Identity – online elections and e-residency - National Unique ID Program of India - National Digital Identity in Malaysia – study (Samion & Mohamed, 2020)	Protected data privacy

identification and biometric data on integrated chips as national identity cards and is close to introducing a national digital identity (Samion & Mohamed, 2020).

35.3.2   Blockchain Technology Use Cases across Project-Based Sectors

Only 16 articles were on blockchain and project management. Nevertheless, applications from other key sectors described above are relevant to various areas of project organising. At a closer look, these studies relate to mainly applications in construction project management. Li et al. (2019) and Kiu et al. (2020) performed systematic literature reviews on blockchain in the construction sector, and Hunhevicz and Hall (2020) systematised an approach to categorise use cases and designed a decision framework for DLT. The intended aims and benefits of blockchain in construction, creative and research and development (R&D) sectors are: (1) eliminating distrust; (2) eliminating late payments; (3) enabling record-keeping; (4) proving ownership; (5) improving data security and transparency; (6) immutability for preventing forgery; and (7) improving trust in goods traceability. The main blockchain uses cases in construction and R&D projects are:

- supply chain management;
- Building Information Modelling (BIM);
- contract management;
- document management;
- real estate management;
- funding management;
- workers' identity validation;
- anti-counterfeit mechanism in R&D and creative projects; and
- business-to-consumer product authenticity verification.

The construction industry is a highly project-based industry characterised by its fragmentation, decentralisation and uniqueness of each project. Construction supply chains are very long and complex and, therefore, blockchain technology can significantly improve the processes around construction supply chain management as it improves trust between chain stakeholders (Kiu et al., 2020). Many use cases of blockchain in construction relate directly to the commercial interface. Elghaish et al. (2020) developed a framework to allow core project team members to automatically execute financial transactions, such as reimbursed costs, profit and cost savings, through smart contracts coded on Hyperledger to automate transactions. Das et al. (2020) proposed a mechanism to automatically initiate, validate and disburse interim payments according to general contract conditions that enabled selective transparency in payment records. Other applications include project bank accounts, a ring-fenced bank account from where payments are quickly made directly and simultaneously to supply chain members. Tezel et al. (2021) developed a payment model, integrated with Ethereum, for owner organisations where upon creation and approval of a payment for a work package by the owner, the payment is executed instantly using cryptocurrency to the supply chain members. This process renders transactions more secure by keeping the payment in an escrow account, which is only released when all the terms of an agreement are met as overseen by the escrow agent. Blockchain-based crowdfunding platforms could also be a solution for raising funds for some public projects in a transparent and open manner (Kiu et al., 2020).

The adoption of BIM is currently a driver for digital transformation in the construction industry (Chapter 32). Its implementation could be enhanced by introducing blockchain that can improve some inherent weaknesses of BIM, such as cybersecurity, interoperability and proving data ownership (Nawari & Ravindran, 2019). Blockchain can tackle trust and transparency issues in BIM-based collaboration by allowing the recording of all changes in BIM models in a traceable and immutable manner thanks to transaction time-stamping (Kiu et al., 2020).

Blockchain facilitates contract and document management in construction management such as enormous numbers of documents, difficulties proving ownership rights of files and an overall lack of transparency that is often a cause of disputes between project stakeholders (Kiu et al., 2020). In contract management, and especially contractual disputes, Li et al. (2021) suggested blockchain technology to provide convincing evidence for parties to construct and define accountability in claims and disputes and improve the efficiency and effectiveness of their management. Amaludin and Bin Taharin (2018) used blockchain technology for workers' identity validation and notarisation of construction personnel to allow for daily remittance of construction workers based on their completed work.

Similarly, in R&D industries where forgery prevention is important, Lee et al. (2020) proposed an anti-counterfeit mechanism in R&D and creative projects to ensure their immutability. Anti-counterfeit tracing is also applied in supply chains for e-commerce for creative retail industries where Liu et al. (2020) suggested the combination of data tampering and transaction traceability on blockchain to solve the problem of fake and inferior products circulating and to protect the rights and interests of consumers. These use cases relate to developments such as non-fungible tokens (NFT) applied in digital art, which has long been undervalued and freely available. NFTs are a scarce, usually one-of-a-kind, digital asset that represent real-world objects like art, music, in-game items and videos and can be bought and sold online encoded with cryptocurrency software. Topological representation of physical buildings can also be used to generate an NFT that could be used as legal proof of ownership of a building. This could facilitate smart transactions of property ownership and could completely transform real estate operations (Dounas et al., 2021).

35.4   OUTLOOK

This chapter conceptualised project organising following the logic of the three domains of project organising (Winch, 2014) where the three interfaces of commercial, resource and governance reveal important connections with blockchain technology. The three domains and interfaces were useful in structuring this chapter and seeking ways to break down complex project organising in easy-to-study parts. First, we framed blockchain technology through the theory of information and thereafter through digital technologies, defining blockchain as a digital technology trend. The analysis above showed that blockchain has numerous applications but that it also works in isolation and some of its use cases are coupled with other technologies, such as IoT in physical assets, manufacturing and logistics. Table 35.2 summarises the data collected and analysed through the SMS and meta-review.

First, blockchain technology opportunities for the commercial interface between owners/operators and PBFs abound, especially regarding financing. For instance, smart contracts automate financial transactions and payments when conditions are met and firms have faster

Table 35.2   Blockchain technology use cases applicable to complex project organising

Project-organising interface	Domain(s) of project organising	Relevant industry	Key use cases
Commercial	Owners/operators and project-based firms	Finance	- Payment and transfer platforms - Lending platforms - Derivatives platforms - Asset management platforms
		Energy	- Metering, billing and security - Cryptocurrencies, tokens and investments
		Construction	- Project bank accounts - Crowdfunding project financing - Funding management
Resources	Projects/programmes and project-based firms	Logistics	- Supply chain initiatives to track goods - Vaccine cold chains
		Manufacturing	- Pre-production purchase and procurement - Distribution and marketing for warranty, recalling actions or demand analysis
		Healthcare	- Decentralised record management, authorisation and data sharing among healthcare stakeholders - Non-intermediated customer relationship management between patient and provider - Secure data management
		Construction	- Building Information Modelling document management - Workers' identity validation
		Research and development	- Anti-counterfeit mechanisms - Business-to-consumer product authenticity verification
Governance	Projects/programmes and owners/operators	Government	- Estonia Digital Identity: online elections, e-residency - National identity programmes in India and Malaysia

Project-organising interface	Domain(s) of project organising	Relevant industry	Key use cases
		Energy	- Green certificates and carbon trading - Smart grid applications and data transfer – Internet of Things, smart devices, automation and asset management - Grid management - Electric e-mobility
		Construction	- Building Information Modelling ownership rights and provenance - Real estate and asset management

accessibility to finance through tokenisation, crowdfunding and auctions. However, there has been little evidence about the creation of new business models to support the new financial institutions put together through blockchain applications. This shows the potential for new types of organisations emerging or consolidating. Second, the resource interface benefits from various promising applications in logistics – together with IoT – and associated material flows. However, there are only scarce use cases that can support human resources, for example related to non-intermediated customer relationship management and workers' identity verification systems. Third, there are also a few blockchain use cases in governance, related to identities, certificates, ownership rights and asset management. This gap analysis shows that digital technologies cannot yet be fully exploited to support the interfaces with the project domain.

REFERENCES

Amaludin, A. E. & Bin Taharin, M. R. (2018). Prospect of blockchain technology for construction project management in Malaysia. *ASM Science Journal*, 11(3), 199–205.

Andoni, M., Robu, V., Flynn, D., Abram, S., Geach, D., Jenkins, D., Mccallum, P. & Peacock, A. (2019). Blockchain technology in the energy sector: A systematic review of challenges and opportunities. *Renewable and Sustainable Energy Reviews*, 100, 143–174.

Brady, T. & Davies, A. (2014). Managing structural and dynamic complexity: A tale of two projects. *Project Management Journal*, 45(4), 21–38.

Catalini, C. & Gans, J. S. (2016). *Some simple economics of the blockchain*. Working paper 22952. National Bureau of Economic Research.

Das, M., Luo, H. & Cheng, J. C. P. (2020). Securing interim payments in construction projects through a blockchain-based framework. *Automation in Construction*, 118, 103284.

De La Pena, J. & Papadonikolaki, E. (2019). From relational to technological trust: How do the IoT and Blockchain technology fit in? In J. O'Donnell, A. Chassiakos, D. Rovas & D. Hall (Eds), *Proceedings of 2019 European Conference on Computing in Construction* (pp. 415–424). European Council on Computing in Construction, July 10–12, Chania.

Dounas, T., Jabi, W. & Lombardi, D. (2021). Topology generated non-fungible tokens: Blockchain as infrastructure for architectural design. In A. Globa, J. van Ameijde, A. Fingrut, N. Kim & T. T. S. Lo (Eds), *Projections – Proceedings of the 26th International Conference of the Association for Computer-Aided Architectural Design Research in Asia* (Vol. 2, pp. 151–160). Association for Computer-Aided Architectural Design Research in Asia, Hong Kong.

Elghaish, F., Abrishami, S. & Hosseini, M. R. (2020). Integrated project delivery with blockchain: An automated financial system. *Automation in Construction*, 114, 103182.

Frizzo-Barker, J., Chow-White, P. A., Adams, P. R., Mentanko, J., Ha, D. & Green, S. (2020). Blockchain as a disruptive technology for business: A systematic review. *International Journal of Information Management*, 51(C), 102029.

Higgins, J. P., Thomas, J., Chandler, J., Cumpston, M., Li, T., Page, M. J. & Welch, V. A. (2019). *Cochrane handbook for systematic reviews of interventions*. John Wiley & Sons.

Hobday, M. (1998). Product complexity, innovation and industrial organisation. *Research Policy*, 26(6), 689–710.

Hunhevicz, J. J. & Hall, D. M. (2020). Do you need a blockchain in construction? Use case categories and decision framework for DLT design options. *Advanced Engineering Informatics*, 45, 101094.

Kitchenham, B. & Charters, S. (2007). Guidelines for performing systematic literature reviews in software engineering. EBSE Technical Report, Keele University and University of Durham.

Kiu, M. S., Chia, F. C. & Wong, P. F. (2020). Exploring the potentials of blockchain application in construction industry: A systematic review. *International Journal of Construction Management*. DOI: 10.1080/15623599.2020.1833436.

Lee, E., Yoon, Y., Lee, G. M. & Um, T. W. (2020). Blockchain-based perfect sharing project platform based on the proof of atomicity consensus algorithm. *Tehnicki Vjesnik*, 27(4), 1244–1253.

Li, J., Greenwood, D. & Kassem, M. (2019). Blockchain in the built environment and construction industry: A systematic review, conceptual models and practical use cases. *Automation in Construction*, 102, 288–307.

Li, W., Duan, P. & Su, J. (2021). The effectiveness of project management construction with data mining and blockchain consensus. *Journal of Ambient Intelligence and Humanized Computing*. DOI: 10.1007/s12652-020-02668-7.

Liu, A., Liu, T., Mou, J. & Wang, R. (2020). A supplier evaluation model based on customer demand in blockchain tracing anti-counterfeiting platform project management. *Journal of Management Science and Engineering*, 5(3), 172–194.

Morris, P. W. G. (2013). *Reconstructing project management*. John Wiley & Sons.

Nakamoto, S. (2008, October 31). *Bitcoin: A peer-to-peer electronic cash system*. https://nakamotoinstitute .org/bitcoin/.

Nawari, N. O. & Ravindran, S. (2019). Blockchain technology and BIM process: Review and potential applications. *Journal of Information Technology in Construction*, 24(12), 209–238.

Papadonikolaki, E., Krystallis, I. & Morgan, B. (2020, May 5). *Digital transformation in construction: Systematic literature review of evolving concepts*. Conference presentation, Engineering Project Organization Conference, Boulder, CO.

Perera, S., Nanayakkara, S., Rodrigo, M., Senaratne, S. & Weinand, R. (2020). Blockchain technology: Is it hype or real in the construction industry? *Journal of Industrial Information Integration*, 17, 100125.

Petersen, K., Vakkalanka, S. & Kuzniarz, L. (2015). Guidelines for conducting systematic mapping studies in software engineering: An update. *Information and Software Technology*, 64, 1–18.

Pournader, M., Shi, Y., Seuring, S. & Koh, S. C. L. (2020). Blockchain applications in supply chains, transport and logistics: A systematic review of the literature. *International Journal of Production Research*, 58(7), 2063–2081.

Qian, X. A. & Papadonikolaki, E. (2020). Shifting trust in construction supply chains through blockchain technology. *Engineering, Construction and Architectural Management*, 28(2), 584–602.

Raj Kumar Reddy, K., Gunasekaran, A., Kalpana, P., Raja Sreedharan, V. & Arvind Kumar, S. (2021). Developing a blockchain framework for the automotive supply chain: A systematic review. *Computers and Industrial Engineering*, 157, 107334.

Ramasesh, R. V. & Browning, T. R. (2014). A conceptual framework for tackling knowable unknown unknowns in project management. *Journal of Operations Management*, 32(4), 190–204.

Salmons, J. & Wilson, L. (Eds) (2008). *Handbook of research on electronic collaboration and organizational synergy*. IGI Global.

Samion, N. A. & Mohamed, A. (2020). Innovation of national digital identity: A review. *International Journal of Advanced Trends in Computer Science and Engineering*, 9(1.2), 151–159.

Sarrami-Foroushani, P., Travaglia, J., Debono, D., Clay-Williams, R. & Braithwaite, J. (2015). Scoping meta-review: Introducing a new methodology. *Clinical and Translational Science*, 8(1), 77–81.

Shenhar, A. J. & Dvir, D. (2007). *Reinventing project management: The diamond approach to successful growth and innovation*. Harvard Business Review Press.

Stepanova, V. & Eriņš, I. (2021). Review of decentralized finance applications and their total value locked. *TEM Journal*, 10(1), 327–333.

Swan, M. (2015). *Blockchain: Blueprint for a new economy*. O'Reilly Media.

Tapscott, D. & Tapscott, A. (2016). *Blockchain revolution: How the technology behind bitcoin is changing money, business, and the world*. Penguin.

Tezel, A., Febrero, P., Papadonikolaki, E. & Yitmen, I. (2021). Insights into blockchain implementation in construction: Models for supply chain management. *Journal of Management in Engineering*, 37(4), 04021038.

Unalan, S. & Ozcan, S. (2020). Democratising systems of innovations based on blockchain platform technologies. *Journal of Enterprise Information Management*, 33(6), 1511–1536.

Wang, J., Wu, P., Wang, X. & Shou, W. (2017). The outlook of blockchain technology for construction engineering management. *Frontiers of Engineering Management*, 4(1), 67–75.

Whyte, J. & Levitt, R. (2011). Information management and the management of projects. In P. W. G. Morris, J. Pinto & J. Söderlund (Eds), *The Oxford handbook of project management* (pp. 365–388). Oxford University Press.

Winch, G. M. (2014). Three domains of project organising. *International Journal of Project Management*, 32(5), 721–731.

Yaqoob, S., Khan, M. M., Talib, R., Butt, A. D., Saleem, S., Arif, F. & Nadeem, A. (2019). Use of Blockchain in healthcare: A systematic literature review. *International Journal of Advanced Computer Science and Applications*, 10(5), 644–653.

Yoo, Y., Henfridsson, O. & Lyytinen, K. (2010). Research commentary: The new organizing logic of digital innovation: An agenda for information systems research. *Information Systems Research*, 21(4), 724–735.

36. Big data analytics and project organizing

Weisheng Lu and Jinying Xu

36.1 INTRODUCTION

Since the emergence of the first Gantt chart, our knowledge of projects and project management has progressed remarkably through enriched related theory, practice, and technology. There are prolific perspectives regarding what exactly a project is. It may be viewed from various perspectives as a form of temporary organization (Turner & Müller, 2003), a system for managing information flows (Winch, 2015), or a set of formal and informal institutions imprinting and controlling behavior (Wang et al., 2018). However they are defined, it is widely agreed that projects are characterized by temporality (Chapter 5), uncertainty (Chapter 2), heterogeneity, and discontinuity (Bakker et al., 2016; Hanisch & Wald, 2011). These features sometimes combine advantageously and on other occasions work against project value delivery. Investigating the organizing mechanisms of a project to improve project performance is at the kernel of complex project organizing (CPO).

CPO can be viewed as temporary organizing or temporary configurations of permanent organizations (Winch, 2014). Encompassing project thinking, formation, configuration, management, optimization, and even dissolution, it is wider in scope than project management. Just as 'no project is an island' (Engwall, 2003), CPO takes place in a rich social context that is constantly changing in line with interdependences, interfaces, interactions, and infrastructures. CPO involves adapting to turbulent environments within a predefined time frame (Bakker et al., 2016); making an array of decisions per se. Such decision-making is bound to the features of the projects. In facilitating better decision-making, information plays a crucial role by reducing uncertainty (Citroen, 2011). The potential of big data analytics has not been explored in CPO or project organizing more generally, although it is heatedly explored in other management areas.

Big data is a collection of data sets so large and complicated that they are difficult to process using traditional data management tools (Padhy, 2013). With larger, more diverse, and better-quality data, e.g., in tera-bytes or even zeta-bytes, one can do things that cannot be done at a smaller scale, creating new value (Mayer-Schönberger & Cukier, 2013). Big data analytics can uncover hidden patterns and unknown correlations, thereby allowing better business prediction, more informed decision-making, and more precise interventions, *inter alia* (McAfee et al., 2012). However, the development of big data in CPO is stagnant. Researchers attribute it to the uncertain, temporary, heterogeneous, and discontinuous nature of projects.

We argue in this chapter that CPO is an area where big data is highly pertinent. Big data sets are intentionally or unintentionally created and left over in projects. We first review the definition, scope, and characteristics of project organizing and the features of big data and its analytics. The review leads to two streams of theoretical perspectives underpinning our argument: project organizing as a data-intensive decision-making process inherently constrained by 'bounded rationality', and big data analytics as an emerging technological instrument to unbind this bounded rationality. We then provide two examples of big data use in CPO, discuss the prospects, and finally draw conclusions.

36.2 CPO AS DATA-INTENSIVE DECISION-MAKING

According to Bakker et al. (2016), existing research investigates project organizing from three aspects, namely process, form, and perspective. Project organizing as process implies the central role of temporariness and dynamics of change, whereby a more dynamic and temporary project-organizing process leads to more unanticipated developments and outcomes (Bakker et al., 2016). Project organizing as form focuses on project organization, forms of which include project-supported organizations (Chapter 30), project-based organizations (Chapter 17), project networks (Chapter 13), or project management offices (Bakker et al., 2016). Project organizing as perspective emphasizes the fundamental differences in organizing logic of projects. This branch of research explores the causation, impact factors, and contingencies of project organization from behavioral, processual, multilevel, and relational aspects (Bakker et al., 2016; Söderlund, 2011).

Another view is that project organizing can be better understood through decision science, where project organizing in essence involves using available information and knowledge to make a web of decisions across the project lifecycle. Human decision-makers, according to Simon's (1997) bounded rationality theory, are inherently bound by three limits: (1) the decision-support information they have; (2) the cognitive limitations of their minds; and (3) the time available to make the decision.

The limitations of current research methods also call for big data analytics in project organizing. To consider the constant dynamics of project organizing and its social contexts, longitudinal and ethnographic studies are desired (Bakker et al., 2016). However, such studies are difficult to undertake owing to the temporary nature, limited time frame, and changing characteristics of projects. While case studies are commonly used to study project organizing, the risk is that these methods may only record a window of time. Big data offers a way to record project organizing as it progresses. As Bakker et al. (2016) suggest, digitally recorded activities have increased the availability of secondary, empirical data for more comprehensive quantitative studies using mixed methods.

36.3 BIG DATA AND ITS ANALYTICS

Big data has three defining characteristics, namely volume, variety, and velocity (McAfee et al., 2012). Volume is the quantity of data in the form of records, transactions, tables, or files; velocity can be expressed in batch, near time, real time and streams; and variety can be structured, unstructured, semi-structured, or a combination thereof (Russom, 2011). In a project, data is generated relentlessly by sources such as web logs, sensor networks, unstructured social networking, and streamed video and audio. Big data analytics can be applied to these data in order to uncover hidden patterns, unknown correlations, and other useful information that will guide better business predictions and decision-making (Wang et al., 2016), leading to suggestions that value is the fourth 'V'.

Big data analytics is the application of advanced analytic techniques, such as predictive analysis, data mining, statistics, machine learning, deep learning, and very big data sets (Russom, 2011). Big data analytics has the potential to 'unbind' bounded rationality and supplement human cognitive limitations. Analyzing big data, one can identify latent or actionable knowledge (Agrawal, 2006), which can be utilized for future decision-making. Compared with small data analysis, big data analytics can account for the totality of the subject it describes and provide more authentic information. As a result, big data analytics has become a differentiator for organizational performance and competitive advantage, and a reconstructing power for project management (Whyte et al., 2016).

Despite the enormous potential of big data and its analytics, there is a perception among the project-organizing community that these cutting-edge domains are largely irrelevant to project organizing. According to this perception, a project is temporary so data are gone after the project is dissolved; heterogeneous data are specific to a project and have little referential use to others; and discontinuous so data are siloed among project members. While these statements are reasonable, one should note that project organizing generates a great deal of human, material, machine, money, method, activity, and environmental data. It increasingly uses digital technologies such as sensors, portable devices, and 5G technologies, which generate enormous amounts of data. Thus, there is great potential for the application of big data analytics in project organizing.

36.4   EXAMPLES OF BIG DATA ANALYTICS FOR CONSTRUCTION PROJECT ORGANIZING

Winch (1989, p. 970) asserts that 'construction projects are amongst the most complex of all undertakings', while Gidado (1996) underlines the continuous and rapid growth in complexity of construction projects against a backdrop of cost, quality, safety and efficiency demands, new technologies, and fragmentation of the industry. Construction projects are also characterized by large investment, long duration, multiple stakeholders, non-linear relationships, temporality, and many other challenges (Stark et al., 2014). As common practice, project organizing is adopted in construction to rethink, form, configure, optimize, and manage projects in broader social contexts such as project-based organizations and beyond. Big data analytics can offer a way to navigate the uncertainty, complexity, and sophistication of construction project organizing (LaValle et al., 2011).

36.4.1   Big Data-Enabled Social Network Analysis for Construction Project Organizing

Social network analysis (SNA) is gaining popularity in project-organizing research. Researchers (Chinowsky et al., 2010; Pryke, 2012) tend to consider project organizing in a socially embedded context which can be visualized and analyzed in various social networks. SNA is a new language for representing and understanding project organizing. However, mapping social networks, particularly comprehensive ones, is a difficult, data-demanding process traditionally performed using questionnaires, interviews, participant observations (Vinten, 1994), and ethnographic methods (Hartmann et al., 2009).

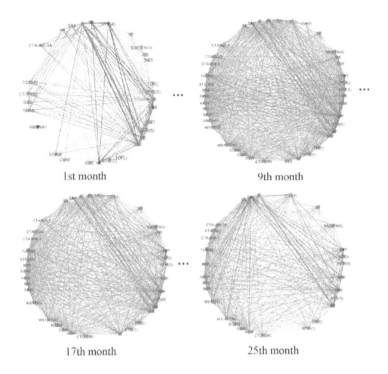

Figure 36.1   Dynamics of project organizing via a big data-enabled social network analysis

The authors (e.g., Lu et al., 2020; Xu et al., 2022) have adopted an innovative method by exploring big data for SNA to investigate how building information modeling (BIM; Chapter 32) can impact construction project organizing. Some project clients (e.g., construction clients, main contractors, and consultants) record the work done by project teams in project timesheets. This somewhat bureaucratic practice leaves behind a rigorous timesheet of the projects to keep a record of almost every non-trivial project activity with individual actors' ranks and time to conduct these activities alongside the construction processes. They contribute a very good data source for SNA.

Even a single practice of timesheeting generates hundreds of thousands of data entries related to a specific project. If considering all the trades, communications, and technologies related to the project, they can generate a big data set accumulated unintentionally as the project activities are done. With over 3 million records of timesheet data from 27 projects, Lu et al. (2020) constructed social networks and analyzed their interactional dynamics. Figure 36.1 selects four of the 25 monthly social networks to demonstrate the results of a longitudinal SNA of project organizing based on big data. It shows just one non-BIM project over its lifecycle. Looking at the changes of nodes and the connections between them helps us visualize the dynamics of social networks along a project lifecycle. By comparing BIM and non-BIM projects, it was found that BIM can enhance human interaction efficiency and information delivery at an early stage in construction projects while such impact varies among different professionals when a project progresses (Lu et al., 2020; Xu et al., 2022). Furthermore, the authors applied a similar big data-enabled SNA method to measure the human-organization-technology (HOT) fit levels in organizing construction projects (Xu et al., 2022). The HOT fit model emphasizes the congruence among human, organization, and technology in project organizing.

36.4.2   Big Data Analytics for Construction Waste Management

Big data analytics is also emerging for construction waste management (CWM), a key aspect of CPO. Unlike social networks, solid waste from construction activities is tangible and easy to measure. Researchers in this field commonly use waste generation rates measured by weight or volume per square meter of construction floor area as the CWM performance indicator. From the early days of Skoyles (1976), researchers have suffered from notoriously erratic 'small' data, with a relatively small sample size or relatively small sites sampled. One explanation is the temporary nature of projects, which, once complete, cease to generate construction waste closing the window of opportunity to collect data. Researchers in the field have also tended to use on-site sorting and weighing of waste (Kazaz et al., 2020), tape measurement (Skoyles, 1976), and truck load records (Poon et al., 2004) as data collection methods, all of which are widely perceived to be costly and disruptive.

The authors have collected big data from the Hong Kong Environmental Protection Department, which records almost every truckload of construction waste dumped in government waste disposal facilities over the past decade. This big data set comprises more than 10 million well-structured data records (Figure 36.2). Big data has allowed the research team to do studies that would be extremely difficult, if not impossible, with small, ethnographic data. By analyzing the big data, the research team has uncovered meaningful information for decision-making related to CWM. Lu et al. (2016) illustrated that statistical results of CWM

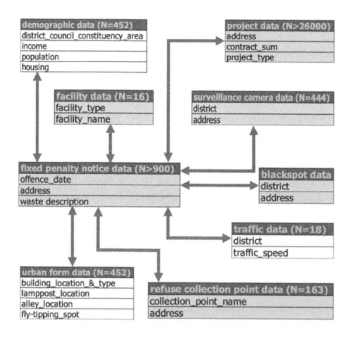

Figure 36.2   Structure of big data sets for construction waste management studies

performance based on big data can be accepted with a higher level of confidence. Xu et al. (2020a) found that although all projects generate waste following an S curve, foundation projects generate waste more slowly in the early stages than building and demolition projects. Xu et al. (2020b) further found that the public sector has better performance than the private sector in managing construction waste. They analyzed the bulk density of construction waste and discovered its correlation with waste classification (Lu et al., 2021) and waste composition (Yuan et al., 2021) and investigated the correlation between prefabrication and construction waste generation.

Such findings can provide undiscovered knowledge for project managers. For example, they can better plan for the waste management at different stages for different types of projects. They can just use bulk density to decide which facility the waste truck should go to for a more efficient decision. They can decide whether prefabrication or modular construction will help with carbon deduction.

36.5   DISCUSSION

The above cases vividly demonstrate that CPO is far from a 'small data' area. Throughout its lifecycle, project organizing generates numerous heterogenous data sets to form a big data set. Compared with small data, big data captures a fuller picture of the different aspects of project management, enhancing the credibility of results and findings. It can also uncover hidden patterns to better support project-organizing decisions. For example, project managers can use big data to forecast project performance, and introduce proper interventions when there is a warning deviation. Nevertheless, it is an unfortunate fact that the project-organizing professions are yet to foster a culture of respecting, accumulating, and sharing data across different projects, as well as harnessing data for future decision-making.

Existing big data applications mine the data left over when business is done, called passive big data. Due to the advocacy and success of information and communication technology (ICT), many institutions have started to adopt proactive technologies, ranging from Global Positioning System, Geographic Information System, Radio Frequency Identification, cameras, sensors, and others for further uses (Kitchin, 2014; Lv et al., 2019). This is increasingly becoming a healthy culture in project organizing, through its conscious adoption of ubiquitous sensors, portable devices, and ICT on- and off-site. The wide adoption of BIM, digital twins, and cyber-physical systems in the construction industry provides a rich source of big data that forms a de facto platform for project organizing.

Even though big data analytics is agreed to be applied in CPO, there are many challenges to be overcome. The first hurdle is the extra cost of big data collection, storage, and analyses (Chen et al., 2014). Collecting data can be expensive because extra man-hours are required to record project activities. The implementation of ICT may reduce the data collection cost but is itself expensive. Furthermore, while storage cost is more affordable due to rapid advancements in data-storing capabilities, there are no handy toolkits for big data analytics. Another hurdle is that stakeholders need to see a virtuous circle (Davis, 2012). A company can invest some initial resources but their longevity will be determined by the perceivable value instigated by big data analytics. Besides, the need to improve skills, numerical literacy, and collaboration between project management experts and big data analysts is critical for big data analytics implementation in project organizing.

A more challenging part of big data analytics for CPO can be related to classic dilemmas such as empowerment and disempowerment. Big data can change the current power landscape. Increasingly, arithmetic equality in big data is a concern in many business fields, including project organizing. This has triggered the question of whether simply the availability of big data means it is legitimate to exploit it, even for good causes (e.g., to improve occupational health and safety of workers). Big data in project organizing relates to the business secrets of multiple stakeholders, making data ownership, use right, and profit sharing confusing and contested. Given this changing power landscape, whether data owners are willing to share the big data in their respective domains is an increasing concern. In addition, there are many issues related to big data ethics. In contrast with the advocate of open data movement is the ever heightened data and privacy protection. Although it is agreed that big data analytics is an irreversible trend, how to ensure privacy and data security is a major concern. For example, the General Data Protection Regulation as the toughest privacy and security law in the world has been passed by the European Union. However, how to protect data security and management ethics is still a problem that awaits more research. All these issues must be resolved in the heterogeneous context of CPO.

36.6   CONCLUSIONS

We argue that big data analytics could be applied to CPO, a research field that is traditionally deemed as data-intensive but heterogenous data are always left over without fully exploring their value. We adopt the theoretical perspective of decision science to view CPO as a series of decisions to be made. We further demonstrate, by using two case studies, that big data analytics can be used to analyze the impacts of facilitating technologies and waste management in construction project organizing. It is illustrated that project organizing generates a great deal of data along the way, and they form big data if joining different projects together. We also illustrate that analyses of big data can enable many value-added applications that cannot be done in small data scenarios.

Currently, big data is passively left over when business is done. However, it is envisioned that people, like project managers, will be more conscious in collecting and harnessing big data for their project organizing-related decision-making. Nevertheless, a series of issues related to big data analytics should be addressed carefully in the future. Big data is able to empower a new field and disempower a traditional field. This empowerment and disempowerment will be further linked to data ownership and liability. Currently, whether big data is owned by data creators or the central depositors, and its respective liabilities, are under heated debate without a consensus. In parallel with the open big data movement is the tightening of data and privacy protection around the globe. Big data analytics is set to move forward by breaking through all these thorns and roses.

REFERENCES

Agrawal, A. (2006). Engaging the inventor: Exploring licensing strategies for university inventions and the role of latent knowledge. *Strategic Management Journal*, 27(1), 63–79.
Bakker, R. M., DeFillippi, R. J., Schwab, A. & Sydow, J. (2016). Temporary organizing: Promises, processes, problems. *Organization Studies*, 37(12), 1703–1719.

Chen, M., Mao, S. & Liu, Y. (2014). Big data: A survey. *Mobile Networks and Applications*, 19(2), 171–209.

Chinowsky, P. S., Diekmann, J. & O'Brien, J. (2010). Project organizations as social networks. *Journal of Construction Engineering and Management*, 136(4), 452–458.

Citroen, C. L. (2011). The role of information in strategic decision-making. *International Journal of Information Management*, 31(6), 493–501.

Davis, K. (2012). *Ethics of Big Data: Balancing risk and innovation*. O'Reilly Media.

Engwall, M. (2003). No project is an island: Linking projects to history and context. *Research Policy*, 32(5), 789–808.

Gidado, K. (1996). Project complexity: The focal point of construction production planning. *Construction Management and Economics*, 14(3), 213–225.

Hanisch, B. & Wald, A. (2011). A project management research framework integrating multiple theoretical perspectives and influencing factors. *Project Management Journal*, 42(3), 4–22.

Hartmann, T., Fischer, M. & Haymaker, J. (2009). Implementing information systems with project teams using ethnographic–action research. *Advanced Engineering Informatics*, 23(1), 57–67.

Kazaz, A., Ulubeyli, S. & Arslan, A. (2020). Quantification of fresh ready-mix concrete waste: Order and truck-mixer based planning coefficients. *International Journal of Construction Management*, 20(1), 53–64.

Kitchin, R. (2014). The real-time city? Big data and smart urbanism. *GeoJournal*, 79(1), 1–14.

LaValle, S., Lesser, E., Shockley, R., Hopkins, M. S. & Kruschwitz, N. (2011). Big data, analytics and the path from insights to value. *MIT Sloan Management Review*, 52(2), 21–32.

Lu, W., Chen, X., Ho, D. C. & Wang, H. (2016). Analysis of the construction waste management performance in Hong Kong: The public and private sectors compared using big data. *Journal of Cleaner Production*, 112, 521–531.

Lu, W., Xu, J. & Söderlund, J. (2020). Exploring the effects of building information modeling on Projects: Longitudinal social network analysis. *Journal of Construction Engineering and Management*, 146(5), 04020037.

Lu, W., Yuan, L. & Xue, F. (2021). Investigating the bulk density of construction waste: A big data-driven approach. *Resources, Conservation and Recycling*, 169, 105480.

Lv, Z., Li, X., Lv, H. & Xiu, W. (2019). BIM big data storage in WebVRGIS. *IEEE Transactions on Industrial Informatics*, 16(4), 2566–2573.

Mayer-Schönberger, V. & Cukier, K. (2013). *Big data: A revolution that will transform how we live, work, and think*. Houghton Mifflin Harcourt.

McAfee, A., Brynjolfsson, E., Davenport, T. H., Patil, D. & Barton, D. (2012). Big data: The management revolution. *Harvard Business Review*, 90(10), 60–68.

Padhy, R. P. (2013). Big data processing with Hadoop-MapReduce in cloud systems. *International Journal of Cloud Computing and Services Science*, 2(1), 16–27.

Poon, C. S., Yu, A. T. W., See, S. C. & Cheung, E. (2004). Minimizing demolition wastes in Hong Kong public housing projects. *Construction Management and Economics*, 22(8), 799–805.

Pryke, S. (2012). *Social network analysis in construction*. John Wiley & Sons.

Russom, P. (2011). *Big data analytics: TDWI best practices report*. Data Warehousing Institute.

Simon, H. A. (1997). *Models of bounded rationality, Vol. 3: Empirically grounded economic reason*. MIT Press.

Skoyles, E. (1976). Materials wastage: A misuse of resources. *Batiment International, Building Research and Practice*, 4(4), 232–243.

Söderlund, J. (2011). Pluralism in project management: Navigating the crossroads of specialization and fragmentation. *International Journal of Management Reviews*, 13(2), 153–176.

Stark, E., Bierly, P. & Harper, S. R. (2014). The interactive influences of conflict, task interdependence and cooperation on perceptions of virtualness in co-located teams. *Team Performance Management*, 20(5/6), 221–241.

Turner, J. R. & Müller, R. (2003). On the nature of the project as a temporary organization. *International Journal of Project Management*, 21(1), 1–8.

Vinten, G. (1994). Participant observation: A model for organizational investigation? *Journal of Managerial Psychology*, 9(2), 30–38.

Wang, H., Xu, Z., Fujita, H. & Liu, S. (2016). Towards felicitous decision making: An overview on challenges and trends of Big Data. *Information Sciences*, 367, 747–765.

Wang, H., Lu, W., Söderlund, J. & Chen, K. (2018). The interplay between formal and informal institutions in projects. *Project Management Journal*, 49(4), 20–35.

Whyte, J., Stasis, A. & Lindkvist, C. (2016). Managing change in the delivery of complex projects: Configuration management, asset information and 'big data'. *International Journal of Project Management*, 34(2), 339–351.

Winch, G. M. (1989). The construction firm and the construction project: A transaction cost approach. *Construction Management and Economics*, 7(4), 331–345.

Winch, G. M. (2014). Three domains of project organising. *International Journal of Project Management*, 32(5), 721–731.

Winch, G. M. (2015). Project organising as a problem in information. *Construction Management and Economics*, 33(2), 106–116.

Xu, J., Lu, W., Ye, M., Webster, C. & Xue, F. (2020a). An anatomy of waste generation flows in construction projects using passive bigger data. *Waste Management*, 106, 162–172.

Xu, J., Lu, W., Ye, M., Xue, F., Zhang, X. & Lee, B. F. P. (2020b). Is the private sector more efficient? Big data analytics of construction waste management sectoral efficiency. *Resources, Conservation and Recycling*, 155, 104674.

Xu, J., Lu, W. & Papadonikolaki, E. (2022). Human-Organization-Technology (HOT) fit model for BIM adoption in construction project organizations: Impact factor analysis using social network analysis and comparative case study. *Journal of Management in Engineering* 38(3), 04022004.

Yuan, L., Lu, W. & Xue, F. (2021). Estimation of construction waste composition based on bulk density: A big data-probability (BD-P) model. *Journal of Environmental Management*, 292, 112822.

37. A management flight simulator to catalyse learning about complex projects

Burak Gozluklu and John Sterman

37.1 SIMULATING THE DYNAMICS OF COMPLEX PROJECTS

Projects large and small are chronically LEW: late, expensive, and wrong (fail to meet quality standards and customer requirements). These problems persist even though organizations have never had more frameworks, tools, and data to help manage projects more effectively. The prevalence and persistence of poor project performance, spanning projects large and small, commercial and military, hardware and software, mean the problem cannot be due to the peculiarities of any particular technology or industry, and cannot be blamed on the poor decisions of a 'few bad apples'. Chapter 7 describes the feedback processes that lead to poor outcomes, including productivity and quality decline from failure to account for, and delays in, the discovery of errors and rework, rapid unplanned hiring, fatigue and employee turnover from excessive overtime, work done out of sequence, and corner cutting in project work, quality assurance, and testing. The system dynamics perspective, consistent with decades of research in the social sciences, emphasizes that the structure of the systems in which we are embedded powerfully conditions our behaviour. But the complexity of the systems in which we are embedded far exceeds our ability to understand the many feedbacks and interactions that create their dynamics. Instead, people facing intense pressure to hit aggressive cost, schedule, and quality targets often make decisions in good faith that, while helpful in the short run, worsen performance later, further intensifying the pressures they face.

To explore these hypotheses and provide insight into effective policies to manage complex projects, here we examine results from the *MIT Sloan Project Management Simulator* (https://forio.com/app/mit/project-management). In this interactive management flight simulator individuals play the role of managers for a complex project. Users can select projects representing a new consumer product, software, or construction, and the simulation can be customized to other settings. The simulation represents two main phases, design and prototype/build. In each simulated week, participants make decisions including schedule and staffing for each phase, whether to accept late customer feature requests or reduce scope, alter the degree of concurrent development, or pressure the workforce for faster progress or higher quality. Figure 37.1 shows the main interface. The tabs provide users with detailed feedback on key performance indicators including progress, current and projected costs, productivity, and rework, along with emails from the simulated organization's engineering, quality assurance, human resources, and marketing departments – and the chief executive officer.

Here we report the results with managers using the version of the simulation calibrated to represent the development of a new consumer product. The deadline is 48 weeks and the initial budget is $33 million – goals that can be achieved while delivering excellent quality. To capture late specification changes, we assume marketing proposes new features stochastically at a rate averaging 20 per cent of the initial project scope per year (the budget rises for each

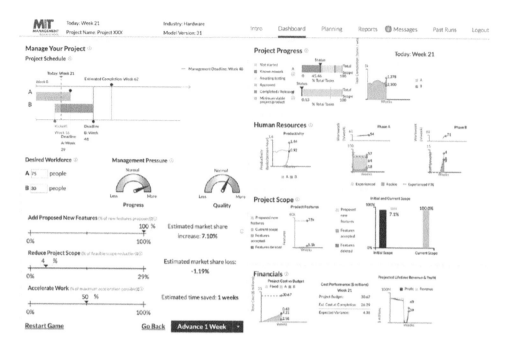

Figure 37.1   Top-level interface of the MIT Sloan Project Management Simulator

new feature accepted). The commercial success of the product depends on time to market, the scope delivered, and product quality: releasing the product late, without the latest features, or with many defects erodes revenue; cost overruns raise development costs, and low quality drives up warranty costs.

37.1.1   A Tale of Two Managers

To illustrate, we simulate two project managers: reactive and proactive. Both use the same information to manage their projects. The simulated managers cannot use information about the future, such as when marketing will demand late specification changes, or how many team members will quit each week. They do not know how large the stock of unknown defects is until testing discovers them. Neither simulated manager is assumed to behave optimally. Instead, they use behavioural decision rules (Sterman, 2000) to make decisions.

The reactive manager staffs initially at the level indicated by the initial scope, deadline, and worker productivity, then continuously monitors the project, adjusting hiring to meet the deadline given the work remaining, time remaining, and reported worker productivity. The reactive manager expects the team will handle any rework that may be discovered with overtime, and does not account for the reinforcing feedbacks that can result from fatigue, corner cutting, cuts in testing, increasing concurrency, and so on. The reactive manager accepts all new features proposed by marketing.

The proactive manager anticipates the possibility of late changes and unplanned rework and therefore staffs initially with more people, for both phases, than initially indicated. The proactive manager also monitors the project closely, including known rework, schedule pressure,

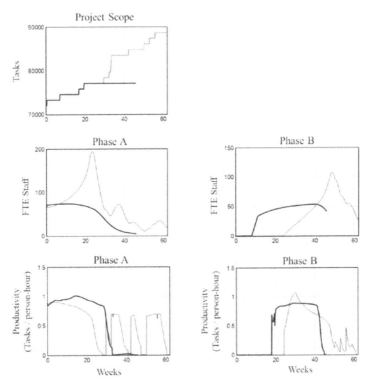

Note: Phase A: Design; Phase B: Prototype/build; FTE = full-time equivalent.

Figure 37.2   *Project evolution for simulated proactive (black) and reactive (grey)*
managers

and the workweek, and adjusts staffing to avoid pressure on workers to cut corners or testing. Finally, the proactive manager accepts new feature requests early in the design phase but, to avoid excessive rework, rejects them as design proceeds.

Figure 37.2 shows the dynamics. By accepting late change requests, the reactive manager finds the design staff is inadequate, and hires more people to stay on schedule. But the unplanned hiring increases the rookie fraction, lowering productivity and increasing errors. Progress slows, requiring still more hiring, further eroding experience. Schedule pressure builds. In response, the design team works longer hours, causing fatigue that eventually erodes productivity and quality, and increases worker attrition. Progress slows further, forcing still more hiring. High schedule pressure causes the team to cut corners and testing, speeding apparent progress but increasing defect creation and slowing defect detection. The eventual discovery of these defects forces even more late hiring. The design staff peaks many times above the initial level late in the design phase, quality is low, and cuts in testing cause many defects to be released to the prototype/build phase. The dynamics there are similar: with so many defects inherited from design, the prototype/build staff proves to be too small, forcing overtime and unplanned hiring. The reinforcing feedbacks described above work as vicious cycles, and the project finishes late, over budget, with poor quality and many defects released to the customer.

In contrast, the proactive manager immediately builds the design staff above the indicated level to create the capacity to handle rework and late feature requests without excessive overtime, corner cutting, or cuts in testing. Late feature requests are accepted only until most of the high-level design work is done, but none afterwards. The proactive manager also builds the staff for the prototype/build phase early and above the initially indicated level. The better-rested, more experienced team is more productive and does higher-quality work. They also inherit fewer defects from design, boosting their productivity and speeding progress as fewer tasks are returned to the design team for rework. Consequently, the prototype/build staff peaks at about half the level of the reactive manager's project. The feedback structure in the two cases is the same, but the vicious cycles triggered by the reactive manager remain far weaker, or entirely dormant, for the proactive manager.

Comparing project outcomes (Figure 37.3), the reactive manager delivers the project 13 weeks late, a 27 per cent schedule overrun, at a cost of $50 million, 40 per cent over the final budget. Final product quality is low, with about 5.3 per cent of the features in the project scope defective. Being so late to market with such poor quality causes the product to flop in the marketplace. The company loses approximately $38 million. In contrast, the proactive manager delivers the project more than a week early, about 1 per cent under budget, and with a defect rate of 1.67 per cent, 69 per cent lower than the reactive manager. As a result the product does well in the market and is highly profitable, netting $45 million in lifetime profit.

The results are illustrative, and represent particular assumptions about the project, workforce, and the market's response to delivery times and quality. Extensive sensitivity analysis, not shown, shows these patterns to be robust across a wide range of these assumptions.

Note that the proactive manager's results are not optimal. Rather, they arise from realistic behavioural decision rules, based on information available to real project managers. The

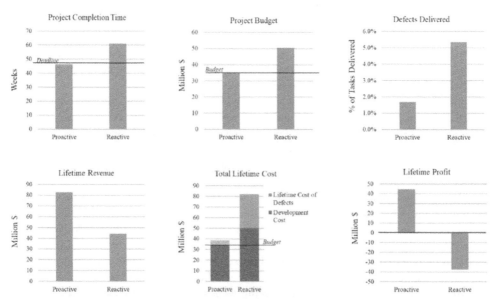

Figure 37.3   Reactive versus proactive project outcomes

simulated proactive manager's results thus represent a realistic benchmark for performance. Optimal performance is even higher.

37.2 EXPERIMENTAL RESULTS WITH EXPERIENCED MANAGERS

We use the MIT Sloan Project Management Simulation to help people, from undergraduates and MBA students to experienced managers, learn about the dynamics of complex projects. Here we report the performance of seasoned managers and engineers, many with extensive experience with complex projects in successful organizations. The participants were enrolled in an online executive education programme on systems thinking offered by MIT. After exposure to various approaches to systems thinking and systems engineering, including the management of complex projects, they ran the project simulation using the product development scenario. Participants could play as many times as they liked, then summarized the lessons they learned in a memo to their superior describing how their real organization should scope and manage projects in the future.

Figure 37.4 reports the results from a session with 269 participants held in July 2020. We focus on results from the participants' first simulation, as it best reveals their initial mental models about how to manage projects effectively. Overall, participants did poorly. For time to market, 85.5 per cent performed worse than the proactive benchmark, and 2.6 per cent were worse than the reactive benchmark. Approximately 73 per cent had costs higher than the proactive benchmark, and 4.8 per cent had higher costs than the reactive benchmark. Only 15.6 per cent released the product to the public with fewer defects than the proactive benchmark, and 58.7 per cent released the product with more defects than the reactive benchmark.

Of course, there are tradeoffs among schedule, cost, and quality. Delivering the project earlier through extensive overtime and corner cutting degrades quality; improving quality may raise costs. Overall performance on schedule, cost, and quality determine the success of the project. Shockingly, none of the participants outperformed the proactive benchmark on all three metrics. Fewer than 12 per cent did better on two. Worse, the reactive manager outperformed 64.3 per cent of the participants on at least one metric.

Critically, participants focused on schedule and cost at the expense of quality. On average, participants' projects were 4.5 per cent late and 8.2 per cent over budget, but the average project was launched with an 11.3 per cent defect rate, more than twice the rate achieved by the reactive manager and nearly seven times higher than the proactive manager. Such poor quality dooms the product in the marketplace. Schedule and cost are highly salient and feedback on them is continuously available, whereas quality is harder to assess. Like the reactive manager (Figure 37.2), participants who focused on controlling cost and hitting the schedule caused initial understaffing, excessive overtime, late hiring, corner cutting, inadequate testing, and other impacts that trigger the vicious cycles that lead to significant delay, disruption, and quality degradation.

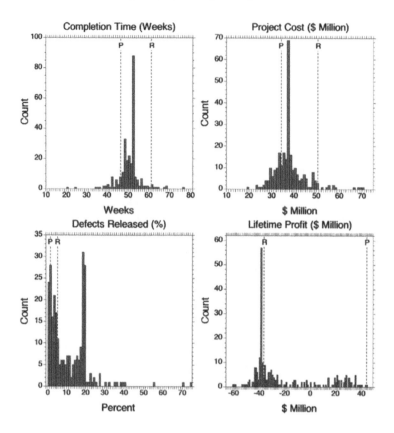

Figure 37.4   Participant results (N = 269) for schedule, cost, quality, and lifetime profit, compared to the reactive (R) and proactive (P) benchmarks

37.3   IMPLICATIONS FOR COMPLEX PROJECT ORGANIZING

Project managers commonly overestimate productivity and work quality, often assuming there will be little or no rework, and request budgets and timelines that are inadequate. Relentless cost pressure means project managers are given smaller budgets and less time than they request and told to 'do more with less'. Consequently, projects often begin with unrealistically aggressive deadlines and inadequate resources and staff. The rush to complete the project as quickly as possible leads the project to start with an ill-defined scope, increasing the number of late scope changes imposed by customers, marketing, and project team members themselves. Schedule pressure builds, leading to excessive overtime and rapid unplanned hiring, triggering fatigue, corner cutting, inadequate testing, more work done out of sequence, and other impacts that slow progress, further eroding progress and leading to still more overtime, late hiring, and so on. These reinforcing feedbacks, described in Chapter 7, become vicious cycles causing extensive delay and disruption. The project is delivered late, over budget, with low quality, and often, serious, even life-threatening defects released to the customer. Examples abound, including GM's defective ignition switches, Merck's Vioxx, Pfizer's Bextra, the Samsung Note 7, and the Boeing 737 Max 8.

Facing pressure to control costs, managers tend to rely first on overtime, hiring additional people only later. Doing so harms the project in multiple ways: extended overtime leads to fatigue, higher error rates, less effective testing, and increased attrition, requiring even more late hiring. Late, unplanned hiring dilutes experience, increases coordination problems, and leads to worksite congestion, degrading project performance before people can gain sufficient experience, build new networks of collaboration and trust, and optimize the worksite.

In contrast, superior performance requires decisions that are highly counterintuitive. Projects should be staffed initially at much higher levels to provide the resources needed to address rework and late specification changes, and thus limit overtime, corner cutting, inadequate testing, and other harms these actions trigger. Detailed design should not start until the scope is firm, and late changes should not be accepted at all, or, if accepted, only during high-level design. Costs are initially higher, but lower overall.

Cutting corners or testing should never be tolerated. But building norms for high quality requires resources and staffing sufficient to prevent pressures causing people to cut corners and compromise testing, and then hide these decisions from others, creating a 'Liar's Club' (Ford & Sterman, 2003).

Why don't people learn to avoid these pathologies? Why don't more organizations provide their projects with sufficient resources and realistic schedules, avoid late changes, and create incentives, norms, and systems that prevent corner cutting and inadequate testing?

First, project performance depends on the non-linear interaction of multiple feedbacks, accumulations, and time delays. The mental models and software tools people use to manage projects often fail to include these critical feedbacks. Even if they did, the complexity of these interactions is far greater than people's ability to simulate them mentally. Instead, people tend to blame trouble on suppliers, customers, poor-quality workers, or other 'bad apples', not the complex feedback system in which well-intentioned, capable people are embedded, a system that creates powerful pressures that shape people's behaviour.

Second, the outcome feedback people receive systematically perpetuates poor mental models and blaming behaviour. Projects in trouble often trigger firefighting, with a few workers and managers working heroically to save the project (Repenning, 2000, 2001). Such heroes are likely to be promoted, reinforcing culture and norms that reward firefighting. But where do these heroes get the time and resources needed to fight the fire? The answer is often cutting corners, testing, and quality; poaching people from other projects; and failing to document their work, coordinate with others, coach and mentor trainees, and invest in the capabilities needed for long-run success. The benefits of firefighting are immediate and highly visible, while the costs are diffuse and delayed. Firefighters who succeed will be rewarded and promoted, while the organizational capabilities needed to prevent future fires erode further, creating a capability trap (Repenning & Sterman, 2002). In contrast, building the capabilities for effective project management increases short-run costs to individuals, even as doing so prevents costly project failures later. As one executive explained, 'Nobody ever gets rewarded for solving problems that never happened' (Repenning & Sterman, 2001).

These pathologies cannot be solved solely by more sophisticated tools that improve the productivity and management of complex projects, including automation, digitization, and artificial intelligence. Without a paradigm change in the mental models and behaviours of managers and workers, productivity and cycle time gains from technological innovation will simply lead to even more complex projects, more aggressive schedules, and tighter budgets. No matter how good our technology, pressure to 'do more with less, faster' will keep causing projects to be launched with inadequate resources, triggering schedule pressure, unplanned overtime and hiring, fatigue and skill dilution, corner cutting, and insufficient testing.

Indeed, despite unprecedented technological progress since the age of the pyramids, projects today continue to be late, expensive, and wrong, often with disastrous consequences. The designers of the Swedish warship Vasa, which sank 1638 minutes into its maiden voyage, drowning approximately 150 people, would hardly recognize a modern vessel, and would be amazed by our aircraft. But they would understand well the intense pressures to meet aggressive targets that led to the crash of two 737 Max 8 aircraft minutes after takeoff, killing 346.

What is required to catalyse that paradigm change? Important questions for research and education remain. How much management simulation experience is needed to catalyse meaningful learning? How can people learn generalizable lessons that transfer from one project to settings with different scope, timeline, budgets, and market pressures? What kinds of feedback and coaching will help participants improve their understanding of complex project dynamics and use those insights in real projects? Simulation has long been essential to design and test complex systems, and to train people to operate them safely. It is even more important to use simulation to design better project management processes and help people learn how to manage complex projects safely and effectively. System dynamics provides the framework, simulation methods and models, and successful examples to help organizations transform the management of complex projects.

REFERENCES

Ford, D. & Sterman, J. D. (2003). The Liar's Club: Concealing rework in concurrent development. *Concurrent Engineering: Research and Applications*, 11(3), 211–220.

Repenning, N. (2000). A dynamic model of resource allocation in multi-project research and development systems. *System Dynamics Review*, 16(3), 173–212.

Repenning, N. (2001). Understanding fire fighting in new product development. *Journal of Product Innovation Management*, 18(5), 285–300.

Repenning, N. & Sterman, J. (2001). Nobody ever gets credit for fixing problems that never happened: Creating and sustaining process improvement. *California Management Review*, 43(4), 64–88.

Repenning, N. & Sterman, J. (2002). Capability traps and self-confirming attribution errors in the dynamics of process improvement. *Administrative Science Quarterly*, 47(2), 265–295.

Sterman, J. (2000). *Business dynamics: Systems thinking and modeling for a complex world*. Irwin/McGraw-Hill.

38. The digital revolution and complex project organizing: towards Project Management 4.0?

Jennifer Whyte, Karim Farghaly and Shanjing Zhou (Alexander)

38.1 INTRODUCTION

Digital information is now pervasive in project organizing, and changing how projects are delivered (Whyte, 2019). Consider how a project manager works at their laptop, checks details on their smartphone, talks to the designer, and texts the site manager. The exponential growth in computing power since 1950 (Brynjolfsson & McAfee, 2014) has profoundly changed project delivery practices. Today, project professionals all use digital information in their individual and collective work, continually adapting and incorporating new hardware, software, standards and data into their ongoing practice. Digital innovation becomes self-referential and is, according to some scholars, accelerating (Dodgson et al., 2005; Yoo et al., 2010). Here, we consider the question: What challenges and opportunities are posed by digitalization in complex project organizing?

There is increasing interest in the idea of Project Management 4.0 (PM4.0). In this chapter, we seek to explicitly engage with the World Economic Forum narrative of Industry 4.0 (Schwab, 2015) to critically examine PM4.0's explanatory and performative power, and consider the primary theoretical and practical challenges of complex project organizing in this era. Thus, we extend the work on digitally enabled project management, discussed in Whyte and Levitt (2011), Levitt (2011) and Whyte (2019). However, given the differing origins of work characterizing a shift from PM1.0 to PM2.0, and this work on Industry 4.0 and PM4.0, we do not try to extend the previous schema.

Section 38.2 discusses the different framing and understanding of increasing digitalization. Section 38.3 examines how, in the context of Industry 4.0 and PM4.0, digital information helps and hinders in addressing uncertainty, complexity, temporality and productivity, and ultimately in delivering good outcomes. Section 38.4 discusses the new forms of integration that we see arising, and we conclude by summarizing the major challenges and opportunities we see as posed by digitalization in complex project organizing and suggest directions for further research.

38.2 FRAMING AND UNDERSTANDING INCREASING DIGITALIZATION

There are a number of approaches to framing and understanding increasing digitalization of organizational practice. With a focus on projects, and how their delivery is changing, Levitt (2011) and Whyte and Levitt (2011) characterize the growth of formal project management techniques in the mid-twentieth century as PM1.0. Formal methods such as the Program

Evaluation Review Technique and the critical path method were developed using early computing on complex projects. These formal methods relied on up-front planning, hierarchical work breakdown structures and tracking variance from plans to manage complexity. However, Levitt (2011) and Whyte and Levitt (2011) suggest that increasing digitization in the early twenty-first century enables a reformulation of project organizing and management as PM2.0, using the more agile decentralized digitally enabled approaches enabled by the Internet, and particularly Web2.0 and associated technologies.

An alternative framing at the level of an economy is as a digital era, wave, revolution or age, where such patterns of technological change can be traced across a broad time horizon back to the (first) industrial revolution. Economists of innovation articulate and delineate the contours of such technological eras (where these may span across years, decades or centuries), using diverse numbering systems. For example, in work on the long waves of innovation, digital innovation is characterized as the fifth of five long waves since the industrial revolution (Freeman & Louçã, 2001; Freeman & Perez, 1988). Here, each wave involves a general-purpose technology having a pervasive impact across economic sectors over many decades.

More recently the notion of 'Industry 4.0' has grown in international interest, taken up by the World Economic Forum (Schwab, 2015), and with origins in German industrial policy (Xu et al., 2018). Like the work of Freeman and his colleagues, this framing sets out a number of eras. These are initiated by industrial revolutions, with a first revolution of mechanization, steam and water power (~1760–1840); a second of mass production and electricity (late nineteenth–early twentieth century); a third of electronic and information technology systems and automation (1960s onwards); and a fourth, currently experienced, of cyberphysical systems (CPS) (Schwab, 2015, 2017). Such a framing does not only purport to explain the past, but it is also used instrumentally as a call to government and industry action, attracting resources toward the development of particular futures. In project management, work has begun to explore the relationships between projects and Industry 4.0.

While such temporal bracketing can be useful in theorizing change over time (Langley, 1999), there are significant areas for evidence-based contestation around interpretations of the history of technology-enabled organizing.

First, work to enumerate and characterize technological change as observed in eras, waves, revolutions or ages has been criticized for its inconsistency in the number and labelling of different episodes of change. For example, Brynjolfsson and McAfee (2014), who Schwab approvingly cites, characterize ours as a second machine age, with brilliant digital technologies (with the first machine age being the industrial revolution). Hence, innovation scholars characterize technological history since the late eighteenth century, in relation to five waves (Freeman & Louçã, 2001; Freeman & Perez, 1988), four revolutions (Schwab, 2015, 2017) and two ages (Brynjolfsson & McAfee, 2014). This lack of agreement does not matter where individual studies are insightful, but suggests that scholars do not agree on a set of criteria for identifying what is historically significant, seeking instead to characterize and draw attention to different phenomena.

Second, and more substantively, this approach to economic history is also criticized by Edgerton (2011), who argues these characterizations of history wrongly suggest inevitability of outcomes, overemphasizing progress, homogeneity and novelty, and under-recognizing the rich mix of generations of technologies-in-use over time (with technological choices and contestations and a diversity of practices across industries, some also becoming less high tech over time). Third, and relatedly, there is growing recognition that the field of innovation studies needs to question assumptions of progress, where such work under-recognizes the detrimental effects of innovation (Coad et al., 2021), and also the potential for agency and technological choice in directing the nature of technological change.

There is a need for social scientists to unpack these narratives, particularly where they are influential in shaping futures. Such work has begun in industries that are organized through complex projects, such as construction, with critical scholars asking questions about the relationship between Industry 4.0 and social equity, for example regarding gender inclusivity (Barrett, 2020), and the changing balance of power between the 'technology owner', professionals and trade unions (Sherratt et al., 2020). At different levels of analysis – from the overall economy or innovation system to particular economic sectors, industries, practices or projects, there is a need to move beyond single narratives to better understand the differentiated effects of digitalization of organizing, and the performative as well as descriptive role of characterizations of technological change in policy.

38.3   PROJECT ORGANIZING IN AN ERA OF PROJECT MANAGEMENT 4.0

In an era of PM4.0, digitalization is integrating and transforming practices within the project, across organizational and project boundaries, and into the use of the systems delivered by the project. In this section, we present the timeline of digital technologies and techniques adopted and implemented on mega projects over the past six decades (Table 38.1) as an organizing device for initiating a conversation about how these technologies – especially the ones associated with Industry 4.0 – can benefit project organizing. Before we turn our attention to their integrative role, in the next section, we are interested here in how, in the context of Industry 4.0 and PM4.0, digital information helps and hinders in addressing uncertainty, complexity, temporality and productivity, and ultimately in delivering good outcomes.

38.3.1   Outlining the Developments in Hardware, Software and Capabilities

Information management technologies and techniques have played a core role in the history of the development of project management. Whyte and Levitt (2011) defined information management as the activities involved in shaping the flow of data, information and knowledge, not the physical materials. Table 38.1 illustrates developments in the hardware and software technologies and capabilities for information management in projects over the last six decades.

The last two columns for the last two decades are an extension of the table presented by Whyte and Levitt (2011). In 2010, the hardware technologies concentrated on capturing real-time data through smartphones, point cloud scanners, and sensors. The software technologies were mainly to integrate the data from different sources and systems, and analyse and visualize the data for data-driven decision making (Brynjolfsson & McElheran, 2016). In 2020, the wave of technology concentrated on connecting the physical asset and digital asset and the use of information to drive the design and build of our economic and social infrastructure and the operation and integration of the services they deliver (Chen et al., 2021).

The capabilities of these hardware and software technologies associated with Industry 4.0 have stimulated project managers' requirements towards their project information manage-

Table 38.1   Developments in hardware, software and capabilities

	1970s	1980s	1990s	2000s	2010s	2020s
Hardware	Bitmapped screens; computer graphics	First personal computers	Laptops; Internet; first mobile computing	Mobile computing; sensors; electronic paper	Smartphone; 3D printers; point cloud scanners; sensors; 3G evolution	Control rooms; autonomous robots; drones
Software	Standards, protocols, and processes, e.g. IDEF0; capability maturity model	PC-based computer-aided design and project management; simulation; Internet	Automated digital search; expert systems; project extranets	Visual decision-making tools; shared workspaces	Semantic web and linked data; data mining and machine learning tools and techniques	Platforms; digital twin; streaming and integrating real-time data; blockchain
New capabilities	Text processing; widespread engineering automation; sharing of information	Diffusion of computers to smaller firms and individuals; knowledge formalization	Share information and knowledge across teams and firms	Agile, decentralized development methods; using centralized data storage and applications	Data analytics and data mining; instant communications; managing cyberphysical systems; simulation of process and product	Extensive remote, and hybrid (in-person and remote) working; insights definition; data-driven decision making; resilient platforms

Source: Adapted and extended from Whyte and Levitt (2011).

ment. Digital innovation is increasingly integrating practices across organizational and project boundaries. As digital information is shareable, accessible remotely, searchable and updateable (Whyte, 2019), it is enabling new forms of integration across project boundaries, including with other projects and with stakeholders in the innovation system, such as standard providers, government and technology providers.

38.3.2   Technologies Associated with Project Management 4.0

Within this landscape, some recent technologies that are in widespread use in projects have become associated with PM4.0. Reviewing the literature, we find that for Industry 4.0, the underlying technology is represented by CPS, which provides an ability to interact with and expand the capabilities of the physical world through computation and control (Baheti & Gill, 2011). Certainly, when CPS connect over the Internet of Things, they connect physical assets, human actors, machines and processes across organizational boundaries and enable the blend of the physical and virtual worlds for decentralized decision-making processes (Trappey et al., 2017).

   There are also other digital technologies that have emerged as Industry 4.0 enablers. For example, Ciano et al. (2021) utilized big data and analytics and specifically descriptive diagnostics to store, manage and display key performance indicators updated in real time on visual boards. This has been used during five-minute meetings to empower employee commitment. Despite that, project managers can argue that most of the problems faced pertain to people rather than technology, and artificial intelligence and analytics applications could still help to overcome these problems by (1) reducing the repetitive tasks, (2) tracking and suggesting particular communication with engaged stakeholders and (3) tracking the network structure of internal communications looking for gaps and issues (Niederman, 2021). Another enabler technology is blockchain, which shifts the nature of trust in supply chains (Qian & Papadonikolaki, 2021), sources of real-time and trustworthy information (Lee et al., 2021) and a valuable secured source of lessons learned and future analysis.

Despite all the proposed benefits of Industry 4.0 enablers technologies can provide to project organizing, scholars also raise concerns about uptake. Niederman (2021) argues that managers of non-information technology projects are unlikely to create an environment for adopting artificial intelligence enablers technologies and they will not learn the intricacies of implementing these technologies. Consequently, Industry 4.0 remains on the abstract level with few implementations in mega projects (Zheng et al., 2021). Therefore, there is a need for scientists and software vendors to overcome this challenge by providing: (1) more agile project management approaches, with shortened planning horizons and more involvement and communication with the stakeholders (Camci & Kotnour, 2019); (2) a solution including both the technologies and processes including a transversal and integrated use of digital technologies (Zheng et al., 2021); and (3) awareness of the solution utilized by the entire project delivery team to the extent necessary to ensure the solution is integrated and enables automation of the overall project delivery process (Whitmore et al., 2020).

In an era of PM4.0, the digitalization enabled by these technologies is integrating and transforming practices within the project. Thus, rather than focus on how digital information is transforming specific stages or practices in project delivery, we argue for the need for work that broadly considers digital practices across complex projects and their impact on project management.

38.4   PROJECT MANAGEMENT 4.0 AND NEW FORMS OF INTEGRATION (AND DISINTEGRATION)

New forms of integration are arising. We see pervasive digital information as generally integrative, enabling new forms of connectivity, such as enhancing traceability across supply chains or connecting data from operators, owners and users into project analytics. In this section, we use example practices to discuss how emerging digitally enabled forms of integration (and disaggregation) break the assumptions of traditional models, and to characterize the new questions that arise.

While there is substantial work on how digital innovation transforms work within a project delivery stage or task, we are interested in how it integrates across multiple practices. These practices increasingly involve combinations of emerging technologies such as digitally enabled product platforms, Internet of Things, artificial intelligence and blockchain. Separately and together, such technologies have implications for project delivery models, changing organizational, contractual and governance structures. Depending on the technologies used, and how they are implemented in practice, digital innovation may increase managerial control (Çıdık & Boyd, 2020; Çıdık et al., 2017; Whyte & Lobo, 2010) or lead to greater decentralization

(Hunhevicz & Hall, 2020; Li et al., 2019). We thus consider what we know about the practices of using these technologies, and the potential empirical questions that arise from a digital construction practice perspective.

38.4.1 Across Project Delivery Stages

As digital innovation integrates practices across project delivery stages, what is done within each project stage cannot be assumed to be fixed. Contrasts, contradictions and tensions arise between contractual arrangements, which agree in advance the work and when it is done, and how work is practised. Thus, empirical questions arise about how the product delivery stages are and might become reordered, integrated and transformed, as digital practices change the relative difficulty and duration of different tasks. Extant work describe how technologies such as building information modelling (BIM) shift the locus of work, enabling more information to be generated earlier, ahead of critical design decisions, and how distributed ledger (or block-chain) technologies can enable more decentralized decision making, as they enable tracing and keeping a distributed record of transactions (Li et al., 2019).

The boundaries of the digital infrastructure for delivery become important. Where digital systems are shared across first-tier suppliers, and more tightly couple their work, they may still exclude the supply chain (Whyte, 2013). They may alternatively bring new forms of collaboration across customers and supply chains (Lindgren & Widén, 2018; Love et al., 2002; Papadonikolaki & Wamelink, 2017; Papadonikolaki et al., 2016). For example, smart contracts driven by distributed ledger technologies can also potentially reinforce trust and transparency, and reduce transactions costs in procurement and suppliers (Li et al., 2019). Rather than describe how BIM should be a 'single source of truth' or single model on a project, the work on digital practice shows how diverse practices continue to proliferate and become more or less aligned with mandated technologies on projects.

38.4.2 Across Organizational and Project Boundaries

Digital information is becoming shared across projects. For example, the practices around digitally enabled product platforms enable modules to be reused and recombined across projects. Digitally enabled product platforms are defined as 'a set of assets organized in a common structure from which a company can efficiently develop and produce a stream of derivative products' (Gawer & Cusumano, 2014, p. 418). In construction, we are beginning to see uptake of these product platforms for industrialized construction, as these become used to create and configure a kit-of-parts of modular components using digital technologies. An example of a firm adopting such product platforms to reuse design effort across projects is the design firm Bryden Wood. Rather than putting design effort in at the project level, this firm has been developing platforms for schools, offices and health and residential facilities using digitally enabled workflows and tools (Bryden Wood, 2018, p. 69). A similar approach is being taken by the Construction Innovation Hub, which was set up with government funding in the United Kingdom (UK), and is developing new kinds of integrated software to support the use of product platforms (Mosca et al., 2020) in government-funded projects.

Digital innovation also brings projects into contact with other stakeholders in the innovation system. Work on the adaptation of the industry process standards shows both their transformation effects, but also the unstable nature of their adoption because the systemic linkages across a set of evolving standards introduces contradictions, which have to be worked out in practice, where one standard mandates one process for using BIM and another a different process (Maradza, 2015). These connections are not always anticipated by software developers and implementers, and may bring different stakeholders into view. Whyte and Levitt (2011) give the example of how a global community was mobilized in the social media campaign to rehouse wild cats in the London 2012 Olympics site.

Digital innovation is also mandated and promoted by the public sector, and projects have to respond to these developments. New approaches to construction are advocated in many countries, with modern methods of construction using a range of modular design, product platforms and off-site (near-site and on-site) manufacturing methods as well as increasingly automating on-site assembly. There are policy initiatives to promote such innovative new forms of delivery in many countries, for example in the UK (HM Government, 2018, 2020), China (MOHURD, 2020) and Singapore (BCA, 2018, 2020), as well as through the World Economic Forum (WEF, 2016). Digital innovation is central to these initiatives, and the policy interest recognizes that systemic innovation requires new forms of integration across organizational boundaries.

38.4.3   Across Projects and Use

Digital innovation is integrating practices across the boundary between projects and use, enabling new forms of integration with a richer dialogue across, and integration between, operations and delivery, and with clients and end users. For example, OFWAT, the UK water regulator, encourages companies such as Anglian Water to take an 'outcomes' rather than an 'outputs' focus by considering the operational outcome that may be solved through a project first, and then deciding the nature and scope of the project.

Project deliverables are now dual – physical and digital – where physical deliverables embed sensors and devices and digital data becomes a valuable deliverable for use in operations as well as construction. There is increasing practical interest in digital twins (e.g. Lu et al., 2020; Zhang et al., 2022), which we define as extending BIM by modelling the performance as well as geometry and asset information and updating either in real time or in ways that allow experimentation with future scenarios.

With the data bridging across project construction into operations (Whyte et al., 2016), the use of a digital twin in operations has implications for delivery, and raises new questions about how the information is structured for use in, and made useable within, practices.

38.5   DISCUSSION AND CONCLUSIONS

In this chapter we extend work on paradigms of digitally enabled project management, from PM1.0 and PM2.0 discussed in Whyte and Levitt (2011) and Levitt (2011), to consider the key characteristics of PM4.0 and primary challenges of project organizing in the era of PM4.0. Project processes and their outputs and outcomes are now conceptualized first in the computer and then materialized.

In an era of PM4.0, digitalization is integrating and transforming practices within the project, across organizational and project boundaries, and into the use of the systems delivered by the project. This integration is both a challenge and an opportunity posed by digitalization in complex project organizing, with far-reaching consequences, as information becomes stored across the 'cloud' and as information becomes used with project stakeholders and to address questions of resilience, climate change and adaptability.

Thus, rather than focus on how digital information is transforming specific stages or practices in project delivery, we argue for the need for work that broadly considers digital practices across complex projects and their impact on project management, where the project delivery stages are not fixed but may become reordered, integrated and transformed through increasing digitalization.

This work suggests some directions for further research on complex project organizing, for example, there is a need for work on how the global software industry interacts with project-based industries, tracing the ensuing power dynamics and asymmetries of information. As well as technical work on the algorithms and approaches for project analytics, there is also a need for work on how to visualize information to make decisions on projects, on the carbon footprint of digital technology itself and on how such technologies can be used across ecosystems of innovation in project-based industries.

REFERENCES

Baheti, R. & Gill, H. (2011). Cyber-physical systems. In T. Samad & A. M. Annaswamy (Eds), *The impact of control technology* (pp. 161–166). IEEE Control Systems Society.

Barrett, J. (2020). Choose your future: A feminist perspective on Construction 4.0 as techno-utopia or digital dystopia. *Proceedings of the Institution of Civil Engineers – Management, Procurement and Law*, 173(4), 153–157.

BCA (2018). *Media factsheets: BCA continues its digitalisation push with industry partners*. Building and Construction Authority.

BCA (2020). Good progress made in key transformation focus areas for the built environment sector, supported by a skilled and competent local core. *Media Release*, 4 March. Building and Construction Authority.

Bryden Wood (2018). *Platforms – bridging the gap between construction + manufacturing*. Bryden Wood Technology.

Brynjolfsson, E. & McAfee, A. (2014). *The second machine age: Work, progress, and prosperity in a time of brilliant technologies*. W. W. Norton & Company.

Brynjolfsson, E. & McElheran, K. (2016). The rapid adoption of data-driven decision-making. *American Economic Review*, 106(5), 133–39.

Camci, A. & Kotnour, T. (2019). Agile approaches for successfully managing and executing projects in the fourth industrial revolution. In A. Camci & T. Kotnour (Eds), *How to manage projects in Industry 4.0 environment: Aligning management style with complexity* (pp. 20–39). IGI Global.

Chen, L., Xie, X., Lu, Q., Parlikad, A. K., Pitt, M. & Yang, J. (2021). Gemini principles-based digital twin maturity model for asset management. *Sustainability*, 13(15), 8224.

Ciano, M. P., Dallasega, P., Orzes, G. & Rossi, T. (2021). One-to-one relationships between Industry 4.0 technologies and lean production techniques: A multiple case study. *International Journal of Production Research*, 59(5), 1386–1410.

Çıdık, M. S. & Boyd, D. (2020). 'Shared sense of purposefulness': A new concept to understand the practice of coordinating design in construction. *Construction Management and Economics*, 38(1), 18–31.

Çıdık, M. S., Boyd, D. & Thurairajah, N. (2017). Ordering in disguise: Digital integration in built-environment practices. *Building Research and Information*, 45(6), 665–680.

Coad, A., Nightingale, P., Stilgoe, J. & Vezzani, A. (2021). Editorial: The dark side of innovation. *Industry and Innovation*, 28(1), 102–112.

Dodgson, M., Gann, D. & Salter, A. J. (2005). *Think, play, do: Technology, innovation, and organization*. Oxford University Press.

Edgerton, D. (2011). *Shock of the old: Technology and global history since 1900*. Profile Books.

Freeman, C. & Louçã, F. (2001). *As time goes by: From the industrial revolutions to the information revolution.* Oxford University Press.

Freeman, C. & Perez, C. (1988). Structural crises of adjustment, business cycles and investment behaviour. In G. Dossie, C. Freeman, R. Nelson, G. Silverberg & L. Soete (Eds), *Technical change and economic theory* (pp. 39–62). Francis Pinter.

Gawer, A. & Cusumano, M. A. (2014). Industry platforms and ecosystem innovation. *Journal of Product Innovation Management*, 31(3), 417–433.

HM Government (2018). *Industrial strategy: Construction sector deal.* Department for Business, Energy and Industrial Strategy.

HM Government (2020). *The construction playbook: Government guidance on sourcing and contracting public works projects and programmes.* Cabinet Office.

Hunhevicz, J. J. & Hall, D. M. (2020). Do you need a blockchain in construction? Use case categories and decision framework for DLT design options. *Advanced Engineering Informatics*, 45(August), 101094.

Langley, A. (1999). Strategies for theorizing from process data. *Academy of Management Review*, 24(4), 691–710.

Lee, D., Lee, S. H., Masoud, N., Krishnan, M. S. & Li, V. C. (2021). Integrated digital twin and blockchain framework to support accountable information sharing in construction projects. *Automation in Construction*, 127, 103688.

Levitt, R. E. (2011). Towards project management 2.0. *Engineering Project Organization Journal*, 1(3), 197–210.

Li, J., Greenwood, D. & Kassem, M. (2019). Blockchain in the built environment and construction industry: A systematic review, conceptual models and practical use cases. *Automation in Construction*, 102, 288–307.

Lindgren, J. & Widén, K. (2018). Diffusing building information management–knowledge integration, mechanisms and knowledge development. *Architectural Engineering and Design Management*, 14(5), 347–362.

Love, P. E. D., Irani, Z., Cheng, E. & Li, H. (2002). A model for supporting inter-organizational relations in the supply chain. *Engineering, Construction and Architectural Management*, 9(1), 2–15.

Lu, Q., Parlikad, A. K., Woodall, P., Ranasinghe, G. D., Xie, X., Liang, Z., Konstantinou, E., Heaton, J. & Schooling, J. (2020). Developing a digital twin at building and city levels: A case study of West Cambridge campus. *Journal of Management in Engineering*, 36(3).

Maradza, E. N. (2015). *Adaptation of industry BIM process standards in a large construction firm.* Doctoral dissertation, School of Construction Management and Engineering, University of Reading.

MOHURD (2020). 住房和城乡建设部等部门关于加快新型建筑工业化发展的若干意见 [Several views from the Ministry of Housing and Urban-Rural Development and other departments on accelerating the industrialization development of new types of construction]. Ministry of Housing and Urban-Rural Development, Beijing.

Mosca, L., Jones, K., Davies, A., Whyte, J. & Glass, J. (2020). Platform thinking for construction. *Transforming Construction Network Plus Digest Series*, 2.

Niederman, F. (2021). Project management: Openings for disruption from AI and advanced analytics. *Information Technology and People*, 34(6), 1570–1599.

Papadonikolaki, E. & Wamelink, H. (2017). Inter- and intra-organizational conditions for supply chain integration with BIM. *Building Research and Information*, 45(6), 649–664.

Papadonikolaki, E., Vrijhoef, R. & Wamelink, H. (2016). The interdependences of BIM and supply chain partnering: Empirical explorations. *Architectural Engineering and Design Management*, 12, 476–494.

Qian, X. (A). & Papadonikolaki, E. (2021). Shifting trust in construction supply chains through blockchain technology. *Engineering, Construction and Architectural Management*, 28(2), 584–602.

Schwab, K. (2015, 12 December). *The fourth industrial revolution: What it means and how to respond.* Foreign Affairs. www.foreignaffairs.com/articles/2015-12-12/fourth-industrial-revolution/.

Schwab, K. (2017). *The fourth industrial revolution.* Crown Business.

Sherratt, F., Dowsett, R. & Sherratt, S. (2020). Construction 4.0 and its potential impact on people working in the construction industry. *Proceedings of the Institution of Civil Engineers – Management, Procurement and Law*, 173(4), 145–152.

Trappey, A. J., Trappey, C. V., Govindarajan, U. H., Chuang A. C. & Sun, J. J. (2017). A review of essential standards and patent landscapes for the Internet of Things: A key enabler for Industry 4.0. *Advanced Engineering Informatics*, 33(C), 208–229.

WEF (2016). *Industry agenda: Shaping the future of construction, a breakthrough in mindset and technology*. World Economic Forum, with Boston Consulting Group.

Whitmore, D., Papadonikolaki, E., Krystallis, I. & Locatelli, G. (2020). Are megaprojects ready for the Fourth Industrial Revolution? *Proceedings of the Institution of Civil Engineers – Management. Procurement and Law*, 174(2), 49–58.

Whyte, J. (2013). Beyond the computer: Changing medium from digital to physical. *Information and Organization*, 23(1), 41–57.

Whyte, J. (2019). How digital information transforms project delivery models. *Project Management Journal*, 50(2), 177–194.

Whyte, J. & Levitt, R. (2011). Information management and the management of projects. In P. W. G. Morris, J. Pinto & J. Söderlund (Eds), *The Oxford handbook of project management* (pp. 365–388). Oxford University Press.

Whyte, J., Lindkvist, C. & Jaradat, S. (2016). Passing the baton? Handing over digital data from the project to operations. *Engineering Project Organization Journal*, 6(1), 2–14.

Whyte, J. & Lobo, S. (2010). Coordination and control in project-based work: Digital objects and infrastructures for delivery. *Construction Management and Economics*, 28, 557–567.

Xu, L. D., Xu, E. L. & Li, L. (2018). Industry 4.0: State of the art and future trends. *International Journal of Production Research*, 56(8), 2941–2962.

Yoo, Y., Henfridsson, O. & Lyytinen, K. (2010). Research commentary: The new organizing logic of digital innovation: An agenda for information systems research. *Information Systems Research*, 21(4), 724–735.

Zhang, J., Cheng, J. C. P., Chen, W. & Chen, K. (2022). Digital twins for construction sites: Concepts, LoD definition, and applications. *Journal of Management in Engineering*, 38(2), 04021094.

Zheng, T., Ardolino, M., Bacchetti, A. & Perona, M. (2021). The applications of Industry 4.0 technologies in manufacturing context: A systematic literature review. *International Journal of Production Research*, 59(5), 1922–1954.

Index

Printed and bound by CPI Group (UK) Ltd, Croydon, CR0 4YY

16/04/2025

14658396-0004